Academe

Dynamic Decisions deepens managers' insights into how humans interact and shape decisions under evolving industry and policy ecosystems. As the author posits in *Energy Investments*, his previous book, scenarios and analytical tools inform managers but cannot prescribe a decision. In placing the person at the core of decision-making, how managers respond to uncertainties, extreme events such as pandemic, or risks, could turn gloom into lucrative niches that firms could pivot into the next boom.

Bernardo M Villegas, Co-founder, University of Asia and the Pacific, Former Member, Constitutional Commission, Philippines, and Board of Advisers, Rolls Royce, United Kingdom

Ricardo's *Dynamic Decisions* should be thought-provoking for a wide range of energy professionals. In highlighting the risks that energy transition poses, Ricardo's work presents plenty of relatable case studies supporting that dynamic decision-making is required to reap the opportunities, and succeed in the energy sector of today and tomorrow.

Rosalind Archer, Head, School of Engineering and Built Environment, Griffith University, Australia, and President, Engineering New Zealand, New Zealand

Energy markets are very volatile because of both the nature of markets and the geopolitical conditions that assert their influence. By making explicit how human behaviour could influence decisions, Ricardo's effort adds a lot of value. In particular, he analyses the interactions of technology and how it shapes market evolution. Ricardo's works provide insights into how appropriate decisions should be made under ambiguous conditions.

Narendra K Rustagi, Professor and Director, Centre for Global Business Studies, School of Business, Howard University, Washington DC, USA

Prof Barcelona integrates insights from human behaviour, business, and policy, to highlight a need to deepen stakeholders' leading and learning cycles — from reacting and "quick fixes" to tackling profound reinvention and rapid change. By providing a way around the complexity of ambiguous decision contexts, a more robust access is made feasible to analytical tools and mindsets for navigating the evolving decision ecosystem. Prof Barcelona, the educator and mentor that he has also chosen to be, guides leaders to combine scenarios, option games, and behavioural economics to "make sense" of emerging futures.

Maria Nieves R Confesor, Professor, Asian Institute of Management, Philippines, and Former Chair, International Labour Organization, Switzerland

The energy markets used to be highly regulated and predictable. With liberalising markets, participants often would live in fear of facing risk. Leveraging in Ricardo's deep knowledge of the energy market, and a broad interest in economic literature, he carefully deconstructs this myth. He argues that risk offers upside potential while allowing market participants to curtail adverse developments, when there is managerial flexibility.

Benoît Chevalier-Roignant, Co-author, Competitive Strategy: Options and Games *(with Lenos Trigeorgis), and Professor, emlyon business school, France/International*

Practice and Policy

Ah, finally we are all discovering everything affects everything else and business must honour this. Managers who give priority to the common good can have all the stakeholders getting more than what they would have gotten otherwise. That is the mission of Ricardo's book.

Terry Möllner, Chair, Stakeholders Capital, Founder of the Calvert Funds, and Former Board Director of Ben & Jerry's for Sustainability, USA

Bringing his deep understanding of the most important strategic issues, Ricardo offers us ways to address constructively the dilemmas we face, as business leaders. This enables us to help create a prosperous and economically sustainable future, in a world characterised by uncertainties and rapid changes. In an accessible manner, with humour, he illustrates how some management thinking come to life by testing it against the "voices of the real world" from battle tested leaders operating in dynamic energy markets. *Dynamic Decisions* tracks multiple aspects of energy transitions, recommend convincing and actionable approaches, to inspire day-to-day as well as strategic actions of managers.

Michael Laengle, Chief Financial Officer, and Member, Management Board, RAG Austria AG, Austria

As the world starts to experience the consequences of climate change, energy companies are under extreme pressure from stakeholders to develop new business strategies to cope with the new dynamics of energy markets. This book is very relevant and a highly recommended read for anyone in the energy industry today.

Stephen A Paradies, Chairman, MORE Electric & Power Company, Philippines

Ricardo's *Dynamic Decisions* examines in a direct and straightforward manner how infrastructure investment and financing could be reframed under rapidly changing conditions in Indonesia, as well as globally. In highlighting the inconvenient realities of continual renegotiations, rigid long-term obligations could create risks that are often ignored. In re-examining how policy and managers could positively interact, I recommend *Dynamic Decisions* for business leaders and practitioners to inform our strategic dialogues.

Ir Montty Girianna, Deputy Minister, Coordinating Ministry for Energy and Mining, Indonesia

Through *Dynamic Decisions*, Ricardo gives energy professionals deep insights, supported by his research, into the interplay among policy, technology and business. It provides a framework that energy leaders may use to maximise utility, mitigate risks, and optimise stakeholder returns in an industry that is uncertain, volatile and ambiguous.

Jorge A Consunji, President and Chief Executive Officer, D M Consunji Inc., and Member, Board of Directors, Semirara Mining and Power Corporation, Philippines

This book is timely and insightful. In the post pandemic world, strategic agility and operational excellence, combined with stakeholder alignment, will be of even greater importance for those who strive to recover and succeed. *Dynamic Decisions* proposes a human-centred approach to addressing these cultural and leadership challenges.

Gary Steel, Former Member, Group Executive Committee, ABB, Switzerland

The energy transition is gathering strong momentum globally, and will require bold decision-making and strategic pivots among industry participants. Prof Barcelona's *Dynamic Decisions* couldn't have come at a better time to help equip decision-makers with a fresh and innovative approach to navigate the dynamic and disruptive environment.

Eric Francia, President and Chief Executive Officer, ACEN, Asia-Pacific/Philippines

Ricardo's take on a resource company's strategic advantages provokes in depth re-examination of managers' business assumptions. How leaders respond, and how they create opportunities from challenging markets, arise from their beliefs and values that guide their strategic actions. In *Dynamic Decisions*, Ricardo offers an adaptive and resilient take on sustainability where firms can *repurpose*, *reframe*, and *reconfigure* their resources to flourish amidst the ambiguities of changing markets.

Maria Cristina C Gotianun, President and Chief Operating Officer, Semirara Mining and Power Corporation, Philippines

Dynamic Decisions offers multiple perspectives on energy transition policies, and effectively caters to regulators, business practitioners and the academe. A masterful blend of theory and practice weave into the ambiguities arising from imperfect humans and markets.

Francisco L Viray, Former Secretary of Energy, Philippines, and Former Dean, College of Engineering, University of the Philippines Diliman, Philippines

These times have indeed been extraordinary and unexpected. And all of us have had no choice but to step up to the plate, or perish. To have an impact, as the Aboitiz Group, our continued commitment in aspiring to do well by doing good, is sustained by our mindset to consistently innovate, improve and inspire. Our passion to help drive change for a better world by advancing business and communities, is underpinned with hope, realism and optimism. In this context, Dr Ricardo Barcelona's book is a great and insightful read. He gives us practical examples as to how we can adapt, and win, in this remarkable time of our nation's history.

Ana Margarita "Ginggay" Hontiveros Malvar, Vice President, Reputation Management, Aboitiz Equity Ventures Inc., and Member, Board of Trustees, UN Global Compact Network, Philippines

Modest in tone, sharp in his observations, Ricardo articulates the human dimension of doing sound sustainable business: Intriguingly timeless, priceless.

Bas Kloppenborg, Director, shpKlop, The Netherlands, and Former Commercial Effectiveness Lead, Shell Exploration & Production, Nigeria, Africa

In *Dynamic Decisions*, Dr Barcelona provides a fresh perspective that policymakers, industry practitioners and civil society stakeholders can use in creating a roadmap for advancing the goals of sustainability. His mastery of the subject matter combining actual experience in the energy industry and finance with deep insights honed in the halls of academia shines through this work. As an advocate for international public-private collaboration in promoting the role of lenders and investors in incentivising progressive alignment of emerging market companies' practices with sustainable development goals, I have benefited from Dr Barcelona's analysis in formulating practical and actionable recommendations from the business sector to political decision-makers and government leaders in the Asia-Pacific region. I wholeheartedly encourage anyone who has genuine interest in this subject, especially those sincerely seeking ideas to promote sustainable development goals, to read this book.

Julius Caesar Parreñas, Coordinator of the Asia-Pacific Financial Forum, and Senior Advisor, Daiwa Institute of Research, Daiwa Securities Group, Japan

Dynamic Decisions goes behind financial and economic data to explicitly surface assumptions, uncertainties, and human biases, to inform decision-makers' judgement. This often better prepares us to tackle future threats and challenges, and to act on opportunities hidden from plain sight.

Anton Perdices, Chief Operating Officer, Distribution Utilities, Aboitiz Power, Philippines

Dynamic Decisions

Energy *PIVOT*, Adaptive Moves, Winning *BOUnCE*

Dynamic Decisions

Energy *PIVOT*, Adaptive Moves, Winning *BOUnCE*

Ricardo G Barcelona

with a foreword by
Franz Heukamp
Dean, IESE Business School, Spain

NEW JERSEY · LONDON · SINGAPORE · BEIJING · SHANGHAI · HONG KONG · TAIPEI · CHENNAI · TOKYO

Published by

World Scientific Publishing Europe Ltd.
57 Shelton Street, Covent Garden, London WC2H 9HE
Head office: 5 Toh Tuck Link, Singapore 596224
USA office: 27 Warren Street, Suite 401-402, Hackensack, NJ 07601

Library of Congress Cataloging-in-Publication Data
Names: Barcelona, Ricardo G., author.
Title: Dynamic decisions : energy PIVOT, Adaptive Moves, Winning BOUnCE /
    Ricardo G Barcelona ; with a foreword by Franz Heukamp, Dean, IESE Business School, Spain.
Description: Hackensack, NJ : World Scientific, 2023. |
    Includes bibliographical references and index.
Identifiers: LCCN 2021058962 | ISBN 9781800611962 (hardcover) |
    ISBN 9781800611979 (ebook) | ISBN 9781800611986 (ebook other)
Subjects: LCSH: Management--Technological innovations. | Creative ability in business. |
    Business enterprises--Technological innovations. | Strategic planning. | Organizational change.
Classification: LCC HD30.2 .B3627 2023 | DDC 658.4/0380285--dc23/eng/20220120
LC record available at https://lccn.loc.gov/2021058962

British Library Cataloguing-in-Publication Data
A catalogue record for this book is available from the British Library.

Copyright © 2023 by Ricardo G Barcelona

All rights reserved.

For any available supplementary material, please visit
https://www.worldscientific.com/worldscibooks/10.1142/Q0353#t=suppl

Desk Editors: Nimal Koliyat/Shi Ying Koe

Typeset by Stallion Press
Email: enquiries@stallionpress.com

To
my wife

Jonelyn "Bing" Ortega Carballo

whose informed choices and adaptive moves created a world of evolving possibilities for us and our children such that the next generation can freely access choices and exercise their options.

Jasmine Carballo Barcelona and her husband, James Harry Ellis Greenhalgh
Ainhoa Itziar Carballo Barcelona and her husband, Peter Meehan McClay
Chantal Beatriz Carballo Barcelona

Family and friends

Foreword

In my interactions with business and policy leaders, I come face to face with what appears to be intractable problems that decision-makers are confronted with. To some, a lack of information is what stopped them from taking action. To others, one takes calculated bets that could hopefully turn out right.

In both cases, they have to deal with decision contexts that are at best ambiguous and even uncertain or unknown. Indeed, these are very uncomfortable backdrops for most managers to stake the future of their firms. To add to the conundrum, the future is never going to be any more certain at a time a decision has to be taken. Inaction is a conscious strategy that hopes the status quo could be perpetuated.

The question of energy transition, and how managers could flourish under an uncertain future, is a case in point. These are wicked contexts to wicked problems, where no known solutions would suffice.

Energy matters because it is central to how our modern economies operate. It touches every aspect of our lives and communities. At an individual level, we power our computers or phones. With energy being so ubiquitous, at least in developed economies, we expect that at a flick of a switch, a darkened room is lit. By turning on a vehicle's ignition and driving safely, we expect to reach our destination in no time.

In emerging markets, the challenges are more basic and fundamental: access to reliable energy, institutional integrity, and available infrastructure and resources, to name a few. Added to this, the social dynamics and how energy systems could transition would draw decision-makers to questions of social equity and equitable access. To these two factors, the environmental question comes full circle to affect all people — rich or poor, of all races, beliefs, and states in life.

Having access to reliable and safe energy sources is one of the key factors that contribute to economic growth and development around the world. After all, energy powers everything from our health care facilities, transportation and essential industries, to our communications, and the latest innovations. As such, modern sources of energy can help us open up access to better health and social conditions as well as economic and educational opportunities across the globe. This is the extent to which energy plays a crucial role in our efforts to forge a better, more sustainable, and equitable society.

Decades of economic progress, and unprecedented prosperity, are fuelled by fossil fuels. In its infancy, coal and oil were seen as humanity's salvation from the curse of animal waste. A little more than a century ago, the convenience of modern cities relied on horse-drawn carriages to ferry people and goods. Animal power moved industries until the curse of horse manure threatened to overwhelm human society to extinction with no solutions in sight. While policy and business leaders were busy looking for solutions, it was the few at the periphery that changed the world.

I have Henry Ford's Model T in mind that introduced mass production to car assembly, a major advancement in making car ownership widely affordable. By replacing horse carriages, animal power was made obsolete in transport. With the Industrial Revolution, mechanical power ushered in unprecedented prosperity, punctuated by a Great Depression and two World Wars. Human innovations propelled this age of wealth creation that relegated the intractable "Horse Manure Crisis" to a footnote for a thriving society.

In today's conversations around sustainable societies, coal and oil as the precursors of our economic prosperity come under question and serious challenges. Fossil fuels are no longer the clean substitutes to animal waste or purveyors of economic wealth.

With more tools on hand and advanced technologies at their disposal, policy and managers continue to follow the 19th century narratives. To transition to a low-carbon energy system, massive expenditures are contemplated. Government plays a primordial role: It plans centrally, mandates the pathway, and funds through subsidies or public expenditures for the required investments. The "all knowing, all powerful" policy holds a monopoly of presumed wisdom.

Here lies my discomfort, which I suspect is shared by a vast majority of managers, in how some environmental advocates would frame climate challenges and their solutions. After three decades since the Rio Earth Summit, the fear of catastrophic climate consequences has only escalated rather than subsided, judging from the polarised political discourse.

Against this backdrop, I am comforted by the greater convergence in recognising the role that individuals play. After all, humans are the very reason societies exist — an obvious fact perhaps, although a reality often presumed, if not ignored, when taking managerial and policy actions.

Today's conversations on low-carbon energy transitions could benefit from what history has to offer and what human ingenuity could achieve to propel society to a prosperous future. This is the essence of Ricardo's work, encapsulated in this book entitled *Dynamic Decisions*.

In questioning a number of the basic presumptions, Ricardo takes us to a different track in framing the managerial and policy challenges of energy transition. For instance:

> In lamenting the lack of progress, why does policy continue to pursue big mandate approaches that failed and continue to choose to make bigger publicly funded bets?
>
> While major strides are achieved to bring energy efficiency to unprecedented levels, why are CO_2 emissions continuing to rise globally?
>
> With sustainability taking its well-deserved focus, why are some managers locked into a mindset that sees profits and sustainability as irretrievably incompatible?

In Ricardo's formulation, he sees a decision ecosystem that is inherently dynamic. In this world, how managers shape their business and respond to policy actions and their rivals' strategic moves interact to influence the outcomes. This is a reality that any battle-tested manager would recognise and use as their starting points when deciding what to reshape in their businesses or markets.

Unfortunately, these same managers are hardwired with a "financial wisdom" that value what is known and predictable. Inadvertently, proven technologies are preferred over innovative approaches that may disrupt a status quo. Partly, the unknowns are to be feared and mitigated as risks, not as a source of opportunities to create tomorrow's profitable niches.

The more enlightened, and evolving, environmental narratives are gaining traction with decision-makers. The good news is policymakers, regulatory bodies, and business leaders around the world *are* listening and paying attention.

Larry Fink, Chief Executive Officer of BlackRock, one of the largest institutional investors, has a practice of outlining his thoughts on issues of societal import in his annual letters. In January 2021, he affirmed how BlackRock aims to influence companies they invest in to move towards a net zero economy by 2050. To achieve these objectives, "there is no company whose business model won't be profoundly affected by the transition to a net zero economy."

This aspiration to refashion the global economy away from traditional sources of energy, in theory, represents a huge opportunity for business leaders around the world. The shift in consumer preferences combined with a growing awareness of climate risk and scrutiny from regulators also means that issues and opportunities related to low-carbon sustainable solutions will be at the forefront of making managerial choices. Yet, it also poses an enormous challenge to firms and society.

Larry Fink challenges managers to reframe how they think about what they invest today and what feasible futures they are contributing to shape. With this mindset shift, ambiguities will have to be made explicit, making conventional financial tools inadequate to do the job. Human values, strategic purpose, and the imperfections of human decision-makers (complete with their biases) would have to be understood as sources of and form part of how these ambiguities are clarified.

In addressing these issues, *Dynamic Decisions* turns the uncertainties into avenues for creating arenas for emerging opportunities to flourish. Ricardo illustrates the way managers could *repurpose*, *reframe*, and then *reconfigure* their way to tomorrow's profitable niches.

In focussing on the decision-maker as a human person, Ricardo humanises the investment process by making explicit the behavioural aspects that are often ignored. Departing from what financial conventions prescribe, ambiguities and uncertainties are examined deeply to shed light on its sources and potential causes. Consistent with behavioural economics and finance, using real-life cases, Ricardo illustrates that the obvious problems are at times not always the challenges that matter. By framing the questions differently, managers and policy often pivot to create opportunities that were previously unimaginable.

The question arises: What does a manager do when they are confronted with uncertainties, while rivals are in the wings ready to pounce or offer the hand of collaboration?

In connecting complex theories to practice, Ricardo builds on his previous works in *Energy Investments* and links the logic of real options and game theory to informing investment decisions. In his previous book, he simplified how the math and the complex logic are made intuitive and accessible, so that managers can quantify their analysis in a simple spreadsheet.

To gain practical insights and incorporate the behavioural aspects of decision-making, Ricardo offers his take on how profits and sustainability are indeed compatible as well as how firms and societal interests often converge. In recognising energy transitions as often protracted and tentative processes, managers could address the strategic imperatives of the firm operating under ambiguous and uncertain ecosystems.

What is often within the manager's greater influence is *repurposing* their extant resources. This may involve a process of divesting or investing or acquiring, together with reskilling people, to gain greater flexibility and resilience to respond profitably to changing markets. Managers *reframe* what matters to markets and consumers, which could lead to a very different approach to fulfil these emerging opportunities. Once the purpose and what propels firms to transform are made clearer, at least in the managers' minds, firms *reconfigure* adaptively to shift emerging advantages through innovation.

Ricardo asserts that "innovation is what sustains humanity and the society it creates. Set free, practical and intelligent people tend to make the right choices for themselves and their communities."

He also observes: "History is replete with policy becoming unworkable when it seeks to regulate against the market. By inhibiting people to deploy their innovative solutions, because the government is supposed to know best, big mandated measures to enforce sustainability are predestined to fail. Instead, if government chooses to regulate the market, by expanding access to opportunities, with people profiting from the choices they made, society can prosper and are likely to be made more sustainable."

In reframing their strategic approaches, managers would use their deep understanding of their business and markets and the results of their analyses to inform their decisions. These decisions are often taken under imperfect and uncertain conditions or even with asymmetric information. This may appear obvious. However, that managers are greatly surprised at how actual outcomes often deviate from policy and their strategic expectations tells us something. Perhaps, how the real world operates is far from what financial tools abstracted in their analytical models.

As managers, being able to take advantage of the opportunities created by this global drive towards modern energy sources necessarily means your day job will get more complex and even more exciting.

First, it will mean having to get quickly up to speed with a variety of different technologies and, in a broader sense, being comfortable with technological complexities and uncertainties. Here, it is less about needing to understand the details of individual technologies and more about understanding *how* these developments and *how* your firm's rivals' actions can fundamentally transform your business. It is about developing the frameworks that can help you identify the vital information and separate it from the background noise.

On a personal note, I can count on Ricardo to come up with counterintuitive insights. With his sharp wit and good humour, Ricardo offers perspectives that provoke an in-depth re-examination of our fundamental premises. Managers and policy are challenged to rethink their "tried and tested" approaches, particularly when there is sparse evidence to support that their approaches actually worked.

Reshaping our businesses and industries as part of wider global efforts to tackle climate change is hard work. Yet, we must not forget the fundamental reason *why* this work needs to be done. Beyond any long-term economic reasons, at its core, this is about securing the long-term future of the people around us and our communities. While we should not downplay the scale of the climate challenge, there are strong grounds for optimism. We have seen in our own lifetimes the power of business to drive positive change around the world. I believe in the potential of business to come up with creative, innovative, and scalable solutions to tackle the challenges before us.

As Ricardo would say in jest to colleagues and friends: By making the humans in managers relevant, there is a great future ahead for managers and business schools that nurture their full person. Some may even change the world they live in and create a better one. The next Model T may just be lurking in the peripheries. To a betting person, innovation is unlikely to emerge from big mandates that policy appears bent on pursuing.

Franz Heukamp
Dean and Professor of Decision Science
IESE Business School
Barcelona, Spain

About the Author

Ricardo G Barcelona authored *Energy Investments*, a ground-breaking book that values renewables as real options under interacting energy portfolios and oligopolistic rivalries. Through his research and interactions with academe, businesses, and policy experts, he contributes to conversations around energy transitions and sustainability, decisions under uncertainties, and how imperfect humans creatively reshape their businesses and society. His insights benefit from his academic rigour, senior leadership experiences at Shell plc, Netherlands and London, and the City of London. As an investment banker, he was consistently voted the top-rated equity analyst and adviser for European utilities while at SBC Warburg and ABN AMRO/Rothschild. He obtained his PhD in Management from King's College London, United Kingdom, MBA from IESE Business School, Spain, and BA from the School of Economics, University of the Philippines.

LinkedIn **ResearchGate**

  Scan the QR code to access the author's LinkedIn and ResearchGate pages.

About the Book

Dynamic Decisions
*Energy PIVOT, Adaptive Moves,
Winning BOUnCE*

Dynamic Decisions highlights how some managers and policymakers sleepwalk into decision paralysis. Strategically, they partly recognise their world is changing radically as energy systems transition. In deciding what to invest in, they default to rewarding the predictable and proven, often misdiagnosing the ignored risks of innately ambiguous markets. To remedy this, the author frames ambiguity as a source of opportunity. As extant advantages obsolesce, new entrants could disrupt to gain dominance. Some managers could *repurpose*, *reframe*, and *reconfigure* their resources and processes to create tomorrow's profitable niches *today*. To profit from these emerging business landscapes, managers can **PIVOT** and **BOUnCE** to win by transitioning into a dynamic *mindset*. Endowed with a creative mind to innovate, humans could reshape their firms and their societies. Armed with these capabilities, albeit partial, managers could choose to adapt *responsive* strategic actions that are *tangible, actionable, and achievable*, with policy sustaining societal benefits by expanding people's access to opportunities.

Dynamic Decisions is written for managers and policymakers that seek to benefit their firms and communities in how they conduct their business and themselves. Connecting theory to practice with actual business cases, this book is organised into four clusters that act as building blocks to structure the reader's decision-making process. Through experimentation, learning, and adaptation, the reader of *Dynamic Decisions* will redirect their strategic actions that are necessary to nurture tomorrow's profitable niches *today*.

 Scan the QR code to access the webpage of *Dynamic Decisions*.

Author's Related Book

Energy Investments
An Adaptive Approach to Profiting from Uncertainties

This book examines what lies behind the uncertainties surrounding the fuel and power markets. Exploring the role of renewables and how they potentially disrupt or create opportunities, it challenges widely accepted wisdoms in investment. The author asks questions such as: Are "business as usual" strategies that favour fossil fuels the best route to future prosperity? What prospects do firms face when their competitors diversify into renewables? Why do generous subsidies to renewables often fail to achieve wide-scale deployment? Illustrating how real options and option games reasoning yield vastly different insights from those gained from NPVs, *Energy Investments* offers case studies and simulations to demonstrate how firms can benefit from the methods it showcases.

Contents

Foreword   xiii
About the Author   xix
About the Book   xxi
List of Boxes   xxv
List of Charts   xxvii
List of Tables   xxxi
Introduction   xxxv

I	**Understanding Energy *PIVOT***		**1**
	Chapter 1	From Impasse to *PIVOT*	3
	Chapter 2	Policy and Managerial Actions	75
II	**Adaptive Moves**		**135**
	Chapter 3	Articulate a Purpose	137
	Chapter 4	Bounded Possibilities	189
	Chapter 5	Calibrate	241
	Chapter 6	Take Actions to De-risk	295
III	***BOUnCE* to Win**		**357**
	Chapter 7	Cost of Energy	359
	Chapter 8	Levers of Value	413
	Chapter 9	Price Taker	469
	Chapter 10	Oligopolistic Rivalries	511

IV Winning Actions   583
   Chapter 11   *PIVOT* and *BOUnCE* to Profit   585

Glossary   641
Index   673

List of Boxes

Box 0.1	Lluis Bertran Rafecas	lxii
Box 1.1	Antonio Brufau Niubó — Moving Boldly to a Low-Carbon Future	45
Box 1.2	RAG Austria AG — The Missing Link in Decarbonising Energy	58
Box 2.1	A Policy Process under Ambiguous Conditions	113
Box 2.2	Learning from Impact Investing	121
Box 3.1	Living *PW One Three* with Bas Kloppenborg	176
Box 4.1	Views from the Inside	226
Box 4.2	Charles Edward Payne II	232
Box 5.1	Conversations with Rama Velamuri	285
Box 6.1	Resolving Indonesia's Geothermal Paradox	341
Box 6.2	Recouping Revenue Losses via Social Innovation	348
Box 7.1	Geothermal — Evidence from the Field	397
Box 10.1	Binomial Model and Processes	552
Box 11.1	ACEN Corporation — New Entrant's Pivot to Green Value	613
Box 11.2	Semirara: Adaptive Pivot by Redeploying Strengths	622
Box 11.3	Getting to Low Carbon with Data Analytics	630

List of Charts

Chart 0.1	Making *PIVOT* and Winning *BOUnCE*	xliv
Chart 1.1	Varied CO_2 Emissions Performance, 1965–2020	15
Chart 1.2	Dynamic Power Market	23
Chart 1.3	Dynamic Displacements and Shifting Advantages	26
Chart 1.4	Strategic Approaches under Ambiguous Conditions	30
Chart 1.5	Rethinking *Tactical* and *Strategic* Moves	34
Chart 1.6	*Reframing* Strategic Moves	38
Chart 1.7	Reconfigured Hydrogen Value Chain and Industry Coupling	41
Box Chart 1.1.1	Repsol's Strategic Plan 2021–2025	46
Chart 2.1	Policy and Managerial Spheres of Influence	85
Chart 2.2	Normative Anchors of Policy	89
Chart 2.3	Money Flows — Intermittent Renewables vs. Fossil Fuels Subsidies	96
Chart 2.4	Subsidies under Volatile Coal and Gas Prices	98
Chart 2.5	Subsidies under Declining Costs and Volatile Prices	100
Chart 2.6	Comparative CO_2 Abatement Costs	103
Chart 2.7	Feasible Policy Choices and Firms' Actions under Different Systems	106
Box Chart 2.2.1	Asset Classes and Return Expectations	121
Chart 3.1	Evolving Notions of the Firm	144
Chart 3.2	Rethinking the Energy Ecosystem	157

Chart 3.3	Feasible Roles for Energy Firms	162
Chart 3.4	Shifting Roles and Strategies	165
Chart 3.5	Energy Financial Returns and CO_2 Abatement Costs	170
Chart 4.1	Untangling Webs of Interacting Factors	196
Chart 4.2	Expected Outcomes–Variations Matrix	200
Chart 4.3	Climate Policy and Expected Outcomes	206
Chart 4.4	Policy Instruments and Market Orientation Matrix	210
Chart 4.5	Enabling Mindsets and Decision-Making Ecosystem	214
Chart 4.6	Organisation Agility and Innovations	218
Chart 4.7	Uncertainties, Organisational Agility, and Profits	223
Box Chart 4.1.1	ABB Leadership Ladder and Shell Comparative	229
Chart 5.1	Human Biases and Possible Remedies	248
Chart 5.2	Schematic Overview of a Funnelling Process	258
Chart 5.3	Human Judgement in Prospects-to-Opportunities Funnel	261
Chart 5.4	Levers of Value Creation and Policy Actions	265
Chart 5.5	Invested Capital — Historic vs. Market Price Bases	269
Chart 5.6	Financial Economics and Investment Conditions	274
Chart 5.7	Linking Theories to Inform Practice and Policy	275
Chart 5.8	Value–Risk Trade-off Framework	279
Chart 6.1	PPA Revenues and Risks	303
Chart 6.2	Grid Price Parity under Ambiguous Conditions	308
Chart 6.3	Expected Risks and Payoffs of Fuels and Power Investments	311
Chart 6.4	Comparative Values of Contracting Strategy	319
Chart 6.5	Sequential Value Capture	322
Chart 6.6	Late-mover's Benefits in Solar Power	330
Chart 6.7	Interacting Supply Decisions and Volume Re-allocation	336
Chart 7.1	Building Blocks of Financial and Economic Costing	364
Chart 7.2	Costs–Returns Nexus	366
Chart 7.3	Lifecycle Costs of Energy Calculations	374
Box Chart 7.1.1	EDC and Pertamina Geothermal Performance	400
Chart 8.1	Investment Cycle under Static Conditions	415
Chart 8.2	Linkages of Financial Information	420
Chart 8.3	Spot Power Prices under Gas System	425

List of Charts

Chart 8.4	Comparative Valuations	450
Chart 8.5	Evolution and Appropriation of Equity Value	455
Chart 9.1	*BOUnCE* and Financial Analyses	475
Chart 9.2	Iterative Interactions of Value Creation	479
Chart 9.3	Comparative Costs and Profiles	482
Chart 9.4	Comparative Power Prices and Cash Margins	484
Chart 9.5	Comparative Financial Indicators — $Coal_M$ vs $ACCGT_M$ Systems	486
Chart 9.6	How Revenues and "Cash Margins" Differ	490
Chart 9.7	Working Capital Requirements under $ACCGT_M$	494
Chart 9.8	Working Capital under $ACCGT_M$	496
Chart 9.9	Credit Strength and Cash Accumulation	498
Chart 9.10	Comparative Cash Flows and Profiles	499
Chart 9.11	Levers of Returns	504
Chart 9.12	Comparative Residual Value Accretion	506
Chart 10.1	Comparative Approaches of NPV and Binomial Processes	518
Chart 10.2	A Feasible Dynamic Thought Process	522
Chart 10.3	Comparative Cost Volatilities	530
Chart 10.4	Volume Reallocation and Value of MCPX — $ACCGT_B$ and $Coal_B$	532
Chart 10.5	Volume Reallocation and Value of MCPX — $ACCGT_B$ and $StoHydro_B$	537
Chart 10.6	Volume Reallocation and Value of MCPX — $ACCGT_B$ and $ANuke_B$	545
Chart 10.7	Summary of Dynamic Interactions of Rivals	550
Box Chart 10.1.1	Interacting Volumes, Payoffs, and Maintenance Capex	572
Box Chart 11.1.1	ACEN Corporation Financial Performance and Portfolio Shift	617
Box Chart 11.2.1	Semirara's Historic Performance	624
Box Chart 11.2.2	Proposed National Grid Interconnections	626

List of Tables

Table 1.1	Static Lifecycle Costs of Energy	20
Box Appendix 2.2A	Five Projects with Different Strategies for Funding Renewables Projects	128
Table 5.1	Value Creation under Historic or Market Invested Capital Value	270
Box Table 6.1.1	Comparative Costs of Geothermal Drilling Technologies	342
Table 7.1	Financial Periodic Costs of Energy	370
Table 7.2	Comparable Total Overnight Costs Equivalence	376
Table 7.3	Fuel Costs Volatilities and LCOEs	380
Table 7.4	Volatile Fuel Costs and Impact on Relative Costs of Energy	381
Table 7.5	Location Specificity and LACEs of $Wind_{ON}$	383
Table 7.6	Comparative Costs of LCOEs and FPCOEs	389
Table 7.7	Implied Costs of CO_2 Abatement	395
Box Table 7.1.1	Comparative Actual Capacity Factors and Contract Tenors	402
Appendix 7A	Fixed Cost Recovery C_{FX}	408
Appendix 7B	Variable Operating Cost — C_{VAR}	410
Appendix 7C	Fuel Cost C_{FUEL}	412
Table 8.1	Threshold for Financial Feasibility	424
Table 8.2	Threshold for Financial Viability	427
Table 8.3	Financing and Taxes	429

Table 8.4	Funding of Long-term Commitments	432
Table 8.5	Working Capital Requirement	434
Table 8.6	Operating and Cash Cycle	436
Table 8.7	Cash and Rebalancing Capital Structure	438
Table 8.8	Operating Cash and Its Genesis	441
Table 8.9	Investing and Calls on Cash Flow	443
Table 8.10	Appropriating Residual Cash	444
Table 8.11	Reconciliation of "Cash Flows" Measures	446
Table 8.12	Deconstructing Residual Income and Value Creation	452
Appendix 8A	$ACCGT_B$ under Gas System — Balance Sheet	460
Appendix 8B	$ACCGT_B$ — Cash Flow Analysis	462
Appendix 8C	$ACCGT_B$ Gas System — Profit & Loss Analysis	463
Appendix 8D	$ACCGT_B$ under Gas System — Financial Ratios	465
Appendix 8E	$ACCGT_B$ under Gas System — Residual Income Analysis	467
Table 9.1	Comparative Payback Periods under $Coal_M$ and $ACCGT_M$	501
Table 9.2	Comparative NPVs	502
Table 10.1	$ACCGT_B$ and $Coal_B$ under Symmetric Cost Volatilities and Stable Volumes	527
Table 10.2	$ACCGT_B$ and $Coal_B$ under Asymmetric Cost Volatilities	529
Table 10.3	$ACCGT_B$ and $StoHydro_B$ with Asymmetric Costs under $ACCGT_M$, Stable Volumes	535
Table 10.4	$ACCGT_B$ and $StoHydro_B$ with Asymmetric Costs under $ACCGT_M$, Growth-Biased Volumes	538
Table 10.5	$ACCGT_B$ and $GeoS_B$ with Asymmetric Costs under $ACCGT_M$, Stable Volumes	540
Table 10.6	$ACCGT_B$ and $GeoS_B$ with Asymmetric Costs under $ACCGT_B$, Growth-biased Volumes	541
Table 10.7	$ACCGT_B$ and ANuke with Asymmetric Costs under $ACCGT_M$, Stable Volumes	543
Table 10.8	$ACCGT_B$ and $Wind_{ON}$ with Asymmetric Costs under $ACCGT_M$, Stable Volumes	546

Table 10.9	$ACCGT_B$ and PVT_M with Asymmetric Costs under $ACCGT_M$, Stable Volumes	548
Box Table 10.1.1	Comparative Lifecycle Costs of Energy and Assumptions	553
Box Table 10.1.2	Market and Rival Firms' Volumes	555
Box Table 10.1.3	Power Prices under $ACCGT_M$	558
Box Table 10.1.4	Economic Cash Margin	562
Box Table 10.1.5	Payoffs and Strategic Option Value	565
Box Table 10.1.6	Call Value with Maintenance Capex	569
Box Table 10.1.7	Residual Economic Value	574
Appendix 10A	$ACCGT_B$ and Geo_B with Asymmetric Costs under $ACCGT_M$, Stable Volumes	580
Appendix 10B	$ACCGT_B$ and Geo_B with Asymmetric Costs under $ACCGT_M$, Growth-biased Volumes	581
Appendix 10C	$ACCGT_B$ and $Coal_B$ with Asymmetric Costs under $ACCGT_M$, Stable Volumes	582
Box Table 11.3.1	Comparison of Conventional Database and Blockchain	631

Introduction

Dynamic Decisions emerged from these phenomena I often encounter: Working to enhance people's well-being, managers and policy are divided by a common purpose. Within firms, strategy and finance aim to create value but fundamentally differ in their mindsets towards risk. Inadvertently, the controllers' aversion to risks and the strategists' tolerance for ambiguities are set to collide.

There is also a deep-seated belief in some quarters that managers (and policy) are driven by greed. Sowing doubts on people's inherent goodness, the vast majority of managers are caught in the crossfires among ever-polarising advocacies. As opposing ideas compete for influence, *energy transition* and *sustainability* become a politicised process, leaving managers to bear most of the responsibilities without a direct voice. This is indeed far from satisfactory for managers and businesses.

In writing *Dynamic Decisions*, I have in mind the managers residing in a world that is ambiguous and uncertain. While some may encourage the myth, managers' control and influence on markets and society are far from categorical. Policy and advocates seldom stake their financial fortunes in the outcomes of what they promote. In contrast, managers commit resources that could be lost or multiplied, subject to how their investments work out. However, under the constant gaze of policy and advocates, risk-averse managers are continually caught by "surprise" by adverse outcomes. This occurs when managers abdicate judgement to follow the imagined certainty of the algorithms of their analytical tools.

This is symptomatic of some managers working to resolve the irrelevant problems. A remedy is to recognise *real-life markets* populated by *real people* for what it is. In effecting *energy transition* and the *sustainability agenda*, how financial economics and strategy influence managerial actions needs to be specified and made explicit:

> Economics hold up competitive markets as the ideal to make resource allocation efficient. Without barriers or distortions, the most economically rational path is pursued. Policy, in asserting its influence to manifest society's "preferences", chooses to subsidise renewables. This is in the hope of creating niches for socially valuable energy resources to displace "unsustainable" fossil fuels. On their part, managers employ strategy to secure their competitive advantages by going around policy constraints, erecting barriers against rivals, or collaborating to strengthen their market power. These actions are anathema to the adherents of competition and the proper workings of the market economy.

The observed contradictions run deeper. A strategist recognises that what they do alters how firms compete by changing the very sources of their competitive advantages. Finance and economics, however, would mimic certainty *under ceteris paribus* by assuming to know the *unknowns* and *the unknowable* future. This is manifested in how managers assume the *knowns* and the *knowable* as largely unchanged when evaluating the venture's payoffs or policy's costs and benefits.

Allowing these contradictions to fester and persist, managers and policy are stuck: To play it safe, a vast majority would go with the herd and hope to outcompete rivals but would usually fail. Without attempting to swim against the currents, people would try with futility to solve the wicked problems. A few mavericks, working at the periphery, would first reconcile the opposing *mindsets* and *ambitions*. This they do by recognising ambiguities as offering some paths to tomorrow's opportunities *today*.

Counterintuitive and Contrarian Moves

In a *real world* populated by *real people*, solutions to *real problems* are pursued under ambiguous and uncertain markets. To flourish, people may need to "look forward and reason backward" (Dixit and Nalebuff, 2008) and sideways, I would add. This enables managers to see how "rivals could block or ease their way in order to open other routes should markets turn out differently" (Barcelona, 2017). Imperfect humans seldom act with total rationality: The *strategic mindset* seeks to change the game, to the point of disrupting extant systems that present risks, making the path to the future ambiguous.

A *controller's mindset*, to which some finance professionals adhere to as its ideal, would see risks as something abhorrent that needs to be avoided or even neutralised. In promoting this *mindset*, managers would ignore opportunities that are risky but offer a prospect for greater wealth. In the hands of more enlightened rivals, the foregone opportunity may just disrupt the very business that the *controller's mindset* was supposed to protect.

This is where the human virtues, often ignored by managers, become relevant. To profitably transition into an unknown future, managers endowed with *humility*, *integrity*, and *generosity* could engender openness that enables innovation. This facilitates strategic dialogues to identify the arenas in which ambiguities could pave the way to nurture emerging opportunities. More importantly, as *integrity* builds trust, *humility* and *generosity* replace an imaginary omniscience with a readiness to learn and to receive feedback as a gift. Here are a few examples:

Privatisation and deregulation transformed the "solid but stolid" power utilities into firms with divergent financial and regulatory exposures. One prominent area where rival firms differ was in their capital structure and in their capacity to sustain their capital expenditures. Consequently, one has to question the homogeneity in their valuations prescribed by their dividend yields and earnings ratios. Our equity analysts proposed a different approach to make these differences explicit.

The City of London found our enterprise value[1] methodology too novel, with many deciding to stick with "the old reliable price-to-earnings ratio (or its variants)". *Institutional Investors* reported on how equity investors responded:

> "At one time, investors used to think of electric utilities as one big interest play. But in October 1993, S G Warburg's Ricardo Barcelona ingenuously

---

[1] Chapter 8 explains how this was introduced and goes into details on its logic and math, as a way to value firms with different capital structures, returns, and value creation potential.

split the sector into three: cyclical, regulatory beneficiaries, and classics. He directed fund managers into the first two types of utilities and told them to dodge the third" (II, 1995). Barcelona "introduced another wrinkle to his enterprise value analysis: the implied equity value of his stocks. 'It simplified cross-border comparisons and gives a cross-check to the enterprise value approach', says an investor" (II, 1996). As his approach gained traction, Barcelona was "so influential, says a proponent, that 'you can't afford to ignore what he says'" (II, 1997).

Admittedly, our team members were flattered by these accolades, with Pablo Diaz Megias singled out for recognition. The methods extended to our work in mergers and acquisitions, and corporate advisory. The deeper insights, however, were lessons in *humility*, *integrity*, and *generosity*. Deeply embedded in the equity investors' psyche, utilities and bonds were indistinguishable. No amount of counterfactual evidence would likely change that, particularly to those who elevated their wisdom to an unassailable belief.

Instead of openly challenging the hardcore beliefs, we chose to work closely with some fund managers and industry stalwarts to truly understand how the world is changing and how a different way of valuing firms would help. This opens the way to re-examine embedded biases, the extent to which valuation methods form part of the solution, and how dialogues recognise the merits that opposing views hold. With positive outcomes, profits and informed counterintuitive views became inextricably linked at least for some fund managers and energy managers.

Liquified natural gas (LNG) was reserved for large volume markets supplied by well-capitalised firms. As a fuel, LNG is liquified at a source at less than −160°C atmospheric pressure to enhance its transportability. Loaded on specialised vessels, LNG is converted back to gas at the destination through a regasification facility at the import terminal. The gas is distributed through a pipeline network to end users. The whole setup costs a lot of money to operate, requiring advanced engineering capabilities. With high capital commitments, the volume thresholds for reserves and markets tend to make LNG beyond the reach of smaller resource holders and fragmented gas markets. Colleagues at Shell plc *reconfigured* the logistics to make LNG more widely available to decarbonise fuels:

Small reserves, instead of being left unexploited, benefited from gas-to-liquids technology (RDS, 2021). By converting natural gas into cleaner petrol-like fuel, conventional oil carriers could transport the fuel, thereby reducing logistics costs and the minimum volume thresholds to achieve a viable scale. Gas-to-liquids are unloaded and stored like conventional petrol, eliminating the need for capital-intensive logistics.

Smaller volume markets and reserves are made financially viable by reducing the capital expenditures. A solution was in prospect with a glut in LNG shipping. Instead of mothballing expensive ships, excess vessels were *repurposed* into floating regasification and storage units (FRSU). This cuts deployment time and reduces capital expenditure by more than half. Previously unviable small markets became a source for growth by making them accessible (Battersby, 2021). Extending this concept, *bunkering* is an extension that opens small regional markets or refuels ships safely with LNG (Trelleborg, 2021).

Technical innovation and its benefits are tangible and easier to see. It is, however, in financial economics where the *mindset transitions* would yield counterintuitive insights of value to managers and policy.

Capital budgeting is heavily influenced by economic and financial tools, such as net present values (NPVs) and its variants or cost–benefit analysis (CBA), that managers and policy rely heavily on. In rewarding predictable cash flows, payoffs are made certain through a complex web of rigid obligations. Inadvertently, the value of flexible pricing or volumes is foregone. Project financing is an example:

Supported by webs of complex contracts, "cost–benefit analysis of the complete life cycle of project is used to determine if the economic benefits of a project are larger than the economic costs" (CFI, 2021). Practitioners, however, while grudgingly accepting this premise, fully realise that in a changing world, rigid obligations are bound to be continually renegotiated. To avoid this expensive exercise, a good legal mind is deemed a necessity to ensure contracts are ironclad against parties reneging on their commitments.

Piqued by curiosity, I cannot help but question why upright people would even consider reneging. In looking at investments and the decision ecosystem, as they operate in real life, modern financial economics offers a logical explanation. The problem is not legal or the way contracts are drafted. It is how financial economics shapes and informs human decisions. In contracting implicitly under *ceteris paribus*, changing prices or costs would yield benefits (or penalties), and when large enough, would outweigh the cost of reneging. Under this "*cost–benefit*" comparison, ignoring reputation and its impact on trust and human relations, amoral positivist economics would prescribe a point when reneging is a rational economic decision.

This is where the inconvenient nuances of decision-making would rediscover the ignored *mutatis mutandis*, the flip side of *ceteris paribus*. Operating under uncertainty, Avinash K Dixit and Robert S Pindyck (1994) see value in changing course when market conditions change. In combining real options and game theory, Benoit Chevalier-Roignant and Lenos Trigeorgis (2011) extended my understanding of how interacting actions would alter the decision contexts and feasible investment outcomes. This insight allows for a dynamic and adaptive response to shifting strategies and, to a large extent, quantifies the value of managerial flexibility.

What I started in my previous book — *Energy Investments* — dynamically informs the decision-making process under ambiguities and uncertainties. Instead of relying on complex webs of rigid obligations, managers opt to adaptively act on evolving market information. They rely on their agility and judgements, and employ innovations to adapt to evolving opportunities or disrupt extant networks and relationships.

One area where strategy and finance met in agreement is in redefining optimality from a portfolio perspective. Unlike making each asset maximises its cash flows, managers learn to combine assets with different cost structures and volatilities to optimise returns at minimum risk, a notion founded on diversification. This approach moves finance away from a *controller's mindset*, where adaptive moves and the ambiguities in outcomes that ensue would wreak havoc on their well-ordered and structured world, as they imagine in their financial models. In the *controller's mindset*, chaos is avoided by making as much of the variables predictable, usually by committing to rigid long-term obligations. With the gain in certainty in cash flows, the firm foregoes any upside should markets prove better than expected. By moving to a portfolio approach, how the technologies' financial merits are evaluated would yield a very different decision, often for the better.

Here's how the academe and practitioners have evolved in their portfolio thinking:

In the aftermath of the 1973 Arab Oil Embargo, gas was expensive and unproven relative to oil and coal. Dan Bar-Lev and Steven Katz (1976) came up with this novel idea: Stable priced gas, because it was hardly traded, tempers the volatile prices of coal and oil. Faced with regulated fixed power prices, utilities could minimise fuel costs variance by diversifying with gas. It worked for a while until gas prices became pegged to oil as it became more widely traded as an alternative to coal and oil.

The *fuel cost minimisation* took a new lease of life with zero fuel costs renewables, following Harry M Markowitz's (1991) portfolio principles. Shimon Awerbuch (2006), in assuming fixed power prices, showed how renewables and fixed costs nuclear could stabilise and reduce the marginal cost of incumbent power portfolios comprising fossil fuels. In tackling wind power's volume intermittency, Fabien Roques, David M Newberry, and William Nuttal (2006) argued for geographic integration of wind supplies. With wind flows varying regionally, integrated supplies in markets with reliable infrastructure would reduce volume volatilities as uneven or opposing variations would offset each other. Combined with Awerbuch's logic, the diversification benefit to the costs of wind power is demonstrated.

In a practical and tangible way, Spain pioneered the renewables subsystem. This involves managing the entire wind and solar assets as a single portfolio, dominated by wind. Juan Rivier Abbad of Iberdrola, a global leader in renewables headquartered in Spain, observed that the wind blows at different times in various locations. Taking advantage of the uncorrelated volume volatilities across regions, the subsystem is found to mimic the variability of supplies exhibited by hydro power (Rivier Abbad, 2010). With Spain being a major hydro power user, wind power's intermittency is managed similar to hydro, with its load balancing obligation. By 2021, as illustrated in Chapter 1, wind power is not only a mainstay of supply, it has displaced coal with gas, a subject for substitution when demand falls sharply. The COVID-19 lockdowns, seeing drastic volume reductions, are occasions to prove this proposition works under dynamic energy markets.

In working with David Parker, Cranfield School of Management, and Tarik Driouchi, King's College London, both in the United Kingdom, for my doctoral dissertation, we encounter a very different energy market. Prices, costs, and volumes are all volatile, which requires a re-examination of the *fuel cost minimisation* proposition. In employing William F Sharpe's (2007) *state-preference portfolio choice*, combined with the Cox–Ross–Rubinstein binomial trees (Rubinstein, 1994), I posit that renewables confer *call options* to fossil fuel portfolios when power prices are increasing. Under fixed power price regimes, *put options* on fuel liabilities are instead embedded, which are repetitively exercised. In turn, by making these option values explicit, subsidies when still needed are seen as ways to hasten investments, not as *sine qua non* to committing to renewables (Barcelona, 2015).

Learning effects are used to justify early commitments and payment of generous subsidies to renewables. In doing the sums, I came up with a counterintuitive logic: For technologies with rapidly declining costs and modest foregone revenues, a paradox occurs. With little to forego, waiting would reap greater benefits from cost savings that accrue to late movers (Barcelona, 2017). Such is the fate that awaits aggressive investors that moved quickly into solar, only to be competed out by new entrants with significantly lower costs.

In an evolving world, what becomes obvious is the futility of aiming to change the world head on by keeping undisturbed what we have become accustomed to. Particularly, in effecting *energy transition sustainably*, how *mindsets* transition with *ambitions* may take Mark Rubinstein's (2006) advice to heart: "Ideas are seldom born clothed, but are gradually dressed in an arduous process of accretion." It is with a perspective, particularly in the spheres of social science and human well-being, that knowledge can "affect the social evolution that follows discovery, which through reciprocal causation largely determines the succeeding social theory".

Adaptive Actions by Real People

The decision thought process takes a different turn when Richard H Thaler's (2015) behavioural economics and Amartya Sen's (2000) equitable access to opportunities are considered. In equating development with freedom, Sen made governance a principal plank of policy and management, while Thaler places humans, and how they make their choices, at the core of decision-making. Elinor Ostrum (2015) offers empirical evidence on how humans and their communities are seen to respond to higher social ideals to govern the commons for the common good.

That humans can only be driven by greed takes a very dim view of humanity and the society they inhabit. Fortunately, this notion is debunked by the good deeds a vast majority of people do. In recognising this human reality, managers and policy can make the intractable and wicked human problems into an arena where *real people* seek *real solutions* to *real problems* that matter. This is where integrity serves as the foundation for human discourse and interactions, as an antidote to the "post-truth" denial that objective realities exist.

In examining what binds people, alignment is given an inordinate amount of importance. However, what propels people is a convergence of virtues that serves as the foundation for common action. I come across *humility*, *integrity*, and *generosity* as virtues which cement trusting relationships that sustain markets and society. In respecting *freedom of choice* and enabling people, access to opportunities is expanded, with innovation enabling people to flourish.

Dynamic Decisions is written for managers and policymakers who seek to benefit their firms and communities in how they conduct their businesses and themselves. Operating under dynamic, transitioning energy markets, imperfect humans make firms and society sustainable by adapting to change. This calls for a *mindset transition* that shifts the managerial decision focus as follows:

Manager effects change by recognising the ambiguities of its decision ecosystem. Instead of projecting the *status quo* to understand the uncertain future, managers gain insights from their analytical tools to inform their options, not to blindly follow what the tools prescribe as a decision. Using the levers of value, managers adaptively *repurpose*, *reframe*, and *reconfigure* their resources and approaches to shift competitive advantages in their communities' favour.

Policy recognises its greater service as enabling markets to function dynamically. In the process, subsidies and social capital are enablers to de-risk or kickstart investments, not as direct support to promote technological or market "champions". In acting as an arbiter, policy seeks to reconcile colliding interests that are bound to occur on occasions among imperfect humans.

Civil society advances their cause by converging on interests, rather than advocating unassailable beliefs with imaginary omniscience, to formulate *tangible actions* to achieve specified outcomes as ways to coalesce with managers or policy or both.

Cognisant of these different roles and interests, I organise the book into four clusters, as outlined in Chart 0.1. The clusters may be used to inform specific aspects of the decision process or as building blocks to structure a decision-making process for policy or managers.

Each cluster corresponds to an area of strategic focus. By deconstructing into its bite-sized components, the complex problems managers and policy aim to *really* tackle become tractable. This requires, with deep knowledge and insights, to **know** what and why an energy *PIVOT* is worth embarking on. Using this appreciation, one can *frame* in a *tangible, actionable*, and *achievable* manner how one would move adaptively under the ambiguities and uncertainties of evolving policy and market contexts.

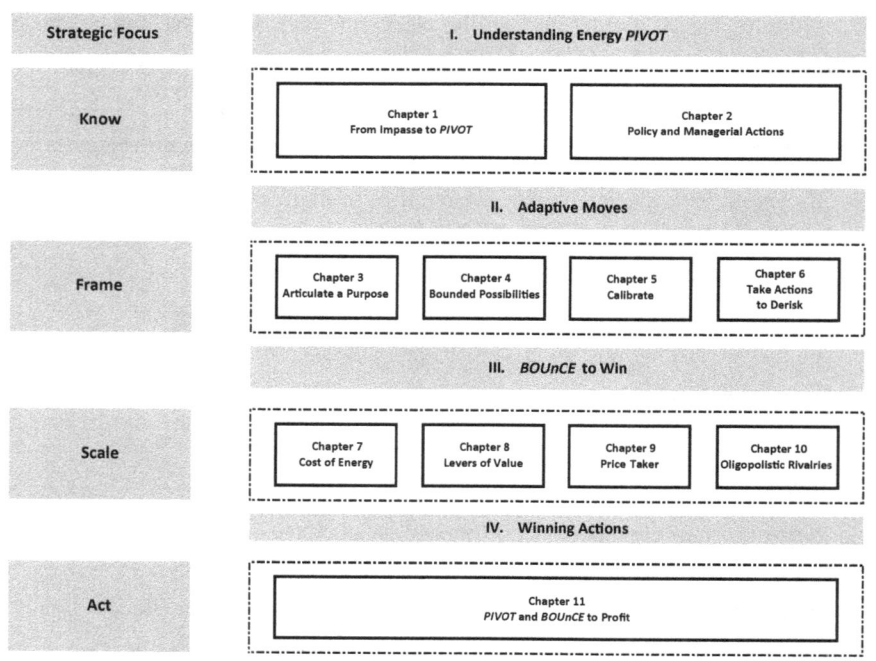

Chart 0.1: Making *PIVOT* and Winning *BOUnCE*

Through experimentation, learning, and adaptation, one gains information and insights to create arenas to nurture tomorrow's profitable niches *today*. In preparing to *BOUnCE* to win, one can **scale** the commitments according to the pace, rivalries among firms, and shifting policy actions. One can **act** with managerial flexibility to profit from each *PIVOT* with orchestrated moves to shift emerging opportunities to one's advantage, following the *PIVOT* and *BOUnCE* playbook of *repurpose, reframe,* and *reconfigure*.

I provided a glossary of selected terminologies to clarify their context and usage while excluding those that conform to popular definitions. Economic and financial variables, and acronyms describing energy technologies, are defined separately in the appendices and narratives of Chapters 7, 8 and 10.

I. Understanding Energy *PIVOT*

Energy transition and how it is understood evolved from fuel substitutions to environmental remediation to extend its scope to ensuring a sustainable society as its eventual outcome. The prescribed routes to *PIVOT* vary, a reality that strategists recognise. Going beyond technology and economics, one needs to recognise how imperfect and at times highly opinionated humans configure their choices. As such, how humans view *energy transitions* and *sustainability* is influenced by the virtues and philosophy that they adhere to as manifested in their ideological leanings. To better understand how firms and society could profitably *PIVOT* to tomorrow's profitable niches *today*, I posit that "accepted wisdoms" will have to be re-examined:

Ambiguous and uncertain markets could create opportunities as obsolescing technologies, hence extant advantages are displaced. New entrants and incumbents respond according to their perceived advantages that are made explicit. In recognising the innate ambiguities of transitioning energy systems, managers could *repurpose* their resources and capabilities, *reframe* the challenges or opportunities they choose to resolve or seize, and *reconfigure* the networks and markets they choose to operate under. As a result, managers focus on creating arenas where emerging opportunities are nurtured rather than on engaging in a futile exercise of making the uncertain predictable (Chapter 1).

Antonio Brufau Niubó, Chair and Chief Executive of Repsol, reflects on how Repsol strategically pivoted as a strengthened company amidst adverse geopolitical actions. Tested by adversities and surmounting obstacles, Repsol is proving its mettle in creating its future niches today (Box 1.1). Michael Laengle, Chief Finance Officer, RAG of Austria, offers a different take on how Austria's largest gas storage company could thrive in a low-carbon energy system. Energy storage sees a different twist in their *Underground Sun Conversion and Storage Initiative* (Box 1.2).

In the sphere of normative economics, policy is a mechanism to effect an equitable distribution of benefits. However, equitable and equal distribution of goods is often confused, placing business and policy at odds that polarise policy prescriptions, at least from a "progressive" perspective. Adhering to principles of market economies, policy seeks to expand access to opportunities by people (Sen, 2000) and enhance governance of the commons for mutual benefits of the community (Ostrum, 2015) under the guiding hand of enlightened policy or libertarian paternalism (Thaler, 2015) (Chapter 2).

Raphael "Popo" PM Lotilla, Philippine Energy Secretary (prior to his appointment for the second time), examines how competing interests shape the restructuring and deregulation of the Philippine energy industry. Ideology and pragmatic compromises make policymaking an exercise in "optimising the feasible" (Box 2.1). Alexandre Moreira, an American climate advocate, shares his insights on how social capital, working with a policy push to decarbonise energy, could play a transformative role in financing emergent technologies and de-risking renewables investment (Box 2.2).

II. Adaptive Moves

In embarking to **PIVOT**, managers and policy comprising *real people* define the firm's *purpose* from a vantage view of deep *insights* to form part of its decision ecosystem. The firm's *raison d'etre*, and how it is understood, is deepened by making explicit why firms and markets exist and how people interact and alter outcomes. Managers respond adaptively by creating feasible pathways to achieve desired outcomes. Conferred with authority to allocate and deploy resources, managers are influenced by how they see their realities from the optics of their morals, customs, and beliefs. In promoting profits as the means to achieve social and economic ends, Terry Möllner, former Board Director, Ben & Jerry's, introduced the idea of objective reality: A red hot stone burns the hand that touches it, regardless of how managers would choose to believe it as being harmless. This is what Terry and I refer to as a "red hot stone phenomenon". In placing *purpose* at an objective level, Bernardo M Villegas, renowned Asian political economist, sees how a baker at Harvard Square taught managers how profits and kindness tangibly manifest the notion of common good (Chapter 3). Bas Kloppenborg, a colleague at Shell plc, reflects on how strategic dialogues and storytelling taught us these lessons: The obvious problems are often the least relevant because the real problems remain hidden from plain sight. To surface what is hidden, ***P W One*** as a framework is employed to evolve and embed a living *purpose* that people can adhere to (Box 3.1).

In preparing firms to *veer* from and *overcome* obstacles, strategic dialogues provide managers with the benefit of harnessing people's diverse talents to meaningfully contribute towards some solutions. This requires honesty for managers to recognise *what they know* and *what they do not*. This encourages open dialogues to create pathways to access learning from others and expand knowledge by learning from one's own experiences and those of others. In this context, the *unknowns* or the *unknowable* are turned into learning opportunities in order to bridge what divides strategy and finance. In bridging this chasm, managers could move from persisting in one's ignorance into making enlightened choices.

Two frameworks are proposed: *TECOP* presents the multiple skills and resources needed to orchestrate work on complex, capital-intensive investments; *Expected Outcomes–Variations Matrix* deconstructs the broad notions of uncertainties in order to specify the sources of uncertainties, ways to gain information, and feasible strategies firms could employ under each market context (Chapter 4). To enable firms to benefit from managerial flexibility under ambiguous contexts, Gary Steel, former member, ABB Group Executive Committee and Paul Collin, former Vice President for Talent, ABB Group, examine the leadership traits and practices that work to enable a successful transformation (Box 4.1). Charles Payne II, veteran in Afghanistan and alumnus of West Point Academy, explains how the US military injects through training and drills certainty in how their units could respond to "surprises" or adverse events. This is a contrarian concept that challenges what some managers do, which is to try to make the uncertain certain (Box 4.2).

Avinash K Dixit and Barry J Nalebuff (2008) describe how some managers behave like woodcutters when evaluating their investments. In cutting trees, they singularly focus on chopping wood and chopping more, until they maximise the pile of wood, as they have conceived in their plan. By ignoring competing claims, managers deem as irrelevant how people could react and respond in kind. In the same token, rival managers would put on their strategic hat and start to behave like generals who aim to cut down an opposing army. Under this mindset, no general would expect the opposing side to stand still and do nothing as the tree did with the woodcutter. Logically, rivals would fight back, work to outmanoeuvre and frustrate the general's moves or scatter to inflict a thousand wounds on a superior force.

In recognising human judgement as the core of decision-making, managers investing large sums on energy assets encounter similar dilemmas. In expanding supplies or divesting, one firm's actions are bound to induce changes that impact rivals' strategic positions and value. Guided by their *purpose*, managers pick the battles by funnelling prospects subject to scrutiny and see how each one, or in combination, could facilitate the firms' **PIVOT**. Supported by enabling *mindsets*, to promote the person's integrity, openness, and commitment, people could enable a decision ecosystem conducive to innovative thinking (Chapter 5). *Veering* in order to avoid adverse outcomes is often mistaken as a licence to engage in constant change or perpetual revolution. On the contrary, working with clarity on the firm's *purpose*, managers seek to gain new information and insights as they *experiment, learn, adapt,* and *act* to inform their investment choices. Towards this end, Rama Velamuri, Dean, Mahindra School of Management, illustrates how such insights could specify to managers what they could *repurpose* and the approaches that they may need to *reframe* as a way to outcompete their rivals or to swim against the biases within (Box 5.1).

In acting like a general, managers frame their decisions to gain strategic and operational flexibility so as to avoid making a loss when conditions go against what they expected or move to profit when markets turn out better than anticipated. This turns risk management on its head: Minimising risk is no longer to reduce variability in outcomes. It is the creation of *real options* where choices of technology or assets, and how they are combined within a portfolio, could embed a *call* on rising returns or a *put* option on expanding liabilities. This requires of managers active management of assets, which contrasts with a one-off "now or never" commitment promoted by conventional capital budgeting.

In employing this dynamic framework for decision-making, managers and policy would tend to diverge in their evaluation: Policy pushes to deploy more renewables, ready to back such effort with generous subsidies or public funding. Managers, on the other hand, would weigh the value of moving early or gain any benefits from deferring investments. Examining within the context of different regulatory and market structures, risk mitigation by making payoffs predictable paradoxically may turn rigid contract obligations, or long-dated subsidies, into the very sources of adverse outcomes.

To remedy this, I propose a strategic de-risking of the value chain: Managers can explicitly quantify the potential deviations of outcomes, where risk reverts to its neutral notion as deviation from what was expected. In some instances, investments are not funded because certain risks are too enormous for markets to provide a satisfactory range of feasible returns. By unpacking the sources of risks and their potential magnitudes, firms and policy could identify how social capital, sovereign aid, and mainstream financing could combine to unlock the benefits from a socially and economically desirable investment (Chapter 6). Working with Antonie de Wilde, former adviser, and Hanan Nagruho, Chief Energy Planner, at Indonesia's BAPPENAS, we illustrate how a value chain *de-risking* could potentially unleash private capital to fund geothermal development. In unlocking specified risks with social capital to fund the "first loss" with resource insurance or sovereign aid, revenue sharing introduces the principle of impact investing to blend social and commercial financing (Box 6.1). Moving risk management from the comforts of the managers' offices, social innovation seeks to involve the community in resolving power thefts in a number of countries, an approach Manweb of Liverpool, United Kingdom, employed four decades ago when the company was privatised. In giving a name and a face to corruption, Anton Perdices, Chief Operating Officer, Aboitiz Power Distribution Utilities, Philippines, provided real-life examples today on how social innovation works and remains relevant (Box 6.2).

III. *BOUnCE* to Win

Managers and policy place too much faith in their numbers, believing that numbers do not lie. As fundamental financial and economic analyses are essential to decision-making, both heavily reliant on the numbers that are used, a closer examination of energy costs is called for. Without a doubt, the concepts behind ***PIVOT*** are operationalised and calibrated by combining human behaviour and the analytical outcomes when

1 Dynamic Decisions

using the tools of financial economics. In adding ***BOUnCE*** to the managers' alphabet soup, I *reframe* how financial and economic analyses are used to inform managerial decisions or policy actions. ***PIVOT*** helps people to understand how the individual's *beliefs* would influence their *outlook*. A generally optimistic disposition may choose to *understand* the world for what it could be rather than start with what it really is. In contrast, a cautious person may let pessimism cloud their outlook so as to see risk aversion (and inaction) as a safe and virtuous trait of managers. Outside these two extremes, most people alternate between bouts of optimism and pessimism to guide them through life's vicissitudes by translating these human traits as gut issues (or *gut feel*).

In this human context, a structured decision process supported by sound strategy informed by rigorous economic and financial analytics would be ideal. However, with advances in techniques and analytical sophistication, managers and policy are nowhere near the savvy demanded by stakeholders. If anything, I posit that with increasing analytical sophistication, managers tend to forego human judgement to become more heavily reliant on algorithms to produce the decisions for them. To partly regain the use of human judgement, I propose validating human *gut feel* with how financial economics could frame how people respond to *incentives*, to *create* and *capture* value, in order to *effect* a commitment.

Lifecycle cost of energy (LCOE) is generally accepted by practitioners as a way to compare costs across different technologies. As a static measure, it experiences similar limitations as net present value (NPV). In essence, it assumes full utilisation of a given capacity. On this basis, the *status quo* is projected to hold true over the life of the asset held to maturity. To its credit, I see in LCOE a useful framework to understand how specific variables fit into the calculation and how each change could alter the lifecycle costs. This offers an alternative use for my purpose: It helps identify principal sources of cost variations as well as the effects of price and volume volatilities. Understanding how the cost structures differ and vary, the benefit of portfolio diversification is made quantifiable. By making the costing explicit, grid price parity's flaw is made apparent in setting "correct levels" of subsidies, resulting in a *green paradox*. Extending the cost comparisons, the cost of CO_2 reduction through supply substitutions is made explicit while serving as a basis for subsequent evaluation of the value to the firm of deferring or accelerating commitments (Chapter 7). Making sense of the complexities of many moving parts, the valuation of geothermal and its many moving parts is made tractable. Antonie de Wilde, credited for expanding Indonesia's geothermal supplies while advising BAPPENAS, illustrates how steam flows and output varies to influence a geothermal field's performance (Box 7.1).

Moving to value investments, I reframe the valuation process as an artful dialogue that seeks to understand the levers of the firm's value. By rearranging how financial information is presented, I aim to connect (even partially) the impact of strategic actions to how the firm's risks, returns, and the stakeholders' value appropriation are impacted. This approach facilitates, in an intuitive manner, answering some of the wicked and inconvenient questions: Are assets mispriced when market value is divorced from its financial performance as the 1990s "dot com" bubble defied gravity for a while? Why are some fast-growing firms, such as aggressive solar companies, going bust? Or why are cash-rich oil and gas companies averse to debt, while cash-strapped start-ups embrace debt with gusto?

In my years in the City of London and the energy industry, the answer may lie in the "theory in use" that drives managers to invest. The "accepted wisdom" faults the methods for the failures of managers, a view which is only partially true but less important. I came around to realising that the deep-seated belief of managers in the power of the herd has more to do with managerial misjudgement.

Driven by what they observe as a "consensus" or "new normal", some managers take leave of the "hard work" in doing and understanding the numbers. In wading deep into this "paradigm", managers miss out on the essential insights on what their actions imply for their finances. As a result, the diligent managers who did their sums would gain these advantages: In understanding their operational hurdles, such as managing their working capital, an eye on receivables could avoid the paradox of excessive cash burns with aggressive growth. Operating under volatile revenues, as oil and gas firms do, prudence would make managers peg their debt at lower levels to provide cash buffer against unexpected disruptions. As a result, with a better understanding of how they monetise and appropriate value, managers could make informed judgements on the trade-offs, paving a way to reconcile or even make compatible competing claims on the firm's cash among stakeholders (Chapter 8).

Managers *believe* that under dynamic energy markets, a competitive system gives limited scope for firms to influence prices or volumes. As a price-taker, firms optimise their value by maximising volume to expand revenues and controlling costs to grow cash margins. Given this *outlook*, managers value a predictable cash flow, where their relevant task is *understood* to avoid risks and continually spend on maintenance capex to ensure optimal operating efficiency and availability. In employing capital budgeting's preferred tool — net present value (NPV) — innovation takes a backseat in favour of securing payoffs with long-term commitments that often come with rigid obligations. In foregoing pricing or volume flexibility, managers abdicate their judgement to the algorithm of the financial tools, making decision-making a "now or never" proposition.

This is when managers would miss a few tricks: In behaving like fund managers, they relegate themselves as "spectators" where NPV conforms to the ideals of bounded risks and value that work well with bonds. However, this becomes problematic when evaluating capital-intensive energy assets that have unbounded risks and returns. To salvage the financial tools' contribution to decision-making, financial analyses are seen to inform managers, not to prescribe decision rules. Used as part of simulations, the discipline that financial analyses possess could help managers to think through these issues: how revenues and costs are earned and interact to produce a profit; the degree to which choices in technology lock in cost structures or provide strategic and operational flexibility; how prospective changes and its impact on the firm's value could be partially understood. In many respects, a simple exercise in doing and understanding the numbers could already go a long way in ascertaining a "natural owner" of an opportunity (Chapter 9).

Energy markets are characterised by oligopolistic rivals. They differ from price-takers in substantive ways. Each rival is large enough to influence volumes, and as they assert their market power, prices are altered by their investments or actions to curtail or expand supplies. In acting like the general, managers recognise that rival firms are directed by people that respond to their actions or even aim to frustrate their moves, with the odd occasion of extending the hand of cooperation. Their *incentives* revolve around gaining strategic advantages by pacing their moves, where the virtue of incremental approach to outflank rivals is valued. To *understand* the battlefield and terrain, they probe and gain information to ascertain how to *create* and *capture* value. Unlike the price-taker, spending on maintenance capex is contingent upon the firm's positioning and prospect to monetise the incremental supply. Operating under this decision ecosystem, managers actively manage their strategic and operational moves to add value. One way to value this managerial flexibility is to use the binomial tree analysis (Chapter 10). To elucidate how this is simplified, I illustrate how managers could adopt this approach using a basic spreadsheet to simulate their scenarios and quantify the outcomes. A *call option value* indicates how much the asset is worth under prevailing conditions if divested prior to maturity (Box 10.1).

IV. Winning Actions

Managers prepare for the unexpected because they seldom possess complete information. What people call *luck* asserts its influence on how managers choose to tackle their challenges to create opportunities. Managers could equip themselves and create their own luck by building the ability to recognise opportunities from the unexpected and adaptively act on their *lucky breaks*. This they do by integrating **PIVOT** and **BOUnCE** to configure their strategic actions. In re-examining the foundations under which the business is built and how it pursues emerging opportunities, a *foundational pivot* serves as a starting point to (re)build resilience. Before firms could successfully transform itself, managers need to understand the resources it possesses, what it could access, and some inkling as to how it could be redeployed.

The kneejerk response, however, is to cut and reduce rather than *repurpose* to the extent possible. Through a process of experimentation, new sets of information are gained to clarify, at least in the managers' mind, what *transitional pivots* may pave the paths to a future characterised by success, however one may define it. In planning for such transitions, managers look at alternative paths that result from how they seek to *reframe* their *purpose* as a firm. This differs from the cost-cutters who tend to dwell on making their business cost-effective, often losing sight that the market had moved elsewhere. In making some of the more decisive moves, managers are confronted with the dilemma to *adapt for longer* or to *disrupt by reconfiguring* one's market. In making extant goods or services obsolete, the sources of strategic advantages are redefined, also shifting the way people think the value they would attribute to a business (Chapter 11).

In my interactions with three Chief Executives, they see in *energy transitions* from their vantage perspectives how they aim to create their profitable niches: Eric Francia, ACEN, complements their project structuring and financing advantages with what technical partners could bring to enhance their regional reach and ability to monetise low-carbon opportunities (Box 10.1). Jorge Consunji, DM Consunji and Cristina C Gotianun, Semirara Mining and Power, focus on how the largest Philippine coal company could *repurpose* its resources adaptively, with an eye on coal's evolving prospects and the pace that emerging opportunities mature (Box 10.2). Anjaney

Borwankar, Navozyme, brings lessons from the maritime industry on how digital technologies and data science are changing the market by providing real-time feedback to consumers and suppliers. Applied to energy, together with his colleague Giulio Toscani, they posit that a similar transformation is in store for energy by enhancing the suppliers' capacity to shape their offerings to meet how consumers would feedback their preferences through real-time purchases and procurement decisions (Box 10.3).

My Reflections

The process of committing my thoughts to paper is in itself a process of learning and enlightenment. Reconnecting with people of greater intellect and benefiting from their generosity, I managed to incorporate their insights and their counterfactual experiences to enrich specific aspects of *Dynamic Decisions*.

I focus on the managers in their human capacity as the object of my study in managerial decisions. Drawing on the various academic disciplines, I benefited from the works of intellectual giants in political economy, behavioural economics, financial economics, and management. Their contributions are cited in each chapter, together with the practitioners I highlighted in feature articles, and those I quoted directly based on my conversations and exchanges. Taken together, their thoughts and insights moved me to see decision science as an artful judgement by humans of goodwill, redefining what it could and should encompass.

In the specific arena of *energy transition* and managerial decision-making under ambiguities, I propose the following spheres that encourage managers and policy to *re-examine* the "accepted wisdoms" and even *reframe* the way decisions are undertaken. Specifically:

1. The obvious problems are probably not always the most relevant challenges managers and policy would need to resolve. A deeper understanding of why things are what they are and how humans interact could uncover the real problems worth resolving.

    Society and politicians have apparently formed a "consensus" that climate change is an existential threat. In looking for a solution, "one political solution that fits all" flows naturally as a given, finding its way to the doorsteps of energy firms awaiting actions. Most managers would buckle at the enormity of the tasks. The adept managers would seek to work around this burden with innovations that *repurpose*, *reframe*, and *reconfigure* and how they produce and serve humanity's needs for energy as a way to create these profitable future niches *today*.

This requires a heavy dose of realism or the ability to recognise what objective reality encompasses. In an era of post-truth, an oxymoron in my view, people learn the hard way when they fail to recognise what Terry Möllner and I refer to as the "red hot stone phenomenon".

In promoting technology champions, policy chooses to ignore the benefits of dynamic markets as an effective arbiter of resource allocation. In leaving managers to freely respond to emerging opportunities, the inherent values of technologies within a supply portfolio are decided within the contexts of markets, available resources, and the interactions of rival firms. Consequently, value chain de-risking, as I illustrated with geothermal exploration and development, could unleash private and social capital more effectively than direct subsidies set by policy with (non-existent) omniscience.

2. In the company of committed and credible rivals, how markets operate and how firms choose to respond among oligopolists form a contextual decision ecosystem that alters "accepted wisdoms" in optimising energy investments.

In a world of dominant energy incumbents, the actions of one firm impact the value of others, even if managers choose to do nothing. In these evolving dynamics, what holds true before may no longer work today or in the future. For this reason, as the energy system incorporates more renewables, the continued relevance of coal or gas cannot be taken for granted. Obsolescence is a prospect that managers and policy would need to evaluate explicitly and incorporate into their expectations.

In the good old days when regulation "protected" the financial viability of energy firms, incurring maintenance capex was a must to maximise output by ensuring operational efficiency of assets. In a dynamic and transitioning energy market, this decision is now contingent on the asset's continued viability. In my simulations, benign neglect is as valid as spending on maintenance capex, depending on the asset's continued role in the supply mix. An obsolescing asset, such as coal in a decarbonised European energy market, is hardly despatched and left underutilised. Improving its operating efficiency would simply expand its unused capacity, thereby using good money to chase after an elusive opportunity that has little prospect of being monetised.

3. To undertake a transition in energy systems, managers and policy may have to first embark on re-examining their basic beliefs and understanding of ambiguities, so that enabling *mindsets* could facilitate business and market transformation.

   Strategy and finance are on a collision course in bringing firms to a future of promise. While strategy acts to change the course of a firm's trajectory, a process fraught with uncertainties, finance follows a prescribed path dictated by capital budgeting that rewards the certain, the *known*, and the *knowable*. Market ambiguities, however, would reward managerial flexibility so that managers could pursue alternative pathways to profitability when circumstances demand.

   Moorburg hard coal power station in Hamburg, Germany, is a case in point. Designed and built in 2015, managers anticipated to earn handsome payoffs from the most modern facility for at least three decades. With tightening regulation (Wehrmann, 2021), the 1,600 MW power plant ceased commercial operations by 2020 and was shuttered on July 7, 2021, for good (Renew Economy, 2021). Looking back to my simulations conducted around 2015, I observed a disturbing pattern from the outcomes: Coal supplies are eased out of the power market as gas displaces coal in setting power prices. Coal suffers in two ways: revenues fall from lower power prices, given that gas is cheaper; volume supplied from coal declines disproportionately as to render coal financially unviable (Barcelona, 2017). That this simulated outcome is played out in full view, sooner than I anticipated, is indeed a sobering thought for me.

   In Moorburg's case, extant facilities and infrastructure are planned to be *repurposed* to produce green hydrogen from wind power. The jury is still out on how this pivot would work out, subject to how managers would adaptively respond to changing policy moves.

4. Innovation starts at the periphery where "mavericks" pursue alternative ways to get things done. Operating outside the mainstream, change occurs out of

sight, nurtured by neglect by policy and rivals, only to evolve to gain substance to disrupt or successfully *reconfigure* the market.

"Horse Manure Crisis" of the 19th century vintage is often cited for its abject lessons in the limits of the "expert's foresight". In projecting the status quo to the future, managers and policy act by tinkering at the margins, often to preserve what is known. With policy relentlessly aiming to deliver on an objective, whatever that may be, people are seen to settle for "one political solution that fits all" to simplify the advocacy. Adept managers would weigh the cost of compliance, examine the scope for bypassing the constraints that such policy imposes, and pursue strategic actions that remove their businesses from the scope of regulatory actions.

In recognising what the creative human mind can conjure, one would only fully comprehend how opportunities are created under the ambiguities of transitioning energy systems by simulating how actions among rival firms and policy would interact. In testing a number of feasible combinations, I come to the view that strategic advantages are transient and amenable to being shaped (and reshaped) by human actions. To evaluate these adaptive actions and incorporate them in strategic decisions, I benefit from the works of Benoit Chevalier-Roignant, who kindly commented on how real options and game-theoretic reasoning could inform managerial decisions, which is described in his book co-authored with Lenos Trigeorgis. Connecting this to behavioural economics and decision science, how imperfect humans tackle their life challenges rest with individual initiatives, made feasible and impactful when undertaken in functioning and dynamic markets.

5. To make markets work, people are guided by principles and a minimum of trust, where a modicum of acceptable behaviour is understood and expected from participants.

In promoting an adaptive approach to decision-making, some have approached me to know if this is a formula for chaos and anarchy, given that managers and policy can simply change their minds as circumstances warrant. On the contrary, a minimum set of principles are required to engender trust among the market participants. Humans, as Amartya Sen and Elinor Ostrum recognise, are capable of informed judgement. While some may nitpick on the relativism of virtues, Bernardo M Villegas would remind people as to how people instinctively behave according to what natural law prescribes as a way of tempering human excesses. In many ways, humans are seen to forego immediate ingratiation, or even work against their obvious interests, to achieve higher goals, as Richard Thaler would propose.

The question of subsidies and the exploitation of the commons come to mind. While subsidies are subject to abuse and the commons are at times overexploited, human communities act to temper such greed. When subsidies are patently losing their purpose, people coax regulators to rescind as they did in Europe and the United States with solar power and some renewables. The dim view of human greed proves to be an exception, with more initiatives succeeding in reversing environmental damage or quietly "greening cities" (Alexandra, 2019). In the midst of the polarised climate advocacies, the substantive progress some firms and industries are making, with nations greening barren land or deserts, is at times lost in making a case for or against climate actions. In the realities where managers reside, how one could turn such "existential threats" into viable opportunities is what pushes people to innovate and pursue pathways with informed judgement.

In the course of writing *Dynamic Decisions*, I benefited from standing on the shoulders of intellectual predecessors, whose reputation looms large in their fields and paves the way for my work. The insights I gained I credit to them for pointing the way for me. How I proceed, at times faltering, is down to my own limitations and imperfections as a practitioner–scholar.

I made a conscious effort to open my thoughts to different perspectives. In reaching out to the youth, I find my interactions with Margarida Madaleno enlightening with her queries while reviewing a number of chapters. After completing her PhD in Economics at the London School of Economics, United Kingdom, Margarida joined as a post-doctoral fellow at the Catolica Lisbon School of Business and Economics, Portugal. Our daughter Ainhoa Itziar, Contents Managing Editor at *Hello* online, provided a reality check on how intelligible my writing is to her generation and audience outside my usual haunts in the energy industry, investment banking, and academe. James Greenhalgh, doing work on marine conservation, gives his perspectives on how environmental issues are tackled in the frontline.

Rene Domingo and Nieves Confesor, professors at the Asian Institute of Management, Philippines, Benoit Chevalier-Roignant, emlyon business school, a global business school based in France, and Bernardo M Villegas and Rolando Dy, professors at the University of Asia and the Pacific, Philippines, provided useful suggestions and comments on some chapters. I enjoyed my chats with Pedro Nueno, my professor while pursuing my MBA at IESE Business School and Founding President of China Europe International Business School, China. From his vantage perspective, his long experience in China injects a commercial reality check on some of the West's ambitions on rapid decarbonisation of energy systems. In different contexts, Jesus Estanislao, Chair, Institute for Solidarity in Asia, and former Finance Secretary, Philippines, himself a prolific writer on good governance, is always generous with his time and wisdom. During his visits to Spain at IESE Business School or during my stays in Manila, Philippines, we endeavour to catch up and spend time for an update. Romeo Bernardo, former Undersecretary of Finance, Philippines, can be relied on to update me on the pace of change in his nick of the wood. Ricardo Mollo, Founder of Brain Business School, Brazil, is always quick to encourage me to give a Latin twist to the ambiguities of how decisions are made at Latin American businesses. Luis Jover, always patient and attentive, ensured the timely completion of the various iterations of Franz Heukamp's Foreword.

In the political and regulatory spheres, numerous politicians work to uplift their people. I am fortunate to come in contact with people of all persuasions and ideological inclinations. In the midst of delivering on their agenda, I find those I engage with stand ready to extend a helping hand. In varying degrees, their instinct is to expand the realms of possibilities, making diplomacy an important plank of international and intranational relations. Among regulators, similar aplomb is essential to reconcile colliding interests, or at the very least, to get opposing parties to agree to disagree while keeping open the doors for small steps to be taken. Without naming them individually, politics gave me a more realistic appreciation of what economics can optimise and how politics could maximise possibilities.

I had ample opportunities to test some of the ideas that I propose in *Dynamic Decisions*. Albert G Mateo, as Head of the school and Mary Grace S Reynoso, Managing Director, School of Executive Education and Lifelong Learning, Asian Institute of Management, are early enthusiasts. Roderick M Planta, Assistant Secretary, National Economic Development Authority (NEDA), Philippines, agreed to include these ideas in a custom programme that I directed for their technocrats, with Asian Development Bank's generous support. The interactions with participants enriched my views as well as those with the participating faculty: Nieves Confesor, Rene Domingo, Christopher Monterola, Fernando Y Roxas, and Manuel de Vera. Acting as resource persons, Cesar Antonio V Purisima, former Philippine Finance Secretary, Raphael PM "Popo" Lotilla, Philippine Energy Secretary, and Vaughn Montes, former Board Director, Development Bank of the Philippines, provided me with an inside view on how policymaking works in an emerging market. Frency C Importado and Criselda V Candelaria, through administrative contributions, made the programme run smoothly for participants and professors.

Julius Caesar Parreñas, Daiwa Institute of Research, Tokyo, Japan, made some of my counterintuitive ideas accessible to Asia-Pacific Financial Forum — Sustainable Finance Development Network and Asia Pacific Economic Cooperation (APEC) Business Advisory Council. Richard Mills' Asia CEO Forum facilitated my interactions, with Mitzi Borromeo moderating, to explore viable approaches to sustainability with practitioners. Across the Atlantic, Narendra Rustagi, Director, Centre for Global Business Studies, School of Business, Howard University, Washington DC, created a platform that facilitated my engagement with academics, including scholars from emerging markets.

A benefit that academics enjoy is the openness that they are received by people who are sincerely interested in making intellectual pursuits relevant to their life and to those in their communities. I benefited from the gift of feedback, with a number of people contributing their wisdom through interviews or writing articles that are featured in this book. A number of them also manifest their encouragement by offering their early praises and describing how *Dynamic Decisions* is relevant to them and their communities. Their contributions are specifically cited in the relevant areas.

A number of people facilitated my work with the featured companies: Jorge Soley, Professor at IESE Business School, Spain, helped in making the arrangements with Antonio Brufau Niubó of Repsol, Spain. Angel Bautista and Jalal Chakkour Akhrif coordinated the work within Repsol. Tatjana Hödl ensured that my communications with Michael Laengle, RAG of Austria, was promptly attended to. Antonie de Wilde kindly made sure Montty Girianna, Indonesia, was up to date with my progress and latest views on his country's efforts in developing alternative sources of energy. Ricardo

S Consunji, DM Consunji, Philippines, ensured that the contributions from Jorge A Consunji, Chief Executive Officer, DM Consunji, and Cristina Consunji Gotianun, Chief Operating Officer, Semirara Mining and Power Corporation, Philippines, hurdled the appropriate internal reviews. Vincent Tobias, Ayala Corporation, Philippines, helped in arranging the feature article with Eric Francia, Chief Executive Officer, ACEN, Philippines, with Irene Maranan and Lenie Lectura assisting.

Chua Hong Koon, publishing director, together with the editors of World Scientific, Jane Sayers, Koe Shi Ying, and Nimal Koliyat ensured the meticulous review of the manuscript, and its copy editing and formatting. The book cover was designed by Lionel Seow with suggestions provided by our daughters, Jasmine and Chantal Beatriz, together with a number of those who contributed their works to this book. Lee Hooi Yean for coordinating the book's promotion and marketing.

I continue to benefit from the wisdom imparted by my late professors at various stages of my academic formation: Patrick H "Paddy" Miller, IESE Business School, whose choice architecture places leadership at the centre of employing finance, strategy, and decision science to inform the managers' strategic moves; Harry L Hansen, Harvard Business School and IESE Business School, for his lasting influence on my perspectives on business and society, particularly in making the complex simple and profound; Alan Harrison, Cranfield School of Management, United Kingdom, for sharing his experience in transitioning from practice to academe; Ruperto Alonzo, School of Economics, University of the Philippines, for entrusting his course on project evaluation. In his final days, we re-examined how economics, finance, and strategy, could and should contribute to informing managerial and policy actions. Jesus M Zulueta, late Chair of ZMG Ward Howell, and late ambassador Jose V Romero, left their legacies marked by humanistic ideals.

From their celestial banquet, my late parents Santiago A.T. Barcelona and Magdalena Go Lieng, and late parents-in-law, Antonio Viason Carballo and Clotilde Diaz Ortega, have left deep imprints that set a high bar for today's sustainability practitioners.

Box 0.1: Lluis Bertran Rafecas

Energy is a strategic factor for the economy. Ricardo G Barcelona is an economist who understands this relationship since his early professional life, where he specialised in energy. Ricardo lives between Manila, Philippines, and Barcelona, Spain. This gives him an in-depth international perspective that cuts across the developed and emerging economies.

I met Ricardo in October 2018, courtesy of our common friend, Luis Calvo. I knew Luis professionally at Naturgy, a major Spanish energy group and through our work at International Gas Union (IGU). Through our travels and in confronting the day-to-day challenges, Luis and I became true and inseparable friends. In a similar way, this is how I befriended Ricardo, through Luis, where our common efforts and interests in energy matters united us. Ricardo is a friend who does his work well. He is prepared to contribute to orient policy that facilitates economic development. The desired outcome that society aspires to is achieved with the stakeholders' contribution, particularly to equitably appropriate its benefits. This is facilitated under a strategic and political ecosystem whereby the energy policy aims to benefit society as a whole.

Energy policy is important to achieve economic development because it multiplies the capacity to produce goods and services. We can place this in the context of two centuries ago when the steam engine was invented. Up to that point, human work was performed with animal power, which was the basis for production and wealth creation. I refer to this as the age when muscular energy — "in-corpore" power — was relied upon to get things done.

This is a source of energy that each individual possesses. With eight hours of daily work, one can quantify how this energy is converted into products. A simple example is to gather firewood in the forest during the Middle Ages. The energy one expends is converted into its equivalent in quantity of firewood that is later burned to keep a feudal castle or household heated at 21°C. The feudal lord would need between 200 and 300 subjects to enjoy this convenience at the manor.

With the introduction of "ex-corpore" power, which no longer employs muscular energy, that relies on inanimate sources of energy, two effects on society and human well-being occur: Capacity to produce expanded dramatically. Human efforts are substantially reduced, thereby liberating human labour for other more fulfilling pursuits.

To put this transformation in today's context, an average European household consumes 45,000 kWh of energy yearly, the sum of electricity, gas, and petrol for vehicles used. This is equivalent to the feudal lord's energy consumption that required the work of 200 subjects to fulfil. In effect, the luxury that a feudal lord enjoyed during the Middle Ages is within reach of an average European household.

It is evident that how "ex-corpore" energy is managed, how labour is employed, how economic prosperity is accessed by people, and how society evolves are inextricably linked. This prospect of liberating people, such as the medieval subjects from providing muscular energy, to pursue with greater freedom and prosperity could indeed be transformative if not disruptive to the hold on the reins of societal authority and power structures. This is the context that a transitioning energy market could provide to governments to pursue policies that improve their citizens' well-being. This is at the core of what is being proposed in this work.

The transformation of how energy is going to be managed is multifaceted and is of great complexity. It affects a large number of industries, where the processes and their effects are of a long-term nature. This is where a policy-driven transformation is problematic under modern democracies where governments are changed every four to eight years. In contrast, some of the changes in the energy sector may take decades, if not longer, to achieve.

The changes in energy activities are progressive rather than drastic or abrupt. The first motive lies in how managers make decisions involving investments. In a democracy, the contributions and opinions of minority groups are respected. At a minimum, they are consulted on available alternatives. The second reason recognises the influence of past decisions where investments in infrastructure and assets have a long operating life, usually ranging from 20–50 years. For this reason, the decisions that political leaders can take today are unlikely to be fully realised during their years in office. These are long-term strategic decisions whose outcomes could only be realised in the distant future. Partly for this reason, day-to-day political decisions in a democracy tend to prioritise decisions with immediate impact and results instead of tackling uncertain and difficult strategic decisions. This approach often results in sub-optimal decisions.

An example of the slow pace of energy transition is to examine how energy usage evolved from firewood to today's hybrid system. Firewood was replaced by coal, which was displaced by oil. Oil was replaced by natural gas and, in parallel, nuclear and renewables displace both oil and the remaining use of coal in power generation. Throughout this evolutionary process, the primary energy mix comprises the older fossil fuels coexisting with the more recent use of renewables. The process of displacing coal, however, appears as a never-ending task even after 150 years since oil was introduced and a century since gas was used to light London's streets.

In emerging energy markets, firewood has not been totally replaced. In India and in some African countries, firewood remains an important fuel for cooking and source of heat. The Western world, having largely used fossil fuels and power, has not totally abandoned firewood. Sunday barbecues still use wood, while log cabins in isolated areas are still heated by burning logs in the fireplace.

These observations underline the reality that the transition to renewables, which was started several decades ago, is unlikely to happen rapidly. In thinking about energy transition, one should consider how the productive capacity of the economy is sustained, while not impairing extant assets' profitability, when moving forward with renewables. The balancing act involves reducing carbon emissions, sustaining growth, and promoting society's well-being.

This complex problem is well identified under the Paris Agreement that signatories promised to adhere to in 2015. Subsequent climate-related agreements continue to clarify or even suggest some approaches to meet the carbon emission reduction targets. The reality, however, is a continually evolving set of suggested actions that individual contracts may, or may not, incorporate into their climate action programme. This is where governments should tackle the challenges of how to combine economic development, with climate change impact, and more globally, how energy usage would impact the environment.

Ricardo's works propose some useful tools to understand the policy and financial conditions around energy transitions that governments and managers may consider in formulating their strategies. There is no single formula that would satisfy everybody and every market. For this reason, each market and the firms operating within those markets would need to combine their strategic approaches according to the resources that are accessible and their respective capabilities.

Seen within the context of the Paris Agreement, specified targets are set for reducing carbon emissions by 2050. Cognisant of the long gestation and operating life of energy assets, today's investment decisions leave very limited scope for error. What is invested today is likely to be around in the next 20–30 years, a period that brings the timeframe to 2050, when all reduction targets are to be met.

I concur with Ricardo on his observations about how energy markets tend to transition. I would highlight two basic propositions:

> The energy industry has always been undergoing transition and is prepared for the next phase of its evolution. This would, as it had in the past, follow a pace that will be driven by economic as well as policy actions, the latter encompassing measures related to climate change.
>
> The supply mix, in varying degrees, is likely to combine all available sources of primary energy that would provide the bases for a sustainable future.

In my view, the set of policy actions would be preferably conducted with an eye on financial viability and another on the virtues of coordinated moves by firms and governments, as needed. In this context, dynamic markets and how they interact with regulatory processes may allow managers (and policy as well) to see that cooperation is compatible with rivalries among firms.

These perspectives are pragmatic and realistic. Each primary energy has its pros and cons. In the same manner that humans do not eliminate the firewood used by their ancestors and repurpose it for a more leisurely application such as Sunday barbecues, fossil fuels may continue to serve future energy needs. Admittedly, the proportion of coal and oil may fall as well as natural gas, as they are replaced by renewables, synthetic gases, and biofuels. The variations in their use are subject to how costs, technology, and resources would evolve and how managers would respond to policy actions.

The case for natural gas is compelling. I posit that natural gas is not a transition source of energy. Rather, it would facilitate the major energy transformation that humanity has ever experienced. Gas forms part of the present energy mix. It will form part of the mix during the evolving transition that has already started. It will continue to be a part of a sustainable energy mix of the future. I offer the following evidence to support my assertions:

- Natural gas emits significantly less CO_2 after combustion. This provides advantages when coal or petrol is substituted. It reduces CO_2 emissions by up to 60% relative to coal, while keeping fuel costs roughly unchanged. Hence, through substitution, environmental performance is significantly improved.
- Chemical composition of natural gas is similar to renewable sources of gas such as biogas, synthetic gas, methanisation of hydrogen, organic and agricultural waste, or hydrogen. This trait allows renewable sources of gas to replace natural gas, with minimal adaptation of equipment.

This substitution provides enormous flexibility for the continued presence of natural gas in a sustainable energy future. The risk of technological or economic obsolescence is also reduced substantially.

The future of human society would continue to evolve. The energy sources that will be available will depend on the energy policy that governments would choose to develop or adopt in this decade. The energy mix will likewise evolve during this transition according to the pace of economic development and the policy stance on climate action. It is clear to me that wind, hydro, photovoltaic power, and gases will play significant roles. In equal measure, I see both natural and renewable gas playing a central role in ensuring society's economic viability and in limiting the impact of climate change.

*****

This article was contributed by Lluis Bertran Rafecas while serving as the Secretary General of the International Gas Union (IGU). In our various conversations, Lluis advances the proposition that natural and renewable gas will be principal contributors to a sustainable energy future. Prior to assuming his post at IGU, Lluis held senior leadership roles at Gas Natural Fenosa, renamed as Naturgy, based in Barcelona, Spain. Lluis was Director of Planning for residential markets and small- and medium-sized firms and Director General for Europe.

Bibliography

Alexandra, J. (2019). For green cities to become mainstream, we need to learn from local success stories and scale up. *The Conversation*, July 8, 2019.

Awerbuch, S. (2006). Portfolio-based electricity generation planning: Policy implications for renewables and energy security. *Mitigation and Adaptation Strategies for Global Change*, 11, 693–710.

Barcelona, R. G. (2015). Renewable energy with volatile prices: Why NPV fails to tell the whole story. *Journal of Applied Corporate Finance*, 27(1), Winter 2015, 101–109.

Barcelona, R. G. (2017). *Energy Investments: An Adaptive Approach to Profiting from Uncertainties*. London: Palgrave Macmillan.

Bar-Lev, D., and Katz, S. (1976). A portfolio approach to fossil fuel procurement in the electric utility industry. *Journal of Finance*, XXXI, 3, 933–947.

Battersby, A. (2021). Shell advances Philippines LNG dream. *Upstream*, March 30, 2021.

Chevalier-Roignant, B. and Trigeorgis, L. (2011). *Competitive Strategy: Options and Games*. Cambridge, MA: The MIT Press, Massachusetts Institute of Technology.

Corporate Finance Institute (CFI) (2021). *Project Finance — A Primer*. Vancouver, Canada: Global Corporate Finance Society.

Dixit, A. K. and Nalebuff, B. J. (2008). *The Art of Strategy: A Game Theorist's Guide to Success in Business and Life*. New York, NY and London, UK: W. W. Norton & Company.

Dixit, A. K. and Pindyck, R. S. (1994). *Investment under Uncertainty*. Princeton, NJ: Princeton University Press.

Institutional Investors (II) (1995). The 1995 All-Europe Research Team. *Institutional Investors*, February 1995.

Institutional Investors (II) (1996). The 1996 All-Europe Research Team. *Institutional Investors*, February 1996.

Institutional Investors (II) (1997). The 1997 All-Europe Research Team. *Institutional Investors*, February 1997.

Markowitz, H. M. (1991). *Portfolio Selection: Efficient Diversification of Investments*, second edition. Oxford, UK: Blackwell Publishing.

Ostrum, E. (2015). *Governing the Commons: The Evolution of Institutions for Collective Actions*. Cambridge: Cambridge University Press.

Renew Energy (2021). German coal plant closes after just six years, to produce green hydrogen from Wind, *Renew Energy*, July 9, 2021.

Rivier Abbad, J. (2010). Electricity market participation of wind farms: The success story of Spanish pragmatism. *Energy Policy*, July 2010, 38(7), 3174–3179.

Roques, F., Newberry, D. M. and Nuttall, W. (2006). Chapter 11: Portfolio optimisation and utilities' investments in liberalised power markets. *Analytical Methods for Energy Diversity & Security*, 2008, 219–246.

Royal Dutch Shell (RDS) (2021). *Gas-to-Liquids*. https://www.shell.com/energy-and-innovation/natural-gas/gas-to-liquids.html. Accessed: June 20, 2021.

Rubinstein, M. (1994). Implied Binomial Trees. *Journal of Finance*, 49(3) (July 1994), 771–818.

Rubinstein, M. (2006). *A History of the Theory of Investments: My Annotated Bibliography*. Hoboken, NJ: John Wiley & Sons, Inc.

Sen, A. (2000). *Development as Freedom*. New York: Anchor Books.

Sharpe, W. F. (2007). *Investors and Markets: Portfolio Choices, Asset Prices, and Investment Advice*. Princeton, NJ and Oxford, UK: Princeton University Press.

Thaler, R. H. (2015). *Misbehaving: The Making of Behavioural Economics*. New York and London: W. W. Norton & Company.

Trelleborg (2021). LNG Vessel Bunkering. https://www.klawlng.com/lng-applications/lng-vessel-bunkering/. Accessed: June 20, 2021.

Wehrmann, B. (2021). Bumpy conclusion to Germany's landmark coal act clears way to next energy transition chapters. *Clean Energy Wire*, July 3, 2021.

I
Understanding Energy *PIVOT*

Chapter 1
From Impasse to *PIVOT*

Energy transitions follow recursive processes that are tentative, operating in systems under flux and subject to ambiguities. Notwithstanding this reality, managers and policy default to mitigating risks by reasserting predictability in outcomes rather than creating arenas to nurture emerging opportunities. As networks and resources are continually *reconfigured*, managers and policy err in employing *static tools* and *mindsets* to inform their strategic or policy moves. Perhaps, not surprisingly, outcomes deviate from what managers expect, while policy produces results opposed to its objectives. To remedy these paradoxes, a *mindset transition*, often ignored, would be needed. This enables managers to adaptively navigate the vagaries of interacting factors within dynamic markets, logistics, and technologies. To strategically respond to these challenges, managers can *PIVOT*. By informing their decisions with strategic insights, managers could *repurpose* resources, *reframe* strategic moves, and *reconfigure* processes and networks to outcompete rivals. By making these moves, managers could create arenas in which emerging opportunities could flourish.

1
Introduction

Three chief executives may have the date May 26, 2021, indelibly etched in their minds. Shareholders made Darren Wood of ExxonMobil and Michael Wirth of Chevron reckon with their climate impacts (Saiyid, 2021). A Dutch local court ordered Shell plc, with Ben van Beurden at its helm, to cut its carbon emissions by 45% by 2030 relative to its 2019 levels (BBC, 2021). How the whole saga reframes climate accountability is described as follows (Crowley, 2021):

> Just five years ago, environmental activists were limited to waving placards outside of annual meetings and to the odd shareholder proposal, inevitably rebuffed by the boards and management teams. On Wednesday [May 26, 2021] by contrast, stock investors ousted two ExxonMobil Corp directors seen as insufficiently attuned to the threat of climate change, while Chevron Corp shareholders voted for a proposal to compel the company to reduce pollution by its customers. Shell plc was ordered to slash emissions harder and faster than planned by a Dutch court.

Roger Harrabin, a multi-awarded journalist at London's *Financial Times*, recognised that Shell plc may as well appeal the judgement and could win. Shell plc did appeal the judgement within weeks (Shell, 2021), while announcing a series of low carbon initiatives to reduce its carbon footprint (Krauss, 2021; Hall, 2021). However, the precedent was unmistakable: It is "not good enough for firms to comply with the law on their emissions — in an extraordinary case like this, they have to comply with global climate policy too" (BBC, 2021). While not violating any Dutch law, Shell plc is made responsible for fulfilling the Dutch government's undertakings under the Paris Agreement (Baazil and Lombrana, 2021).

For managers, a new facet of climate liability is introduced by the Dutch District Court of the Hague ruling. The "concrete effect on the international community is yet to be seen. With that said, the lack of perfection does not diminish the significance of the decision; not only has it opened the doors of the legal arena to corporate climate liability, but has also invited climate justice to the table — and just in the nick of time"

(Aurer, 2021). On the corporate front, Shell unified its structure, dropped "Royal Dutch" from its name, and moved its domicile to the United Kingdom (Hurst, 2021).

Arguably, stakeholders are empowered to monitor compliance, even in the absence of agreed guidelines (Reuters, 2021). An aggressive *Net Zero by 2050*, proposed by the International Energy Agency (2021), bolstered these claims in spite of serious reservations on the roadmap (Yuka and Paul, 2021; PEI, 2021). What is certain is that managers and climate advocates are in for interesting times, with their work cut out for them.

To some, *energy transition* is now understood as a singular pursuit of *the net zero carbon* agenda (EC, 2019). Popularly understood, this is achieved when fossil fuels are replaced by renewables (S&P, 2020) and growth is decoupled from resource use. Add to this social equity and inclusiveness and society's success is judged from an amorphous notion such as "leaving no one behind" whose outcomes are "harder to see" (Esty, 2017).

Today's framing of *energy transition* is no longer simply a "change in the primary form of energy consumption of a given society" (Cleveland and Morris, 2014). What remains unchanged is this reality: Given its "technical and infrastructural imperatives, and because of numerous social and economic implications, energy transitions are generally protracted affairs … *demanding* persistent dedication and considerable patience" (Smil, 2010, *italics added*). Under this nuanced decision ecosystem, the "ideological underpinnings that define the managers' or policymakers' world views" have to be made explicit (Barcelona, 2017).

Three decades of slow progress have brought the climate conversation back to where it started: In making renewables and electric vehicles (EV) competitive with fossil fuels, a transition to sustainable energy is needed. However, with claims of solar power outcompeting coal (Chrobak, 2021), one is made to wonder why a *sustainable energy system* remains elusive. One answer is found in how "humans tend to associate *growth* with *progress*, and with growth, more carbon emissions would follow." To reverse this unsustainable practice, "individuals and society have to downshift its consumption of carbon-intensive products and services by curtailing its use, say to the 1950's level" (Krumdieck, 2020).

Counterfactual evidence, however, offers a more optimistic view of humanity's creative power to shape a prosperous future.

The 19th century "Horse Manure Crisis" in London (Johnson, 2021) saw the replacement of animal with mechanical power to do work that ushered in the Industrial Revolution. Mobility saw horse carriages give way to Henry Ford's Model T and cut short the inroads of Ferdinand Porsche's popular electric vehicles (DoE, 2014). Rather than be buried in horse manure, London and most major cities grew and even prospered.

A century and a half of dynamic human innovation, aided by the freedom of markets, made societies flourish while getting cleaner and healthier. These contrasts are striking:

In abdicating control to an "all-knowing" regulator, a central authority is seen to permit, prohibit, or enforce the rules (OECD, 1997). Policy mandated change usually fails to combat "existential threats" (Howes et al., 2017; Harvey, 2021) with partial measures that prove insufficient (Chouinard et al., 2011). In reengineering the environment (Sinn, 2012), policy produced paradoxical outcomes (Ploeg, 2012): Generous subsidies hindered widescale deployment of renewables (Amram and Kulatilaka, 2009) or slowed technological innovations (Barcelona, 2017).

Human innovation (Reader et al., 2016) creatively resolved societal challenges (Llardo and Nielsen, 2018) when people are free to pursue appropriate solutions. When new capacity permits for renewables were auctioned, bid prices for solar and wind power fell sharply, while volumes grew rapidly (IRENA, 2019b). More aggressive bids and higher volumes are seen in markets that adopted an auction of new permits (Rossell and Sanchez, 2021).

While great strides are achieved by managers by innovating, particularly from a strategic and technological aspect, old habits die hard. Policy and some managers eerily default into grand gestures that mandate "one political solution fits all". Reliant on sophisticated economic models, omniscience is assumed by ignoring uncertainties, particularly for models that specify the effects of temperature on economic growth (Newell et al., 2021).

This is where policy and managers diverge in their prescriptions for a sustainable future. As policy takes a linear path to an aspired outcome, managers innovate around policy and other constraints to best resolve the human challenges that they face (The Heritage Foundation, 2021). As the "Horse Manure Crisis" has taught, what policy saw as insurmountable challenges, adept managers were able to innovate their way through to profits and wealth.

What divides them is a *mindset* that veers away from locking-in rigid obligations. In valuing managerial flexibility, managers embrace ambiguity. In applying this strategic view, *Porter's Innovation Offsets* (Clarke *et al.*, 1994) resonate with what I see as enabling managers to ***PIVOT*** to tomorrow's profitable niches. I posit that when faced with stringent demands on carbon emissions, managers are well advised to adapt new technologies and even *reconfigure* their business. In this way, they take the business out of the regulatory scope, by reducing their carbon footprint while ensuring their financial viability, as Repsol aims to do (see Box 1.1).

To achieve this, how managers respond to the diffused notions that describe sustainability (Jones, 2018) and *energy transition* would need a serious rethink. Managers could start to articulate a purpose that is informed by insights derived from a deep understanding of the context of decisions and the markets. In transforming the business, managers could expand opportunities by looking "outward toward the health and vitality of market and society in which the organisation operates" (Hoffman, 2018). Recognising the ambiguities, agile managers veer and adapt, in order to overcome obstacles, before taking irreversible commitments. Rather than seeing policy as a "nuisance", managers could constructively shape how business and society could work as mutually reinforcing forces for good.

In adapting to a *dynamic mindset*, managers will have to recognise that the world does not stay constant. Unfortunately, some classical economists premise their propositions under *ceteris paribus*. By doing so, they implicitly believe the future will be unchanged so that what they assume today will remain true tomorrow. Under transitioning energy systems, where the future is likely to be different from the present, managers are bound to err in their decisions if they adhere to what classical economists prescribed as an "accepted wisdom".

Under transitioning energy systems, managers may have to get accustomed to *mutatis mutandis* or employing the ability to change when circumstances vary. Responding strategically, managers could *repurpose* their resources and capabilities, *reframe* the challenges they choose to resolve, and *reconfigure* the networks and markets that they choose to operate under. In spurring innovation, policy enables rather than dictates, by ensuring energy markets work effectively to allocate resources and confer rewards to risk takers who made their business work.

2
An Essential Mindset Transition

The deference to science to bolster one's arguments on climate change, the COVID-19 pandemic, or energy transitions, is indeed refreshing. For a change, one would have thought that with scientific methods underpinning the conversations, the capacity to coalesce around *facts* is enhanced. My optimism, however, was proven short-lived and unwarranted.

The *Net Zero to 2050* roadmap (IEA, 2021) benefited from works contributed by scientists of different persuasions. In true scientific tradition, one postulates hypotheses, makes explicit the methodologies, validates, and explains the outcomes and their limitations, complete with ranges of uncertainties. My formation in economics and management, and a fleeting moment in the physical sciences, made me appreciate the *humility* and *integrity* that come with the territory.

What caught the headlines, presented with mathematical precision, were the following prescient points (Layke *et al.*, 2021). To achieve the target, 630 GW PV and 390 GW wind will have to be installed, which is three times the 2020 levels. To phase out fossil fuels, no new investments in coal, oil, or gas will be made. This shift to clean energy would create 14 million jobs, against a loss of 5 million from oil and gas. To fuel future transport and industry, green hydrogen with carbon capture would do the job. Bioenergy, to make it work, would require a hundred exajoules of feedstock or fivefold the present global wood harvest. This latter point is, perhaps, what unites climate advocates and managers in questioning bioenergy's role in decarbonisation (Simon, 2021).

How did intelligent and practical people, supposedly working with science as a common framework, fall so far apart?

Ignored *mindsets* that drive people to prescribe "solutions" is where I would start. Different perspectives make people compete with their ideas and their resources to shape how society could evolve. What prevents people from tearing at each other, although at times they do, is a modicum of *reason*, *trust*, and enough *goodwill*. With this small dose of *good sense* and adhering to natural law, human society is made viable. Within this human reality, *energy transition* operates along two complementary spheres that I see as pertaining to the *economic* and *technological* arenas. Science asserts its influence with economics and finance providing the frameworks to evaluate what works and what doesn't. With imperfect people, their beliefs (and biases) which they hold dear would heavily influence the choices that they see to legitimise changes in the *social* and *political* spheres.

How these two spheres interact to effect change in society, and how both continually reshape markets, are sources of ambiguity and uncertainty. With each reconfiguration, extant advantages would shift with obsolescing resources displaced by emerging technologies and relationships.

2.1 Policy and climate advocates' imperatives

In translating science to support a broader acceptance of policy objectives, the language has to make plain its benefits and how people could coalesce around it. In simplifying the nuances of science, policy emphasises objectives and often downplays uncertainties. Picked up by advocates and promoted by interest groups, the ambiguities around the scientific findings are blurred. Before long, with frequent repetition, the narratives become a "settled science" that now has formed as the foundation of policy action.

In revisiting how their work is used, some scientists may fail to recognise the "consensus". That much is asserted by Steven E Koonin (2021), former US undersecretary of energy during Barack Obama's presidency:

> Policymakers too have to rely on information that's been through several wringers by the time it gets to them. Because most government officials — and others involved in climate policy for public and private sectors — are not themselves scientists, it's up to scientists to make sure that non-scientists making key policy decisions get an accurate, complete, and transparent picture of what's known (and unknown) about the changing climate, one undistorted by "agenda" or "narrative". Unfortunately, getting that story straight isn't as easy as it sounds.

A physicist by training, Steven E Koonin warns against the state of polarised discourse and the pursuit of an elusive "consensus" around the climate conversation. What is reported in the media may not always bear resemblance to what the scientific findings suggest. Far from a "consensus" on the science, to his surprise, climate science is far more immature than he thought. To lament the state of climate mitigation, Dieter Helm (2020) adds his voice:

> If this failure to achieve anything much in the last 30 years had been the consequence of not trying, it would be bad but at least understandable. But this is not the case: A huge amount of political capital and money has been spent in the name of mitigating climate change. Many people have been led to believe that current policies are working and that we are making good progress. They are not and we are not.

For two prominent scientists, among a number of others, to go against the popular narratives that policy considers as resolved science calls for serious re-examination. In historical context, today's dilemmas are little changed from those policy was grappling with in the 19th century.

While debunked on previous occasions (Sen, 1981), the *resource scarcity fallacy* continues to persist in policy thinking (Scanlan *et al.*, 2010). In trying to solve the wrong problem, climate policies have erred in rallying around approaches that do not work (Helm, 2020). At the root of policy thinking is the apparent durability of what Thomas Robert Malthus (2018) postulated in his 1803 treatise on population and food:

> Population grows at geometric rates as a consequence of lust where more children are born unnecessarily. Food production expands arithmetically given the state of agricultural technology and farming methods. The gaps will progressively widen, with famine as the eventual fate of human society, unless population growth is tempered to avoid such catastrophes. The alternatives are to rely on vice to shorten longevity, or a disaster could strike to wipe out a part of the population.

By ignoring the human capacity to innovate, the neo-Malthusians' pre-occupation with the limits of human systems' carrying capacity has led policy to persistent errors. Specifically:

- Horse-drawn carriages were the mode of mobility that resulted in the Horse Manure Crisis in 1894. *The Times* predicted that "in fifty years, every street in London will be buried under nine feet of manure" (Johnson, 2021).
- Henry Ford set out to make automobiles that every American could afford, which he achieved by introducing mass production for his Model T (McGarry, 2018). Without intending to, Ford's innovation rendered the "Horse Manure Crisis" irrelevant, when horse-drawn carriages were made obsolete.
- William Stanley Jevons (1865) recognised the social and political consequences "of a partial exhaustion" of the British coal mines, for the British empire's ability to project its power. As more coal was produced, new supplies could only be extracted at ever-increasing cost, given its finite nature.

The "resource scarcity" proposition predicted, and continually revised, the "peak oil" phenomenon (Helm, 2012). After being repeatedly proven wrong, the notion morphed into "peak demand", followed by grim forecasts of humanity's dire future (Lynch, 2018).

To William Stanley Jevons' (1865) credit, he corrected his peers when he asserted: "It is wholly a confusion of ideas to suppose the economical use of fuel is equivalent to a diminished consumption. The very contrary is the truth" following this logic:

"As a rule, new modes of economy will lead to an increase of consumption according to a principle in many parallel instances. The economy of labour affected by the introduction of new machinery throws labourers out of employment for the moment. But such is the increase in demand of cheapened products" *that more of the same labourers are hired back* (italics added). "Now the same principles apply, with even greater force and distinctions, to the use of such a general agent as coal. It is the very economy of its use, which leads to its extensive consumption. It has been so in the past, and it shall be so in the future."

Jevons' paradox on efficiency and consumption laid the foundation for modern economics' understanding of the *rebound effect*. As energy efficiency improves, it raises real income and accelerates economic growth. By using fewer resources to produce similar or greater output, more goods are sold at a nice profit.

Intelligence, or the lack of it, is not a principal cause of the persistence of the *fallacy of resource scarcity* or its variants. The tendency to project the unchanging present into the future is. In following this logic, technological changes and their potential to reconfigure how human society could meet its needs are often ignored. Almost instinctively, a dangerous path is pursued by asserting *order* to the otherwise less orderly human reality.

In a world that is changing at varying paces, while managers and policy are locked in unchanging thought processes, the outcomes are almost predestined. As economics and finance diverge farther away from the realities of markets, managers err in applying solutions of little relevance to enhancing human welfare, much less to sustainability.

An example is how people may respond to the Dutch court ruling on Shell plc. While climate advocates may see a major breakthrough, a reality check is in order. With a small share of global oil output, curtailing Western firms' production may have a limited impact on carbon emissions (Bordoff, 2021). If divesting is opted for by managers, acquirers with less stringent environmental practices may end up degrading environmental, health, and safety performance. Inadvertently, overall carbon emissions may rise, instead of fall, against what the court ruling and climate advocates intended.

Fortunately for managers and policy, *mutatis mutandis* comes to the rescue to ensure the continued relevance of economics and finance. In making the ambiguities explicit, the approach forces policymakers and managers to gain a deep understanding of their business. To achieve this, the nature of science and its limitations will have to be open to challenge. This prospect is not always comfortable, particularly for those who elevated their beliefs and causes to a status of undeserved omniscience.

2.2 (Some) Managers' strategic responses

Presented with a *fait accompli* by policy, managers may opt to march to a different beat. Valuing their freedom to choose, managers would seek to open various pathways to achieve superior performance. Managers would create some contingencies, employing scenarios to provide alternative pathways should the market turn out different from how they expected. Inadvertently, managers sidestep policy constraints or disrupt the *status quo*. I posit:

Managers bear the brunt of policy actions that aim to hasten fossil fuels' demise by making incumbent energy firms' assets obsolete. In contrast, policy that promotes green investments may in theory provide an accommodative ecosystem that potentially benefits investing firms. With some reservations, managers may listen but do a different calculus of benefits and risks that centre around policy's ability to deliver. As realists, managers appreciate that they bear serious losses if by following policy markets turn out differently. Worst, policy is known to change, at little cost to them, leaving managers to pick up the pieces and cover the costs that firms could incur from such a policy shift.

In the managers' chaotic world, history is replete with mavericks that saved human society from the curse of conformity. Without their courage, human society may have foregone the unprecedented prosperity that characterised the latter half of the 20th century. In making their moves pay off, wealth was created for those that innovate and for the society that they served.

The existential threats of climate challenges are well rehearsed in policy circles and climate advocacy. With more than the usual nudge, it has become core to energy firms' strategic actions. CO_2 emissions, a short hand for measuring progress to a sustainable future, are almost *de rigour* in any corporate pronouncement today.

That global CO_2 emissions continue to climb is undeniable. The prescribed cure is not, with no consensus in how managers or policy would deal with the problem(s) they perceived as relevant. For policy to recover lost ground, national commitments to reduce CO_2 emissions "need to be tripled to get back to 2°C and increased five times to align with 1.5°C" maximum increase in average global temperature (Olhoff and Christenssen, 2019). For managers, there is more alignment in their criticisms of the *Net Zero by 2050* roadmap than in the opportunities they find therein (IEA, 2021).

Stephen Comstock, speaking for American Petroleum Institute, asserts:

> Half of the technology to reach net zero has not yet been invented. Any pathway to net zero must include continued innovation and use of natural

gas and oil, which remains crucial to displacing coal in developing nations and enabling renewable energy (API, 2021).

Director General of World Nuclear Association, Sama Bilbao y Leon's reactions resonate:

Net zero puts too much faith in solutions that are uncertain, untested, or unscalable. Proven nuclear technologies have demonstrated their ability to take a much larger role in electricity decarbonisation in many countries around the world and have the potential to lead decarbonisation in many other sectors (WNA, 2021).

To place these managerial responses in context, actual CO_2 emissions are far from uniform, as Chart 1.1 illustrates. Partly recognised, the nuances and varying pace are lost in the political narratives' push for "one political solution fits all". Antonio Guterres, UN Secretary General, reiterates the prospect of an "unforgivable lost opportunity" because rich countries failed to heed their pronouncements on a post-COVID-19 green recovery (Milman, 2021). Examine, for instance, the following:

- In reducing CO_2 emissions, regional performance varies. A developed and emerging world divide is apparent, with Asia Pacific, Africa, and the Middle East as the "hot spots" where pollutants expand exponentially. In absolute terms, North America and Europe are the polluters that need to pay (A). To reduce emissions, global and concerted actions underpin what the United Nation's Intergovernmental Panel on Climate Change (UN IPCC) (IPCC, 2018) sees as "categorical" prescriptions to avoid catastrophic consequences.
- The "categorical" view, when validated against actual data (BP, 2020), is less straightforward. China emerges as the largest contributor of pollutants, with volumes growing unabated. India and other emerging market polluters, while expanding their CO_2 emissions rapidly, pale in comparison (B). Tagged as culprits, the declining emissions from the United States, Germany, and the

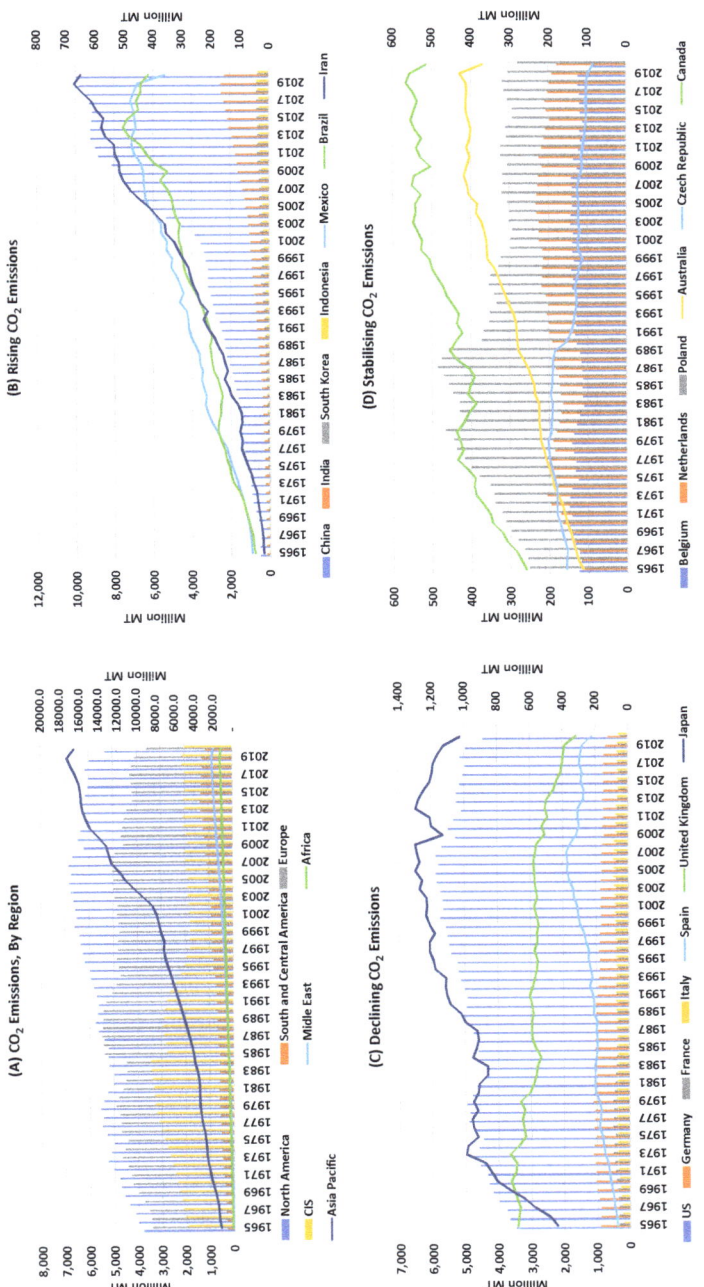

Chart 1.1: Varied CO$_2$ Emissions Performance, 1965–2020

Source: Raw data: BP Statistical Review (2021).

United Kingdom, among others, have been occurring for at least the past decade or more (C). The actual emissions in a number of major "polluters" have mostly plateaued over the same period (D).

As early as a decade ago, Dieter Helm (2012) asserted that "China will go on increasing its CO_2 emissions until 2030". Perhaps prematurely, he declared "coal is the winner in Europe" with Germany investing in new coal supplies while aiming to shut down its nuclear capacity.

3
Environmental Remediation to Sustainability

As policy seeks to reduce CO_2 emissions further, managers grapple with the immediate consequences of balancing reliable supplies and the costs of meeting environmental obligations. Supply reliability becomes a focal issue, with intermittent wind and solar more prominent in the supply mix. With extreme weather now topical, concerns about power outages from extreme heat (DiSavino, 2021) led some to question the ability of intermittent renewables to ensure supply security (Camargo-Renteria, 2021). These concerns are highlighted by energy systems simulations. The results reveal uncertainties in renewable energy supplies that could lead to significant performance gaps (Perera *et al.*, 2020). The European Environmental Agency (EEA) asserts that, in spite of national efforts to address the problem of reliability, there is "limited evidence for the implementation of adaptation actions in the energy sector" (EEA, 2019).

Today's re-emphasis on sustainable development (G7, 2021), as articulated by the Group of Seven (G7), replays the 1980s dilemmas that accentuated the geopolitical framing of climate change discourse: To reduce environmental damage created by industrial and commercial activities, the "United States spent a trillion dollars. By the 1990s, the United States had moved from a position of approximate trade balance on a long-term basis to a position of chronic trade deficit" (Jaffe *et al.*, 1995). By the 21st century, one trillion dollars was the annual price tag, at a minimum, for policy to achieve its low-carbon aspirations by 2040 (Zuckerman *et al.*, 2016).

Extending beyond energy, and energy-intensive steel and auto manufacturing, a vicious cycle is associated with ever-rising costs of environmental compliance. As fewer manufactured goods are exported, the trade deficit worsens. This would result in "polluting industries" employing less labour, with the "less educated" workforce being hit the hardest. Over time, a diminishing American share of industrial output is seen as endangering the nation's economic security (Jaffe *et al.*, 1995).

3.1 The green dilemmas

Given this economic backdrop, "going green" in the 1990s was a choice between surviving financially or complying and going out of business. These popular notions were questioned (Walley and Whitehead, 1994) in the following manner:

> To some observers, "responding to environmental problems has always been a no-win proposition for managers. Help the environment and hurt your business, or irreparably harm your business while protecting the earth." To climb out of this hole people dug for themselves, a new world would have to be *reimagined*. "In this new world, both business and environment can win. Being green is no longer a cost of doing business; it is a catalyst for innovation, new market for opportunity, and wealth creation."

The experts' response was swift and a lively debate ensued (Clarke *et al.*, 1994). Business was seen as on the receiving end of policy action. Specifically:

> To remain in business, managers have to comply with what policy imposes, so as to continue to enjoy its *licence to operate*. The value of compliance is derived from what business would forego for non-compliance. With climate advocates seeing greed as the managers' reason for complying with the minimum, more punitive measures are proposed.

By relying on innovation, Michael Porter sees the challenge of "going green" as providing an impetus to reconfigure a business. Robert N Stavins, however, found "little evidence on environmental regulation stimulating innovation and competitiveness. No evidence supported this view" (Clarke *et al.*, 1994).

Visible progress was scant, but improved energy intensity and efficiency were notable. These advances were drowned by climate advocacies. Politics has hardly moved. It has simply gotten louder and more virulent, with the divide more radical at the extremes. In examining the *ideological* and *philosophical* contexts, Daniel C Esty (2017) noted the American environmental approach alternates as follows: Democrats are seen as the party of big government mandates, with Republicans known to minimise regulatory overreach. With managers seeing policy imposing regulatory burdens, businesses may respond with calculated inaction and await the takeover by a market-friendly regime.

By presenting "science" as resolved and cast in stone, the resulting policies (and even corporate strategies) are treading on dangerous ground, Steven Koonin (2021) warns. As an economist, I see the question of *profits* and *sustainability* as a strategic continuum, where I subscribe to these propositions: Managers commit the firm's resources to meet its aspirational objectives. Choice becomes a trade-off among competing needs and the risks that can be reasonably borne, against the payoffs it could uniquely appropriate. In adapting to changing markets and technologies, managerial flexibility enables firms to innovate and reconfigure resources. Managers shape or respond to policy action and changing consumer preferences, within the interests of the communities it seeks to serve.

To make the link explicit, sustainability is made tangible within the context of business continuity. In essence, firms that are profitable are more likely to generate the resources to fund innovations that would secure their future viability. In framing the decisions that managers prioritise, what matters today and what is relevant to seize tomorrow's opportunities are the questions I would start with. This approach requires managers to ask the meaningful and relevant questions.

3.2 The meaningful and relevant questions

Managers have a habit of asking simple but irrelevant questions and choosing to act in accordance with the answers they like. Praised for their decisiveness, managers (or their successors) live to regret their quick actions *a posteriori*.

The question of what is the cheapest energy source belongs to this genre. Without a context, what is "cheap" today may prove "exorbitant" tomorrow. Dynamic energy markets shift the cost competitiveness of supplies as well as how competing supplies interact. Without understanding the moving parts and the markets in which they operate, the simple answer is precise, but it is often precisely wrong.

Let me illustrate this with how the lifecycle costs of energy (LCOE) changes when specified assumptions are varied. The comparative calculations are shown in Table 1.1, where I used the assumptions from the Energy Information Administration (EIA, 2019) and the International Energy Agency (IEA)/Nuclear Energy Agency (NEA) (IEA, 2020). I use a common methodology (Roth and Ambs, 2004) that a number of regulators and practitioners have adopted.[1]

The two sets of point estimates are considered "correct" within the context of what was assumed. In evaluating the "costs", IEA assumes lower utilisation rates for $Coal_B$ and $ACCGT_B$ and higher total overnight costs. This results in higher "costs" for fossil fuels than those calculated by EIA.

The capital recovery factor, C_{CRF}, is where I introduce a reality check to both agencies' costings. In their calculations, both use a constant recovery factor based on prevailing interest rates. Historically, low interest rates favour the "capital-intensive" renewables. This is where the distortion becomes problematic. Specifically:

- To recover the investment, an amount each year equivalent to a depreciation rate is included, the "cost of money" assumed as the risk-free interest rate, and an attributed risk premium (A.1 to A.11). The resulting C_{CRF} explicitly differentiates between long- and short-dated assets.
- Both agencies assume a constant "rate" roughly equivalent to prevailing interest rates. This practice flatters short-dated assets with "lower" costs, such as intermittent renewables and lithium-ion batteries. Using the "costs" to price the energy output, the internal rate of return (IRR), or net present values (NPVs) would be parlous.

This is indeed problematic for managers expecting to recoup their investments and make a profit. The answer is in the erroneous mathematics: By pegging C_{CRF} at 2.5%, assets would need 40 years (or 100/2.5) to recover the money they initially invested. For an asset with an operating life of 20 years, the "low costs" would imply

---
[1] Chapter 7 goes deeper into the math and how the methodology is applied, the contingency of outcomes, and how it could be used to inform investment evaluation.

Table 1.1: Static Lifecycle Costs of Energy

Column/Row	Technology	Acronym	EIA Data — Median							IEA/NEA Data — Median				
			CCRF %	Total Overnight Costs $/kW	C_{FX} $/kWh	C_{VAR} $/kWh	C_{FUEL} $/kWh	C_{LCOE} $/kWh	CCRF %	Total Overnight Costs $/kW	C_{FX} $/kWh	C_{VAR} $/kWh	C_{FUEL} $/kWh	C_{LCOE} $/kWh
			A	B	C	D	E	F	G	H	I	J	K	L
1	Coal — Baseload	$Coal_B$	9.59%	3,013	0.0389	0.0112	0.0833	**0.1334**	7.00%	1,785	0.0422	0.0167	0.1242	**0.1832**
2	Coal — Baseload, Carbon Capture (CCUS)	$Coal_{BCCUS}$	9.59%	5,764	0.1051	0.0334	0.1103	**0.2488**	7.00%	4,572	0.0808	0.0498	0.1645	**0.2951**
3	Gas Combined Cycle — Baseload	$ACCGT_B$	9.59%	795	0.0100	0.0047	0.0735	**0.0882**	7.00%	955	0.0091	0.0058	0.0914	**0.0163**
4	Gas Combined Cycle — Baseload, CCUS	$ACCGT_{BCCUS}$	9.59%	2,205	0.0278	0.0185	0.0838	**0.01301**	7.00%	2,619	0.0252	0.0230	0.1042	**0.1523**
5	Advance Nuclear	ANuke	8.39%	6,034	0.0643	0.0212	0.0091	**0.0946**	7.00%	3,370	0.0536	0.0224	0.0096	**0.0856**
6	Geothermal — Baseload Conventional	Geo_B	9.59%	2,746	0.0321	0.0203	0.0000	**0.0524**	7.00%	6,647	0.0244	0.0203	0.0000	**0.0447**
7	Pump Storage Hydro — Baseload	$StoHydro_B$	7.71%	2,948	0.0306	0.0098	0.0000	**0.0404**	7.00%	6,647	0.0244	0.0203	0.0000	**0.0447**
8	Onshore Wind	$Wind_{ON}$	10.50%	1,624	0.0527	0.0162	0.0000	**0.0689**	7.00%	1,439	0.0288	0.0119	0.0000	**0.0407**
9	Offshore Wind — Conventional Platform	$Wind_{OFCP}$	10.50%	5,495	0.1393	0.0209	0.0000	**0.1602**	7.00%	2,740	0.0878	0.0209	0.0000	**0.1087**
10	Solar — PV Tracking/Utility	PVT_M	10.50%	1,970	0.0947	0.0111	0.0000	**0.1058**	7.00%	923	0.0605	0.0098	0.0000	**0.0704**
11	Battery	Li-On	16.50%	2,170	0.0664	0.0142	0.0000	**0.0806**	7.00%	655	0.1156	0.0142	0.0000	**0.1298**

Source: Raw data: EIA, IEA/NEA.

only up to half of the initial investment would be recovered. When technological obsolescence is considered, the picture gets worse.

Volatile volumes, which influence costs, were made more explicit when EIA complemented LCOEs with lifecycle avoided costs of energy (LACE). To my mind, the term is a misnomer. What LACE does is "adjust" how variations in volumes during the day impact LCOEs, not the amount of "costs that are avoided". Coming up with "clean" (or unsubsidised) costs is easier said than done.

This is, however, not to say that LCOEs are hopelessly misleading, although they are if applied erroneously. The structure it provides is sufficiently intuitive to guide managers to understand the interacting influences of the different variables. These "moving parts", and how they are linked, could inform how the comparative costs could evolve as volumes, costs, interest rates, and inflation vary. I employ LCOEs as initial inputs in my analyses using binomial trees and dynamic volume allocation,[2] to gain very different strategic insights into what static analyses could provide:

- Comparative advantages are transient, with emerging technologies with superior resilience to volatile prices and volumes likely to displace a prevailing dominant technology. This occurs with $ACCGT_B$ displacing $Coal_B$ and with $StoHydro_B$ or $GeoS_B$ gaining a foothold, as both technologies start to displace $ACCGT_B$.
- $Wind_{ON}$ holds more promise than PVT_M, with PVT_M's rapidly falling costs impairing early adopters' competitive position while rewarding late-movers with lower costs. In ignoring the prospect of obsolescence, early adopters are "surprised" that rapid growth does not redound to high profitability. Instead, mounting losses are more common and a pattern of worsening solar power underperformance persists. For lenders and insurers, the solar risk assessment warns against "elevating default risks, increasing exposure and costs to insurers and insureds" (Matsui, 2021).
- ANuke suffers from a double bind. Long construction periods increase the prospect of cost overruns, with a rigid cost structure rendering payoffs vulnerable to low energy prices. However, just like nil fuel cost renewables, high energy prices provide windfalls.

---

[2] Chapters 8–10 extensively illustrate how these approaches are applied to competitive or oligopoly markets.

Using these insights, managers could act strategically in varying investments and operational configurations. The method continues to evolve, with more externalities for both fossil fuels and renewables (often ignored) made explicit (Rehbein *et al.*, 2020).

Clearly, the insights are more meaningful than a futile debate on which technology is the cheapest. Without a market context, the cost comparisons degenerate into an interesting but futile tinkering of inputs to mould outputs to fit "accepted narratives". This is a weakness that LCOEs share with IRRs and NPVs when misused by managers and in policy.

3.3 Getting to grips with dynamic markets

A highly regulated market follows a "command-and-control" approach. The regulator "commands" through central planning the investment it sees as necessary and "controls" how much suppliers are paid. In this relationship, suppliers are "subcontractors" to the state. In exchange for "secure revenues", because the regulator controls prices and volumes, suppliers accept a cap on their returns. To flourish under this system, managers would deliver value by optimising the volume their firms could supply. Hence, the focus is on operating efficiency.

The progressive deregulation transferred the regulator's pricing and volume allocation functions to a dynamic energy market. As with most functioning markets, suppliers fulfil the demand and take the risk to invest in the assets required to operate in these markets. The fuel market, to a large extent, operates competitively. Power generation, in most developed markets, is liberalised. In emerging markets, the degree of liberalisation varies where energy markets are at different stages of regulatory control. In Chart 1.2, the ways in which different power generating technologies tend to interact is illustrated. Under this dynamic energy market, fungible supplies aided by strong interconnections provide feedback to managers on the state of demand, to inform managers on how to meet this through their operational and investment decisions.

Under this dynamic power market, the singular focus on operating efficiency no longer suffices. Managers have to learn to adapt to a constellation of continually shifting variables that impact cash returns in the following manner:

- Power prices vary periodically where the marginal supply that fulfils the periodic demand sets the power prices. Schematically, the marginal supply

From Impasse to PIVOT 23

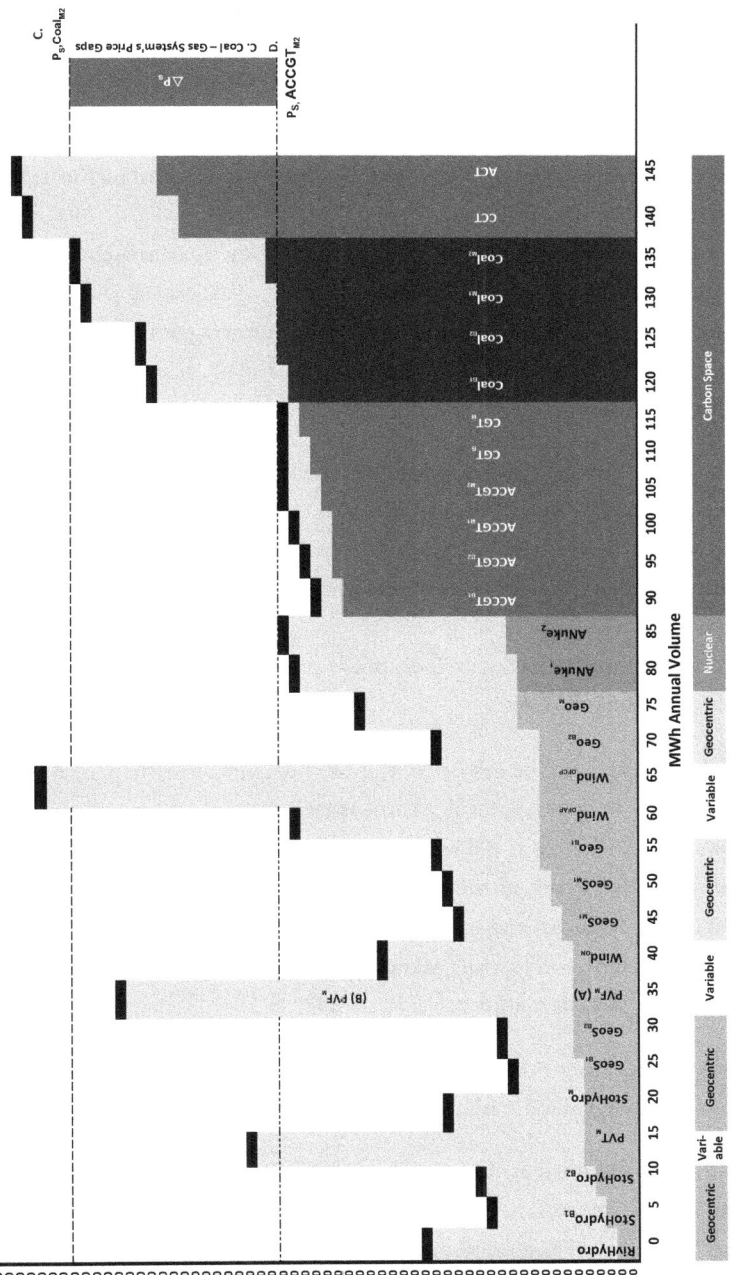

Chart 1.2: Dynamic Power Market

Source: Raw data: EIA.

- could be set by coal or ACCGT depending on the volume of demand, represented as the "carbon space".
- ANuke and renewables, when available, are supplied ahead of coal or ACCGT. Particularly for intermittent renewables, this preferential dispatch minimises curtailment of supplies, which would have otherwise implied nil fuel cost (or low marginal cost) supplies are wasted.
- In using marginal cash costs as the *de facto* "ranking" for dispatch or the sum of the variable costs, C_{VAR}, and the fuel cost, C_{FUEL}, shown as (A) for PVF_M, the power prices, P_s, may prove insufficient to recover the full cost of supply (shown as A + B for PVF_M). In some markets, the C_{FX} is paid separately as a capacity payment.

With consumers paying P_s as equivalent to the marginal supplies' LCOEs, some technologies would fail to recover their full costs at certain periods unless subsidised. A point not lost on Dieter Helm (2020) when he asserted that, when all forms of subsidies are excluded, intermittent renewables would remain more expensive (in most instances) than ACCGT.

The periodic volumes influence periodic power prices, P_s, depending on the extent to which periodic demand varies:

- Under a given coal or gas price, the total demand for the period is, say, 130 MWh. In this case, $Coal_{M2}$ is the marginal supply. Hence, the periodic power price, P_s, is set at (C) which is the LCOE of $Coal_{M2}$.
- Volume falls as part of the usual pattern of demand variations to, say, 100 MWh, with coal and gas prices unchanged. The reduced volumes could only dispatch ACCGTs with coal excluded. $ACCGT_{M2}$ is the "new" marginal supply that sets the market price, P_s, at (D).

From this simple illustration, a number of factors are causing a "nuisance" to how the "true costs" of energy deviate from static LCOE estimates:

- With the falling use of $Coal_{M2}$, the LCOEs would be higher with lower volumes (or vice versa).
- Fuel cost, C_{FUEL}, is significant for coal or ACCGT. With C_{FUEL} as the principal source of power price volatilities, marginal supplies would tend to yield stable cash margins.

The math could be seen to work as follows:

- The cash margin is $P_s - C_{VAR} - C_{FUEL}$, with $P_s = C_{FX} + C_{VAR} + C_{FUEL}$.
- The cash cost of the capacity j that supplies is $C_{VAR,j} + C_{FUEL,j}$, with $C_{FX,j}$ paid separately as periodic capacity payments.
- If $C_{VAR,j} = C_{VAR}$, and $C_{FUEL,j} = C_{FUEL}$, then the periodic cash margin for supplier $j = C_{FX,j}$. For nil fuel cost renewables, j, the periodic cash margins would be $C_{FX,j} + C_{FUEL}$.

The addition of renewables and ANuke, while keeping Coal and ACCGT, and demand volumes, unchanged, means the carbon space is likely to shrink. Recall: By virtue of lower costs of StoHydro, Geo, and GeoS and the preferential dispatch of ANuke and intermittent renewables, Coal and ACCGT become marginal supplies.

As ACCGTs displace Coal, the "carbon space" is gradually dominated by gas. In most markets, power generated from gas is cheaper than that from coal, with the added benefit of significantly reduced CO_2 emissions. This *supply mix transition* has been underway in Europe since the 1990s, accounting for a large part of the decline in CO_2 emissions seen there (Recall Charts 1.1(C) and 1.1(D)).

This is where the simulation may get messy. In theory, under the usual patterns of substitution, the less coal or ACCGTs is dispatched, the higher the costs of the residual supplies. If coal or ACCGTs continue as marginal supplies, one would expect periodic power prices to remain high, in spite of the diminishing share of gas or coal.

The experience of Spain disappoints the economic and market modelling experts (Chart 1.3). What makes Spain interesting is the way fossil fuels and renewables directly compete. The system illustrates how it continues to adapt to meet the twin challenges posed by *energy transition*: A need to create a framework is recognised so that the "private sector can deliver on climate targets at acceptable costs while still supplying reliable power over the short and long term" (Newberry *et al.*, 2018).

Classical supply and demand interactions appear to work, as (A) empirically supports. That is, as volumes increase, so do power prices. Statistically, volume variations may explain up to a third of the price changes, as classic economic theory would predict.

In my formulation, I examine more closely the influence of the supply mix on power prices. The hypothesis is a simple one: With more "expensive" energy sources

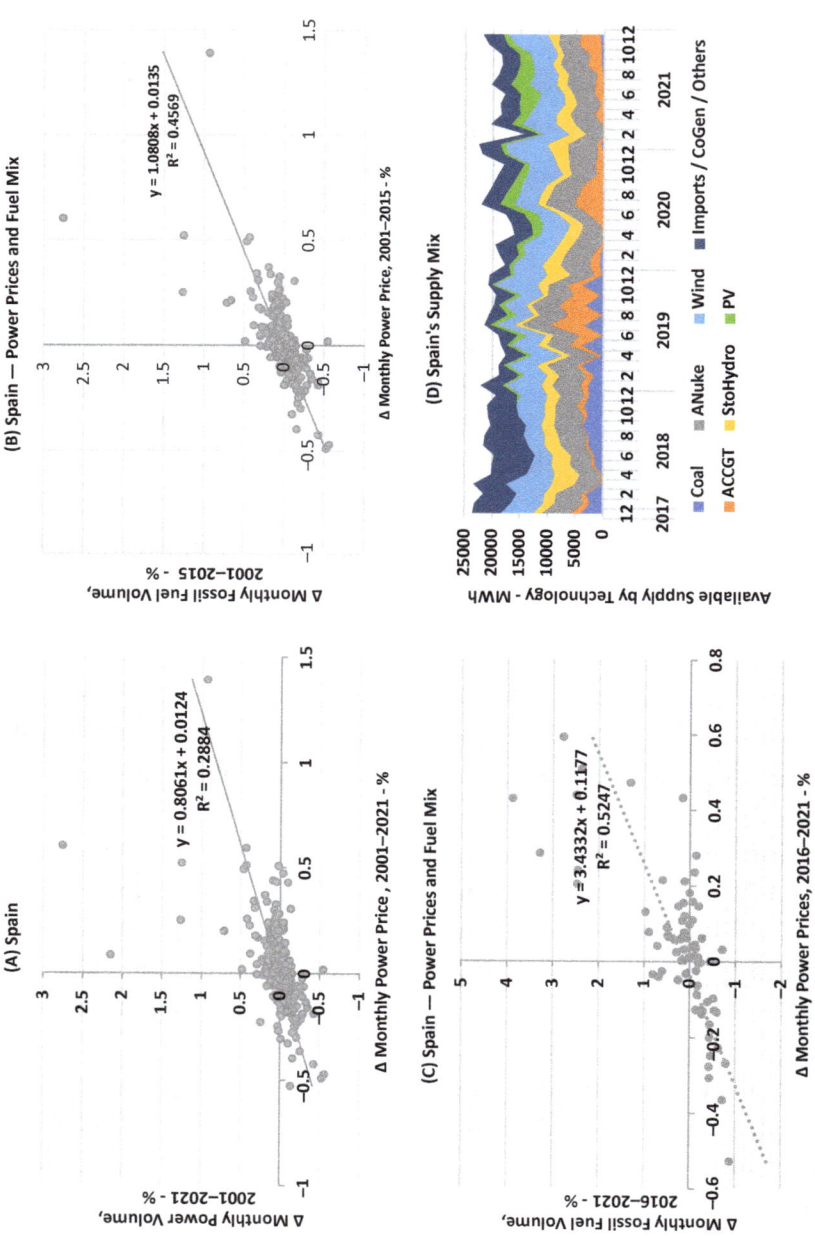

Chart 1.3: Dynamic Displacements and Shifting Advantages

Source: Raw data: OMIE/MIBEL.

displaced by "cheaper" supplies, dynamic volume allocations would eventually reduce power prices, in the absence of any distortions from subsidies. To translate this, in allowing energy supplies to freely compete, reliable and cheaper StoHydro and to an extent, $Wind_{ON}$ and ANuke, would displace coal or ACCGTs. Here's how the Iberian power system operates, with Spain as the major component:

- In its earlier period (B), Coal and ACCGT were providing the baseload supply, complemented by the variable fluvial flows that make StoHydro volumes vary with rainfall. In effect, as hydro supplies vary (by up to +/− 40% from mean), coal and ACCGT take up the slack or are displaced. Operated as a sub-system, $Wind_{ON}$ supplied as a portfolio, starts to mimic the variability and reliability of StoHydro (Barcelona, 2012). This combination alters the influence of volumes *per se*: It is not only how much volume is needed, but how that volume is fulfilled, which has a stronger influence on how power prices vary. For this reason, the share of coal and ACCGT had a stronger influence, explaining more than half of the price variations.
- Wind has been progressively entrenched into the Spanish system, with Portugal contributing its fair share. The carbon space is progressively shrunk, with renewables indirectly displacing Coal and ACCGT, with Coal largely displaced by ACCGT some time ago. From 2016, StoHydro started to displace ACCGT as marginal supplies, hence increasingly exerting downward pressure on power prices (C). This resulted in higher price volatilities, associated with fluvial flows and $Wind_{ON}$ availability. With Coal practically reduced to a marginal supply, sharper swings in ACCGT volumes explained up to 60% of the power price variations.

The conventional wisdom of operating is turned upside down in the Iberian energy system. The idea of Coal and ACCGT operating as baseload supplies does not fit with the realities of market operations. The slump in volumes associated with the COVID-19 lockdowns is instructive: Significantly reduced volumes (D) practically stranded ACCGT and Coal, with excess $Wind_{ON}$ often curtailed (and wasted).

These conditions have been experienced in certain months since 2016, but became exaggerated in 2020. The press would herald these months as "achieving another record" for 100% renewables. While this is factually correct, it could be misleading for the purposes of managerial decision-making. As volumes bounce back, as they did after these "record months" were registered, power prices rose sharply as more ACCGTs are brought back into service to meet rising volumes.

The managers residing in these chaotic markets, however, could no longer rely on regulatory fiat to guarantee the financial viability of their investments. Instead, managers are required to deeply understand their business and its nuances, in order to flourish in more ambiguous conditions. In this context, the overly simplified question — what is the cheapest source of energy — is even less relevant. How managers earn their keep may have more to do with creating the arenas in which emerging opportunities can flourish and devising ways to appropriate the profits they offer.

4
Create Niches to PIVOT

Sustainability is a centre piece of chief executives' agenda, at least going by their public pronouncements. Management practitioners, however, observe significant numbers of sustainability undertakings have failed to live up to their promise. Bain & Company characterises this downward spiral (Davis-Peccoud *et al.*, 2016) as following this pattern:

> Many CEOs want to make a difference. Convinced that companies should play a positive role in environmental stewardship and social development, they declare sustainability a top priority, launch a transformation programme, hire a Chief Sustainability Officer, and commit millions of dollars and hundreds of hours of management time to the effort. Then momentum fades.

At first glance, the CEOs are doing all the right things, as prescribed by the sustainability playbook. However, as *profits* become divorced from *sustainability*, the undetermined benefits of sustainability, other than its lofty aspirations, have come at great expense to firms (Walley and Whitehead, 1994). The *faux* dilemma, unfortunately, continues to haunt managers today.

That sustainability lacks a commonly accepted definition is an understatement and may not even be *the* problem worth solving. I view the issue as going deeper into how *sustainability* is framed in broad and amorphous statements that lack *purpose*. In mistaking lofty ideals as constituting a singular *prescriptive sustainability agenda*, it is predestined to fail: Being vague has its advantages. People can coalesce around notions that are broad enough to be seen as "inclusive". As one moves from "declaring sustainability a top priority", to taking action, people become unsure about what it is that they have signed up for. However, as "inclusive" aspirations unfold and fail to live up to their promise, individuals begin to doubt their very involvement. Momentum fades, and with it, the sustainability agenda becomes "unsustainable" as people drift apart.

At the core of making strategic decisions is the freedom to exercise choice. This requires managerial judgement, not lofty ideals without purpose. Within dynamic markets, policy enables choices by ensuring markets work rather than mandating those choices. Through the various ways people make their choices known, at times implicitly, profit opportunities are created as incentives for risk taking.

Following this logic, I see *energy transition* as a strategic move by which investments seek to create profitable niches that firms could pivot to. For this reason, while *reduce*, *reuse*, and *recycle* raised awareness of the virtue of thrift, the strategic imperative behind sustainable businesses lies in *repurpose*, *reframe*, and *reconfigure*. This relies on a coalition of the willing, not on government generosity with taxpayers' money, to move people and society to a different and a better future.

4.1 Understanding market ambiguities

To translate these aspirations into strategic moves, Chart 1.4 offers a way to link the ambiguous conditions of markets with how managers could frame their strategic approaches. I see ambiguities as occurring at two principal axes: An *economic technological shift* is influenced by how quickly technologies change, and how they impact the economics of energy supply and people's procurement decisions. On the part of society, *socio-political change* is often dictated by how consumers express their preferences, usually through their purchases in dynamic markets or votes via electoral processes that influence policy. The resulting societal change is a confluence of people and policy action.

Schematically, the strategic choices may emerge as these factors interact, often with people influencing the pace of change and how markets migrate from one quadrant to another. As an example: In markets where the state intervenes frequently, the pace of *socio-political change* tends to be slower and more tentative. The political hurdles

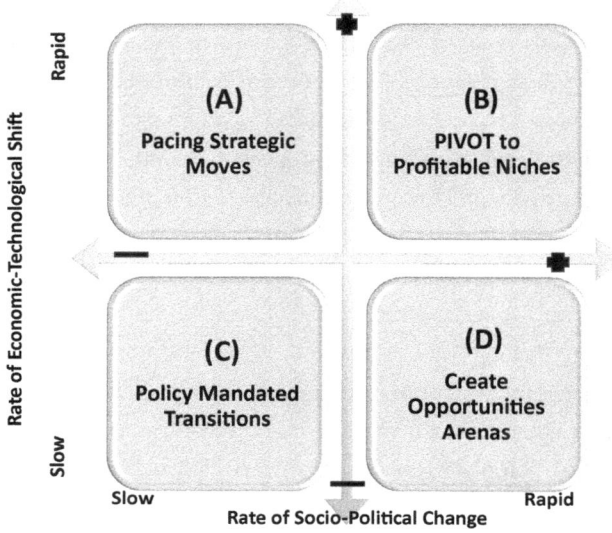

Chart 1.4: Strategic Approaches under Ambiguous Conditions

appear endless, at least in a democracy, while generous subsidies produce green paradoxes (Amram and Kulatilaka, 2009). In a "slow-moving" ecosystem, indexing supply portfolios to the energy system's cost structure could secure predictable returns (A). The incentives to invest in renewables may hinge on a managers' judgement as to the longevity and reliability of regulatory support.

In setting subsidies, renewables' costs are equalised with fossil fuel alternatives, when most are in fact more expensive. However, with volatile prices, the "correct" levels become indeterminate, leading subsidised renewables to "over- or under- recover" the excess costs (Barcelona, 2017). Hence, as renewable costs decline rapidly, investing firms work hard to keep the subsidies. The economics of the project (or investment), when the decision was made, relied on continued receipt of subsidies to make it work. After all, their actual cost did not fall even if investments made at a later date by others are significantly cheaper.

Policy and consumers, however, see the reduced renewables' cost as the basis for expecting how future power prices would evolve. However, when oil prices are low, power prices tend to drop and renewables are left in greater need of subsidies. At this point, consumers are least amenable to "paying over the market" when cheaper alternatives are available (Barcelona, 2017). Coaxed by consumers, politicians scramble to "cut subsidies for current renewables, reinforced by fossil fuel prices which stubbornly refuse to rise as politicians so confidently predicted, and instead follow the inevitable economic path dictated by supply and demand" (Helm, 2012).

When managers choose to diversify into renewables, with fossil fuels as their initial portfolio, or expand extant supplies, they kickstart two phenomena:

- As more investment goes to renewables, a *learning effect* starts to manifest in rapidly declining costs for new investment. With "cheaper" renewables, the case for new entrants becomes more compelling. However, the early movers that aided the *learning effect* may find their investments imperilled by more competitive substitutes.
- Policy is slow to respond. Continuing to promote renewables, the costs it inflicts by making the grid less stable, particularly as more intermittent supplies are incorporated, are borne by incumbent fossil fuel supplies (Barcelona, 2012). In a way, by turning a blind eye, policy tacitly allows intermittent supplies to have a free ride by "socialising" the excess costs to rebalance the system.

Operating under this market imperfection, managers may have to pace their strategic moves (B). I posit that the "quick to commit" may lose out, particularly on solar power, a notion that is counterintuitive to the idea of the "early mover's advantage". This is how latecomers could benefit:

- Solar power costs have been falling by more than 20% annually. The cost of deferring is the foregone revenue (or cash earnings), which for low output solar is lower than the "savings" from capex. The "quick to commit" locked in the higher capex, which is rendered uneconomic within a couple of years or so. With minimal operating costs, the capex disadvantage could not be offset against prospective but limited cost reductions.

In contrast, the "early mover's advantage" continues to work in favour of StoHydro and geothermal, both high output technologies where the cost of deferring could be quite high. Add to this the geo-centricity of the technology: Where locational advantages are important, the early movers could lock out rivals by being there first.

To some extent, Wind$_{ON}$ experiences a similar advantage, particularly on the output side.

Without reconfiguring the networks, subsidising without letting intermittent supplies pay for the excess cost widens the disconnect between policy and managerial action. The prospect, as a result, of another "lost decade" is made more likely. To remedy this, deregulation is resorted to in policy, that could result in the following *market transition*:

- To accelerate network reconfiguration, policy may consider shifting its focus from "leading" to "enabling" managerial actions (C). Moving away from subsidies and introducing carbon taxation, while easing new asset investment, could initiate the reconfiguration of the supply mix and network configuration. In response, managers may move to follow explicit portfolio criteria in evaluating their investments (Barcelona, 2015).
- As the dynamic forces of markets reassert their influence on managerial decisions, the interactions of firms, technological advances, and the commitments that managers make dictate the pace of change that could emerge. In the process, driven by adaptive innovation, a *PIVOT* to low-carbon energy systems would be dynamic and ambiguous (D). Under this dynamic decision ecosystem, managers would seek to *repurpose, reframe,* and *reconfigure* their approach to business.

In giving due credit to climate change advocacy, the merits of cleaner alternatives to coal or some fossil fuels are recognised by policy and managers. In building on these advances, managers and policy can "recast an environmental framework that is simultaneously stronger and lighter (*in its interventionist tendency*), integrating environmental and economic (and social) concerns, and using a policy toolkit that goes beyond command-and-control regulation" (Esty, 2017).

4.2 Rethinking tactical and strategic moves

Managers and policy are overwhelmed by advocates, who appear to have the uncanny ability to categorically pronounce what the future *should* look like. With *energy transitions*, the experts' ability to forecast with accuracy is in doubt: They have mostly underestimated the pace of change and the falls in the cost of intermittent renewables (Wiser *et al.*, 2021).

In framing good strategy, Richard Rumelt (2011) encourages managers to "discover the critical factors in a situation and design ways of coordinating and focusing actions to deal with these factors." To solve the problem that matters, the manager "acknowledges the challenges being faced, and provides an approach to overcoming them".

In tackling the challenges posed by *energy transition*, the critical choices presented to managers often fall under the following *adaptive* or *disruptive* strategies that involve reconfiguring how they do their business. Repsol is a case in point (see Box 1.1).

Smaller than its European energy peers, Repsol emerged from a setback in Argentina post the renationalisation of YPF. What was generally seen as a blow, Repsol took as an opportunity to *reframe* their business by redeploying capital and *repurposing* their resources. On restoring their financial strength, they *prepared to pivot* to expand their low-carbon offerings. Building on a stronger business foundation, managers set their sights to *adapt* their business mix and position themselves to employ technologies to invest in tomorrow's potentially profitable niches.

In examining the challenges that *energy transition* presents, I focus on the initial endowments of firms. The major oil and gas companies, such as ExxonMobil, Shell plc, Total, Chevron, and BP, are large by virtue of their capital and the huge resources at their disposal. In theory, this is an insurmountable advantage they hold over smaller energy firms. In my view, this perspective may prove too optimistic.

The firms' initial endowments are ignored by conventional financial and economic investment evaluation. I view this as a serious omission. The oil and gas majors, faced with transitioning energy markets, have to grapple with these twin challenges: Preserve the value of extant assets that premature obsolescence imperils. Their *PIVOT* to tomorrow's profitable niches may be hindered by being locked-in to extant skills and businesses that may need to be *repurposed*.

Caught in this bind, some managers may opt for inaction or slow the process by resisting change for longer. This stance, however, may prove short-sighted and potentially imperil the firms' prospective viability. Recall: The court judgement against Shell and the inroads shareholder activism is making into corporate boardrooms render managerial inaction a high-risk approach to tackling issues of climate change and sustainability.

In creating the sustainable energy firms of tomorrow, I am inclined to go granular in evaluating how their *strategic actions* are most likely to succeed by keeping an eye on their *adaptive moves*, as outlined in Chart 1.5. The thought processes are generally guided by these approaches:

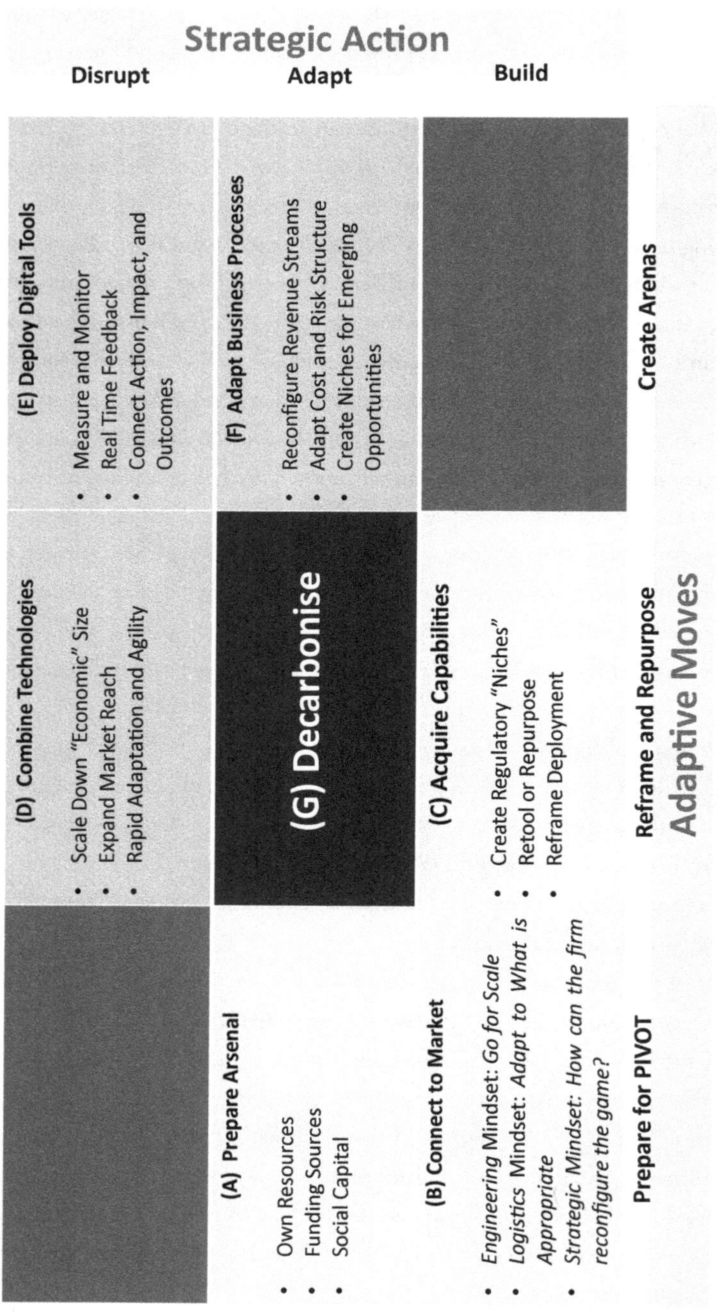

Strategic Action

Disrupt — **Adapt** — **Build**

(E) Deploy Digital Tools
- Measure and Monitor
- Real Time Feedback
- Connect Action, Impact, and Outcomes

(F) Adapt Business Processes
- Reconfigure Revenue Streams
- Adapt Cost and Risk Structure
- Create Niches for Emerging Opportunities

(D) Combine Technologies
- Scale Down "Economic" Size
- Expand Market Reach
- Rapid Adaptation and Agility

(G) Decarbonise

(C) Acquire Capabilities
- Create Regulatory "Niches"
- Retool or Repurpose
- Reframe Deployment

Create Arenas

(A) Prepare Arsenal
- Own Resources
- Funding Sources
- Social Capital

(B) Connect to Market
- *Engineering Mindset: Go for Scale*
- *Logistics Mindset: Adapt to What is Appropriate*
- *Strategic Mindset: How can the firm reconfigure the game?*

Prepare for PIVOT — **Reframe and Repurpose**

Adaptive Moves

Chart 1.5: Rethinking *Tactical* and *Strategic* Moves

- Acting *tactically*, in preparing to *PIVOT*, managers *reframe* the firm's approaches and *repurpose* how its extant assets are employed (or deployed), in order to *create arenas* in which emerging opportunities can flourish.
- Moving *strategically*, firms *build* their capabilities and resources, in order to provide the means by which they can *adapt* to evolving markets. By developing different ways of doing things, firms can *innovate* how their products or services are provided and potentially disrupt markets or adapt to outcompete rivals.

The sequence could vary. Starting with the *knowns*, managers tend to be good at intuitively knowing what they have and what they can *repurpose*. With greater clarity, managers experiment before proceeding to *reframe* their approach. In understanding how policy could evolve, managers may decide to *reconfigure* the way they do business, which may involve *adapting* or *disrupting* the extant networks of markets and relationships.

4.2.1 Repurpose

With just some vague notions of what a decarbonised system may look like, managers are seldom prepared to bet the farm on a single pathway. What is often clear to managers is this reality: *Transformation costs money, with its outcome seldom as visible as one would like it to be.*

In taking stock of their firm's resources, managers *prepare the arsenal* (A) and tend to err on the side of caution. For this reason, conserving cash and financial resources is an *adaptation* in how they manage their capital resources. Optimisation takes on a different meaning; contingency funding and de-risking the new ventures take on a touch of innovation.

Influenced by how weighted average costs of capital (WACC) are calculated, debt is maximised in project financing to employ the benefits of tax shields. This works when interest paid on borrowings is tax-deductible, while dividends are not.[3] Lenders accept this funding approach when they are sufficiently secure contractually. However,

---

[3] In Chapter 8, how the tax shield lowers the WACC is discussed extensively. I added a critic on WACC's application by reacquainting managers with the costs of financial distress and offer some remedies.

when *energy transition* raises the prospect of obsolescing assets, debt financing may become onerous.

Taking a broader look at the value chain, risks are in reality embedded in specified stages of project development. In some cases, subsidies are paid to secure the payoffs which could have been better employed to de-risk aspects of the investment. Increasingly, social capital could enable investments when deployed as part of a risk mitigation package, a point that is revisited under Section 4.2.2.

In a future energy system that seeks to decarbonise, how firms *connect to the market* (B) could be altered:

- An *engineering mindset* tends to value scale, because of the belief that *economies of scale* and, as people learn, the *learning effects* will make production more efficient. As a result, costs are bound to fall, locking in competitive advantages for those that commit earlier, locking in the *early movers' advantage*.
- A *logistics mindset* works to optimise what is available, while being more tolerant with some inefficiencies as trade-offs in order to size the scale of production or provision of services. In effect, smaller units may increase the unit cost of production. However, by minimising redundancy or excess capacity, because the market volume may not be big enough, consistently high utilisation rates could offset higher unit costs.

Cognisant of these different approaches and their impact in determining what technologies to deploy, managers are tested in exercising their *strategic mindset* to harness their firm's capabilities and the resources it can access.

4.2.2 Reframe

To *repurpose* extant resources and capabilities, managers may seek guidance from the firm's goals and aspirations. Armed with these perspectives, managers could *reframe* the *game* they choose to play. The *reframing* could be undertaken at two interacting and related levels:

- Tactically, managers would *acquire capabilities* (C) by hiring new talents, retooling through training or learning programmes, and as a last resort, redeploying people which may imply redundancies. This process requires a

rethink of how human resources are valued: Are people rewarded for their talent or for their agility to adapt or both?
- Strategically, how managers choose to *combine technologies* (D) will impact the tactical actions they have to take. A sudden shift from fossil fuels to renewables may imply divestment of extant assets (and people) or aggressive acquisition of new business. In some cases, managers may choose an adaptive route that sees the firm follows, rather than leads rivals, in committing to specified pathways.

In *reframing* the game, managers and policy approach the adoption of emerging technologies in a very different way. With mature technologies, such as coal- or gas-reliant energy supplies, the focus is on integration into the firm's portfolio and how the technology complies with market rules. How it works is presumed to be proven, given the previous success that the technology may have demonstrated. In this world, social capital plays only a minimal role, if any.

The emergence of environmental, social, and governance (ESG) criteria, which sees environmental remediation moving into the sphere of making society sustainable, makes the boundaries between social and financial returns less clear cut. On a granular level, I illustrate in Chart 1.6 how social capital and mainstream financing could be deployed.

Ideas are generated during the research and development (R&D) phase (A): It is here that the uncertainties as to outcomes and timing are perhaps the greatest. R&D is usually undertaken in academe or laboratories, where the primary funding is provided by social capital (A.1), grants, or subsidies (A.2) subject to the donor's covenants (A.3). In industry, this could be undertaken and funded through specific allocations.

As an idea is tested and undergoes experimentation, prototypes are developed to provide a *proof of concept* (B). Conventionally, private grants or subsidies (B.2.1) are provided as recognition of the social benefits that may accrue to society. In some cases, fiscal incentives (B.2.2) are given to facilitate a technology's deployment. These grants (or aid money) are subjected to the donor's covenants (B.3.1) or the grant's conditions (B.3.2).

Emerging technologies face their first hurdles in commercialisation when they are caught between having no track record and trying to get a first entity to adopt them.

Dynamic Decisions

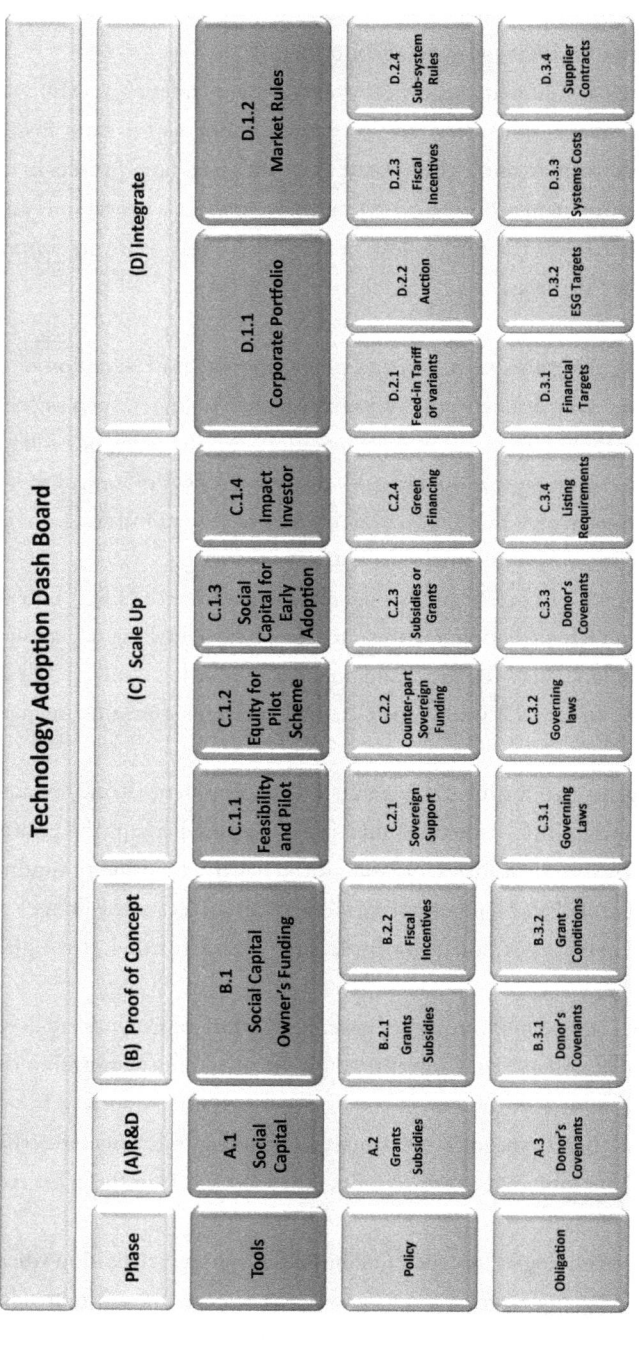

Chart 1.6: *Reframing* Strategic Moves

This is a challenge in *scaling up* (C) the application of the technology, a step necessary to gain early adherents. In this "chicken-or-the-egg" dilemma, I see social capital as playing a different role by applying practices used in impact investing. Examine, for example, the following: Social capital (C.1.3) or sovereign grants are traditionally directed at social initiatives with limited obligation to fulfil a financial returns target. In contrast, impact investment (C.1.4) uses funds destined for social investment with specific "impact" requirements (or equivalent to a financial return in private capital). Combined with private funding, blended finance could fund feasibility studies and the design of a pilot scheme (C.1.1), with private capital providing equity for the pilot scheme.

The tools are varied but most are known or acceptable to financial markets. Their application as part of blended financing is where the adaptation may need to be made.

I cite the example of how slim-hole geothermal drilling *reframes* the managerial challenge (Barcelona *et al.*, 2019):

> Conventional geothermal drilling employs large equipment that requires civil works to be built before any test drilling could commence. With slim-hole drilling, the equipment and drilling tools are made smaller. As a result, no civil works and roads are required upfront, because helicopters can transport the equipment to the drill sites. For this reason, front-end cost is reduced by two-thirds, simply by avoiding building civil works before one knows the site is the right place to drill and develop viable geothermal fields.

By rearranging the sequence of cash outlays, slim-hole technology enables private capital to bear the exploration risks. In reducing the costs of exploratory drilling, new information from test drills can be gathered more cheaply. With better data on the prospective geothermal field, the uncertainties around the size of the well, its structure, and the potential steam reserve it holds are minimised. Add resource insurance to the mix and social capital and aid are employed to enable broader private risk taking when a commensurate payoff is made feasible.[4]

---

[4] Chapter 6 provides more details in Box 6.1.

In this example, *reframing* from a mentality of securing returns, using rigid, long-term supply contracts and state subsidies, to one of attracting the first dollar as a managerial challenge, changes the approach. From an attitude of relying on subsidies and state support, managers work to structure options that blend private financing with social capital and sovereign aid to unleash energy resources.

4.2.3 Reconfigure

In creating arenas for emerging opportunities, managers could *adapt the business processes* (F) and, as needed, *deploy digital tools* (G) or a variant, to enhance product or service offerings. Digital tools have advanced to a point at which real-time feedback on a process' carbon footprint can be measured. Consumer preferences are measured by actual procurement. These data-reliant analytics offer valuable information that aids in product or service design, development, and deployment.

In *adapting the business processes*, RAG of Austria (see Box 1.2) offers an approach for industry coupling to optimise renewables and hydrogen as a clean fuel for industry and transport. Hydrogen is seen as the transport fuel of the future or a wasteful experiment doomed to failure, opposing advocates would propose. These polarised views are perhaps better understood by examining the schematic flow in Chart 1.7, drawn with expert inputs.

Hydrogen is conventionally produced as an energy carrier from feedstock such as coal (A.1), gas (A.2), and methane (A.3). Pyrolysis applies high heat using power (A.5) to a feedstock (A.6) to separate hydrogen and solid carbon or graphite (Renssen, 2020). Graphite is a dominant element in electric vehicle (EV) batteries (Barrera, 2021), with prices set by a commodity market. The other way of extracting hydrogen is electrolysis (B.5), where power currents separate hydrogen from the other elements. In the case of water (C.1), a very stable compound, large amounts of power are needed to split two hydrogen molecules from one molecule of oxygen (H_2O).

As a fuel for power generation, its economics are doubted by Ulf Bossel (2006). A 100 kWh of power, when used to produce hydrogen, has an output between 19 kWh and 23 kWh energy equivalent. In layman's terms, it appears to make little sense to use 100 kWh of power to get 23 kWh of fuel that will be used to produce power *again*. With cheaper ways to decarbonise power generation, hydrogen may struggle to make its mark in this segment.

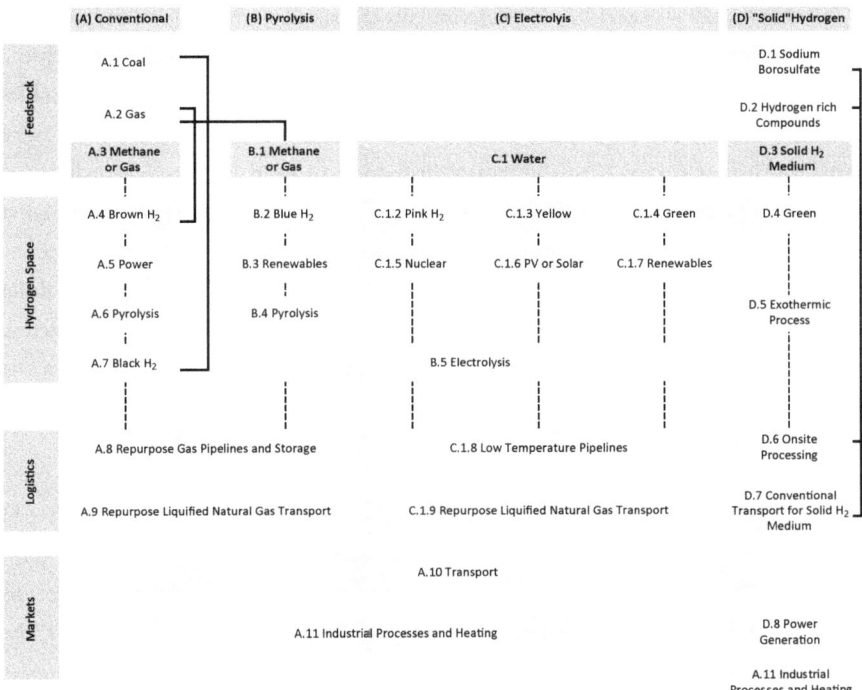

Chart 1.7: Reconfigured Hydrogen Value Chain and Industry Coupling

Transportation and industrial applications (A.10 and A.11) hold greater prospects. With fuels still heavily reliant on oil, decarbonisation takes on a greater challenge. To achieve the ambitious environmental targets, energy firms will have to quickly find pathways to decarbonise transport and industrial processes. However, two factors hinder hydrogen's immediate deployment: Extracting hydrogen uses a lot of energy, with power accounting for a significant share of output cost. Handling hydrogen is expensive, with safety being a major issue. Just like earlier versions of intermittent renewables, the costs hinder wide-scale deployment.

This is where gas companies may hold some advantage over new entrants. Conversion of gas into hydrogen using pyrolysis (B) opens a pathway to clean fuels while drawing on their existing gas production (B.1), logistics and infrastructure, and storage facilities (A.8 and A.9). Building new pipelines or handling facilities would add to the cost of handling a fuel that is not only lighter than gas but also explosive.

The source of power clearly is a determinant to making hydrogen cost-competitive. The Hydrogen Council (2020) pins their hopes on falling renewables costs to achieve their expected 90% reduction by 2030, with 60% accounted for by lower renewables costs. The scaling up of hydrogen usage is expected to account for the rest of the price reductions, thanks largely to the greater utilisation of fixed investments in logistics and distribution networks. Through *economies of scale*, fixed costs are spread over higher volumes, hence reducing the unit costs of hydrogen.

There are at least two approaches that go against this general thread of making hydrogen and fuel cells cheaper. In reconfiguring how hydrogen is used and delivered, the altered network configuration would reallocate the costs and change the way its benefits are appropriated. Examine these two emerging contrarian approaches, albeit at a very early stage of evolution:

- Paul Ronney, a professor in mechanical engineering and aerospace at Viterbi School of Engineering, University of Southern California, chose to adapt internal combustion engines to enable them to use hydrogen as a fuel. In his thinking, the prospect of rapid deployment of hydrogen is likely to be cheaper and quicker than trying to make fuel cells cheaper (Nightingale, 2019).
- Some start-up companies are experimenting on "solid" hydrogen (D). Using an "exothermic process" (D.5), hydrogen is produced from solid compounds (D.1, D.2, and D.3) onsite at customers' premises (D.6). On a small scale, the process appears to work with some obvious drawbacks. Hydrogen-rich compounds are speciality chemicals, which makes the extracted hydrogen fuel expensive. To its credit, transporting solid hydrogen-rich compounds can use existing logistics for common cargo, providing a clear cost advantage.

Paul Ronney's approach could cement the advantages of oil and gas firms and extant automotive firms. At the very least, it provides consumers with a wider choice of future modes of mobility other than electric vehicles. However, the significant power inputs to produce hydrogen at scale may prove a continuing barrier to adoption.

"Solid" hydrogen may hold greater promise if suitable hydrogen-rich compounds could be mass-produced. The disruption to extant gas logistics and infrastructure could prove dramatic. For now, the process remains at a pilot scale with some years to go before it produces the *proof of concept*. At any rate, this is clearly an approach worth watching given its potential to disrupt.

5
Profitably Adapting to Shifting Worlds

When managers examine how the world is changing, they understand that the future is likely to be ambiguous and different from today's world. Hence, the uncertainties around decision-making. However, when investments are evaluated, people tend to project the *status quo* into a changing future that is *known* and *knowable*. In responding to the challenges of *energy transition* and *sustainability*, policy and managers tend to diverge in pursuing a common purpose.

Sustainability initiatives are premised on a jumble of good intentions, cobbled together as policy or strategic programmes. Articulated as amorphous aspirations, people exhibit a surge of enthusiasm to back a big idea, only to struggle to turn this into tangible actions and outcomes. Worse, in navigating ambiguous and uncertain pathways, policy and some managers equate unknowns to "existential threats". This elicits responses that trap people into pursuing "categorical" remedies that do not work.

Instinctively, managers expect to receive generous subsidies because what they do is of great social value, such as saving humanity from extinction. No sum is too great, particularly when taxpayers' money is there to be spent. Unfortunately, in following a big spending mandate, today's "experts" may fall into the same traps that the 19th century policymakers and managers were stuck in when they tried to solve the "Horse Manure Crisis" with approaches that were known but did not work. Working from the periphery, Henry Ford's Model T made automobiles affordable to own. Inadvertently, by making horse-drawn carriages obsolete, a solution to the "Horse Manure Crisis" was found without intending.

In moving the climate agenda from *remediation* to *sustainability*, managers can profit by creating arenas that nurture emerging opportunities. In helping to shape tomorrow's profitable niches, managers adaptively *repurpose* how their resources are employed. As people experiment and learn, managers *reframe* the problem that they truly need to solve. Informed by deep insights and a realistic view, people can creatively *reconfigure* the way they provide for their needs and wants.

Policy expands access to opportunities by making markets work, enabling people to profit from the wise choices they make. In the final analysis, it is the human mind that influences the way people and societies choose to live. In human societies in which people value their freedom, one recognises that there is no monopoly on wisdom or power. For this very reason, "one political solution fits all" is hardly the path to a sustainable future. For odd reasons, some managers and policies default to compelling compliance rather than working to expand choices through competition.

Policy and managers, however, often forget this very human reality. People respond well to incentives, while they resist when forced. Perhaps, not surprisingly, authoritarian regimes fall on their own weight — a lesson that is lost in today's era of "policy and strategic conformity".

Box 1.1: Antonio Brufau Niubó — Moving Boldly to a Low-Carbon Future

Repsol became a pioneer in December 2019, publicly committing to a net zero, carbon-neutral goal by 2050. What distinguishes Repsol from its peers who followed is the mapping out of the principles underlying the company's strategies with tangible short-term targets. This places responsibility squarely on the leadership's shoulders and the Chief Executive's agenda, which raises the commitment of the C-suite. In a nutshell, Box Chart 1.1.1 outlines what these goals entail for the specific businesses and the strategic focus of each going forward.

Antonio Brufau Niubó, Chairman of the Board, Repsol since 2004, explained:

> I had a very clear premise in mind that a strong balance sheet was a must in order to keep our flexibility to cope with a fast-changing, complex world. That was key for a company like ours working in a risky business. Therefore, lowering our financial risk has always been a priority.
>
> Repsol's consistent commitment to sustainability has led us to move boldly into the low-carbon energy sector. Oil and gas will be with us for many decades for these reasons: *First*, there are still millions of people around the world without access to energy, renewables on their own for many of these people are simply not an option, cost being one of the reasons. *Second*, oil is an essential feedstock to petrochemicals. Without oil, many of the basic goods such as detergents may become unavailable. *Third*, renewables still need gas for backup.

How Repsol seeks to turn this into action is outlined in their 2021–2025 Strategic Plan, with the expected outcomes summarised in Box Chart 1.1.1.

What facilitated Repsol's bold moves is deeply embedded in its corporate genetics. Niubó elaborates how he views sustainability as a strategic imperative:

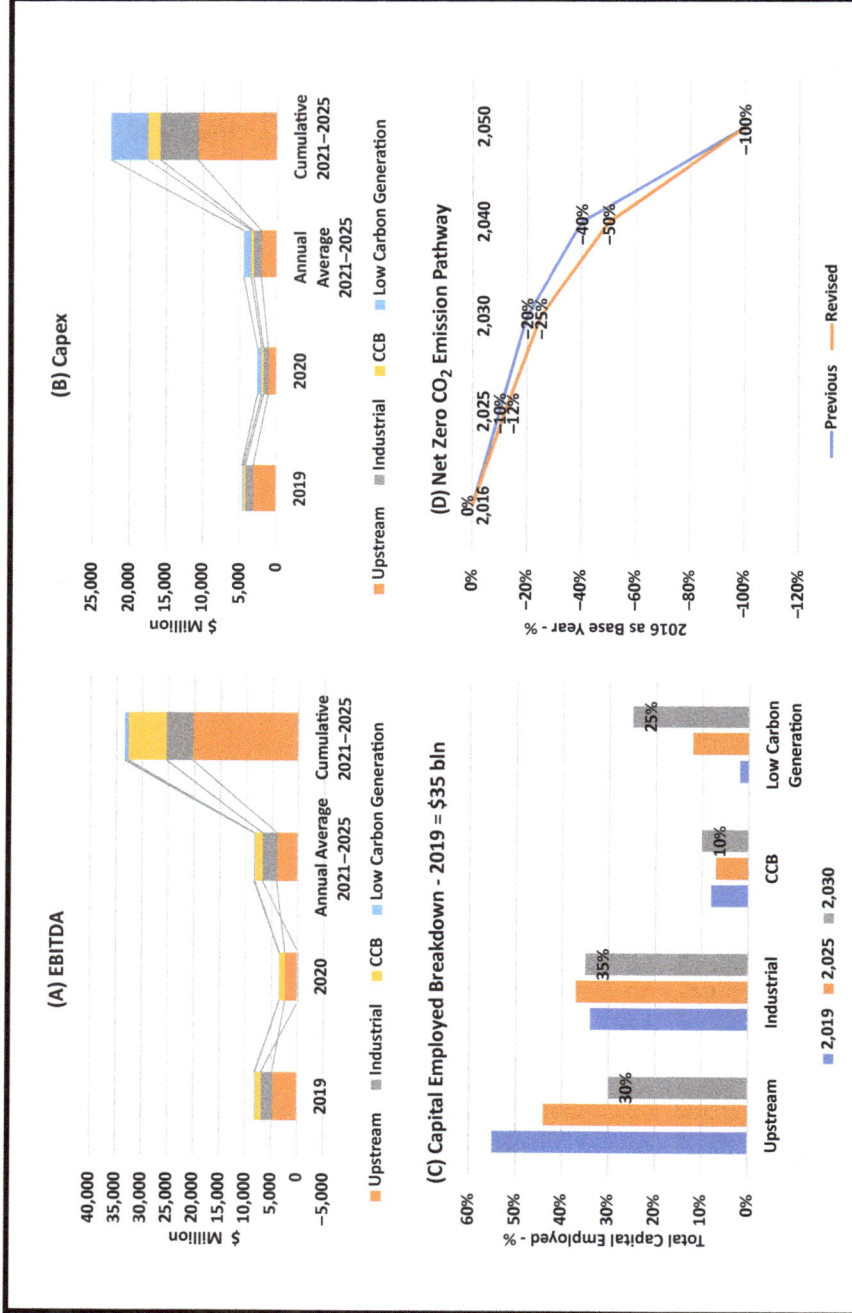

Box Chart 1.1.1: Repsol's Strategic Plan 2021–2025

Note: Capex excludes corporate office capital expenditures.

There are many who think that sustainability is a new phenomenon, something to do with new ways of producing energy, using renewables. In my view, sustainability broadly encompasses environmental, social, and economic parameters. The environmental aspects were already part of our investment and operational standards long before they became fashionable. Since I joined the board in 1996, the board has routinely included environmental criteria in our investments and operational decisions.

As more is known and the means become available, Antonio explains how the sustainability mindset influences the board's strategic approach:

We are conscious that environmental challenges do not have simplistic solutions. However, instead of waiting for someone else to give us the solution, we aim to be part of that solution. This requires commitment from us, proven by our actions, to offer the means to deliver tangible results. To achieve this, we have to sustain our financial viability today and strengthen our agility to pivot to the profitable niches of tomorrow.

1. The capacity to transform profitably

Environmental advocates tar the oil and gas industry with a single brush. The narratives that place environmentalists and some managers in the energy industry at odds with each other have changed little. As early as 1985, Jay D Hair (1985) posed this question to his audience as an avowed environmentalist himself: "Aren't we bone weary of drawing battle lines when we could chart an effective and positive strategy for both economic development and environmental protection?"

One would have thought a decade is a long time to resolve the persistent differences. Apparently not, as Léonie J Archer (1995) observed:

> Environmentalists and the oil industry are not talking to each other. They are addressing a third party that is important *but at cross-purposes*: The governments of OECD[5] countries play the key role. Most of them have the propensity to tax heavily petroleum products. Their main objective is to raise large fiscal revenues. Environmentalists are giving them politically attractive arguments to justify even heavier taxation, which governments use without necessarily believing in their merits.

The 21st century if anything may have sharpened that divide. The climate conversations are seen variously as "techno-fix, Promethean oilman, and climate partnerships *where* defensive responses are facilitated. *This* either entrench well-established understandings that are themselves environmentally harmful or transfer tension from the source of the problem (as producer of fossil fuels) to government or civil society organisations" (Ferns *et al.*, 2019). Seen in this light, Niubó's guiding principles on how Repsol embedded sustainability is given its socio-political context.

Whether or not Repsol's early commitment to sustainability made it unique, it does deviate from the narratives that George Ferns *et al.* (2019) described as the managers' Promethean relationship with more vocal advocates. In Peter Paul Ruben's *Prometheus Bound*, the Dutch master depicts an eagle tearing into the torso of a man to claw into his liver, the liver being the symbol of intelligence. While in deep pain, the man looks at the bird with a fiery glare, ready to fight for his survival. To some advocates, the eagle (read as an avaricious manager) preys on people's weaknesses and inflicts inordinate pain on society for profit. Conversely, managers see themselves as persistently tormented by unelected advocates. The pain comes from some advocates continually but unreasonably demanding, in the name of "science", to comply with vague targets with no grounding in economic or scientific validation, some managers would claim.

Niubó reminds us of a few facts, to his amusement:

---

[5] Organisation for Economic Cooperation and Development groups the developed economies of the world.

> Let us not forget that we were the first from our industry to support the 1997 Kyoto Protocol, a voluntary commitment to tackling rising global temperatures. In 2002, we joined IPIECA,[6] an association that stemmed from a United Nations program to promote sound environmental practices in energy. In 2003, we pioneered the creation of a Climate Change Unit. In 2005, we designed our first Carbon Strategy and joined the European Alliance for Social Responsibility, which saw the inclusion of emission reduction targets in our subsequent strategic plans. From 2006 to 2018, we reduced our CO_2 emissions by 5.1 million metric tonnes. As signatory of the 2015 Paris Agreement, we joined hands with twelve of the major oil and gas companies to pool our know-how and resources under the Oil & Gas Climate Initiative.

After correcting the narrow perspectives that some advocates prefer, Niubó turned to Repsol's own challenges and setbacks in its push to transform itself into a major player, with strengths in Latin America and Spain:

> In our international moves, the acquisition of Argentina's YPF was seen as successful until YPF was "renationalised" by the Argentine government. In Spain, we held controlling interests in Gas Natural, now operating independently as Naturgy, an integrated gas and power company in Spain and parts of Latin America. These changes were significant in turning our strategy on its head. The strategic lessons were invaluable for me and my executive team.

At this juncture of our exchanges, I posed these two questions to Niubó and Repsol:

---

[6] International Petroleum Industry Environmental Conservation Association.

1. What lessons could Repsol apply from your Argentine experiences or "debacle" to some who were less supportive?
2. Given your exit from Naturgy, how would your return to the power business yield different, perhaps better outcomes?

Niubó reflected on these strategic questions. He started with a basic element that is often ignored by observers in financial markets. To wit:

I am proud of how our people successfully overcome the most challenging circumstances. Our humility allows us to recognise our weaknesses and act to remedy them. In turn, we trust each other to do the right thing. Combined, our people never cease to amaze me with their capacity to turn weaknesses into strengths, particularly in times of dire need.

Niubó recounted these examples to illustrate his point:

When I assumed the leadership of Repsol, Argentina through YPF[7] was roughly half of our business. To sustain our integrated business, we needed to expand our oil and gas reserves, which fell far short to cover what we produced. The pace, however, was too slow for me. I was also aiming to diversify to increase the weight of more developed markets. Undoubtedly, YPF's "renationalisation" was a blow to us. The crisis for us, however, may have allowed us to pivot to reposition Repsol's business to refocus on its developed markets.

The recovery of six billion dollars as settlement for our YPF shares was unexpected[8] but helped in accelerating our portfolio repositioning. Almost by a stroke of a pen, cash "windfall" helped in two ways: Reduce Argentine risks, rebalance portfolio to increase oil and gas reserves.

---

[7] Yacimientos de Petroleos Fiscales, formerly a state-owned Argentine oil and gas company that Repsol acquired in 1999. In 2012, after irreconcilable differences with the Argentine government, President Cristina Fernandez Kirchner ordered the renationalisation of YPF.
[8] Equity analysts attributed nil value as a consensus.

We moved to divest assets with premium ratings to maximise proceeds. By 2013, we reached an agreement with Shell plc for the sale of our liquified natural gas (LNG) assets in Perú and Trinidad & Tobago to raise $4.4 billion that accrues to us. We reduced our debt by half to about $2.8 billion. This was fortuitous as the cash pile of more than $10 billion gave us an edge to move on Talisman Energy, a Canadian firm with exploration and production assets in North America, Indonesia, Malaysia, and Vietnam in Southeast Asia, and Norway and Colombia among others. We paid $8.3 billion in cash and assumed $4.7 billion in debt, leaving us with some spare cash.

From Repsol's disclosures, by 2015 the firm had transformed into a leading private energy group well positioned in developed energy markets. Niubó observed: "Equity analysts regained their enthusiasm. Financial markets rewarded us with stellar share revaluation that year."

In emphasising value over size, Niubó added:

We gained the position as a leading exploration and production oil and gas group within three years of our unfortunate Argentine setback. What is often ignored, however, is the focus we managed to instil in the midst of great pessimism that prevailed among investors and some of our stakeholders. We engaged them by creating a focused team within, which dealt with the Argentine "crisis" and any related matters. This gave our operating groups a sense of normalcy in what remained as profitable businesses. As a result, we managed to insulate our business so that they could focus on running the business in the best way they knew how.

2. Priming for *PIVOT*

In preparing for the energy market of the future, Niubó reflected:

> The transition is happening at two levels. Products and operating processes are decarbonising, requiring us to find ways to reconfigure our production and logistics to reduce our CO_2 emissions across our value chain. What our customers would require may have to blend low-carbon energy products with how their use can be facilitated. In a nutshell, we are witnessing a transition from a product-focused business into one that is increasingly service-oriented.

Niubó illustrated how these observations could tangibly impact Repsol's future business:

> In our petrol filling stations, our forecourts fill up the vehicles with fuel, have a tire or vehicle washing service. Some lubricants, accessories, or groceries are retailed, doubling up as a "convenience store". In the future, with electric vehicles (EVs), hydrogen, or alternative fuels becoming ubiquitous, the configuration will have to change.
>
> At residential, commercial, or industrial locations, parking lots may become recharging points for EVs. To retain our retail customers, which is 24 million in Spain alone or capture new business, we may need to supply power. With solar panels getting cheaper, more of these locations are installing solar power to complement their supplies from their utilities. I see this as an opportunity for Repsol to service these needs by managing how their EVs are charged while sitting idle. Perhaps we can offer an operating service to manage their loads for the efficient use of their solar output. We create value by freeing up time for owners to focus on what they do best, while we employ our expertise at their service.

Niubó then addresses my question on Naturgy and why it may not be the most appropriate platform to deliver on Repsol's strategic shift:

Naturgy was premised on the integration of gas with power to lock in value in an integrated gas business. While the logic was impeccable, gas has become more competitively traded, while transmitting and distributing power remains a highly regulated business, even though more choices are given to consumers. In this sense, merging with a gas and power network business gives us scale, although its true benefits are in doubt. Our 24 million customers most probably are also power users that we already access. Hence, my question is, what additional leverage am I achieving with a merger? For me, this remains an open question.

To avoid any doubt, Niubó emphasised:

Naturgy is a great company and we both shared our drive to monetise regional gas chains. With the sale of our LNG assets, and our strategic shift to low-carbon power, a non-operated stake in an incumbent utility may no longer offer similar value. Hence, we decided that Naturgy can be more valuable as an integrated entity with a focus on power and gas distribution.

Niubó elaborated:

In my mind, by moving into low-carbon power supply, with coal and nuclear power explicitly excluded, I foresee two principal advantages. We are not weighed down by legacy assets that need major upgrades. Instead, we can move adaptively and incorporate advanced low-carbon technologies and systems unimpeded. The "prosumers" phenomenon, where customers become producers as well as consumers of energy, is an opportunity to offer our digital advances (through Caleidoscope). We can work with our customers to manage the use and sale of their excess power, which would ease their entry into the "prosumer" arena if they chose.

I do not see, as some people I talk to would naively believe, renewables as a panacea to addressing the dilemmas of climate challenges and economic well-being. I recognise a low-carbon future is an essential part of that solution. While we are wholeheartedly committed to low-carbon technologies, we do recognise renewables, particularly solar panel production, will have to address more explicitly its emerging environmental impact. These challenges revolve around the mining and geopolitics of rare earth metals, an important component of solar panels and battery storage. How we dispose of decommissioned wind turbines and solar and battery systems is something we need to incorporate into our investment evaluation. This is where our long experience in managing the tail-end decommissioning of oilfields would come in handy. In fact, we can probably offer a lesson or two in executing complex, capital intensive, and environmentally sensitive projects to our peers in the renewable world.

An example of this is Repsol's pioneering offshore wind venture at WindAtlantic, where Repsol partners with Energia Do Portugal Renewable (EDPR) and France's ENGIE. Similar pioneering initiatives are employed for Repsol's e-mobility solutions, where recharging is an add-on to their petrol station forecourts. Hydrogen fuel is seen as having the potential to leverage on its extensive know-how in logistics and storage. The latter is often ignored in the re-emerging interests in the hydrogen fuel "relaunch", where debate appears focused on conversion processes and the fuel's green credentials. In Niubó's words:

"I truly believe that without an eye on the entire logistics and value chain, the hydrogen aspiration could be derailed sooner rather than later. This is where I see our oil and gas experience could make a major difference to hydrogen's prospective widescale deployment. This part is the essence of our work with our partners in H4ALL, a fifteen-member group committed to finding solutions to promote hydrogen fuel".

On a broader scale, Niubó continued with how Repsol implements similar approaches to decarbonise their businesses.

3. Pathways to low-carbon prosperity

Niubó reflected on the gravity of the tasks ahead:

> Our commitment to achieve net zero carbon emissions by 2050 implies we have to start our transformation today. This demands of us a change in our mindset from one of sustaining our extant advantages in engineering and operational effectiveness, while continuing to be essential, to one where entrepreneurial pursuit is encouraged and rewarded. As a consequence, we have to broaden our recruitment to a diverse pool of talents. In the male-dominated industry that we operate in, we have to be more creative in attracting and retaining high performing women into our executive ranks. I foresee our women leaders to occupy at least 35% of our leadership roles by 2025.

In contemplating Repsol's choices of the next profitable niches to focus on, Niubó pondered:

> Undoubtedly, the fuel and power markets are more likely to converge. As our 24 million customers drive through our petrol stations' forecourts, some will fill up with gas, hydrogen fuel, or recharge their batteries for their electric vehicles. We may see some who will generate their own power at home, once the technologies and regulation make it worth their while. This is not the stuff of science fiction that happens in futuristic movies. I can see this as a realistic prospect of happening within this decade.

He continues:

> To respond to these evolving scenarios, we need people who can imagine how these futures could evolve, prepare for, and take timely action. This is

the entrepreneurial mindset that we are propagating: Focus on taking calculated risks with informed decisions, less on control for control's sake.

Here's how Niubó sees Repsol evolving:

Our smaller scale compared to our rivals may limit our capacity to capture bigger opportunities. With more limited resources to spare, we are disciplined to be more selective in pursuing only the most attractive opportunities for us. This may not be a bad thing, as we are encouraged to use our wits to outcompete our rivals rather than force our way in and pay over the odds.

Paradoxically, the vagaries of politics may have taken a different turn. While a low-carbon energy system is considered a desired outcome by policy, some advocates call for a total elimination of fossil fuels now. I can choose to ignore these demands as unrealistic and sulk. However, I am one for shaping and constructively contributing to collaborative action to arrive at achieving tangible results.

By 2030, Repsol will lead in providing multi-energy supplies services, with low-carbon power accounting for 25% of our capital employed, while customer-facing services will be around 10%, supported by digital processes to ease our interactions with customers. Increasing digital use in managing production processes explains partly this profit resilience. Capital spending is redirected to biofuels and clean fuels, such as hydrogen, that may become commercially viable, resulting in green fuels replacing gas and petrol products. Including low-carbon processes in our upstream and industrial business, investment in reducing our carbon footprint would comprise about half of our capital employed by 2030.

To prepare to take a leadership role in hydrogen fuel in the Iberian Peninsula, we are on track to produce an equivalent of 400 MW by 2025, rising to 1,200 MW in 2030. Petronor, our plant in Bilbao, is to engage in a number of promising initiatives that could support this ambition.

In moving forward, Niubó emphasises:

> Now that we have taken the lead in going public with our strategic aspirations, we seek to deliver on what we have promised. What started as a hazy vision when I took on the Chairmanship, has given rise to very realistic prospects for our energy system to be decarbonised sooner rather than later. At the core of this confidence, is my recognition of what we are good at, and what others can do better. To broaden our capabilities, we are creating an environment within Repsol where we can embrace those who are better. We invite them to join hands and work with us, as partners, as professionals, members of our community, and as leaders in our common ventures, to bring us closer to our aspired future.

****

Antonio Brufau Nuibó, Chairman, Repsol and Repsol Foundation, is credited for leading Repsol to become a leading multi-energy firm in Spain and Portugal and its pivot to become a leader in low-carbon transition among its peers in oil and gas. Prior to Repsol, Nuibó was Managing Director of "la Caixa" Group, a major financial and industrial European entity based in Spain.

Angel Bautista, Repsol's Director of Institutional Relations, coordinated and contributed to the provision of information included in this feature. Professor Jorge Soley Pujol, IESE Business School, facilitated the exchange of views with Repsol. My appreciation for their contributions.

Box 1.2: RAG Austria AG — The Missing Link in Decarbonising Energy

Battery power storage appears to be the singular missing link for setting humanity on the course to a decarbonised energy system, advocates would assert. By storing excess power in a battery, stored power can balance the grid when needed. The battery can transmit power to balance the load, when power supply dips or decongest the grid when there is oversupply. At night, solar power has nil production, a drawback that is remedied by storing power during the day in a battery for use at night (IRENA, 2019a).

Without battery storage, a novel practice emerged: On a blustery Saturday night, the National Grid paid households 1–5 pence for every kWh they consumed (Ambrose, 2019) in a bid to encourage more use, to avoid having the power grid go down. Germany and California, USA, curtail wind and solar (St John, 2020; Deign, 2020), as do many other systems. The reason is economic: It is cheaper to curtail than to upgrade the grid to accommodate sharper load fluctuations. With affordable batteries, one hopes this would offer a remedy.

Michael Laengle, Chief Financial Officer, RAG Austria AG (RAG), turned this "accepted wisdom" on its head, by making better use of excess intermittent renewables. Intrigued by RAG's approach, Laengle and I discussed his career since his days at EVN, Lower Austria's power and gas distribution utility two decades ago, when Dr Rudolph Gruber chaired EVN.

1. What should be stored — Power or gas?

Laengle posed an intriguing question: What would you rather store — power or gas to conserve energy for future use? For power supplies using feedstock that can be stored, such as coal, gas, or diesel, or water, or geothermal steam, I would stop producing power and store the feedstock. Clearly, with no feedstock to store, wind or solar does not benefit from this prescribed logic. This brings me back to hoping that affordable battery storage would become available soon.

This leaves the grid operator with few options in today's world: Shut down more baseload plants and incur restarting costs. Otherwise, pay consumers to consume more power as National Grid did, whichever turns out cheaper.

In Laengle's mind, that is a complete waste of money and energy. Offering an alternative, he explains: "We recognised this problem. We instead examined what we could use excess the power for that produces economic value." It was not long before RAG zeroed in on electrolysis and pyrolysis, energy-intensive ways of extracting hydrogen from water or methane, respectively. Laengle continues:

Power costs are what impede these technologies from affordably producing hydrogen fuel. With excess renewables having negative economic costs, by avoiding payments to customers, using excess power to extract hydrogen would make economic logic.

Power-to-gas took form and has kept scientists and engineers at RAG gainfully employed ever since.

We did a back-of-the-envelope calculation. A first estimate shows that hydrogen production by pyrolysis may achieve a substantial cost advantage due to lower energy consumption during processing compared to electrolysis. This could have great potential in terms of competitiveness.

"By blending hydrogen with gas in storage, the carbon content was shown to decline", Laengle observed. In another experiment, CO_2 was injected together with hydrogen into depleted gas fields: "What was puzzling was the decrease of CO_2 in the gas field, as well as in the surrounding area." Scientists had no explanation. It was of course too soon to celebrate: If CO_2 can vanish without a trace, had nature offered a natural pathway to reducing CO_2 concentration with minimal human intervention? The jury is still out on this, with RAG's scientists cautiously evaluating the factors that caused CO_2 to vanish.

What transpired is what I refer to as a *Dom Perignon* moment, drawing on the legend around how champagne was supposedly invented. Specifically:

Fray Pierre Pérignon was a Benedictine monk who fermented wine using yeast as catalyst for his monastery. Yeast stopped fermenting in winter and resumed fermentation in spring after the wine was stored in bottles. This caused the bottles to burst from the gas build-up. Indeed, a problem for the monk. Some bottles remained intact. As legend has it, when Fray Pérignon tasted the wine with the problematic sparkle, he supposedly exclaimed: "Come quickly. I am tasting the stars!" In his honour, one of the leading champagne labels bears his name today.

RAG's scientists suspected that bacteria penetrated the depleted gas field. Hydrogen and CO_2 may have activated the bacteria to catalyse the hydrogen to bond with carbon molecules. Without the scientists intending to, the bonding produced "synthetic methane", a carbon-neutral compound of value.

By accident, RAG's scientific and engineering minds may have replicated the environmental equivalent of *Dom Pérignon's moment*. This, at least, is what appears to my simple mind as an economic thinker. In reality, RAG's scientists discovered that the resulting "synthetic methane" imitated nature's way of converting hydrocarbons that would otherwise evolve over millions of years.

2. Cinderella's coming-out ball?

Conventional gas storage's future is overshadowed by uncertain gas prospects (Messeler, 2021) and stringent policy actions, the popular media reports. The demise of gas, which some would like to see as part of a low-carbon drive, would mean less need for gas storage. Policy is lending a hand, as exemplified by UK Chancellor Philip Hammond's banning of gas heaters for new constructions starting from 2025 (Habtsesellasie, 2021).

Paraphrasing Mark Twain, the rumour of gas storage's demise has been greatly exaggerated. Herib Blanco and André Faaij (2018), after weighing the prospects of various ways of storing energy, concluded that battery power storage would struggle to keep up with the demands of an "all renewables" system. An alternative is to store high-density fuel such as hydrogen, which is carbon-neutral and low cost, without the toxic waste that comes with batteries at disposal. With affordable hydrogen becoming feasible, *affordable hydrogen storage is a must, and a low hanging fruit, for wider use of hydrogen as a fuel*, Thierry Trouvé, France GRT Gaz' Chief Executive asserts (Trouvé, 2020).

RAG's *power-to-gas* efforts rearrange the previous logic that prevailed in the gas industry. Used principally as fuel, one explores for natural gas, produces it, and transports it by pipeline (as in Austria) or ship (as with liquified natural gas, or LNG) to end-users. It is used for heating, compressed as fuel, or converted to power. This was how RAG evolved 85 years ago from a gas exploration and production venture into Austria's dominant gas storage and supply company accounting for a storage capacity equivalent to 75% of Austria's gas demand. In contrast, *power-to-gas* uses excess power that would otherwise be curtailed, hence wasted, as feedstock to extract hydrogen as a fuel.

A legacy of its natural gas exploration in Austria, RAG is endowed with depleted gas fields. Before the term "circular economy" was coined, RAG repurposed these fields into affordable, secure, and environmentally sound gas storage facilities. Laengle proudly reminded me:

> We converted about half into underground storage for our gas supplies, which is unmatched anywhere in the world. This leaves us with enough capacity to meet expanding volumes, including new quantities for synthetic gas or hydrogen — a unique advantage for RAG.

Laengle's upbeat outlook may appear at odds with the dim views of fossil fuels favoured by some climate advocates. On closer examination, *power-to-gas* may just offer a more technologically realistic energy configuration that accelerates the pace at which an energy system can decarbonise. Laengle explains:

> Our work in *power-to gas* shows hydrogen can be extracted affordably using pyrolysis. This departs from electrolysis which is very expensive as more energy is needed to break free hydrogen from water, a very stable compound. Our depleted gas fields offer economical storage, and are already connected to extant supply networks to access end-users for energy and heating, industry, and transport.

> Natural gas will remain important. Through our Underground Sun Conversion and Storage Initiatives, we bring together reputed scientists, engineers, and managers to formulate workable solutions to position RAG as leading in integrating renewable gas to a future energy mix.
>
> We bring in our logistics mindset, where we find the most effective ways to link products and services with markets, and feedstock with production. This is how we narrowed our focus to how power and gas would complement each other, and we came to the view that tighter coupling could yield more benefits. Through hydrogen fuel, transport and industrial processes are offered more choices to adopt low-carbon alternatives. This may also kick-start substitution of petrol and diesel in transport with hydrogen fuel in the future, to accelerate decarbonising transport.
>
> The missing link in all the policy efforts is the recognition of gas storage as central to meeting this decarbonisation aspiration. This applies to other forms of energy storage such as pump storage hydro, where limited policy focus is given.

In painting an alternative future, Laengle concurs with a foreseeable endgame of a low carbon-intensive energy system. The path to get there, however, is radically different from a single-minded pursuit of expensive technologies that policy is inadvertently wedded to.

While power-to-gas holds some promise for the future, RAG foresees a world where gas remains an important part of the Austrian (and European) energy mix, albeit in declining proportions. To prepare for this feasible future, RAG examines these possible pathways, as Laengle elaborates:

> Total electrification of the energy system may prove less likely. In fact, official estimates still place a third of our supplies as coming from gas. Power is a way to transmit energy, it is not a carrier, as some may suggest. In our minds, the solution may lie in converting excess renewables into forms that can be readily transported, particularly over long distances, without excessive losses.

> The solution will have to lie in finding cost-effective energy carriers that are transportable. This is where the focus goes back to importing gas, or gradually making way for similar fluids to take up the slack that lower natural gas volumes would free up in our storage. Wind and solar power alone are unlikely to fulfil the expanding power demand that could only be met using gas, or similar fuels. Instead of seeing the demise of our gas storage business, we see its emergence as a critical component to sustain reliable, secure, and low-carbon energy supplies.
>
> Recent events may conspire to our advantage. Power grids experience excess renewables supplies that vary widely. This makes managing the load more challenging. Paying consumers to use more power to clear up excess supplies works for now. This is a loss to the grid operators and a waste of power. This inspired us to see how we could convert it into an opportunity, as a gas storage operator. For now, it points to storing hydrogen fuel. More immediate-term opportunities lie in creating a Central European gas storage hub and expanding what we have already started to our neighbouring markets.

The principles are fairly simple conceptually. Power is too intermittent and battery storage is expensive and of limited capability. Excess renewables can instead be used to produce useful energy carriers. Out of this concept, RAG evolved its strategy of adapting and innovating in the field of logistics: "Rather than see the emergence of renewables as a threat to our gas storage, we try to offer tangible solutions to the real problem of what to do with excess power."

3. Where firms and policy can meet

Managers agreeing or opposing what politicians say may not be paramount to a firm's performance, except in authoritarian regimes. Judging how policy measures would impact how a business does is essential. Laengle describes how the evolving European Union policy landscape influences managerial decisions, particularly when investing for the future:

European governments are very visible in driving energy transition in the 21st century. Policy supported intermittent renewables with subsidies, using feed-in tariffs for wind and solar power. A price for carbon credits followed by setting up a trading mechanism, keeping pace with deepening energy market deregulation.

In Germany, the push went farther, with coal and nuclear power slated for closures within a decade or so. Ultimately, the costs are spread to all consumers as a levy on power sold by utilities. The price distortions made energy more expensive for everyone, posing serious questions about energy-reliant industries' ability to compete globally. The European Union's *Green Deal* aims to do more of the same, but at a bigger scale, directed by governments.

I offer a view of an energy future grounded in reality. I see an ever-closer convergence of gas and power, in a symbiotic manner. Electrons and molecules, and how they complement each other, will accelerate decarbonisation because it substantially lowers the costs while harnessing the innate advantages of dense fuel and flexible volumes that secure supplies in a stable and reliable way. This is the hallmark of industrial processes and logistics that propel societal prosperity.

Faced with these realities, energy firms responded differently. Laengle reflected:

Some of the major energy firms were very self-confident in their dominant positions. Probably, some of these emerging trends were missed in their strategic assessments, making them slow to respond and even slower to offer solutions to address these geopolitical and societal changes. In failing to prepare in advance, the tasks of transforming their business become more drastic, particularly in changing their corporate structures, processes, and even their culture.

In Laengle's view,

> Governments, with all the best intentions, are not immune to public opinion and their ideological inclinations. For this reason, they may err in prescribing or even prohibiting certain technologies instead of simply defining a framework under which private initiatives can operate. In finding the right mix of policy and private investments, managers and private capital are best left to find the solutions through a functioning market. After all, private capital underwrites the investment and commits to the success, or takes the penalties of failures, that their decisions may entail. In contrast, policy and advocates may offer their "solutions" without as much as risking a penny of their own capital.

4. Pivoting to a low-carbon future

To Laengle, "the future belongs to gas with a twist". In working to find innovative ways to harness the power of the sun and the wind, RAG may have found a novel commercial approach. Laengle explains how this could come about: "Wind + sun = green gas is a simple concept that guides our innovation work. We harness excess power in our hydrogen extraction process." For RAG, these advantages are identified by Laengle:

> RAG's depleted gas fields are crucial to provide the missing link in making hydrogen storage affordable. Reliable power from gas and hydrogen can balance the sharp swings from intermittent wind and solar power. In markets that forego intermittent renewables, hydrogen can fuel power generation, and even offer a clean fuel solution to transportation and industry that to date is elusive at scale. The latter two had hardly moved the needle in reducing their CO_2 emissions as a sector, albeit with specific firms making headway with their own innovations. It is not unthinkable that hydrogen fuel may temper the enthusiasm for gold-plated solutions inherent with battery power storage or the singular push for the sun towards a fully "electrified future".

Fossil fuels are vilified by some climate advocates, who erroneously extend their ire to natural gas, while all forecasts from official sources still point to a 30% to 40% share for gas in the energy mix by 2050. We foresee that some of the natural gas will blend or serve as feedstock for green gas. With *power-to-gas* achieving scale, our gas fields may prove to be the largest "battery" substitute to sustain wind and solar power's economic value. Specifically, gas storage provides a seasonal balance of renewable energy production and demand on a large scale.

In offering affordable hydrogen storage, mobility's transition to low-carbon fuels may just gain pace. Transport's substitution of petrol, bunker, and jet fuel with hydrogen fuel may indeed become a reality.

These pathways can indeed unblock the economy's shift to a low-carbon future. By providing viable substitutes, with a clear path to appropriating financial gains, policy may have found a way to play an enabling role and succeed by intervening less in achieving their low-carbon aspirations.

At this point, I posed this question to Laengle: With some of RAG's larger peers having been slower to act, what made you appreciate these challenges and act earlier?

We do not claim to have a better grasp of the issues, because of our superior intelligence. Far from it! What we have is the humility to recognise that we do not know all the answers. As a specialised service, our fortune is tied to our relevance in enabling the storage and delivery of reliable, secure, and affordable energy that gas is proving versatile in fulfilling. Our strategic questions become pointed and specific, always directed at crafting tangible and workable pathways to a viable future.

As a voice from a distant past, I could almost hear Dr Rudolph Gruber's laughter come to life. At a dinner with his principal stakeholders, I was privileged to join him on the outskirts of Vienna (Austria). The occasion was a gathering, weeks prior to

EVN's 75th anniversary celebration. Dr Gruber enjoined us: "Listen to what politicians say to entertain us. Heed more the policy measures that result from their actions. It could favour or hit us hard — wise managers know how to judge which way it might go."

****

Dr Michael Laengle, Chief Finance Officer (CFO), RAG Austria AG and a member of RAG's Management Board. While working on his PhD in Business Administration, he was Assistant Professor at Vienna University of Economics and Business. After some years in audit and tax consultancy, Michael joined EVN, an Austrian-headquartered utility group, where he eventually served as finance director. He is active in Austrian and international business organisations such as The Federation of Austrian Industries and EUROGAS.

Bibliography

Ambrose, J. (2019). Thousands were paid to use extra renewable electricity on windy weekend. *The Guardian*, December 9, 2019.

Amram, M. and Kulatilaka, N. (2009). The invisible green hand: How individual decisions and markets can reduce green house gas emissions. *California Management Review*, 51(2), Winter 2009, 1994–2018.

API (2021). API Statement on IEA Report on Pathway to Net Zero By 2050. American Petroleum Institute, May 18, 2021.

Archer, L. J. (1995). *Environmentalists vs Oil Producers: Clearing Misunderstandings for Constructive Action*. Oxford Institute for Energy Studies, EV18, 1995.

Aurer, I.L (2021). Guest Commentary: An assessment of the Hague District Court's decision in the Milieudefensie *et al* v. Royal Dutch Shell plc. *Sabin Centre for Climate Change Law, Columbia Law School*, May 28, 2021.

Baazil, D. and Lombrana, L. M. (2021). What a Dutch Court Ruling Means for Shell and Big Oil. *Bloomberg Green*, June 4, 2021.

Barcelona, R. G. (2012). Wind power deployment — Why Spain succeeded? *Renewable Energy Law & Policy*, 2, 146–149.

Barcelona, R. G (2015). Renewable energy with volatile prices: Why NPV fails to tell the whole story. *Journal of Applied Corporate Finance*, 27(1), 101–109.

Barcelona, R. G. (2017). *Energy Investments: An Adaptive Approach to Profiting from Uncertainties*. London: Palgrave Macmillan.

Barcelona, R. G., de Wilde, A., and Nugruho, H. (2019). Indonesia's geothermal resource paradox: Unbundling risks, unleashing private capital. *The Indonesian Journal of Development Planning*, III(1), 1–18.

Barrera, P. (2021). Graphite outlook 2021: Demand from battery segment to grow. *Graphite Investing News*, January 11, 2021.

BBC (2021). Shell: Netherlands court orders oil giant to cut emissions. *British Broadcasting Corporation*, May 26, 2021.

Blanco, H. and Faaij, A. (2018). A review at the role of storage in energy systems with focus on power to gas and long-term storage. *Renewable and Sustainable Energy Reviews*, 81(2018), 1049–1086.

Bordoff, J. (2021). Why Shaking Up Big Oil could be a Pyrrhic Victory. *Foreign Policy*, June 3, 2021.

Bossell, U. (2006). Does a hydrogen economy make sense? *Proceedings of the IEEE*, 94(10), 1826–1837, October 2006.

BP (2021). *Statistical Review of World Energy 2020,* 70th Edition. London: BP plc.

Camargo-Renteria, E. (2021). Extreme weather shows need for diversified power grid that includes natural gas. *Energy In Depth,* April 1, 2021.

Chouinard, Y., Ellison, J., and Ridgeway, R. (2011). The sustainable economy. *Harvard Business Review,* October 2011.

Chrobak, U. (2021). Solar power got cheap. So why aren't we using it more? *Popular Science,* January 28, 2021.

Clarke, R. A., Stavins, R. N., Greeno, J. L., Bavaria, J. L., Cairncross, F., Esty, D. C., Smart, B., Piet, J., Wells, R. P., Gray, R., Fischer, K., and Schot, J. (1994). The challenge of going green. *Harvard Business Review,* July–August 1994.

Cleveland, C. J. and Morris, C. G. (2014) (eds.). *Dictionary of Energy,* 2nd Edition. Walthams, MA: Elsevier.

Crowley, K. (2021). Investors to Big Oil: Energy transition is happening, and there's no going back. *World Oil,* May 27, 2021.

Davis-Peccoud, J., Stone, P., and Tovey, C. (2016). Achieving breakthrough results in sustainability. *Briefs — Bain & Company,* November 17, 2016.

Deign, J. (2020). Germany's maxed-out grid is causing trouble across Europe. *gtm,* March 31, 2020.

DiSavino, S. (2021). California tells public to prepare for heat wave; power prices soar. *Reuters,* June 12, 2021.

EEA (2019). Adaptation challenges and opportunities for the European energy system: Building a climate-resilient low carbon energy system. EEA Report 01/2019, European Environmental Agency.

Energy Information Administration (EIA) (2019). *Energy Outlook 2019.* Washington D.C.: Energy Information Administration.

Esty, D. C. (2017). Red lights to green lights: From 20th century environmental regulation to 21st century sustainability. *Environmental Law,* 47(1), 1–80.

European Commission (EC) (2019). A European green deal. https://ec.europa.eu/info/strategy/priorities-2019-2024/european-green-deal_en. Accessed on May 20, 2021.

Ferns, G., Amaeshi, K., and Lambert, A. (2019). Drilling their own graves: How the European oil and gas supermajors avoid sustainability tensions through mythmaking. *Journal of Business Ethics,* 158, 201–231.

G7 (2021). G7 climate and environment Ministers' communiqué, London, 21 May 2021. Accessed on June 12, 2021: https://www.gov.uk/government/publications/g7-climate-and-environment-ministers-meeting-may-2021-communique/g7-climate-and-environment-ministers-communique-london-21-may-2021#contents.

Habtesellasie, M. (2021). Your boiler could be extinct by 2025 — And here's what experts say. *Ideal Home,* January 22, 2021.

Hair, J. D. (1985). An environmentalist's view of the oil industry. Paper presented at the Annual Meeting Papers, Division of Production, Dallas, Texas, March 1985.

Hall, M. (2021). Shell buys solar and storage company Savion. *pv magazine*, December 14, 2021.

Harvey, F. (2021). Global green recovery plans fail to match 2008 stimulus, report shows. *The Guardian*, February 12, 2021.

Helm, D. (2012). *The Carbon Crunch: Revised and Updated Edition*. New Haven and London: Yale University Press.

Helm, D. (2020). *Net Zero: How We Stop Causing Climate Change*. London: William Collins.

Heritage Foundation (2021). The 3 big differences between conservatives and progressives. www.heritage.org/conservatism/heritage-explains/the-3-big-differences-between-conservatives-and-progressives. Accessed on May 8, 2021.

Hoffmann, A. J. (2018). The next phase of business sustainability. *Stanford Social Innovation Review*, Spring 2018.

Howes, M., Wortley, L., Potts, R., Dedekorkut-Howes, A., Serrano-Newmann, S., Davidson, j., Smith, T., and Nunn, P. (2017). Environmental sustainability: A case of policy implementation failure? *Sustainability*, 9(165), 2–17.

Hurst, L. and Baazil, D. (2021). Shell Ditches "Dutch" from Name and Makes Britain its HQ. *Bloomberg*, November 15, 2021.

Hydrogen Council (2020). *Path to Hydrogen Competitiveness: A Cost Perspective*. Brussells, Belgium: Hydrogen Council, January 20, 2020.

IEA (2020). *Projected Costs of Generating Electricity 2020*. Paris: International Energy Agency.

IEA (2021). *Net Zero by 2050: A Roadmap for the Global Energy Sector*. Paris: International Energy Agency.

IPCC (2018). Summary for Policymakers of IPCC Special Report on Global Warming of 1.5° C approved by governments. New York: United Nations Inter-governmental Panel on Climate Change, October 18, 2018.

IRENA (2019a). *Utility-Scale Batteries: Innovation Landscape Brief*. Abu Dhabi: International Renewable Energy Agency.

IRENA (2019b). *Renewable Energy Auctions: Status and Trends Beyond Price*. Abu Dhabi: International Renewable Energy Agency.

Jaffe, A. B., Peterson, S. R., Portney, P. R., and Stavins, R. N. (1995). Environmental regulation and the competitiveness of U.S. manufacturing: What does the evidence tell us? *Journal of Economic Literature*, XXXIII132–163, March 1995.

Jevons, S.W. (1865). *The Coal Question: An Inquiry Concerning the Progress of the Nation and the Probable Exhaustion of Coal Mines*. London: Macmillan.

Johnson, B. (2021). The Great Horse Manure Crisis. Historic UK. Accessed on May 1, 2021: www.historic-uk.com/HistoryUK/HistoryofBritain/Great-Horse-Manure-Crisis-of-1894/.

Jones, G. (2018). *Varieties of Green Business: Industries, Nations and Time*. Northampton, MA: Edward Elgar Publishing Inc.

Koonin, S. E. (2021). *Unsettled: What Climate Science Tells Us, What It Doesn't, and Why It Matters*. Dallas, TX: BenBella Books Inc.

Krauss, C. (2021). Royal Dutch Shell sells Permian Basin Oil Holdings for $9.5 Billion. *The New York Times*, September 20, 2021.

Krumdieck, S. (2020). *Transition Engineering: Building a Sustainable Future*. Boca Raton, FL: CRC Press.

Layke, J., Jaeger, J., Pastor, K., Levin, K., and Searchinger, T. (2021). 5 things to know about the IEA's roadmap to net zero by 2050. *World Resources Institute*, May 21, 2021.

Llardo, M. and Nielsen, R. (2018). Human adaptation to extreme environmental conditions. *Current Opinion Genetics & Development*, 53, 77–82, December 2018.

Lynch, M. (2018). What ever happened to peak oil? *Forbes*, June 29, 2018.

Malthus, T. R. (2018). *An Essay on the Principle of Population: The 1803 Edition. Edited and with an Introduction by Shannon C Stimson*. New Haven, CT: Yale University Press.

Matsui, R. (ed.) (2021). *Solar Risk Assessment 2021: Quantitative Insights from Industry Experts*. San Francisco, CA: kWh Analytics.

McGarry, S. (2018). Moving the millions: How Henry Ford made the automobile affordable for every American. *Autodeck*, September 5, 2018.

Messeler, D. (2021). The future for natural gas is far from certain. *OilPrice.com*, January 7, 2021.

Milman, O. (2021). Antonio Guteres on the climate crisis: "We are coming to a point of no return". *The Guardian*, June 11, 2021.

Newberry, D., Pollitt, M. G., Ritz, R. A., and Strielkowski, W. (2018). Market design for a high-renewables European electricity system. *Renewable and Sustainable Energy Reviews*, 91(2018), 695–707.

Newell, R. G., Prest, B. C., and Sexton, S. E. (2021). The GDP-Temperature relationship: Implications for climate change damages. *Journal of Environmental Economics and Management*, 108(2021), 1–26.

Nightingale, S. (2019). Hydrogen fuel is getting the buzz, but here's why it hasn't gone mainstream. *USC TorjanFamily*, University of Southern California, Autumn 2019.

OECD (1997). *Glossary of Environmental Statistics, Studies in Methods, Series F*. New York: United Nations.

Olhoff, A. and Christenssen, J.M. (2019). *Lessons From a Decade of Emissions Gap Assessments.* Nairoibi, Kenya: United Nations Environment Programme.

PEI (2021). IEA's bold net zero report yields mixed reactions from industry. *Power Engineering International*, May 19, 2021.

Perera, A. T. D., Nik, V. M., Chen, D., Scartezzini, J.-L., and Hong, T. (2020). Quantifying the impacts of climate change and extreme events on energy systems. *Nature Energy*, 5, 150–159.

Ploeg, F. van der (2012). Is there really a green paradox? *Journal of Environmental Economics and Management*, 64(3), 342–363, November 2012.

Porter, M. E. (1985). *Competitive Advantage: Creating and Sustaining Superior Performance.* New York: The Free Press.

Reader, S. M., Morand-Ferron, J., and Flynn, E. (2016). Animal and human innovations: Novel problems and novel solutions. *Philosophical Transactions of The Royal Society B, Special Issue*, 371(1690), 1–11.

Rehbein, J. A., Watson, J, E. M., Lane, J. L., Sonter, L. J., Venter, O., Atkinson, S. C., and Allan, H. R. (2020). Renewable energy deployment threatens many globally important biodiversity areas. *Global Change Biology*, 2020, 1–12.

Renssen, S.V. (2020). Hydrogen is the next renewables story. *Energy Monitor*, August 14, 2020.

Reuters (2021). Explainer: What the Dutch court carbon emissions ruling means to Shell. *Reuters*, May 26, 2021.

Rossell, A. D. and Sanchez Molina, P. (2021). Winners, prices of Spain's latest renewables auction. *pv magazine*, January 28, 2021.

Roth, I. F. and Ambs, L. (2004). Incorporating externalities into a full cost approach to electric power generation lifecycle costing. *Energy*, 29(12–15), 2125–2144.

Rumelt, R. (2011). *Good Strategy, Bad Strategy: The Difference and Why it Matters.* London: Profile Books.

Saiyid, A. (2021). Oil majors forced to reckon with climate impacts. *IHS Markit*, May 26, 2021.

Scanlon, S. J., Jenkins, J. C., and Peterson, L. (2010). The scarcity fallacy. *Contexts*, February 17, 2010.

Sen, A. (1981). *Poverty and Famines: An Essay on Entitlement and Deprivation.* Oxford: Oxford University Press.

Shell (2021). Shell confirms decision to appeal court ruling in Netherlands climate case. Press Release, July 20, 2021.

Simon, F. (2021). IEA criticised over growing shore of bioenergy in net-zero scenario. *EURACTIV.com*, May 18, 2021.

Sinn, H.-W. (2012). *The Green Paradox: A Supply-Side Approach to Global Warming*. Cambridge, MA: The MIT Press, Massachusetts Institute of Technology.

Smil, V. (2010). *Energy Transitions: History, Requirements, and Prospects*. Santa Barbara, CA: Praeger.

St John, J. (2020). California Renewables Curtailments Surge as Coronavirus Cuts Energy Demand. gtm, April 2, 2020.

S&P Global (2020). What is energy transition? S&P Global, February 24, 2020.

Trouvé, T. (2020). Energy system integration: What role for gas infrastructure and renewable and low carbon gas? *The European Files*, July 7, 2020.

US Department of Energy (DoE) (2014). The history of electric cars. *Energy.gov*, September 15, 2014.

Walley, N. and Whitehead, B. (1994). It's not easy being green. *Harvard Business Review*, May–June, 1994.

Wiser, R., Rand, J., Seel, J., Beiter, P., Baker, E., Lantz, E., and Gilman, P. (2021). Expert elicitation survey predicts 37% to 49% declines in wind energy costs by 2050. *Nature Energy*, April 15, 2021.

WNA (2021). World nuclear association response to the international energy agency's net zero by 2050 report. *World Nuclear Association*, May 18, 2021.

Yuka, O. and Paul, S. (2021). Asia snubs IEA call to stop new fossil fuel investments. *Reuters*, May 19, 2021.

Zuckerman, J., Frejova, J., Granoff, I., and Wilson, D. (2016). Investing at least a trillion dollars a year in clean energy. In *Seizing the Global Opportunity: Partnerships for Better Growth and a Better Climate*. London and Washington, D.C.: New Climate Energy.

Chapter 2
Policy and Managerial Actions

Regulatory risks are inadvertently heightened when policy (erroneously) perceives business as "innately evil," as "progressive" advocacies would claim to justify direct actions. Drawing on political economy and guided by the wisdom of its leading thinkers, managers and policy are offered alternative pathways to positively navigate the vagaries of polarised political discourse. These reflections lead policy and firms to harness their respective strengths to enhance individual and societal good. To turn policy aspirations into reality, business can meaningfully contribute and mobilise its resources, when asymmetries in incentives and rewards are reconciled, even when the perceived gaps are only partially bridged. Through *tangible*, *actionable*, and *achievable* strategic initiatives, managers can work with policy to turn ambiguous conditions into arenas of emerging opportunities to create tomorrow's profitable niches, starting *today*.

1
Introduction

Why do managers take regulatory developments seriously? What is it with policy and regulation that business pays attention to?

Energy investments are characterised by lumpy initial commitments, whereby managers expect to recoup over time through the cash flows that the investment would earn. In this context, policy plays various roles in making this possible. By authorising the investment, usually through permits and regulations, the firm's rights to receive the returns are governed by law. By taxing or subsidising, policy influences how much accrue to private capital or the state.

The allocation is a normative process that is not immune from ideology or public opinions. Within this context, formulating policy becomes a contest of opposing interests and prescriptions on how best to meet society's perceived needs. This is accentuated by sharper divides between the so-called "progressive" and "conservative" perspectives of business.

Kevin Williamson (2017), in *National Review*, noted that "in the 'progressive' lexicon, the word 'corporation' is practically a synonym for 'evil'. Corporations are so stoned on greed and ripped on ruthlessness that they present an existential threat to democracy as we know it."

In my view, this "progressive" perspective is so off the mark that managers may be inclined to dismiss them outright. However, this is where the peril lies. The soundness of policy becomes secondary once it is in effect. The labels "progressive" or "conservative" or "populist" lose their descriptive significance. To managers, they have to contend with the effects of policy actions, not adequately captured by their designated labels, to navigate through its pitfalls or reap its benefits.

How the "conservatives" are seen to react is asymmetric to the actions the "progressives" tend to take on issues they care about. Kevin Williamson continues with his discourse: "Conservatives may roll their eyes a little bit at promises to build wind mills that are so efficient that we'll cease needing coal or oil, but the 'progressives' (at least a portion of them) believe using fossil fuels may very well end human civilisation."

"Conservatives" would usually weigh the merits of climate initiatives before devoting resources to them. In contrast, "progressives" would spare no expense to avoid humanity's extinction. The results? Gargantuan spending bills, exemplified by the Green New Deals, are "must do" to make economies carbon-neutral by 2050 (Friedman, 2019; Politico, 2020).

Populists have ambiguous affiliations, when they alternate between their association with left leaning "progressive" and ultra right "conservative" rhetoric. This depends on who the political or governing elite happens to be, or perceive as, in power.

The realities on the ground raise these nagging questions to managers: With large numbers thrown randomly, what opportunities are on offer? Why is business slow to adopt and prefers to wait for policy's cue or act reluctantly when pushed by climate advocates?

Part of the wisdom CEOs acquire is to learn to focus on policy actions that matter, not so much on the political discourse that entertains the "talking heads." To prioritise, CEOs choose the contests they would want to take on. The norms that policy rewards define how players are to behave to remain in the game and flourish.

Intelligent humans do not always agree, and this is not necessarily a bad thing (see, for example, Johnson, 2010). Without this human penchant to explore new ways of seeing things, often by rejecting "accepted wisdoms," human society would not have been enriched — culturally, socially, and economically.

It is these continual challenges that move scholars to question the notions that humans respond only with self-interests. In Amartya Sen's (2000) notion of equitable access to opportunities, he equates development with the freedom that enables people to choose a life that enhances their well-being as well as the welfare of those around them. The capability to make informed judgements counters Garrett Hardin's (1968) dim view of people. Driven by self-interest (Scott, 1954), people are destined to a "tragedy of the commons." To Garrett Hardin, people extract more of the common resources to satisfy their insatiable appetite to consume until the resources are exhausted or damaged.

Amartya Sen is joined by Elinor Ostrum (2015) in offering a more optimistic view of human nature. Ostrum sees humans as capable of working collectively to benefit each other. This paves the way for good governance to temper the drive for individual gains by expanding and sustaining societal gains to benefit more people.

In the process, policy and managers may harness the power of markets, with imperfect people complete with their biases working together. They are bound by recognising the value of the guiding hand of an enlightened policy. People's freedom is enhanced to make choices to pursue their well-being — individually and collectively. This notion is promoted by Richard H Thaler (in Thaler and Sunstein, 2008) under *libertarian paternalism*.

Aesop's fable of *The Hare and The Tortoise* comes to mind. The lesson was supposedly one around persistence. The tortoise won the race, with all its innate drawbacks — slow to move — against the hare's nimbleness and speed because the hare chose to take a nap. Meanwhile, with the tortoise persistently inching towards the finish line, the hare woke up and dashed to catch up. The hare was too late, letting its innate advantages lay to waste because of poor judgement. The hare recklessly let overconfidence take leave of one's better judgement.

Aesop may have inadvertently given a lesson or two to policy and managers alike. In a world that Amartya Sen (2000) describes in *Development as Freedom*, by redefining the contests to their advantage, they could create conditions for each to flourish. Examine these contrasting scenarios:

In a world that is unfree, the hare and the tortoise can only race on land because that is how things have been and will continue to be. With its inherent drawbacks — the tortoise can run (crawl is more like it) up to 18 km/h against the hare at 72 km/h — the tortoise is left with hope as a means to win. The hare would remain irredeemably stupid and recklessly overconfident to never learn its lessons. The tortoise may hope that some misfortune may befall the hare and prevent it from reaching the finish line. That is the article of hope that the foolhardy would pin as their "strategy" to win.

In a world with freedom, the hare and the tortoise may choose contests where their innate traits, put to good use, would give them a fair shot at finishing ahead of rivals. While outracing the tortoise on land, the hare would be reluctant or even fearful of swimming in water. In managerial (and perhaps in policy as well) parlance, this is what choosing your battle would actually mean in real life.

The hare's drawback was made apparent when people taking a stroll by the river saw a hare trapped in a rock amidst rising tide. It was forced to jump as the water engulfed the rock where it stood while trying to overcome its fear of the rushing water.

That was the last people knew of the hare (*The Irish Times*, 1997). In contrast, in open water, a tortoise can swim up to 35 km/h, giving it a fair chance to outrace its rivals. For a change, the tortoise can win by outwitting its rivals — a feature of what it takes to craft and execute a good strategy.

Raised and formed in a Judeo-Christian milieu, I have greater confidence in the innate goodness of human nature. To do good is as much a choice as to do bad. Endowed with free will and a predilection to behave according to natural law, a higher calling for human actions is conceivable. Examine how "rational" people can choose to work against their self-interests in an economic sense, by learning from Richard H Thaler's story on resisting temptation (Thaler and Sunstein, 2008):

"Many years ago, Thaler was hosting dinner for some guests and put a large bowl of nuts to nibble on the first bottle of wine. Within a few minutes it became clear that the bowl of nuts was going to be consumed in its entirety, and that the guests might lack sufficient appetite to enjoy all the food that was to follow. Leaping into action, Thaler grabbed the bowl of nuts, and (while sneaking a few more nuts for himself) removed the bowl to the kitchen, where it was put out of sight."

"When he returned, the guests thanked him for removing the nuts." This would appear odd in the company of fellow economists. Thaler continues: "*Before the bowl was removed*, the group had the choice of whether to eat the nuts or not — now they didn't."

In the company of "rational" economists, they behave like "irrational" humans. Instead of maximising their "utility" by consuming more nuts until they are bloated, curtailing present consumption removes the prospect of a bum stomach. Tempering consumption of nuts leaves some room for them to savour the sumptuous meal that came next.

With free will, at least in the Judeo-Christian context, comes mindfulness that makes temperance a virtue against overindulgence (or excessive consumption). In the context of society's common pool resources, I see nothing "rational" about reasonable people wilfully taking actions that inevitably lead to self-destruction. Within reasonable bounds, people's "self-understanding of their roles and their conceptions of proper and acceptable behaviour in particular contexts" (Grant, 2016) could find alignment within a given community.

Bernardo M Villegas, a prominent economic thinker in Asia, weighs in: "For those following Judeo-Christian principles, freedom is actually oriented to the good and not to evil. In adding a supernatural level to human existence, redemption is an aspiration that helps believers to choose good when there are forces within people that tempts humans to do what is evil. For the faithful in the Christian faith, it is hardly surprising for people to want to contribute to the common good and when necessary, to sacrifice personal interests in favour of achieving higher ideals."

In conferring greater confidence on the magnanimity of the human spirit, Ostrum (2015) illustrated that "communities of individuals have relied on institutions resembling neither the state nor the market to govern some resource systems with reasonable degrees of success over long periods of time." That humans are and can choose altruism over greed is repeatedly shown as consistent with the notion of rewards and incentives, when broadened to include social as well as economic well-being.

Guided by these principles or beliefs, managers are better positioned to engage policy of a wide range of political persuasions. To sustain their firms' viability *today* and position to pivot to tomorrow's potentially prosperous niches, managers can formulate strategies premised on the realities of life. Specifically:

What arenas can their business and policy play to leverage on each other's distinct strengths to serve their communities?

Why are the state's benevolent interventions creating outcomes that are diametrically opposed to its objectives?

How could managers and policy interact to formulate common frameworks to undertake, on its own or jointly, *tangible*, *actionable*, and *achievable* actions within the specified timeframe?

In this chapter, I propose to examine these fundamental questions that remain open questions in academe and practice. In the face of more aggressive advocacies of all stripes, the actions of activists are no longer isolated domains that managers could simply ignore. One may agree, or choose to be dismissive, that the question of a sustainable future where humans can continue to thrive is primordial. For this reason, a return to fundamental principles is a necessary first step.

2
Why Freedom and Choices Matter?

Freedom, and its exercise by individuals to make choices freely, as a foundation of societal well-being is far from a theoretical musing of academics. Over the years, the annual surveys on economic freedom conducted by *The Heritage Foundation* yield consistent insights: In good or adverse economic conditions, greater economic freedom (admittedly a narrow notion of well-being, according to Martha C Nussbaum (2011)) tends to create conditions for societies to prosper — economically as well as socially. For its 2021 survey, it concludes: "Citizens of 'free' or 'mostly free' countries enjoy income that are more than double the global average and more than six times higher than 'repressed' economies" (Miller *et al.*, 2021). The report continued to highlight that people in "free" or "mostly free" societies live longer, healthier, with access to "higher quality" education, healthcare, and cleaner environment.

2.1 Freedom, choice, and spheres of influence

Vox populi, vox dei is now deeply embedded as an ideal of governance among adherents to freedom under a democracy. The power of the state emanates from the consent of the people. In *Law and Judicial Duty*, Harvard Law's Philip Hamburger (2008) traced its popular use to Archbishop of Canterbury, Walter Reynolds. In 1327, Reynolds promoted the ideal that the *voice of the people is the voice of God* to oppose King Charles II of England's increasingly repressive reign.

As with great ideals, some would oppose and even fear its prospect to upstage an established order. Alcuin, a royal adviser to Charlemagne (or Carlo Magno), dissuaded the king in 739 A.D. against promoting such ideas to people that could turn against him. Democracy's ideals are no different: With each Walter Reynolds promoting a bold idea, many Alcuins are in the shadows working to strengthen the powers of kings.

The role of ideals is made more important, not diminished by a need to compromise in a political sense. Philip Hamburger (2008) provides an answer to this vexing question:

> "Through their ideals and particularly *their ideals*, people responded to their circumstances — both to sort out their impressions of the world and to act in it — and although they frequently recalibrated and even adjusted their understandings of their ideals, they tended to do so because they relied on these conceptions of themselves and their conduct to get them through the difficulties they saw ahead."

To Amartya Sen (2000), setting freedom and its expansion as the object of development, he sets an ideal for any social arrangement. Does it provide people with real opportunities to do what they value?

This freedom is used to acquire the capabilities to function in a society where rewards are predicated on merits. For this reason, unless a person can voluntarily gain the capabilities, with society lending a hand as needed, the notion of making choices to achieve well-being is hypothetical. Amartya Sen uses his bicycle example to illustrate his point:

> When one sets out to enjoy a bike ride, one first has to learn how to ride. Initially, the fear of falling and getting hurt impedes the pleasure of riding, with some choosing to give up. For those that persist, they fulfil a function of (or achieve) the capability to ride. For those that fail to learn or by choice did not want to learn how to ride, enjoying a bike ride is a theoretical prospect for the simple reason that one is not equipped to do so.

In examining real-life dilemmas, Amartya Sen's focus on access to opportunities by building internal capabilities is seen as a better framework for thinking about human well-being. Sen offered an explicit link between utility (happiness or pleasure) and resource-based well-being (good form of life) (Clark, 2000). Recognising the *free will* that humans are endowed with, development becomes an increase in freedom and citizens have to choose from among the preferred development options (Jacobson and Chang, 2019).

Inextricably linked to well-being is how political and economic freedoms help to reinforce each other. To this end, Amartya Sen (2000) posits that individual freedom is seen as a social commitment. To wit:

> "To be generically against markets would be almost as odd as being generically against the conversations between people (even though some conversations are clearly foul and cause problems for others — or even for the conversationalists themselves). The freedom to exchange words, or goods, or gifts, does not need defensive justification in terms of their favourable but distant effects; they are part of the way human beings in society live and interact with each other (unless stopped by regulation or a fist). The contribution of the market mechanism to economic growth is, of course, important, but this comes only after the direct significance of the freedom to interchange — words, goods, gift — has been acknowledged."

The translation to practice is not obvious to some. An example is an attempt to empirically measure "capabilities" and test its relationship to making choices in health care. As the researchers rightly pointed out, "questionnaires and people's responses run the risks of highlighting only an aspect of capabilities and ignoring others, resulting in an inaccurate description of reality" (Karimi *et al.*, 2016). In a narrower notion of capabilities, Martha Nussbaum (2011) emphasises social justice in how human well-being is achieved.

In a policy context, Amartya Sen (2000) offers a framework that provides a wider latitude for actions. In his approach, rather than prescribing how human well-being would be achieved, Sen provides a framework to help structure policy formulation to facilitate these ends:

> "Development requires the removal of sources of unfreedoms: poverty as well as tyranny, poor economic opportunities as well as systematic social deprivation, neglect of public facilities as well as intolerance or overactivity

of repressive states. Despite unprecedented increases in overall opulence, the contemporary world denies elementary freedoms to vast numbers — perhaps even the majority — of people. Sometimes the lack of substantive freedoms relates directly to economic poverty, or to achieve sufficient nutrition, or to obtain remedies for treatable illnesses, or the ability to be properly clothed or sheltered, or to enjoy clean water or sanitary facilities."

To my mind, people with intelligence and practical inclinations could be moved to actions by their ideals in whatever way it is understood. However, even the most altruistic of spirits would have to pick their battles. This is where Aesop's *The Hare and The Tortoise* may trigger some thoughts on who best could undertake these *functions* according to their innate capabilities.

2.2 Innate strengths of firms and policy

Policymakers, with their good intentions, may see it upon themselves to do good as a mantra for their governance. In this aspect, policy may seek to do more than what is prudently within their means. For example, in raising literacy, policy may go beyond providing guidance to facilitate how schools could achieve these objectives. In some cases, in the absence of private providers, the state takes on, by default, this role. Over time, as the state becomes entrenched and a constituency develops around this arrangement, reverting to the private provision of education is made more difficult. In the oil and gas industry, the stakes in extant assets and livelihoods experience similar entrenched interests and resistance from a segment that struggles to adapt (Gross, 2020), with coal having similar constituencies, particularly in policy (Genscu *et al.*, 2019).

Not that this development is problematic *per se*. Poor delivery, combined with lack of facilities, as some markets would experience, may turn the state complicit in limiting its people's capabilities. Almost by neglect, poor standards result in unemployable graduates, leading to poor prospects for accessing opportunities.

In some cases, the state's role in undermining people's capabilities could be through active coercion such as denying political and civil rights. In more subtle forms, these are manifested by restricting education to gender or religious affiliations or using family size to deny social services (under China's previous one child policy) or "pay to play" in corrupt regimes. By denying targeted people from meaningfully participating in economic and social pursuits, these restrictions could consign some to unescapable poverty. In practice, opulence for the few coexists with the misery of the many.

This brings Martha Nussbaum's (2011) challenge into focus to classicists: Why are some opulent countries, with high gross domestic products (GDPs), also experiencing poor health care, mediocre literacy, or unescapable poverty for some (or a vast majority)?

Economic measures such as GDPs are incapable of highlighting the nuances of how economic benefits accrue to people. The deeper causes lie with how misunderstood the innate strengths of policy and business are. I propose, as a way of crafting a "division of labour," a schematic framework in Chart 2.1 for policy and managers to consider when structuring their thought processes.

In the policy context, to pay for the provision of services, governments raise taxes or collect levies. In theory, people pay taxes for the state to provide services to society that are social in nature because their benefits accrue beyond the provider. In effect, these benefits are positive externalities that public goods possess (D), with the state taking on the role of provider as the agent acting for the people.

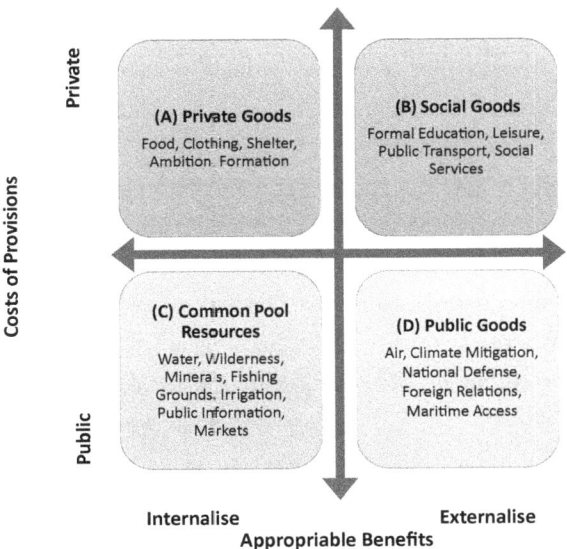

Chart 2.1: Policy and Managerial Spheres of Influence

Private goods (A), in contrast, can more directly relate costs to benefits (as revenues or income) of the provider. When one sells a pair of pants, the buyer pays the seller. The costs and the benefits are internalised, with the seller earning their revenue, while the buyer enjoys the "utility" (or enjoyment) of owning the pair of pants. This is the trait of a private good, where private exchanges are transacted among willing parties. Each party decides on how best to satisfy their needs (or even their wants) without needing the state to intervene except in resolving disputes, as needed.

Social goods (B), in my usage, are to distinguish goods or services whose social benefits are significant, ambiguous in how the benefits could be appropriated, and amenable to private or state provision. This is an arena where government, social enterprises, and private capital, among others, co-exist and usually collaborate to work for the common good. In some countries, this is an arena for ideological contests: The lines between forming future citizens, and indoctrinating future advocates (or ideologues), are played out in designing curriculums and recruitment of students and professors to funding scholarly works, among others.

Common pool resources (C) pertain to cultural and natural resources accessible to all in society. Its private exploitation could prove lucrative to private capital. Perhaps, for this reason, a dim view of human nature would lead people to suspect that avarice would deplete a finite resource. As a result, the finite resources are depleted in due course because private capital could gain without incurring any financial costs from a degraded resource (or environment). The costs to remediate fall on society to collectively bear.

It is in the area of governing common pool resources that clarity in the spheres of influence of policy and managers is critical. This leads Elinor Ostrum (2015) to assert: "The issues of how best to govern natural resources used by many individuals in the common are no more settled in academia than in the world of politics. Some scholarly articles about the 'tragedy of the commons' recommended that 'the state' control most natural resources to prevent their destruction. Others recommend that privatising those resources will resolve the problem. What one can observe in the world, however, is that the state nor the market is uniformly successful in enabling individuals to sustain long term, productive use of natural resource systems. Further, communities of individuals have relied on institutions resembling neither the state nor the market to govern some resource systems with reasonable degrees of success over long periods of time."

3
Reframing Policy and Managerial Actions

In an African safari, one can observe how herds instinctively follow some order in behaving to ensure the propagation, and survival, of the species. A lioness cares for the young, while the Lion King perched over a vantage point keeps watch over its pride. In some cases, bears organise a sleuth of migrating members by positioning the guide up front to pace the walk, with the weaker and elderly members in the middle. The strongest stays at the back to protect the flank from hostile attacks or adverse events. It also allows the strong to assist the weak who may occasionally falter. Wolves hunt in packs, with fish swimming in schools, as birds tend to fly in flocks.

Unfettered by rationalisation, animals in the wilds are endowed with instincts that conform to natural law. In many human endeavours, a similar order is observed. A stone thrown into the air is more likely to fall back to earth by virtue of gravity. When a person punches somebody in the nose, the one receiving the blow is likely to bleed if the punch was strong enough. While some would punch back in retaliation, others may consider how best to respond. This brings in human judgement into play in understanding how people are likely to behave in the face of stimuli for reaction. What appears certain is for Newton's *Third Law of Motion* to operate: *For every action, there is an equal and opposite reaction*. However, what that reaction constitutes would remain uncertain, even to the person contemplating such reaction. In the heat of the moment, the person receiving the punch may choose to fight, take flight, or even freeze in a daze.

3.1   Governing the common pool resources

In designing how the commons are governed, the assumption on how humans behave and how society comprises "rational" humans is seldom made explicit. With the ascendancy of classical economic theories and quantitative analytical tools, policy appears to forego human judgement as it finds comfort in the sanctity of numbers. This approach accounts for policy falling into the traps of extrapolating its analytical "conclusions" as panaceas for what ails society. For some, it is "justified" to assert its "unique" solution as the only correct and narrow path (Basurto and Ostrum, 2008) to "prosperity" in whatever way it is (mis-)construed.

Richard H Thaler (2015) illustrates how this could upstage policy's best intentions. To wit: "Economists get into trouble when they make a highly specific prediction that depends explicitly on everyone being economically sophisticated." In examining how farmers respond to modern farming techniques, scientists noted that crop yields tend to improve with the use of fertilisers. Thaler noted that "if everyone can be assumed to get things right as long as they have the proper information, then there is no appropriate policy prescription other than making this information freely available. Publish the findings, make them readily available to farmers, and let the magic of the markets take care of the rest."

Such a well-intentioned policy stance is laudable, but it is bound to fail. Part of the reason is when basic realities are ignored. In focusing on the elegance of analytical models, one is blindsided by the very nature of models as abstractions that "describe the behaviour of imaginary *Econs*."[1] While such models serve to simplify one's understanding of how a system may work, Thaler advises that "we should stop assuming that those models are accurate descriptions of behaviour, and stop basing policy decisions on such flawed analyses. And we have to start paying attention to those supposedly irrelevant factors." Human beliefs, and their influence on individual preferences, are irrelevant factors that are best ignored, as rationalists would advocate.

Managers may start by examining the normative anchors that underpin policy formulation by comparing the opposing dynamics under a market- or policy-directed system. I summarise its salient points in Chart 2.2.

Under a policy-directed ecosystem, societal good is presumably entrusted to the hegemony of experts. Given their "expertise," some people know better than the rest as to how they can guide the others. With benevolence, an enlightened ruling elite will work for the common good, as conceived by a privileged few. This notion has the following implications for how energy systems could be governed. Specifically:

---

[1] Richard H Thaler uses Econ to refer to rational beings conceived by economists as the norm of how people should behave as dictated by economic logic.

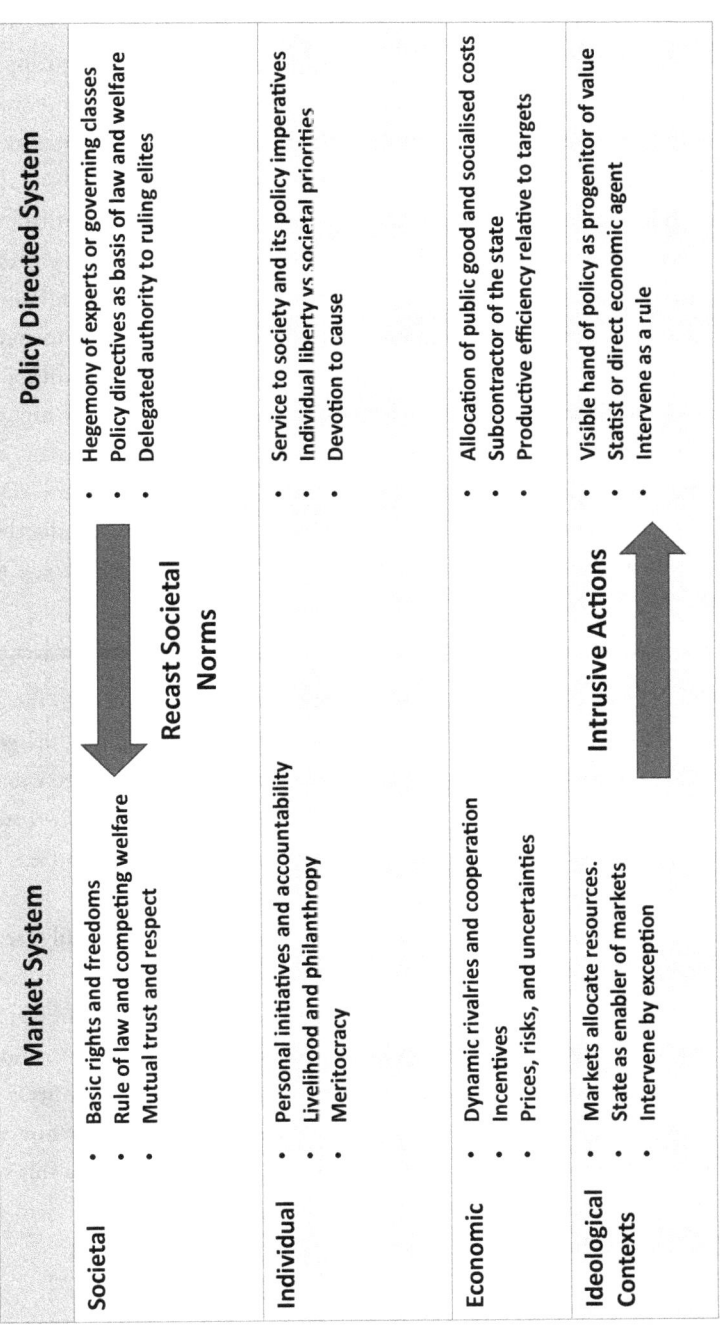

Chart 2.2: Normative Anchors of Policy

Entrusted to a regulator, policy would set the prices and the basis that supply is given access to a "regulated market." Using planned management, a command-and-control system is put in place and directed, often centrally, where investments and allowed returns are regulated.

The individuals or firms are at the service of society, effectively turning each player as sub-contractors to the state. The visible hand of policy is the progenitor of value because policy sets the price and creates demand. Policy becomes an omniscient and omnipotent creator of profitable niches for preferred firms. Direct regulatory interventions correct undesirable outcomes.

Individual liberty and the firms' actions are subsumed under higher "societal priorities," often set by a governing coalition of interests. Operating under these conditions, firms conform to centrally set targets and meeting these in the most cost-effective manner. Hence, the focus on productive efficiency as a regulated system would enable the primordial strategy to flourish.

In an era of interventionist regulation, energy prices are set to recoup the costs. What easier way than to sum up all the costs to supply and add a profit margin on top to calculate the total costs. Divide this sum by the volume one expects to need and the unit price of energy emerges. Deviations at the end of each period are corrected to keep the firms "whole" — or earn what they were expected to at the outset. Thus, the cost-plus pricing regime was deeply entrenched.

Over time, why did highly regulated firms do poorly under these highly "secure" policy-supported ecosystems?

I venture to offer a different view on what "optimisation" meant under regulated systems. "Productive efficiency" took on a very different meaning. When piling up costs was rewarded and no penalties were imposed from overspending, firms were rewarded to sustain high costs. On the same ratio of profit margin (i.e. 10% of costs), earnings growth expands by growing the costs (e.g. from 100 to 150). In this sense, being "productively efficient," the firm increases their profit margin from 10 to 15 or shows a 50% increase in money terms.

It took years to correct this "novel" view of "efficiency" to mint cash. In principle, with the certainty of profit without, in theory, taking substantial risks of a loss, firms are prepared to have their returns cap. To incentivise firms to be truly efficient, some forms of standard costs were applied. In essence, if a firm produces power at less than the standard costs, the firm could keep the "excess profits" from "efficiency gains." To an extent, this encouraged managers to work towards cost improvements, usually by tinkering at the margins, to be ahead of possible cuts in regulated prices.

3.2 Glacial pace to deregulation

The centralised "command-and-control" approach to energy regulation evolved from a bygone era of fragmentation in 19th century Chicago, USA. Leonard S Hyman (1985) characterised the city council as the sole issuer of franchises and as notoriously corrupt. Energy suppliers — mostly private power utilities generating and distributing power — gain a franchise that gives them exclusivity to supply an area. With franchises individually agreed, no standards existed. As a result, "it made it difficult to develop standardised products, limited the mobility of large users of power, and — it later became apparent — prevented the utilities from achieving the benefits of load diversity and economies of scale," Hyman added. Jumping a few decades, as technology evolved and with better measurements of energy output (and costs), firms managed to "compete" to takeover struggling monopolies. Standardised products and regulation almost came through the back door.

World War II shattered the economies of many countries. Capital was largely concentrated in the government, with few private enterprises ready to invest on their own to rebuild their communities. Public ownership became entrenched and extended to any economic sector considered "strategic," which is almost all that required large capital to get started. This condition was broadly intact, with private firms co-existing with state-owned or controlled enterprises, conducting their business under some form of regulation.

The ubiquitous presence of some form of dynamic energy markets originated from the deregulation that the late Margaret R Thatcher promoted as UK Prime Minister. In today's evolved form, particularly in developed markets such as Europe and a number of US regional markets, a return to Chart 2.2 is in order.

From the "comforts or travails" of state regulation, energy firms and policy have to adapt to their newfound roles and freedoms, a process that is proved to be more nuanced than classical economic logic had hoped for. Specifically:

> In seizing the opportunities of liberalised markets, managers focus not only on achieving cost-competitiveness but also aim to be more alert about what their competitors are doing. The object is to outflank rivals to gain strategic dominance, a trait that is believed to confer advantages.
>
> In its ideal conception, markets allocate resources and arbitrate the creation of value, with the state strengthening the institutions. Under this incarnation, the state ceases to be the progenitor of value. Instead, the state sets the rules and monitors its compliance. Regulators intervene to correct market failures in exceptional cases.

The energy industry, as a user of natural resources and contributor to societal well-being, has generally flourished under a market system, particularly for fuels. One could even point out that today's comforts and prosperity reached unprecedented levels because of advances in how energy is extracted and made available to humanity. However, the greater awareness of its environmental impact, particularly for fossil fuels and nuclear waste, increasingly turned energy firms from hero to villain. At the root of this change in sentiments is a perception that energy firms extract profits without bearing the full costs of the resource to society.

The conversion process generates employment, profits, and reallocation of wealth and income. However, it produces pollution as well as harmful materials to human health as in nuclear waste, soil or water contamination. These costs are not readily measured, much less recognised, but society (or affected communities) suffers from its consequences. For Richard H Thaler and Cass R Sunstein (2008), this is a source of failure of market mechanisms to align social costs or benefits. Specifically:

> "It helps to think of the environment as the outcome of a global choice architecture system in which decisions are made by all kinds of actors, from consumers to large companies to governments. Markets are a big part of

this system, and for all their virtues, they face two problems that contribute to environmental problems.

Incentives are not properly aligned. If you engage in environmentally costly behaviour next year, through your consumption choices, you will probably pay nothing for the environmental harms that you inflict. This is what is often called a 'tragedy of the commons'."

To add to people's consumption choices, Thaler and Sunstein added, "people do not get feedback on the environmental consequences of their actions. If your use of energy produces air pollution, you are unlikely to know or appreciate the fact, certainly not on a continuing basis. Even if you know about the connection, it is probably not salient to your behaviour."

The missing links to govern common pool resources lie in linking incentives with actions that explicitly reward "good environmental behaviour." In this area, private initiatives, more than the state, have proven to be more innovative in devising instruments that can move people to change or reframe their perspectives. To scale how these innovations are in mobilising capital, structuring investments, and accessing potentially profitable niches, the approach to policy-supported incentives will have to be recast. More importantly, sorely needed early indicators that could signal links between actions and pollution may offer some lucrative niches with the help of digital technology.

4
From Green Paradoxes to Green Bucks

In examining the record of subsidies, used broadly to cover state-sponsored incentives, a few strands of realities are apparent. Specifically:

1. Intended beneficiaries of subsidies may be the last to profit from the payments from the state. As taxpayers and consumers, they may inadvertently benefit

others rather than the intended beneficiaries or their communities as contemplated by policy.
2. *Feed-in tariffs*, a popular tool to "equalise" the costs of fossil fuels and intermittent renewables, diminish in value as it fails to achieve wide-scale deployment. The opposite happens: Generous subsidies paradoxically could disincentivise technological innovations or early deployment — a green paradox.
3. "Innovations" are inspired from an erroneous belief that policy as well as managers are endowed with omniscience that they do not possess, but entrusting them with omnipotence can help pursue single-mindedly policy-mandated "champions."

A place to start is to trace the money trails in order to connect the source to the ultimate beneficiaries.

4.1 Who actually gains from subsidies?

In subsidising intermittent renewables, taxpayers in theory fund part of the cost differences between supplying energy from the more "expensive" intermittent renewables and "cheaper" fossil fuels. The cost differences are equalised by "paying" a feed-in tariff to renewables. In practical terms, the differences are derived from the respective lifecycle costs of energy (LCOEs)[2] of the various technologies.

As early as 2011, the multilateral funding agencies recognised the need to address the paradoxes from subsidies. Grzegorz Peszko (2011) noted: "For a few years now, increased in demand triggered by these *subsidised* tariffs and insufficient competition on the supply side kept prices in solar panels high." This is contrary to what was expected with learning effects, where more capacity installed would progressively reduce costs of supplies. Grzegorz Peszko added, referring to the rounds of significant subsidies cuts in Europe, that the "solar bonanza has contributed to fiscal crises."

The usual culprits are easy to identify: poor execution; high probability of support policy reversals; abuse of subsidies scheme that encourage frauds. To add to these factors, I posit that misaligned incentives and policy objectives may have more to do

---

[2] Chapter 11 explains in great detail the calculations for different power generation technologies.

with the deeper flaws in some policy-supported deployment of intermittent renewables.

I compare schematically how generic cash transfers in Chart 2.3 differ between subsidies paid to intermittent renewables and to mineral or feedstocks for fossil fuel energy.

At a high level, intermittent renewables receive subsidies by investing and operating the asset, with subsidies paid as capital grants (A.1) on acquiring the equipment or feed-in tariffs (A.3) as power is produced or delivered to consumers (E) to earn the subsidies as part of its payoffs (B.2). The payoffs may enjoy tax incentives (A.4) or be "secured" by some "guaranteed" volumes under portfolio standards (A.5) that prioritise intermittent renewables. The investment is usually funded with equity and debt at varying proportions in exchange for paying dividends to equity and interest as the cost to borrowing with a repayment of the principal borrowed. Capital expenditures (B.1) are funded accordingly, with any grants (A.1; A.2) reducing the financing needed from equity or debt.

In contrast, oil and gas, coal, or geothermal steam may enjoy some subsidies or tax incentives (A.4), principally in exploring and developing new resources (H). The front-end capital expenditures are usually funded by equity or debt or a combination (K), with the payoffs to recoup capex (G.1) earned from producing and distributing the outputs (G.2; G.3) sold to customers (I). The contractors (H) are usually paid from own financing, given that any policy support usually comes in the form of tax incentives (A.4). Any fiscal incentives would reduce taxes accruing to the state, thus increasing what the private capital would appropriate. Unlike with intermittent renewables, the state usually receives as much as 70% of the revenues from the production of fossil fuel resources such as oil and gas (Gross, 2020) or coal (Genscu *et al.*, 2019) as royalties. Consumers separately pay up to 80% (in some markets in Europe) of pump prices for their petrol products.

4.2 Why the green paradoxes?

The feed-in tariffs are calculated under the *grid price parity* principles. Initially, the idea of a subsidy was not difficult to fathom. When intermittent renewables were seen as more "expensive" than fossil fuels, the easier way to give them a chance to compete is to "equalise" the cost differences. Take the "cost difference" between fossil fuel-based

Dynamic Decisions

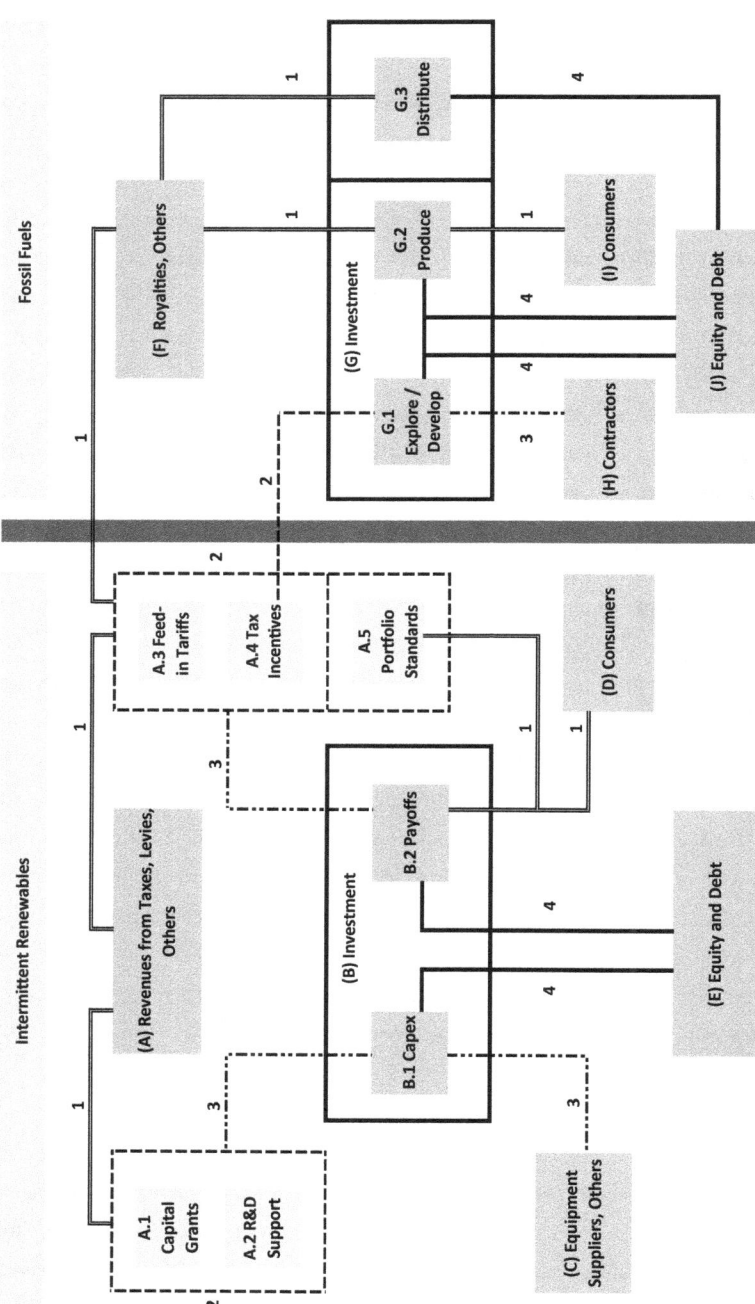

Legends: 1. Sources of cash transfers; 2. Incentives; 3. Transfers of Cash to ultimate beneficiary; 4. Dividends and debt repayment.

Chart 2.3: Money Flows — Intermittent Renewables vs. Fossil Fuels Subsidies

supplies and those supplied by an intermittent renewable and you have the "correct" number. Nothing could have been made simpler than arithmetic.

Under highly regulated pricing, this was indeed the case. However, when energy markets were liberalised, the arithmetic started to become more nuanced. At this point, it is worth recalling how competitive markets operate from Chapter 1. In summary, the relevant changes and how subsidies calculations are affected revolve around the following:

In comparing fossil fuel costs that vary periodically, with stable costs of intermittent renewables — because of its nil fuel costs — the cost differences will also vary periodically.

By setting subsidies using an assumed cost for fossil fuels (that is made constant artificially), the *grid price parity* may over- or undercompensate most (if not all) of the time.

In a paradoxical way, what was intended to secure the investments from private capital has now become the very source of risks that policy tries to minimise. Here's how these scenarios play out in real life under deregulated and dynamic power markets, with Chart 2.4 illustrating how the required subsidies (to equalise costs) would vary:

High coal or gas prices would provide a benign environment for intermittent renewables. In (C), only $Solar_B$ and MSW would require subsidies. In contrast, under ACCGTs-dominated system, more intermittent renewables would require (and higher) subsidies to be at parity.

Some market realities become apparent in explaining why a *green paradox* could result when applying grid price parity principles to determine "correct" subsidies. With volatile coal or gas prices, the "correct" subsidies become indeterminate. By setting the initial subsidy based on LCOEs (or some assumed costs for coal or ACCGT), varying fuel prices would also vary the "correct" subsidies. When actual fuel costs are above those assumed in LCOEs, the "correct" subsidies would be insufficient to recover the excess costs of subsidised supplies (or vice versa). Policy, in theory, could adjust the subsidies as fuel costs vary. However, frequent changes in subsidies schemes would be seen as too much regulatory interventions that tend to erode confidence in the

Dynamic Decisions

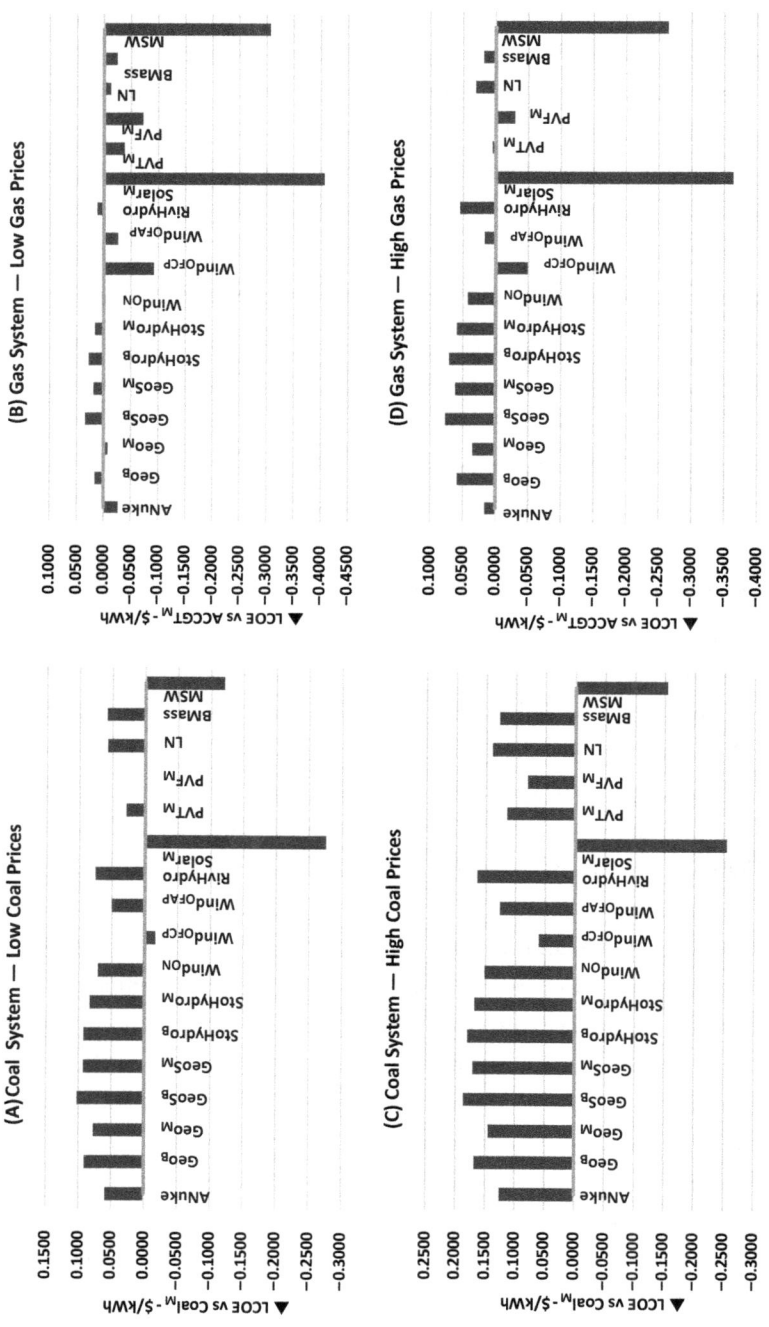

Chart 2.4: Subsidies under Volatile Coal and Gas Prices

system. As energy markets become more dynamic (read as volatile), policy is ill equipped to respond quickly (and correctly).

Faced with this prospect, unless subsidies are set very generously, investors would tend to focus on what they could lose (when subsidies are too low). In a few cases, investors may appreciate the opportunity to gain from higher power prices (given their nil fuel costs), but a foregone gain is less visible than incurring an actual loss.

4.3 Learning effects – Confused logic, flawed euphoria

The *learning curve effects*, or simply the learning effects, are popularised in mainstream business press. The hypothesis is simple. Winfred B Hirschmann of Harvard Business School (1964) observed: "The industrial learning curve … has evolved from experience in airframe manufacture, which found that the number of man-hours spent on building a plane declined at a regular rate over a wide range of production. Such continuing improvement was so common in the aircraft industry that it became normal expectation in the war time mass production of aircraft; thus, production and other types of performance were customarily scheduled on some basis of progressive betterment."

The wind farm developers had their first shock in 2004. With tight manufacturing capacity for wind turbines, the surge in demand induced by a more stable feed-in tariff regime in the United States created a significant shortage. Using data from Ryan Wiser and Mark Bollinger of Lawrence Berkeley National Laboratory (2015), the sharp spike in turbine prices did not reverse until well into 2012, as I illustrated in my book, *Energy Investments* (2017). This "setback," at least for windfarm developers, did not dim the optimism of experts. Recognising underlying uncertainties, the 24–30% cost decline expected by 2030, and 35–41% by 2050, attests to this optimism (Wiser *et al.*, 2016).

How the learning effects influence the assessment of renewables' prospects is illustrated in a simplified way in Chart 2.5. The comparisons of the implied subsidies required — simply a difference between the LCOEs of $Coal_M$ (or $ACCGT_M$) and a given renewable technology — are made. A positive number implies no subsidies are needed (or vice versa) as renewables are cheaper.

With $Coal_M$ setting the power prices, most renewables would outcompete coal even at low coal prices (A), when capex costs are falling rapidly. In contrast, with $ACCGT_M$ setting the power price, intermittent renewables together with ANuke and Geo_M would struggle to remain competitive when gas prices plunge (B).

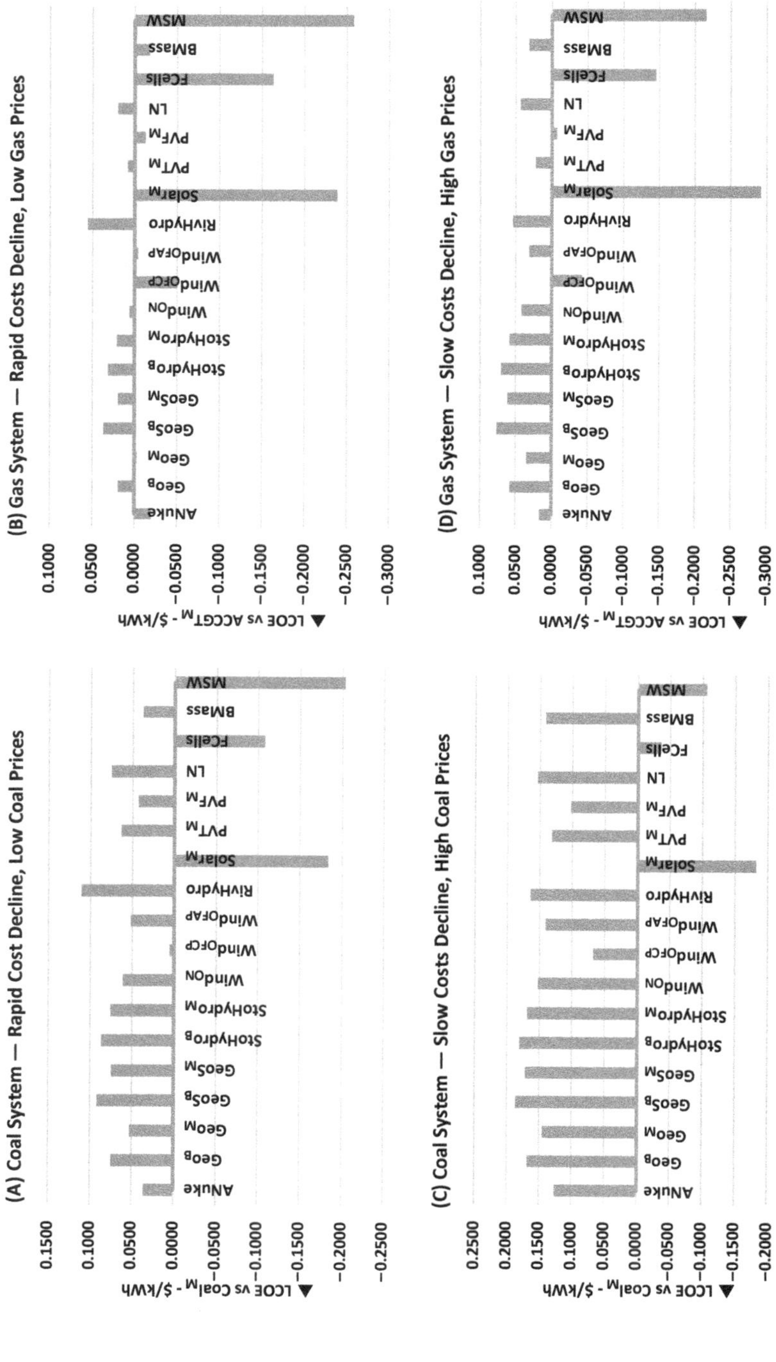

Chart 2.5: Subsidies under Declining Costs and Volatile Prices

With rising tides lifting all boats, including the leaky ones, high coal (C) or gas (D) prices would offer a more benign ecosystem, even when capex costs are lagging behind the expected falls.

In the absence of an explicit context, a claim that one technology is necessarily cheaper than another is not always true. But how much damage does this confused logic inflict on investors and society?

An anecdote on how a "drunken sailor" offered a fixed price of less than $0.02 kWh on its power purchase agreement (PPA) is a case in point.

In preparing their costing, using the most heroic (or optimistic) assumptions on costs, a bidder made a calculated bet. The winning bid has four years to make the first delivery from the date the contract is signed. Judging they could build the wind farm in two years and the award is a year away, they estimated at least a three-year window for them to procure the equipment. The developer confidently believed that this is very tight but within their possibilities. This implies that their wind turbine would cost 20% less if procured later.

They did win the bid. However, instead of minting a bundle, the wind farm was never completed. Cost overruns and delays in issuing permits doomed the project. Caught out in the turbine supply squeeze, capex costs doubled before they could blink. Indeed, it was difficult to imagine that there was an era wind turbine cost fell below the levels seen in 2021.

Policy suffers from a similar malady. In pushing for more volumes, generous subsidies were at times spent on projects with little prospect of enabling public interests. In this example, a failed wind farm casts doubts or dampens prospective investors' enthusiasm when economic "good sense" is penalised. By falling in love with the headlines — *cheapest wind farm on record* — financial prudence is ushered through the exit door. But then, the *cheapest wind farm* that fails to produce a single kWh is an exorbitant ointment to suave the ego.

In closely examining what policy is trying to achieve, the problem is not the scale of renewables deployment *per se*. In an indirect way, CO_2 emissions are reduced when less polluting energy is used to generate power. As a logical extension, the more cost-effective low polluting technologies become available, and widely deployed, the higher and faster are the levels and the rate of reduction. This reasoning has two elements:

The *level* of coal or "dirty fuels" avoided preferably should be high. In this case, a "less dirty" fuel such as gas with high fuel usage and power output may be more effective in reducing CO_2 released into the atmosphere than PVT_M with lower output despite its nil fuel input.

The *pace* of reducing CO_2 emissions is partly dictated by how fast "CO_2 displacing" supplies are made available. This is where policy's interest in encouraging more and faster additions of renewables is justified.

The cost of installing low polluting technologies becomes the capex spent for renewables, for example. This cost is compared to how much one would spend for $Coal_B$, for instance, a reference cost that I use to estimate the relative costs. In effect, a negative cost implies that the less polluting technology is cheaper to build than $Coal_B$, with $ACCGT_B$ as an example.

The implied returns are the inverse of LCOEs, a shorthand made popular by the late Shimon Awerbuch (2006) in promoting a portfolio approach to capacity planning. To minimise cost variations, he proposed combining volatile coal with nil fuel cost renewables. This works when power prices are fixed or constant, while costs freely fluctuate, as in a number of regulated regimes.

The comparisons shown in Chart 2.6 offer interesting reading. In general, subsidies may have benefited the low output intermittent renewables. High output ACCGTs, Geo, GeoS, StoHydro, and ANuke are the cost-effective means to reduce CO_2 emissions, according to my calculations using EIA data (2019).

Subsidising intermittent renewables is seen by the state as a way to bridge the cost gaps. However, improving the technology's efficiency in increasing the MWh per MW is essential to bridge the gap.

Following this reasoning, carbon pricing through a traded mechanism may hold more promise. Leaving the choice of technology to managers to decide gives a better

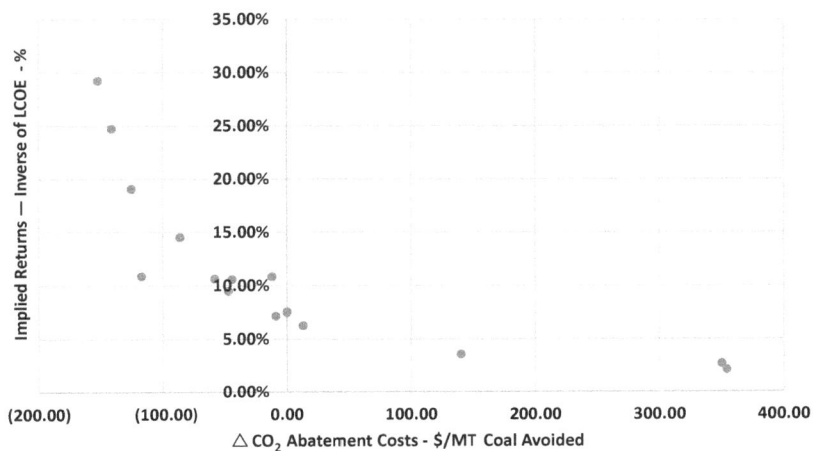

Chart 2.6: Comparative CO_2 Abatement Costs

Note: The math and the calculations behind the estimated CO_2 abatement costs are described in Chapter 10.

chance of instilling economic criteria in investments. The *cap-and-trade* is an example. Richard H Thaler and Cass R Sunstein (2008) have an accessible description of this system. To wit: "In such systems those who pollute are given (or sold) a 'right' to pollute in certain amounts ('the cap') and these rights are then traded in the market. Most specialists believe that such incentives-based system as these should usually displace command-and-control regulation."

In Thaler and Sunstein's (2008) perspective, "This basic approach is compatible with *libertarian paternalism* because people can avoid paying the tax by not creating pollution." They continued: "Liberty is much greater when people are told, 'you can continue with your behaviour, so long as you pay for the social harm that it does' than when they are told 'you must act according to what the government says'. Companies prefer cap-and-trade systems to rigid government commands, because such systems allow more freedom and impose lower costs."

4.4 Why are market structures crucial but ignored?

When policy confers benefits to specific niches, one encounters the question of equity. In some contexts, as some classic welfare economic notions would prescribe, equity is equivalent to a quantitative equalisation of burdens or benefits. Without going into the minutiae of the theories, practical managers may suffice to appreciate the deep theoretical underpinnings of welfare economics that seep into the business and policy lexicon. For example:

> The very notion that economic prosperity and welfare are closely linked dates back to Adam Smith's *Wealth of Nations* (1982) where the "invisible hand" directs people to allocate resources in an efficient manner. This evolved into the *Pareto Optimality* (2014) where resources are allocated to those who care for (or value) a given resource because it maximises their utility. Hence, a person who likes papayas but does not care much for apples could trade their apples with papayas to someone who cares a lot about apples. The trade results in a "win–win" for the parties, leading to Jeremy Bentham's (1890) *social utility*, which is the sum of all the individuals' utility in a given society. To expand welfare therefore is to "make the pie bigger" by going back to meeting Vilfredo Pareto's optimality criterion. Pareto's other enrichment to business lexicon is the "80/20 rule" that extends to other disciplines and policy. That is, Pareto observed that 80% of the output or outcome results from 20% of the input or effort.
>
> Jeremy Bentham made happiness the only pursuit that produces something of value under his utilitarianism (1890). This equates pleasure or happiness to a value where the "ends justify the means" under a system where everyone's pleasure counts equally, a seminal notion of equality. With succeeding economic theorists working on human welfare, Kenneth Arrow's (2020) impossibility theorem broke new grounds on social choices. In examining voting systems, Arrow posited that social choice rule can only be operated when restrictions are placed on individual choices or the neutrality of the constitution to feasible alternatives. For this reason, unfettered individual preferences expressed through majority rule may fail to achieve a stable result. This notion resonates with operating concepts such as "constrained optimalisation" or "second best" from Lipsey and Lancaster's (1956) *General Theory of Second Best*. Formally, the theory posits that if one of the conditions to achieving *Pareto Optimality* can no longer be met, then one

can find a "second best" solution that may not fulfil all the Pareto conditions, hence considered "sub-optimal."

With common usage, at least the familiar ones to business and policy's language, strategic actions and policy measures are purportedly pursued following one or another of the "welfare economic theories." One area where this dominates is in justifying subsidies and in how it should be "correctly" determined. In my book (Barcelona, 2017) — *Energy Investments* — I describe an alternative framing of subsidies:

"Subsidies play a decision-switching role in technology adoption. Through technology-specific subsidies, providing a 'correct' level can be estimated, the adoption of a preferred technology can be promoted by policy over another by seeking to penalise through carbon tax or neglect. Hence, by equalising the costs, as grid price parity attempted to achieve, a switch in preference is expected to occur. By extension, what works in one market is expected to work in another — notwithstanding the evidence to the contrary."

"Failures to transplant a successful scheme to another market are plentiful. Part of the reason for this is in the industry structures, where economic incentives differ between a price-taker and a firm operating under oligopoly. These differences are highlighted in the works of Grenadier's (2002) option premium (OP) formulation. If, under specific market structures (i.e. a monopoly or a multi-player game), an option premium for waiting can be specified, then applying that premium to a reference power source (i.e. Coal or ACCGT) allows us to estimate an adequate level of subsidies or carbon tax."

I then propose that "for a monopoly, without the threat of pre-emption, the OP for waiting to commit (or deferral option) is valuable," a view that resonates with economic literature (for example, Majd and Pindyck, 1987). In contrast, with a credible threat from a rival (or many rivals) to pre-empt, the value erodes rapidly.

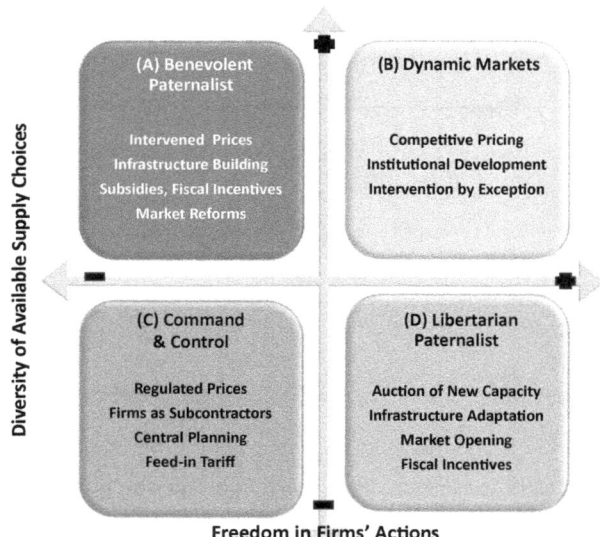

Chart 2.7: Feasible Policy Choices and Firms' Actions under Different Systems

This is not surprising: Under dynamic markets, rivals seek to outcompete one another, where an optimal condition is no longer achieving the full value of the option premium. Instead, a rival is more interested in reaping part of the value (a second best, sort of) rather than losing an attractive opportunity to a rival that could lock out the party that was slower to act. This case applies to access to energy resources, such as water sources or geothermal reserves, that are part of the "commons," as Elinor Ostrum (2015) describes (recall Chart 2.1).

That different policy measures and corporate strategies are required to meet specified challenges appears obvious. However, the predominance of one size fits all, particularly in policy prescriptions, also appears to find favour for climate-related policy interventions. Perhaps, what was assumed as "obvious" may in reality be errors in framing: By believing subsidies are applied and could work everywhere, one wakes up to realise it does not always deliver as expected.

In aligning policy actions and the realities of the energy market policy seeks to regulate, it is essential to test against "what supplies are available" and "how much freedom are firms provided" to comply and respond productively. I propose a framework that I describe in Chart 2.7, where I focus on two factors: "Diversity of Available Supply Choices" and "Freedom in Firms' Actions."

Recalling Amartya Sen (2000), the state is endowed with unique powers to sequester through taxation or confiscation or to promote profitable niches by providing incentives or enabling access (e.g. concessions). I would suggest the following usage of the framework:

In systems that confer limited freedom for firms to act, often found in closed economies or sparsely endowed, energy markets may be regulated under tight "Command-and-Control" (A) or for those endowed with abundant and varied resources, managed by a "Benevolent Paternalist" state (B).

The state's control is considered primordial. Policy in (A) would tend to ensure effective regulation of prices, reducing firms to sub-contractor status. The system thrives or falters on the competence (or lack of) of a controlling agency (e.g. regulator) or bureaucracy (e.g. state enterprises). To encourage sub-contracting firms to pivot to renewables, feed-in tariffs are effective because all the pricing and costing variables are fairly known and predictable.

The state's control is seen as a necessity to harness the abundant and varied resources in (B). Exhibiting benevolence, policy focus is aimed at allowing the system to pivot to a more dynamic system, as described in (D). With this resolve, the state may intervene in pricing to gradually guide a transition to greener futures. Policy would tend to focus on strengthening its infrastructures and employ incentives and subsidies to guide firms to invest in their preferred technologies. Through market reforms, the system may accommodate a more diverse supply mix and withstand the demands on infrastructure of a more dynamic market.

In systems that recognise the firms' freedom to act, a market approach is usually employed, as in many advanced energy systems. With the regulator morphing into an enabling role, scarce diversity of feasible resources may leave firms with little choice but to entrust their fortune to a "Libertarian Paternalist." For the well-endowed systems, "Dynamic Markets" ease the allocation process by harnessing the strengths of the firms and policy.

With the state's control delegated to a market, a "Libertarian Paternalist" would tend to conserve its resources and open the market to other supplies or give access for alternative resources to develop. While occasionally intervening, new capacity or supplies are attracted through auctions of permits to build, while ensuring access to the market stays open. Fiscal incentives may be offered to redirect investments to a preferred path.

As the system matures into a form that approximates "Dynamic Markets," competitive pricing tends to prevail. Policy would shift more and more to policing and institutional development roles to safeguard the integrity of the market. Policy intervenes by exception.

To managers and policy, their respective roles and responsibilities are more clearly delineated. Without this clarity, systems are beset by *ad hoc* actions that often overlap (and cancel out). Inadvertently, policy's best intentions are seldom met, as managers and stakeholders tend to work at cross-purposes to preserve their "perceived gains" (see Box 2.1).

Worst, policy may promote carbon taxation to phase out coal while providing no avenues where firms could pivot to low-carbon alternatives, which apparently is what policy intended. Such avenues become open with access to international supplies and technologies. Hence, unless import facilities are available and capital is given access — the state may fail to open the capital market — the carbon tax becomes a punitive penalty to firms that serves no other purpose but to raise revenues. Unfortunately, by killing extant supplies which are coal-based, energy shortage may be in prospect, while little tax revenues are likely to be raised.

5
Feasible Policy Focus Areas to Pivot

An interesting phenomenon is occurring with policy and some managers. In some ways, both agree that the world *will* change and is already changing. Observing how policy is conducted and the resulting measures that emerge, it varies little from old practices. The same could be said of how some managers choose to evaluate their investments. The world is changing, too fast for some, with some managers seeking comfort in what could be made predictable. Unfortunately, while old habits die hard, successful policies and investment approaches that worked before may prove to be major drawbacks under changing market conditions that make ambiguity a persistent feature. Of course, I am not suggesting that the past was in any way less ambiguous. It has always been, but policy and managers selectively succeeded in getting things done by choosing to sidestep, and getting adept at it, the formal constraints of static and rigid policy and investment evaluation process.

In reframing policy approaches, Richard H Thaler and Cass R Sunstein's (2008) contention on human response to policy may be taken to heart. Intelligent people, and any person for that matter, would tend to act positively when given a choice. When told to comply, and compelled to do so, people often resist, and at times resist violently. In my mind, this is in no small measure how the climate conversation become so polarised when reasonable people would have resolved their differences on approaches amicably.

This brings me to propose specified areas on how choices are enhanced by reframing how policy could facilitate to widen the access to opportunities for all:

Policy could employ principles from social investing and use them broadly, where policy aims to unblock barriers to capital flow. Privately raised "social capital" is making effective inroads into funding emergent technologies, which are too risky for mainstream finance to fund, and aiding them to pilot and scale (see Box 2.2).

Sovereign aid or grant, which is usually disbursed on a government-to-government basis, may need to be relaxed or reframed to broaden its application. Its direct support for private initiatives, usually requiring revisions to its restrictions, may expand its impact. Some grants already do this in funding private research and engineering, with strict provisions against beneficiaries directly profiting from the grants.

Policy's principal contribution is not to cuddle struggling firms to survive by subsidising them. That is the managers' responsibility and a dynamic market's function to weed out failing ventures. *Making an energy market function effectively under the rule of law is.* In the various examples on how subsidies failed, and created green paradoxes, building the institutions and mechanisms that make a market work proves to sustain better most investments' viability. That is, an enabling policy works best when managers are offered the choice to manage their own affairs, knowing the rule of law is on their side.

A clear view on how the energy value chain works, and how it is shifting, offers a common arena for policy and managers to formulate mutually reinforcing loops for business and policy to deliver on a common good, as mutually understood.

An immediate need is some agreed streamlining of reporting standards. A hard and fast rule similar to Sarbanes–Oxley (required for accounting) is not what is needed, it may even prove counterproductive to prescribe hard rules on an evolving and ambiguous issue. An approach similar to the Equator Principles (EPFI, 2020) in project finance may progress and enhance the value of environmental reporting substantively. After all, one cannot have an intelligent conversation to resolve climate-related issues when the parties are talking at cross-purposes.

In pursuing these worthy endeavours, policy and managers may also have to recognise the innate magnanimity of the human spirit. Humans may not have all the answers and may not have an answer at all. What they possess is the capacity to frame a problem, find ways to resolve issues, and work towards some solutions. Underpinning this effort is a deep-seated desire to leave an imprint — mundane or substantial or even evil to some, but to the person, it is all the world of difference *to them.*

This brings me to suggest how policy may shift its focus. Policy should not only become overly obsessed with controlling and penalising the "environmental sinners." Policy could start to learn to appreciate the progress some firms are making in spite of policy's control focus by rewarding the tangible traits comprising "environmental virtues."

Policy and managers may learn from how sports revenues are managed at the stadium, the usual arena for competition and the spectators to converge. I offer these contrasts:

Policy and financiers follow some form of a "first past the post" in rewarding the qualifying environmental practitioner. In a sports event, this is like giving access to the stadium for those who paid for a ticket, being charged a single price. Once inside, the spectator could sit anywhere they choose to. Perhaps, not surprisingly, by paying the minimum, people would go early enough to choose the front rows closest to field, where the best view of the game could be had. This system is no different from how policy and multi-lateral development agencies disburse funds or subsidies to support "clean energy investments."

The managers of sports arenas have long learned that people devoted to their clubs, or to the sports, would be willing to pay more to secure their preferred seats. By applying tiered pricing, the club's ticket revenues went up significantly without adding more seats. The stadium for some clubs is usually filled to the point that reselling tickets for popular games could in itself be a lucrative alternative to watching the game — for the ticket holders.

In operating like the arena manager, policy may shift to differentiating their support, or at least their recognition, of firms with a record of practising "environmental virtues" with consistency. By rewarding them to do more, rather than coming down like a tonne of bricks for non-compliance, managers may surprise even the staunchest critics of "corporate greed" at the magnanimity of the human spirit to innovate and do good.

In a political and enterprise milieu with heightened consciousness on a climate challenge, I find the conditions *now* as more conducive, ironically because of the polarised politics, to tackling real issues with real solutions. This change in attitudes and receptiveness I credit to the works of some environmental advocates with a hard-nosed appreciation of the managers' quandaries. By offering real alternatives that business could take seriously, some climate advocates succeeded in getting the C-suites to act and commit.

Some managers are far along in their execution, while others are on the starting block or are barely getting started. One thing is clear from several of the energy majors' strategic initiatives: Commitments to *net zero* carbon targets are part of the mainstream strategic actions, no longer a nice luxury to varnish one's green credentials.

The slew of "net zero aspirations" announced by major energy and resources firms are no accident or coincidence. C-suite executives did not wake up one day to find their conscience. They now have realistic pathways to realise a tangible opportunity, with all its risks and ambiguities included.

The path is long and treacherous, but inaction may no longer provide a safe haven for managers, *not that inaction without a purpose ever did by design.*

Box 2.1: A Policy Process under Ambiguous Conditions

Over the years, Raphael PM Lotilla and I would catch up whenever I am in the Philippines or on his visits to Europe. He is Energy Secretary, and prior to this, was an Under-Secretary for the National Economic Development Authority (NEDA). It is always a privilege to get a first-hand view on how Philippine energy policy continues to evolve at its own pace. The country has honed into a fine art the ability to adapt policymaking to "optimise the possible." Imperfect as it appears, and even too *ad hoc* for the ideological purists, the system continues to evolve under very ambiguous political and economic conditions.

1. Colliding aspirations and political realities

When I look back to what we proposed, as bankers to the government, almost three decades back, restructuring the Philippine power industry took many different turns from its initial intent. The power supply crisis having just been addressed, President Fidel V Ramos took on the task of opening the industry to private capital by accelerating the roll-out of the build–operate–transfer (BOT) (and its variants) scheme.

Secretary Raphael PM Lotilla, Popo to friends and peers, reflected: "A market-based power sector constitutes the core of Philippine industry reforms under EPIRA, the Electric Power and Industry Restructuring Act (RA 9136) legislated in 2001. The reform has produced positive outcomes, among which are the emergence of financially viable Philippine entities, albeit in a very round-about way. Some form of competition is occurring with the wholesale electricity spot market (WESM),[3] but retail competition remains limited to those consuming a monthly average of 1 MW or above as the Supreme Court has failed to resolve the issue of whether retail competition is mandatory or voluntary. Briefly, WESM was designed to provide a market for power supplies to be traded, where market prices could be set periodically. In

---
[3] A description of WESM is provided in Maria Joy Abrenica's paper in *The Philippine Review of Economics* (2009).

practice, WESM became a market for *contract for differences*, where excess supplies to contracted requirements are sold, or contract shortfalls are covered by spot market purchases. The predominance of long-term supply obligations remains to this day, even though distribution utilities are free to choose between the spot market and bilateral supply contracts."

How the Philippines came to where they are today, Popo recalled: "We started with a perfectly *imperfect* market: Power supply (i.e. power generation) was nearly monopolised by a state-owned enterprise, and demand (i.e. distribution, or wires and supplies to customers) was overwhelmingly dominated by a private utility controlled by politically well-connected interests. Under those circumstances, one would expect frequent setbacks. But by hewing close — by and large — to the main direction of the reforms, attrition has not been on the side of those who oppose them. We tried to move as fast as possible to commence commercial operations of WESM despite the inherent risks in an imperfect market. With WESM starting to operate, we believed that we could promote transparency, provide an alternative market to privatised power generation assets, and enable a space for regulators and market participants to 'learn as you go'. While not fully meeting our aspiration of a fully functional energy market, the piece meal sales of power assets was made feasible, cross-subsidies were largely removed, and market efficiency and transparency introduced. These facilitated the entry and growth of intermittent renewables several years later with the passage of the Renewable Energy Law."

2. Private governance, public regulation

In the political milieu that Philippine policy operates, "optimising the possibilities" takes on a very "inclusive" practice. This often involves making compromises to accommodate all political persuasions that are indistinguishable from specific interests. In the process, the "diverse" but often conflicting rules that result are not always reconciled prior to adoption. Popo cited the following examples:

"The governance of WESM was lodged in the Philippine Electric Market Corporation (PEMC) whose board members were to come from the ranks of the 'Electric Power Industry Participants'. For a limited period, the Energy Secretary was to chair the PEMC board to shepherd its transition to a fully private entity. But the interim period dragged on for more than a decade with the Secretary remaining as the

PEMC chair. In the meantime, a new law created the Government Commission for GOCC[4] (GCG) whose mandate was to oversee the operations of parastatals particularly through the vetting of appointees to their boards by the President of the Philippines. The GCG, in a largely self-serving move, classified the PEMC as a GOCC. The consequences would have been far-reaching. At a stroke of a pen, all the reforms leading to an independent WESM would have been reversed, and nationalised the energy trading system without meaning to, had the government interpretation been allowed to stand." All officers would have been classed as government employees, subject to civil service rules, and government procurement and budgetary rules would have applied.

"To backtrack, the GCG equated the leadership of the Energy Secretary and the presence of National Power (NPC) and TRANSCO, both GOCCs, in the PEMC board as indicating that the PEMC is also a GOCC. This of course ignored existing laws, because nowhere in EPIRA and PEMC's statutes is government ownership or control over the WESM ever contemplated. The DoE, NPC, and TRANSCO's presence in the interim board was in their capacity as representatives of industry participants that awaited privatisation, making their presence transitory and did not in any way constitute government control."

In Popo's mind, "the GCG could have avoided this distorted view of the restructured electricity sector had it, with more diligence, looked at similar examples. Popo cited the Philippine Stock Exchange, a private securities market entity, that exercises powers and responsibilities recognised by the Securities and Exchange Commission (SEC). Other jurisdictions have similar power market entities that are well publicised and extensively studied by academics and practitioners. PEMC is no different, with its fees recovered through a cost recovery basis approved by the regulator pursuant to EPIRA."

Thankfully, the Energy Secretary in 2018 turned over the chairmanship of the PEMC to one elected by representatives of private electricity industry participants.

A related issue concerned the Market Operator of the WESM. "Two distinct phases in creating WESM was contemplated: A 12-month preparatory period was intended to initiate and test the system, undertaken by the autonomous group market operator (AGMO), followed by regular operations under an independent market operator (IMO).

---

[4] Acronym for Government owned and controlled corporation, or generically referred to as state owned enterprises in academic and policy literature.

Had the original timetable been followed, only a foreign entity would have qualified as an IMO as no Philippine entity had the requisite experience. By the time the transition to an IMO was to have happened, the AGMO personnel had chalked up an uninterrupted track record of more than 12 years as market operator. An adjustment had to be made for AGMO to transform into the IMO."

In 2018, the DoE Secretary effected the transfer of WESM market operation to an independent entity, the *Independent Electric Market Operator of the Philippines* (IEMOP) with seasoned market professionals formerly serving with the AGMO. Popo explained the significance of this development:

"The private corporate form that was chosen under EPIRA for WESM is no longer in question. The discipline of the market, unhindered by political considerations, is crucial to the long-term sustainability of the sector. Operated and privately governed, PEMC can better attract and maintain professionals based on merit, adopt advances in technologies unhampered by government rules such as those on appropriations and procurement, and focus on building its capabilities to enhance efficiency and in ensuring the energy market works under dynamic conditions."

"The regulator, Energy Regulatory Commission (ERC), continues to exercise oversight functions over the WESM. These areas are: approval of pricing methodology, market fees, and eligibility for WESM membership, enforcing rules and regulations governing the spot market, and monitoring and enforcing competition rules. The DoE continues to exercise its power to approve any changes to WESM rules and regulations, and issue formal appointments of the PEMC board of directors. More importantly, even as private entities, WESM and industry participants are subject to DoE's judicious exercise of its power to issue rules and regulations pursuant to EPIRA, and to implement government policy in the energy sector."

From an outsider's perspective, I made these observations: In many respects, the Philippines aspired to introduce competition. However, the government chose to remain in control of pricing rather than leave the wholesale market to freely set the periodic prices. The temptation to intervene is not limited to pricing. In certain instances, direct political interventions prior to the turnover of governance to the private sector prevented PEMC from suspending non-compliant market participants. This resulted in the generation companies absorbing financial losses and adversely affecting the credibility of the market to enforce its rules.

3. Intermittent renewables: Net social cost of FiT ALL

Joyce Marie P Lagac and Joseph Yap (2020) question the efficacy of Philippine subsidies scheme to renewables under the feed-in tariff (FiT) scheme. The premise is simple: Renewables benefit society because they abate pollution from coal and fossil fuels. These social benefits, however, cannot be uniquely appropriated by investors. The private costs, which were higher than fossil fuels, are borne by private capital. To correct for this mismatch, the cost differences are recovered through subsidies.

Popo summarised their findings: To estimate the environmental benefit of the FiTs, the actual generation of FiT-eligible plants from 2015 to 2019 was used. The CO_2 emissions avoided were estimated at 9,694,318 MT coal equivalent, giving an environmental benefit of $480 million[5] using the social cost of carbon emissions. The "merit order" benefits added another $997 million to provide combined social benefits of $1,477 million. This arose from curtailing coal and even geothermal power (the latter further reduced carbon emissions from coal) to decongest the grid when wind and solar power supplies are high, given their priority in dispatch. Compared to what was collected from consumers, to fund FiT ALL amounting to $1,580 million, the "net social cost" was $103 million for the period.

In my view, what was seen as a "social cost" is in reality a direct cash transfer from consumers to renewables developers. With most of these cash transfers used to fund solar panel purchases, the ultimate beneficiaries are in reality solar panel producers.

Examining the crowding out of coal and conventional renewables, geothermal and hydro power, Popo cited Asian Development Bank's (2018) report: Curtailment risks arise when some supplies are not sold in the wholesale market because they exceed the transmission capacity of the grid. To maintain the balance, some of the load will have to be "shed" to prevent the collapse of the grid. Negros Island attracted 57% of solar capacity additions in 2016, when 279 MW was added to an island system with a peak demand of 316 MW. Experiencing serious oversupply, with Negros Island also a major geothermal producer, even solar power had to be curtailed. In effect, as Lagac and Yap (2020) pointed out, when these are included in the social cost of intermittent

---

[5] The Philippine peso amount was converted to its US dollar equivalent, using an exchange rate of P50/$1.00, to ease comparisons with international studies.

renewables, which they are not, the $103 million "social cost" is seen as a minimum.

In my conversations with Popo, I offered my prognosis. The Philippines will have to recognise the need to adapt legislation to how archipelagic systems operate. With weak inter-island interconnections, planning for future power capacity additions has to recognise these geographic realities. An excess supply in one area cannot always offset shortages in another unless the grid is sufficiently integrated and robust to handle sharp swings in supplies.

This reality was not lost on policymakers. In 2016, when the initial quota for qualifying FiT-ALL assets was set at 400 MW, there was a strong clamour for its expansion. The government refused to the disappointment of environmental and intermittent renewables advocates.

4. Biofuels and the coconut and sugar industries

The Philippines was the first in southeast Asia to require biofuels blending with petroleum-based fuels through the passage of the Biofuels Act of 2006. Popo reflected: "The government saw biofuels as a way to assist its moribund coconut and sugar industries. Rural poverty was to be reduced by creating alternative markets for coconut and sugar. Policy aimed to raise rural income while enhancing energy security and addressing the effects of climate change through the reduction of CO_2 emissions."

Popo recalled: "The mandatory blend for sugarcane-based ethanol is 10%. However, with limited local production, imports became the easy route to comply by oil companies and independent fuel importers. What was designed to alleviate poverty ended up rewarding importers and foreign suppliers."

On the other hand, the mandatory 1% blend of coco-biodiesel and diesel was raised to 2% in 2009, with a view to raise this to 5% in 2013. The late Ruperto Alonzo (2016) observed the following:

The negative economic impact far outweighs the positive health and environmental net loss, with a net loss amounting to $65 million in 2016 alone, based on a biodiesel price of $0.80/ltr. Judging by the trends in diesel and coconut oil prices, as forecasted by the World Bank, blending "cheaper" diesel with "more expensive" coconut oil would lead to even higher blended diesel fuel cost. Raising the blend to 5% would adversely affect consumers and local producers alike. Even with the Philippine Coconut Authority's optimistic projections, the projected "surplus" coconut oil would not be enough to locally cover the proposed 5% blending rate.

Popo noted that the government, faced with relative price trends favouring coconut oil and limited local production, decided to freeze the required blends at 2% subject to review (DoE, 2018).

5. Competitive supply procurement (CSP)

In most of the developed power markets, retail competition means that consumers could choose their supplies from any qualified power generators. Distribution utilities access suppliers competitively through the wholesale power market, where prices are set periodically. The Philippine government and the public are not fully comfortable with the volatilities in this dynamic market. Price spikes often become sensitive political issues with accusations of regulatory capture. Nor does the public trust the distribution utilities, in a market where bilateral supply contracting is the preferred choice, to deal with related parties at arm's length. Government has instead put in place a novel competitive supply procurement (CSP).

Essentially, long-term contracts between power generators and utilities are subjected to competitive comparison based on prices. In theory, the lowest long-term price offered at the time of signing the contract is deemed to be the most favourable. This creates practical problems similar to rigid long-term power purchase agreements: What is deemed competitive today may appear expensive in a few months if fuel prices fall (or vice versa), but the public appears more comfortable with price stability.

The Supreme Court has upheld the power of the DoE under the EPIRA to require a CSP process. In the latest supply procurement through CSP, the ERC (that used to review bilateral supply contracts on the basis of costs rather than price) has respected the bidding outcome of the CSP. If this becomes the accepted practice, the bulk of ERC resources and attention could be focused on more strategic concerns. It would also do away with ERC's indirect price regulation of the generation and retail supply subsectors which were clearly deregulated under the EPIRA.

Reflecting on how the Philippine energy could be made to work better, Popo shared these thoughts: "Policy's best intentions are insufficient to solve all the problems that plague an energy market that took an eternity to even transition to a workable market. In committing to a market economy, policy will have to learn to recognise that it does not have all the solutions, and neither is it expected to. By playing an enabling role, policy would have to let market participants freely conduct their business within the framework of a rule of law. For this reason, the less policy intervenes, and the more market players and consumers rely on their freedom of choice, the more likely we are to meet our societal objectives. In this context, the government and the public have to first recognise the specific needs of our archipelagic and fragmented system, rather than simply copying what works in contiguous markets with strong interconnectivity."

****

Raphael PM Lotilla is an independent Director at Aboitiz Equity Ventures, First Metro Investment, ACE Enexor, and Petron Foundation. Previously, Popo was a Professor of Law, University of the Philippines. In July 2022, he was appointed for the second time as Secretary of Energy, Philippines. This article was contributed prior to Popo's appointment for the second time as Secretary of Energy.

Box 2.2: Learning from Impact Investing

The dramatic growth in wind and solar energy (IRENA, 2020) is attributed to their environmental merits, with investor financial costs falling in part because of subsidies and policy incentives and in part from scale and innovation. In certain applications and markets, for example, Rwanda's rooftop solar and wind power in Mongolia, catalytic capital has played a significant role in facilitating early deployment through impact, blended, and development financing schemes. Private corporations are also increasingly making their sustainability commitments visible. Microsoft's procurement of 500 MW solar power from Sol Systems in 2020 (Clancy, 2020) is an example where achieving social returns are ranked as a priority.

1. Impact investing: What can it offer?

Renewables are one of the more traditional areas of impact investing. The practice has come a long way over the past 25 years as government incentives, research and development, and de-risking strategies enabled the adoption of various renewable technologies. This ranges from wind, solar, geothermal, bioenergy, hydrogen, small-scale hydro to emerging technologies such as tidal energy in advanced or emerging markets.

Wind and solar benefited, seeing its costs progressively decreased with scale, as private capital favoured its adoption. For these investors, in spite of its intermittency, solar is seen as a paragon in the race to deliver affordable renewables. This assertion is supported by the 85% decrease in solar power's installed costs in the past decade, with wind following closely. A range of finanical instruments employed by impact investors are shown in Box Chart 2.2.1.

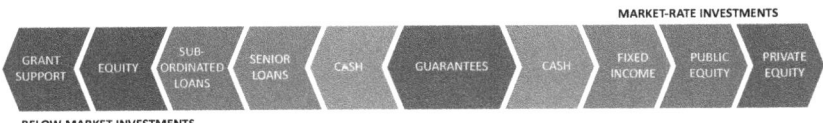

Box Chart 2.2.1: Asset Classes and Return Expectations

Encouraged by this performance, coupled with tighter environmental standards progressively adopted by some countries, some assert that wind and solar are the future of a low-carbon energy system.

These welcome technological and policy advances, while raising a fundamental question: If renewables such as solar and wind are financially competitive, why is concessionary capital still needed to support wider adoption?

The reasons are perhaps more obvious than it appears to some who find this paradox puzzling. In certain markets, particularly in emerging markets with weak institutions, the ability to access capital is limited. This is hindered by the financial system's limited know-how or the absence of appropriate regulatory mechanisms to support private capital. In some cases, some technologies are new, at least to the early adopters in specific markets, hence they are considered as unproven or untested under local conditions. With the reluctance of private capital and the state lacking resources, social capital steps in by taking first losses, fund early deployment, and orchestrate technical assistance during the earlier or riskier phases.

2. How does impact investing work?

Impact investing is defined as "investments made with the intention to generate positive, measurable, social and environmental impact alongside a financial return" (GIIN, 2020). Central to impact investing, therefore, is the concept of social and environmental yields that ought to be "measurable." That is, specific positive outcomes are expected beyond good intentions or "check-in-the-box" exercise that pass as complying with economic, social, and governance (ESG) criteria. Impact investing generally has four elements:

1. **Intentionality:** The purpose of the investment is to tangibly contribute to positive social and/or environmental outcomes, which is different from passive screens present in ESG or socially responsible investing. Investors, more than investees, have the intent to create impact (IFC, 2019).
2. **Financial returns:** Capital must be paid back along with a financial return at or below risk-adjusted market rates. Otherwise, it is considered grant-making or philanthropy.
3. **Range of asset classes:** Impact investing can take place in a wide range of asset classes (practically all) and through a variety of financial instruments

and structures. It can also be performed via private placements or public offerings in capital markets.
4. **Impact measurement:** There must be a clear set of metrics and transparent methodologies to measure the social and environmental outcomes of the investments.

Impact investing can materialise via private placements, such as private equity, venture capital, project finance, bonds, and other debt facilities. It can take place, in addition, through publicly traded securities markets such as stocks and funds which tend to be managed on a portfolio basis. All in all, they make up a wide spectrum of asset classes, objectives, and mandates stipulated by the provider of social capital.

In its most recent survey, the Global Impact Investing Network (GIIN) estimated the size of the impact investing market to be in the order of $702 billion as of 2020, with 20% allocated to energy and infrastructure. Among organisations engaging in this type of investing are asset managers, foundations, banks, family offices, development financial institutions, pension funds, and insurance companies.

3. Impact investing and blended finance

Blended finance, or a combination of social and commercial funding, was in common use among development financial institutions (DFIs) and foundations. The UN Sustainable Development Goals broadened its use when a funding gap of about $3 trillion was estimated to fully meet the ESG initiatives by 2030 (Convergence, 2020). According to Convergence, social capital from public or philanthropic sources can facilitate private investment in sustainable development initiatives. Convergence sees that social capital is incorporated as a funding source according to how the project is structured to delineate how returns are allocated to various fund providers.

Blended finance enables impact by incorporating concessionary (or social) capital to take on non-bankable risks. This can be done in a variety of ways. First loss capital, for example, is typically provided by non-profit entities, concessional funds, and governments. It represents an efficient way of doing philanthropy (De Schrevel, 2020). Instead of donating to a certain cause, the non-profit can take on the "first loss" role in a given investment. In essence, if the investment fails, social capital absorbs the losses that it was designed to cover (e.g. exploration failure for geothermal). When successful, social capital is paid back with or without a return so that it can be redeployed to other socially beneficial investments. In this way, a dollar towards impact investing can mobilise several dollars from private finance. Examples of these mechanisms are described as the following, including public–private partnerships (PPPs) (OECD, 2018):

- **Direct investments** may take the form of concessional capital applied to projects or companies to boost private investment.
- **Credit lines** are extended to banks and other financial institutions in support of specific niches such as small-holder farms and Small and Medium Enterprises (SMEs).
- **Green bonds** are raised for projects as well as companies to provide longer-term financing backed by DFIs and MDBs in specific risks such as political and liquidity-related risks.
- **Guarantees and insurance for credit enhancement** are among the earliest forms of blended finance. It seeks to safeguard investors against certain types of commercial or political risks that the private markets would not have an appetite for. A traditional player is the World Bank through its Multilateral Investment Guarantee Agency (MIGA).
- **Grants and technical assistance** take the form of non-refundable money, often extended by DFIs geared towards technical capacity, feasibility studies, and other types of assistance to improve the chances of success of the project.
- **Local currency loans and investments** expand the sources of funding that better align with local currency revenues that the venture is expected to generate. Multilateral financial institutions and specialised funds may come in to provide the cross-currency hedge to make the transaction work (OECD, 2018).

Some of the cases discussed in the following sections show how blended finance, and more broadly impact investing, supported renewables deployment in various markets.

4. Broadening access to renewables

Five projects represent different strategies on how impact investing is employed for funding renewables projects. Two projects use blended finance to de-risk, the other two use development finance to catalyse investments with social and environmental benefits, and one project showcases social commitments attached to a clean energy procurement process. The details are summarised in Box Appendix 2.2A.

The Subnational Climate Fund (SnCF) is a novel private equity fund targeting mid-sized climate mitigation and adaptation projects ranging from $5 million to $75 million. The Green Climate Fund brings a $150 million first loss, catalytic capital in a $750 million fund. There is in addition a Technical Assistance Facility of $28 million designed to help projects in the early stages of planning, the aspect which makes the fund unique. The consortium of companies is led by New York-based impact investor Pegasus Capital Advisors and includes names such as BNP Paribas, R20, and the Gold Standard. The name SnCF derives from the fact that the fund targets projects at the subnational level and therefore does not depend on federal governments for approvals. Such projects, given their size and focus, usually fall outside the scope of mainstream commercial financing. The ultimate goal is to attract up to $3.8 billion in private capital from institutional investors, such as insurance companies, pension funds, sovereign funds, and various modalities of impact investors, among others.

Crossboundary Energy Fund (CBE) was constituted with the proposition that commercial clients in Africa would pay for distributed solar energy (Pothering, 2020). This approach, however, was untested when CBE was created. Unlike remote rural areas in Africa, companies that were targeted by the fund were already connected to the grid, although an unreliable one, which threatened business continuity. CBE accessed a $1.3 million first loss recoverable grant from the US Agency for International Development (USAID) and its Power Africa initiative in 2015. With that in place, and supported by grant capital to cover the fund's early operational costs, CBE was able to raise $6 million from investors and break into a market that was not yet established but had a potential for positive impact. CBE sold its portfolio to ARCH Emerging Markets Partners for $40 million while yielding investors a 15% annualised return and a successful exit.

Salkhit Wind Farm was conceived 10 years ago as a $120 million, 50 MW project consisting of the installation of 31 wind turbines in Mongolia. The wind farm serves Ulaanbaatar, the capital of Mongolia with 1.5 million people, representing 46% of the country's population. The migration from rural areas to the city happened quickly, resulting in almost tripling the population of Ulaanbaatar, Mongolia's capital, compared to its population in 1990 (WHO, 2019). This quick influx resulted in informal housing called "gers" being built north of the city. A "ger" typically has a stove used for cooking and heating in the middle of the dwelling that burns wood, dung, and unprocessed coal. In winter months, the preferred material for heat stoves is coal, which burns for a longer period of time, resulting in emissions of a wide range of substances from sulphates to black carbon, carbon monoxide, and nitrous oxide, representing serious long-term health hazards. Given the absence of local capital markets to finance an undertaking with clear social and environmental benefits, the wind farm was constructed with debt and equity financing from the European Bank for Reconstruction and Development and the Dutch development bank FMO (Pyrkalo, 2013). The availability of electricity replaced the stove for cooking and to provide heating.

Pacific Islands Renewable Energy Investment Program was designed to replace diesel generators with renewable power as the islands' primary source of power. Premised on plentiful sunlight and ample wind, the Small Island Development States (SIDS) in the Pacific were chosen as recipients of the $29.9 million grant from Green Climate Fund and Asian Development Bank.

Microsoft and Sol Systems partnership was considered a landmark agreement in establishing corporate power purchase agreement (Corporate PPA) as a way of funding solar power projects. In July 2020, Microsoft agreed to purchase the output of a 500 MW solar farm developed by Sol Systems as a way for Microsoft to fully offset by 2025 its power usage derived from non-renewable sources. Sol Systems are to locate their solar installations in disadvantaged communities as a way to foster energy equity and justice. Through their corporate PPAs, Microsoft enables access to affordable clean energy, alongside a $50 million in grants, to these communities for education and community welfare (Merchant, 2020).

5. Impetus from a necessity

The widespread deployment of renewables is seen as crucial to a world that grapples with the Herculean task of reducing CO_2 emissions from energy generation. In many ways, this rush to decarbonise to keep global warming between 1.5°C and 2.0°C will have to occur with unnatural speed and scale. Climate change is considered to represent an unnatural evolution of earth's conditions in the Anthropocene, a period described as a shift in the geological cycle impacted by human activities (Kolbert, 2014).

Following this logic, a wide range of energy solutions, both large and small, will be employed — from solar, wind, microgrids, small hydro to other sources, including nuclear power. Some of these will take place in markets that lack the capacity to mobilise capital and access to specialised finance, expertise, or appropriate regulatory mechanisms. That is when non-conventional finance will be needed. Organisations such as Regions 20, the Climate Finance Access Network, and Convergence, among many others, work to try to unblock bottlenecks. They may focus on specific aspects in the investment process (R20), training in-country advisors to broaden the access to climate finance (CFAN), or providing a platform for deal origination and conversations among the various stakeholders, including governments, investors, project sponsors, and financial intermediaries (Convergence, 2020).

Out of necessity, mainstream financing tools are reframed, or adapted, to suit local circumstances. The consensus is that public capital alone will fall well short of the $3 trillion SDG financing gap (Convergence, 2020). Thus, alternative ways are being devised to attract private capital to align their aspirations with the Sustainable Development Goals.

Grants and non-reimbursable capital are likely to coexist with impact investing. Perhaps, the marriage of financial necessity and social aspirations may influence policy to learn a few principles from impact investors. With these lessons learned, accountability and performance follow the demand for money that may surprise even the hardcore socially inclined policymaker that firms indeed can do good for far less.

****

This feature article was written by Alexandre Moreira. He is Managing Director at International Financial Consulting Ltd, a Canadian firm working with the leading Development Financial Institutions globally. He is also Founder at Aska Impact LLC through which he advises on financing of renewables, environmental, and social impact projects.

Appendix

Box 2.2A Five Projects with Different Strategies for Funding Renewables Projects

Project	Main Sponsors	Year of Inception	Countries	Activities Supported	Size and Financial Structure	Impact Obtained/Sought	How Do They Differ?	Follow on Benefits
Sub-national Climate Fund	• Green Climate Fund • Pegasus Capital • R20	2020	42 developing nations	• Small- and medium-scale renewables, restorative agriculture/aquaculture, waste optimisation, water and sanitation, and energy-efficient lighting	$750 million private equity fund with $150 million first loss, catalytic capital from the GCF. In addition, $28 million in technical assistance for project development contribute to its uniqueness	• Climate mitigation and adaptation. No specific metrics in the aggregate but each project will be assessed separately for impact	First private equity fund for climate mitigation and adaptation with a built-in technical assistance facility	• Mobilisation of up to $3.8 billion in private investment
Crossboundary Energy Fund	• Crossboundary Energy • USAID	2015	Kenya, Rwanda, Ghana, Madagascar, Uganda, Sierra Leone, Zambia, and Nigeria	• Commercial rooftop solar	$7.3 million with $1.3 million first-loss, recoverable grant from USAID	• 30 MW of energy between solar generation and storage • Lower cost of energy • Most importantly, reliability in the energy supply	Rooftop commercial solar was an untapped market in many African countries. The USAID grant was instrumental to jump start the market	• Crossboundary sold its operating assets for $40 million and is now putting together a $100 million fund to continue its work

Policy and Managerial Actions

Box 2.2A: (*Continued*)

Project	Main Sponsors	Year of Inception	Countries	Activities Supported	Size and Financial Structure	Impact Obtained/ Sought	How Do They Differ?	Follow on Benefits
Salkhit Wind Farm	• EBRD • FMO	2012	Mongolia	• Wind power — 50 MW • Carbon credits	$123 million debt and equity financing (50% EBRD, 50% FMO) complemented by €366K grant from Japan and Luxembourg for regulatory framework and assessment of impacts	• 178,000 tons of CO_2 emissions avoided per year • Saving of 1.6 million tons of fresh water annually • Creation of over 3,000 local jobs	Development banks stepped in to create a new market and regulatory framework for renewable power	• 41 MW distributed wind solar project financed by the ADB • Opened the market for exploration of Mongolia's vast wind generation potential
Pacific Islands Renewable Energy Investment Program	• GCF • ADB	2016	Small Island Developing States (SIDS)	• Renewable energy generation	$29.2 million in grant financing	• Three million tons of CO_2 emissions avoided	Allows small island nations to transition away from diesel electricity generation	• 100% renewable energy by 2025
Microsoft/Sol Systems	• Microsoft/Sol Systems	2020	United States	• Solar energy generation — 500 MW • Empowerment of women, minority-owned businesses, and disadvantaged communities	~$600 million + $50 million grant for education, career training, land restoration, clean energy, and efficiency programs	• Unspecified	First of its kind. It attaches a social component to a corporate net zero pledge	• It is expected that the market will follow suit in similar undertakings

Bibliography

Abrenica, M. J. (2009). Detecting and measuring market power in the Philippine wholesale electricity spot market. *The Philippine Review of Economics*, 46(2), 5–46.

Alonzo, R. (2016). An economic and environmental analysis of the impact of higher-blended biodiesel on the Philippine economy. Working Paper 2016–2017, Energy Policy and Development Programme, US Agency for International Development (USAID) and UPEcon Foundation, October 2016.

Arrow, K. J. (2020). *Social Choice and Individual Values*. Reprint: Barakaldo Books.

Asian Development Bank (2018). Philippines: Energy Sector Assessment, Strategy, and Road Map. Manila, Philippines: Asian Development Bank.

Awerbuch, S. (2006). Portfolio-based electricity generation planning: Policy implications for renewables and energy security. *Mitigation and Adaptation Strategies for Global Change*, 11, 693–710.

Barcelona, R. G. (2017). *Energy Investments: An Adaptive Approach to Profiting from Uncertainties*. London: Palgrave Macmillan.

Basurto, X. and Ostrum, E. (2008). Beyond the tragedy of commons. *Economia delle Fonti di Energia e dell'Ambiente*, January 2009.

Bentham, J. (1890). *Utilitarianism* (Reprint). London: Progressive Publishing Company.

Clancy, H. (2020). Behind Microsoft's bold plan to build social equity into clean energy buying. *Greenbiz*, August 6, 2020.

Clark, D. A. (2000). Sen's capability approach and the many spaces of human well-being. *The Journal of Development Studies*, 41(8), 1339–1368.

Convergence (2020). Blended finance. https://www.convergence.finance/blended-finance. Accessed on April 7, 2021.

Department of Energy (DoE) (2018). *Philippine Energy Plan 2018–2040*. Metro Manila, Philippines: Department of Energy.

Energy Information Administration (EIA) (2019). *Energy Outlook 2019*. Washington, D.C.: Energy Information Administration.

EPFI (2020). *The Equator Principles*. Equator Principles Financial Institutions, July 2020.

Friedman, L. (2019). What is the green new deal? *New York Times*, February 21, 2019.

Genscu, I., Whitley, S., Roberts, L., Beaton, C., Chen, H., Donkas, A., Geddes, A., Gerasimchuk, I., Sanchez, L., and Suharsono, A. (2019). *G20 Coal Subsidies: Tracking Government Support to a Fading Industry*. London: Overseas Development Institute, June 2019.

Gordon, H. S. (1954). The economic theory of a common property resource: the fishery. *The Journal of Political Economy*, 62, 124–142.

Grant, W. (2016). Feature essay: Elinor Ostrom's work on governing the commons: An appreciation. London School of Economics Review of Books, August 9, 2016.

Grenadier, S. R. (2002). Option exercise games: An application to the equilibrium investment strategies of firms. *The Review of Financial Studies*, 15(3), 691–721.

Gross, S. (2020). *Why are Fossil Fuels as Hard to Quit?* Washington, DC: The Brookings Institution.

Hamburger, P. (2008). *Law and Judicial Duty*. Cambridge, MA: Harvard University Press.

Hand, D., Dithrich, H., and Sunderji, S. (2020). *Renewable Capacity Highlights: 2020 Annual Impact Investor Survey*. Abu Dhabi: International Renewable Energy Agency, March 31, 2020.

Hardin, G. (1968). The tragedy of the commons. *Science*, 162(3865), 1243–1248.

Hirschmann, W. N. (1964). Profit from the learning curve. *Harvard Business Review*, January 1964.

Hyman, L. S. (1985). *America's Electric Utilities: Past, Present, and Future*. Second Edition. Arlington, VA: Public Utilities Report.

IFC (2019). *Operating Principles for Impact Management*. Washington D.C.: International Finance Corporation, February 2019.

IRENA (2020). *Renewable Capacity Highlights*. Abu Dhabi: International Renewable Energy Agency, March 31, 2020.

The Irish Times (1997). How far can a hare run? *The Irish Times*, August 25, 1997.

Jacobson, T. and Chang, L. (2019). Sen's capabilities approach and the measurement of communication outcomes. *Journal of Information Policy*, 9(2019), 111–131.

Johnson, T. (2010). Alternative views on climate change. *Council on Foreign Relations*, February 23, 2010.

Karimi, M., Brazier, J., and Basarir, H. (2016). The capability approach: A critical review of its applications in health economics. *Value in Health*, 19(6), 795–799, September–October 2016.

Kolbert, E. (2014). *The Sixth Extinction: An Unnatural History*. New York: Henry Holt and Company.

Lagac, J. M. P. and Yap, J. (2020). Evaluating the feed-in tariff policy in the Philippines. Ateneo School of Government Working Paper 20-004, January 2020.

Lejano, R. P. (2019). Ideology and the narrative of climate scepticism. *American Meteorological Society*, 415–421, December 2019.

Lipsey, R. and Lancaster, K. (1956). The general theory of second best. *The Review of Economic Studies*, 24(1), 11–22.

Majd, S. and Pindyck, R. S. (1987). Time to build, option value and investment decisions. *Journal of Financial Economics*, 18, 7–28.

Merchant, E. F. (2020). Sol Systems, Microsoft partner on 500MW of community-based solar projects. *Institute for Energy Economics & Financial Analysis* (IEEFA), July 24, 2020.

Miller, T., Kim, A. B., Roberts, J. M., and Tyrrell, P. (2021). *Highlights of the 2021 Index of Economic Freedom*. Washington, D.C.: The Heritage Foundation.

Nova, N. (2020). *Global Impact Investing Network*, June 11, 2020.

Nussbaum, M. C. (2011). *Creating Capabilities: The Human Development Approach*. Cambridge, MA: Belknap Press.

OECD (2018). *Making Blended Finance Work for Sustainable Development Goals*. Paris: Organisation for Economic Cooperation and Development.

Ostrum, E. (2015). *Governing the Commons: The Evolution of Institutions for Collective Actions*. Cambridge: Cambridge University Press.

Pareto, V. (2014). *Manual of Political Economy: A Critical and Varorium Edition*, Monetsino, A., Zanni, A., Bruni, L., Chipman, J. S., and McLure, M. (Eds.), Oxford: Oxford University Press.

Peszko, G. (2011). Information Note on Subsidies for Renewable Energy Technologies under SREP. Meeting of the SREP Sub-committee, November 1, 2011. *Scaling Up Renewable Energy Programme (SREP)*, Washington, DC: Climate Investment Funds, October 26, 2011.

Politico (2020). What is the green deal? *Politico*, October 20, 2020.

Pothering, J. (2020). CrossBoundary energy's fund exit is a proof point for Africa's commercial solar market — And catalytic capital. *Impact Alpha*, November 30, 2020.

Pyrkalo, S. Salkhit wind farm in mongolia starts production. *EBRD — European Bank for Reconstruction and Development*, June 30, 2013.

Republic Act 9136 (RA 9136) (2001). An Act ordaining reforms on the electric power industry, amending for the purpose certain laws and for other purposes, The Electric Power Industry Reform Act (EPIRA), Republic of the Philippines, June 8, 2001.

Republic Act 10149 (RA 10149) (2011). GOCC Governance Act of 2011, Republic of the Philippines, June 6, 2011.

Sacchetti, D. (2008). Contrarian views on climate change: Daring to zig. *International Atomic Energy Agency, IAEA Bulletin*, 49(2), 20–21.

Schrevel, de, J. P. (2020). How blended finance can plug the SDG financing gap. *OECD Development Matters*, Organisation for Economic Cooperation and Development, January 22, 2020.

Sen, A. (2000). *Development as Freedom*. New York: Anchor Books.

Smith, A. (1982). *The Wealth of Nations: Books 1–111*. New York: Penguin Classics.

Sparkman, G. and Attari, S. Z. (2020). Credibility, communication, and climate change: How lifestyle inconsistency and do-gooder derogation impact decarbonisation advocacy. *Energy Research & Social Science*, 59, 1–7.

Thaler, R. H. (2015). *Misbehaving: The Making of Behavioural Economics*. New York and London: W. W. Norton & Company.

Thaler, R. H. and Sunstein, C. R. (2008). *Nudge: Improving Decisions About Health, Wealth, and Happiness*. New Haven & London: Yale University Press.

Williamson, K. (2017). Why corporate leaders become progressive activists. *National Review*, March 13, 2017.

Wiser, R. and Bollinger, M. (2015). *2014 Wind Technologies Market Report*. Washington, D.C.: Department of Energy.

Wiser, R., Jenni, K., Seel, J., Baker, E., Hand, M., Lantz, E., and Smith, A. (2016). Expert elicitation survey on future wind energy costs. *Nature Energy*, 1(10), 1–8.

WHO (2019). Air pollution in Mongolia. *World Health Organisation*, January 31, 2019.

II
Adaptive Moves

Chapter 3
Articulate a Purpose

In articulating the firm's purpose, managers tend to presume that why firms exist is well understood. However, the very role of modern corporations is increasingly being questioned and continually reframed. Operating within this market context, managers would need to articulate their *raison d'être*. Through this understanding, managers are in a better position to define a *purpose* (or vision) that inspires commitment to deliver the results. In this chapter, why firms exist is revisited as a premise for defining its purpose. To operationalise the emerging "vision," the firm's purpose is examined as to how it seeks to carve a role under a continually changing energy landscape when markets are transitioning to a low-carbon economy. This would require of managers to understand how their business could be disrupted in order to identify feasible pathways to create shared value for its stakeholders. In an uncertain world, how to move forward is as important as knowing when to change course when things work out differently from what was expected. Once formulated, the vision will need to be communicated, assimilated, and embedded among stakeholders' actions towards achieving some commonly understood objectives.

1
Introduction

In a number of strategic planning exercises, I observed managers seldom question why they are called to participate. By their presence, their relevance is presumed. To illustrate my point, I pose this question to participants in an executive education programme: *Why are you here?*

With few exceptions, I was met with thoughtful looks followed by deep silence. To relieve the unease, I asked the participants to imagine the setting of a board room. The handful of managers are entrusted to decide on matters that range from profound to mundane. As participants recovered their bearing, I posed this question: Why are you in the business that you are engaged in?

Espoused with confidence, most default to Milton Friedman's (1970) shareholder principles, as popularly understood: *The purpose of the firm is to maximise profits for shareholders.* To an overwhelming number, this is their accepted wisdom in management.

Real people do not always agree. Taking issue with Friedman, Jeb Brugmann and C.K. Prahalad (2007) were brought in to offer alternative views. For example:

To flourish in today's world, some would assert that businesses should seek to co-create social value for their communities. Ben & Jerry's linked prosperity is an iconic example. Bob Michalak, Global Director of social impact, describes what this meant: When Ben & Jerry's flourishes in its business, it makes sure that its community of stakeholders also benefits (Michalak, 2019).

That community gets extended when multinational firms are brought into the conversation. Operating under globalised markets, they expect rules to be consistent according to international standards. Planning for success, they see their business plans crumble in plain sight as they encounter bumps, or gaping holes, that managers choose to ignore.

Without meaning to, as a prominent firm in local communities, managers of multinational firms are drawn into "nation-building" that are traditionally of purely public concerns (Scherer *et al.*, 2014). Inadvertently, firms take on political roles that some are reluctant to assume.

In an inter-connected world, social demands are placed on firms to fulfil under *The Triple Bottom Line* (Elkington, 2008). With climate concerns intertwined with sustainability, managers alternate between earning a profit to stay afloat and demonstrating their environmental credentials. While few would oppose their responsibility for *planet*, *people*, and *profits*, they differ in how to achieve this (Norman and Macdonald, 2004).

Up until this point, I am an observer in the conversations of people who direct the future of their firms. They orchestrate resources, decide on their use, and create the conditions for their teams to flourish. They interact with people (or firms) as customers, suppliers, or peers within their community as stakeholders. In its broadest sense, at various levels of authority, these are the people collectively referred to as managers.

I am encouraged to note that managers of all stripes and persuasions could agree on one notion. Business serves a *common good*, in whichever way this is understood through the different means managers choose to achieve this. Curiously, this dilemma continues to divide managers: Why is making a profit and doing good for society seen by some as irreconcilable objectives?

In the safety of the classroom, the discomfort of battle-tested managers is palpable: The firm's *raison d'être*, once beyond question, is now the very subject of public challenge, if not outcry. Bewildered, managers tend to wonder: Have firms and markets not ushered in unprecedented prosperity under capitalism?

In answering these questions, I choose to frame the answers from a managerial perspective under the optics of *dynamic decisions*. In real life, managers are humans relating to real people. In these interactions, how people act elicit responses, making most managerial decisions contingent on people's reactions, and how these alter markets as rival firms aim to outcompete each other.

Variously seen as the employer of first (and last) resort, firms' actions directly impact people's lives through employment, trade, and investments. They buy from people or other firms to produce their goods or services. In this ecosystem, the firm performs multiple roles that are economic and social in nature, where people are linked through transactions or intermediation.

To simplify the theory, economic theorists construct a notion of the ***firm*** with "human" traits as a juridical person. Seen as quasi-"human," firms are bestowed with rights and responsibilities as a human person would, separating real people acting as managers from legal obligations. Increasingly, interactions among firms are impersonal, making ambiguous how people and firms would tackle their accountabilities.

In this transactional world, some managers start articulating their *vision* as a statement of lofty ideals, made "specific" by its *mission* expressed as generic aspirations. Perhaps, not surprisingly, most firms are indistinguishable in their stated *visions* and *missions*. I see this as a contradiction.

If each firm aspires to be the "best in class," managers would need to articulate how they could set their firm apart from rivals. This, they hardly do when lofty ideals substitute for *purpose*.

Enron comes to mind. A major gas company, it was the darling of Wall Street analysts (Kunen, 2002). Going solely by its *vision*, *mission*, and what its *Code of Ethics* encapsulated (Nilsen, 2013), Enron should be, and at one time, was among the world's leading enterprises. However, the truth emerged in 2001 when regulators discovered revenues were inflated, hence flattering the value of stock options and equity. Bankruptcy ended the myth (history.com, 2001). In spite of the regulator's best efforts, as memories blur, Enron's flawed financial tinkering re-emerged in the 21st century as "innovative financing" *sans* the controls and transparency. To Enron's credit, managers at least kept the pretence of following some form of internal controls amenable to external audits.

The lesson that Enron conveyed to me is simpler. To articulate a *purpose* is to live its full import in one's professional as well as personal life. This unity is a must. If a *purpose* is a unifying expression of principles that managers adhere to, it should at least be coherent with their personal virtues. Otherwise, schizophrenia would make a manager's life in the firm impossible.

Some managers would find this aspiration as too idealistic, if not far-fetched. In fact, it is commonly thought that one's personal ethics and beliefs should not infringe on the professional expediency of business. I disagree and here's why:

Let us consider setting a manager's just compensation. When managers are rewarded based on the profits they report, are they justified to fiddle the books to flatter what they report as profits? After all, no one is supposed to get hurt, advocates would assert.

Students of agency theory would see through this as posing moral hazards, leading to conflicts of interests. Managers gain when more profits are reported. To achieve this, jobs are cut, wages frozen, required expenditures delayed, or suppliers and contractors are not paid on time. The latter may bloat working capital that may reduce borrowings, hence lowering interest expenses. In a very tangible way, these actions hurt stakeholders to benefit managers.

Bernardo M Villegas, co-founder of the University of Asia and the Pacific, Philippines, sees the profit motive as a means to an end. The emergence of stakeholder capitalism sees profit as the creation of resources to support a higher social purpose. This, in essence, emphasises not only how profits are earned but also how it is allocated for the benefit of stakeholders. For this reason, human beliefs, virtues, and formation have as much of an influence as that of economic criteria in defining what is considered equitable among the claimants of the goods that firms produce. Translated, that firms should earn a profit is a given and a necessary condition to financially sustain themselves. What is optimised is the capacity of the firm, and its managers, to equitably expand the shared value of its stakeholders and the communities that it serves.

In this chapter, I put forward this proposition: To articulate a firm's purpose and live it, managers contribute to society's well-being and legitimise its claims on common resource by knowing why firms exist in organised markets. Firms gain their *licence to operate* when, at a minimum, they adhere to the laws of nature and humans to sustain order. Operating under changing circumstances, managers are likely to respond by shifting their priorities, guided by the *purpose* that they commit to adhere to.

Firms are more likely to flourish when there is a coherence of purpose and actions. More often than not, managers could create the conditions that promote boundless possibilities, when stakeholders commit themselves to a common future. The basic ingredient is trust, which is strengthened by personal integrity and commitment, with humility as its outward manifestation.

2
Why Do Firms and Markets Exist?

Articulating a *purpose* starts with self-knowledge because "to know thyself is the beginning of wisdom," as Socrates asserted two and a half millennia ago. While it is almost *de rigour* for managers to publish a vision, only to let it gather dust, few would probably sit back to ask themselves: Why do I wake up each day to attend to my *business*?

Managers could use this to reflect on the *raison d'être* of why firms and businesses exist and their role in it. I propose the following questions could structure the thought processes:

1. Under a market economy, why do firms exist and what purpose do they serve?
2. Why does profit play such a central role in managerial decisions?
3. How does a firm's purpose influence the pathways it seeks to traverse?

In the 21st century, few communities exist in isolation where some forms of organised markets do not exist. Because people engage in business, they create firms to invest, produce, intermediate, or co-create the means through which they and their communities could prosper. With firms taking on different roles, how these exchanges occur is through a market. In a small community, chances are people would know each other well enough to trust in what the sellers purvey and in what the buyers could pay.

In this world, few regulations are needed, because word does get around when a buyer defaults or a seller sells faulty goods. One can be sure, someone who plays foul too often would be excluded from the market at a great personal loss. Ostracised or expelled, recalcitrant members could no longer participate in the market, hence denied of income or livelihood.

Living in this functional market confers convenience. To get a bowl of fruit cocktail ready with the meal, a short trip to the grocer is sufficient.

Behind the scenes, a complex network of logistics, humans working with one another and the organisation is hidden from plain sight. They come to mind, often when supply chains are disrupted or panics occur that would empty the grocer's shelves. In times like this, people are given stark reminders as to how inter-related human communities have become.

Almost instinctively, pandemics push humans to take immediate action. In extremis, supply autarky is proposed by well-intentioned people. They advocate to "grow your own food to supply your own needs." I caution against this with a reality check:

A fruit cocktail is a mixture of different fruits, usually grown locally. In the absence of an organised market, households would need to grow different kinds of fruit trees to harvest a variety of fruits. When milk is added, to satisfy some Asian palates, cows will have to be bred to supply the milk.

Some trees bear fruits seasonally or throughout the year. To gather enough varieties of fruits, one would wait before the fruits are ready for harvesting. With prior planning, enough varieties hopefully could be harvested at *the same time* to prepare a bowl of fruit cocktails.

At this stage, the person living in an autarkic world would soon appreciate the utter inefficiency of this system. Endowed with a dose of creativity, one encounters a solution in specialisation.

The idea of dividing the work, and relying on their neighbours, began to take shape. In its rudimentary form, a household with an excess of strawberries may barter with neighbours who just harvested kiwis, melons, and apples in excess of their needs. Through this exchange, several neighbours now are able to prepare their fruit cocktails ready for meal time. As more neighbours join in, the community created money and organised a market to facilitate the exchange of goods. Instead of bartering, they price each good in their money equivalent. The money received could be used to purchase inputs, pay wages, or settle the trade in goods. Thus, the seminal notion of a market economy was born, based on exchange and trade.

As neighbourhoods grew into towns or cities, trade was increasingly made with strangers. To facilitate the exchange, aside from the growing importance of money, merchants vouched for their peers from other cities. Increasingly, intermediaries and financiers (e.g. bankers) began to grease the wheels of commerce. Fast forward, nations and trading blocs brought more strangers into the transactional economy.

This is when rules, regulations, and creditworthiness entered the lexicon of business. Embedded within these notions is the idea of trust. In a world among strangers, reputation began to play a part in associating integrity with trustworthiness. In time, credit rating agencies took on this role. In effect, businesses began to entrust to these agencies to give an opinion, based on specified criteria, as to how likely is a stranger going to default on their obligations.

As managers ponder the future, how relevant is an economic theory and understanding the firm's purpose in crafting a strategy for a world that emerges the morning after a crisis?

In outlining my thoughts in Chart 3.1, I see theories and the contexts that lead to their formulation as instructive. In the first instance, what some managers instinctively refer to as "new paradigm" is a rehash of an old idea. Informed by history, however, managers could see what truly emerge as ideas that could shift the world to

Dynamic Decisions

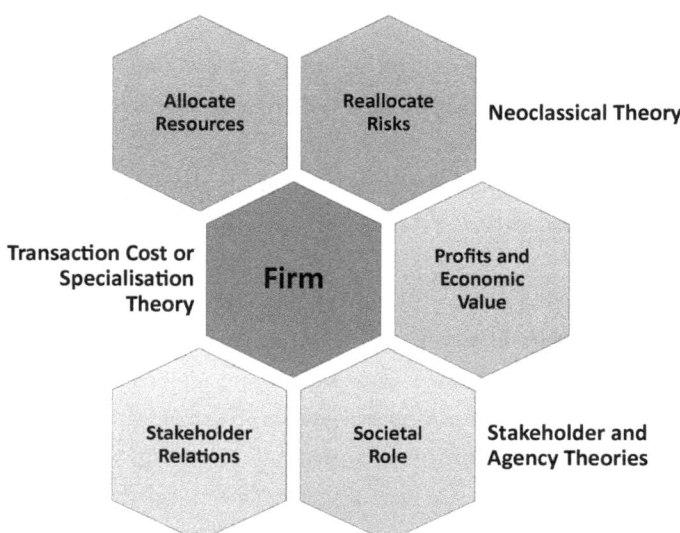

Chart 3.1: Evolving Notions of the Firm

a new place. This latter case is what constitutes an opportunity to breakthrough from a faltering system.

A modern firm transcended the neoclassical theory's narrower construct. To a neoclassical economist, a firm is a "notional construct of a self-contained producer of goods and services for others, the others being the households. In this market, price is what moves supply and demand, where the firm is precluded from any self-consumption," Harold Demsetz explains (1995).

Under this narrow market conception, producers and consumers are diametrically opposed in relation to price. Producers would want the highest price possible for their goods. Consumers, in contrast, would seek the lowest price. With perfect information, repeated auctions would eventually match what producers are willing to supply with what consumers are willing to pay. The common price achieved is the equilibrium or a condition that could be sustained unless the market condition changes. This works when people are rational, as microeconomics (or the price theory) would assume. As rational people will *always* respond to reason, how resources and institutions are organised will naturally fall into place, a big presumption in my view. Increasingly, how prices would influence choices is the focus, until Ronald Harry Coase (1988), Nobel laureate, raised his objections.

Coase posits that by losing sight that humans are the ones making choices, the price theory has placed less emphasis on the human person as the object of their study of consumer choices. As a result, "the consumer is not a human being but a consistent set of preferences. The firm to an economist, as Slater[1] has said, 'is effectively defined as a cost curve and a demand curve, and the theory is simply the logic of optimal pricing and input combination'. Exchange takes place without any specification of its institutional setting. We have consumers without humanity, firms without organisation, and even exchange without markets."

Bernardo M Villegas, one of Asia's renowned economists, shared his story of the benevolent baker from his days at Harvard. While providing sustenance for the young talents at Harvard square, the baker added that extra touch of love and quality to the bread that was purveyed. By selling at a discount, quality bread was made accessible to the future leaders on student budget. The rewards came with the memories that these scholars brought back to their homeland. These intangibles are ignored, particularly the very humanity that marked the benevolent baker apart.

2.1 From profit maximisation to risk reductions

The premise of pure competition rests with perfect information, where goods and services could be priced accordingly. With all factors known *a priori*, how quantities and prices interact could be understood as following a cause-and-effect relationship. To produce these goods, how inputs are combined and sold follows a ranking process. With all information known beforehand, costs are compared against the sale prices that competitive auctions establish.

While this is a common conception, the insertion of utility and its maximisation as an objective introduces the idea of welfare. In its broadest sense, welfare represents the surplus that an economy generates (e.g. consumer and producer surplus) and how it is allocated. Thus, the idea of income distribution and inequality gained prominence in economic discourse. With this "advance" in neoclassical theory, the firm's purpose is to arbitrate the exchange of goods through the market so that utility is maximised. With this comes the idea of satisfying wants, as something that detracts from societal welfare by first fulfilling individual human needs.

---

[1] Coase quoted Martin Slater's foreword to Edith Penrose's work on *The Theory of the Growth of the Firm*. Penrose was a pioneer in stakeholder theory that is discussed later in this chapter.

Frank Hyneman Knight (2009), an influential voice in neoclassical economics, recognised this as a problem that economists spent their energy debating. He noted: "It is not on any sentimental or idealistic ground but as a plain question of the facts as to how ordinary *persons* conceive their wants and interprets their conduct that we shall argue this matter. Wants, it is suggested, not only are unstable, changeable in response to all sorts of influences, but it is their essential nature to change and grow; it is an inherent inner necessity in them. The chief thing which the common-sense individuals actually want is not satisfactions for the wants which they have, but more and *better* wants."

With imperfect information, Knight would add, "comes uncertainty. But because uncertainty cannot be priced into a known production function, its rewards for committing capital is to gain profit because the entry or exit from markets cannot rationally construct an anticipation of these events."

Demsetz (1995) extends this contention: "Being unpredictable, profits cannot rationally influence resource allocation decisions. Yet, what makes profits an important variable in neoclassical theory, and in Adam Smith's *Wealth of the Nations* (2019), is the guidance it gives to resource flows." In the eyes of Demsetz, by "constructing uncertainty, Knight deviates from the firm's existence as maximising profits, to one on redistribution of risks."

The implications of how modern corporations are organised are far-reaching at first glance. Following Knight's logic, an employee may enter into a wage agreement for some fixed payments. In effect, wages are received with some certainty in the backdrop of fluctuating profits. The same thing could be said of suppliers. They receive a known payment for their inputs. Under this commercial relationship, the owner (or the firm) by "supervising" the inputs gets to keep a surplus known as profit for bearing the risks.

Demsetz (1995) would disagree. He posits that wages, in the same way as input costs, should adapt to accommodate the actual distribution of risks, "the firm is not needed to perform a risk redistribution function in a price-guided market." Translated, lower wages or input prices are paid when risks borne by labour or suppliers are low. Through this adjustment, labour and suppliers are presumed capable of self-organisation and coordination as to efficiently produce the goods at the least costs.

Short of this market perfection, Knight's proposition could be seen as reducing risks through coordination and managing the interactions of suppliers. In this formulation, the manager as a human person is given the due recognition that neoclassical theory tends to ignore.

It is not far-fetched to consider freelance or outsourced work as an application of what Demsetz proposes. For a fee, the worker accepts jobs according to conditions that satisfy their risk preferences. In its generic forms, long-term employment is preferred by those who want some predictable income and security. In contrast, consultancy is accepted by those who could tolerate some slack or uncertainty in employment, usually for a higher fee.

2.2 Minimise costs of production through specialisation

In the post-World War II industrial boom, the distinction between firms and markets came into greater focus. This departs from the neoclassical theory where at times, markets could supplant the firm, as Demsetz suggested. This distinction is important to clarify their individual roles.

Firms are units of production where their emphasis is on their cost curves. To produce their goods and to sell them through a market, a transaction cost is incurred. By recognising the transaction costs, the modern-day dilemma of *produce or purchase* (or outsource) is better understood. That is, if managing the inputs in-house becomes prohibitive relative to external suppliers, the firm is better off outsourcing some or all of their production. In due course, as firms specialise, they presumably become "experts" in their sub-units of production that reduce the cost curves. Thus, was born the learning curve, suggesting that costs fall as more units are produced (Hirschmann, 1964).

Unlike in neoclassical theory, with markets and firms having distinct roles, firms will continue to produce (and specialise) without being replaced by the market. Instead, the role of management (and managers) is made explicit rather than assumed to occur naturally with prices as the mechanism to make coordination happen. That is, as Demsetz pointed out, while prices move firms to supply or not, a functioning market could reduce the cost of coordination. However, a larger number of specialised firms would require more central management to facilitate the flow of goods and services.

In parallel, the firm is given, as a juridical person, quasi-human obligations and benefits. Through this legal construct, the formation of modern corporations allows a separation of roles, functions, and liabilities between the entity as a contracting party and the shareholders as owners. Under Anglo-American jurisprudence, people transact with firms while limiting the legal liabilities of people acting as shareholders or managers. Managers earn their remuneration, while shareholders gain from dividends or any cash distributions that the firm may allocate.

This notional separation of the firm and its owners brings the conversation back to Milton Friedman (1970) and Frank H Knight's previous thoughts on maximising utility (1923). In this construct, the firm could focus on maximising profit so that more could be distributed to the shareholders. In turn, the shareholders would choose to save or spend what they receive (usually in cash), where such a decision is made within their households (in neoclassical theory's usage).

The purpose of the firm evolved to form the basis of how modern corporations are managed. The fruit cocktail analogy illustrates how neoclassical theory downplays managerial action: When people offer their harvest for sale, they need to organise to bring goods to market. In a world with perfect information, buyers and sellers would organise themselves without the need for a firm. As Demsetz observed in neoclassical thinking, "inputs are put into the right places to work with an appropriate batch of other inputs solely by the independent actions of input owners responding to prices."

When Knight's concerns about market imperfections are considered, and the uncertainties it gives rise to, the role of ethics and management is reinforced. Conferred with the authority to allocate, managers are expected to act in accordance with a set of principles that seeks the common good. This is where morals, customs, and beliefs would influence how managers resolve the dilemmas that confront them, almost on a daily basis.

In modern firms, where ownership and management are usually separated, managers are entrusted by shareholders to act in their best interests. As humans, managers could be tempted to promote their interests ahead of those of the shareholders. When shareholder and managerial interests diverge, a conflict of interest could arise. The same issue could arise with suppliers and other contractors. The question of moral hazard was in prominent display in the Great Recession triggered by the 2008 financial crisis (Bernstein, 2009).

Coase (1988), for instance, sees the firm's purpose as a reduction in costs through productivity enhancement. Within the context of a team, as Demsetz would suggest, managers would coordinate so that the costs are minimised while retaining the quality of the goods (e.g. as technically specified). This involves comingling machines, labour, and intellectual properties, where the value of critical assets or skills for production that is in short supply could be inflated. People's propensity for opportunism is heightened when substitutes are limited, enabling the input supplier to hold the firm hostage. This only worsens when feeble legal recourse allows errant managers or people to act with impunity or to get away with "murder"!

As a consequence, the notions of teams and how they are coordinated, motivated, and rewarded give rise to labour relations and labour unions, at one level, and management to enter into collective bargaining. Supply chain management also became part of the business lexicon.

2.3 Stakeholder theory and community relations

Digging deeper into the historical contexts, Friedman's view that a firm's social responsibility is to maximise profits was an attempt to delineate what rightly is the firm's obligation and the shareholder's choices in the use of the proceeds.

The 1969 Moon Landing (NASA, 2019) unleashed boundless optimism in what humanity can achieve. This was preceded by President John F Kennedy's peace corps, which was attracting young Americans to spend time abroad to uplift people's lives (history.com, 2009). Inadvertently, making a profit and doing philanthropy were intertwined in business, often with a blurring of boundaries. Some in business found this ambiguity unsatisfactory. With Friedman's voice commanding the Chief Executives' full attention, they enshrined this in their Principles of Governance in their association, *The Business Round Table*. This was later broadened to include stakeholders (BRT, 2019).

In my view, the American Chief Executives have reconciled themselves to Friedman's corollary proposition that was generally downplayed: *Once profits are distributed, shareholders may do with whatever they choose with the money*. True to his calling as a free market advocate, Friedman left shareholders to decide on what is equitable to their chosen beneficiaries.

In a world where stakeholders take centre stage, how would the *purpose* of the firm change, if at all?

My conversations with Terry Möllner were fortuitous. We met in May 2019 in Miami, Florida, when we both spoke at a sustainability conference. He is the Founder of the $21 billion Calvert Social Funds and former Board Director of Ben & Jerry's.

Managers are intelligent and practical people. They have uncanny ways of recognising the reality that confronts them. This trait does not always sit well with theory and academic discourse.

To a manager, they would instinctively understand what Terry describes as objective realities: "You see a piece of 'red-hot stone' in a burning grill. You can pretend that it is cold and harmless, because that this how you perceived (or imagined) your 'reality'. To prove your point, you pick it up with your bare hands. When you burn your hands very badly, you hopefully learn what objective reality is, the hard and painful way."

In a nuanced way, business and how it understands social responsibility may suffer from "red-hot stone" phenomena. There is a school of thought that sees profits and achieving societal well-being as inherently incompatible. It is a zero-sum game of sorts. An emerging counter-factual notion is the integration of socially responsible values as the core of the firm's strategic actions. Here's how some firms manifest this approach to doing business:

Firms operate within socially inter-related communities, a notion that is real and undeniable. By contributing to the common good, however it is understood, the whole is usually made better off. For this reason, Terry goes a step farther than Friedman: "Firms may choose to cap the profits that they distribute to capital as a fair return. Any excess is invested in perpetuity to funds that prioritise the common good."

Ben & Jerry's, founded on socially responsible principles, is a case in point. Terry shared his experience in negotiating with Nestle for the company's sale. In the course of the due diligence, he sensed that Ben & Jerry's *raison d' être*, values and culture would not survive the onslaught of the acquirer's push for standardisation. In the end, with the Nestle deal falling though, Terry and the board concluded a deal with Unilever.

The difference? Unilever agreed to keep intact the social contracts with suppliers, employees, and their community. In effect, by keeping its culture intact, Ben & Jerry's continues to flourish under Unilever. Terry served on the board in the following 18 years and has recently retired.

In 2000, observers were wary: "Did Ben & Jerry's sell out, or is the Ben & Jerry's culture invading the corporate world? A scoop of each, perhaps," the headline proclaimed (Hayes, 2000).

The question itself is self-evident. Social enterprises were perceived to downplay profits over their social objectives. By selling to Unilever, the founders Ben Cohen and Jerry Greenfield were thought to have "surrendered" principles to profits (Page and

Katz, 2012). The fear was in conforming to Unilever's push for profit maximisation, critics presumed that Ben & Jerry's would succumb. Consequently, its uniqueness in not only espousing but also living social responsibility will be a distant memory.

Terry recalled: "After some difficult years, Unilever has fully embraced support for Ben & Jerry's legal agreement with them that allows it to annually spend on social activism as much as the year bought. It allows it to speak out on social issues even if Unilever disagrees, and for the board to continue being a self-perpetuating board, electing its own future board members."

Two decades later, the news is more upbeat: Ben Cohen and Jerry Greenfield continue to guide Ben & Jerry's on its social mission, seeing their company flourishing under Unilever. In addition, both founders have extended Ben & Jerry's culture to Unilever, a $45 billion behemoth consumer goods enterprise (Hadden, 2020).

Back to Terry, Ben & Jerry's represents an epochal shift in business thinking about profits and social responsibility. Here's how the business landscape is changing:

With firms failing to account for their behaviour, people seek to redress the very personal consequences they see when markets "misbehave." They do, as Richard Thaler (2015) explains, when economists assume markets to work with people acting rationally. However, humans often err in their decisions because what they assume may not always reflect what reality is. Thus, while positivist economics has guided managerial thinking for generations, finance is paid scant attention in macroeconomics, as Justin Fox observed (2012). The 2008 Great Recession brought to the fore the attempts of financial economists to "wrestle with some of the broader consequences of what they've learned about market misbehaviour."

The actions of managers impact the firms' stakeholders. Without a voice in the decision-making, some advocate stakeholder participation in line with what they understood of R Edward Freeman's stakeholder theory, first proposed in 1984. Some managers see this "over-reach" as a problem: "One can thoroughly support legislation constraining corporations or seeking to prevent age discrimination, market monopolies, and externalities and regret the extent that capitalism is heir to such shortcomings. All of this could be done without following that business beneficiaries should be changed from stockholders to stakeholders, and the latter should be given serious decision-making power" (Stieb, 2009).

Freeman *et al.* (2018) proposed an approach could bridge the varied interests of people. A dominant mindset among managers is to accept that firms have limited liabilities for their effects on others. In a largely domestic economy, governments could abrogate any adverse effects in a way that is fair to all. However, when fairness plays a part to resolve an allocation of benefits, neoclassical economics is at a loss. As an economic allocation process, questions of value and ethics are "extra-theoretic" or outright irrelevant. Cognisant of this "red-hot stone" phenomenon, how firms affect the lives of people are at the core of how managers are called to account. Recognising this reality, how social responsibility, ethics, and sustainability, influence economic decisions would forge different ways of formulating strategies and purpose.

One such change is for managers to instead focus on the relationship of business and the groups and individuals that are affected by it, collectively referred to as stakeholders, asserts Freeman *et al.* (2018). A consequence of this way of thinking is to integrate purpose with responsibility, which gives up the separation fallacy (of firms and managers) that plague neoclassical notions of firms, reinforced by law that limits shareholder (and managerial) liabilities. In focusing on relationships, it corrects two prevailing misconceptions:

1. Representatives of stakeholders should sit on governing boards, as some would demand.
2. Shareholders do not have rights, as neo-liberals would suggest under socialised distribution of benefits that favours stakeholders over capital.

What it means is that interests of each group are joint and that to create value, one must focus on how value is created for each and every stakeholder. To this I would add, shareholders and through their agents, the managers, are among the stakeholders. They coordinate, orchestrate, and organise, so that their firms could flourish so that by expanding the economic pie, the stakeholders' prosperity is greatly enhanced.

3
Reshaping Thinking on Energy Firms

Resource minerals, which include oil, gas, uranium, and coal, fuelled rapid material progress that humans have experienced. In economies where markets operate, competition and free enterprise systems are seen as the backbones of prosperity. It is not by coincidence that access to these resources, through trade and investments, unlocks society's material wealth.

Throughout this expansionary phase, energy firms played varied roles. Their wealth is variously associated with "ownership" of resources, "control" of access and markets, and exerting undue influence on politics through their "monopoly" of production, marketing, and logistics. With power supply equally concentrated under state monopolies, or private oligopolists, consumers are seen as the "milking cows" of energy firms. From the purveyors of prosperity, oil and gas behemoths (The Economist, 2019) and fossil fuel-based power companies (BBC, 2016) are firms that environmentalists love to hate. How did this change in some people's attitudes come about and why does it matter to managers?

In no small measure, extractive industries (of which energy is a big part) bring in capital, employment, and economic prosperity (at least to some) wherever they choose to operate. This places managers in an enviable position.

Seen as bearers of riches, politicians in resource-owning communities ("resource holders") would welcome them with open arms. In short order, local communities buoyed by high expectations may feel short-changed when the expected riches take longer to materialise. With increasing unease, people may call for a greater share of resource revenues (Joffe *et al.*, 2009) or outright expropriation. This is characterised by an *obsolescing bargain*, as negotiating power shifts from the investing firm, as they are more invested, to the sovereign (Inadomi, 2010).

To a manager, this shift in perception is baffling. How can they be marked as "evil" when they have made resources available to make societies prosperous? For these managers, fulfilling the rising demand for minerals is pivotal in sustaining the material wealth of people. However, managers may have missed how the conversation had changed: "Resource production is seen as fundamentally about our moral commitment and the role of minerals in the kinds of lives we desire for ourselves and *for* others" (Smith, 2019).

The environmental conversation is plagued by what this "moral commitment" means in real life. To some managers, it is one's livelihood at stake and perhaps the embodiment of their life's purpose that define who they are. To an environmentalist, one commits to a world without fossil fuels as a matter of human conviction about how salvation is obtained. Between these two extremes is a place characterised by uncertainties, ambiguity, and compromises, where most people reside.

In this imperfect world, in more subtle ways, managers encounter numerous "red-hot stone" phenomena. Unexamined and blindly accepted, managers get burned badly from time to time. Specifically:

Energy firms are valued by the resources they own, hence the more mineral reserves a firm holds, the more valuable it is (Mercer Capital, 2019).

Sunlight, wind, and water are free and widely available. Following in Lewis Strauss' thinking[2] on nuclear, these renewables are clean and getting cheaper (IRENA, 2020) and would soon be "too cheap to meter" (Ketchell, 2015).

Wind and solar power dominate new capacity additions, resulting in rapid volume expansion. With supportive power prices, returns are secured (IRENA, 2020).

Dynamic markets would see prices and volumes fluctuate, making cash flows volatile. To restore stable cash flows, rigid long-term take-or-pay contracts are preferable to secure stable cash flows (World Bank, 2020). By entering into a fixed price and volume contract, with limited flexibility, the buyer commits to purchase whether or not they use the fuel or power.

To promote and accelerate renewables deployment, rebalancing subsidies away from petroleum products to favour renewables are needed (Taylor, 2020).

Oil and gas super majors are destined for extinction similar to the dinosaurs (Stevens, 2016; Reed, 2018).

In failing to recognise these "red-hot stone" assertions, managers misdiagnose the problem that they should address. The consequences, among which are to pursue bad strategies, are far from trivial. Specifically:

When managers believe more reserves would secure their future, they would go to great lengths to explore for oil and gas in highly uncertain and risky

---

[2] Lewis Strauss was Chair of Atomic Energy Commission, USA, in 1954 renowned for claiming nuclear power was "too cheap to meter." Branko Terzik (2018) reinterpreted this to mean that, by comparing nuclear power's low variable and fuel costs against the high cost of metering, it was not worth metering the power consumption.

areas such as the Arctic (Turner, 2020). Past forays ended in tears and shortened managers' careers (Cunningham, 2015). In some cases, fiddling with reserves reporting worked for a while until it caught up with the erring managers (Cummins and Barrionuevo, 2004). These misdiagnoses extend to energy policy. Just as resource-rich economies may underperform and lag their less endowed peers (Frankel, 2010), firms and countries could equally suffer from a natural resource curse.

Cheap and getting cheaper, combined with expanding volumes, should be a formula for reaping riches in renewables. However, as nuclear suffers from phase-out (Jarvis *et al.*, 2019), the high number of solar firms going bankrupt in Australia (Infinite Energy, 2020) is puzzling. China's world-leading panel producers are faring no better (Shaw, 2020).

Capital budgeting embeds a bias for cash flow predictability. In the manager's view, this could be achieved in one of the two ways: Fix the prices, costs, and volume obligations contractually or secure a minimum revenue through subsidies or corporate power purchase agreements.

The latter is a long-term supply contract, where a corporate buyer agrees to pay a fixed price for the renewables volumes it consumes. The supplier sells what it actually generates to a wholesale power market. If the prices the supplier achieved are higher than the fixed price, they pay the buyer the difference. If the market price is lower, the buyer pays them the contracted price.

One would think that a way around price and volume volatilities has been resolved. However, instead of securing cash flows, take-or-pay has kept lawyers and regulators busy in resolving buyer–seller disputes (Doane, 1987). Corporate power purchase agreements are proving not to be a walk in the park (Maloney, 2016). Subsidies, either to fossil fuels (Sovacool, 2017) or renewables (Kalkuhl *et al.*, 2013), tend to produce outcomes that are contrary to policy objectives.

Equinor took a different route to addressing its dwindling reserves by refocusing the investments on renewables (Guthrie, 2019). It is making a big bet on offshore wind where it is establishing global leadership.

News headlines herald a new era that foresees the demise of fossil fuels, and with it, big oil and gas. To support this view, mounting losses are cited which arise from write-downs of assets and lower demand because of the

COVID-19 lockdowns (Turak, 2020). A common theme is an aspiration to transition into low-carbon fuels, which justified some of the big write-offs of fossil fuel assets that BP (Blackmon, 2020) and Shell plc (McFarlane, 2020) announced. ExxonMobil's write-down of reserves is a statutory requirement to adjust down the value when oil and gas prices are expected to be lower (IEEFA, 2020) for longer.

Are the oil and gas supermajors caught between the hard rock and the devil in the deep blue sea? To an extent, they are not because of the managers' inaction. It is mistaking lofty ideals for a *purpose* that is hoped to secure their place in a transitioning energy market.

Over the past decades, oil and gas firms have outspent any clean technology ventures in investing in renewable energy (Pickl, 2019). Instead of being recognised, incumbent energy firms are subjected to criticisms for doing "too little, too late" (Johnston *et al.*, 2020).

To an environmental activist, ploughing profits back to sustain the oil and gas business is tantamount to prolonging "dirty" fuels' existence. For managers, investing in extant business and renewables is a way to gain flexibility to adapt to uncertainties in pace and outcomes of a transitioning energy market. This dichotomy is likely to persist in the foreseeable future. With it, the prospect is very real of a polarised market or at best an uneasy co-existence.

3.1   What the business of energy is really about

Energy is, according to science, freely available in nature. How did a "free resource" command premium prices?

The origins of energy resources may provide an answer. Minerals, such as coal, oil, gas, (e.g. fossil fuels), and uranium, are as natural as water, geothermal steam, wind, or the sunlight, which are considered as renewables. In their raw form, they are freely available to be found and exploited.

In Chart 3.2, I offer this proposition: To make raw energy resources useful for humans, it needs to be converted using technology and conveyed to markets. This costs money, manpower, and logistics. For this reason, the *business of energy* is to convert raw feedstocks into goods that fuel machines to move people and goods (transport), warm (or cool) abodes and workplaces, and energise production, work processes, or

Articulate a Purpose

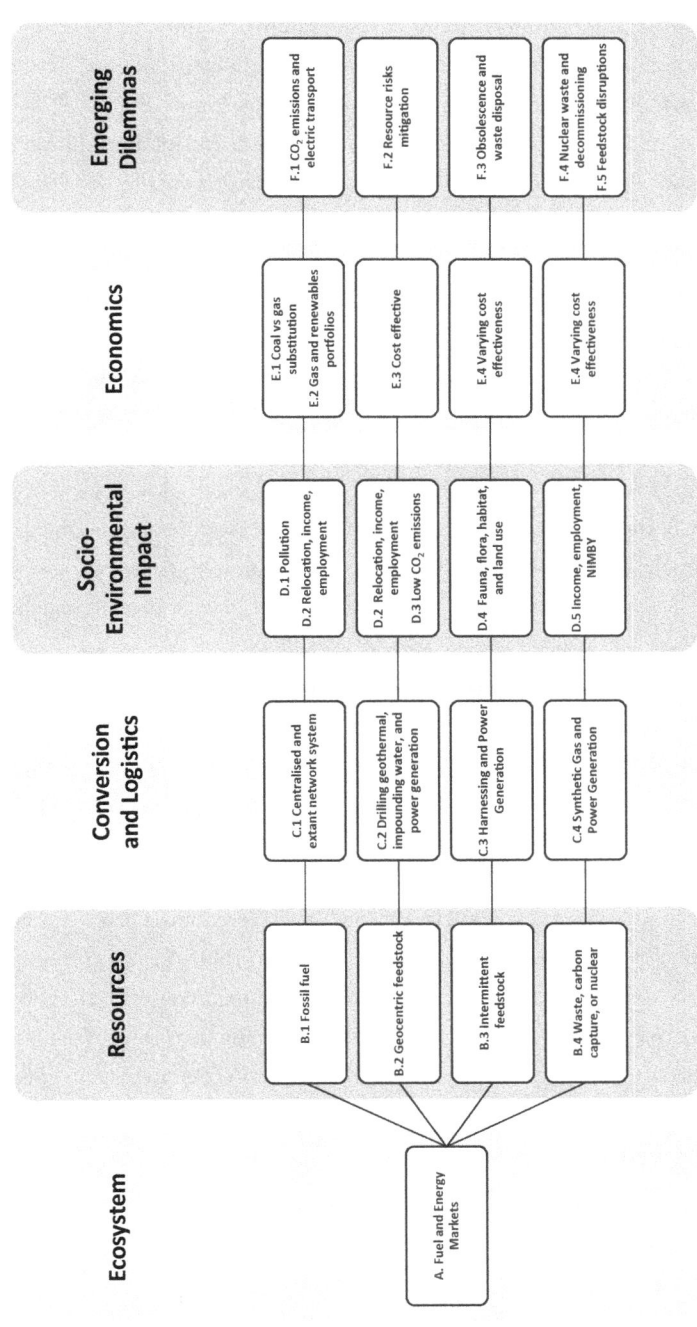

Chart 3.2: Rethinking the Energy Ecosystem

communications, among others. In the course of human history, how energy is converted has substantially changed because technology and consumer preferences have also changed. Curiously, the sources have remained largely unchanged.

Coal, oil, and gas (B.1) have remained buried for centuries, until humans "discovered" a way to use them as fuels (C.1). In the days of steam engines, coal was loaded and burned on trains to produce steam that runs the engines. Oil replaced coal when internal combustion engines were widely adopted by transport, ushering in the age of oil followed by gas as a cleaner fuel. Uranium became useful with nuclear fusion technology as a way of generating power, aside from its use for weapons.

Water is plentiful with the exception of the arid desert. Water's (B.2) strong flow can turn the turbines to generate power, as in waterfalls or rivers. In some cases, human ingenuity found ways to impound water and funnel its flow to generate power more reliably (C.2).

The core of the earth has always been hot, with steam springing through the earth's mantle. Humans found hot springs soothing. In due course, geothermal steam (B.2) was used to turn turbines to generate power, enough to meet a few centuries' consumption.

In the same way, wind, and sunlight (B.3) have always been plentiful. These energy resources nourished life on earth in its raw and dispersed form. Humans found more use when they discovered ways to harness these resources to produce power.

What makes fossil resources different from other energy sources? The pollution they emit when converted to fuels or power.

Using existing technologies, coal and gas emit CO_2 and other pollutants when "burned" to produce energy, popularly referred to as "greenhouse gases."[3] According to US National Aeronautics and Space Administration (NASA), "greenhouse gases" are needed to keep the earth warm enough so that humans can live on it. By their name, these gases trap the warmth from the sun. The ozone layer absorbs the radiation from the sun, particularly the ultraviolet (UV) rays, to protect humans from its harmful effects. However, beyond a certain threshold, too much heat may be trapped to cause warming that imperils human life, vegetation, or fauna.

---

[3] "Greenhouse gases" comprise water vapor (H_2O), methane (CH_4), ozone (O_3), nitrous oxide (N_2O), and chlorofluorocarbons (CFCs).

Given this backdrop, two climate-related problems keep scientists awake at night. One is the ozone hole that came to light in 1987 and global warming.

The ozone hole arises when the ozone layer is depleted by gases such as CFCs, which are emitted by industrial and human activities. The banning of CFC's usage in refrigeration and industrial processes aided in the recovery and eventual closing of the "ozone hole" (Merzdorf, 2020).

Global warming is seen to arise when greenhouse gases accumulate to dangerously high levels. By some estimates, to limit temperature rise to 1.5°C, the "carbon budget" is equivalent to 25 gigatonnes, which is the maximum amount of CO_2 that could be added to the atmosphere to be within target. By some estimates, human activities are on track to add 56 gigatonnes.

The question is: are humans set for toasting as they are hopelessly incapable of mending their ways?

Almost all climate models are remarkable for their consensus: As more CO_2 is accumulated in the atmosphere, temperatures tend to rise proportionally. However, as to how much of the carbon budget is still left, the forecasters are divided: "It has been used up" or "at present rate of emissions, humanity has fifteen years to mend their errant ways" (Hausfather, 2018). The difference lies in a wide range of the carbon stock's initial estimates. To add to the uncertainties of estimates, how temperatures vary with CO_2 emissions are influenced by how methane and nitrous oxide vary or how quickly the climate-cooling aerosols are reduced (Hausfather, 2018).

Against this backdrop, practical managers weigh the large investments civil society demands against the prospect of benefits that may come too little or never materialise because humanity is beyond redemption.

Before one would despair, when interests and the basic principles by which people adhere to are understood, the chasm is far narrower than it initially appears. Examine how these two "opposing camps" end up on the same side of the climate divide insofar as principles are concerned:

One camp sees the end game of climate action as costly and ineffective (see Hausfather, 2018), thus hailing the US withdrawal from the Paris Agreement under then President Donald J Trump. Costly and ineffective, because climate-related investments end up funding corrupt governments, achieving little. Instead, governments should look to their firms to innovate and compete in markets for solutions (Loris and Stubb, 2017).

In issuing the *Liberal Manifesto* (Kluth, 2020), advocates distance themselves from draconian government interventions. They rely on liberal economics of an earlier era, associated with minimum government and a general distrust with big government or corporates (and even mafias) that exert excessive control over markets. What they propose are market-based solutions to climate change, not too different from what conservatives propose.

To emphasise, Andreas Kluth laments the polarised conversations around climate between "liberals" and "conservatives," as presently understood in American politics: It "spooked the loony right into denying the problem (and indeed science) and the loony left into just shaming generally, reminiscent of France's Jacobins in 1793, or China's Red Guards in 1966."

Serving as the backdrop to decision-making, managers will have to evaluate the trade-offs for each technology. Given inherent uncertainties, these dilemmas are presented as follows:

By sticking to fossil fuels, pollution may not abate causing CO_2 to accumulate in the atmosphere. With policy push towards reducing CO_2 emissions and electrification of transport, incumbent oil and gas firms may face punitive carbon taxes or obsolescence.

Geocentric resources, such as geothermal and hydro power, which are clean and cost-effective, are seen as environmentally destructive when forests have to be cleared or large tracts of land are flooded to impound water.

Intermittent renewables, such as wind and solar power, are not spared. With increasing usage, the disposal of mothballed wind turbines and solar panels has to be costly. Overly optimistic lifespan estimates may shock investors when obsolescence comes sooner, as costs decline rapidly thanks to "learning curve" effects.

Costs of waste disposal, as nuclear power would attest, are a well-known problem. Emerging issues are ignored, partly because people tend to project the present into the future linearly. The human capacity to innovate or the ability to develop solutions is at best considered as a complication by forecasters. In some, it is a nuisance for making their forecasts inaccurate or erroneous.

If there is a "consensus" of sorts, managers recognise the disruptive potential of renewables under a low-carbon economy. Vaguely, to achieve the Paris Agreement's 2050 targets, some technological breakthroughs would be desirable. What needs changing is not only how managers try to understand the future. It would also involve redefining the roles of energy firms and regulation in a low-carbon economy.

3.2 Changing roles of energy firms

In linearly projecting the present to the future, managers err in presuming that the centralised network of energy supply would survive intact. By visualising how the energy system is evolving, as illustrated in Chart 3.3, one can appreciate how much it changed since energy supply was "mechanised." The shifts coincided when machines replaced work animals and human muscle to fulfil the needs to energise mobility, shelter, and work processes. Working backwards, how a fuel becomes dominant is largely driven by the technology and portfolio choices firms would adopt (D.1) and the strength of consumer preferences (D.2). As technologies evolve, the substitution of one technology by another occurs, which tends to alter fuel use (D.3). In some cases, regulatory actions may facilitate or hinder adoption. Throughout these interactions, prices and volumes are altered under dynamic markets.

Looking at the supply side, coal's use in transport ceded to oil when internal combustion engines became widespread. Power generation (A.2) took longer, but as gas supplies became reliable and combined cycle turbine technologies emerged, gas became the preferred fuel. As the oil market achieved a sufficient scale, centralising oil refining (A.1) enhanced cost-effectiveness. With this development, logistics (A.3) became part and parcel of competing in the age of oil.

The incorporation of gas into the fuel mix saw some changes. Natural gas is generally transported by pipelines, which limits its market reach. To extend its market reach, gas was first liquefied, stored at below freezing temperatures in specialised ships, regasification occurs at the destination, before being conveyed by pipelines to users. The infrastructures are specific, with limited flexibility for use to transport oil, partly explaining why oil and gas remained separate for a while. In exploration, oil and gas converged given the technologies and location overlapped. That is, in the same field, firms may find oil or gas, or both. To secure financing, liquefied natural gas (LNG) was sold by suppliers (A.1) under long-term contracts to power generators (A.2).

Dynamic Decisions

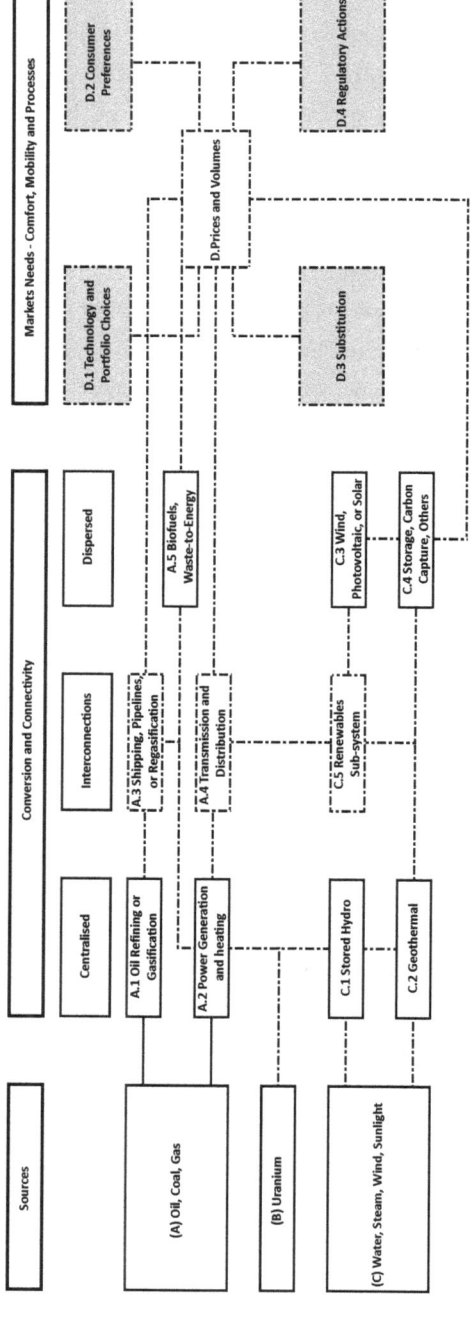

Chart 3.3: Feasible Roles for Energy Firms

Source: Adapted from Barcino Advisers, Hong Kong and Author's work.

It is in heating and power generation (A.2) where gas is widely used, with nuclear finding favour in specific countries. It took the 1973 Oil Crisis to highlight the supply risks emanating from political actions. While the political impetus to replace oil was strong, power generation is more successful than transport in weaning itself from oil.

The next transition, characterised by the entry of renewables, is triggered by forces that are latent in the energy market. Pollution from the conversion of coal and oil pushes regulation (D.4) to tighten environmental standards. With technologies (D.1) available, hydro and geothermal power became features in power generation. Eventually, more renewables were promoted through subsidies, with some rapidly achieving economic viability as costs fell. The combination of consumer preferences for clean energy (D.2) and the firm's portfolio choices (D.1) saw a process of substituting coal with renewables (D.3).

As renewables coexist with fossil fuels, their interactions and how they influence power prices and volumes render conventional valuation tools inadequate. However, just like the forecasters, some managers prefer to ignore[4] the limitations. With the emergence of electric vehicles, increasing electrification of transport may erode volumes for oil, while expanding power demand. Hence, oil and gas firms are buying their presence in power-related assets and infrastructures, as Shell plc and BP are doing through acquisitions.

What can managers deduce from past transitions that remain relevant towards a low-carbon economy?

Incumbents are heavily invested in infrastructures and logistics. Much as society and firms would want to accelerate a transition, change follows an evolutionary process. This opens a window for firms to adapt, while those opposing could use to mobilise and resist to derail the transition.

When this happens, advocates of change may present a flurry of data and findings, which may convince some or strengthen the resolve of those that oppose. Managers would recalibrate and pace their commitments as technologies and markets evolve. Those that flourish would build the agility and the means to co-create an energy system that continues to be affordable and reliable, one that serves humanity's needs.

---

[4] I have illustrated the interacting effects in Chapters 8–10, where the limitations of conventional valuation tools are re-examined and reframed.

4
Inspiring Commitment with a Purpose

My conversations with managers and civil society taught me some lessons in paradoxes. Both are committed to serve society, and in their own mind, are conscious of the challenges to fulfilling these good intentions. I am not alone, however, in this quandary. In any public discourse, the consensus on caring for the environment is almost universal. When these conversations involve specific renewable investments, there is as much local opposition as there is national support. The reason, managers would assert, is the notorious NIMBY[5] or the technologies' relative lack of merits compared to a status quo. Research, however, points to a perceived lack of influence by affected communities in decision-making as causing apathy or resistance (Barry *et al.*, 2008).

In the corporate world, a new strategy or an innovation is met with similar resistance. In an uncertain world, a transition to low-carbon technologies qualifies, where people may associate change with disruptions. It disrupts their life, redundancies are among its features, or simply, the fear of the unknown. Fortunately, engagement and information and a clearly articulated purpose to guide the transition journey may soften some of the reasons for resisting.

I propose mapping the business realities according to capabilities and markets, as I do in Chart 3.4. In its generic form, by sticking to a status quo (A), one hopes that markets remain stable and the capabilities that have been built for years would remain relevant. One's niche is supposedly secured through operating efficiency.

When managers are lulled into complacency, the perils of obsolescence are insidious. Managers may be rudely awakened and find their business in distress. In some cases, a quick retooling of capabilities may save the day, albeit unlikely. More probably, divestment or filing for bankruptcy is the only available recourse (B).

When faced with a shifting market, managers invoke innovation as an instinctive defence. Within the usage of Chart 3.4, sustaining innovation involves improving the offering, which may include combining fossil fuels and renewables under a supply

---

[5] "Not in my backyard" is popularized when explaining how people could support building nuclear plants, for as long as it is done elsewhere.

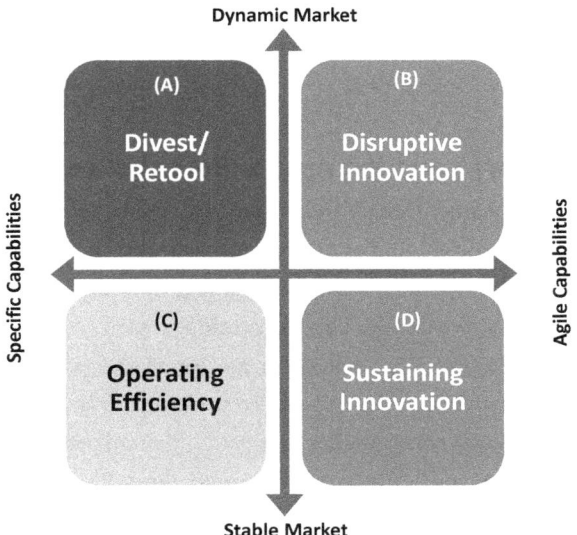

Chart 3.4: Shifting Roles and Strategies

portfolio. This is said to improve the cost-effectiveness while reducing the carbon footprint by lowering CO_2 emissions. The other is disruptive innovation that evolves unnoticed in ignored segments to build an ecosystem that potentially displaces the incumbent's offering (Christensen *et al.*, 2015).

What a number of energy firms do is to solidify their hold on their most lucrative markets (C). These are usually their customers that generate the more profitable volumes. In Christensen's formulation, firms would offer higher quality products or services or bundle these into an offering that "overshoot the needs of mainstream or low-end customers."

In the energy market, a truly disruptive innovation should be feasible, particularly in areas where centralised networks work with a scale that impedes incumbents from serving fragmented or disconnected segments (D). Distributed generation, micro-grids, or scaling down of capital expenditures as slim-hole geothermal generation has achieved, opens isolated (or off-grid) segments for commercialisation.

Seen in this context, weak infrastructures and feeble regulation in emerging markets may counterintuitively open the way for disruptive innovation to work. Intermittent renewables (e.g. wind and solar), however, are directed at replacing coal in developed systems with very slim pickings. Deployed in underserved systems, its small scale may fit with the small volumes that would be too expensive to supply by larger power generation units.

4.1 *PW One Three* and the *Bust to Best* challenge

How the *purpose* (or *vision*) of the firm is embedded within teams is as important as articulating an actionable vision. For this reason, the ability of managers to engage in disruptive innovation in tandem with its sustaining innovation depends to a large extent on the clarity of its purpose. Here's an example:

A struggling commercial fuels division in a major oil and gas firm was given three years to reverse its mounting losses or face divestment. This is a "burning platform" with personal and business consequences. Failure could mean people lose employment and income, as the firm cedes a large market to competitors. The rallying call was *From Bust to Best* in 1,000 days.

In a paper on *Inspired Commitment* (2002), I described how "storytelling can be a powerful way of crafting a vision. Just like a story, a vision has plots and characters, and the characters interact with one another in the context of their environment." When I engaged the business leaders and their teams, "phrases such as 'partnerships', 'winning teams', 'understand customers', 'value today … value tomorrow', 'operational excellence', 'robust profitability' were among the most repeated at various stages of the discussions."

Prior to this conversation, the team followed a textbook approach to buoying profits: When revenues fall, prices are discounted for fuels and lubricants to boost volumes. Costs are cut, particularly making people redundant until it cuts close to the bone. What managers could show was progressive loss of market and a pool of red ink. The dialogue that follows, as I described in *Inspired Commitment,* paved the way to a very different narrative. I quote:

PW One Three

Business Leader: *A lot of things were discussed in our strategy meeting … still a number of uncertainties to be clarified but I am confident about one thing. We did crystallise a vision that I can fully commit to. That is PW One Three.*

Colleague: *Interesting ... but what is PW One Three?*

Business Leader: *Partnerships that win — this is the basis of our business success. We win by being a top tier partner. This we can achieve by helping our customers become top tier players in their own game. We can achieve this by making a difference in the three areas that matter most: network configuration, payments and billing, and shorter delivery cycle. We have the next 1,000 days to deliver ...*

Colleague: *Let us see how this can help me with my large transport customer ...*

Business Leader: *Your customer spends about $10 mln a year in goods and services that our company provides. We are a second-tier supplier and make about $500,000 a year. The top tier, comprising the top three suppliers, average about $2.5 mln a year each.*

Colleague: *So, if I become a top tier partner, my revenue potential can go up five times. That is a real prize worth going for ...*

Business Leader: *Yes, that is precisely the point why I can see a strong alignment is possible between vision and actions. I gather that what makes our customers win is to reduce the delivery cycle — that is, the time spent in picking up their cargo at origin, fuelling, maintenance downtime, and turnaround after delivering their cargo at the destination. Each hour lost on the road is potential revenue loss for our customer.*

Colleague: *I think I know where we are heading... My customer mostly takes routes where only half are accessible to our refuelling and supply points. As a result, the drivers travel another 100 km outside their normal route to refuel. So, if we can reconfigure our refuelling network, they can cut the delivery cycle by 20%. If we provide a convenient payment system, our dealers and customers can minimise time spent on administration. With such savings for the customer, whatever discounts we offer on our products will pale in comparison.*

Business Leader: *Exactly. You may be interested to know that your customer is not unique in what they need. About 60% of our revenues come from customers with a profile similar to the one you described.*

Colleague: *I will go through each customer and work out with my team how we can realise PW One Three.*

In a brief exchange, the two colleagues managed to pinpoint a time-bound *prioritised set of actions*, know *where they are, what they aspire*, and *how to get there* in a concrete way.

As the dialogue suggests, "more work, of course, needs to be done to *PW One Three* to convert the vision into a working plan. Repeated a number of times, the dialogue could take a life of its own, making the vision a living one." The power of storytelling lies in the following, as paraphrased from *Inspired Commitment*:

Iterative process: In engaging in a dialogue, business leaders' insights are enriched by people's feedback. It revalidates or questions the premises on which the foundation of the *purpose* is laid.

Deep understanding: Conducted prior analyses that deepen people's understanding of what and how their business *really* works enhance the credibility of leaders. Conversely, a discomforting realisation is, with ignorance, the myth of the "emperor's new clothes" is laid bare for the world to see.

Focus on the essentials: When a *purpose* clarifies what is essential to succeed, it also presents in plain sight (hopefully) what the team should discard or avoid. Scrutinised in this way, one appreciates most "opportunities of a lifetime" come knocking every other day. More importantly, not all opportunities fit, as someone's beef is another's poison.

Tangible actions: The story inspires — with the prize clearly articulated and actions aligned. The pathways that the three leverage points identify serve to guide how an also run business can become top tier, by making their customers win.

A simple idea can pack power if it is derived after deep reflections that result in greater understanding. Creating a story that explains the vision is just the beginning of a journey. What I aim is that the *purpose*, throughout its evolution, is converted into actionable plans.

4.2 Disruptive innovation and agility

To complete the envisioning of feasible futures, managers may need to turn their thinking around and answer this question: How can new entrants spoil the apple cart of incumbents?

Clayton M Christensen (1997) offers some answers. In my view, policy and managers tend to believe the extent of their influence and control of extant markets. While conscious that a transitioning energy market brings with it change or even disruptions as markets reconfigure, dangerously linear thought processes persist. In creating "technology champions," the chosen few are generously supported, as wind and solar power are today's flavour of the month.

In examining the static "hierarchy of costs," albeit in a stylised manner, Chart 3.5 would find the excitement curious (at least judging from press coverage). On its own merits, without any subsidies, only $Wind_{ON}$, and to some extent, PVT_M[6] may turn its potential into economic reality soon. The comparison holds for dynamic markets that are functional, where access and pricing for on-grid energy supplies are verifiable. In these markets, while the costs are falling fast, wind and solar (and its variants) are struggling to flourish, attested by bankruptcies as its continuing feature.

Counterintuitively, markets with weak infrastructure and feeble regulation are shunned by investors and struggle to access financing. I refer to emerging but isolated communities in Asia, Africa, and Latin America, where access to energy is intermittent (or hypothetical). In archipelagic markets, small island systems are ignored by incumbents because they are too small and uneconomic to serve. This characterisation fits what Clayton (1997) describe as segments ripe for disruptive innovation: "By focusing on these segments, a disruptor, usually with less resources, could gain footholds because incumbents typically try to provide their most profitable and demanding customers with ever improving products and services, and they pay less attention to less demanding customers. In fact, the incumbent's offerings often over-shoot the performance requirements of the latter. This opens the door to a disrupter focused (at first) on providing low end customers with 'good enough' product" (Christensen *et al.*, 2015). In the case of new markets, they added: "disrupters create a market where none exists. Put simply, they turn non-consumers into consumers."

---

[6] Onshore wind ($Wind_{ON}$) and photovoltaic tracking (PVT_M) are among the closest on present lifecycle costing to achieve the potential of delivering financial returns to meet capital's thresholds and policy's goal of reducing CO_2 cost-effectively. The details of the calculations are shown in Chapters 7 and 8.

Dynamic Decisions

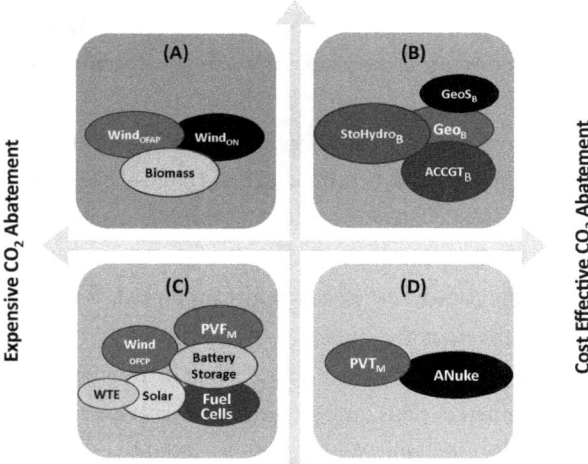

Chart 3.5: Energy Financial Returns and CO_2 Abatement Costs

Technologies clustered in quadrants (D) and (B) could selectively reposition themselves as "disruptive innovators" in off-grid markets (e.g. unconnected to a centralised network) where lack of access to energy hinders their economic advances. Here are some thoughts to consider:

PVF_M or PVT_M combined with battery storage can operate with a flexible scale that is adapted to how volumes evolve. With exorbitant interconnection costs, incumbents are likely to rush in and outcompete the new entrants. This could improve returns (move from D to B), while CO_2 abatement costs are improved by higher power output.

Coastal areas may benefit from $Wind_{ON}$ or rapid cost declines for offshore wind employing cheaper advanced platforms, $Wind_{OFAP}$. Power costs to supply islands or isolated coastal areas are prohibitive. To connect small communities to centralised networks makes little economic sense. However, by eliminating these costs, microgrids combined with battery storage may prove feasible in moving them from quadrant (B) to (A).

Slim hole geothermal is the Cinderella that awaits its prince. Cost-effective even in dynamic centralised markets, its lower capital expenditure makes it financially viable for small communities that microgrids serve. In areas with access to geothermal steam, a cheap, clean, and reliable energy supply becomes available to unlock its economic potential. This reinforces the position of $GeoS_B$ in quadrant A as a disruptive innovator.

A word of caution is in order when I reframe how "learning curve" effects (Hirschmann, 1964) can cut both ways. In manufacturing, Hirschmann posits that the costs of producing a good fall as workers become more proficient as more units are produced. In renewables, this logic explains why wind turbines and solar panel costs are rapidly falling as more units are installed. This process is in no way a one-way bet.

In theory, one would invest in cluster (A) technologies where high financial returns are achievable, while significantly reducing CO_2 emissions at lower costs. Sustaining innovation is worth pursuing in (B), particularly in expanding output and reconfiguring costs to lower CO_2 abatement costs. In contrast, lowering capital expenditures could be a focus for (C) by scaling down and shortening time-to-build for nuclear or enhancing output for PVT_M. This is a probable (and reasonable) perspective one would take under dynamic and centralised energy markets.

In a curious way, policy appears to intervene more decisively in promoting cluster (D) in centralised systems. The belief that firms should invest now, in technologies that could be significantly cheaper tomorrow, is indeed novel. I would instead posit that making choices on which technology to adopt is a managerial decision, not for policy to "champion":

Rapid costs decline as experienced by PVT_M, PVF_M, solar, and battery storage places managers in a bind. By investing now, the investment could be obsolete when rivals commit to assets that are substantially cheaper (and more profitable, hopefully). For this reason, an option to defer and reconsider a later entry is a managerial prerogative.

Markets with feeble regulation and inefficient infrastructure may offer scope for an earlier deployment that could be profitable, albeit with higher risks. In these markets, power prices are heavily subsidised, hence set too low for any commercial venture to survive. The "cheap" prices are hypothetical because recurrent power outages increase the actual cost of accessing a reliable power supply. This occurs when standby power, usually diesel generators, is needed to sustain commerce and industrial processes.

Some lessons could be learned from *PW One Three*. While reducing costs is a laudable effort, renewables' future may not rely entirely on it being the "cheapest" source. By matching technologies to the appropriate markets, a reconfiguration of the offer may break the insurmountable barriers of costs and intermittency in centralised energy markets.

The question that managers would need to ask is not about how quickly costs would fall, albeit an important one. Rather, to create a foothold in an underserved energy market, managers may ask this question instead: What do I need to reconfigure, if any, to give technologies in cluster (D) a fair shot at disrupting an incumbent's market long overdue for a shake-up?

5
A Chief Executive's Next Moves

In mobilising people and resources, Jim Collins of the *Good to Great* renown (2001) advised managers: To deliver on the business agenda is akin to organising a journey. Rather than select people to fit a chosen destination, you choose people who can share your passion for greatness.

Collins' advice runs counter to how managers tend to recruit the team for their projects. Some start by looking at the tasks, line up the skills required, and match them with the people possessing the capabilities. While rational, the resulting team may lose part of its agility (or flexibility). The first lesson is learned the hard way when circumstances change. To reach its destination, a different route or mode of travel may have to be taken. Instead of riding the bus, people may have to hike the rest of the way. Clearly, some become redundant (as in the bus driver or mechanic) or those unprepared to tackle the physical demands of a long hike. In using the bus metaphor, Collins explains his reasoning which I paraphrase from *Inspired Commitment*:

Begin with who rather than what: If people join the bus primarily because of where it is going, a detour would see some wanting to get off. But if people are there because of who else is in the bus, one can be more agile in redirecting the journey.

Self-motivate: The right people motivate themselves by their inner drive to produce the best results and to be part of creating something great with little supervision.

Remember that great vision without great people is irrelevant: When people put their minds and hearts to achieve a common purpose, the fruits of sound purpose are realised. In its absence, it gathers dust before the ink is dry in someone's dust bin.

I posit that people jump out of bed each morning to attend to their business for a simple reason. Making the *purpose* into a personal quest, managers lead by example. People derive their "authority not from the power of position, or the barrel of a gun, but it comes with credibility to inspire and influence." I asserted this when the world was recovering from the Asian Financial Crisis and the dot-com collapse. It was the time when confidence in governance and traditional authority was wearing thin.

In the polarised world that managers encounter today, energy firms are perceived by environmental advocates as hindering progress towards a low-carbon economy (UCS, 2019). Greenpeace is equally adamant about big oil's responsibilities for its role in climate destruction (Shapiro, 2020). Michael Shellenberger (2019), Time *Hero of the Environment*, blew their cover: "Environmentalists advocate nuclear in the 1960s, turned their backs on it in the 1990s, and espouse renewables only to preside over the expansion of fossil fuel use."

The apparent contradictory moves of big oil, that of investing in renewables and spending more on "dying" fossil fuel, represent the dilemmas of energy firms. "They want to profit from their gas business, while expanding plastics and power. By 2050, Shell wants to be the world's largest power company" (Worland, 2020).

Clearly, business and civil society will need to come to terms with each other's existence. To move the conversations and for managers to meaningfully craft their strategy, I paraphrase from *Inspired Commitment* the leadership traits that may unlock the impasse.

Trust: Partnership is what the journey is all about. Without the ability to build trust, partnerships are at best founded on shifting interests that result in fragile alliances.

Openness: The ability to face the brutal facts of the business allows leaders to adapt to its realities. This avoids managers from falling into Terry Möllner's "red-hot stones" traps, where leaders build sandcastles as their bunker, easily blown away by the slightest breeze.

Persuasion: First win the mind, then the heart, and the hand will follow. Self-righteous claims convince no one but the advocate.

Shared commitment, individual accountability: We are all in this together … each one seeks to understand what the commitment entails. Once this is clarified, take responsibility for achieving your end of the bargain.

Clearly, articulating a *purpose* that withstands the scrutiny of stakeholders enhances the prospect of adhering to it. In overcoming the test of reason, the merits of a *purpose* are amplified. Not all will be sympathetic. However, when a *purpose* is well understood, the protagonists will at least appreciate where they could meet and the chasm that they need to bridge (if at all).

It becomes apparent that managers operate under uncertainties of an economic, socio-environmental, and political nature. In these situations, what managers plan for may be derailed by those that oppose their ambition for reasons only known to adversaries.

Cognisant of these uncertainties, a manager's next moves would comprise bounding to the extent feasible the scope of their ambitions. Once the ambitions are *bounded*, the prize and risks are *calibrated* and a *contingency* is planned for. As a result, managers develop agility in their capabilities and resilience by *de-risking* the business in a manner that is sensible. When *articulating* a purpose is followed by these managerial actions, the firm is more likely to come prepared to surmount severe crises or disruptions.

Having a living *purpose*, managers may embed its contingency in a business continuity protocol. This connects the abstract notion of the firm and its purpose to real people. The protocol is not designed to totally eliminate risks. It is a set of actions that managers continually test to respond to emergencies or crises, simulated or actual. Continual exercises build confidence, and with greater confidence, trust among managers and colleagues is strengthened. That trust is founded on knowing that colleagues would pitch in when needed. That capability is proven when people demonstrate repeatedly without fail their capacity to respond and assist each other.

With stakeholders, the same principles apply. When there is integrity, opposing views are reconcilable because people are sincere. Integrity is demonstrated repeatedly by actions, which are visible manifestations of what managers do. The managers' intentions, undoubtedly well-meaning, are invisible and are probably known only to the individual. Even that, however, is a presumption.

In the absence of integrity, any commitment is as fluid as flowing water. It is of little practical use to build a lasting and sustainable relationship that *really* matters.

Box 3.1: Living *PW One Three* with Bas Kloppenborg

Bas Kloppenborg, Dutch by nationality and a global native by choice, combines personal principles with leadership traits to drive transformation at Shell plc. A product of Delft University, renowned for engineering programmes, Bas describes his journey: "After twelve years in reservoir engineering, reservoir operations, and field development, which form the core of upstream business, I encountered LEAP in Brunei Darussalam. That encounter eventually led me to make choices that brought me to paths seldom taken by my technical peers."

LEAP was a small group operating globally. Each member of the *Leadership and Performance* team was drawn from various talent pools. Inspired by Noel M Tichy's (1997) *The Leadership Engine*, RDS embarked on a transformational journey. Bas described his LEAP experience as "not only had a big impact on business performance, it also had a profound personal influence on those involved." For Bas personally, he would "depart from a structured, technically-based, and proven career progression to start anew in a field that would stretch his leadership competence beyond his comfort zone."

Working with accomplished professionals in their own disciplines, everyone was brought together to learn and contribute meaningfully to emerging challenges. It was under this crucible that our friendship was formed. An offshoot of this was our contribution to strategy and leadership's "alphabet soup." Bas saw coherent language and principles as necessary ingredients to make effective all of his organisational development interventions.

Bas describes LEAP's approach as operating within a triangle comprising strategy development, business improvement, and personal development. To align personal development with business, Bas employed the following programmatic interventions:

1. Develop the *I* with *Shell Leadership Challenge* to instil a common ethos, language and to mould behaviour that defines how individuals would relate with each other.

2. Create a relationship of *you* and *me* through *Coaching for Performance*, where feedback is a gift. Managers learn how to tap into the natural interests of a person to motivate and orchestrate resources to support a team to succeed.
3. Elevate to *we* to work towards a common purpose by *Creating Winning Teams* to deliver results that the team embraces and owns.

Bas continued: "Apart from the corporate programs, individual approaches were developed, effectively articulating practices which are successful. One of them was developed by Ricardo Barcelona — *PW One Three*. This is a mnemonic for *Partnerships that Win*, one works to make customers *first in their business*. As a partner of choice, you are your *customer's first choice*. To deliver on this aspired position, one needs to focus on *three priority areas*. In case it turned out that managers need to work on a fourth area, the mnemonic is adopted to become *PW One Four*."

After two decades, Bas and I caught up on where *PW One Three* has brought him. He briefly summarised: "After LEAP, I went back to the operating business where I initiated transformations in Europe and Africa, patterned after my journey at LEAP. I later decided to set up my own advisory firm, where I continue to intuitively use *PW One Three* to formulate my diagnoses and plan the appropriate interventions."

1. ONEgas offshore academy

"When I was appointed as ONEgas transformation manager," Bas started to explain, "I was presented with a challenge by Anthony Charnley, business head of ONEgas, to integrate the Dutch and UK upstream offshore assets held under two country organisations."

In this high-stake transformation, the personal and business stakes are significant: Succeed and the prize of a flourishing integrated European business awaits, opening more opportunities with global streamlining. Fail and European assets would be divested, cutting short careers nurtured over decades.

In guiding his thoughts with *PW One Three*, Bas started by understanding what his challenge meant: "The integration operationalises the Offshore Rationalisation Project. This involves reducing unit operating costs within three years, from 2004 to 2006. To achieve this, assets may have to be merged, divested, or refurbished.

This would imply radical restructuring of businesses, the way they organise, and how they are to account for their success (or failures)."

Bas continued: "To initiate the transformation process, I set up with two colleagues what we referred to as Offshore Operations Academy ('Academy'). Through this Academy, we undertook personal and leadership competencies development in line with thorough business reviews. Anthony orchestrated the resources to rationalise the South North Sea."

To rally the business behind ONEgas, Anthony and Bas identified three immediate tasks:

1. ***Engage positively on the merits*** of an integrated cross-border vision and how people could deliver and benefit.
2. ***Speed up execution*** to demonstrate its tangible financial benefits as "quick wins."
3. ***Enhance support*** for employees given foreseen job cuts, while minimising disruptions from industrial actions.

Anthony saw the Academy as a vehicle to roll out the change management programme. Bas was tasked with co-creating an execution plan with engineers from Nederlandse Aardolie Maatschappij (NAM), a joint venture exploration company of RDS and ExxonMobil, with Shell Exploration and Production, United Kingdom (E&P UK). Service providers, forming the AJS consortium, comprised Amec, Jacobs and Stork.

Patterned after LEAP, Bas combined active engagement with employees and service providers with personal development. Once equipped and empowered, people were provided avenues to actively participate in formulating, reviewing, and executing the relevant actions. One of the more effective means was the "Thirty Hours Workshops." Bas explains how it works:

Engineers work on a two-week shift. At the end of each shift, engineers were invited to an overnight stay at a hotel where they could directly engage with Anthony and his leadership team. It is a "pressure cooker" environment. We started with good meals, games, and fun.

As all participants settled into their cross-functional groups, we started with some exercises to signal the start of extensive work ahead. Together with colleagues from the academy, we facilitated the small group conversations or plenary discussions. In guiding the conversations, I saw my role as enabling colleagues to freely express their views without the constraints of hierarchy. The purpose was to align around some common understanding of the challenges ahead. In effect, what I contributed was enabling a learning environment where engineers felt safe to contribute, reinforced by a trusting relationship among all of us and the willingness to listen, adopt ideas, and take action as needed.

To demonstrate commitment, Anthony and his leadership team received the ideas presented by colleagues. Anthony usually commented, challenged, or supported specific proposals as appropriate. As the workshop's repository of knowledge, I collated in a living document the great ideas that were contributed, codified the actions agreed, and followed through with Anthony on resources and funding. In a way, I acted as the conscience that made sure business leaders would put "their money where their mouth is." Conversely, I ensured each one "delivered on what they promised to do."

After a few iterations, a vision as to what *PW One Three* meant evolved. In outlining their thoughts, Anthony and Bas came up with the following:

P W: Cost leadership will make ONEgas a preferred supplier to RDS' European gas customers and downstream business.

One: Expand cash margins and reduce capital expenditures to enhance profitability across the gas pricing cycle.

Three: Three areas of focus in delivering results are as follows: (a) streamline and simplify work processes; (b) adopt new technologies to enhance efficiency; (c) improve reserves recovery and operating life.

Dealing with mature fields and assets, ONEgas fell under RDS' "make the most of assets" strategy. By achieving cost leadership, low costs offer advantages against competing supplies from liquefied natural gas (LNG) in a high-volume gas market.

As a profitable venture, jobs could be secured while opening new opportunities for new skills to be added with the adoption of advanced technologies. In streamlining and simplifying work processes, resources are redeployed where skills and opportunities are better matched. In managing extant wells more efficiently, following flexible operating systems, gas could be sold optimally according to how volumes and prices evolve.

Encapsulated in a concise narrative, what ONEgas and its success meant to each person was internalised. While full alignment was seldom achieved, nor was it necessary, there was sufficient understanding of what matters. As a result, EP Europe was advanced following the success of ONEgas with Tom Botts at its helm. By a process of diffusion, the spirit of ONEgas mutated into similar academies (e.g. project management, commercial, among others).

Bas reflected a decade and a half later: "By creating a learning environment, people can thrive under conditions where real dialogues and exchange of knowledge consolidated great practices and new ways of working. As trust is strengthened, with people knowing that their voice matters, people were motivated to go that extra mile to make a difference. In aligning around *PW One Three*, a compass was provided to navigate through treacherous terrains."

Anthony appears to concur. Asked how he consolidated great ideas and converted them into actions, his simple answer was: "Just listen to your people and work with their personal and professional priorities," and the rest that follows may positively surprise you, Bas attested.

2. Cross-cultural cooperation

Bas was appointed as gas integration manager in Nigeria in 2006, where he served until 2010, with the prime task to put gas more prominently on the business agenda. To start off, gas was flared as a by-product to oil production, resulting not only in an environmental issue and thereby reputational exposure, but revenues were also foregone. With domestic gas demand growing and its export potential well recognised, flaring was increasingly an expensive way to dispose a by-product.

To commercialise flared gas, the oil and gas production has to undergo a revamp of the logistics and delivery system. Crude oil is simply pumped into tankers at ambient temperature. With raw gas, it has to be subjected to high pressure before it could be loaded to ships as liquefied natural gas (LNG) or conveyed through pipelines as gas.

While building the logistics was a technical problem with an engineering solution, the change had to overturn a 60-year oil operating culture. As Bas soon realised, his more immediate challenge involved an obscure problem that tested his cross-cultural capabilities to the limits.

Before gas could be monetised, Bas was confronted with an age-old problem of unpaid bills by a local district. Over the years, $15 mln was accumulated and rising. RDS always treated the problem as a credit and collection issue. By enforcing the contract, the local government should pay up or face litigation. However, the local government has an entirely different view. From their perspective, the associated gas reserves were owned by Nigerians. As owners, they do not see why they should pay for its use.

Bas appreciated the contractual obligations. It was tried and led nowhere. He started looking for avenues where the balance of influence is better understood. After several iterations, he identified these elements to develop local gas into a viable business:

1. ***(Foreign) technology and capital*** were essential to explore and drill for reserves.
2. ***Local permits and access*** were needed to unlock the reserves to get an exploration and drilling programme started.

To bring all these elements in place, a secure legal framework would need to be seen to function. For this reason, the unpaid bills had evolved into a broader problem that could potentially derail investments. Without the gas, the loss to the local community could mean foregone revenues, employment, and taxes.

As a global native, Bas appreciated the value of dignity and stature of local officials within their community. Pressing for payment, while RDS was legally entitled to, could prove damaging to local relations. In condoning, a bad precedent would be set that would encourage future, and perhaps bigger, defaults. Unresolved, RDS would be operating in a legally unstable business environment. In turn, the local community may not attract much in the way of investments or business.

Recalling his experience with ONEgas, Bas started structuring his thought process to frame the problem RDS is in reality trying to solve. It was far from collecting $15 mln from an errant debtor. Rather, it was setting the conditions for gas development to proceed under a legally secure market environment. Bas started outlining the basis for such a venture:

> *P W*: Build a venture that monetises flared gas and develops more domestic gas reserves.
>
> *One*: The winning proposition is Venture converts gas into a major financial contributor to stakeholders.
>
> *Three*: Three areas to focus on are as follows: (a) well-governed joint venture; (b) demonstrated respect for contracts and obligations; (c) community outreach.

Bas appreciated that lecturing the local community on integrity, or contracts and obligations, would lead to a blind alley. What he did was to introduce these ideas by co-creating a learning environment. The objective was to let stakeholders develop a *modus vivendi* that commits people to a minimum standard of governance.

Over the years, Bas reflected on what he learned: "I looked at the situation from the Nigerian's perspective, place myself in their shoes, so to speak. By posing the question, what would give the Nigerians a 'victory' that does not compromise the integrity of contracts or good governance? In answering this question, I came to appreciate that I need to trust the Nigerians to solve an essentially local problem. For this reason, I assigned one of my most senior Nigerians to lead the discussion and to facilitate the co-creation of the gas venture's governance."

"Through iterative engagements, a local solution developed by the locals emerged. The receivables? It was offset against the local share in the venture's revenues. In the end, RDS got their gas organisation, and Nigeria became a major gas exporter. Revenues and employment grew, with the local community doing better economically," Bas concluded.

****

On reflection, what is obvious as a "problem" to solve may prove to be illusory, Bas contemplated. To avoid falling into traps of solving the wrong problem with the "right" solutions, visualise alternative approaches to test the initial diagnosis. In the final analyses, problem-solving is about bringing people to acknowledge the wisdom of a solution that they themselves have a hand in crafting. This is the discipline of thought and actions that *PW One Three* facilitates.

****

Bas Kloppenborg evolved from his technical formation into leadership and change management consultancy. As Director, shpKlop, he serves clients globally, with a focus on corporate transformation and leadership development. At Shell plc, he served as Commercial Effectiveness Lead, Exploration & Production, Africa; Opportunity Delivery Manager, Gas Commercial Nigeria; Change Manager, Leadership and Performance (LEAP); Change Manager and Petroleum Engineer at NAM, The Netherlands, and Shell Exploration and Production, United Kingdom.

Bibliography

Barcelona, R. G. (2002). Inspired commitment: Vision that delivers on business agenda. *Policies and Issues in Perspective Staff Memos 19*, University of Asia and the Pacific, 1–8.

Barry, J., Ellis, G., and Robinson, C. (2008). Cool rationalities and hot air: A rhetorical approach to understanding debates on renewable energy. *Global Environmental Politics*, 8(2), 67–98, May 2008.

BBC (2016). UK funding of overseas fossil fuel projects: A necessary evil? *British Broadcasting Corporation*, March 2, 2016.

Bernstein, P. L. (2009). The moral hazard economy. *Harvard Business Review*, 1–5, July–August 2009.

Blackmon, D. (2020). BP's big write-down: A harbinger for a declining industry or of a struggling company? *Forbes*, June 16, 2020.

Brugmann, J. and Coimbatore Krishnarao Prahalad (2007). Co-creating business's new social compact. *Harvard Business Review*, February 2007.

Business Round Table (BRT) (2019). https://www.businessroundtable.org/business-roundtable-redefines-the-purpose-of-a-corporation-to-promote-an-economy-that-serves-all-americans. Accessed on July 29, 2020.

Christensen, C. M. (1997). *The Innovator's Dilemma: When New Technologies Cause Great Firms to Fail*. Boston, MA: Harvard Business School Press.

Christensen, C. M., Raynor, M., and MacDonald, R. (2015). What is disruptive innovation? *Harvard Business Review*, December 2015, 2–13.

Coase, R. H. (1988). *The Firm, the Market, and the Law*. Chicago: The University of Chicago Press.

Collins, J. (2001). *Good to Great: Why Some Companies Make the Leap ... and Others Don't*. New York: Harper Business.

Cummins, C. and Barrionuevo, A. (2004). Former Shell officials clashed as they hid reserves problems. *The Wall Street Journal*, April 20, 2004.

Cunningham, N. (2015). With Shell's failure, US Arctic drilling is dead. *OilPrice.com*, September 28, 2015.

Demsetz, H. (1995). *The Economics of the Business Firm*. Cambridge, UK: Cambridge University Press.

Doane, H. C. (1987). Take-or pay: FERC's Regulatory Dilemma. *Natural Resources & Environment*, 2(4), 18–21.

The Economist (2019). The truth about big oil and climate change. *The Economist*, February 9, 2019.

Elkington, J. (2008). The triple bottom line: Sustainability's accountants. In *Environmental Management: Readings and Cases*, Russo, M. V., Los Angeles: Sage Publication.

Frankel, J. (2010). The natural resource curse: A survey. Faculty Working Paper Series, RWP 10-005, Kennedy School of Government, Harvard, February 2010.

Freeman, R., Harrison, J., and Zyglidopolous, S. (2018). *Stakeholder Theory: Concepts and Strategies*. Cambridge: Cambridge University Press.

Friedman, M. (1970). The social responsibility of business is to increase its profits. *The New York Times Magazine*, September 13, 1970.

Fox, J. (2012). What we've learned from the financial crisis. *Harvard Business Review*, November 2013, 2–9.

Guthrie, C. (2019). Equinor buffeted by transition winds. *Petroleum Economist*, March 22, 2019.

Hadden, J. (2020). Meet the founders of Ben & Jerry's, who started their company in a converted gas station and built it up into an ice cream empire. *Business Insider*, June 14, 2020.

Hare, B., Rowing, N., Schaeffer, M., and Schleussner, C.-F. (2016). Implications of the 1.5C limit in the Paris agreement. *Climate Analysis*, April 2016.

Hausfather, Z. (2018). Analysis: How much "carbon budget" is left to limit global warming to 1.5C? *Carbon Brief*, April 9, 2018.

Hayes, C. L. (2000). Ben & Jerry's to Unilever, with attitude. *The New York Times*, April 13, 2000.

Hirschmann, W. B. (1964). Profit from the learning curve. *Harvard Business Review*, January 1964.

History.com editors (2001). Enron Scandal I Summary, History & Facts. https://www.history.com/this-day-in-history/enron-files-for-bankruptcy. Accessed on July 31, 2020.

History.com editors (2009). President Kennedy signs Peace Corps legislation. https://www.history.com/this-day-in-history/president-kennedy-signs-peace-corps-legislation. Accessed on July 25, 2020.

IEEFA (2020). ExxonMObil Warns of possible 20% Write-down in Oil and Gas Assets. *Institute for Energy Economics and Financial Analysis*, August 6, 2020.

Inadomi, H. M. (2010). *Independent Power Projects in Developing Countries*. The Netherlands: Wolters Kluwer.

Infinite Energy (2020). Why do so many solar companies go bankrupt? January 6, 2020. https://www.infiniteenergy.com.au/why-do-so-many-solar-companies-go-bankrupt/. Accessed on August 5, 2020.

IRENA (2020). *Renewable Power Generation Costs in 2019*. Abu Dhabi: International Renewable Energy Agency.

Jarvis, S., Deschenes, O., and Jhe, A. (2019). The private and external costs of Germany's nuclear phaseout. NBER Working Paper (26598), National Bureau of Economic Research, December 2019.

Johnston, R. J., Blakemore, R., and Bell, R. (2020). *The Role of Oil and Gas Companies in the Energy Transition*. Washington D.C.: Atlantic Council, January 2020.

Joffe, G., Stevens, P., George, T., Lux, J., and Searle, C. (2009). Expropriation of oil and gas investments: Historical, legal and economic perspectives in a new age of resource nationalism. *The Journal of World Energy Law & Business*, 2(1), 3–23, March 2009.

Kalkuhl, M., Edenhoffer, O., and Lessmann, K. (2013). Renewable energy subsidies: Second-best policy or fatal aberration for mitigation? *Resource and Energy Economics*, 35(3), 217–234, September 2013.

Ketchell, M. (2015). Sun and wind could finally make electricity "too cheap to meter". *The Conversation*, January 7, 2015.

Kluth, A. (2020). A liberal manifesto in a time of inequality and climate change. *Bloomberg*, January 18, 2020.

Knight, F. H. (1923). The ethics of competition. *The Quarterly Journal of Economics*, 37(4), 579–624, August 1923.

Knight, F. H. (2009). *The Ethics of Competition*. New Brunswick, NJ: Transaction Publishers (Third Printing).

Kunen, J. (2002). Enron's vision (and values) thing. *The New York Times*, January 19, 2002.

Loris, N. and Stubb, K. (2017). 4 reasons Trump was right to pull out of the Paris agreement. *The Heritage Foundation*, June 1, 2017.

Maloney, P. (2016). Mutual needs, mutual challenges: How corporate PPAs are remaking the renewables sector. *Utility Dive*, September 1, 2016.

McFarlane, S. (2020). Shell takes $20 billion write-down, expecting lower oil and gas prices. *The Wall Street Journal*, June 30, 2020.

Mercer Capital (2019). The fair market value of oil and gas reserves. *Energy Valuation Insights*, Mercer Capital, October 1, 2019.

Merzdorf, J. (2020). NASA data aids ozone hole's journey to recovery. National Aeronautics and Space Administration, April 15, 2020.

Michalak, B. (2019). Ben & Jerry's continuing to turn values into value through linked prosperity. In *Perspectives on Purpose: Leading Voices on Building Brands and Businesses for the Twenty-First Century*, Montgomery, N. (ed.), Oxon: Routledge, 172–180.

NASA (2019). July 20, 1969: One giant leap for mankind. *National Aeronautics and Space Administration*, July 20, 2019.

Nilsen, S. R. (2013). The Enron code of ethics handbook from July 2000 is a fascinating read. *CFA Institute*. https://blogs.cfainstitute.org/investor/2013/10/14/the-enron-code-of-ethics-handbook-from-july-2000-is-a-fascinating-read/. Accessed on August 1, 2020.

Norman, W. and MacDonald, C. (2004). Getting to the bottom of the "triple bottom line". *Business Ethics Quarterly*, 14(2), 243–262, April 2004.

Page, A. and Katz, R. A. (2012). The truth about Ben & Jerry's. *Stanford Social Innovation Review*, 39–43, Fall 2012.

Pickl, M. J. (2019). The renewable energy strategies of oil majors — From oil to energy? *Energy Strategy Reviews*, 26, 1–8.

Reed, S. (2018). Climate change drives oil dinosaur to invest in a friendlier face. *The Seattle Times*, June 1, 2018.

Rumelt, R. (2011). *Good Strategy, Bad Strategy: The Difference and Why It Matters*. London: Profile Books.

Scherer, A. G., Palazzo, G., and Matten, D. (2014). The business firm as a political actor: A new theory of the firm for a globalised world. *Business & Society*, 53(2), 143–156.

Shapiro, J. (2020). Don't let oil companies design climate policy; say yes to renewables. *The Washington Post*, February 27, 2020.

Shaw, V. (2020). Main shareholder of Chinese module maker ET Solar files for bankruptcy. *pv magazine*, February 3, 2020.

Shellenberger, M. (2019). Why renewables advocates protect fossil fuel interests, not the climate. *Forbes*, March 28, 2019.

Smith, A. (2019). *The Wealth of Nations*. New York: Ixia Press (Republication of the 1789 fifth edition published in 1904).

Smith, J. M. (2019). The ethics of material provisioning: Insiders' views of work in the extractive industries. *The Extractive Industries and Society*, 6(2019), 807–814.

Sovacool, B. K. (2017). Reviewing, reforming, and rethinking global energy subsidies: Towards a political economy research agenda. *Ecological Economics*, 135(2017), 150–163.

Stevens, P. (2016). International oil companies: The death of the old business model. Chatham House Research Paper, May 2016.

Stieb, J. A. (2009). Assessing freeman's stakeholder theory. *Journal of Business Ethics*, 87, 401–414.

Taylor, M. (2020). *Energy Subsidies: Evolution in the Global Energy Transformation to 2050*. Abu Dhabi: International Renewable Energy Agency.

Terzik, B. (2018). Is power ever too cheap to meter? *Atlantic Council*, July 3, 2018.

Thaler, R. (2015). *Misbehaving: The Making of Behavioural Economics*. New York: W. W. Norton & Company.

Tichy, N. and Cohen, E. (1997). *The Leadership Engine: How Winning Companies Build Leaders at Every Level*. New York: Harper Business.

Turak, N. (2020). Oil and gas companies set to lose $1 trillion in revenues this year. *CNBC*, April 30, 2020.

Turner, J. (2020). The cold thaw: Inside Russia's $300 bln Arctic oil and gas investment. *Offshore Technology*, May 5, 2020.

Union of Concerned Scientists (2019). Holding major fossil fuel companies accountable for nearly 40 years of climate deception and harm. *Manifesto* updated on June 20, 2019.

Worland, J. (2020). The reasons fossil fuel companies are finally reckoning with climate change. *Time*, January 18, 2020.

World Bank (2020). Public private partnership legal resource centre. https://ppp.worldbank.org/public-private-partnership/sector/energy/energy-power-agreements/power-purchase-agreements. Accessed on August 6, 2020.

Chapter 4
Bounded Possibilities

Some managers see uncertainties as indistinguishable from risks. This is attributed to the popular notion of risk as an exposure to danger or losses. With the fear of unknowns eliciting a similar response, avoiding uncertainties equates to minimising losses. Unfortunately, this is a stance that leads managers to misdiagnose opportunities. For this reason, when disruptions or crises strike and profits are squeezed, managers default to cost-cutting to keep the firm afloat. As managers cut and cut more with each down cycle, they lose sight of emerging technological shifts that lead to a strategic paradox: Why aim to be the best horse whip maker in the age of automobiles? Unresolved, managers persist in this contradiction that is hidden in plain sight: Dynamic markets are inherently volatile and uncertain in spite of managers' best efforts to create an imagined predictability around their investments. A remedy is to understand, rather than ignore, the nature of uncertainties. As a result, by learning from others and converting the *unknowns* to *knowns*, managers could bridge the chasm between "complete ignorance" and "enlightened choices." In tackling *deep unknowns*, managers can visualise and experiment to gain knowledge and experience, while nurturing enabling mindsets within the decision ecosystem.

1
Introduction

Some managers equate uncertainties (*unknowns*) with risks that should be avoided. Partly for this reason, some managers would spend endless efforts and time to gather more data. Just how the additional data would make the *unknowns* known could only elicit an ambiguous answer from its practitioners.

I argue that ambiguity between uncertainties and risks originates from popular usage. Extrapolated to managerial decision-making, the consequences for the firm could be dire. To see how this could pan out, let me start with how uncertainty and risks are popularly understood. Specifically:

Uncertainty is "something that is unknown" (Cambridge, 2020). To a strategic mind, this immediately elicits a query — "to whom" and "why" the unknown is unknown?

Risk is feared because of its association with "exposure to danger, losses, or something bad" (Oxford, 2020).

As the unknowns instil fear, uncertainties and risks become indistinguishable. In short order, aversion to the unknowns is hardwired into people's psyche when deciding on matters that are mundane or of great import. For this reason, as the perceived uncertainty grows, people would opt to take no action, unless a sure deal is offered. This popular "wisdom," however, could imperil a firm's prospect to prosper under transitioning markets. Here's how this could happen:

Acting as strategist-in-chief, the Chief Executive Officer (CEO) seeks to change, or even disrupt, the status quo to create a future that is yet to emerge. In this brave new world, past experiences or previous strategic advantages may become obsolete. The CEO and those that follow instinctively entrust their future to a venture whose "outcome and their probabilities of occurring are yet unknown" (Knight, 1921).

To most managers, this is beyond what they are accustomed to. Cast erroneously as a bean counter, the Chief Finance Officer (CFO) demands precision in evaluating investments that are not forthcoming. In persisting down a path of precise estimates, financial analyses lose their relevance, when dynamic markets continually "prove the numbers wrong."

Perhaps, for this reason, only half of CFOs feel that they fully enjoy their CEO's confidence (Russell Reynolds, 2016), a feeling that is mutually shared by CEOs (Bunting, 2016).

The energy industry appears to fall into these dynamics of managerial interactions. How managers respond to supply disruptions, volatile prices, or perceived profit squeeze is illustrative.

The energy system is characterised by networks of infrastructures and relationships, designed around extant technologies that are of specific use and capital-intensive (Hirst and Zeitlin, 1991). These initial endowments, combined with what new technologies could be integrated, predetermine the costs structures and confer or limit the strategic and operational flexibility accorded to managers.

When markets are stable or unchanging, incumbents tend to benefit from their prior commitments that lock-in access to extant networks (or lock-out late entrants). As new technologies emerge and networks are reconfigured, the world is seen by incumbents to turn uncertain (Dosi *et al.*, 1988). As the known world becomes unknown, CEOs have to grapple with the "big picture" as to how the future energy industry would look like.

I recall my professor at business school, the late Harry Louis Hansen.[1] He was known for his incisive wit and ability to focus on the essentials. In tackling complex problems, he would pose these simple questions (Verstringhe, 1992) to guide people's thought process:

"What is the problem?"
"What can we do about it?"
"Where lies the opportunity?"

---

[1] During my MBA at IESE Business School, Spain, I made the friendship of Harry L Hansen, my Professor in general management and strategy, and marketing. He was the first Malcolm P McNair Professor of Marketing at Harvard Business School. He was remembered for his contributions to management education, and I count myself as a beneficiary of his wisdom and mentoring.

Unfortunately, some managers choose to jump straight into finding solutions to problems they have not fully understood or articulated. The resulting quagmire is often the only predictable outcome.

In persisting with the same analytical tools, some CFOs may highlight their inability to incorporate into their evaluation the vastly altered contexts of their investments. To respond to eroding profits, firms default to what they have almost always done: *cut costs*, *delay capital expenditures*, and *divest peripheral assets*. The immediate relief, as shown in a profit uplift, may prove to be short-lived. In tough markets, however, this may still be a cause for undeserved celebration, some CFOs would rationalise.

Strategically, fledgling but pivotal new ventures become under-resourced or are aborted. Belatedly, as the market cycle turns for the better, old ideas are revived, while capabilities that were lost are restored at a higher cost. Meanwhile, new entrants or rivals surge ahead and frustrate the incumbents' vaunted aspirations.

Faced with this setback, some managers would point to the absence of opportunities in uncertain times. I can almost hear Harry whisper in the CFO's ears: *If you keep your eyes wide open, and really see, you may find the pearl in an oyster hidden under the rocks.*

Indeed, by relying on their own perceived advantage, some managers assume that they possess all the answers. In failing to cast their net wider, they fail to appreciate that others who possess the answer have not been asked. Consequently, what managers consider as unknowns, because they lack familiarity, are actually known by others but remain hidden to them in plain sight.

The inability to access a wider pool of knowledge or experiences, I propose, is largely caused by human behaviour and a failure to recognise the virtues that enable effective decision-making. To a manager who sees no real need for others to contribute, one becomes limited by the knowledge one possesses, vast as it may seem. More importantly, to accept the possibility that managers, as well as advocates and policy, may be wrong, becomes unthinkable.

Fortunately, astute CFOs acquaint themselves with the business and its associated unknowns. What they harness first is their humility and honesty to recognise what they know and what they do not know. They seek to open dialogues to co-create pathways to access learning and to encourage people to expand their knowledge by learning from their own experiences and those of others. In the process, the CFO and their team could leapfrog the chasm between "ignorance" and "enlightenment" by humbly and sincerely seeking help.

Through iterations and astute questioning, reasoned guesses (or estimates) of possible outcomes start to form by employing informed assumptions. This process differs from a single-minded push for precision of forecasts, where a "magic number" emerged for people to latch on to make their choices. That is, when prices are up, they commit (or vice versa). This of course ignores a fundamental fact: Managers seldom exert full control over market prices. By using price level as a trigger to commit "now or never," managers are held hostage by the vicissitudes of external factors to invest in an often irreversible and lumpy investment.

An astute mind would seek to understand the reasoning behind certain estimates, the contexts and conditions under which these could be achieved. As a result, investment evaluation departs from a "pass–fail" approach that engenders a mindset that blames others as "accountable" for adverse outcomes. The alternate path encourages people to understand what they could achieve, what they need to learn, and how they could respond when reality turns out different from what they expected (or fail to anticipate). In recognising this ambiguity, trust and openness are essential for this decision ecosystem to operate effectively. The resulting conversation replaces advocacy with strategic dialogue where managers suspend judgement, leaving ego out, listening more and directing less.

In the process, managers commit to what they aspire to deliver and get it done. This demonstration of integrity through action holds greater value than unfulfilled intentions. Tony Simons (2008) encapsulates succinctly the value of integrity in business: "Few would deny that a broken promise lowers the morale of employees, but what is the dollar cost — the bottom-line impact? Or what is the payoff of keeping a promise? It should be simple to align your words and actions in a way that employees can see. But if it's so simple, why do most employees say their managers do not do it? Maybe it is not so simple."

In concurring with Simons, CEOs cited that "our greatest challenge in leadership, and in life, is not honesty with others — though that is tough too — our greatest challenge is being honest with ourselves" (Bunting, 2016). This is where a neutral perspective of how uncertainties could be managed is essential.

A manager could start by recognising uncertainty for what it really is. Humans, in their brilliance, are not expected to know everything there is to know. In embracing this mindset, the unknowns become a learning opportunity. As one becomes familiar with its nature, some unknowns can be bounded as to its impact on outcomes.

In effect, the deviations from an expected outcome are amenable to being quantified as a risk. In this context, risk is simply the variation from an expected outcome, which could be higher or lower than what was expected (Park and Shapira, 2017).

In translating these notions of uncertainties and risks, I reach back to my conversation with my father, Santiago Barcelona, as a very young boy. During our rare walks in his twilight years, I admired the majesty of the mountain peaks with the rising sun as its backdrop. Feeling my excitement, he said: "The view from the top is even more far reaching and wonderful. You can choose one of two ways to get there." He elaborated:

"Race ahead and speed to the top full of energy and excitement. When you reach the top, you can singularly claim credit as a lonely man. You may of course fall from the cliff on your way to the top, and break your bones, or left alone to die.

You may instead choose to gather your friends, climb a few hills to test your capabilities, stumble, learn, and pick yourself up a few times. When you are all ready, and sturdy, scale the peak together, and look after each other."

When I turned to my father and asked: "What would you do?" He simply replied, "You have to find your way and make those choices when your time comes." It was years later when I assimilated its full significance to managing life's circumstances and the choices that I make.

As I learned to roll with every punch life served, it was my mother Magdalena Go Lieng's unorthodox philanthropy that taught me how to learn and pick myself up from every stumble. Her example was an eye-opener: *She gave generously to help people to the point that they can pick themselves up, stand on their own two feet, and move on.* What she refused to do was to cuddle people from pain, so as not to deny them the opportunity to unshackle themselves from dependency.

In this chapter, I aim to provide my slant on dealing with uncertainties. If climate change occurs because of human activities, as advocates would assert, uncertainties often arise from human (mis)behaviour when the knowns become unknown because of managerial ego. In this context, human virtues (or lack of it) may have to be made explicit as to how it influences strategic and financial choices. This may bridge what divides strategy and finance by crossing the chasm between persisting in ignorance and making enlightened choices.

2
Why Uncertainties Persist?

When uncertainty is a problem that managers seek to resolve, they often err in their strategic choices. Implicitly, what would drive managers is to minimise variations in their cash flows, which in their mind, is a source of "uncertain payoffs." To reduce the variations, long-term "take-or-pay" supply contracts (Holland, 2016) are used to secure the cash flows.

While arguably the contracts are legally "air-tight," its continual renegotiations (Medina, 1991) may negate its original intent of securing cash flows. Worse, renegotiation appears to gain urgency when drastic oil price falls make investments uneconomic (NRF, 2015) or major disruptions such as a pandemic occur (Khanna, 2020).

To some managers, it is pointless to incorporate the unknowns into decision-making. After all, unknowns are uncertain that cannot be known *a priori*, a logical tautology. In some exceptional cases, half in jest, some would ease their guilt by asserting that what one does not know cannot hurt them.

Business realities may not sit well with these assertions. Indeed, by ignoring uncertainties, managers are akin to driving through the curving roads in mountains in a straight line without a steering wheel. Worse, the driver may look at the rear-view mirror to drive the car forward. In both cases, the manager is traveling oblivious of the car wreck awaiting to happen.

By its very nature, energy investments are complex, capital-intensive, and require cross-functional competencies. An overview of how the decision-making process operates is illustrated in Chart 4.1, where the Energy TECOP framework is used as an example.

Evaluated under five inter-related criteria, a selection of performance indicators and competencies is listed. These are by no means exhaustive. A way of illustrating the interactions is to consider an investment in a new power plant:

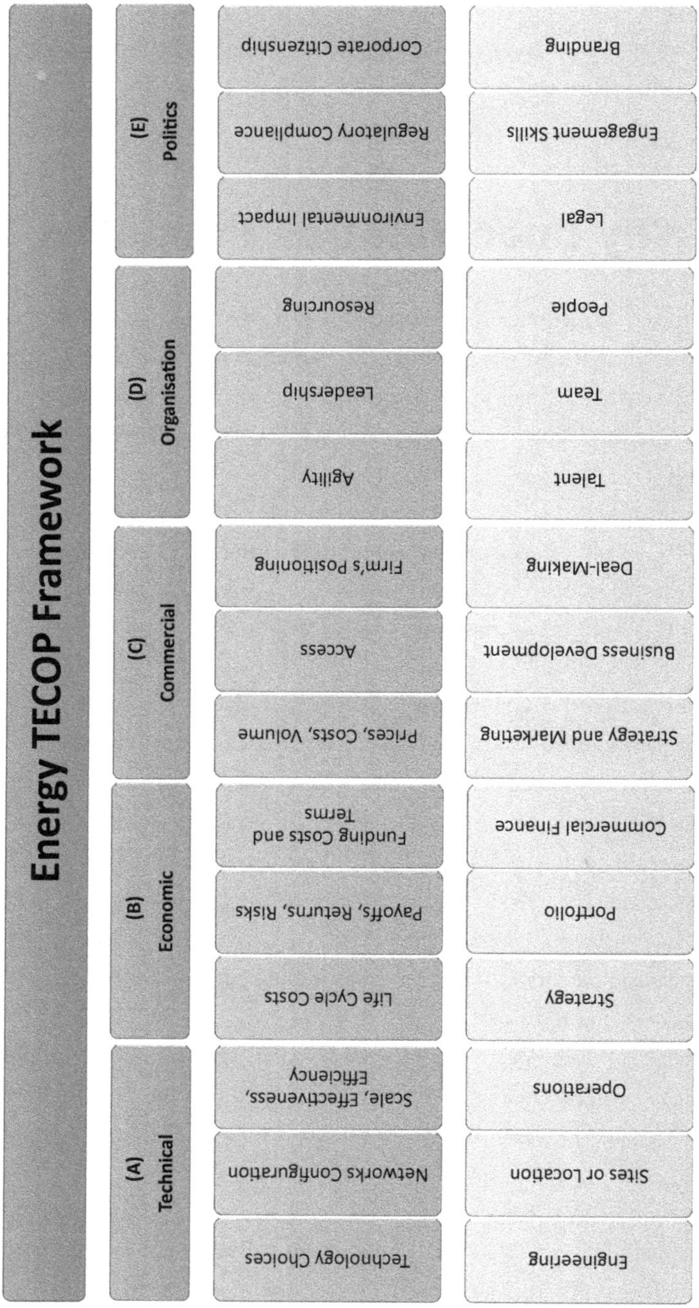

Energy TECOP Framework

(A) Technical
- Technology Choices
- Networks Configuration
- Scale, Effectiveness, Efficiency
- Engineering
- Sites or Location
- Operations

(B) Economic
- Life Cycle Costs
- Payoffs, Returns, Risks
- Funding Costs and Terms
- Strategy
- Portfolio
- Commercial Finance

(C) Commercial
- Prices, Costs, Volume
- Access
- Firm's Positioning
- Strategy and Marketing
- Business Development
- Deal-Making

(D) Organisation
- Agility
- Leadership
- Resourcing
- Talent
- Team
- People

(E) Politics
- Environmental Impact
- Regulatory Compliance
- Corporate Citizenship
- Legal
- Engagement Skills
- Branding

Chart 4.1: Untangling Webs of Interacting Factors

Source: Author as adopted from Project Management Institute.

The CEO of an oil and gas firm sees the future for her business in power generation. In choosing between a gas-fired and slim-hole geothermal power plant, managers would compare the *economics*[2] where slim-hole geothermal would potentially prove more profitable. However, the uncertainties around drilling for geothermal steam may prove prohibitive. Advances in drilling *technology* have reduced front-end costs, hence rebalancing the cost rewards in favour of slim-hole drilling. In addition, its smaller scale, together with advances in power generation technology, opens access to smaller markets. This improves the *commercial* viability of the technology. *Politically*, as a renewable resource, geothermal power is sufficiently flexible to generate power when needed. This is an advantage over intermittent renewables in terms of reliability and affordability. *Organisationally*, oil and gas exploration skills are partly transferable to geothermal drilling, with some retraining and adaptation.

What becomes apparent is how the framework enables the CEO to concisely communicate the team's decision in choosing slim-hole geothermal over gas. From a decision-making perspective, TECOP helps to focus the manager's efforts on what is essential to their business.

What is given less focus is the value of human interactions and how virtues facilitate informed choices. To a manager trained in finance, how deeply should one drill or what equipment to deploy probably is part of one's unknowns (or incompetence). Some managers may pretend otherwise. A more sensible move, however, is to ask technically competent people. Hence, the technical unknowns are clarified and become known within the team.

In one of my visits to Harry L Hansen in Boston, USA, we caught up about my life in investment banking. This was more of a continuation of our breakfast conversation in Jakarta, Indonesia, a couple of years before when we met. He gently reminded me:

---

[2] Chapters 9 and 10 provide the detailed analyses and calculations under competitive or oligopoly markets.

One of the core skills people tend to forget is the ability to work with and through people. In becoming very adept at quantifying everything, people forget that without good people to do the work, not much good will happen. This is where the political skills will have to be acquired, to convince others of the merits of your ideas. Without forming a coalition, the top is indeed going to be a very lonely place.

As I departed, he reached for a book that two of his colleagues at Harvard Business School published — *Leadership and the Quest for Integrity* by Joseph L Badaracco Jr and Richard R Ellsworth. He signed it and gave it to me as a reminder of our conversation. That was the last time I saw Harry from the steps of Mellon Hall, as he wished me god speed.

As I boarded my flight home to London, I began reading a chapter on *Values-Driven Leadership* from the book Harry gave me. These passages from Badaracco and Ellsworth (1989) piqued my curiosity:

"The company's goals have to be accepted by employees within the company; they should also help the company meet competitive challenges. Potentially, these two objectives can conflict. If the company's common purpose embraces shared values, however, these conflicts are substantially reduced. Fundamental — and thus more powerful — shared values and purposes, such as creativity and a contribution to something worthwhile, dominate parochial self-interest. *Localitis* yields to the pursuit of a common purpose."

In quoting Walter Wriston, former Chief Executive of Citicorp, "leadership is being able to articulate your value system and where you are going in ways people understand. In the corporation, as in your life, you have to have some benchmarks by which to operate. A corporation is a collection of individuals. Without a framework, you don't know what you are doing. The only thing that draws our cultures together is our common value system. For example, collegial management is a value. You have to have trust between people, and that's based on a common set of values and a common set of procedures."

In real life, managers are conscious that not all that they set out to achieve will work out according to plan.

Following Wriston's advice, managers will have to go back to some framework with which to think through their dilemmas. In the energy industry, TECOP is added to the managers' menu of their alphabet soup.

At first glance, TECOP would make the managerial tasks daunting and fraught with uncertainties: How could a manager be on top of all things when there are far too many moving parts? In effect, how could managers tackle the uncertainties that could emerge from any place in the value chain?

In recalling my conversation with Harry, the complexity is made tractable when a coalition of people understands the problems they are aiming to solve. In multifaceted problems that characterise energy investments, a coalition of talents and the willing could pool their resources, knowledge, and experiences to unbundle the opportunities hidden within uncertainties. I adapted from project management (Kim, 2012) an expanded *Expected Outcomes — Variations* matrix shown in Chart 4.2. In this matrix, uncertainties, to a large extent, are examined as a series of binary events to see how volatilities alter outcomes. Admittedly, deep uncertainties are exceptions, where its nature and sources are more nuanced, even if its impact could be understood following binary logic.

Within this managerial context, TECOP allows managers to break down the uncertainties into smaller bite sizes. By first isolating the discrete effects of specified factors, their influence on a subset of uncertain events could have a higher chance of being deciphered. Recombining how discrete variables interact with each other has a better prospect of being untangled and understood.

2.1 Predictable extant world (A. *Known–Knowns*)

Continuing from Chart 4.2, there are few instances where all the factors that are relevant for making choices are known with certainty. In this rare occasion, the expected outcomes are **known**, and the sources of variations (to outcomes) are identified (or **known**). One may say that managers operate in a relatively predictable world. In effect, when prices, costs, and volumes are known and how they vary are within known ranges, conventional capital budgeting tools may prove adequate.

This was the world that managers inhabited when energy markets were highly regulated. In today's markets, long-term contracts, such as *take-or-pay*, usually with

Dynamic Decisions

Chart 4.2: Expected Outcomes–Variations Matrix

	Expected Outcomes			
Variations or Uncertainties	**Certain (Known)**	**Uncertain (Unknown)**		**Prior Actions or Endowments**
		Impact	**Occurrence**	
Identified (Known) — Consequences	**A** Seasonal Rainfall and Tidal Flows; Seasonal Temperature Ranges; Seasonal Geothermal Steam Flows; Seasonal Sunlight	**B.1** Volume Volatilities; Prices or Costs; Losses or Gains; Access to Logistics	**B.2** Periodic; Strength; Duration; Temporal	**B.3** Technology Choices; Network Configuration; Strategic and Operational Flexibility; Policy Orientation
Unidentified (Unknown) — Consequences	**C.1** Revenue Losses; Cash Earnings Variations; Price or Volume Volatilities; Cost Overruns	**D.1** Network Disruptions; Obsolescence; Losses or Gains; Defer or Accelerate Investments	**D.3** Duration; Human or Geological Time; Imminent or Decades; Non-occurrence	**D.5** Loss Avoidance; Pivot; Adaptive Moves; Call or Put Options
Unidentified (Unknown) — Event	**C.2** Network Breakdown; Dry or Wet Spells; Unplanned Downtime or Delays; Rivals' Expansion or Contraction	**D.2** Pandemic; >+/- 1.5 C or <+/- 1.5 C; Regulatory Actions; Learning Effects or Substitution	**D.4** Rarely; Timing; Pace; Temporal or Multi-generational	**D.6** Asset Mix; Cost Structure; Contigency; Strategic or Operational Agility

Source: Author with features partly adapted for energy investments from Kim (2012).

the state, are the closest to a "predictable" way to earn one's payoffs. Under this relationship, the firm *de facto* acts as a contractor to the state. In exchange for secure profits, the firm foregoes any upside from higher prices, while avoiding making a loss when prices are low (assuming costs are inflexible).

The manager's principal tasks revolve around tracking the seasonal or cyclical patterns of its costs and how its volumes are maximised. More importantly, engaging its regulator and keeping consumers satisfied may prove to be of strategic importance.

Conversely, a change in government or regulation, particularly one that encourages more competition, could raise uncertainties around the incumbents' business approach. As more energy commodities are freely traded, this world becomes an exception rather than the rule.

2.2 Strategic or operational flexibility (B. *Unknown–Knowns*)

A more common situation that managers encounter relate to outcomes that may be ***unknown***. However, given the manager's instincts and experiences, the sources of variations that are observed such as volatilities in prices, costs, or volumes could be simulated or made ***known*** from historical patterns. An example is how weather plays a role in setting the level of pump storage hydro reserves. Cloudy days may lower the output of solar or photovoltaic power. Through observations, some patterns could be known of the consequences (B.1), although the timing of the occurrence (B.2) or its magnitudes may remain unknown.

The initial endowments such as how the network is configured, the extant technologies, and the policy orientation of the state could allow managers to bound uncertainties and convert them into quantifiable risks (or deviations).

Operating under conditions of managerial flexibility, managers may opt to curtail supplies, if by supplying they incur a loss. Conversely, they may ramp up volumes when markets are short.

When investing, managers may defer commitment when market conditions become adverse, accelerate when things improve or abort (or divest) when firms decide to pivot from fossil fuels to renewables. Strategically, when costs for wind or solar are rapidly declining, the question is radically reframed: Managers may consider a solar investment today that appears attractive when tax incentives and subsidies are included. Instead of committing outright, they may defer and wait for a couple of years.

If costs are falling by more than double digits a year, surely two years down the road, solar would yield an even more compelling return if the trend continues. By investing now, the manager locks in a cost structure that would be uncompetitive two years hence. With low yearly power output, the foregone earnings are less than the reduction in capital expenditures.

2.3 Insurable consequences (C. *Known–Unknowns*)

Insurers make a living by betting against the prospect of their clients making a loss. A client would opt to offload the burden of incurring a loss to an insurance firm for a fee. The insurer would spread their "bets," using actuarial calculations that estimate an adverse event occurring, to determine how much they should charge for their services (and risk-taking). In effect, the insurer is working with outcomes that may be ***known*** when the effects of volatility on results are well understood. What are ***unknown*** *a priori* are the timing, pacing, or severity of disruptions from unknown sources.

To ascertain how the unknowns may impact the business, managers may reverse the process. In anticipating a range of outcomes, managers may assess the conditions under which those outcomes may be realised. In doing so, the dependency on identified factors may provide an initial view as to their effects. A second round of information gathering, and re-examining experiences, may deepen managers' understanding of the relevance of the identified factors.

A long drought may drain the pump storage as to impair power output (Herrera *et al.*, 2018), thereby eroding stored hydro power's revenue and cash flows. Dust may accumulate that may cover the panels of a solar farm in a desert, rendering it unproductive for an extended period (Adinoyi and Said, 2013).

Any contingency plan would cost money, and the prospect of overinsuring is no different from gold-plating assets. The latter is a practice where assets are overspecified to withstand a disaster at a cost that may exceed replacing the asset. This is where I apply what I learned from my mother's unorthodox philanthropy: *Prepare for a duration that covers a period when alternative power supplies could be made available, or the problem could be fixed.*

2.4 Learning through options and games (D. *Unknown–Unknowns*)

Managers making strategic choices are often confronted with a future that is unknown, compounded by an ever-changing calculus of events and actions by rival firms. This is what managers refer to as deep uncertainties, where the outcomes are unknown as well as the sources of the variations in outcomes. This is what characterises transitioning markets, where the known networks of relationships are shifting. What evolves are tentative and often recursive outcomes. This is a function of competing policies interacting with people's preferences and choices to shape future demand and supply configurations.

The ***unknown*** outcomes may be examined in terms of their occurrence and impact of certain events, with an eye on how prior decisions may influence the scope for actions by managers. The sources of uncertainty of outcomes are dependent on the event and its consequences to the firm's viability.

Recall the CEO's narrative under TECOP. How would her prior decision on slim-hole geothermal power stack up under the uncertainties of a transitioning energy market?

In a dramatic reversal of a technology-neutral policy, the state chooses to accelerate the closure of coal-fired power by imposing a massive carbon tax. Her success with geothermal drilling allowed her firm to build a sizeable portfolio of geothermal supplies. The tax favoured the portfolio: Coal supplies have to be replaced with reliable and affordable renewables that only pump storage hydro and geothermal could provide. Unaffected by the carbon tax, her initial position is favourable (D.6).

The event, a regulatory action (D.2), is of a multi-generational nature as a "permanent tax" (D.4) that would occur over a long duration, perhaps over the remaining life of the assets (D.3). The impact could accelerate coal's economic obsolescence while accelerating investments in pump storage hydro or geothermal power (D.1). This train of events is triggered largely by the imposition of a massive carbon tax.

Rare events give rise to serious managerial dilemmas. In planning for contingency for each event, the costs would be prohibitive to make it untenable. This is where past rare events, such as a pandemic, may provide some clues. In the final analysis, a similar principle may be applied, using my mother's unorthodox philanthropic principles: *Prepare enough to give time for the firm to reconfigure its resources to adapt to a changing business environment.*

Deep uncertainties are characterised by situations where no known precedents may be relevant or of limited direct application. In this case, new information and learning may only be available through experimentation.

Recalling my father's advice, one climbs small hills with friends, rolls with every punch, gets up, learns, and moves on. With friends looking after each other, one becomes adept at navigating through pitfalls. In the process, one minimises the prospect of breaking some bones and left alone on the way to the peak.

3
Unpacking Policy Uncertainties

In my interactions with senior business leaders, some expressed frustrations over the direction the climate change conversations are evolving. For managers who are prepared to commit cash, political uncertainty would give them pause from proceeding.

Political uncertainties arise when there is no decisive resolution of the issues, which engenders a situation of continual recasting of policy and the state's priorities. Given this vacuum, firms are drawn inadvertently into shaping policy prerogatives that may or may not achieve broad public support.

Climate policy is a case in point. While advocates claim consensus exists within policy circles, managers are less certain about how one could translate policy aspirations into a business proposition. Here's why:

A majority sees climate change as a major threat to their nation, Pew Research reported in their survey. Diving deeper into the data, however, still shows substantial proportions of people rate climate change as a minor or no threat at all. People with more years of schooling, and those younger, tend to show more concern. It is in the United States where people are more polarised along the partisan divide. A quarter of

Republicans see climate change as a major issue compared to 83% of Democrats (Fagan and Huang, 2019).

The US partisan divide influences people's thinking, with party affiliation as a determinant (more than knowledge) of their views on climate change. More Americans see climate change as a federal priority for the Congress and the President who are more prepared to assume the costs as worth bearing. However, 85% of Republicans still consider spending too much on climate change mitigation as harmful to the economy or makes no difference. This is compared to 47% of Democrats who sees such spending as doing good than harm (Funk and Kennedy, 2020). Extended to respondents from advanced economies, the divide remains deep albeit a greater willingness to change their lifestyle to abate the effects of climate change (Bell *et al.*, 2021).

The divergent views are far from trivial. The value chain of energy and its components are influenced by political factors. This is manifested through the policy orientation that would emerge from the shifting political discourse that influences the choice of policy measures that will be employed. I outline in Chart 4.3 how linear thought processes turn ideas into policy measures.

In formulating a low-carbon policy, people tend to focus on the specific knowledge that is required to craft a good policy. In this case, knowledge of environmental science, energy economics, and redistributive justice, among others, may prove essential. However, the policymaking knowledge, which seeks to inform how the policymaking system works is often assumed to be known (Dror, 2017).

By focusing on specific knowledge to understand policy, managers may similarly err, as they do with neo-classical economics, in believing that humans rationally adopt a policy that is on paper. However, competing advocacies and interests would result in compromises where politics aims to "maximise the possible." How this plays out in real life may resemble tentative, recursive processes that vary with shifting ideological dominance. For long-term energy assets, it is conceivable that an investment is committed under one policy stance, built under another, and may operate commercially under yet another set of policy measures. Specifically:

In the sphere of economics (A), policy may create a demand pull for renewables by penalising polluters with carbon taxes. Levied high enough, polluting supplies such as coal and oil may exit (A.1.2) that, in theory, would reduce fossil fuel quantity (A.1.3) from the supply mix. In contrast, policy in its omniscience would choose to follow a supply push approach by subsidising preferred renewables technologies (A.2.1).

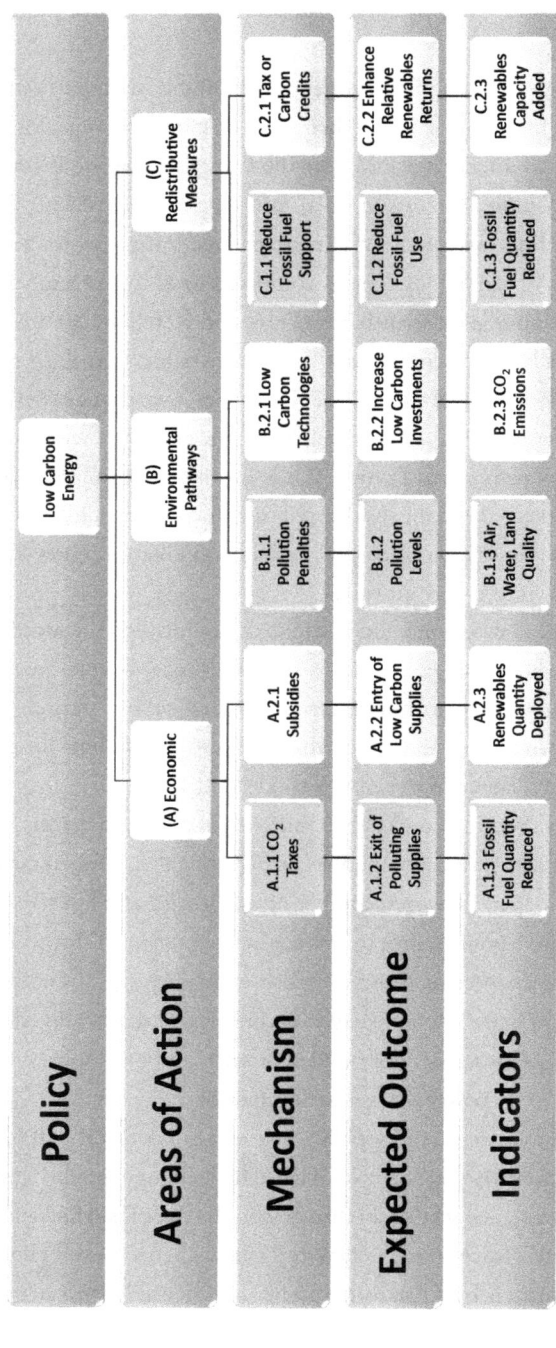

Chart 4.3: Climate Policy and Expected Outcomes

By making subsidised non-polluting technologies financially "cheaper," investors may opt for entry into low-carbon supplies (A.2.2) by foregoing fossil fuels, thereby increasing renewables deployment.

The environmental pathways (B) follow a quasi-taxation and a technological route. By imposing punitive pollution penalties (B.1.1), pollution levels are expected to fall (B.1.2). This happens when firms chose to exit polluting industries or substitute dirty with cleaner technologies. Consequently, air, water, and land quality could improve (B.1.3).

The operative notion is technological substitution. To make pollution penalties work, substitute technologies should be available for firms to migrate their industrial processes or replace their extant "dirty" with low-carbon technologies (B.2.1). In theory, investments in low-carbon technology would increase (B.2.2), which could reduce CO_2 emissions.

Without making the low-carbon technologies available and affordable, pollution penalties (or carbon taxes) degenerate into a revenue-raising measure without reducing pollution. This loses the moral high ground that environmental advocates use to push their agenda.

Policy initiatives tend to create "winners" or "losers" in applying redistributive measures. This is where distributive justice plays prominent roles in arbitrating among competing interests. The way the benefits or costs are reallocated is heavily influenced by policymakers' ideological orientation.

Market-friendly policies weigh their success in intervening less, often by exception, while leaving private capital to organise resources. In this context, carbon tax is usually accompanied by measures that mitigate its impact on poorer consumers. The decision to invest or not is entrusted to managers, where higher carbon tax in theory would enhance the relative returns of renewables investments. This is expected, under markets with secure legal and property rights, to encourage more renewables capacity to be added.

Policy-directed systems see policy's role as directly pushing firms towards a green future. This may be achieved by recasting the support system by reducing fossil fuel support and offering carbon credits to renewables. Both approaches would aspire to reduce fossil fuel use while enhancing renewables' relative returns. The dual penalty on fossil fuels — loss of public support and hit by carbon tax — is hoped to accelerate a transition to low-carbon energy markets.

At this point, a reality check on the rationalist reasoning of policy formulation and its expected outcomes is required. In my various works, I highlighted the persistent occurrence of green paradoxes. I posit that as subsidies are generously given to achieve wide-scale renewables deployment, it tends to deter investments and hinder innovations that accelerate the decline in costs.

In a tangible way, managers grapple with the mixed financial records of policy promoted champions in the case of wind and solar power. For example:

Wind farms are cheaper to build in 2020 compared to 2008. The decline was interrupted from 2004 to 2012 when wind turbine costs surged because the subsidy created a demand that caused a shortage in turbines and critical components. After having fallen to $1,300/kW in 2001–2004, costs surged to $2,000/kW before it plateaued in 2011 (IRENA, 2012).

Solar farms' rapid expansion is accompanied by shrinking cash margins, causing bankruptcies among suppliers (Zaremba, 2020) and investors (Puko and Randles, 2020), largely as falling asset costs led to falling prices that compressed profits for manufacturers. This follows similar patterns since Solyndra's scandal (Fehrenbader, 2015) set back the US government by $500 mln.

The math appears simple: To build a solar panel factory, one needs hundreds of millions of dollars. When the solar panels come to market, prices fall rapidly, resulting in paltry returns with most turning in losses (Hoium, 2017). Developers are not in better shape, with volumes collapsing in 2020.

Rate of costs decline accelerated for wind and solar power as markets move from subsidies-induced demand to competitive auctions of new capacity. Partly because of excess solar panel supplies and improved economics of wind farms, the prices achieved are substantially lower than what policy-induced deployment expected (IRENA, 2019).

Some managers look at the energy market and blame competition for the uncertainties. However, it is more important to understand how policy formulation and the policy measures it promotes would impact markets. This ultimately influences how the rival firms would perform.

Connecting this to corporate strategy and finance, I recall Harry L Hansen's thought process. In tackling the problem, what is the problem that policy or managers are trying to solve?

Policy sees climate change as the problem. They believe that carbon emissions cause temperatures to vary (or warm). Humans using fossil fuels are the cause. In equating climate change to CO_2 emissions, there is a need to limit climate variation to within +/- 1.5 °C by displacing fossil fuels with renewables. The opportunity, under policy mandated transition, is the creation of a green market that runs into several trillion dollars. Advocates see this as a sure bet to mint money.

The paradox, however, puzzles climate advocates. Large numbers appear to elicit a lukewarm response from managers. Notwithstanding the billions spent by oil and gas firms on renewables, outpacing any clean technology ventures, advocates still see this as too little, too late.

I see this as a dichotomy in how managers see the problem. In committing to meet their future energy supplies, managers see the problem as a trade-off between the cost today of investing against what they could gain in the future. Compliance with environmental standards, its financial costs and payoffs form part of this calculus. Hence, they see policy actions as part of the uncertainties in pursuing a strategic path. In this case, before managers would part with the firm's cash, they would assess the costs or opportunities that shifting policy priorities would imply.

To inform the managerial thought process, I use Chart 4.4 to ascertain the types of instruments that policy may employ, how firms may respond, and more importantly, how managers could adapt when policy changes its stance.

I see policy may try to engineer a transition from fossil fuels to renewables by influencing the market. A *policy push transition* relies on direct subsidies or aids to make renewables financially more attractive than fossil fuels. Under this world, policy is omniscient on what society needs, and with its omnipotence, drives a transition as a mandate of the state. A *market pull transition* entrusts managers to make their choices according to their firm's *purpose*. The state nudges as a paternalistic enabler that encourages firms to opt for clean technologies (Thaler and Sunstein, 2008). In effect,

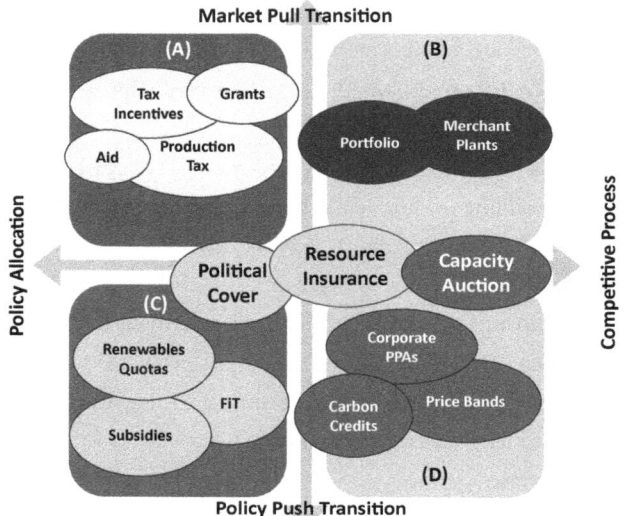

Chart 4.4: Policy Instruments and Market Orientation Matrix

policy seeks to influence how managers decide and the choices they would eventually make. This differs dramatically from the state dictating through regulatory fiat what the firm should commit while reserving policy's prerogative to change their mind. The costs? It accrues to the firm and its stakeholders.

The other aspect is how the benefits (or subsidies) are allocated. *Policy allocation* follows a similar omniscient approach where the state knows what is best for society and firms. The other approach is through a *competitive process* where firms opt to rely on or ignore any state support. In either case, firms compete to gain access to state support, with policy taking an enabling role.

In understanding the policy dynamics, managers may adapt more effectively to influence policy and actively shape the future of the energy market as a stakeholder. Specifically:

Policy Push and Champions (A), in policy's greater wisdom (omniscience) and power (omnipotence), instruments are used to push the deployment of technology "champions." These are common among early-stage adopters of renewables as their principal pathway to low-carbon energy systems. The objective is to install enough capacity to push a specified technology along the path of declining costs, premised on the learning effects,[3] so that the technology could compete with coal or gas.

Policy Enabled Market Pull (B) deployment shifts the policy role to one of enabler. This they achieve by using taxation or grants that are technology agnostic. Consequently, managers make the choice as to which technology to deploy according to their objectives.

Policy Enabled Competitive Process (C) moves policy towards trusting market mechanisms to push energy transition. Policy may employ a competitive process to access capacity permits, carbon credits, or create a more flexible energy pricing based on a specified range of variation. Capacity auction is a more recent scheme, together with corporate power purchase agreements (PPAs) that I see as a bridge towards a fully market-based system.

Markets with Regulatory Intervention by Exception (D) are supported by institutions that govern the smooth functioning of energy markets. Regulator intervenes usually to correct market failures. Otherwise, managers and rival firms freely decide their investments, usually with limited monetary support from the state.

Multilateral agencies contribute to the transition by providing political risk cover or resource insurance. These are instruments that are usually employed for emerging markets to strengthen the country's credit or partly de-risk specified aspects of investments.

These decisions are reached through a political process where competing interests would continually shift the priorities of the prevailing government. Paradoxically, with regime change being a reality and with it the prospect of policy changes, reliance on policy guarantees may in fact increase the uncertainties.

When firms take a conscious effort to see politics and its potential for good, the political uncertainties surrounding energy transitions are more reassuring. After all, the political process in a democracy allows a period of public discernment before policy is adopted and implemented. This period enables managers to make their adaptive moves into winning actions.

---

[3] Learning effects assume that as more units are installed, the costs would decline as people become adept at producing and installing the systems.

4
Managerial Responses to Deep Uncertainties

In uncertain times, with the future largely unknown, some managers are tempted to keep their options open. By keeping their options open, they could adapt their action as new information becomes available. In some cases, the problem may simply resolve itself with time.

There are those that choose to engage in perpetual change because transformation by itself is a desirable outcome. Managers see "organisational agility is often treated as an immutable quality, implying that firms need to be in a constant state of transformation. However, this ignores that such transformation, while often essential, come at a cost. They are not always necessary, and may not even be possible" (Teece et al., 2016).

Underlying these beliefs is a thought process that is heavily influenced by rational choice and vested interests in decision-making.

When making choices, be it in consumption or investment or in life generally, people are assumed to choose what is in their best interest. The criteria are economic, where expected value (or utility) is ordered to allow managers to choose prospects that maximise returns. The choices are "purely rational and calculative. All social action, it is argued, can be seen as rationally motivated, however much it may appear to be irrational" (Scott, 2000).

While logical and readily understood, rationality is in itself ill-defined in mainstream economics and hence opens the way for much confusion. This happens, as in neoclassical theories when *payoffs* and *utility* are assumed to be equivalent. An example is when rational people are said to act for reasons or do their utmost to achieve the "best goal." This falls foul when how people interpret their situations and what they understand as their "best goal" are unknown or ignored by managers. In certain cases, people respond to incentives, which could be economic or take other forms (e.g. honour, awards, among others) or adapt to circumstances (Hodgson, 2012).

Taken in the context of business, managers that subscribe to rationalist approaches would also adhere to a consistent response to incentives. This tends to happen when payoffs, which is economic, are ascribed equivalent "value" to utility, which is psychological in nature. That is, payoffs add to one's balances, say in a bank account, while utility could add to one's joy or self-esteem. In some circumstances, when the bank balances give an equivalent "value" in joy, one may argue that the two are equivalent.

In real life, I would tend to subscribe to the idea that payoffs and utility may not always coincide in value. There are rich people who are miserable or poor who are happy. It is also true that there are some of the rich who are happy and poor who are miserable. This is where the rationalist foundations of investment evaluation come under serious questions.

The consequences are important to decision-making and how managers respond to opportunities. When people's perceptions are asymmetric, their attitudes to economic (e.g. payoffs) or psychological (e.g. utility) stimuli are likely to differ. In this context, multiple outcomes are feasible (Arsenio, 2008) from the interactions of people, firms, and the rivalry that may ensue in dynamic markets.

Recognising this context, I learn from colleagues at Shell plc[4] that unravelling the mysteries of deep uncertainties is akin to embarking on a transformation journey. This requires a change in the way I attempt to access knowledge beyond what is readily available. More importantly, how discrete forms of knowledge could be assimilated to inform decision-making would require a learning ecosystem different from how technical or specific skills are imparted. I outline in Chart 4.5 how I see managers could structure a response to deep uncertainties.

In embarking on a journey of discovery, the individual (or ***I***) starts with a personal transformation in order to create an enabling learning ecosystem for the team (or ***We***). By opening with *I accept what I do not know*, one invites others to contribute while signalling the willingness to engage with humility. In setting an expectation, *I recognise ambiguity* encourages curiosity to explore and consider approaches beyond one's comfort. In reinforcing one's openness, *I accept others may differ* makes it explicit that divergent ideas are freely considered. In working with others, experimenting with ideas or approaches may not always work as one would expect. The "failure" becomes a learning opportunity when one takes this attitude: *I fail, learn,*

---

[4] See Box 4.1 for a discussion of the role of leadership and team dynamics in successful transformations.

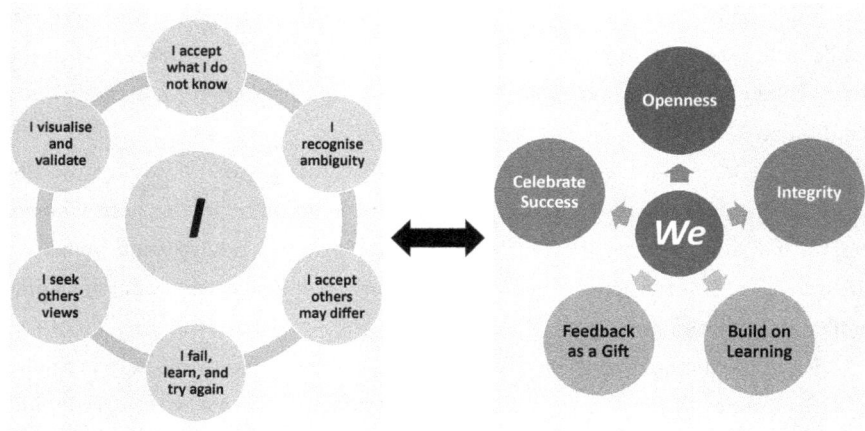

Chart 4.5: Enabling Mindsets and Decision-Making Ecosystem

and try again. In the process of learning, *I seek other's views* challenges one's own thinking with the benefit of others' wisdom. As one starts to uncover what could work, *I visualise and validate* a narrative with people and together, one co-creates viable approaches to resolving uncertainties.

In harnessing the collective wisdom of the team, the **We** would have to create the decision ecosystem wherein people feel safe to express their views truthfully, inconvenient as it may seem to others. Building on the enabling mindset around *I*, the effectiveness of the **We** is reinforced when there is *openness*. In the spirit of honesty, sincerity is facilitated to strengthen trust among team members. This environment, underpinned by *integrity*, could create a working approach where people *build on learning* with each experience. Failure is seen as an opportunity to learn by eliciting honest *feedback as a gift*. Among my colleagues at Shell plc, this was often delivered as a "hard love" whose sole purpose is to improve the individual by making the person a valuable contributor to the team. It goes without saying that the teams *celebrate success* to recognise outstanding performance as well as to demonstrate what works well for the team and for others to emulate as appropriate.

In effectively tackling deep uncertainties, the team's ability to identify emerging changes, prepare for them, and take action will have to follow an adaptive approach.

This is where finance and strategy would tend to collide, and popular notions of uncertainty are proven wrong.

Finance, of the bean counter type, errs in relying on their financial tools to follow a prescribed decision rule. Tools are inert instruments that give predetermined answers according to the assumptions and inputs that are provided. People are entrusted to use the information to inform their judgement to make a choice among competing opportunities. *In extremis*, CFOs seeking more data become pointless because none are likely to make certain what are inherently ambiguous.

CEOs in contrast would accept the imperfection of knowledge. They may grudgingly admit that those who may know are out of reach. Hence, they may satisfy themselves that what they are missing, in terms of information or knowledge, may only be known after the initial outcomes are known. This is the case for adopting new technologies, untested processes, or innovations. To balance what they aspire with what they know and do not know, astute CEOs tend to rely on organisational agility.

Contrary to a perpetual revolution, organisational agility is seen as an "ability of the organisation to renew itself, adapt, change quickly, and succeed in rapidly changing, ambiguous, turbulent environments" (Aghina *et al.*, 2015). Some managers, to succeed, (erroneously) see this as an organisation that flourishes in perpetual turmoil.

Quite the contrary, people's ability to move fast is enabled when there is a stable platform. This stability is not achieved by the managers' ability to foresee with perfection when adverse events would strike. This is perhaps impossible, and even if feasible with sophisticated forecasting tools, the exercise may have limited value. That is, unless the team is equipped to respond to the consequences, it may not matter if managers knew what was coming or are caught by surprise. Equipped with specified rules of engagement, teams are empowered to act when *rare events* or adverse changes to markets occur.[5]

In modern energy firms, oil and gas and power companies are usually large, structured, and capital-intensive behemoths that are perceived by some as slow-moving supertankers. To turn them around, enormous force is applied to break the inertia. For this reason, change comes slowly where the initial force of change is imperceptible. This is followed by accumulating small changes until momentum is built from within. Once this is reached, the transformation could take a life of its own.

---

[5] An example is illustrated in Box 4.2, learning from how the US military designs this agility within their units.

The perceived absence of agility is attributed to how the energy business, as people know it, evolved from capital-intensive projects. With so much cash committed to assets, the extant networks of infrastructures and interactions lock in a pattern of doing things. As projects are completed, business processes settle into a routine that makes things somewhat predictable.

In focusing on how humans effect change, I posit that works on the innovation economy hold many parallels to understanding why energy transitions tend to be tentative and recursive. "In the innovation economy, new futures emerge with new players (business firms and banks) owning different assets playing within a broadly circumscribed (by regulation and competition law) set of rules. New entrants are not only combining and recombining technological elements, but also creating entirely new ones. Surprises and 'Black Swans' become the norm, particularly when fundamental technological breakthroughs occur and when economic and monetary policy begins traversing uncharted territory, as it has in recent years" (Teece *et al.*, 2016).

For these reasons, when managers let their financial tools, rather than their judgement, make the choices for them, they would err in their commitments. When *unknowns* are evaluated by the same metrics as the *knowns*, the tools give predetermined answers that are precise, but are often precisely wrong.

To remedy this unfortunate situation, managers will have to configure an enabling environment where hierarchy is dispensed with. The logic is, when people trust that their views will be valued and opposing perspectives are welcome, this gives life and value to diversity of thinking. This is the key to unlocking the opportunities hidden in the *unknown–unknowns*.

4.1   Organising adaptively for uncertain outcomes

When a *purpose* is understood and adhered to, firms are in a position to mobilise their people to embark on a journey. In planning the way forward, the energy market appears to follow two visions of what a low-carbon energy system would look like for incumbents:

> The liquid fuels, comprising the oil and gas firms, see in power a new segment that offers growth. Perhaps, this is not a coincidence. Power generation is a major user of gas. Transport, while fossil fuel still dominated, could

increasingly move to electric vehicles. Acquisitions of power generation and electric recharging business are attracting top dollars (Coren, 2019).

Power firms are hardly seen to integrate backwards to fuels. Instead, focus is on divesting coal and nuclear assets (Lacey, 2014; Walton, 2019), expanding in intermittent renewables, and modernising outdated transmission and distribution infrastructure. The future is seen as more renewables and digitising networks to better accommodate variable loads.

The focus is largely on the hardware and how to make it work better when loads from gas-fired power supplies, a more flexible capacity to supply fluctuating demand, are combined with intermittent wind and solar power. How people are deployed and empowered with new capabilities are not made explicit.

What is amiss in the energy firms' actions is the rarity of mergers of oil and gas firms and power utilities. The obvious answer is it was done before and the marriage was often a difficult one. The businesses were very different, where the "synergies" between fuel suppliers and power generators were not obvious. Germany's E.ON and RWE disposed their oil and gas assets, as they restructured their business to focus on power (RWE, 2014; Reuters, 2015).

The less obvious reasons could be deduced from the uncertainties surrounding both the fuels and power markets. As a new entrant in power, acquiring an incumbent power utility would achieve scale and access to market. However, one also inherits legacy assets such as coal and nuclear and ageing network infrastructures. Under a transitioning energy market, one may opt to focus on bypassing obsolescing assets by leapfrogging to microgrids or renewables.

A similar logic is more compelling for power utilities. As their power generation decarbonises, the strategic logic of integrating backwards to fossil fuels is not obvious. As networks potentially move to decentralise distribution, this may prove a better way to leverage its capabilities.

In both instances, rival firms from fuels and power try to converge towards electrification of energy and transport. In making this transition, organisational agility is demanded of managers to sustain the viability of extant assets, while shedding or adding assets to its extant portfolios.

While firms are transitioning, managers are faced with the challenge of retaining as much of the value of extant assets. This task is combined with evaluating the technologies or opportunities that would propel them to a low-carbon future, and delivering on their stakeholders' needs.

To organise the firm's resources, I propose using Chart 4.6 to guide how managers could focus their efforts on innovation and building organisational agility. Schematically, businesses are clustered around the returns from innovation and the corresponding need for organisational agility.

Innovation returns are incremental when the outcomes revolve around efficiency improvement achieved from tighter control of costs or increases in outputs from the same assets. In contrast, reconfiguring the network of relationships and infrastructures may yield significant enhancement to returns.

Organisational agility follows the pace and complexity of change. Incremental changes are unlikely to disrupt resource allocation and industrial processes. In this case, the need for organisational agility is low, whereas a focus on operational efficiency may prove financially rewarding. Rapid changes or complex transitions that may render some assets obsolete, while locking in future costs and operational flexibility based on today's decisions, would benefit from a more agile organisation to respond to an ever-changing calculus of outcomes from human interactions.

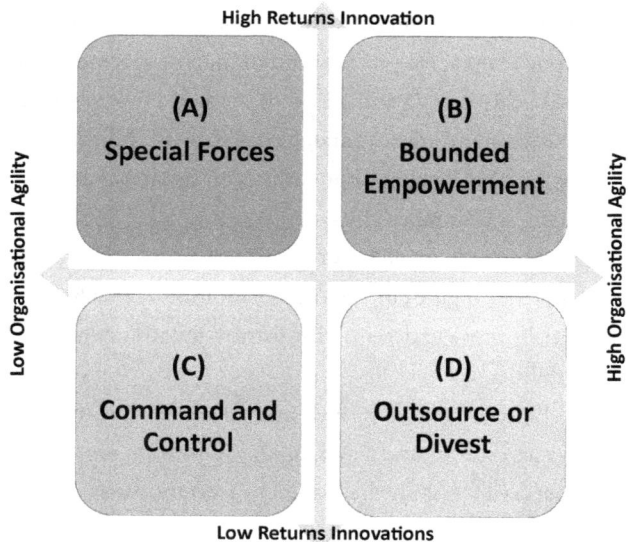

Chart 4.6: Organisation Agility and Innovations

Seen in this context, managers may employ different approaches to manage their resources. I propose the following as an illustrative approach for an oil and gas firm:

1. ***Command-and-Control*** features specialised assets with limited flexibility to adapt. To optimise, production efficiency under stable demand is largely achieved from standardisation, or specialisation, with incremental returns from innovation.

   The team may singularly follow a designated leader with well-trained specialists. Each team member is designated their tasks, with specified rules of engagement in how they relate to each other. When markets remain stable and predictable, the efficiency is optimal as the team "delivers like clockwork." To sustain this efficiency, leadership succession is crucial to mitigate disruptions from "regime change."

2. ***Outsource or Divest*** may occur when the firm's organisational agility is limited, while under a different owner, others may better manage the assets under a dynamic (hence volatile) market.

   Comprising deal-makers, the team focuses on short-term performance to maximise the value of assets for divestment. They are usually adept at valuing assets, from the buyer's perspective, and negotiating the best terms for the sale of assets.

3. ***Special Forces*** work with small opportunities, usually as projects, to experiment, learn, and scale, focusing on low hanging opportunities yielding high returns from innovation of processes, organisation, or logistics.

   Inspired from the military, a team of gifted talents are deployed, with enthusiasm and imagination as their principal strengths. They pursue the best way they could to find alternative ways of getting things done. When mishaps occur, they regroup, discuss, and agree on an alternative course of action, undeterred to drop out when deemed necessary.

4. ***Bounded Empowerment*** involves the deployment of cross-functional teams, with specified mandate, to undertake new ventures. They initially operate outside the mainstream business.

   The team recognises uncertainty for what it is. One can hardly predict when adverse events could occur. By understanding its nature, its effects could be predicted. While having an eye on reaching the summit, a collegial team prepares themselves by acquiring the skills needed for survival. In the process, team agility is developed alongside an ordered command structure, conferring capabilities that adaptively reconfigure themselves to surmount obstacles that come their way (see Box 4.2).

Within dynamic markets, each team configuration could work for as long as they are matched to the appropriate challenges. This matching process requires judgement, informed by a deep understanding of capabilities, the factors that make markets dynamic, and the nature of uncertainties.

In effect, the persona of an entrepreneurial manager comes to mind. They are entrusted with two principal tasks: As the orchestrator of resources and capabilities, the manager coaches and cheerleads the team to higher performance.

"When confronting such circumstances, entrepreneurial managers are needed to redeploy not only financial capital, but also technical expertise while balancing shareholder interests both within and beyond the organisation" (Teece *et al.*, 2016). To achieve this, organisational agility is embedded in decision-making within a stable framework of the firm's purpose (Aghina *et al.*, 2015). Specifically:

Governance mandates *a priori* what the teams are empowered to do, how they interact with others, and how they escalate decisions (or consult). In effect, a *modus operandi* confers greater agility within their scope of authority.

Structure and Competency provides a "home" where skills and expertise are developed and deployed. They are the repository of pools of talents where project teams are drawn from.

Processes pertains to managing the interfaces among skill pools, information and resource flows, and how opportunities are accepted, evaluated, and prioritised. Rules ease the way to do the right things, not to restrict actions.

"The entrepreneurial manager is an 'orchestrator' giving direction to and coordinating amongst activities. Superior skills as an entrepreneurial manager result from not only more experience and better learning opportunities, but also superior managerial and social capital" (Teece *et al.*, 2016). In differentiating how uncertainties and risks are managed, they added "the role of organisational agility in modern management cannot be assessed separately from a consideration of risk, uncertainty, budgets, costs, commitment, and strategy."

4.2   Recombining resources to move ahead

One needs to appreciate how human behaviour contributes, or impedes, a resolution of uncertainties. In some cases, human attitudes such as a mistaken notion that "all there is to know are known" would fail to access the lessons from others' experiences and knowledge. This belief is often centred around the individual. In complex investments such as energy, one can indeed become very limited by what the manager knows, vast as that experience and knowledge may prove to be.

At a more mundane level, people are predisposed differently to how they choose to respond to uncertain events. For this reason, asymmetric responses may cause behaviour to deviate from what are thought as rational responses by the neoclassical theory. Specifically:

> When people are given a description of what they are investing, such as investment trusts or prospectus, investors tend to focus on the prospect of losses, hence "end up overweighting risks" (Hertwig *et al.*, 2004). In contrast, for rare events that may have higher impact (such as pandemics), people would instead underweight the probability (Ungemach *et al.*, 2009). With its rare occurrence, it is recognised but often ignored.
>
> Human perceptions of value are at times confused with utility. While an economic value is often resolved by arithmetical calculations, the notion of attaching utility makes the choices subjective. What was seen as an objective (economic) value is now subjected to the vagaries of human preferences that may "differ from one context to another, or from one decision-maker to another" (Savage, 1954).
>
> This is where human behaviour may clash with theory that underpins rational decisions. People's aversion to ambiguity would lead them to seek clarity, often relying on their experiences, limited as it may be. The eventual choices are "moderated by the decision-maker's confidence in his or her judgement and skill" (Heath and Tversky, 1991). The choice is between "clear and vague prospects" (Fox and Tversky, 1995), which refers to conditions between clearly understood risks or complete ignorance.

The apparent ambiguity, however, is a product of the limits of one's experiences. By focusing on "different elements in people's conceptualisation of such events may lead to a better understanding of the creation of subjective estimates of probabilistic events" (Ülkümen *et al.*, 2016).

When teams are set up, how could they build the capabilities that are potentially self-reinforcing directed at achieving superior results? I propose a possible approach in Chart 4.7.

Managers would usually aim for *risk-weighted returns*, where they balance how much unknowns are tolerated in their decisions against the potential gains financially and socially. I see this as a managerial ability to orchestrate how they acquire knowledge (A), build capabilities (B), use their experiences (C) when relevant, understand what remains as unknowns (D), and why.

To avoid being swamped, managers may choose to bound the uncertainties and experiment with a few approaches in order to validate and learn from the initial results. This is where I recall my father's advice to me as a young boy: *Before scaling the peak, climb a few hills with friends, stumble, learn, get up, and move on.* In a business context, particularly in undertaking complex and capital-intensive energy investments, I see the following as a feasible way of unbundling the team's actions:

When lack of **knowledge** is at the root of the unknown, one may gain clarity by outsourcing (A.1), using advisers, to provide the expertise. The firm may acquire (A.2) by purchasing firms as oil and gas companies are doing with renewables and battery recharging firms. The knowledge gained will have to be shared more widely by knowing how to interface (A.1.1) with extant systems or onboarding (A.2.1) new talents into the organisation. The process of assimilating the new knowledge (A.1.2) or integrating new talents will have to be managed, validated, and learning extracted to enhance capabilities.

Capabilities are usually bounded by how people are formed (B.1), formally through their academic qualifications and the virtues they acquire at home and from peers or others. Specific skills are gained through training (B.2).

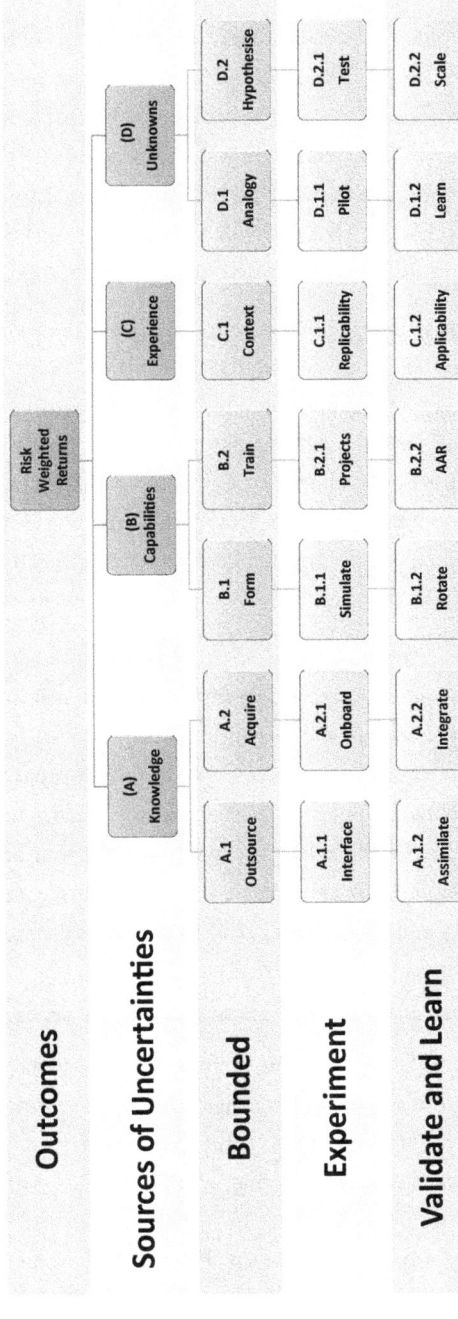

Chart 4.7: Uncertainties, Organisational Agility, and Profits

To deploy their capabilities, people may simulate (B.1.1) to test how certain approaches could pan out under specified conditions. From this safe environment, where actual damage could be minimised, people may turn an idea into projects (B.2.1) as a first approximation prior to scaling up (or down). To broaden people's competencies, they may rotate (B.1.2) across different or related roles. A practice that proves effective is to undertake an *After Action Review* (AAR) (B.2.2), where outcomes are examined and understood, and capture and disseminate the lessons learned.

Experience is often assumed as essential to the firm's successful transition. I see this as a double-edged sword that cuts both ways. Amidst the uncertainties of transitioning markets, what was of value in a prior situation may be irrelevant. When pursued as a basis for moving forward, the team may flounder when generals choose to fight the present battles with tools and tactics from a previous encounter. This is where managers may scrutinise the context (C.1) of experience, understand the conditions under which it could be replicated (as to outcomes) (C.1.1), to know its relevance and applicability (C.1.2) to an evolving situation on hand.

What remains are the persistent ***unknowns*** that I see as requiring the creative minds of managers to seek out a viable approach. Committing to a low-carbon strategy falls under this category. One common approach is to use an analogy (D.1) to approximate a narrative as to how managers could learn from other industries. One could gain information by piloting (D.1.1), observe its results, experiment and learn (D.1.2). Alternatively, managers may frame a strategy as a hypothesis (D.2) that could be tested in markets (D.2.1), before scaling up (D.2.2).

In tackling investments facing great uncertainties, managers may look into buying an option. In buying an option, it gives managers the "right to buy an asset at a particular price in the future. Forming a joint venture, or acquiring a small stake initially, with an option to increase future control, may achieve the purpose of learning about an unfamiliar business."

"In decision-making, it means taking a small step to learn more, before making a call that could significantly impact your people or the organisation" (Davenport, 2019).

5
A CFO's Role in the Strategic Dialogue

The push by policy for a rapid transition to low-carbon energy systems is premised on the certainty of science, advocates for climate action would assert. The CFO plays a pivotal role, albeit a difficult position, to inform the CEO and the board on the strategic alternatives that are realistically open to them.

An important challenge is how to incorporate how climate actions would influence the firms' options going forward. Policy premised their stance on the science of climate change, a matter that is settled as advocates would assert. One can question this belief, but how this translates into policy measures is more relevant to managers to ascertain.

Policy as an outcome of competing ideologies and interests may provide some guideposts for managers. However, its full effect will continue to evolve and remain a source of uncertainty. By no means will its trajectory take a linear progression. It is more likely to be tentative and recursive. For this reason, managers cannot entirely pin their hopes on a stable framework. Instead, a tolerance for ambiguity and building organisational agility may better serve the CFO's longevity in the modern corporation.

A clearer appreciation of the nature of uncertainty, and how it differs from risks, is a source of strategic advantage to firms. It enables astute managers to see opportunities, while the herd takes fright (and flight) in the face of the unknowns. By harnessing their enabling mindsets and creating an ecosystem that facilitates sound decisions, managers can unbundle the sources of uncertainties. In the process, managers can segregate and prioritise actions to focus on the deep uncertainties, while setting the rules of engagement for tackling recurrent uncertainties such as price, cost, or volume volatilities.

Ultimately, the bean counter may be relied upon to bound these uncertainties, convert them into risks, and manage them accordingly. The deep uncertainties? Managers will have to learn to calibrate their effects, equip their team to respond effectively, and plan the appropriate contingencies. This is where the CFO could prove a worthy partner to the CEO, acting as a sparring partner, a trusted adviser, and as a conscience to reach sound judgement.

Box 4.1: Views from the Inside

Corporate transformation is variously seen as a shock treatment for survival, a boot camp to instil the discipline that sustains change (for the better, hopefully) or a passing fad of little lasting consequence. While none of these views truly encapsulates the change process, these views persist even within executive teams that aim to deliver on similar agenda.

Cognisant of these divergent responses to change, executing corporate transformation is akin to a political process. In essence, there is supportive leadership to initiate change, managers who are committed to role model the enabling change behaviour, and people who are empowered. These elements are often ignored, particularly in strategy, finance, and economics. While focusing on outcomes and how they deviate from expectations is important, what essentially drives people to take action holds the key to success.

My unexpected involvement with *Leadership and Performance* (LEAP), at Shell plc in London and The Hague, was an eye-opener. Not one to be enamoured with the "soft" aspirations, I was challenged by the assertion of Gary Steel, then Director of LEAP succeeding Mac MacDonald: *Transformation is about delivering the hard and harder goals of Shell*. It was over some reflections when I truly grasped what Gary was driving at. The hard goals were the financial and strategic objectives of Shell, which were readily measured and quantified (so one would often believe). The harder goals were embedding the human traits that drive behaviour that crystallises actions towards a common purpose. It was *harder* because it involved personal transformation that was a constant struggle. With collegial support, it required openness to receive as well as to give feedback that are both positive or negative. Given in the spirit of honesty, feedback becomes a gift for one who is intent on improving oneself and others within their spheres of influence.

Intuitively, one would suspect that corporate transformation is as much about the firm as well as the manager. In changing the firm and its culture and values, one would need to start with the people influencing its destiny. Paul Collin reflected on his experiences:

"When Chief Executives assumed their position, they aspire to leave a better place than what they found coming in. They would often articulate 'visions' that would span their full term, or the decade ahead. Circumstances, however, may conspire to cut short their tenure."

Gary Steel recalled: "When I joined ABB in 2003, Juergen Dormann was the newly appointed Chief Executive replacing Jorgen Centerman. Dormann also retained the Chairmanship of ABB. At this time the ABB group was a struggling engineering conglomerate despite having been previously held in high esteem by analysts at the City of London's financial market during the time when the charismatic Percy Barnevik was their Chief Executive. In challenging times Dormann set to work on two fundamental objectives: Operational Excellence to deliver streamlined costs thus making ABB more competitive and alignment of all employees to focus externally on customers rather than internally on my business unit.

Operational Excellence meant doing better with less by simplifying and removing work processes. Alignment required a mindset shift throughout the organization away from customisation to standardisation. Many deeply held beliefs and hobby horses had to be sacrificed and as a result, over a period of 18 months, $1.2 billion was taken out of the cost structure and, within 5 years, ABB was a thriving $40 billion revenue company. In 2006, Dormann brought in Fred Kindle as CEO whilst retaining his role as Chairman."

Paul added: "Fred Kindle followed through with the transformation programme. With more leeway to expand, Kindle faced a different challenge. Shareholders longed for ABB's former dominance in the global arena. Awash with cash, he resisted calls to aggressively acquire rivals in what he deemed as an over-inflated equity market. His adversaries won the argument, and Kindle prematurely departed on his third year as Chief Executive."

Dormann organised cohorts of early adopters comprising senior change leaders. To execute, he relied on his executive committee that included himself, his Chief Finance Officer, two business heads, and Gary Steel, his Chief Human Resources Officer. He communicated through his weekly Dormann letters, which was eventually broadened to the whole organisation. The other plank is to embed his transformation agenda through the groupwide learning and development architecture.

The agenda of Shell's LEAP and ABB's Core Values Transformation share a common approach to learning, as compared in Box Chart 4.1.1. I drew the parallels by juxtaposing the programmes against what I considered as the purpose of the training.

At Shell and ABB, we use short programmes that use consistent language and content that addressed the strategic agenda. This was not unusual given that the challenge was similar: Shell refers to their objective as *doing the most with what we have* which resonated with ABB's focus on *operational excellence* and *delighting the customer*. In common parlance, they both sought to maximise the benefits from their assets, customer relations, and making their people more productive.

To ensure consistency, similar learning programmes were adapted to their specific focus to a combined 180,000 workforce. At ABB, it was essential that external learning programmes were aligned to enhance coherence and eliminate duplications. To my horror, I discovered that there were 140 external providers of *Time Management* training with the least in coherence to what they were offering to managers. By streamlining, costs were cut while demonstrating to the ABB ranks that *Group Learning and Development* walked their talk on operational excellence.

One of the failings of corporate transformation is to assume that having a well-written "vision statement" is the key to success. For this reason, a number of firms spent an enormous amount of time aligning around a vision and mission statements. Unfortunately, without embedding the message and making the managers and people own and personalise it, the "vision and mission" gather dust while people carry on with their lives as if nothing had or will change.

How the message is communicated varies with the individual styles of the managers. In Shell, workshops and town hall meetings were the norm in engaging a broad range of people. At ABB, with the focus on operational excellence and delighting customers, the message was made considerably simpler and straightforward. As managers at the C-suite, or people at the shop floor, learn to develop a common language, alignment of purpose was facilitated in time. This multi-pronged approach was without doubt the most successful I have seen. People at ABB were in tune and made aware of the changes that are occurring and what their roles are under this unfolding change.

To shift the conversation, I recalled with Paul how the gift of feedback was embedded in learning programmes at Shell. Within large organisations, there is a tendency to become insular, particularly for those in support functions with minimal external

Bounded Possibilities   229

					Executive	ELT - Shell Executive Leadership Programme
				Senior Managers		
			General Manager		GBLP - Shell Global Business Leadership	SLDP - Senior Leadership Development Programme
		Middle Manager			MMP - Middle Management Programme	
	First Line Manager				MDP - First Line Managers Programme	
Individual Contributor						

| Shell Job Groups 6/5/4 | Shell Job Groups 4/3 | Shell Job Groups 3/2 | Shell Job Groups 1/A/B | Shell Senior Executive Group |
| ABB Grades 14/13/12 | Grades 12/11/10 | Grades 10/9/8 | Grades 7/6 | Grades 5/4/3 | Grades 2/1 |

Mentoring Programme - Mentees | Mentoring Programme - Mentors

| ABB Life/Shell Life | Manager Onboarding/Shell Coaching for Performance | HRBP | Country Manager Essentials | Action Learning/ABB Results Delivery |
| ABB Tool Box/Orientation | | | | Shell Focused Results Delivery |

Leadership Challenge Programme/Shell Leadership Challenge
ABB Leadership Competency Model/Shell Leadership Competency

Development for Advancement
Development for Performance

Box Chart 4.1.1: ABB Leadership Ladder and Shell Comparative

Source: Paul Collin.

customer interactions. How does learning offer opportunities to broaden the perspectives of future leaders?

Paul offered his insights on how ABB cooperated with other firms under the *International Consortium Programme*. Among the participants were Boeing, TATA, ABN AMRO, and ABB working with leading business schools. Each participating firm provided about five of its senior rising stars. They were assigned to teams from other firms, where they explored ways in which they would tackle various opportunities under different markets and industries.

Unconstrained by rank or hierarchy, which were made irrelevant by how the teams were formed, participants were given liberty to challenge, support, or offer alternatives to their team members or other participants. These free-flowing interactions not only produced innovative ideas but also taught participants the virtue of humility.

By learning to listen, opening oneself to be challenged, and developing the ability to acknowledge a good idea when one is offered, would take a lot of humility. For future or even present leaders, a trait often ignored is the character to nurture environments where people can flourish and develop.

In contrast, some managers have the misconception that their positions allow them to coerce or control people because they are the only font for knowledge and competence. These managers often fail, as dictators fall in time. By being unable to assimilate new ideas or innovations that run counter to their beliefs, the errors they persist in committing remained unchallenged.

As a final word, Paul added: "Issues of ego, positional power, or lack of engagement, all contribute to a failed leadership. Inability to see what may destabilize their business or themselves will also lead to failure. Stopping learning and thinking they know best will certainly lead to failure. I was often exposed to the cost cutting of HR to channel resources into the business, where the business actually didn't know better. Business results are of course critical to any organization. But well-motivated and well-developed staff will generally outperform those who are not and senior leaders must recognize this and believe and invest, if they are to succeed."

****

Gary Steel, former member of ABB Group Executive Committee, has broad-based global business experience at both non-executive and executive levels. He has focused on cultural transformation, personal leadership, and business growth, with direct managerial experiences in various markets globally. He retains a passion for all aspects of inclusive leadership.

Paul Collin was Group Vice President for Leadership and Talent Development at ABB. Previously, he held similar roles at Shell plc, UBS, and Yara International.

Box 4.2: Charles Edward Payne II

On an autumn morning, Charles Edward Payne II and I had breakfast in Sarria, a bohemian enclave in Barcelona, Spain, behind the imposing 7th century Catholic church. The church stood as a silent witness to the Black Plague, Napoleonic wars, and civil war. In happier times, artists and writers congregated in its plaza.

Charles directed operations for two *Route Clearance Patrols* in Afghanistan, shortly after West Point. His unit was tasked with eliminating threats from enemy mines, securing paths for troop movements, and reconnaissance. After serving in the US Army, he enrolled at IESE Business School, Spain to prepare for his corporate career. This is where our paths crossed.

Charles offered a different take on uncertainties. Instead of aiming to make the uncertain certain, he injects some certainty into how soldiers tackle the effects of unexpected events. This is premised on the following:

That soldiers stake their lives to accomplish their mission is a known fact. Why soldiers do this is because they trust that their comrades and commander are equipped to do the job. With confidence, they serve a higher purpose for the country and self. For this reason, in the heat of battle, commands are followed with little room for questions or debates. As Charles puts it, the *military deals with uncertainty by building certainty into how the team could respond.*

Concretely, "when a bomb explodes, it destroys a vehicle, and takes the lives of soldiers. Within the command structure, the commander knows who to call upon to act," Charles explained. To do this, the commander must "know the capabilities of their remaining team members, vehicles, and weapon systems. In this way, he can give orders to the right people to take action." The soldiers respond when each is empowered to take the place of fallen comrades to continue the fight.

Charles cited the example of his unit, the *Route Clearance Patrols*. "In the event of an explosion, my mine-detection vehicle would scan the ground around the attack site for any remaining explosives. Then, we block off the area before sending a team to rescue injured soldiers, or recover casualties. This procedure ensures that soldiers are out of harm's way and can execute their tasks speedily."

"This is where the hundreds of drill-hours make a difference. When and where the bombs would hit the unit is unknown. What is certain is the aftermath: There will be casualties. We will need to work together, and the speed of our rescue makes the difference between survival and death. With the right training, soldiers instinctively respond with objectivity to commands given under pressure."

How exactly do you train the soldiers to be battle-ready? I queried.

Charles started with how the US Army spends significant amounts of time and money preparing its officers to lead soldiers under extreme conditions. For his unit, they started with troop movements: "Our *Route Clearance Patrol* usually consisted of 8 to 10 vehicles, spaced 10 to 15 meters apart. Spread over 150 to 200 meters, effective radio communication is the primary way to unify command and provide instantaneous feedback."

To test the unit's coordination, Charles underwent a training programme within the safe confines of the National Training Centre in California, USA. Shortly after arriving, he failed his first two missions as his radio communications were stymied by technical issues. "Our performance was terrible. No one could hear my directives, and my squad leader was overwhelmed by a barrage of information."

The training was a safe environment, where mistakes could be corrected. Charles added: "What made the situation worse was a crucial personal mistake. I forgot to give the map's coordinates to our lead vehicle to reach our destination. While I assumed that we all knew where we were going, the lead vehicle took a route unknown to the driver. As a result, we got lost in the sand hills and I was thoroughly embarrassed. Although I did not want to admit it at first, eventually I came to terms with my situation. I was lost."

In battlefield conditions, this error could have added to the uncertainties. Not knowing where the unit was, it was impossible to anticipate an attack and its severity. Not knowing the terrain, the unit was unable to tell whether or not they were in hostile or friendly territory.

Returning to camp finally, Charles made a few changes to subsequent drills. His first move was to switch his position in the convoy to the Mine-resistant Ambush Protected Buffalo (MRAP Buffalo), the most protected and targeted vehicle by enemy fire. With its best communication system, it provides a front seat view to exploring for bombs. It is also the first vehicle enemies would hit to paralyze the convoy. For this reason, Charles' co-commander expressed reservation over his move.

New to the battlefield, Charles learned to appreciate what his battle-hardened soldiers could offer. Humbled by his embarrassments, he changed his approach. "I began all my mission planning by sketching out a map of the terrain and our objectives, and providing my insights. I then ask the squad leaders how they would execute their part of the mission. This is where the debates and astute questioning happen, not in the thick of battle. Through this collaborative process, I leveraged their expertise and created a sense of ownership in the mission. I was no longer telling them what to do, they were co-creating the tactics that they instinctively execute."

After perfecting the troop movements, Charles elevated the tactical capabilities of his patrols. By looking at his convoy's capabilities from the enemy's perspectives, he observed that "it allowed him to better prepare his counter-attacks should the worst happen." His thinking was guided by these questions: "Where would I place an explosive to disable the convoy? Where would I place my gunners to attack the unit while maintaining a path of escape? What vulnerabilities would I create to inflict the maximum possible damage?

Thinking like the enemy, I was hoping I could shed light on where we can be made vulnerable. This was a struggle for me. Puffed up by my success in training, I overlooked basics of operational planning and potential weaknesses of my plans. On the other hand, I am conscious that I may overestimate how much I knew of my enemies. This is where I rediscovered the value of collegial insights by eliciting my team mates' perspectives."

We have thus far covered how you evolved as an officer fit to command for battle. How do you build your unit to be battle-ready? I queried.

Charles continued: "Great soldiers are not created by coddling. They are trained under stress and held to a new set of standards. One such capability is the speed of rescue. A squad is sent to rescue an injured comrade. They are timed to an exacting target. The squad repeats the exercise by following this procedure: Initiate rescue, extract injured soldier, and transfer from damaged vehicle to ambulance. After each round, the squad assessed their performance, refine their tactics, experiment, learn, and repeat, until they perfected the routine."

To instil confidence, Charles added: "I have to demonstrate my competence of command to earn my unit's trust through sound decision-making. By demonstrating and fine-tuning my abilities in combat conditions, my soldiers knew they could count on me in real-life situations."

And, in the final analysis, how do you test that you and your unit are ready to face the enemies? I enquired.

Charles quipped: "Every organization can use small crises to see how well their systems function under stress. This complements what we learn from planning and the drills we routinely conduct. It may appear pointless but when a real crisis hits, the team's readiness is appreciated."

Clarity on how the unit is organised is essential. The US military forms a *command team* comprising the commanding officer and the sergeant. Charles described the "sergeant is the senior soldier in the platoon. His technical expertise is proven by experience. This endows the sergeant with leadership authority that empowers the person to train the soldiers." Charles added: "If you want to know how well the unit is performing, how the soldiers truly feel, the platoon sergeant would probably know better."

The *command team* possesses the "brains, motivation, and experience, that produce mission and training plans that are both aspirational and practical." Charles added: "We execute the training plan as a team. Through our 'After Action Review' (AAR), we extract what we learned, refine our tactics, and assess how we perform against specified objectives."

To provide clarity of mandate, Charles added: "Each mission has a statement which is called the *Commander's Intent*. It clarifies the overarching goal behind the mission. It is our north star in ambiguous circumstances."

On his part, Charles seeks to contribute by providing tactical and strategic guidance to his unit: "I think through the decision from the opposite party's perspective. I imagine their goals, desires, and reactions. How are they likely to react to my entering their zone of influence? What is their most desired outcome? As I envision the decision from this standpoint, I am better prepared to conduct operational planning with my team."

I posed this question to Charles: How would you extricate your unit from an error of judgement or situations you were unprepared for?

Charles recalled when he was lost in the Californian desert. Reluctant to admit his error, he finally harnessed enough humility to own up to his mistakes: "I stopped, accepted, and acknowledged the mistake. After acknowledging the situation, I began to gather our resources to return to the last known safe-point. This retreat may set us back temporarily, but it is better than hiding the mistake to assuage my ego. In combat, such pride may endanger the patrol."

In engaging others, it "helps to (a) have ideas of possible solutions, (b) take ownership of the mistake, even if it was committed by one of your soldiers, and (c) begin taking appropriate actions to mitigate the damage as soon as possible," Charles concluded.

To wrap up, in taking up his post-MBA role at AB InBev, I asked Charles what lessons he would bring to his managerial life. Without hesitation, he cited the following:

1. Never take the people you work with for granted

"I will never forget the day I yelled at one of my mine-detection vehicle drivers ('Husky') for making a mistake. My First Sergeant pulled me aside and said, 'Lieutenant, if you ever yell at a private like that again on the radio, I'm going to call you out the next time you make a stupid decision. And you are not going to like it'."

At first, I was shocked. Then, I saw the error of my ways. Did I think about how exhausting that job was when I yelled at him? Did I think about how stressful that role was, searching for bombs?

No. I didn't. Belatedly, I forgot that the person I yelled at was a twenty years old soldier. He carried the patrol's fate on his shoulders, without fully comprehending the gravity of his position. More importantly, I appreciated the courage and care of my First Sergeant for giving me the gift of feedback."

2. Keep it simple but do not forget the details

"*Keep it simple, stupid* is a way to *kiss* confusion good bye. Simple ideas are powerful. Simplicity often requires a deep level of understanding. Most importantly, simple means that people will be able to receive, ponder, or act on the information I am providing. If an idea is too complicated, it does not matter how smart I am or what my rank is, I will lose my audience and my ability to influence people. In the process of simplifying, pay attention to details such as the map's coordinates or weapons checks."

3. "Hard decisions, easy life" or vice versa

Quoting Olympian Jerzy Gregorek, these choices underpin *we train even when it rains*. "I recalled a rainy day in West Point. As squad leader, I had to train new cadets on military movements that involved crawling in the mud under barbed wire. Since the task was optional, the cadets were reluctant to soil their fresh uniforms. Cadet Michael J Thury was the exception. Hesitantly, I said: 'You know what Thury, let us do this'. Before long, the whole squad crawled, burst into laughter, got trained, and had a blast from a miserable situation.

That mud was the same feeling I encountered at AB InBev, when I crawl in negative customer feedback, struggle to gain insights from data, or take time to talk to and understand my co-workers. Get your boots dirty. These are the hard work that inform sound decisions. I realised that the shortest route to getting results is to get it right the first time around. This comes with preparedness, competence, and empowerment of people."

****

As Charles and I continued our correspondence, I expressed this sentiment: Did the US Army lose a potential Chief of Staff or did business gain a Chief Executive in waiting? True to form, Charles responded: "I simply aim to contribute the best I can wherever life brings me. I trust my transition to business would encourage other veterans to take the leap. They could bring their experience to the commercial world."

****

Charles Edward Payne II graduated from West Point Military Academy and obtained his MBA from IESE Business School, Spain. He is a third-generation US military veteran. As an army officer, Charles served as Operations Director for a route-side bomb detection company. After his service, he was a non-profit team leader where he discovered business as a vehicle for social good. Charles lives in Europe and works for AB InBev, the world's largest brewer, where he is Head, Commercial Operations for Expansion, Middle East, and Retail Travel.

Bibliography

Adinoyi, M. and Syed A. M. Said (2013). Effect of dust accumulation on the power outputs of solar photovoltaic modules. *Renewable Energy*, 60, 633–636, December 2013.

Aghina, W., de Smet, A., Murarka, M., and Collins, L. (2015). The keys to organisational agility. McKinsey & Company, December 2015.

Arsenio, W. F. (2008). Psychological limits of economic rationality: Relational contexts and cognitive irrationality. *Human Development*, 51, 268–273.

Badaracco, J. L. Jr. and Ellsworth, R. R. (1989). *Leadership and the Quest for Integrity*. Boston, MA: Harvard Business School Press.

Bell, J., Poushter, J., Fagan, M., and Huang, C. (2021). In response to climate change, citizens in advanced economies are willing to alter how they live and work: Many doubt success of international efforts to reduce global warming. *Pew Research Center*, September 14, 2021.

Bunting, M. (2016). Honesty: The single most important leadership value. *CEO Magazine*, March 4, 2016.

Cambridge English Dictionary (2020). Definition of uncertainty, August 26, 2020. https://dictionary.cambridge.org/us/dictionary/english/uncertainty. Accessed on August 30, 2020.

Coren, M. J. (2019). This is why oil companies and utilities are buying into renewables. *World Economic Forum*, February 15, 2019.

Davenport, T. H. (2019). When to stop deliberating and just make a decision. *Harvard Business Review*, July 9, 2019.

Dosi, G., Freeman, C., Nelson, R., Silverberg, G., and Soete, L. (eds.) (1988). *Technical Change and Economic Theory*. London: Pinter.

Dror, Y. (2017). *Public Policymanking Reexamined*. London: Taylor and Francis.

Fehrenbader, K. (2015). Why the Solyndra mistake is still important to remember. *Fortune*, August 27, 2015.

Fox, Craig R., and Amos Tversky (1995). Ambiguity aversion and comparative ignorance. *Quarterly Journal Econometrics*, 110 (3), 585–603.

Funk, C., and Kennedy, B. (2020). How Americans see climate change and the environment in 7 charts. *Pew Research Center*, April 21, 2020. https://www.pewresearch.org/fact-tank/2020/04/21/how-americans-see-climate-change-and-the-environment-in-7-charts/.

Heath, C. and Tversky, A. (1991). Preference and belief: Ambiguity and competence in choice under uncertainties. *Journal of Risk and Uncertainty*, 4(1), 5–28.

Herrera-Estrada, J. E., Diffenbaugh, N. S., Wagner, F., Craft, A., and Sheffield, J. (2018). Response of electricity sector air pollution emissions to drought conditions in the western United States. *Environmental Research Letters*, 13(12), 1–10.

Hertwig, R., Barron, G., Weber, E. U., and Erev, I. (2004). Decisions from experience and the effect of rare events. *Psychological Science*, 15(8), 534–539.

Hirst, P. and Zeitlin, J. (1991). Flexible specialisation vs post-Fordism: Theory, evidence and policy implications. *Economy and Society*, 20(1), 2–56, February 1991.

Hodgson, G. M. (2012). On the limits of rational choice theory. *Economic Thought*, 1, 94–108.

Hoium, T. (2017). Bankruptcies continue in solar industry. *The Motley Fool*, May 19, 2017.

Holland, B. (2016). Enforceability of take-or-pay provisions in English law contracts — Resolved. *Journal of Energy & Natural Resources Law*, 2016, 1–11.

IRENA (2012). Renewable energy technologies: Cost analysis series. IRENA Working Paper, 1(5/5), 1–64.

IRENA (2019). *Renewable Energy Auctions: Status and Trends Beyond Price*. Abu Dhabi: International Renewable Energy Agency.

Julio, B. and Yook, Y. (2016). Policy uncertainty, irreversibility, and cross border flows of capital. *Journal of International Economics*, 103, 13–26.

Khanna, D. (2020). COVID-19 Energy: Pandemic-hit LNG supply contracts — Rights, remedies and price-re-openers. *Clyde & Co.*, April 24, 2020.

Kim, S. D. (2012). Characterising unknown unknowns. Paper presented at Project Management Institute Global Congress 2012 — North America, Vancouver, British Columbia, Canada.

Knight, F. H. (1921). *Risk, Uncertainty, and Profit*. Boston, MA: Houghton Mifflin Company.

Lacey, S. (2014). Germany's biggest utility, E.ON, is divesting fully from centralised power plants. *gtm*, December 1, 2014.

Medina, J. M. (1991). The take-or-pay wars: A cautionary analysis for the future, 27 *Tulsa Law Journal*, 27(2), 283–312.

NRF (2015). Oil price volatility: 10 points to consider when facing termination or renegotiation of a contract. *Norton Rose Fulbright*, September 2015.

Oxford Learner's Dictionary (2020). Definition of risk. https://www.oxfordlearnersdictionaries.com/us/definition/english/risk_1. Accessed on August 30, 2020.

Park, F.K., and Shapira, Z. (2017). Risk and uncertainty . In *The Palgrave Encyclopedia of Strategic Management*. Augier, M., and Teece, D.J. (eds.), London: Palgrave Macmillan.

Puko, T. and Randles, J. (2020). Energy department poised to lose up to $225 million on solar project bankruptcy. *Wall Street Journal*, July 30, 2020.

Reuters (2015). E.ON agrees 1 billion pound sale of North Sea assets to Fridman. *Reuters*, October 14, 2015.

Russell Reynolds (2016). Leadership squared: The power of industry-leading CFO — CEO relationships. https://www.russellreynolds.com/insights/thought-leadership/leadership-squared-the-power-of-industry-leading-cfo-ceo-relationships. Accessed on August 29, 2020.

RWE (2014). RWE entered into an agreement to sell RWE Dea. *RWE Press Release*, March 16, 2014.

Savage, L. J. (1954). *The Foundations of Statistics*. New York: John Wiley.

Scott, J. (2000). Rational choice theory. In *Understanding Contemporary Society, Theories of the Present*, Browning, G., Halcli, A., and Webster, F. (eds.), London: SAGE Publications.

Simons, T. (2008). *The Integrity Dividend: Leading by the Power of Your Word*. San Francisco, CA: Jossey — Bass.

Teece, D., Peteraf, M., and Leth, S. (2016). Dynamic capabilities and organisational agility. *California Management Review*, 58(4), 13–35.

Thaler, R. H. and Sunstein, C. R. (2008). *NUDGE: Improving Decisions About Health, Wealth, and Happiness*. Newhaven and London: Yale University Press.

Ülkümen, G., Fox, C. R., and Malle, B. F. (2016). Two dimensions of subjective uncertainty: Clues from natural language. *Journal of Experimental Psychology: General*, 145(10), 1280–1297.

Ungemach, C., Chater, N., and Stewart, N. (2009). Are probabilities over-weighted or under-weighted when rare outcomes are experienced (rarely)? *Psychological Science*, 20(4), 473–479.

Vestringhe, M. (1992). Obituary: Professor Harry Hansen. *Independent*, August 14, 1992. https://www.independent.co.uk/news/people/obituary-professor-harry-hansen-1540386.html.

Walton, R. (2019). PSEG on track to reduce emissions 80%, will divest all remaining coal interests. *Utility Dive*, July 25, 2019.

Zaremba, H. (2020). US solar industry wants government bailout as Bankruptcies Loom. *OilPrice.com*, March 30, 2020.

Chapter 5
Calibrate

To succeed financially, managers learn to adapt and pivot to an evolving market with uncertain payoffs that demand agility. However, risk-averse managers shun taking risks to avoid mistakes or incurring losses. This risk aversion inadvertently could lead to inaction. The causes lie in human biases and the methods managers used to evaluate investments. By ignoring how *humans* actually decide, managers misdiagnose the firm's value by ignoring how managerial flexibility and the actions of rival firms alter competitive advantages. To partly remedy this, managers could better calibrate their investments' value by funnelling their pipeline of prospects to convert tangible (or actionable) opportunities. By clustering prospects, financial tools are deployed to match against the appropriate contexts of the decisions. Through this structured thought process, managers can harness the diversity of human capabilities and pursue profitable solutions under ambiguities. This becomes feasible when managers can better align their business pursuits with a purpose rather than profit from problems that business helps to create.

1
Introduction

After a few rounds of conversations, managers would have landed on some understanding of their firms' ***purpose*** and the uncertainties that they are confronted with. At this stage, it is well recognised that dynamic markets are inherently volatile and fraught with complexities. However, when managers turn intents into actions, they reflexively yearn for *the* predictable outcome.

Almost by instinct, managers would rather "get the numbers right," with the expected cash flows laid out neatly as "accurately as possible." The "gut feel" takes precedence when "accuracy" is judged as "feeling about right," which is achieved after iteratively estimating a "right answer." The strategic insights inadvertently are consigned to the back burner. This evaluation process clearly is problematic: Why "calibrate" when the answers are already predetermined?

Managers err into thinking that getting to *the* answer is their ultimate objective no matter what. On the contrary, by knowing how managers exercise their options and how these actions could influence outcomes, managers can improve the odds of successfully navigating through uncertain terrains. Here's how:

In an open-ended investment process, managers set out to seek some answers and identify the conditions under which an opportunity could work or the circumstances which could make it fail. Throughout an iterative process, assumptions are tested and various hypotheses are experimented and validated or discarded. With each iteration, managers deepen their understanding, and with the learning, the investment proposition is continually improved.

Managers, as Avinash K Dixit and Barry J Nalebuff (1991) contend,[1] often behave like a woodcutter when evaluating their investments. Managers assume that they operate in the woods as an allusion to markets. They chop wood and chop more until they maximise their pile of firewood. Ignoring competing claims, managers deem as "irrelevant" how people could react and respond in kind to their actions.

In operating under markets with real people, to succeed, managers would need the acumen of a wise and lucky general (with apologies to Napoleon Bonaparte).

---

[1] Chapter 10 goes deeper into applying these analogies to business and investment evaluation.

Imagine a general who aims to cut down an opposing army. The opposing side will not stand still (like a tree). They will fight back, outmanoeuvre to frustrate the general's moves, or scatter to inflict a thousand wounds on a superior force.

The Vietnamese army may have a lesson or two for managers. Through persistence, they caused the French colonial power to withdraw, with the Americans following suit decades later. The Vietnamese also repelled a superior Chinese army from crossing past their border.

In business, as in one's personal life, humans interact and respond to the actions of others. They lead, follow, cooperate, or compete, as appropriate. Underlying these actions, human qualities such as integrity, openness, and sincerity build trust that influences how humans choose to relate to one another. Consequently, humans form a judgement by following reason, complete with their biases.

In recognising human judgement as the core of decision-making, calibrating value and how this expected outcome is monetised would take a different turn. A decision no longer relies entirely on what the prescribed rules that financial models dictate. It encompasses a coalition of views and some resolution, albeit partial, of what unites people rather than what divides them. For this reason, managers would seek to understand what matters to people who are affected by a given decision or policy.

Without this ability to engage, managers would find that at the root of many conflicts, "communication failures and cultural misunderstandings" could prevent people from framing a common understanding of the problem (Schein, 1993).

How do people avoid being trapped, where they end up working at cross-purposes?

A feasible answer may lie in understanding how humans think prior to taking action. Intuitively, some managers may take a quick look, decide, and rely on their guts to screen opportunities. Others may take longer and employ a more deliberate approach to selecting the opportunities they wish to support.

In either case, managers are asked to simultaneously process opposing traits, set up criteria (albeit implicitly for some), and pick a winner. Unnerved by this prospect, "ordinary mortals" may see this trait as reserved for the truly gifted managers who are beyond their reach. But how exclusive is this club? I would wonder. The answer is hidden in plain sight.

Roger L Martin (2007) asserts this much: "We were born with opposable minds, which allow us to hold two conflicting ideas in constructive, almost dialectic tension.

We can use that tension to think our way towards new, superior ideas." In contrast, if the human mind can only deal with one idea at a time, its ability to compare and contrast is non-existent.

Anticipating the unasked question, Martin reflected: "Why is this potentially powerful but generally latent tool used so infrequently and to less than full advantage? Because putting it to work makes us anxious. Most of us avoid complexity and ambiguity and seek out the comfort of simplicity and clarity. To cope with the dizzying complexity of the world around us, we simplify where we can. We crave the certainty of choosing between well-defined alternatives and the closure that comes when a decision has been made."

Martin's assertions remain eerily familiar more than a decade after they were proposed. Under a transitioning energy market, the complexity calls for reframing how managers could harness the creative power of people. This starts with a recognition that the artifice of strategic insights and wisdom is no longer the exclusive domain of the highly gifted individuals. In this complex world, a financial whiz may prove inadequate to develop the technology to harness the energy of the future. In a similar way, a narrowly focused specialist may lose sight of the broad arrays of strategic alternatives or opportunities. To complicate matters more, an opportunity for one firm may prove to be someone's path to downfall — a question that managers often fail to ask themselves: *Who is the natural owner of such an opportunity?*

To bring together a wide array of capabilities, a structured and integrative approach such as a funnel process may be more conducive to creating a supportive decision-making ecosystem. To improve the odds of flourishing under ambiguous conditions, prospects are funnelled to select a set of opportunities to pursue. By clustering the prospects and creating the ground rules for accessing resources, the diverse capabilities are brought to bear, to mature, defer, or discard prospects according to specified criteria. By design, rather than by accident, opposing ideas coexist within a team where managers of varying expertise cocreate pathways to monetising a business idea.

In this chapter, I examine how human biases could be explicitly recognised and incorporated into calibrating the competing opportunities. With humans recognised as the decision-makers, a funnelling process is reframed to consider the interacting actions of the firms and their ambiguities rather than ignore them. As a result, managers could use the funnelling process to inform how to calibrate and examine the dynamic shifts in an investment's value under conditions of uncertainties.

2
Harnessing the Creative Power of Humans

F. Scott Fitzgerald describes exceptional leaders to possess the "ability to hold two opposing ideas in a mind at the same time and still retain the ability to function" (Martin, 2007).

In a modern firm (or policy circle), there is no shortage of highly gifted individuals. However, there is also no shortage of successful firms that failed in the hands of highly gifted managers. Chris Argyris (2008) attributes such failures to an inability to learn as an organisation. Specifically:

> Consider the automation of temperature control. People believe that 20°C is an ideal room temperature to enhance productivity. In winter, when the temperature falls below 20°C, the system would turn on the heater automatically. In the tropics, the air conditioning turns on when it gets too hot (e.g. above 20°C). Arguably, the benefits would be significant from such a system, assuming that the convenience and the enhanced productivity could be monetised.
>
> A cluster of managers, employing *single loop learning*, would narrowly focus on identifying and correcting errors ascribed to the external environment. They are likely to tinker with the sensitivity of the sensors to trigger the switches for the heater (or air conditioning). In single-mindedly pursuing perfection, managers would aim to hone their tools with precision.
>
> Another cluster, applying *double loop learning*, would introspectively reflect critically on how their behaviour and methods are inadvertently contributing to the problems of the organisation. What they learn from these reflections is used to inform how they could change and act differently to resolve the problems worth addressing. Instead of honing their tools, they would most likely question why 20°C should be set as the ideal. What would deviations from this ideal lead to as an outcome?

The consequences of these divergent thought processes are radically different when managers formulate their strategic decisions under dynamic conditions. Here's how:

Single loop learning moves managers to reinforce the status quo. In pushing for perfection, extant processes are improved by enhancing the precision of outcomes. In investment evaluation, value is optimised when the payoffs are predictable (and stable). Deeply invested in extant processes, managers would be inclined to stick it out rather than change, which may lay to waste years of cumulative experiences.

In contrast, *double loop learning* encourages managers to explore alternative futures. Discovery is an exciting adventure that pumps the adrenaline. Managers thrive in an ecosystem where dialectic tensions are harnessed to create and select exceptional opportunities (Terwiesch and Ulrich, 2009).

In such an open-ended process, the outcome is ambiguous, which causes discomfort to some managers. Instead of rushing headlong to adopt a funnel process, managers would first have to learn how to deal with human biases and the decision traps that they lay for managers. Then and only then could any structured funnelling of prospects to opportunities meaningfully achieve its objective of selecting the gem among the dirt.

2.1 How managers fall into decision traps

Behavioural economics contrasts with the rational behaviour that the classical theory espouses. In practice, managers are supposed to behave rationally as "cold-blooded optimisers," as Richard H Thaler (2015) described according to the classicists' notion of economic agents. Under this rationalist notion, the classical theory struggles to dismiss empirical evidence that suggests humans may not always be as *rational* when they decide to invest. For instance, if a valuation is premised on established science, where outcomes are replicated with consistency, how would one explain people's penchant to repeat similar mistakes?

After each economic disruption, there is no shortage of prescribed solutions to avoid repeating the pain. However, Thaler noted that we continue to experience a "series of booms, bubbles, and crashes we have observed in financial markets beginning on October 19, 1987, a day when stock prices fell more than 20% all around the world in the absence of any substantive bad news. This was followed by a bubble and crash in technology stocks that quickly turned into a bubble in house prices, which in turn, when popped, caused a global financial crisis."

Just as economics "was raised to a pinnacle of influence which it now rests," Thaler added, "critiques over the years have been brushed aside with a gauntlet of poor excuses and implausible alternative explanations of embarrassing empirical evidence." Finance suffers from a similar fate when it encourages managers to opt to elevate net present value (NPV),[2] at least judging by its popular usage, as a "gold standard" (of sort) in investment evaluation.

John S Hammond *et al.* (2006) assert that some of the pitfalls managers fall into include their "tendencies to stick with the status quo, to look for evidence confirming one's preferences, and to throw good money after bad because it is hard to admit *having made* a mistake." A broader examination of how human biases, according to Hammond and his co-authors, influence managerial decisions is outlined in Chart 5.1.

In *framing* a problem, the obvious is often taken as the problem worthy of solving. In one of my economics lectures in Southeast Asia, I used an irrigation project as one of the many ways to boost farm productivity. Not surprisingly, the graduate students jumped straight into a conversation about the width of the canals, the size of the pumps, and the problem with water sources.

Realising that the students behaved in *single loop learning* mode, I turned around and asked: Why do you need an irrigation system when water is scarce?

After recovering from an initial surprise, the students quickly realised that enhancing farm productivity in water-scarce areas is the problem that they need to address. With a simple reframing, the class of highly talented economists cast their net wider. Drip irrigation was seen as a feasible alternative. At a fraction of the costs, and with a significant boost in productivity, the students applied *double loop learning* without even being conscious about it.

The ***status quo trap*** displays the managers' predisposition to perpetuate extant systems or ways of doing things. By following *single loop learning*, the damage it inflicts is there for all to see. Farm productivity was always associated with irrigation systems. Framed in this way, the solution has to be more canals and dams, with water sources becoming an afterthought!

---

[2] As described in Chapter 8, this is the difference between the present values of the expected payoffs (or cash flows) and the capital expenditure. In a transactional perspective, managers pay by committing to spend (e.g. capital expenditure or capex for short), with the expectation of appropriating the expected payoffs, which is fraught with uncertain outcomes.

Dynamic Decisions

	Type of Decision Trap	What Is It?	How It Influences Actions?	Possible Remedies
1	Framing	Articulating the problem that one is trying to solve.	The default choice is often chosen.	Test against different default choices or problem definition.
2	Status Quo	Preference for existing conditions. "If the clock is not broken, do not fix it"	Resist change, defend extant strategy or structures.	Connect actions to purpose. Assess implications of inaction.
3	Anchoring	The first data or information is assumed as the correct starting point.	Project future linearly, and use sensitivity analysis to ascertain range of variations of outcomes.	Use different starting points, or scenarios, instead of sensitivity analysis.
4	Sunk Cost	Justify past actions or errors.	Good money chasing bad investment.	Get views of those not involved in original decision or policy.
5	Confirming Evidence	Limit evidence to those who took similar actions to justify own decision.	By listening to one's echo chamber, mistakes are repeated and spread among "like-minded people".	Listen honestly to opposing arguments. Weigh with an open mind the merits of alternative actions.
6	Estimating/Forecasting	Placing confidence in what was estimated as what will be the outcome. This could result in the following traps: • Over-confidence • Over-prudence • Recallability	Over-confident manager spotentially ignore adverse events, or exposure to excessive risks. Over-cautious managers may miss growth opportunities, or over-provide for contingencies. Project the present to the future as a linear progression.	Examine opposing or contrasting scenarios. Make assumptions and assessment of probabilities explicit. Focus on what to do under each scenario, rather than on making forecasts accurate to the last decimal point.

Chart 5.1: Human Biases and Possible Remedies

Source: Adapted from Hammond *et al.* (2006) and Thaler and Sunstein (2008).

Investments in intermittent renewable energy are evaluated as if they confer the certainty of volumes that coal- or gas-fired power generators could provide. Combine this with what NPV prescribes, where predictable cash flows are worth more, managers build their financial models around long-term power purchase agreements (PPAs) that fix prices and volumes. As they crunch their numbers, a range of returns are estimated. An academic proudly proclaimed:

After a massive drop in costs, photovoltaic power (PVT_M) earns between 8% and 12% internal rate of return (IRR). At this rate, with low interest rates, PVT_M is a steal. Why are you not jumping into the opportunity?

I queried: Why are these numbers relevant? After a period of silence, the academic said in a low voice: It is financially attractive, is it not?

I illustrated how the IRRs could be negative or barely turning positive with a few changes in assumptions. Further, I surmised that by fixing contract prices today, while future PVT_M costs continue to fall, today's contract would prove exorbitant. With increasing pressure to cut prices or eliminate subsidies, falling revenues would make the high IRRs elusive.

In disbelief, the academic nodded. With a worried look, the academic heaved a sigh — I will stick to NPV and IRR. It is *known to me* and *looks about right*.

Anchoring is described by Thaler and Sunstein (2008) as "starting with some number you know (or guessed) and adjust in the direction you think is appropriate. The bias occurs because the adjustments are typically insufficient."

When asked how far oil and gas prices I expect to fall (or rise), I'm inclined to come clean. It could be higher or lower than today's prices. However, this is not a useful question, with the answer equally being of limited value. What matters is what one will do under different price scenarios. With forecasters often wide off the mark, betting the farm on the forecast outcome may prove to be costly.

Sunk costs trap managers into "making choices that justify past choices, even when the past choices no longer seem valid" (Hammond *et al.*, 2006). For capital-intensive investments, cost overrun is a common feature. The culprits are plenty, such as cost inflation, faulty designs, reworks, and delays, but it is seldom the managers' errors, one would conveniently assert.

The responses of managers are almost predictable. Instead of reassessing cost overruns, particularly as to its effects on the investment's continued viability, more cash is disbursed to "correct" the deviations. Unless the roots of cost overruns are well understood, solving the problem with more money is like throwing good money after bad.

Prior to falling into the sunk costs trap, managers fall into the ***confirming evidence*** trap that precedes it. In a number of instances, managers recruit like-minded people to work for them. With people thinking alike, one would assume that alignment is facilitated that enables efficient decision-making. Without much opposing views, the team could focus on getting the job done. However, what that job is or how desirable the outcomes are is not made explicit.

At this stage, one can recall Chris Argyris's example of how a team would work perfectly with precision to maintain an ideal room temperature of 20°C. Without anyone challenging this objective, the team precludes the possibility that they can be dead wrong. Within the echo chamber of like-minded people, one could walk straight off the precipice.

Most decision traps converge towards compounding ***estimating and forecasting*** errors. In *anchoring* revenues and costs to today's prices, future cash flows are escalated linearly, assuming the *status quo* remains true two decades hence. However, if and when energy markets transition, today's *status quo* may prove to be of little relevance to a radically different future. Yet, managers would continue to project from today's realities that are likely to be irrelevant for the future.

2.2 Improving the managers' odds at succeeding

Short of relegating, and perhaps even centralising, decision-making to the wisdom of a singularly intelligent individual (a "charismatic leader"), a collaborative approach is a viable alternative. While offering no guarantees, the odds are significantly improved for achieving desired outcomes when the creative power of humans is harnessed. Specifically:

1. In vying for resources, proponents undergo a process of challenges and tests that often sharpen how the opportunity is seen, surface the decision traps, and ultimately improve how the opportunity is defined and understood.
2. Teams experiment prior to fully committing to pathways and integrate opportunities into the business' portfolio of assets.

In maturing prospects as a gradual build-up, ideas can be tested as a pilot (or experiment) on a small scale. With minimal commitments, several ideas are allowed to fail (and fail fast) or lay their claim on resources after some prospect for success is demonstrated. This competitive process is akin to a tournament (Terwiesch and Ulrich, 2009).

That resources are limited may appear obvious, at least in theory. However, in the thick of staking a claim, managers may be blindsided into thinking that theirs is the obvious and "must-do" investment. Paradoxically, the slack in financial discipline is more pronounced when capital and human resources appear to be in abundance.

Firms with copious money at times err in believing that their capacity to pursue investment prospects is unbounded. Prospects are expectations of future events occurring. In an investment context, a prospect is an unpolished idea subject to many unknowns. Just like a raw stone, it needs to be polished to reveal the gem that it is in order to verify its value (or lack of). The value of any gems, as people in the trade would be keen to point out, depends on how it is cut. Applied to investing, an idea could be polished to show its brilliance by refining its premises and establishing its relevance and how it could contribute to delivering the firm's purpose and strategy.

Clearly, not all brilliant ideas would be relevant to the firm. In pivoting to a low carbon future, the best idea to make a horse whip may be interesting but of little relevance to the firm's strategy. For this reason, pursuing ***all*** prospects with the firm's full resource commitment is not only imprudent but also reckless.

The prospects that hurdle the first barrier — relevance — are matured into potential opportunities to invest. In orchestrating the resources, ideas are structured so that the circumstances are created to enable managers to do something with the idea (or prospect). These circumstances involve ascertaining when to move, stall, or commit and take action. In this contingent decision, managers no longer see investment as a "now or never" proposition. Instead, commitments could be altered, at some costs, to avert losses or accelerate to gain strategic advantages.

By incorporating this decision-making approach to funnelling prospects to opportunities, managers treat an investment as an option that gives a right to commit, but not as an obligation to proceed, subject to how markets are expected to evolve (Dixit and Pindyck, 1994). Here's how this approach differs from conventional capital budgeting:

To commit to an investment, immediate costs are incurred with an expectation of earning a future return. This is a notion shared by the policy when public expenditures are evaluated on their social cost–benefit (Florio, 2014). With limited flexibility to alter or correct prior commitments, any deviations would result in a loss or excess gains in relation to what was assumed.

Managers are given the flexibility to alter the course because investments seldom deliver *exactly* according to the plan. If by altering a prior commitment, excess value accrues, then there is value in adapting to the market's evolving circumstances. The ability to defer, accelerate, or abort an investment is valued using real options reasoning.

Managers may make a mistake, as they often do. A technological breakthrough may render an asset or system obsolete. A pandemic could turn an industry, or economies, upside down. In response, would closing a business, or aborting a prior commitment, qualify as investing?

Avinash K Dixit and Robert S Pindyck (1994) would argue it is, albeit causing some managers to look bewildered. In applying real options reasoning, when one closes a failing business, owners (or shareholders) incur the immediate costs of extracting themselves from any contractual commitments. Among these immediate expenses are severance pay, winding down costs, and what are owed to third parties. The "rewards" are to avoid future losses and continuing claims to conserve the owners' patrimony (or whatever is left to start anew).

To invest in energy, the immediate costs are lumpy and often irreversible. A way to execute such a commitment is to start with small expenditures, such as doing a pilot project, before scaling up. This allows managers to experiment, test, reframe, scale, or defer, which are all subject to relevant information becoming available. In this way, losses are minimised if expectations prove to be overly optimistic (or unrealistic) as to warrant aborting the investment. In contrast, the pace could be accelerated when there is managerial flexibility to respond to robust markets.

Human imperfections subject managers to errors and biases. Failing to recognise this, managers single-mindedly pursue a *right and narrow path* that disregards the uncertainties around outcomes. Two contrasting approaches may result:

1. Risk aversion is a virtue that managers equate to preserving the firms' asset values (at times mistaken for accounting costs) by avoiding incurring losses. With loss avoidance as the paramount objective, inaction follows, which inadvertently forego new (and seen as risky) opportunities.
2. Risk-taking is seen by some managers as essential to growing or pivoting away from the obsolescing business. They see errors as learning opportunities, hence the mantra — "fail fast and sooner."

In its purest form, each approach could have dire consequences for the firms' continued viability. Dismissed for being overly cautious, risk-averse managers may err in producing the best horse whip in the age of cars. The overly confident risk taker may only see the blue sky, ignoring that they too could underperform. In brushing failures as learning opportunities, the risk taker may inadvertently morph into a perpetual learner.

In persisting with the known and familiar, a transitioning energy market poses imminent risks when managers fail to recognise how markets are changing. Two types of decision errors occur:

1. *Error of omission* ensues when managers ignore the effects of volatilities and the unknowns by conveniently assuming them away. A dynamic market does not become stable because managers imagined them to be through their financial or economic models.
2. *Error of commission* happens when managers knowingly commit to rigid obligations that have no way of being known *a priori*. A contract that fixes prices or volumes, while the market is inherently volatile, could only burden one party to benefit another, a distortion that is only corrected by continual renegotiations or defaults.

A deeper question is left unasked. With the best intentions of managers, the apparent trade-offs are seldom made too explicit or could come only as an afterthought. For example, the pressure of meeting short-term earnings targets could blur the priorities of managers. When rewards favour meeting (or surpassing) targets, managers may pursue actions that come at the expense of strategies designed for the long term (Sneader *et al.*, 2020).

3
Ecosystem for Prioritising Opportunities

One of the strategies designed for sustained value creation is to invest in opportunities that can be made exceptional. This is easier said than done. Out of the many prospects, or business ideas, only a handful could build the foundation for today's prosperity and tomorrow's viability.

To convert a collection of raw prospects into actionable opportunities, firms would draw from a collection of competing prospects to create a pipeline. In identifying the prospects, managers would often realise that the opportunities are at different levels of maturity. Some are simple ideas, holding out some promise. Others are more advanced and could be ready for further development.

Within this diverse pipeline, a tournament process funnels the prospects through a series of filters (or decision gates). At each stage, a winnowing process narrows the opportunities that will be allocated resources by dropping the less promising prospects (Terwiesch and Ulrich, 2009). As in any tournament, some rules and criteria are adhered to by the players and umpires to provide the bases for advancement. Generically, the following may serve as bases for calibrating opportunities:

Validity of the opportunity defines its fit with the firm's purpose, which in turn defines the conduct that a modern corporation expects its managers to adhere to (Mayer, 2013). In pursuing this coherence, investments seek, in Mayer's view, to offer "profitable solutions, not profiting from a problem."

Clarity of a business case for commitment, where pathways to the desired outcome(s) can be articulated, and as necessary, calibrated with explicit recognition of the opportunities' risks (or uncertainties).

Delivery involves an explicit process for allocating and mobilising resources, including partnering and financing options, for achieving specified objectives.

Operationally, calibration involves how managers would organise the process of valuing prospects. On acceptance, how these prospects are converted into opportunities, hence scaling up the commitment and resourcing, would form part of the rules and criteria for the tournament. Specifically:

Investment funnel organises the pipeline of prospects and clusters them into stages of evaluation, subject to peer challenge. This is the "ground" under which the tournament is conducted.

Matching of tools to evaluate prospects to simplify the calibration of their strategic fit, and how such prospects could impact the firm's value as a portfolio of opportunities. The tools are selected and matched to the stage of play in the tournament.

Stress testing and experimentation is a process of validating or debunking what works, or what does not, and why. This is an iterative process underpinned by competitive challenges to establish the prospect's robustness. Prior to engaging rivals in a tournament, the prospect may test various ways to outdo an adversary or validate the virtue of collaborating with rivals or peers.

In each of these processes, managers often fall into decision traps when they ignore a basic fact. Humans are the ones making the decisions, who are creatures of habit that can be brilliant albeit imperfect, even irrational at times. This contradiction is observed as dichotomies in human actions by Thaler and Sunstein (2008) that affect the best of the human race. Specifically:

"The workings of the human brain are more than a bit befuddling. How can we be so ingenious in some tasks, and so clueless at others? How can people be simultaneously so smart and so dumb? Many psychologists and neuroscientists have been converging on a description of the brain's functioning that helps us to make sense of these seeming contradictions. The approach involves a distinction between two kinds of thinking, one that is intuitive automatic, and another that is reflective and rational."

These human realities are what managers need to recognise and take into account when aiming to harness the best from their teams. One way this could be satisfied is to design a funnelling process that is human-centric.

3.1 A prospects-to-opportunities funnel

When humans are seen to drive the decisions, an investment funnel can be made as dynamic as people are prepared to subject their ideas to external challenges. This becomes a process of discovery where human judgement is juxtaposed against the rigour of financial analyses.

There is no singular funnelling process that works perfectly all the time for all managers and all firms. This is bad news to managers who may pin their hopes that somehow automation and machines would become "intelligent" enough to do the job. With machines taking over, humans may be spared the boredom of sifting through multitudes of data on each prospect. With machines "objectively" ranking the prospects, the politics around selecting, and then justifying those choices, could be avoided. At least, this is what some managers would (erroneously) believe.

Going back to Richard H Thaler and Cass R Sunstein (2008), humans are prone to make decisions relying on their gut feel. In a series of cognitive tests, while gut feel may be accurate at times, it could prove wrong in many instances. In a decision-making context, a manager may feel in their guts that committing to an opportunity is the right thing. Without pausing to validate, disbursing a sizeable sum to build a solar farm must be the right move because it feels right. After all, media reports extol the sun's virtues as a clean source of energy that has become affordable.

Finance, often criticised for being cautious to a fault, would tend to pause and do the sums to verify the claims of proponents. The human brain, in Thaler and Sunstein's proposition, is said to operate in a deliberate and reflective mode. They take time to quantify, and instead of taking heed from their guts, they default to what their analytical tools would prescribe.

These divergent approaches would need a common ground where opposing views could be considered and possibly reconciled. On its own, each mode of thinking and the decision approach that follows are problematic. Specifically:

In following their guts, humans are susceptible to letting their biases rule the way they decide. With a superficial or feeble attempt to validate, managers are in for some big surprises when outcomes deviate from what their guts are leading them to expect.

Quantification is a virtue when more of the unknowns are made known. For some prospects, particularly those that could disrupt extant systems, the ability of financial tools to meaningfully evaluate their value is indeed very limited.

I propose that a human-centric investment funnel could facilitate how managers go about making their choices, as outlined in Chart 5.2. Imagine a manager swamped with multitudes of investment prospects to choose from. Without any criteria for selecting which ones would warrant immediate attention and what types of actions, the tasks appear insurmountable.

Life becomes easier apparently when managers start clustering their prospects according to their maturity and identifying the actions that are needed under a pipeline of prospects and opportunities. However, no sooner has the clustering been done, managers competing for resources would jockey for a first shot at what is available for disbursement. The intensity of the competition is not surprising. Going by some experiences, the venture capital world showed that about 1% of the original proponents made it to the final round of funding (equivalent to the final investment decision) (PGF500, 2018).

For capital-intensive prospects, I see the funnelling process as an aid to formulating sound decisions. It is **NOT** a silver bullet that assures financial success at *all* times. What it does is put some structure and focus into the formulation of a decision. Under this system, a manager starts by understanding what is critical at each stage to assess, select, and move the prospects forward to the next stage of resourcing and development. At each decision gate, managers exercise their judgement, as humans would, as to how the firm's resources are best deployed.

That humans make the judgement appears obvious. However, it is not unusual to observe that funnelling becomes another bureaucratic hurdle or an arena to compete single-mindedly for the money to continue working. To shift the way funnels could be used strategically, the humans in managers will need to take centre stage. Translated, financial tools aid the human mind to guard against its own biases by providing a framework through which people would conduct a strategic dialogue.[3]

---

[3] In Chapter 8, how strategic dialogue connects financial analyses to managerial actions are discussed and illustrated.

258 Dynamic Decisions

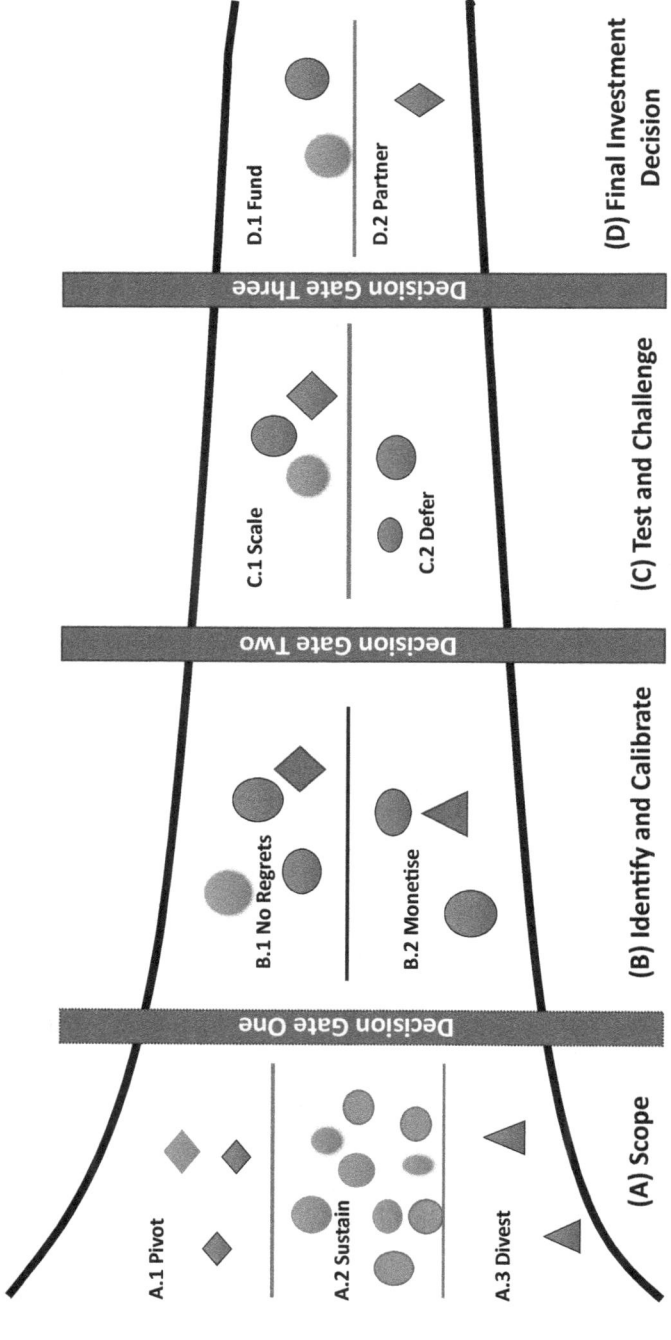

Chart 5.2: Schematic Overview of a Funnelling Process

Starting with an overview, extant energy firms are faced with a dual challenge: In a decarbonising world, carbon-intensive assets are bound to experience obsolescence. In backing this belief, managers would need to pivot by investing in low carbon energy supplies, while divesting its carbon-intensive assets such as fossil fuels. Under this scenario, the pipeline of prospects will be dominated by investments to pivot with renewables, while divesting fossil fuels to recycle capital.

The investment funnel follows the logic of real options reasoning. Prospects are clustered as real options that confer managers a *right*, but not an *obligation* to commit. In practice, the commitment of resources is usually sequential, with future spending contingent on information or expectations that justify continuing, deferring, scaling, or aborting the investment. Specifically:

Scope represents the early stages of a prospect entering the funnelling process. By its very nature, the raw concepts are insufficiently developed. To fine-tune the prospect, some resources are committed to ascertaining, at a high level, how it could deliver on the firm's purpose (e.g. pivot or sustain) or how it could enable other prospects to become an opportunity for investment. Often, managers ignore the strategic value of divesting assets as a way to enhance the firm's value (e.g. obsolescing or marginal assets).

In some cases, a prospect is amenable to being structured as a project entity that can accrue some value. Such value may arise from holding permits, licences, or concessions that are transferable.

Identify and calibrate build the case for moving the prospect to a stage where more resources are committed to identifying how the prospect could create value and how such value could be initially estimated. At this stage, some technical designs are initiated, financial modelling is done, and organising for a pilot scheme as appropriate is readied. At this stage, a prospect may be assessed for its complementarity (or duplication) with more mature prospects.

Tested against the firm's strategic aspirations and the uncertainties around the prospect, prospects may appear robust under most scenarios. Such prospects are considered as "no regrets" commitments that are usually adequately resourced for further development. In some cases, partially developed prospects are seen as doubtful as to their fitness for the firm.

However, because of the way the prospect was structured as a project entity, divesting such prospects is a form of "investment," following Dixit and Pindyck's proposition (1994).

Test and challenge follow iterative processes where assumptions, inputs, and expectations are rigorously checked against alternative views. What is essential is to answer a simple question: What happens if the manager's expectations happen to be off?

At this point, the process could become uncomfortable. After spending endless hours "getting the numbers right," as if it is the only *right and narrow* way forward, managers have to entertain the possibility that they could be wrong.

Final investment decision involves a commitment to proceed with the opportunity. The obvious decision that managers would take is to go for it alone or partner up. Whichever option is chosen, the managers would need to embed flexibility to alter the course when circumstances justify. Valuation, at this advanced stage, is bound to be fully developed.

A potential distraction to managers is the exhaustive financial analyses that accompany the decision-making. Inadvertently, getting to the value takes precedence over extracting strategic insights that inform decisions. As managers converge towards *getting the number right*, the conversations take a turn to advocacy. Inadvertently, very few numbers would inspire such passionate debates as NPVs to convince others of the investment's compelling case.

3.2 Interactions of human judgement and financial analyses

At this point, two very imperfect tools — human judgement and financial analyses — could combine to harness the benefits of the analytical discipline of financial analyses and the power of human wisdom and virtues. I reframe the investment funnelling to introduce an iterative, albeit tentative process, outlined in Chart 5.3, to formulate a selection decision.

Consider an incumbent energy firm assessing its options to pivot to a low carbon system. Endowed with ample cash, but saddled with assets that could become obsolete, a major oil and gas firm is faced with the following dilemmas:

Calibrate | 261

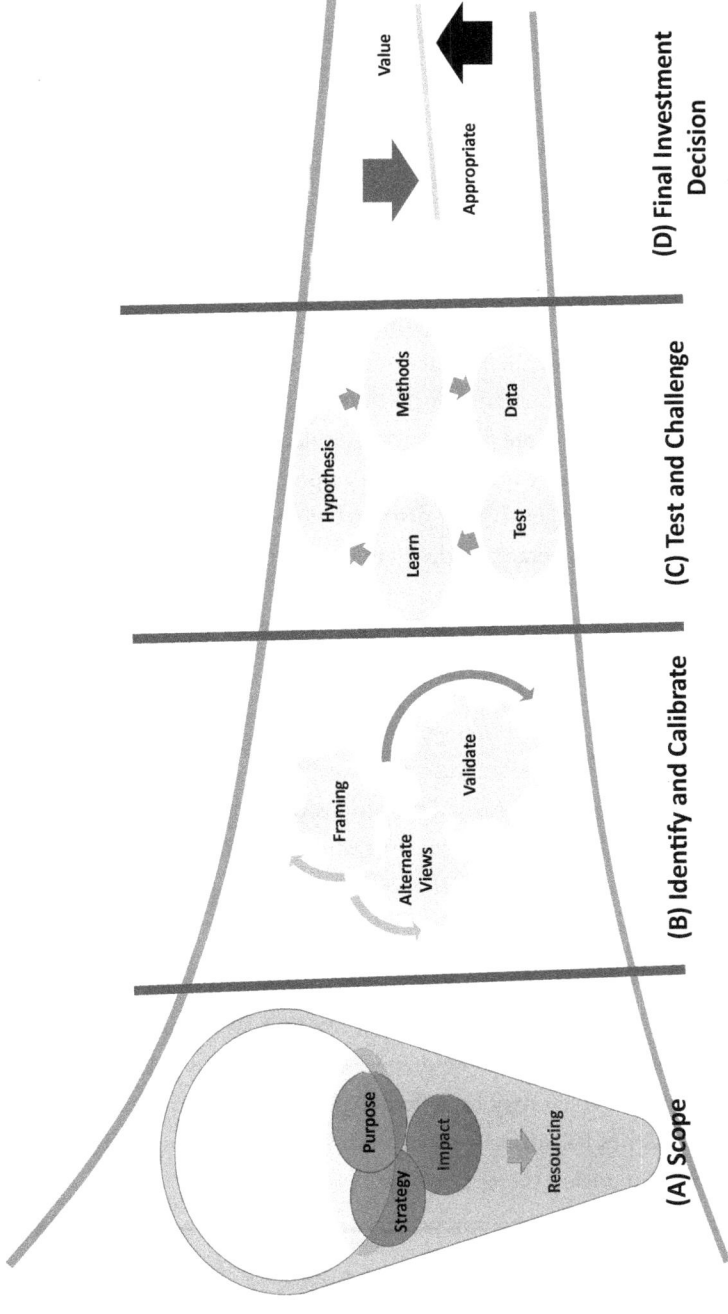

Chart 5.3: Human Judgement in Prospects-to-Opportunities Funnel

In *scoping* its prospects, investing in hydrogen fuel, geothermal and offshore wind power, or electric charging offers some obvious fit into its extant competencies. Hydrogen fuel could leverage on its logistics and distribution network that other rivals may find expensive to replicate. Geothermal power could retool the firm's exploration capabilities (e.g. from looking for oil and gas to steam deposits), with offshore wind offering scope for redeploying its offshore engineering to redesign platforms to reduce costs.

In *identifying and calibrating* the prospects, small investments are undertaken to test how the transfer of skills, and how it impacts the firm's ability to pivot, would actually work. In deciding to pilot specific schemes, prospective hypotheses are formulated, simulated to test their workability, and validated against experiences in the prospective applications. For example, how hydrogen fuel is distributed could be compared to how petroleum logistics operate. In designing wells for geothermal steam, how much of the capabilities are transferable from oil or gas? In designing platforms for offshore wind, a major cost item, how could it benefit from the experience of offshore rigs?

Progressing to *test and challenge,* some capital expenditures are incurred to build experimental assets. This process, with low initial commitment, is designed to test the hypothesis and the proposed methods to test the concept, gain data and information from the tests, and extract learning. This iterative process creates an accumulation of knowledge that could inform the possible (almost likely) reframing of the hypotheses.

A *final investment decision* is reached to initiate major commitments to capital-intensive ventures. At this stage, the team is prepared to scale up how they manage their team or prepare to transition development to an execution team (which may be different). In most cases, the development team relinquishes its primary responsibility to a team that would assume the lead in monetising the opportunity.

In parallel, with new opportunities being pursued, a reshuffling of the portfolio may become necessary. As the strategy pivots to exploiting opportunities offered by a low carbon system, some assets may no longer fit. In divesting assets, a pivoting energy firm disposes potential liabilities from carbon penalties should punitive taxes be imposed on polluting technologies. Obsolescence could create future streams of losses that could be avoided. Hence, by divesting these assets, managers exercise their *put* option (by selling these liabilities) to optimise today's value. This is balanced against the cost of erring: A future that continues to favour fossil fuels may forego the continuing profits that would accrue to the succeeding owners.

4
Judgements and Financial Discipline

In calibrating the value of investments, how do investments create value? In a subliminal way, managers hardwired into *single loop learning* would look for a silver bullet as the holy grail. In many situations, managers would default into "perfecting" their NPV or refine their estimates of economic value added (EVA).

While this is as good as any place to start, I would focus on understanding the levers that managers can use to enhance value creation. As these factors are identified, the "qualitative" factors such as rivals' actions, competitive interactions within a given market structure, and policy measures can be explicitly examined.

In adopting this stance, value creation is seen as an iterative process examined at various levels of analyses, where managers could alter or reinforce prior decisions in response to the business' changed circumstances. By understanding how value varies, managers could formulate dynamic strategies that recognise how human judgement is informed by internally coherent financial models (or vice versa).

4.1 Calibrating value creation under complex choices

John Graham and Campbell R Harvey (2001), in their survey of corporate executives, observed a widespread practice of gaming the earnings expectations. This sets the earnings target low so as to "exceed" it. The incentives to *game* the system increase, the more remuneration is directly linked to meeting budget or "exceeding targets." To remedy this, Alfred Rappaport (2006) reiterated his value creation proposition, a condition that is met when, generally, financial returns exceed the costs of capital employed.

Shareholder value has its share of critics and advocates. Rappaport (2006) encapsulates these as follows: "It's become fashionable to blame the pursuit of shareholder value for its ills besetting corporate America: managers and investors obsessed with next quarter's results; failure to invest in long-term growth; and even in accounting scandals that grabbed headlines." At the root of these failings, Rappaport asserts that "the reality is that shareholder value principle has not failed management. Rather, it is management that has betrayed the principle" by misapplying it.

In my view, the problem starts with the partial application of the principles outside the context of how the levers of value interact. Worst, stock options are used to lure talents, but cease to motivate value-creating behaviour when it is vested shortly after being awarded. This contradicts the principle of rewarding managers when value is delivered, which for capital-intensive investments may take a few years after completion.

What underpins value creation could be traced to residual income theory, which dated back to the 19th century (Magni, 2009). In its recent incarnation, value creation connects management accounting, corporate finance, and financial mathematics to create a framework for evaluating investment prospects prior to final investment decisions being taken. Its use is extended to monitor performance and even influence the setting of managerial remuneration (Kaplan, 2001). In its various forms, the firm value is understood as the book value of the investment (e.g. amount historically spent) and any present value of residual income (e.g. cash returns less attributed cost of capital) (Myers, 1999). This is popularised as economic value added (EVA) (Stewart, 1991) or shareholder value added (SVA) (Rappaport, 2006). To differentiate my usage, as specific to decision-making, I return to the theoretical roots of residual value added (RVA).

To frame a decision, I identify through Chart 5.4 the levers of value creation[4] and how "qualitative" factors could influence RVA. Value creation is broadly measured as the RVA (A) or the difference between *Return on Invested Capital (RoIC)* (B) and the *Weighted Average Cost of Capital (WACC)* (C). The levers of value are the variables that directly impact these two measures. Through these levers of value, the impact of how policy measures and market factors interact could be quantified. Specifically:

---

[4] Chapter 12 illustrates the calculations of RVA (or EVA) using data usually available from financial statements and publicly published sources.

Calibrate

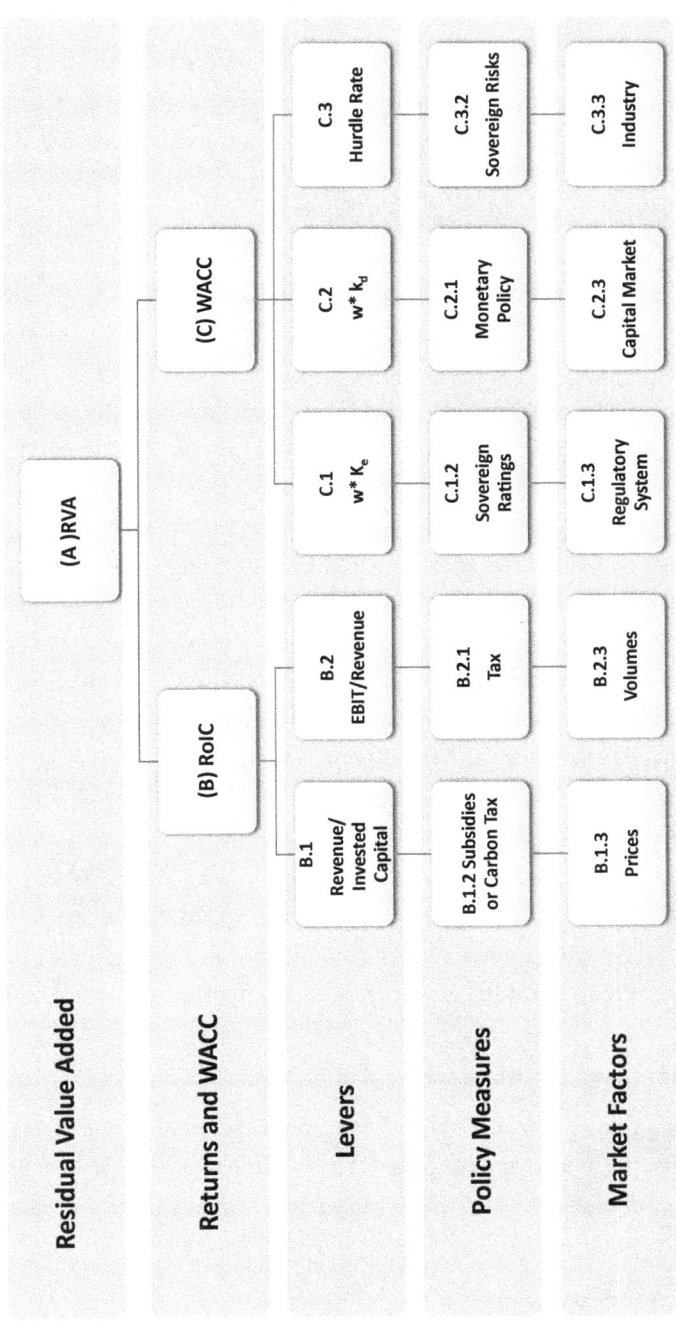

Chart 5.4: Levers of Value Creation and Policy Actions

RoIC (B) is a function of how the assets are used efficiently (B.1) and profitably (B.2). In this disaggregated form, one can surmise that some technologies are more asset-intensive to generate similar revenues while earning higher periodic cash margins (e.g. zero fuel cost renewables). Policy measures, when specified as subsidies or carbon taxes, may add to revenues (thus improving asset efficiency), or penalise profitability (when carbon taxes cannot be passed on to consumers), or reduce invested capital (when capital expenditures are subsidised). Periodic demand and supplies, under a functioning energy market, would set periodic prices and volumes.

WACC (C) is where monetary and fiscal policies manifest their influence on the cost of capital. The cost of equity (C.1) is usually measured as a risk-free rate, with a risk premium, to remunerate equity providers for risking their capital. The cost of debt, in contrast, is the interest rate paid on borrowing, which is set according to the credit rating of the investment. As an expense, the interest paid is tax-deductible. Weighted, the sum of the costs gives the WACC. In many respects, how the government sets taxes and interest rates would have a direct impact on WACC. Managers would influence to the point of how much debt they choose to borrow against the equity shareholders provide. The liquidity of the capital market and the confidence investors have on the regulatory system could influence the risk premium.

In some cases, a hurdle rate[5] (C.3) is used instead of WACC as a way of explicitly differentiating assets with varying operating life spans. In a way, a hurdle rate may indicate the minimum returns that should be earned in order to recoup its capital expenditure and its opportunity costs (relative to cash).

By breaking down the analyses, one can immediately appreciate the extent to which value creation is influenced by factors that are market- or policy-driven. Revenues are driven by prices and volumes that are inherently exogenous to direct managerial

---

[5] Chapter 11 explains the calculation of hurdle rates. This is the sum of the risk-free rate, risk premium, and the depreciation rate of the asset.

actions. How firms appropriate the potential revenues is where prior managerial decisions are relevant. Consider the following example:

> A manager is deciding to invest in gas ($ACCGT_B$) or photovoltaics (PVT_M) to generate power.[6] $ACCGT_B$ requires a lower invested capital (IC) than PVT_M for each MW installed while generating more power (MWh), given $ACCGT_B$'s higher utilisation rate. To its advantage, PVT_M has zero fuel costs, and at the same power price, it would earn a higher cash margin than $ACCGT_B$ for each MWh sold.
>
> Applying the RVA analytical framework, a manager is making the following trade-offs. By opting for $ACCGT_B$, it is investing in an asset with higher asset efficiency (B.1) but lower cash margin (B.2). The opposite is true for PVT_M. This narrows the choice to the quantity of power each is able to generate, which in this case favours $ACCGT_B$. Taking volume into account, $ACCGT_B$ would prove a more attractive financial investment on the basis of its RVA.
>
> Going back to management accounting, the value of equity post investment could be estimated. The book value of the invested capital is used as a starting point. The value created for the firm is the present value of RVA. For an ongoing concern, one may assume to simplify the calculation that the firm could reinvest and earn similar returns in perpetuity. If this were true, dividing RVA (A) by the WACC (C) would yield the perpetual value of the RVA or the amount of value created. Adding this to the invested capital, the sum represents the enterprise value (EV) of the firm (e.g. debt + equity + cash). The equity value, recognising the value created that accrues to shareholders, is simply EV — debt.

The extent to which detailed calculations are performed is adapted to the availability of data. For this reason, as the prospect matures in the funnel process, the estimates could be continually revised as new information becomes available. In many instances,

---

[6] Chapter 7 shows the cost calculations for each type of power generation technology using data provided by Energy Information Administration (EIA), United States. Chapter 8 compares the RVA (or EVA) of the competing technologies.

with investments evaluated as a discrete (or individual) commitment, projected estimates serve a specific purpose: as a way to gain insights on how variables interact, and impact value creation, under different investment and financing strategies.

Roger L Martin (2020) brings the conversation closer to situations that managers are more likely to encounter. With some investing firms listed in stock exchanges or when investment vehicles are listed, the use of historic or market value of IC is raised as a valuation question.

A basic financial structure is presented in Chart 5.5. Management accounting would view, using historic costs (A), the asset side as comprising the fixed assets (A.1) and the working capital requirements (A.2), the latter being the difference between current assets (e.g. what the firm funds its customers) and current liabilities (e.g. what suppliers finance the firm). This is identical to how much the firm borrows as debt (A.3) and the equity the shareholders provide (A.4).

When firms are listed in stock exchanges, the equity gains a valuation that is often different from its historic costs. Examining how this impacts the financial structure, one can use the market prices (B) to evaluate the firm's prospects to create value. To simplify, the principal difference is the equity revaluation (B.4.1). This reflects the value creation (or destruction) that is implied in the share price. In real life, the pace of the adjustment in equity value is dependent on how quickly financial investors may recognise (or ignore) management's capacity to deliver the value — a somewhat subjective process.

If one is to assume that the market is omniscient, although there are some doubts on this, one can attribute the equity "revaluation" to the asset "revaluation" (B.1.2). The other variables, such as debt or working capital, are not affected by the equity "revaluation," as these are usually expressed in their cash values.

Assuming further, no other changes are considered, such as a different WACC could result, the picture painted is completed by adding the asset "revaluation" (A.1.2) to the historic cost of invested capital (A) (or the equity "revaluation" to debt and equity calculation). An example is given in Table 5.1.

Consider any energy investment. By applying the RVA calculations, using the historic data A.1 to A.11, a "fair value" for equity is estimated as $2,359 mln (D.10). Now, if this equity value is fully recognised in the share price, the fair market value of equity can be substituted for equity (B.7), instead of the historic value of $300 mln (A.7). This adjustment has two immediate effects:

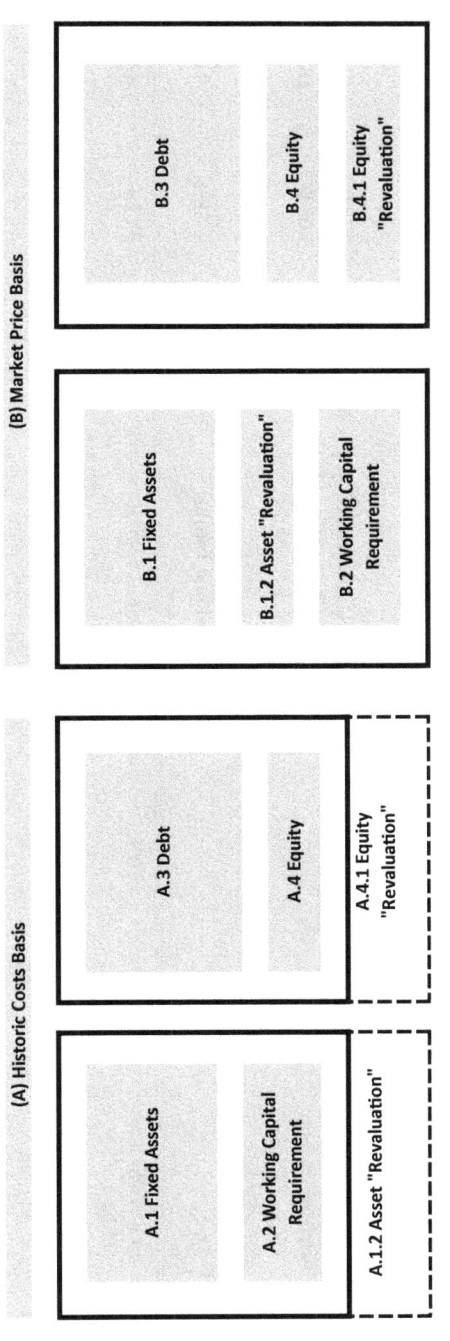

Chart 5.5: Invested Capital — Historic vs. Market Price Bases

Table 5.1: Value Creation under Historic or Market Invested Capital Value

	Invested Capital — IC	Unit	Historic Cost A	Fair Market Value B	Premium Market Value C	Return on Invested Capital — RoIC	Unit	Historic D	Fair Market Value E	Premium Market Value F
1	Fixed Asset	$ mln	1,000	3,129	3,770	Revenue/IC — Asset Efficiency	%	22.73%	7.74%	6.46%
2	Working Capital Requirement	$ mln	100	100	100	EBIT/Revenue — Cash Margin	%	70.00%	70.00%	70.00%
3	IC	$ mln	1,100	3,229	3,870	RoIC net of Tax	%	11.14%	3.79%	3.17%
4	**Weighted Average Cost of Capital — WACC**					WACC	%	3.92%	5.07%	5.18%
5	Debt	$ mln	770	770	770	**Residual Income — r**	%	7.22%	-1.28%	-2.01%
6	Cost of Debt Net of Tax	%	4.50%	4.50%	4.50%	Invested Capital	$ mln	1,100	3,229	3,870
7	Equity	$ mln	330	**2,359**	3,000	Residual Income	$ mln	79	-41	-78
8	Cost of Equity	%	5.70%	5.70%	5.70%	Residual Value Added	$ mln	2,029	-814	-1,505
9	WACC	$	3.92%	5.07%	5.18%	**Enterprise Value**	$ mln	**3,129**	**2,415**	**2,365**
10	**Tax**					**Equity Value**	$ mln	**2,359**	**1,645**	**1,595**
11	Tax Rate	%	30.00%	30.00%	30.00%					

1. Market value of IC increases, resulting in a significantly lower asset efficiency (E.1). With cash margin remaining unchanged, RoIC net of tax declines from 11.14% (D.3) to 3.79% (E.3).
2. The weight of equity in WACC increases. Without the benefit of tax shield, equity returns would push WACC higher from 3.92% (D.4) to 5.07% (E.4).

The combined effects would turn the investment from a value-creating (D.5) to a value-destroying (E.5) venture. A common error is to adjust the invested capital by simply adding the historic RVA (D.8) while failing to recalculate the WACC. Had no adjustment been made to equity, the WACC remains unchanged, hence the equity value for both will be equivalent (e.g. D.10 = E.10).

What does this recalculation imply for taking any decision on the portfolio of assets?

For listed firms, a gap in how capital markets value equity could offer arbitrage. In this example, with "fair value" (D.10 = B.7) fully recognised in the share price, managers may consider divesting and reinvesting the funds into alternative ventures. However, if by some managerial actions, RVA could be enhanced, then there may be a case for retaining the asset. In the case of a premium valuation, where the share price (C.7) substantially exceeds the "fair value" of equity (D.10), divesting the asset may prove lucrative for shareholders.

To complete the illustration, managers may choose the hurdle rate as a proxy for "cost of capital." This separates the financing decision — proportions of debt and equity in funding — from the operational evaluation of the investment. In this case, whether one chooses to use historic or market value for equity, the RVA will not be directly affected. In this case, the equity values in (D.11) and (E.11) will be equal. The relevance of share price is to give an indication to investors as to how much of the value creation potential is recognised (or ignored) by the equity market.

4.2 Valuation under ambiguous conditions

The object of investing is to create value by earning payoffs that exceed what was invested. While simple as a concept, managers face ambiguities on two fronts:

1. Payoffs are readily calculated when investments work according to expectations. However, volatile markets could wreak havoc to forecast revenues and

costs, with policy and rivals' actions dynamically altering how payoffs would evolve.
2. The amount planned to be spent on capital expenditures is generally more predictable. However, managers may encounter "unforeseen" events that would incur additional costs or work revisions that would result in deviating from what was budgeted.

While not intended as an exhaustive list, Chart 5.6 attempts to map how different financial tools may be used under different investment conditions and decision contexts.[7] A matrix of how expected outcomes could vary, against the investments' degree of complexities, would yield the following matches:

In a world where *all variables are largely known (A)*, conventional tools such as NPV would yield about the right answers for single asset valuation, isolated from the influences of competitor's actions. In the best of circumstances, narrowly focused obligations work for bonds or borrowings, where interest and capital repayments form the expected cash flows for the lender.

In energy supply contracts, this predictability is attempted for replication under *take-or-pay* obligations, where a seller undertakes to deliver a quantity of supplies at a specified price. The buyer takes on the responsibility to receive the supplies at an agreed schedule and pay for the periodic volumes whether they need it or not. Translated to policy, a popular tool is to evaluate the cost–benefit of public investment by introducing the social costs or benefits to complement the financial evaluation. Implicitly, managers are seen to write the cheque, sit back, and hope for the best that everything works out according to plan — a prospect that is unrealistic.

Markets are inherently volatile and dynamic (B). With plans likely to change as markets vary, managers are given the flexibility to change course following real options reasoning. That is, under a functioning energy market, prices are set according to periodic demand and supplies. The managers' *a priori* choice of technology sets the cost structure that may be higher or

---

[7] Chapters 8–10 explains in detail the math behind each valuation approach using different types of power generation technologies.

lower than the prevailing market prices. When there is managerial flexibility, supplies are curtailed to avoid making a loss when supply costs exceed prevailing prices. In contrast, more volumes are supplied when prices are going up in order to lock in higher cash margins (if costs lag price increases). In this more dynamic ecosystem, managers actively manage volume and pricing decisions. To evaluate its effects on valuation, volatile prices, costs, and volumes are modelled using binomial tree analysis.

As firms operate under multiple assets portfolio, the question of how fossil fuels and renewables interact becomes relevant. Unfortunately, this is also the reality where NPV (and cost–benefit analysis) is ill-equipped to provide informed guidance to decision-makers (and policy). Quoting from my previous works (Barcelona, 2017), I highlighted this observation:

"Capital budgeting's focus on discrete technology optimisation is not aligned with the uncertainties that come with dynamic energy markets. Conceptual and practical gaps clearly exist when experienced decision-makers struggle to articulate the following: (a) how their investments contribute to their firms' returns; (b) why a strategic premium can uniquely accrue to their firms' gains. To compound this problem, capital budgeting often draws a blank when it comes to providing practical guidance on how the inherent uncertainties surrounding energy investments can best be tackled. By incorrectly valuing energy supplies portfolios, renewables' diversification values and embedded options are often mispriced."

4.3 Portfolio diversification and firms' rivalry

In the evolving world of energy markets, the disconnect between presumed reality and what dynamic markets are causes managers to miss out on three decision dimensions:

1. *Concept* of energy value optimisation fails to provide for explicitly evaluating the influence of volatilities and how managerial flexibility, competition, and dynamic actions interact to alter investment outcomes.
2. *Methods* dictate a "now or never" passive stance that optimises single investments while changing markets require adaptive commitments that benefit from complementation within the portfolio or reversal of prior actions.

Dynamic Decisions

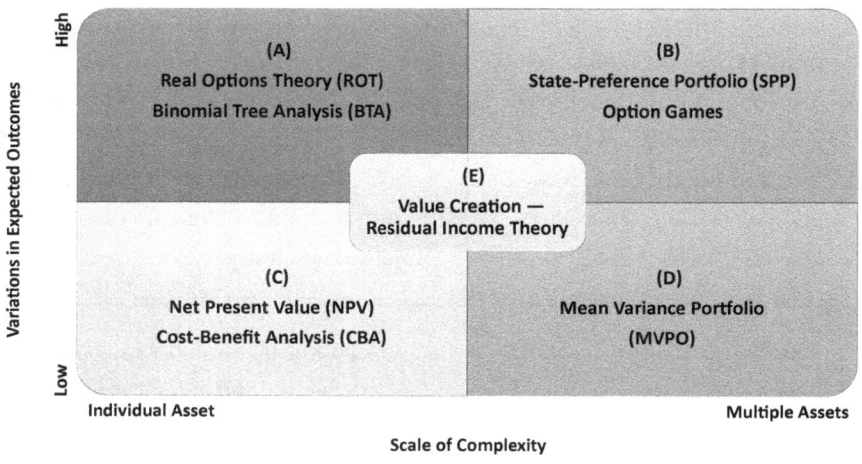

Chart 5.6: Financial Economics and Investment Conditions

3. ***Adaption*** requires commonly understood approaches that managers and policy can use in framing their decisions and actions.

When changing energy markets operate under uncertainty, while managerial decisions follow prescribed or assumed certainty, the outcomes are almost predictable. Asset-intensive energy industries experience inordinately high proportions of commitments that fail to deliver on their expected returns (Gale, 2011).

Managers in modern energy firms, particularly the major oil and gas and power companies, seldom invest in isolation. To remedy the limitations of NPV, financial economics offers a myriad of tools that managers can employ. I map these tools in Chart 5.7 to deepen the insights gained in Chart 5.6 by bringing theory to life in practice.

The "accepted wisdoms" are premised on single (or discrete) asset investments, with NPV serving as its bedrock (A). It involves an inter-temporal context (A.1) when expected payoffs could materialise in the future, while capital expenditures are disbursed upfront. When both quantities are discounted to the present, a net present value (NPV) (A.2) is estimated. In essence, this is like paying now by exercising an option to invest, to acquire the right to appropriate future cash flows (A.3). In taking no notice of competition (A.4 and A.5), managers decide "now or never" to invest. Hoping that everything works out according to plan, managers choose investments with the

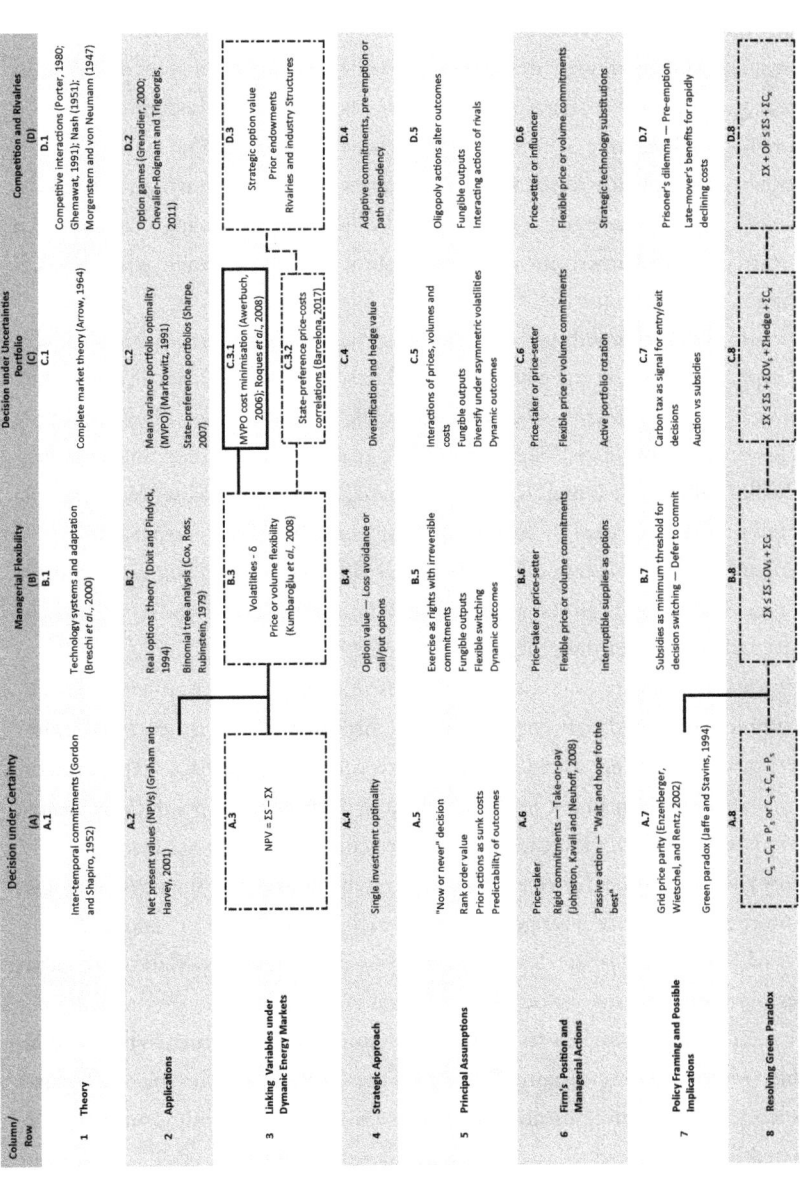

Chart 5.7: Linking Theories to Inform Practice and Policy

Source: Adapted from Barcelona (2017).

highest NPV (A.6), with policy following a similar using grid price parity logic (A.7). However, when dynamic markets disturb this tranquil life, outcomes often turn out to be vastly different from expectations. As a result, the security that rigid long-term obligations, and subsidies, were designed to provide has become a source of risk. In the process, green paradoxes emerge when measures to secure early commitment no longer provide the incentive to commit now rather than later (A.8).

A remedy is to explicitly recognise how managers operate under dynamic markets. In the chaotic world where managers reside, the flexibility to change course when markets shift, or correct an erroneous prior decision, confer some value when the cost of reversing is not exorbitant (B).

Real options theory, combined with binomial tree analysis, extends NPV's evaluation by explicitly assessing the effects of volatilities (B.2 and B.3). Intuitively, when two approaches are considered — a rigid, inflexible obligation and a flexible supply contract — the *delta value* (or the difference in payoffs) results from managerial flexibility. The flexibility value is manifested when managers can avoid losses (when supply costs exceed prevailing prices) by curtailing supply or gain more by increasing supply when demand and price increase (B.4, B.5, and B.6). Under this market, subsidies become a residual amount aimed at providing a floor return to encourage managers to commit early instead of deferring investment (B.7).

When investments are evaluated from the firm's perspective, Kenneth J Arrow's (1964) complete market theory comes in handy. Among practical people, a complete market exists when there are sufficient assets, with volatilities and risks that are uncorrelated, that investors can invest in. By combining these assets, a portfolio is created that minimises large swings in outcomes. This is achieved when losses from one asset are offset by gains in another (or vice versa). In effect, by diversifying the risks, outcomes become more predictable at a range of volatile market prices (C, C.1, and C.2).

Harry M Markowitz (1991) describes how diversification works. Markowitz asserts that investors want "returns" to be high, in whichever way returns are defined, with more of it seen as better than less. In addition, investors want this return to be "dependable, stable, not subject to uncertainty." To satisfy these criteria, reinforcing Markowitz's previous works (1952), diversification entails investing in assets with returns that are uncorrelated in order to reduce their variance (as a proxy for risk) (C.3.1).

Translated, when a firm possesses two assets, where returns for one go up when fuel price increases (e.g. renewables), while the other asset's returns tend to fall (e.g. coal), the portfolio's returns are less volatile than either one, taken individually. The variance, or the range of changes in returns, is observed to revert to some average over time. In combining these observations, the mean variance portfolio optimality (MVPO) was proposed.

MVPO gained popularity in energy economics when Dan Bar-Lev and Steven Katz (1976) reframed cost as the criterion for selecting an energy source. In the midst of the 1973 oil shock, seeking alternatives to oil was of great urgency, with gas holding some promise. However, gas was an "expensive" fuel then. Using MVPO principles, Bar-Lev and Katz observed that in highly volatile coal prices, when combined with stable gas prices, the cost variability of power generation is diminished. This notion was picked up by H Brett Humphreys and Katherine T McClain (1998) two decades later, with Shimon Awerbuch (2006) expanding this notion to nuclear and renewables' ability to minimise portfolio costs of generation. Fabien A Roques *et al.* (2008) reinforce the cost minimisation approach as a way to satisfy Markowitz's portfolio returns criteria. In a later work, Fabien A Roques *et al.* (2010) extended the cost minimisation logic to argue for a European wind portfolio. They argue that managed as one portfolio and assuming unconstrained fungible supplies, variations of wind flow in one region (e.g. France) could be offset by uncorrelated volatilities in another (e.g. Spain or Germany) (C.3.3).

The cost minimisation strategy work when power prices were fixed usually by regulation or rigid supply contracts. Logically, with costs variance minimised, in theory, the cash returns (e.g. revenues less the cash costs of supply) expand. However, as energy markets liberalise competition and volatile prices, costs or volumes invalidate the cost minimisation proposition.

At this point, William F Sharpe's (2007) state-preference portfolio theory offers a generalised notion (C.3.2). Sharpe visualises a state of the world as the probable scenarios or futures that could result from discrete events or actions and how they interact. In making the underlying interactions transparent, linking individual preferences with the probable scenarios, and the combination of events that underpin the analyses, becomes easier to follow. The math involved is far simpler as well.

The complex combination of variables, when examined individually, could be simplified as binary moves as previously applied to evaluate managerial flexibility. The Cox–Ross–Rubinstein binomial tree (1979) comes to the managers' aid (B.2).

A binomial tree is a series of up or down moves that enables managers to model price, costs, volume, or any form of binary moves (C.4). Volatilities indeed are simply that variables could move up or down, the magnitudes may differ, and could vary at each period. These assumptions are incorporated, with each periodic event (or node) in the binomial tree explicitly shown. The individual variable, and their influence on other related variables, could be modelled separately, with the results recombined to estimate the eventual payoffs under each scenario (C.5). An essential element to monetise the resulting values is the presence of managerial and operational flexibility (Näsäkkälä and Fleten, 2005) (B).

By employing binomial trees, how energy markets transition, or how technological evolution rearranges the use of resources (Eliasson and Taymaz, 2002), can be explicitly considered in modelling a portfolio of assets under uncertain and dynamic conditions. In my formulation, I propose an explicit *Value–Risk Trade-off* that aims to make portfolio choices more transparent. Extracted from my previous work (Barcelona, 2015), I posit:

"The value of the physical asset portfolio approach to operating companies is not only diversification. Shareholders can diversify on their own to satisfy their risk preferences. Rather, the value comes mainly from 'real options' provided by different assets. The existence and value of such options become evident only when examined within a framework that recognises that various inputs are likely to vary significantly over the lives of power generating assets. In the face of this uncertainty, managerial flexibility provides a way to seize opportunities or avoid losses."

To illustrate an example of how the *Value–Risk Trade-off Framework* operates, I replicate the results of my analysis of various combinations of fossil fuel and renewables. A more extensive treatment of the math is included in my paper (Barcelona, 2015). What I aim to illustrate is encapsulated in this conclusion:

The results shown in Chart 5.8 "shows how decision-makers could trade-off their returns with risk. Such option-based strategies would allow firms to make decisions based on deep strategic understanding of their business. This replaces the implicit hope that the simple set of assumption in traditional NPV analysis would come to pass. This strategy encourages managers

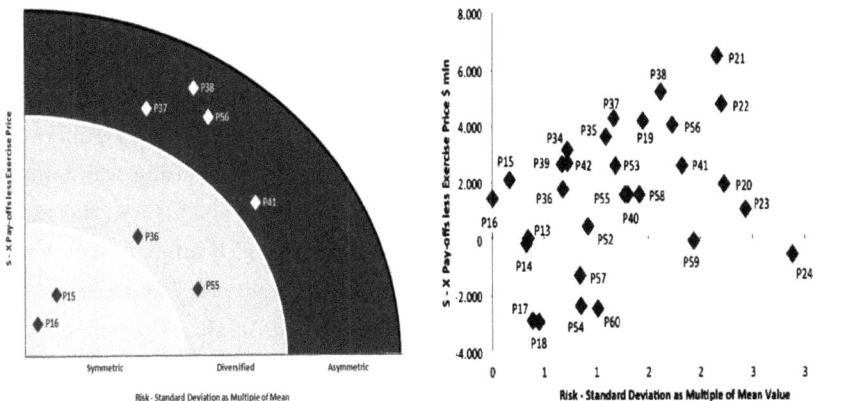

Chart 5.8: Value–Risk Trade-off Framework

Source: Barcelona (2015).

to become familiar with uncertainties and comfortable with reasonable levels of risk to exploit opportunities presented by volatile prices and volumes."

An example of how a portfolio could shift the strategic approach of the firm is to combine $ACCGT_B$ (P15) and $StoHydro_B$ (P21) to form a portfolio (P38).

Opting for $ACCGT_B$ (P15) expresses a preference for stable and predictable cash earnings. As a price-setting supply, $ACCGT_B$'s costs are indexed to the market. For this reason, volatile power prices, largely induced by fuel cost variations, cancels out.[8]

A supply strategy entirely relying on $StoHydro_B$ (P21) would exhibit volatile cash margins that mimic the price variations. This is largely because of its zero fuel costs.

When both supplies are operated under a single portfolio (P38), it minimises cash margin volatility (in relation to P21) while enhancing returns (in relation to P15). On balance, the portfolio "sacrifices" some returns of $StoHydro_B$ while gaining more stability provided by $ACCGT_B$.

---

[8] If $C_{LCOE} = P_s = C_{FX} + C_{VAR} + C_{FUEL}$ and cash costs of supply is $C_{VAR} + C_{FUEL}$, then the cash margin of $ACCGT_B$ roughly equals C_{FX} under any power prices when market freely sets the prices. A more detailed explanation is shown in Chapter 7.

In a world with rival firms that dynamically alter the *games* and the competitive advantages of each player, managerial flexibility comes to the fore. Within an ever-changing business landscape, managers are well advised to "look forward, reason backwards" (Dixit and Nalebuff, 1991) and look sideways. Looking forward is informed by strategic purpose, with the means to get there informed by using real options reasoning to reason backwards (from an aspired position) (C.5 and C.6). At this stage, the policy takes a back seat by choosing to intervene selectively, often to hasten the pace or dampen enthusiasm when expectations outpace reality (C.7 and C.8).

Along the way, uncooperative rivals may seek to derail a firm's progress. Alternatively, a deep understanding of the imperatives of energy transitions may confer opportunities for firms to convert rivals into fellow travellers. This is where option games could provide the insights needed to understand how rivals are likely to act, in a rational way, and how competing firms could achieve some equilibrium. This follows the logic of *games* that Oskar Morgenstern and John von Neumann (1947) proposed and also found in the works of John Nash (1951) (D).

Confronted with dynamic markets, where not only prices or volumes cause returns to vary (often significantly), "rapid technological changes and intensified competition necessitate an analysis of the project's strategic growth potential that is more dynamic than just a forecast of expected cash flows" (Smit and Trigeorgis, 2017). The valuation of these dynamic aspects could be guided by drawing on the intuition and logic of *real options reasoning* and *games* theory (D.2 and D.3):

Continuing with the example on $ACCGT_B$ and $StoHydro_B$, real options reasoning guides managers strategically in timing and pacing their investments. Managers may commit now to lock in a preferred hydro resource, at times at a cost of having excess capacity. Faced with the prospect of languishing demand, investments may be deferred or aborted. When the assets are operational, managerial flexibility would enable supplies to be ramped up or curtailed. This occurs when markets confer managers the right, by having the supply available, but not the obligation to supply when costs of supply exceed prevailing prices.

Under an oligopoly, the actions of one firm could alter a rival's available alternatives and hence their firms' value. Hydro resources are location-specific, giving the holder of access rights the ability to pre-empt rivals.

The same is true for geothermal steam access. For this reason, a first mover could conceivably lock out competitors.

Managers are said to *game* their moves, contingent upon the actions (or anticipated reactions) of rivals. Thus, a firm with $ACCGT_B$ may opt to diversify with $StoHydro_B$ or $GeoS_B$ to lock out competitors to enhance its value. However, rivals may increase the stakes by bidding up the cost of acquiring access. The value to each bidder is likely to be different, so will the bid prices. Recall: The value accrues mostly to the "natural owner" of the opportunity. A "drunken sailor" will overbid, thus benefiting the "seller."

Acting as oligopoly players, the two firms may influence the intensity of competition. A cosy relationship may not last if a determined competitor could change the *game* and appropriate for itself any incremental gains (or avoid marginal losses). That is, as more competitors enter the market, firms may decide to invest even if the payoffs are "sub-optimal" following Grenadier's proposition (2002)[9] (D.4 and D.5).

In my previous works (Barcelona, 2017), I observe a contrarian logic for adopting rapidly improving technologies, such as PVT_M. I noted: "The 'certainty' of *benefits from* significant falls in equipment costs often exceed any foregone revenues. For this reason, managers are deterred from making commitments now, while encouraging deferrals, because future commitments would be cheaper. Paradoxically, while renewables generally confer early mover's advantage, solar power rewards late-movers by saddling early commitments with expensive assets that could result in stranded costs" (D.7).

From a broader perspective, the transition of European energy markets from the "comforts" of regulated prices to an era of volatile prices, costs, and volumes is a case in point. The strategic responses of firms diverged. Risk-averse managers reasserted predictability through long-term contracts (e.g. take-or-pay) (A.6), while some took a leap to experiment using tools to extract insights into the value of volatilities (e.g. options, derivatives, or physical hedges) (D.6).

---

[9] Steven Grenadier (2002) posits that a monopolist, facing no credible prospect of being pre-empted, would wait before investing until the conditions exist for prospective payoffs are maximised (e.g. tight supplies or shortage). However, this payoff threshold is substantially lowered when one or more credible competitors emerge. That is, the ex-monopolist would rather lock in a lower payoff rather than face the prospect of losing the prospective payoff to a rival.

It did not take long for managers to experience the paradox: Far from securing their payoffs, firms experienced continual renegotiations as contracted prices diverge from what prevailing markets were offering (A.5). As managerial world views diverge, I made the following observations (Barcelona, 2017) on how these affect the managers' strategic choices:

"Neo-Malthusian theory sees energy resources as finite, where scarcity drives the fuel usage transition. This reasoning inspires approaches that William Stanley Jevons (1865) prescribed for coal: *There is no substitute for coal. The only recourse is to spend more to dig deeper to get more so that humanity's demand for coal could be met.* However, coal ceased to dominate as fuel in spite of coal remaining plentiful" (A).

In a tangible way, a *single loop learning* sustains the new Malthusians to err another day. However, a simple reframing to a *double loop learning* takes an innovative mind farther.

"The *innovation system* approach offers a more optimistic narrative of human capabilities to adapt. As technology evolves, and markets change or get disrupted, resources and capabilities are re-arranged to respond to shifting needs" (D.6 and D.7).

The role of policy evolves from an arbiter of value, by setting prices and costs recovery when regulator actively intervenes, to one of enabling firms (and people) to take actions that serve their purpose. These actions include the firms' obligations to their stakeholders, of which society is an important component (D.7 and D.8). A further reflection led me to posit: "These transitions impact the financial viability of firms. As coal mines in Newcastle[10] declined, new wealth was created in the oilfields of Texas, United States. Under this dynamic market, inertia consigns firms, as they

---

[10] In the 19th century, Newcastle was a major coal mining area in the United Kingdom. By the 1970s, the coal mining firms were virtually living on state support, with their eventual closures during the 1990s.

did with coal companies to the dustbin of history, when managers remain blind as to how the world is changing fast."

5
Improving the Odds to Succeed

In an age where investment evaluation increasingly relies on complex financial models, a call to a return to a human-centric decision ecosystem may appear odd. After all, with computing power boasting artificial "intelligence," machines are indeed doing more and more of the routine calculations. This is where I see a present and imminent danger to perpetuate the decline of otherwise flourishing firms.

John S Hammond *et al.* (2006) forewarned: "Our brains are always at work, sometimes, unfortunately, in ways that hinder rather than help us. At every stage of the decision-making process, misperceptions, biases, and other tricks of the mind can influence the choices we make. Highly complex and important decisions are the most prone to distortion because they tend to involve assumptions, the most estimates, and the most inputs from people. The higher the stakes, the higher the risks of being caught in a psychological trap."

This is where a human-centric investment funnelling process provides the common ground for thoughtful human judgement, imperfect as it is, and analytical discipline coexists. The instinct of the human mind, loaded with unescapable biases and emotions, is balanced against the inanimate (and often cold logic) structure that analytical tools provide. These interactions, while proving uncomfortable for some managers, enables a firm to draw on deep expertise and "off-tangent" ideas to challenge "accepted wisdoms." After all, for a market to transition, they evolve into something different. This process opens a prospect that could make some extant advantages into liabilities, or even obsolete, and new capabilities to emerge.

To this focus on human virtues and imperfections, I would add: "Competition, and their effects on portfolio performance, depends on competitors' actions that are often non-cooperative and impacts the competing firms' values. Increased renewables supplies dampen power prices. When there is strategic asymmetry under oligopoly, where one firm diversifies into renewables, while another follows a fossil fuel-based only supplies, the latter's value is eroded while the former gain. Simply put, each firm responds differently to the challenge of technological evolution. As a result, how they rearrange their resources and capabilities also differ, resulting in diverging performances, often as a result of the firm's prior endowments" (Barcelona, 2015).

The regulator, as omniscient as it may consider its (limited) ability to shape the future, is constantly besieged by this dilemma: to continually intervene or to set the economic agents free under transitioning and dynamic energy markets to pursue their future.

Given a choice, I would choose the freedom of the market pursued with responsibility over the concentrated omnipotence of "experts" with presumed (but non-existent) omniscience.

Box 5.1: Conversations with Rama Velamuri

At IESE Business School, Spain, Rama Velamuri was one of the youngest members of our MBA[11] class of 1985. As one of the few from the Indo-Pacific area, we shared a curiosity about how the Western world, and its corporations, operate. Obviously, there were differences that made us stand out for all sorts of reasons. However, there were more traits that we have in common that continue to give meaning to what humans aspire as a common good. While intellect and socio-economic metrics appear to generally set MBAs apart, what bound us was a pursuit for an impactful life. These are the human virtues that one lives and exercises, namely, *Humility*, *Integrity*, and *Respect*.

Rama was among the few that joined the industry instead of management consulting or investment banking. The latter two were the more popular destinations of MBAs of our time. Well-grounded in the realities of real-life European business, Rama deepened his preparation for a life in academe with his doctoral degree at Darden Business School, University of Virginia, USA. After a few years at IESE Business School, Spain, he now teaches entrepreneurship at the China Europe International Business School (CEIBS), Shanghai, China.

Looking back to three decades and a half, Rama and I took stock of where management education has brought us. In tackling real-life business problems, the basic framework for making choices has hardly changed. Rama drew from his interactions with entrepreneurs and managers from across the world to highlight what he learned. Rama explained:

"When presented with a problem to solve, I ask my students to think critically about why that problem is *the problem* to solve. Often, what is presented as a problem is simply a manifestation of an underlying problem, which should ideally be the one that is tackled. This would require them

---

[11] Master of Business Administration is a graduate degree programme that the school offered for young people aspiring for leadership roles in business.

to understand what caused the problem that is presented to them, before jumping in to finding solutions. Let me illustrate this with a simple problem of a major client defecting to a competitor.

The customer accounted for 10% of a business line's annual revenues. The firm historically earned above average profit margins in excess of 50% for their niche product. To the manager, this was clearly a problem that caused sleepless nights. The instinct of the manager was to do whatever it took to claw back the customer from the competitor, including offering significantly lower prices. However, was this the right thing to do?

In digging deeper, the manager realised belatedly that two recurring issues from the past had remained unresolved. Customers, even key accounts, had been experiencing under-deliveries of their orders. It was taking about a month, at its quickest, to make up for the shortfall. This caused delays in the defecting customer's construction schedule, which exposed them to potential penalties. The recurring shortfalls in deliveries had forced the customer to try alternative suppliers, whose products met the technical specifications and cost approximately 10% less."

Rama observed: "Managers would find the pricing issue to be the easiest to solve. By offering a 10% discount, the manager can match the competitor's pricing. However, the deeper problem, which gave the competitor the opportunity of getting a foot in the customer's door, is the late deliveries." In Rama's perspective, this is where some managers misdiagnose the problem that they should be solving and end up not solving it.

I concurred with Rama. I queried him on whether the problems the company was facing with its major customer could be a sign of more difficulties in the future.

Rama continued: "On further reflection, lower pricing from the competitor for an acceptable product could be an early signal of emerging substitutes that could endanger the product line. The internal issues around delivery and customer fulfilment is an immediate issue. If a major customer suffers from such poor attention, others are probably having a worse time. Indeed, this was the case. On realizing this, the manager sat down with each of the customers that accounted for 80% of revenues, revised their delivery system, and just avoided having more customer defects. For those customers that were lost, the manager was still working to win them back with mixed results. He also realized that a margin of 50% would not be sustainable in the face of increasing competition unless he added significantly more value to customers."

1. Diverging paths in market disruptions

This insight into a simple business problem allows a refreshing look into how some managers would tackle their day-to-day problems. If they miss out on emerging threats that stare them in plain sight, what hope would they have to survive disruptions from new technologies or unforeseen events such as pandemics that can create major shocks?

Rama steered our conversation to how two iconic brands in analogue photography and films — Kodak and Fuji Films — approached the disruptive digital technology.

In setting the scene, we recalled how core competences are emphasised in business programmes. This is a notion made popular by C. K. Prahalad and Gary Hamel, who posit that "knowing and mastering core business factors can be leveraged across products and markets. Yet, the ways companies make products, especially electronics, have been disrupted and redesigned. As Nokia's boss noted, Nokia's core competence is in phone design, but the trend in China, where manufacturers buy phone chipsets from vendors, and make phones at unbelievable pace and price, controlling one third of the global market, introduces a new dimension of competition" (Ekekwe, 2011).

Under transitioning markets, or those that are in the process of being disrupted, one would assume that old processes and products become obsolete, incapable of being adapted for new applications. While this is the case for Kodak and Nokia, Fuji Films took a different path and flourished. Yuichi Habashi, General Manager of e-Strategy Management Office of Fujifilm, described their journey:

> "Fujifilm survived disruption of the film and analogue photography. It executed a successful transformation by taking its in-house expertise in chemical compounds and applied it in new markets in cosmetics, healthcare products, pharmaceuticals, computer tapes for data centres, and of course for digital cameras" (Twentyman, 2019).

Rama encapsulated how he saw Fujifilm differed in this observation: "Boldness in investing in new technologies, or turning old expertise into new businesses, contrasted with Kodak's attempts to extend the life of an obsolescing business." When times are good, Rama added: "One should continuously invest in new technologies, new products and new business models, following an *affordable loss philosophy*. That is, one can tolerate making losses from incremental investments, and treat these losses as a cost of learning what works and what does not." To illustrate an incremental trial and error approach, Rama cited Deng Xiaoping, China's former supreme leader: *"Crossing the river by feeling the stones."*

2. Where do strategy and finance meet?

The question of money, and how the *affordable loss philosophy* could be incorporated into resource allocation decisions, raises interesting dilemmas for CFOs. This problem deepens when conventional financial theories are employed to inform investment evaluation. Investments are valued on their capacity to generate cash flows. Relying on the manager's ability to foresee what would happen in the distant future with some degree of accuracy, future cash flows are discounted to today's value. For new technologies or evolving markets with unknown trajectory, the exercise of projecting outcomes (revenues, costs, and cash flows) so far into the future appears rather pointless.

Rama offered his perspective: "Conventional financial tools, such as discounted cash flows (DCF) or net present value (NPV), can lead firms to stop or curtail their exploratory efforts. In times of economic difficulties, when a pivot is perhaps of most value and impact, managers may cut short their investments. They may also forego any advantages when they fail to build upon what they learned ahead of rivals."

Inadvertently, some managers may endlessly debate the elegance of one financial model over another. Rama pointed to a "deeper philosophical question that managers may shy away from. When a firm is still in an exploratory mode (e.g. new technologies, business, or processes), particularly pursuing opportunities outside its core competencies, should NPV even be used at all?"

In reconciling this chasm, strategy and finance may have to recognise the role that luck plays. As Fujifilm's experience illustrated, they sought the opportunity to redeploy a valuable resource that they possessed — expertise with chemical compounds. Rama attributes to luck part of the success of transforming a business. By acquiring potentially valuable skills and capabilities, one could seize opportunities by simply being in the right place at the right time to offer a viable solution. In other cases, one can create a receptive mind among managers to see opportunities in new ideas, a mindset that Richard Wiseman (2003) refers to as turning chance encounters into a profit opportunity.

Rama continues: "The tools of financial analyses lead managers to avoid 'false positives' (or Type I errors). Managers do not want to back an investment project (such as the launch of a new product or new business) and lose money on it. To prepare for transitions and disruptions, managers need to be willing to make Type I errors, and avoid making Type II errors (or 'false negatives'). In other words, mangers need to be willing to lose money (affordable amounts) on a number of new initiatives and show an unwillingness to let great opportunities pass them by. Contemporary accounting systems are able to record accurately the out-of-pocket losses from failed investment projects but are not able to record gains not realized from opportunities not pursued. This biases organizations towards avoidance of Type I errors, whereas the imperative in periods of high uncertainty is the avoidance of Type II errors."

3. Remedies and pathway to prosperity

Management education plays a role in preparing today's aspiring business leaders. The way people are "retooled," for lack of a better term, in the present day may differ from the way previous generations were prepared to tackle future problems.

The energy industry is a case in point. Transition means a reconfiguration of its technological foundations as well as the way logistics and markets are organised. In this evolving strategic landscape, the bestowed advantages that are locked in capital-intensive assets and capabilities to convert raw materials into useful energy are specific and inflexible — at least at first sight. These accepted wisdoms are coherent with the structured approach to investments, insofar as achieving operating efficiency is the route to prosperity that a stable market confers.

Evolving markets, however, do not guarantee such stability. In Rama's view, aspiring business leaders are better equipped if they are imbued with entrepreneurial dynamism. Management education can partly contribute by offering more courses in entrepreneurship.

"This is already happening, with leading business schools offering at least one core course in entrepreneurship, and approximately 25% of electives relating to entrepreneurship."

The era that Rama and I experienced in business school was labelled as the information age, characterised by the rapid speed of communication and information exchange that predated the internet. In less than a generation, the way people communicate, process information, and employ data is unrecognisable to the information technology experts of those days. This age has evolved in tandem with materialism and an individualistic pursuit of gains, tempered by a rediscovery of the virtues of humility, integrity, and respect.

How would the firm in 2040 look like and how could businesses prepare for the advent of a "new age"?

Rama sees a future where "a firm is more attuned to the changing needs of its stakeholders, and proactively responds to them. The present generation of young people, who will be consumers twenty years from now, are much more sensitive to issues relating to sustainability, equality, fairness, diversity, and similar virtues. Firms that build strong cultures that emphasise these values will be more successful."

A wise piece of advice indeed. After all, while one may agree or not with how one's children may choose to live their lives, they are more likely to inherit the future and shape it. At the root of these evolving changes, whether they are creeping or disruptive, the foundations on which human relations are built remain constant — *humility*, *integrity*, and *respect*.

*****

Rama Velamuri is the Dean at the School of Management, Mahindra University. Previously, Rama was the Chengwei Ventures Chair and Professor of Entrepreneurship at the China Europe International Business School (CEIBS), Shanghai, China. He was recognised as among the 100 top entrepreneurship faculty in the world by the technology media platform Hot Topics. Prior to this role, Rama was the Assistant Professor at IESE Business School, Spain. He has facilitated executive programs in innovation and entrepreneurship for leading companies, such as Henkel, Michelin, Tencent, China Development Bank, Telefonica, Goodyear-Dunlop, and SASAC, among many others.

Bibliography

Argyris, C. (2008). *Teaching Smart People How to Learn*. Boston, MA: Harvard Business Review Classics, pp. 1–72.

Arrow, K. J. (1964). The role of securities in the optimal allocation of risk-bearing. *Review of Economic Studies*, 31(2), 91–96.

Awerbuch, S. (2006). A portfolio-based electricity generation planning: Policy implications for renewable and energy security. *Mitigation and Adaptation Strategies for Global Change*, 11, 693–710.

Barcelona, R. G. (2015). Renewable energy with volatile prices: Why NPVs fails to tell the whole story? *Journal of Applied Corporate Finance*, 27(1), 101–109.

Barcelona, R. G. (2017). *Energy Investments: An Adaptive Approach to Profiting from Uncertainties*. London: Palgrave Macmillan.

Bar-Lev, D. and Katz. S. (1976). A portfolio approach to fossil fuel procurement in the electric utility industry. *Journal of Finance*, 31(3), 933–947.

Chevalier-Roignant, B. and Trigeorgis, L. (2011). *Competitive Strategy: Options and Games*. Cambridge, MA: Massachusetts Institute of Technology Press.

Cox, J. C., Ross, S. R., and Rubinstein, M. (1979). Option pricing: A simplified approach. *Journal of Financial Economics*, 7(3), 229–263.

Dixit, A. K. and Nalebuff, B. J. (1991). *Thinking Strategically: The Competitive Edge in Business, Politics, and Everyday Life*. New York: W. W. Norton & Company.

Dixit, A. K. and Pindyck, R. S. (1994). *Investment under Uncertainty*. New Jersey: Princeton University Press.

Ekekwe, N. (2011). Beyond Core Competence. *Harvard Business Review*, February 21, 2011.

Eliasson, G. and Taymaz, E. (2002). Institutions, entrepreneurship, economic flexibility and growth — Experiments on an evolutionary micro-to-macro model. In Cantner, U. (ed.), *Economic Evolution, Learning, and Complexity*, Berlin: Springer.

Enzenberger, N., Wietschel, M., and Rentz, O. (2002). Policy instruments fostering wind energy projects — A multi-perspective evaluation approach. *Energy Policy*, 30(9), 793–801, July 2002.

Florio, M. (2014). *Applied Welfare Economics: Cost-benefit Analysis of Projects and Policies*. Oxon and New York: Routledge.

Gale, S. F. (2011). *Prepare for the Unexpected: Investment Planning in Asset Intensive Industries*. London: Economist Intelligence Unit.

Ghemawat, P. (1991). *Commitment*. New York: Free Press.

Graham, J. R. and Harvey, C. R. (2001). The theory and practice of corporate finance: Evidence from the filed. *Journal of Financial Economics*, 60(2/3), 187–243.

Grenadier, S. (2002). Option exercise games: An application to the equilibrium investment strategies of firms. *The Review of Financial Studies*, 15(3), 691–721.

Hammond, J. S., Keeney, R., and Raiffa, H. (2006). The hidden traps in decision making. *Harvard Business Review*, January 2006.

Humphreys, H. B. and McClain, K. T. (1998). Reducing the impacts of energy price volatility through dynamic portfolio selection. *The Energy Journal*, 19(3), 107–131.

Jaffe, A. B. and Stavins, R. N. (1994). The energy paradox and diffusion of conservation technology. *Resource and Energy Economics*, 16, 91–122.

Jevons, W. S. (1865). *The Coal Question: An Enquiry Concerning the Progress of the Nation, and the Probable Exhaustion of Coal Mines*. London: Macmillan.

Johnson, A., Kavali, A., and Neuhoff, K. (2008). Take-or-Pay contracts for renewable deployment. *Energy Policy*, 36(7), 2481–2503.

Kaplan, R. S. (2001). Integrating shareholder value and activity based costing with balanced scorecard. *Balanced Scorecard*, Harvard Business Publishing, 1–4, January 15, 2001.

Kombaroglu, G., Madlener, R., and Demirel, M. (2008). A real options evaluation model for the diffusion prospects of new renewable power generation technology. *Energy Economics*, 30(4), 1882–1903, July 2008.

Magni, C. A. (2009). Splitting up value: A critical review of residual income theories. *European Journal of Operation Research*, 198(1), 1–22, October 2009.

Markowitz, H. M. (1952). Portfolio selection. *Journal of Finance*, 7(1), 77–91.

Markowitz, H. M. (1991). *Portfolio Selection: Efficient Diversification of Investments*, 2nd edn. Oxford: Blackwell Publishing.

Martin, R. L. (2007). How successful leaders think. *Harvard Business Review*, 1–9, June 2007.

Martin, R. L. (2020). What managers get wrong about capital. *Harvard Business Review*, 1–11, May–June 2020.

Mayer, C. (2013). *Firm Commitment: Why the Corporation is Failing us and How to Restore Trust*. Oxford: Oxford University Press.

Morgenstern, O. and von Neumann, J. (1947). *The Theory of Games and Economic Behavior*. Princeton, NJ: Princeton University Press.

Myers, J. N. (1999). Implementing residual income valuation with linear information dynamics. *The Accounting Review*, 74(1), 1–28.

Näsäkkälä, E. and Fleten, S. E. (2005). Flexibility and technology choice in gas-fired power plant investments. *Review of Financial Economics*, 14, 371–393.

Nash, J. (1951). Non-cooperative games. *The Annals of Mathematics*, 54(2), 286–295.

PGF500. (2018). The venture capital funnel shows odds of becoming a unicorn are about 1%. https://www.pgf500.com/news/the-venture-capital-funnel. Accessed on November 7, 2020.

Porter, M. E. (1980). *Competitive Strategy*. New York: Free Press.

Rappaport, A. (2006). Ten ways to create shareholder value. *Harvard Business Review*, 1–14, September 2006.

Roques, F. A., Newberry, D. M., and Nuttal, W. J. (2008). Fuel mix diversification incentives in liberalised electricity markets: A mean variance portfolio approach. *Energy Economics*, 30(4), 1831–1849.

Roques, F. A., Hiroux, C., and Saguan, M. (2010). Optimal wind power deployment in Europe — A portfolio approach. *Energy Policy*, 38, 3245–3256.

Schein, E. H. (1993). On dialogue, culture, and organisational learning. *Organisational Dynamics*, 22(2), 40–51, August 1993.

Sharpe, W. F. (2007). *Investors and Markets: Portfolio Choices, Asset Prices, and Investment Advice*. Princeton, NJ: Princeton University Press.

Smit, H. T. J. and Trigeorgis, L. (2017). Strategic NPV: Real options and strategic games under different information structures. *Strategic Management Journal*, 38(13), 2555–2578, December 2017.

Sneader, K., Williamson, K. S., Koller, T., Potter, V., and Babcock, A. (2020). *Corporate Long-term Behaviours: How CEOs and Boards Drive Sustained Value Creation*. McKinsey & Co., and Focusing Capital on the Long Term Global, October 2020.

Stewart, G. B., III. (1991). *The Quest for Value*. New York: HarperCollins Publishers.

Terwiesch, C. and Ulrich, K. T. (2009). *Innovation Tournaments: Creating and Selecting Exceptional Opportunities*. Boston, MA: Harvard Business Press.

Thaler, R. H. and Sunstein, C. R. (2008). *Nudge: Improving Decisions About Health, Wealth, and Happiness*. New Haven: Yale University Press.

Thaler, R. H. (2015). *Misbehaving: The Making of Behavioural Economics*. New York: W. W. Norton & Company.

Twentyman, J. (2019). How Fujifilm lives by the maxim: Never stop transforming. *Global Intelligence for Digital Leaders*, January 2019.

Wiseman, R. (2003). The Luck Factor. *Skeptical Inquirer*, 27(3), May–June 2003, 1–5.

Chapter 6
Take Actions to De-risk

De-risking energy investments imply two complementary facets: Avoiding losses from adverse events or profiting from better-than-expected outcomes. This managerial mindset reframes risk management. Under volatile markets, managerial flexibility is valued when prior commitments can be reversed affordably to avoid losses or to appropriate surplus. By employing value chain risk assessment, managers could have a granular and comprehensive view of specified risks and their underlying causes. As a result, risk-taking confers on managers the ability to structure specific commitments as creating options by adaptively managing their strategic and operational moves. Policy's role is likewise reframed as one that facilitates capital flows as opposed to one that guarantees private payoffs.

1
Introduction

Ask a manager how they optimise their investment's value and the answers reflect an almost universally shared consensus. To maximise value, one must optimise payoffs at minimum risks. In managerial parlance, minimising risks equate to reducing volatilities. Partly for this reason, managers spend endless hours, through myriad financial tools, to avoid (or minimise) cash flow volatilities. Inadvertently, the search for returns stability becomes a "holy grail" that crown efforts to mitigate risks. As a result, capital-intensive investments are evaluated, structured, planned for success, and funded, under markets with presumably known (and knowable) risks.

Reduced into a number-crunching exercise, *de-risking* investments is oversimplified as a loss avoidance approach, with inadvertent consequences. Avoiding losses, as a principal preoccupation of some managers, can potentially trap people into living a schizophrenic dual life. Specifically:

1. Energy markets are dynamic, uncertain, and pivoting to low carbon supplies, creating ambiguities for extant players and new entrants alike. To evaluate investments, some managers persist in perpetuating the myth of a static, certain, and predictable world, that exists only as a figment of an imagined reality.
2. High administrative and regulatory barriers, which previously shielded returns from competitive erosion, are largely dismantled. Exposed to an uncertain business landscape, some managers blame "misbehaving markets" rather than examine their prior choices as causes for what ails, or propels to new heights, their business.
3. Obsolescence somehow is a strange notion that is best left to hope or ignored, as some managers advocate. Accustomed to extant technologies' long lifecycles, how innovations have shortened the assets' economic life may surprise some managers.

In misdiagnosing the emerging business realities, some managers inadvertently commit to contradictory actions. While recognising obsolescence as a possibility, some choose to lock in rigid obligations for two decades or more. In the face of obsolescence, firms could be placed in default on these commitments and incur financial losses.

In planning for success, these unasked questions, when ignored, could impair managers' ability to respond: What happens if the asset becomes hopelessly uneconomic a few years after commencing operations? What contingencies are contemplated when things work out differently?

Operating under this state of blissful ignorance, it is hardly surprising that some managers realise, often far too late, how they stumble into a world of paradoxes. Here are a few examples:

Instinctively, some managers see price and volume volatilities as the risk to mitigate. With volatile prices and volumes come the undesirable cash flow variations. To smoothen cash flows, prices and volume commitments can be fixed, more or less, for the long haul contractually. By legal fiat, some managers thought that they can safely look to the next couple of decades with an assured nest egg. What was anticipated as a tranquil existence, some managers may spend their life, unexpectedly, from one renegotiation to the next (or from crisis to crisis).

Policy is initially designed for the long term, consistent with prevailing priorities set by an incumbent government. A change in focus, or a shift in ideology, may shorten the life of a policy designed for the next two generations. At this juncture, the managers' conversations with policy take a radically different twist.

If only policy can accelerate new technology adoption, the costs will decline rapidly as to outcompete its rivals, advocates would point to empirical evidence for support (Elshurafa *et al.*, 2018). As wind and solar power technologies have demonstrated, costs fell sharply as more capacity was installed (IRENA, 2020a). Given this evidence, policy defaults to subsidies to jumpstart private capital participation. However, the results are mixed, giving rise to a *green paradox*. Hans-Werner Sinn (2012) is among the minority that point out how generous subsidies failed to curve CO_2 emissions. On a global scale, this is the case (McGrath, 2020), albeit industry performance is varied. The much-maligned power utilities reduced their CO_2 emissions by a fifth since 2015, with energy firms holding their carbon footprint static (Farnworth, 2021).

Policy's best intentions are stymied when private capital risks its investment under uncertain markets. Wind and solar are both supported by policy for their *greenness*, while hydro and geothermal are too mature to deserve assistance. However, their value to a portfolio of energy assets may differ, with some noting wind as a substitute for solar rather than its complement (Gazheli and Bergh, 2018). Indeed, a counterintuitive view that my own work could only reconcile when managers take the value explicitly of pacing their commitments. That is, wind contributes to portfolio value now, with late entrants to solar the more likely beneficiaries.

Subsidies potentially slow technological innovation when rapidly declining costs are experienced, leading some to question subsidies' ability to accelerate adoption (Torani *et al.*, 2016). This is a continuing theme that arose from misgivings about Germany's *Energiewende,* to quote from Manuel Frondel *et al.* at Ruhr-Universität Bochum (2009):

"Government policy has failed to harness the market incentives needed to ensure a viable and cost-effective introduction of renewable energies to the energy portfolio. To the contrary, the government's support mechanisms have in many respects subverted these incentives, resulting in massive expenditures that show little long-term promise for stimulating the economy, protecting the environment, or increasing energy security."

These sentiments are echoed by Brian C Murray *et al.* (2014) in questioning the US renewables subsidies scheme. Others are more supportive, calling against its "premature" withdrawal (Wyman, 2020). Some credit subsidies for accelerating renewables adoption (Nicolini and Ravoni, 2017) to the point of advocating shifting subsidies from fossil fuels to renewables. The views on how effective such a shift may prove to be are equally divided (Jewell *et al.*, 2018; Bridle *et al.*, 2018). To add a social dimension, falling renewables costs seldom equate directly to cuts in power prices, at least in Europe (Deign, 2020).

With "experts" divided in their prescriptions, managers may have to revisit their reliance on subsidies as a secure source of revenues for renewables. That is, to a manager, one has to navigate between the rhetoric of advocates, who risk none of their capital, and the likely impact the resulting policy measures are likely to produce on the investments' financial viability.

Previous reliance on subsidies by investors proves painful. As priorities change or budgetary pressures made continued payments burdensome, the state cuts subsidies. Once bitten by previous subsidy cuts (IER, 2018), some managers met this with a sense of betrayal. As governments removed subsidies to renewables, some investments saw drastic erosion of value. Particularly hit hard were investments undertaken because generous subsidies made it look financially "compelling."

The notion of *de-risking* energy investments will have to depart from a purely "loss avoidance" endeavour. In observing the pace of change, Benoit Chevalier-Roignant and Lenos Trigeorgis (2011) highlight how corporate managers increasingly incorporate *strategic uncertainty* and market structure in evaluating their investments. By its very nature, reversing or pivoting from a prior commitment adds value. The firm's extant endowments such as assets, capabilities, or resources are reconfigured. With each reconfiguration, the firm's ability to realign its initial endowments to its prospective strategy will prove crucial to its survival. Emerging market opportunities, the sources of its payoffs, and the means to appropriate it would largely shift the firms' strategic advantages.

Operating under these dynamic conditions, I posit that de-risking today's commitments involves two facets:

When risk is seen as a deviation from what was expected, managers benefit from exercising managerial flexibility affordably to change course as its strategic moves require. This implies withdrawing to avoid incurring a loss or committing to appropriate any surplus as market conditions favour.

In sustaining prospective viability, managers may have to employ strategic thinking as a way to understand and anticipate rivals' actions. *De-risking* involves judgement on when to compete or cooperate or identify the conditions to lead or follow rival firms.

Employing strategic moves, managers would seek, as Avinash K Dixit and Barry J Nalebuff (2008) propose, to outdo an adversary knowing that they are trying to do the same to you. As part of these tactical moves, managers may at times "find ways to cooperate even when rivals are motivated by self-interests, not benevolence."

In this context, part of the object of making strategic moves is to convert a rival into a prospective partner. One achieves this by placing oneself in the shoes of rivals, to "predict and influence what they will do," Dixit and Nalebuff assert. Within these dynamic interactions, policy and managerial actions are active elements that shape (and reshape) the advantages and value of firms. Understanding how policy works, and how it impacts business, is a core managerial competence to *de-risk* investments. For this reason, how managers would need to perceive, hence manage risks, cuts across the value chain that goes beyond individual investments. Specifically:

The energy fuel markets are governed by trading hubs, where coal, oil, and gas are traded under relatively transparent rules and freedom. Spot prices result from the state of demand and the available supplies. With fuel largely fungible, fuel supply uncertainty is reduced to volatile prices and volumes and integrity of logistics and supportive institutions.

Renewables are faced with vastly different challenges. Depending on feedstocks that are freely available but dispersed, the whims of nature dictate its availability. Taming nature through technology, engineering, and human creativity, one can monetise (sort of) resources that are freely dispersed but intermittent and otherwise costly to harness.

In this chapter, I examine how conventional risk mitigations create inadvertent consequences. Often, measures to secure payoffs can become the very sources of hidden and often ignored risks. This is partly remedied by deploying one's insights on the value chain, to identify at a granular level, the sources of risks that the firm could offload, as needed, to third parties or convert into profit opportunities. An offshoot of this understanding is the prospect of innovating how investments are structured and combining social and private funding to de-risk portfolios of energy assets.

2
Inadvertent Consequences

Almost instinctively, some managers default into structuring their investment's payoffs to achieve the highest degree of certitude. This is confirmed by the "top wish list" colleagues in investment banking would require managers to satisfy when arranging financing. To make an investment "bankable" (IRENA, 2020b), hence ensuring its access to private financing (Hampl *et al.*, 2011), proponents are expected to show the following:

A robust power purchase agreement (PPA) comprises a long-term commitment by a buyer to purchase a specified volume, at given prices, that ensures a level of cash flows that service debt repayments. To prove the cash flows' predictability, buyers enter into a *take-or-pay* obligation. This simply means that a buyer either chooses to *take* deliveries as contracted or pay just the same, even if they are unable to take deliveries. In its later incarnation, some flexibility is introduced on volume deliveries. The buyer may choose to postpone physical deliveries to a future date or allow the seller to divert the volumes to other buyers (or sell at the spot market). The payment remains due, however, which in effect transfers the volume risks to the buyer (from the seller).

Seen from the lender's perspective, the arrangement makes sense, at least to the providers of debt. Debt providers earn the interest paid for the use of the money. For the privilege, they risk their funds to finance usually up to 70% of the investment outlay over a long period. With interest rates at historic lows, the yield may not fully compensate the risk of borrowers defaulting. This remains true even when interest rates were at their previous highs in excess of 10%.

The equity holders are in a better position. In theory, if all work according to plan, they are on track to mint a fortune. On a 30% share of the funding, which represents the portion not taken up by debt, all residual payoffs accrue to them. That is, as debts are repaid, more of the payoffs accrue to the equity providers.[1] For this privilege, equity holders take on all the risks, including bankruptcy, where they could lose all their equity. To monetise equity returns, one would ideally have the flexibility on pricing and volumes. When prices are high, suppliers would want to sell more. In some cases, supply glut would result in very low prices that could fall below the costs to supply. To avoid incurring a loss, suppliers may choose to curtail temporarily selling to the market. Acting as a quasi-monopoly, this is what OPEC[2] does with their production quotas to seek to balance prevailing supplies according to the strength (or weakness) of crude oil demand.

---

[1] Chapter 8 discusses this question extensively.
[2] Oil Producing and Exporting Countries (OPEC), a cartel of sovereign oil suppliers that sets production quotas and reference prices for oil for its members.

2.1 Ignored risks under rigid obligations

In structuring the power purchase agreement (PPA), a team of lawyers and managers usually take several months to negotiate an acceptable contract that debt and equity providers *can live with*. In real life, few managers are fully satisfied with what they achieved to negotiate.

In the company of reasonable and highly intelligent people, why this level of dissatisfaction?

Part of the reason is the diverse and conflicting demands from stakeholders that a PPA should provide. For the debt providers, an alternative is to keep the money in the bank or in sovereign treasuries to earn interest income. With minimal administrative costs, the cash provider earns a steady flow of periodic income with a low probability of the bank or government defaulting. This is usually the case when one operates in developed financial systems with strong institutions.

The buyers, who bear the brunt of the risk, are asked to secure the payoffs of the sellers for the privilege of getting a steady supply of fuels or energy. Without a functional energy market, this makes sense and is even essential to the buyer, particularly when few suppliers could satisfy the buyers' volume requirements. However, as markets develop and become more efficient in arbitrating supply and demand, the buyer's interest runs counter to that of the supplier. Examine, for instance, the following:

> While the buyer would want supply security, they would seek the most affordable fuels or energy to fulfil their needs. In this case, few managers would willingly concede their flexibility to purchase what they need or forego what is not required. In the absence of a functioning market, contingency inventories are stockpiled to minimise supply disruptions. The level is reasonably pegged to the amount that covers the expected demand for the period before a replacement supply could be delivered.

Using this as a context, the "secure payoffs" that PPAs are expected to provide are far from a tenable agreement that could outlast the first credible challenge. This emerges when contracted and market prices begin to significantly diverge. The shifting positions of buyers and sellers are illustrated in Chart 6.1.

Take Actions to De-risk 303

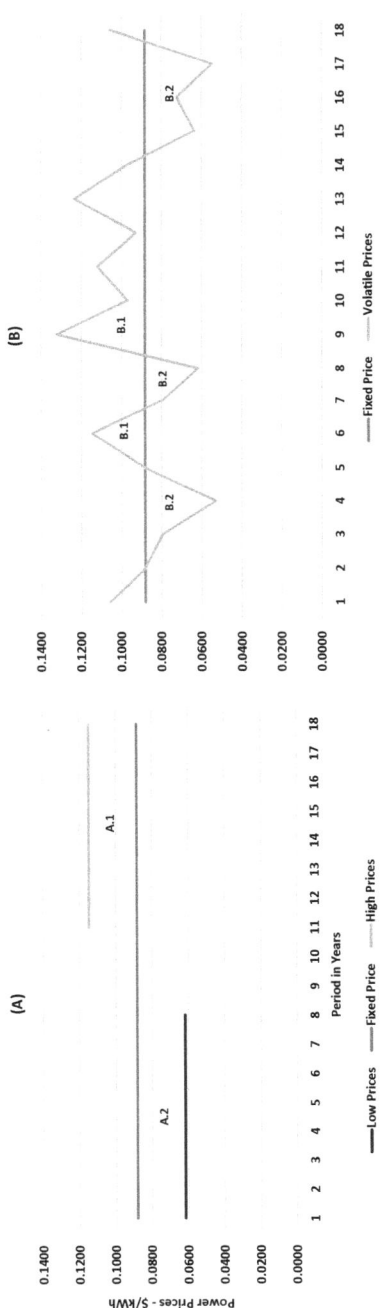

Chart 6.1: PPA Revenues and Risks

Source: Author using EIA data.

In (A), the straight line is the contracted price set at $0.0882/kWh. Soon after committing, a supply shortage was experienced by a severe winter, which caused gas prices to spike by 30%. The resulting gap, which represents the foregone revenues of the seller (A.1), is a transfer of value in favour of the buyer. While both seller and buyer are upright citizens, the price increase alters their respective positions:

For a 300 MW gas-fired power plant, the annual output for $ACCGT_B$ is 2,286,360 MWh (300 MW * 24 hours/day * 365 days/year * 87% utilisation rate), implying an annual foregone revenue of $60.45 mln.

Assuming that the power plant offloaded its fuel risks by entering into a similar *ship-or-pay* contract, the gas supplier would incur foregone fuel revenues of $43.8 mln ($19.16/MWh * 2,286,360). The power generator is, in theory, even given that any fuel price variations are matched by a similar change in fuel costs, with transport and regasification expenses equally passed through to the power buyer.

In this chain of seller–buyer transactions, a default by one party would result in cascading losses. With the financial risks unevenly allocated, the PPA is hardly sustainable. In a reversal of roles, when fuel and energy prices fall, say 30% below the contract price, the gap shown as (A.2) is the foregone savings of the buyer. In effect, the buyer by adhering to the contract is paying more than what they could purchase in the market.

Over the long term, one may argue that the price fluctuations would even out. Hence, what the seller foregoes in one period, they may recoup in another. A similar logic is applied to the buyer. This would work with managers who operate with aligned views of future price movements, with a dose of perfect foresight thrown in. However, with people drawn by opposing motivations, continual renegotiations are in prospect. In reality, firms tend to be saddled with renegotiation risks, long after managers and their lawyers have moved on to other pastures.

Variable renewables developers found solace in corporate PPAs, where a number of adaptations have to be designed into the structures. Intermittent supplies, which characterise wind and solar power, cannot guarantee to deliver the volumes when they are needed. By relaxing this rigid volume obligation, corporate PPAs "fix" the costs to the "buyer". The supplier (or developer) sells their output to the wholesale market. As shown in (B), the seller's position works out as the following:

> When market prices are above what was contracted, the seller takes a "loss" and supplies at the contracted price (B.1). In rare cases, the seller may enjoy some arbitrage when they could sell at market price and somehow find some supplies that are cheaper to fulfil their contracted volume as it falls due for delivery.
>
> Conversely, as market prices fall below what was contracted, the seller may choose to supply the buyer from their own output at the higher contracted price. The buyer continues to pay a "fix" price whatever the energy market does, in theory, that is. The gaps (B.2) represent a gain (or "excess" profit) to the seller.

Corporate buyers have altruistic as well as economic reasons to enter into such agreements. In funding the deployment of green technologies, mostly solar at this stage, some corporates see this as fulfilling their environmental promise. For some, managing energy supply is not seen as a core or strategic activity. By outsourcing this, as many corporates tend to do with their utilities, they can focus on higher value-adding priorities in their strategic agenda.

The seller's "losses" are in principle, hypothetical. Knowing their lifecycle costs of energy (LCOEs), sellers are likely to contract at or above this price. With fuel prices having no influence on their cost of supplies, the "loss" is in reality a foregone revenue. Thus, for as long as the sum of (B.1) is less than the sum of (B.2), the seller could find the agreement to their advantage. In effect, corporate PPAs protect sellers from the adverse financial effects of prolonged low prices.

The secured payoffs that managers hoped to achieve with PPAs are proving more elusive than initially thought. Worse, what was supposed to be secure is turning out to create new sources of risks that are ignored (Kemp, 2019). Specifically:

> Conventional *take-or-pay* in power purchases, or its equivalent in fuels, *ship-or-pay*, is costly to sustain. The opposing interests embed the economic incentives to renegotiate, with the value of the rewards increasing as the deviations (market vs contracted prices) widen.

With each renegotiation, the carefully crafted balance is broken. In theory, sellers give up excess revenues, when market prices exceed what was contracted. As this is reversed, buyers give up their "savings" from lower market prices by adhering to the higher contracted price. As contract prices are adjusted down, which are more likely than up, the "bonus" from rising market prices becomes a fleeting prospect for the seller. Aggressively pushing contracted prices down, the buyer may find their suppliers walk away, leaving them with nil supplies.

Corporate PPAs may experience a similar pressure to renegotiate, although for different reasons. Renewables are in reality a source of fixed costs supply, with some costs incurred to administer (equivalent to operating costs). As costs of wind or solar power continue to fall, corporates may find it to their advantage to bypass PPAs and operate their own assets.

Contrary to the proponents of "win–win" solutions, the certitude of payoffs or the security of fixed costs may prove a bargain too expensive to sustain. This is what India is discovering to their grief (Jhawar, 2020), when state-owned utilities opt to cancel or at times, renegotiate old contracts to benefit from ever-declining costs from renewables. India, of course, is not alone. They simply follow historic precedents from other markets (see, for example, Woolf and Halpern, 2001).

2.2 Secure revenues or embedded default risks?

When investments are dependent on subsidies or the government as guarantor, managers may have taken the state as a counter-party. That is, the investment's financial viability is now subjected to the good behaviour of the state. A government known to comply with its promise is seen as a reliable counter-party that delivers on its obligations. Conversely, frequent interventions by the government, often leading to changes in the incentive schemes, could drastically alter the value of investments.

How the *grid price parity* principles are applied is a case in point. To recognise the benefits of reducing CO_2 emissions that variable renewables deliver, some form of compensation is due to private investors. This is more so if, in some cases, the private costs are in excess of investing in fossil fuel-based supplies. Economists refer to this as externalities, which are social benefits or costs that private capital cannot uniquely appropriate as profits. To equalise, the difference in LCOEs between the two technologies is estimated. This serves as the basis for setting the right level of subsidies.

This formulation, simple as it is, encounters serious problems in practice, as I illustrate in Chart 6.2. Starting with (A), gas-fired $ACCGT_B$'s LCOEs vary with fuel prices. Over a range of assumed gas prices, the LCOEs would be above or below some of the intermittent renewables. In contrast, intermittent renewables have nil fuel costs, which would imply relatively stable LCOEs over its life.

When one takes the cost differences between technologies with variable and stable costs, the answers will vary, as shown in (B). With gas prices as the principal source of volatility, $ACCGT_B$ would be cheaper when gas prices are low (or vice versa) when compared to onshore wind ($Wind_{ON}$), photovoltaic with tracking (PVT_M), or offshore wind with advanced platforms ($Wind_{OFAP}$). The different intermittent renewables, such as wind and solar, have different capital expenditures. This would imply that each technology would need different levels of payoffs to achieve a reasonable return.

From my estimates, at lower gas prices, intermittent renewables would require varying levels of subsidies to achieve *grid price parity* with $ACCGT_B$ (or vice versa). The implications to policy-induced subsidies are the following:

In fixing a technology-specific subsidy, or any *ad valorem* subsidies, the level is bound to over- or undercompensate. Set too high, private capital is earning a "bonus" that consumers are bound to bear the burden in terms of higher power prices. On the other hand, subsidies that are too low to compensate the "excess" costs of variable renewables will prove ineffective. Private capital is unlikely to commit, if by doing so, they are destined to lose or underrecover their investments.

Almost reflexively, private capital would include generous subsidies as a precondition for investing in variable renewables, at least for first-round early adopters. With a secure revenue stream from subsidies, private capital sees the prospect of earning payoffs with minimal risks (of government defaulting).

A second-order problem arises within dynamic energy markets. Volatile energy prices are bound to create temporal and cyclical mismatches between $ACCGT_B$ and $Wind_{ON}$, PVT_M, or $Wind_{OFAP}$. When gas prices are low,

Chart 6.2: Grid Price Parity under Ambiguous Conditions
Source: Author using EIA data.

variable renewables would need the subsidies the most and in large amounts. For consumers, they are likely to resist the "excess" levy. As gas prices rise, intermittent renewables become comparatively cheaper, eliciting a different reaction from consumers. That is, why continue to subsidise technologies that have "come of age" to outcompete fossil fuels?

Under these conditions, consumers are likely to coax regulators to cut subsidies, with some regulators more inclined to side with consumers. At this point, investments that are highly leveraged to subsidies become vulnerable to the state's changing priorities. When this change of heart occurs, subsidies become the very source of risks, manifested by "secure revenues" dissipating into thin air.

3
Adaptive Value Chain De-risking

In one of my visits to a boot camp, I noticed a vertical wall with rocks embedded on its surface. The trainer describes how the trainees perform rock climbing. Each climber, wearing a harness to prevent injury from falling, would secure their grip while balancing their foothold on the individual rocks. Pacing their ascent, they pivot from one rock to the next, at times stepping back to regain their balance. The object of the game is to reach the top of the wall as a team without injuries. The climb mixes individual efforts as well as team coordination to ensure that everyone makes it to the top safely ahead of other competing teams.

I turned to the trainer: "What traits would prove decisive for a team to win the race to the top?" His answer resonated with me: "More than speed, it is *agility* that allows the team to regain their balance when someone missteps, and *awareness* of where each one stands at each moment. Given these two traits, a coordinated move to step forward or retreat, is facilitated."

Rock climbing, seen as a simple use of brute force by some, is to my mind an exercise in strategic agility in deployment. In navigating through a transitioning energy system, progress is seldom linear. Recognising that outcomes are often recursive and tentative, managers would need to broaden their approach to de-risking today's investments to deliver a sustainable future.

So, how does one *de-risk* today's commitments, while traversing the uncertain paths to an aspired future?

Juxtaposing the language of risk mitigation with the lexicon of strategy, *where the firm is* equated to the *initial endowments* that the firm possesses in terms of resources, assets, and capabilities. In this combination, the degree to which firms can pursue, or adapt, to achieve their aspired position of *where they want to be* could be ascertained with a dose of uncertainty. What the future could be, however, is seen as a tangled web of outcomes that arise from how rival firms would interact. Given this range of uncertainties, *how they get there* becomes a contingent series of decisions. In effect, the trajectories to successful outcomes may resemble the steps the rock climbers take to pivot while keeping their balance or to step back to regain their momentum.

3.1 Divergent risks or opportunities

Operating under these recursive and tentative conditions, managers would need to dive deeper into a granular and segmented approach to *de-risking* their investments. By taking a value chain perspective, the extent to which risks are embedded within each component is better understood. As a result, how the risk could be assumed or mitigated can be specified and its impact on the firm's value quantified to the extent possible.

Schematically, an overview of the value chain would identify where the risks reside and how they relate to the other segments of the chain. I attempt to illustrate these interactions in Chart 6.3.

To generate power, one needs to find the fuel (or feedstock) that converts raw energy into useful power. For fossil fuel sources, such as coal, oil, and gas, the market generally separates the value chains for fuel and power generation. In essence, fossil fuels are widely traded as fungible goods, where a molecule of gas of similar specifications can be interchangeably used by power plants with access to these molecules. Consequently, with adequate logistics, fossil fuels are sold separately from power, with each having its own users. Uranium, as feedstock for nuclear plants, possesses similar characteristics.

Mining for coal (A.1, B.1) and uranium (A.6, B.6) is a well-established business, with geologists having proven protocols to explore and develop the mines to extract

Take Actions to De-risk 311

Column/Row	Sources of Risks	Acronym	Fuels or Feedstock					Power Generation				
			Explore A	Develop B	Convert C	Market D	Dismantle E	Select E	Build F	Operate G	Market H	Dismantle I
1	Coal	Coal$_B$	xx	xx	x	xxx	xx	x	x	x	xx	x
2	Advance Combined Cycle Gas Turbines	ACCGT$_B$	xxx	xxx	x	xx	xx	x	x	x	x	x
3	Conventional hydro — Pump Storage	StoHydro$_B$	x	xx	x	x	x	xx	xx	x	x	x
4	Geothermal — Large Hole	Geo$_B$	xxx	xxx	xx	x	x	xx	x	x	x	x
5	Geothermal — Slim Hole	GeoS$_B$	xx	xx	xx	x	x	xx	x	x	x	x
6	Advance Nuclear	ANuke	xx	xx	xx	xx	xxx	xxx	xxx	x	x	xxx
7	Wind — Onshore	Wind$_{ON}$	O	O	xx	x	xx	xx	x	xx	xx	xx
8	Wind — Offshore	Wind$_{OFF}$	O	O	xx	x	xx	xxx	x	xx	xx	xx
9	Photovoltaic — Tracking	PVT$_M$	O	O	xxx	x	xxx	xx	x	x	xx	xx
10	Battery Storage	Li-ON	O	O	O	O	O	x	x	x	x	xx

Column/Row	Sources of Payoffs	Acronym	Fuels or Feedstock					Power Generation				
			Explore	Develop	Convert	Market	Dismantle	Select	Build	Operate	Market	Dismantle
11	Coal	Coal$_B$	O	O	✓✓	✓✓	x	O	O	✓✓	✓✓	x
12	Advance Combined Cycle Gas Turbines	ACCGT$_B$	O	O	✓✓	✓✓	x	O	O	✓✓	✓✓	x
13	Conventional hydro — Pump Storage	StoHydro$_B$	O	O	O	✓✓	O	O	O	✓✓✓	✓✓✓	x
14	Geothermal — Large Hole	Geo$_B$	O	O	✓✓	✓✓✓	x	O	O	✓✓✓	✓✓✓	x
15	Geothermal — Slim Hole	GeoS$_B$	O	O	✓✓	✓✓✓	x	O	O	✓✓✓	✓✓✓	x
16	Advance Nuclear	ANuke	O	O	✓✓	✓✓	x	O	O	✓✓	✓✓	xxx
17	Wind — Onshore	Wind$_{ON}$	O	O	O	✓✓✓	O	O	O	✓	✓✓	xx
18	Wind — Offshore	Wind$_{OFF}$	O	O	O	✓✓✓	O	O	O	✓✓	✓✓	xx
19	Photovoltaic — Tracking	PVT$_M$	O	O	O	✓✓	O	O	O	✓	✓	xx
20	Battery Storage	Li-ON	O	O	O	✓✓✓	O	O	O	✓	✓	xx

Legend: x Low Risk; xx Moderate Risk; xxx High Risk
✓ Low Payoffs; ✓✓ Moderate Payoffs; ✓✓✓ High Payoffs
O Neutral (Shaded areas show that the factor described is not relevant to the technology under consideration.)

Chart 6.3: Expected Risks and Payoffs of Fuels and Power Investments

the raw materials. The technology to convert coal and uranium into energy (C.1, C.6) is equally proven. While the markets for both fuels are equally established and global in scale, tighter environmental standards overshadow coal's prospects (D.1) for continued expansion (D.11). Uranium would depend on how future acceptance of nuclear power, aside from its other uses in defence and civilian applications, would foreshadow its future demand (D.6, D.16). At the end of a mine's life, the area has to be restored to its original state, which could imply expenditures that vary with environmental and regulatory requirements (E.1, E.6). Hence, costs may exceed what was provisioned for (E.1, E.6) or new and stringent costs are levied to reduce payoffs appropriable by investors (E.11, E.16).

Oil and gas have to be explored (A.2), and once the reserves are proven to be commercially viable, the wells are developed (B.2). This is a risky venture, given that money is spent on deploying equipment and people, without the certainty that oil or gas will be found. Fortunately, the sums involved are usually within levels that prospective payoffs from successful wells could recoup with a healthy return.

An established supply and market for coal, oil and gas, and uranium, is a major advantage for investors in fossil fuel-based power generators. With adequate logistical linkages, the selection of sites (E.1, E.2) for fossil fuel technologies poses manageable risks. Nuclear power (E.6, F.6) may encounter challenges on acceptability from the community. Seen as employing hazardous fuels, in spite of a record of safe use and operations for most nuclear plants, people want to enjoy reliable power supplies for as long as it is generated far from their own backyard (or the "not-in-my-backyard," NIMBY phenomenon). Maturing oil and gas wells or fields may be abandoned (E.2) or divested (E.12) with generally accepted protocols.

Renewables pose different challenges and opportunities that fossil fuel and nuclear as conventional feedstocks confer. For this reason, what worked with conventional feedstocks may not always migrate with ease to inform how renewables investments are de-risked.

The feedstocks for renewables vary. Wind and sunlight, while generally available, are dispersed and costly to harness. Water may vary with fluvial patterns, although it could be impounded and stored in pump storage reservoir. Geothermal steam has to be found by drilling, with the subsequent reserves collected through a pipe system.

While wind, water, and sunlight are ubiquitous, they need to be of appropriate speed, flows, or availability, to turn the turbines or windmills, or convert light into power. These energy resources are geocentric, where location counts to determine how abundant or reliable or intermittent their supplies may turn out.

In theory, these feedstocks are "free," particularly for water, wind, and sunlight. It can be tapped at varying quantities from most places on the planet, the arctic excepted. However, the costs to harness it and centralise in sufficient quantities to ease handling or conversion can be hefty in relation to their energy output. For this reason, investors would prefer to locate their investments in places where renewables can operate viably. Hence, site selection (E.3–E.9) and what to build (F.3–F.9) are the most critical choices managers would make.

To differentiate, renewables may come as *modulated* or *intermittent* supplies. Water, when stored in pumped storage, can generate power according to how demand varies. Similarly, geothermal steam can be channelled through pipes that are amenable to being *modulated* with fluctuations in volumes. In effect, managers in a sense have some direct control over how much of the feedstock is supplied and how much of the power is generated at a given time. Given these operational characteristics, energy supplies can be flexibly deployed and generally integrated into conventional power grids with minimal adaptation. For these reasons, the operational risks (G.3–G.5) are considered low, with access to an established power market reducing risks to payoffs (H.3–H.5). Once built, pumped storage hydro power offers the prospect of a low-cost power supply for the long term, with attractive payoffs (G.13) given its fifty years of expected operational life.

Wind is everywhere as well as sunlight. However, while wind can blow the whole day, at varying speeds and strengths, the sunlight is limited to certain hours of the day in specified locations. Without a way to store its power output, energy generated from sunlight will have to be used as it is produced. Battery storage is hoped to become cheap enough in the future to affordably mitigate solar power's drawbacks.

Available only when the wind blows or when the sun shines, extant technologies limit the yields of power, leading to lower output for every MW of capacity installed. In effect, for the same output as fossil fuel-based technologies, wind and solar power would need to install more capacity. In the absence of any subsidies, the resulting payoffs would be lower as well, with wind faring better than solar (G.17–G.19,

H.17–H.19). This remains true, using data from Energy Information Administration (EIA),[3] even after the sharp falls in wind and solar costs once incentives and subsidies are removed.

This creates a conundrum for investors in *intermittent* renewables. Seeking to earn stable payoffs, managers would aspire to replicate a "proven and tested" *ship-or-pay* contract, with the seller's obligation to *ship* relaxed to when power is, and can be, generated (or the wind blows or the sun shines), with a corresponding buyer's commitment to *pay* a fixed price. As previously explained, corporate PPAs emerged as the "compromise" for *intermittent* renewables to gain access to financing.

Geothermal is straddling between fossil fuel and hydro power's ability to *modulate* supplies and the zero fuel costs enjoyed by intermittent renewables. One would think that geothermal would provide the panacea to achieve an affordable pivot to a low carbon system. In theory, and in practice, it can be the missing link in the evolving decarbonisation of energy.

The question is, why is it consigned to the attic, hidden from its Prince Charming, as Cinderella was by her stepmother and stepsisters?

3.2 Resolving contradictions and geothermal paradox

In our paper on Indonesia's geothermal resource paradox, we argued that the constraints to adopting geothermal energy, of which Indonesia overtook the Philippines, as the second producer globally, lie in the following unresolved contradictions:

> "Quick to complain about the government's unreliable and shifting stance, investors look to the same counter-party to guarantee their 'iron clad' power purchased agreements to secure their returns. To unleash Indonesia's geothermal potential, we propose adopting slim-hole drilling technologies to reduce costs, while facilitating sequential commitments. This could enhance strategic flexibility that lowers cost of well failures, while facilitating adoption of resource insurance to de-risk geothermal exploration and drilling. To sustain these benefits, 'cheap' energy policy needs to be phased out" (Barcelona *et al.*, 2019).

---

[3] The detailed calculations for the different power generation technologies are shown in Chapter 7.

To dive deeper into resolving this paradox, let me unpack our principal findings:

> Indonesia pursues a "cheap" energy policy that sells power to consumers at below the cost of supplies. To make this "work," fuel costs such as coal and diesel are subsidised, with any losses of the state-owned power firm, PT Perusahaan Listrik Negara (PLN), compensated through a budgetary contribution by the state. The suppliers of coal and diesel are state-owned entities. We noted that "as the whole chain is cross-subsidised, consumers get their power 'cheap'." Under this system, "PLN's financial ability to report profits, *as well as other state-owned suppliers*, is totally reliant on the government's generosity, as its *de facto* sovereign guarantor for its liabilities."
>
> To reinforce this "cheap" energy policy, regional prices are kept low. In relative terms, the high demand markets — Java and Sumatra — are offered higher power prices, presumably to reduce the overall deficits of PLN. Private investors, not enjoying any of the subsidies that PLN gets, are required by regulation to offer power prices for their supplies that are no higher than the prevailing regional prices.
>
> We noted: "As one may expect, few private investments are pursued, with higher priced Java and Sumatra taking the lion's share, while regional grids are starved of capital." A silver lining is emerging, but only just, when the government is gradually allowing PLN's prices to align with the market.

The more serious consequences that are overlooked are the contradictions that emerged. As the spiralling subsidies become untenable, if kept unchanged as the demand grows, a greater proportion of the Indonesian public expenditures is diverted from other social and critical infrastructure investments. As a result, we noted that "investors may have, and continue to, misdiagnose what ails Indonesia's geothermal development. Rather than finding security in PPAs, the ability to unbundle uncertainties, and finding a structure to bound the financial costs of *exploration and development* failures, holds greater promise."

This is of course not a unique Indonesian problem. Similar misaligned risks, that is, returns, have plagued geothermal developments in Africa, Asia, and most other locations. Turkey and Kenya introduce resource insurance that offers some prospects of reversing this poor performance. Here are some realities that investors may reconsider, as we noted in our analysis of Indonesia's experience that applies more broadly:

"High exploration costs front-load cash commitments when the prospect of finding commercially viable resources is most uncertain, and prospects for revenues being earned are poor.

Each drilling yields information that guides the decision to proceed or abandon. On striking a seam of viable reserves, the subsequent wells are more likely to strike pay dirt. At this point, spending on well testing and validation of reserves could unlock the potential power affordably at lower risks.

Committing to PPAs prior to establishing the viable geothermal reserves, investors take on default risks they may not be able to manage. Inadvertently, investors plan on success by ignoring the costs of failures. In the event of successive well failures, the costs to abandon increase exponentially. Without steam, investors default as suppliers, while buyers could sue for compensation. In this situation, the only resolution is for the investor to pay up or declare bankruptcy.

Arguably, investors may commit to PPAs once they know the viable reserves, hence gaining the ability to bound (or estimate) the steam or energy that they could deliver (more or less). Managers may opt to lock-in prices and volumes to secure stable cash flows. PPAs however, do not provide the cash flow security that private investors and lenders hoped for given the prospect of continual renegotiations.

Continual PPA renegotiations are far from a theoretical exercise. Following Indonesia's price-setting rules, a twenty years PPA signed on March 28, 2018, would fall under the 2017 price caps set at $0.1076/kWh. When the new price cap takes effect on April 1, 2018, the same contract on the same project signed on April 2, 2018, would fetch $0.1700/kWh, because coal prices have gone up (Handiputranto, Hadinoto & Partners,

2018). Applied to geothermal projects, the annual revenue difference is $491,961 ($0.17/kWh–$0.1076/kWh, and the difference is multiplied by 7,884 MWh/year) for each MW installed."

This is where the "private investors' narratives become contradictory. Decrying the government's penchant for arbitrary actions, hence increasing 'regulatory risks', they turn to the same 'unreliable' government to secure their PPAs' cash flows for two decades," we argued.

In conclusion, we observed: "Under these circumstances, increased uncertainties are the likely outcomes. Billions of dollars are committed, trusting in a foresight that hardly exists among investors, lenders, or policy. All these are done in the hope of securing profits through regulatory fiat under volatile fuel and energy markets."

To avoid being trapped in this dead end, a broader assessment of risks and identifying critical constraints to unleashing value lies in a value chain approach to de-risking.

4
Adaptive Moves to De-risking

In a number of instances, *de-risking* is associated with minimising deviations (volatilities) from expected outcomes. This conventional approach is heavily influenced by the notion that capital budgeting encourages. To recall, stable and predictable cash payoffs are worth more than volatile (or risky) future expected cash flows. For similar aggregate amounts cash flows, stable cash flows are discounted by a lower discount rate, while a higher rate applies to more volatile payoffs. The rest is simple math: Lower discount rates would yield higher present values (or vice versa). For this reason, managers tend to err, as described in previous examples, in how they structure their investments and inadvertently forego values that are otherwise embedded as potential gains.

To unlock these embedded values, managers would need to recognise dynamic markets for what they are. When confronted with uncertain and volatile markets, managers veer around its pitfalls to adapt to reap the opportunities that are embedded.

Within this dynamic context, managers adapt to how the market condition is expected to change, and to avoid making a loss, abort or accelerate investments as needed. In essence, this involves the trade-off between exercising managerial flexibility, to keep one's options open, and the benefits of committing to an investment that is lumpy and expensive to reverse. I propose that this trade-off involves two generic types of managerial flexibility, described as the following:

1. *Operational flexibility* is a continuous exercise of periodic options to supply, by how much and under what conditions. The object is to avoid losses or gain when expected outcomes are more favourable than anticipated.
2. *Strategic flexibility* involves a decision on what technologies to choose and their scale, when to invest and how to pace the commitments, and where to locate the asset(s).

A highly simplified example is a decision to commit to rigid obligations to supply or keeping one's options on how much to supply, at what price, open, as I illustrate in Chart 6.4.

Managers may exercise strategic flexibility when they choose to use a technology, which in this case, pump storage hydro (StoHydro$_B$) is chosen as an example. It is seen to offer the advantages of high supply availability with volumes that can be adapted to how demand varies, quickly and cost-effectively. Its fuel cost is nil, which is an added advantage. Its long operating life, with reasonable maintenance costs for half a century or more, makes changing variations in demand expectations less critical to its financial viability.

When constructing the reservoir, the uncertainties relate to social actions by affected communities and how aggressively they would resist the presence of dam(s) in their vicinity. This may cause delays that could result in cost overruns, which is a permanent penalty on the investment's financial returns. In exercising its strategic flexibility, managers may abort to cut their losses or expand if more resources could be channelled to supply the growing demand.

As StoHydro$_B$ becomes operational, the periodic payoffs may mimic the pattern seen previously in Chart 6.1(B). To recall, as power prices vary (with gas prices when

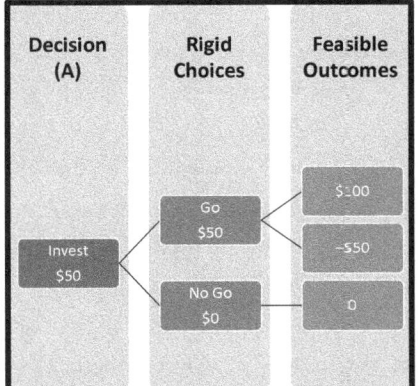 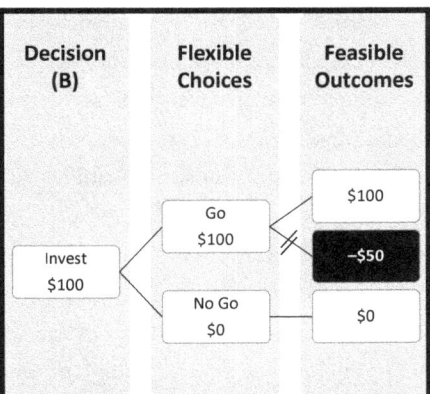

Chart 6.4: Comparative Values of Contracting Strategy

ACCGT$_M$ sets the price), StoHydro$_B$ cash margin will similarly fluctuate. Under this market condition, managers may opt to follow either decision (A) or (B) in Chart 6.4.

With the asset already in operation, some risk-averse managers may choose to "secure" their payoffs by committing to rigid volumes while keeping prices at the market or in effect taking "pricing risks." Following decision (A), the expected NPV may yield $100 mln, after simulating the variations in volumes, partly because of observed climatic patterns, using binomial tree analysis.[4] Without going into the math in the meantime, it suffices to say that when power prices are persistently low, NPV may turn negative, which in this case is −$50 mln.

Acting as rational managers, attributing an even chance of either event occurring, the risk-weighted value is estimated at $50 mln (or, $100 mln * 0.5 − $50 mln * 0.5). One of course is tempted to "fix" the costs as well so that payoffs can be "made predictable," except that there is no reason to do so when fuel costs are already nil. Fixing the price, as previously shown in Chart 6.1(A) could be costly for StoHydro$_B$. The foregone revenues are significant, implying a costly sacrifice of foregone payoffs to attain certitude in financial returns.

Some managers can tolerate ambiguities in their financial payoffs, for as long as they are sufficiently compensated. By following decision (B), managers opt to take

---

[4] Chapter 10 illustrates the calculations using binomial trees under interacting actions of competing firms.

market risks or expose their financial payoffs to both pricing and volume risks (or volatilities). Their conditions? They decide when to supply and when to curtail volumes. In real life, these managers look at interruptible supplies under dynamic markets as a source of value. Here's how it works:

A simple operational rule is followed: When the cost of supply is higher than the prevailing price, curtail. Otherwise, supply at available volume. When volumes are expected to continue to be better than expected, one can ramp up supplies or add new capacities (or exercise growth options).

One is said to follow a loss avoidance tactic when supply is curtailed or exercise a put option on incurring a liability. In aiming to gain more when prices are higher, one is exercising a call option on "excess" payoffs (relative to fix price contracts). Repeated continually, one can avoid the losses (by not supplying) while gaining the "excess" payoffs, resulting in a value gain of $50 mln (or, $0 * 0.5 instead of $-50 * 0.5). The value of the decision is estimated at $100 mln (or, $100 mln *1.0 + $0 * 0.0).

What just transpired is not a mathematical chicanery. It applies the precept of real options reasoning where a manager has the right to exercise, but does not have the obligation to commit. In essence, this is what a dynamic market confers: Managers decide to supply or curtail subject to what their cost curve is. As prices fall, usually because of a glut, high-cost suppliers would exit rather than incur a loss, and more would follow until the periodic supply and demand are in equilibrium.

At this point, the value of operational flexibility may already be obvious: It is the NPV difference between the expected outcomes of decisions (A) and (B).

4.1 Strategically adapting across value chain

Intuitively, managers would seek to commit the minimum resources, particularly cash, at the early stages of assessing prospect(s). The reasons may include any or a combination of the following:

1. In the process of learning how the prospect(s) may have a fit with the firm's strategic purpose, managers may prefer to spend little to gain information relevant for their decision to proceed.
2. Financial payoffs, and how they could be monetised and appropriated, are highly uncertain. Cash, once committed, is a certain expense (or outflow).

3. Cost of compliance or failures may prove prohibitive to proponents, particularly when *ex ante* cash commitments are significant in relation to the firm's financial resources and probability of success.

While these are not exhaustive, the list may provide a starting point to illustrate how value chain *de-risking* could facilitate private capital's participation. Examine, for instance, the following:

Valuation of firms is often conducted that assumes owners will hold their equity till maturity. In theory, equity "matures" when the firm winds down its business or ends up in liquidation. While in business, the firm is an "ongoing concern" where equity has, in theory, an "infinite" life.

An alternative approach is to see equity as a less permanent commitment. Just like debt, the security can be sold or paid down when its "full value" is achieved or the investment (or firm) no longer fits with the investor's aspirations.

Applied to energy investments, an investment may be structured in such a way as to allow the owners the flexibility to sequentially capture the value that accrues at each stage of execution. This structure is illustrated in Chart 6.5.

Consider two energy markets that follow different licencing requirements, designated as (B) and (C). Market (B) follows a sequential commitment, where a permit is issued subject to a time-bound execution of the investments under an agreed plan. In contrast, to ensure maximum visibility (to the permit grantor), a full investment assessment is needed to support the permit application.

Faced with these contrasting approaches, managers may break down the permitting and investment process into binary actions at each stage. Specifically:

Under a sequential permitting (B), the firm may proceed and spend $10 mln to comply (B.1). By exiting or foregoing the opportunity, they spend nil (B.2). On being granted a permit, a basis of design is required, which may call for the submission of technical drawings and other documents to justify the investment's business viability (B.3). Otherwise, the firm loses $10 mln if a permit is not granted (B.4), given that little value accrues to the proponent at this stage.

Dynamic Decisions

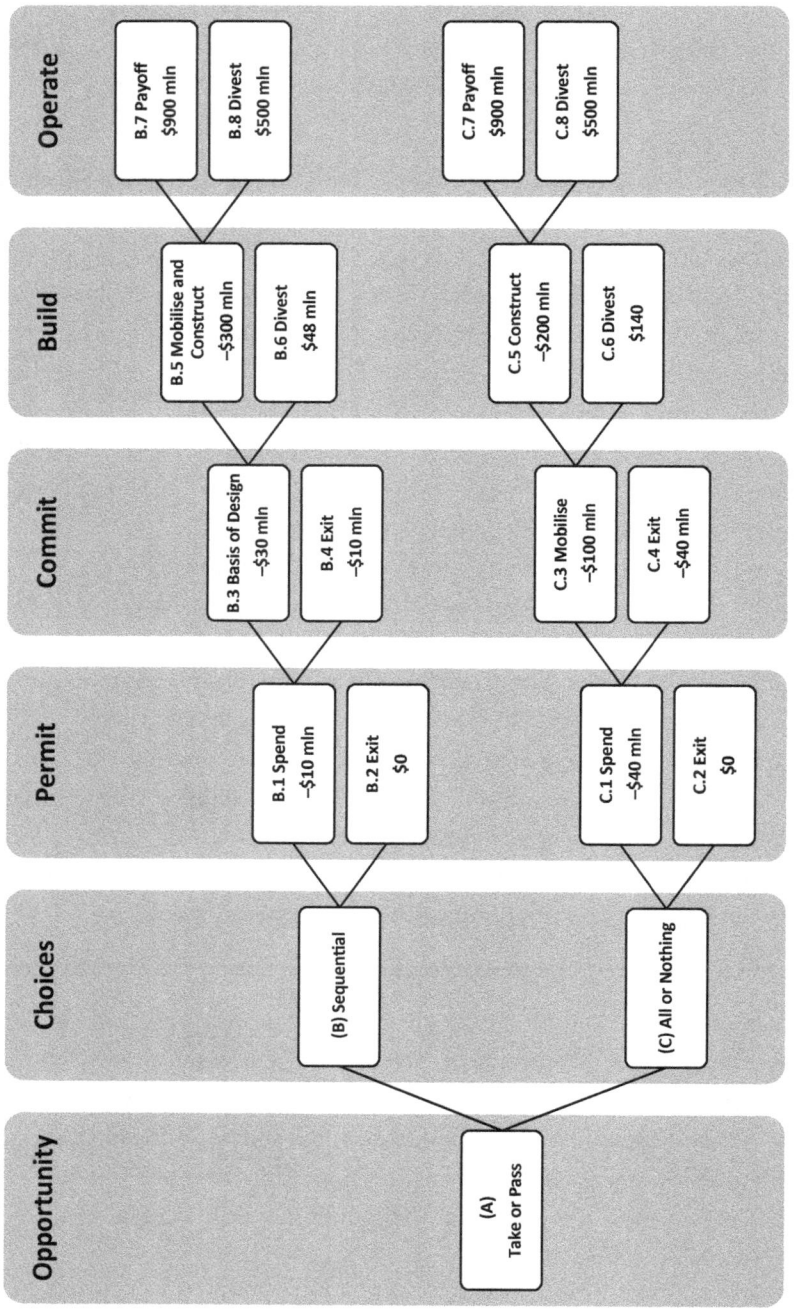

Chart 6.5: Sequential Value Capture

The value starts to accrue once a permit is obtained. At this stage, the proponent (or firm) may proceed and mobilise resources to pursue the investment to its development phase (B.5). Aborting the investment may result in a loss of $40 mln, which could be recovered if someone else would take over the project by paying a development premium, say 20% of costs, to achieve $48 mln as divestment proceeds (B.6). Playing the role of a developer, the firm commits to spend the capital expenditure, which is exercising its option to acquire the expected payoffs (B.7). This implies that the firm is prepared to assume the responsibilities, any risks embedded, and any continuing costs to operate. An alternative strategy is to divest to monetise the value of a completely built asset (B.8), leaving some of the residual value to the operator to monetise.

In contrast, policy may pursue an "all or nothing" approach (C) when handing out permits to develop energy investments. This usually follows a "two envelop system": A technical proposal outlines and is supported with design and engineering plans, why a proponent is qualified to undertake the project (or investment). This is followed by a financial proposal that usually includes how energy prices would be set and how the investment would sustain itself financially.

While the process is similar to (B), it differs in the front-end cash commitments. A decision to apply or bid for the permit would set the proponent back, in this case, by $40 mln (C.1). Technical and financial proposals cost money to prepare. The level of application or bid fees would add to this front-end cash disbursement. The rest follows a similar process and binary choices that a sequential permitting would evolve.

The decision to commit is influenced by the cost of failure, which in this case is failing to obtain a permit in the first instance. Without the permit, the rest of the expected value is unlikely to be realised. In this case, by minimising the front-end cash disbursement, when the risk of failure is also the highest, one reduces the cost.

The adaptive approach that Spain followed in its earlier efforts to deploy wind power is an example of a successful sequential permitting. The government mapped the suitable sites to promote, which was co-created with the agencies of the autonomous regions. Permitting proceeded, usually for a project entity, by complying with minimum requirements to lower the costs. As the project matured, more detailed technical and financial plans were submitted as supporting documents (Barcelona, 2012).

In contrast, Iberdrola's experience with the wind farm it acquired in Scotland painted a different picture. Under its previous owner, which Iberdrola acquired, permitting was a two-tier decision. Under a national mandate, a project was cleared for permitting. To obtain this permit, one would need to submit detailed technical and financial plans. The project is then passed on to the local authority for site permitting, exposing the project to a binary outcome: It is granted, or fails to obtain, a permit. This is where potential misalignment of national and local priorities could expose a nationally mandated project to fail at the local permitting, resulting in a loss.

Over the years, the permitting process is streamlined under the Department of Environment and Climate Change (DECC). Following Iberdrola's experience in Scotland, through the revamped ScottishPower, its subsidiary, the expansion of wind power deployment for onshore and offshore investments is accelerated.

4.2 Unlocking exogenous bottlenecks

Extending the notion of cost of failure, I recall the schematic illustration of the expected risks and payoffs of geothermal resources in Chart 6.3. In essence, the exploration and development risks are front-loaded, particularly when large-hole geothermal drilling is employed. The introduction of slim-hole drilling reduces the initial cash disbursements.

In a similar way to a permitting problem, exploring for geothermal steam is a highly risky proposition for private capital, unless some form of cost of failure mitigants is considered. This is where the introduction of resource insurance, as described in Box 6.1, is a way to unlock the deployment of geothermal power. At a conceptual level, it works as follows:

> Resource insurance covers the developers of geothermal steam fields for their first loss or the first wells that fail in their drilling portfolio. Usually, the state funds the insurance scheme.

Slim-hole geothermal drilling cuts drilling costs substantially compared to conventional large-hole drilling technology. As a result, the cost of failure for each well is also reduced significantly. This allows scope for private capital to self-insure their drilling risks or open the space for private insurance to participate. To build experience and track record, aid or grants to governments, particularly in emerging economies, could be shifted as social capital to fund resource insurance schemes.

In the realities of the world where business operates, what is perceived as risk by some managers, the insurers managed to convert this into an insurance offering. Munich Re's experience in Kenya is informative, as described by Stephan Jacob and Matthias Tönnis (2015), in-house experts on resource insurance:

Multiple Well Risk insurance reframed the insurance coverage from a "doublet of just two wells" into "a portfolio of several production and injection wells. The minimum energy yield of a complete portfolio is consequently insured in several project phases. Parameters for each phase are agreed between Munich Re and the project."

"These determine whether a project is to be aborted as being unsuccessful, thus triggering an insurance payment, or whether promising results achieved merit continuation to the next phase."

Recognising that geothermal risks are loaded upfront, particularly while exploring for and developing geothermal resources, a portfolio of wells could "balance higher risks at the beginning with lower risks at the later phases makes the project insurable and provides investors with comprehensive security for the entire project term." Jacob and Tönnis added: "The option for early exit in the event of failure also serves the interests of both parties, as it limits the investors' risk of financial loss."

Just as sequential permitting reduces front-end cash disbursements, slim-hole geothermal drilling and resource insurance could unlock wider deployment by lowering the financial cost of failure. With more geothermal resources being made available, geothermal power could experience a resurgence as it has in Turkey and Kenya. Having been nowhere in the geothermal power landscape only a few years ago, both countries are approaching the installed capacity of more established players.

How do sequential commitments impact operational risks and their de-risking?

Another "mystery" that confounds managers is the paradox of rapid expansion (or growth). Volume expansion captures the managers' attention when high growth equates to expanding returns. Some assume, by focusing on volumes, that the cash margins will deliver the returns and eventually build up a healthy cash pile to reinvest to sustain the firm's growth.

Operationally, the firm incurs costs to produce energy, which is a certainty as cash outflows. Managers expect to recover the costs by selling the volumes at a price to generate revenues. In some cases, sellers extend "credit" to their customers by funding a receivable on energy sold. That is, payment comes later after the customers received delivery of their energy, a sum that the seller funds (hence reducing cash flows actually retained on hand). The sequence is similar to investing, albeit on a smaller scale than building an asset. Hence, if left to accumulate, receivables may expand as revenues grow as well as the drain on cash on hand.

A more serious issue, often given scant attention by managers, is the operational costs of integrating intermittent renewables. As more intermittent supplies are added, the operational costs of integration are observed to increase significantly. Specifically: Michael Joos and Iain Staffeld (2018) described these phenomena:

> To rebalance the grid, after variable supplies from renewables alter its load equilibrium, it increased by 62% since 2010 in the United Kingdom, as wind and some solar supplies grew fivefold. Germany shows comparable results. In some areas, congestion in access points occurs, which is eased by curtailing supplies from generators or demand of buyers.
>
> To adjust the load of the grid, a balancing mechanism works by having generators bid how much they expect to be paid to vary their volumes or for consumers to offer how much they expect to be compensated for curtailing their consumption.

In a system without subsidies or regulatory intervention, bid or offer prices would in theory mimic the cost to the generator or consumer of the volumes curtailed.

However, with subsidies, particularly those collected on delivery of energy to a market, the balancing costs could spiral. As more interruptible supplies are subsidised, increased penetration translates into higher curtailment rates, resulting in significantly higher curtailment costs, as Joos and Staffeld validated for United Kingdom and Germany.

Value is often lost when firms fail to monetise the volumes they produce because of thefts or faulty metering. The latter could be solved by replacing the meters, where digital metering enables remote reading that substantially reduce the costs to correctly bill customers. Past efforts at controlling thefts varied from policing to community actions.

Social innovation is a relatively "newish" approach that relies on community cooperation, as described in Box 6.2. In its most basic form, firms extend stakeholder engagement by harnessing the cooperation of the communities they serve as partners in resolving problems. One such problem of common interest is recouping non-revenue energy. In my advisory work, I observed two principal sources of this leakage, as outlined in my article (Barcelona, 2018):

Theft from illegal connections, or illicit reselling of power to non-subscribers, is a practice prevalent in a number of low-income communities. The perpetrators may not always be the "poor," as some would blame by default.

A less obvious source is non-payment by otherwise upright subscribers who may experience temporary liquidity constraints or poor management of their household finances.

Theft of power supply results in produced volumes, where costs are incurred, are not billed and monetised into revenues. Left to persist, non-revenue power, as the unbilled supply is broadly referred to, can lead to power suppliers ending up with losses that eventually impair their financial viability. The paying customers would suffer from increasing prices, as regulators allow power suppliers to charge more to recover the costs of unbilled power. As the vicious cycle spirals, with power prices becoming more expensive, the incentive to steal (via illegal connections) is greater.

Payment problems were addressed by understanding the customers' financial circumstances. By doing so, innovative solutions such as those employed by Manweb of Liverpool, United Kingdom, proves more cost-effective and sustainable as a solution to an otherwise recurring problem with no end in sight (see Box 6.2).

Clearly, regulatory actions that raise power prices are proving ineffective to combat the scourge of non-revenue power. On closer examination, as the examples in Box 6.2 illustrate, getting the community onside to work closely with the power suppliers can prove more effective.

4.3 Pacing and counterintuitive learning effects

Today's decisions create the scope for exercising managerial flexibility in the future. In choosing certain technologies, specified costs are locked-in, while the ability to alter volumes is embedded in the asset's design and contractual obligations. This is a pattern in which future outcomes are *path-dependent* or continue to be influenced by past actions (Driouchi *et al.*, 2010; Vergne and Durand, 2010).

Geocentric energy resources, such as hydro and geothermal, are location-specific, which confers "exclusive" access to the resource. In effect, when a pump storage is built in a suitable area, it makes little economic sense to build a similar facility to access the same source of water. In a way, the economics would confer a natural monopoly where competing access to the same resources may result in diseconomy. Similarly, profitable niches are created through concessions or regulation, for resources such as geothermal power to better manage the resource development. Seen in this context, these factors would encourage firms to invest to develop the resources to move first to lock in its financial benefits:

1. Suitable sites, and the firms' access to them, are the scarce resources that define the investment's cost advantage. By locking in the resources, competitors are in effect locked out from gaining access to abundant and cheap supplies.
2. Left to develop less endowed sites, competitors lock in more expensive resources that present a permanent penalty on costs, usually for a generation or more.
3. Cost of waiting, or deferral of commitment, could be prohibitive given the high energy output from these resources. Hence, the foregone revenues could far outweigh any benefits from delaying commitment.

While this holds true for most of the energy technologies, solar power stands out as an exception to this pattern. Wind power, with its significantly higher energy output, albeit lower than hydro and geothermal, is at the borderline.

Solar power and photovoltaic trackers (PVT_M) have a low conversion ratio of radiance energy to power. Over the past few years, costs have been declining at double digits, partly because of greater efficiency in installations, improved designs of solar arrays, and oversupply in solar panels. Conversion rates and the speed at which this is eroded after installation have seen much slower progress. Combined, the lifecycle costs of energy (LCOEs) of PVT_M and other solar installations have fallen dramatically.

While this rapidly declining cost is welcome, it poses a dilemma for managers in pacing their commitments. Should they invest now rather than later?

In pacing their commitments, managers may choose to invest now and lock in the prevailing costs. By doing so, they hope to gain from an early start by earning revenues sooner. However, with the prospect of solar power costs falling by 20% a year hence, the early mover foregoes these potential savings on their capital expenditures. By locking in higher costs, this becomes a permanent penalty.

Managers that wait for a year before committing are faced with a contrasting dilemma. With its ease to install, solar farms could be up and running in a year, more or less. The cost for waiting is the year's revenue, with the reward the prospect of saving on capital expenditures, assuming the expected 20% costs decline is realised. There is, of course, the prospect that costs will stabilise or even surge if policy-induced demand (more subsidies, for instance) would cause a shortage in solar panels.

I examine this trade-off in Chart 6.6 and came to the view that "haste makes waste" is quite apt for pacing investment in solar power. Here's how I came to this view:

Using PVT_M as a basis, a decline rate experienced over the past three years would indicate an LCOE "cost curve" approximating that illustrated in (A). In effect, within the third year, PVT_M would achieve cost parity with $ACCGT_B$ using a reference gas price shown in (B). Beyond the third year, PVT_M could in theory outcompete $ACCGT_B$.

Turning to (C), the annual foregone cash margins using $ACCGT_M$ as setting the market prices are compared with the savings from declining capital expenditures. With PVT_M having nil fuel costs and a stable LCOE for $ACCGT_M$, the foregone cash margins are fairly stable on this comparison. The decline in capital expenditures, however, is at a diminishing level in absolute money terms. On a cumulative basis, the foregone cash margins

Dynamic Decisions

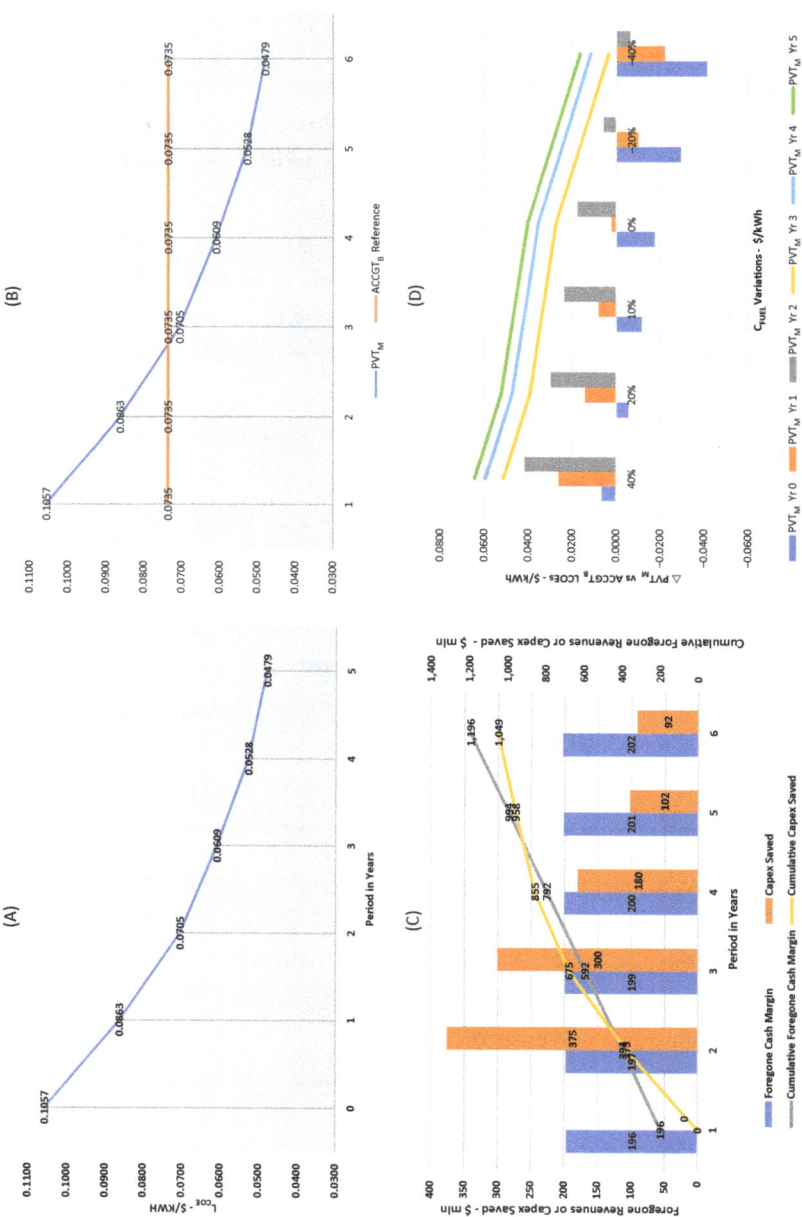

Chart 6.6: Late-mover's Benefits in Solar Power

Source: Author using EIA data.

would exceed the capital expenditure savings by the fifth year. In a loose way, this may suggest that under this stable pricing condition, managers may have the luxury of waiting for a little more than four years before they become indifferent between waiting and committing.

The world, however, does not stand still. If PVT_M benefits late-comers with lower costs, $ACCGT_B$ gains in competitiveness as gas prices fall. This is where the "competitiveness" of PVT_M takes on a different context. As (C) illustrates, the earlier firms to commit to PVT_M lock in higher costs of supplies. As gas prices fall, these assets are not only squeezed, they hardly earn enough to recoup the investments. The late-comers are proving more resilient, although the squeeze on cash margin may paint a vastly different picture: PVT_M may not achieve the lucrative returns it is purported to achieve, just because it "outcompetes" $ACCGT_B$ when gas prices are high.

That a technology is rapidly getting cheaper may prove a boon to society, an outcome that policy aspires (and desires) to accelerate. In dynamic energy markets, however, the first to move may live to regret its haste, as early solar adopters realised belatedly. Taking this into account, the pecking order in choosing to deploy a portfolio of supplies may take on a very different approach from NPV's ranking. The latter chooses to simplify the calculations to the extent that some of its weaknesses, as identified by industry consensus (Richter *et al.*, 2017), are ignored.

When pacing commitments, a more nuanced strategy may seek to lock in resources (such as hydro and geothermal) first, to gain a first-mover's advantage. For technologies with rapidly declining costs, some managers may opt to wait while the enthusiasts rush in, to gain late-mover's benefits.

The obsolescence of earlier onshore wind, and cuts in subsidies, may have opened the way to repowering low output assets (Colmenar-Santos *et al.*, 2015). With the benefit of historic performance, historic patterns of wind flows may identify areas that are most suitable for replacing low output with more advanced wind turbines to upgrade the volume of power generated (Castro-Santos *et al.*, 2016), at lower costs and feedstock risks. As a result, what was seen as a cost that has to be incurred, when earlier wind farms have to be decommissioned, now presents a new lease of life.

In some areas, repowering earlier wind farms may prove more lucrative financially and environmentally, when a significantly higher power output is achieved for the same land area (Martinez-Camara et al., 2018).

The more astute managers may seek social capital to fund, unlock the benefits from learning effects, or de-risk the early commitments, to facilitate and reward earlier adoption to kickstart the virtuous cycle that technological advancement purveys.

Offshore wind farms using advanced platforms ($Wind_{OFAP}$) are a case in point. Potentially operated at energy conversion rates in excess of 50%, the cost of delaying commitments is higher than PVT_M. This implies that the window for waiting is narrowing significantly, as more well-capitalised oil and gas players are choosing to focus on offshore wind. Specifically:

EDPR and Repsol, together with Engie, joined forces to experiment on the viability of offshore wind using EDPR's market presence in Portugal. This resulted in a successful launch of WindFloat Atlantic, as a pioneering venture in the Atlantic using the significantly lower cost advanced platforms (Repsol, 2020).

Iberdrola and Total formed an alliance to exploit Denmark's offshore wind opportunities (Vadillo, 2021) exemplifies combining Iberdrola's advantage with developing and operating wind power, with Total's offshore and marine platform engineering, gained from offshore drilling and production.

Equinor, partnering with BP and the ports of New York, South Brooklyn Marine Terminal and Port of Albany, to develop the largest offshore project, complete with a hub for procuring services (Offshore Engineer, 2021). In scaling up, the project may lock in some of the benefits from declining costs by sequentially adding to more capacity.

Given the scale and complexity of offshore wind, the know-how and expertise gained from scaling are likely to arise from installation and project management, with manufacturing relying on economies of scale. In this case, unlike in PVT_M, the pioneer's ability to appropriate the benefits from learning curve effects is likely to be greater.

4.4 How rivalries impact the firm's value

In facing competition, managers see their rivals as capable of upsetting their game plan to seize markets, particularly when a gain by one is a loss to the other. In other instances, where issues of common concerns are presented, managers may see the scope for cooperation to ally with rivals. In this very human way of interacting, managers recognise the value of each approach under each decision context. This raises questions that conventional approaches to de-risking come short with credible answers. Specifically:

1. When does one lead to change the game, follow rival's moves to minimise losses, or work with rivals to reinforce an established order?
2. At what stage are these decisions sensibly taken, from a strategic perspective?

These decisions are better informed when managers see their actions as potentially eliciting (re)actions. Jean Tirole, Nobel Prize in Economics, made these observations on human interactions and how game theory informs its outcome (Chevalier-Roignant and Trigeorgis, 2011). Tirole sees "game theory aims at describing and predicting behaviours in environments at which actors are interdependent and have potentially conflicting objectives. It deepens our understanding of when the quest for specific goals may lead to inefficiencies and of how players choose actions with an eye on changing other actors' incentives."

Brought to a granular level, how humans react to rivals' actions is important to inform day-to-day managerial decisions. Jean Jacques Rousseau (1974), French philosopher, may have provided some insights. In plain language, Rousseau described the following scenario:

> In hunting for deer, a group of hunters would acquire a crude idea of how mutual commitments and the advantage of fulfilling them align with their present and obvious interests. The best outcome, as the hunters perceive, is to remain at their post in order to succeed. With their catch, the spoils are shared equitably. However, if a hare happens to pass near one of the hunters, one would have no reservations to catch the hare and appropriate it for their individual benefits. The hunter may care little whether or not

one's action would have alerted the deer to take flight and cause others (or everyone) to miss out on the spoils of the hunt.

This coordination failure, as Jahel Mielke and Gesine A Steudle (2018) assert, is what investors see as arising from dynamic trade-offs of gains in an economic or social sense or both. Within policy circles, one may assume and agree with a consensus that climate change is an existential threat. If this belief permeates to the firm and is reinforced with tangible financial outcomes, the "parties are likely to cooperate on the pay-off dominant 'abate-abate' which — if reached — is self-enforcing." In contrast, if climate change and its threat, are seen to be weak, "the object becomes to gain a geopolitical advantage. Hence, the prospect of cooperation is dim," Mielke and Steudle contend.

Operating under dynamic energy markets, the varied interests and motivations of players cannot be fully ascertained with certitude. For this reason, I would rather observe what actions managers are taking and gain deep insights into how those actions potentially alter the rivals' ability to appropriate the spoils. Others' intentions are opaque, or even hidden, to mask the managers' *game*. Their actions, therefore, are one of the few manifestations of how their strategies, by design or implicit (to them), are visible to the rest of the players in the market.

This brings the conversation to how real options reasoning is incorporated into understanding how managers alter their moves and how it impacts the *games* other managers choose to pursue. This combination gave rise to *option games*, an analytical framework that Benoit and Lenos employed in their works that I adapted to evaluating energy investments.

The obvious question needs to be asked: Does a kWh of power, or a molecule of gas, serve the same function regardless of where it came from or how it was produced?

Certainly, at the output level, the product is fungible and undifferentiated. With a functioning energy market and adequate infrastructure and logistics, coal or gas in theory can be traded affordably and substituted to generate power. The same could be said of renewables for mature energy systems. The pre-conditions — adequate infrastructure and logistics — are where the differentiation occurs. Under an energy market organised to cater to fossil fuels, *modulated* renewables would have greater prospect of gaining access, while *interruptible* renewables would require additional adaptation. Those changes would need someone to bear the costs of adaptation or even benefit from disrupting extant networks of market and logistics and relationship. How these factors interact are abstracted in Chart 6.7, where I examine a simplified version of a power system.

A priori, consider two competing oligopolists — GasCo and HydroCo — that aim to supply finite periodic volumes in a given power market. As a rule, the cheaper sources get to supply first, with the residual volume going to the competing supplier.[5] Two supply scenarios are considered — high or low fluvial output — which determines how much hydro power, the cheaper source, is generated.

The inclusion of renewables and how it alters prices and how volumes are re-allocated are often misdiagnosed by managers. In my works over the years (Barcelona, 2017), as renewables deepen their market penetration, power prices tend to fall. These are observed empirically in Spain and the United Kingdom and previously in Scandinavia and the Netherlands (Mulder and Scholtens, 2013). Separated by a few years, similar patterns are observed in Texas, United States (Zarnikau *et al.*, 2019), to wit:

The day-ahead market power prices tend to rise (or fall) with the forecasted prices of natural gas. In the same manner, as power supplies from nuclear and renewables increase, power prices tend to fall (or vice versa).

Firms are not perfect in estimating their day-ahead volumes. For this reason, they may fall short of what they offered to supply. To make up for this shortfall, firms contract additional volumes to balance what they need. At times, this creates a spike in power prices, albeit temporarily, that explains how day-ahead and real-time spot power prices may deviate.

Given this reality, assuming away these interacting effects of prices and volumes are bound to cause great financial pains when managers fail to anticipate its impact

---

[5] A detailed application of the methodology is illustrated with sample calculations in Chapter 10. The results of those calculations are referred to in the discussions that follow in this chapter. The cost of supply is based on the lifecycle cost of energy (LCOE) as described in Chapter 7.

Dynamic Decisions

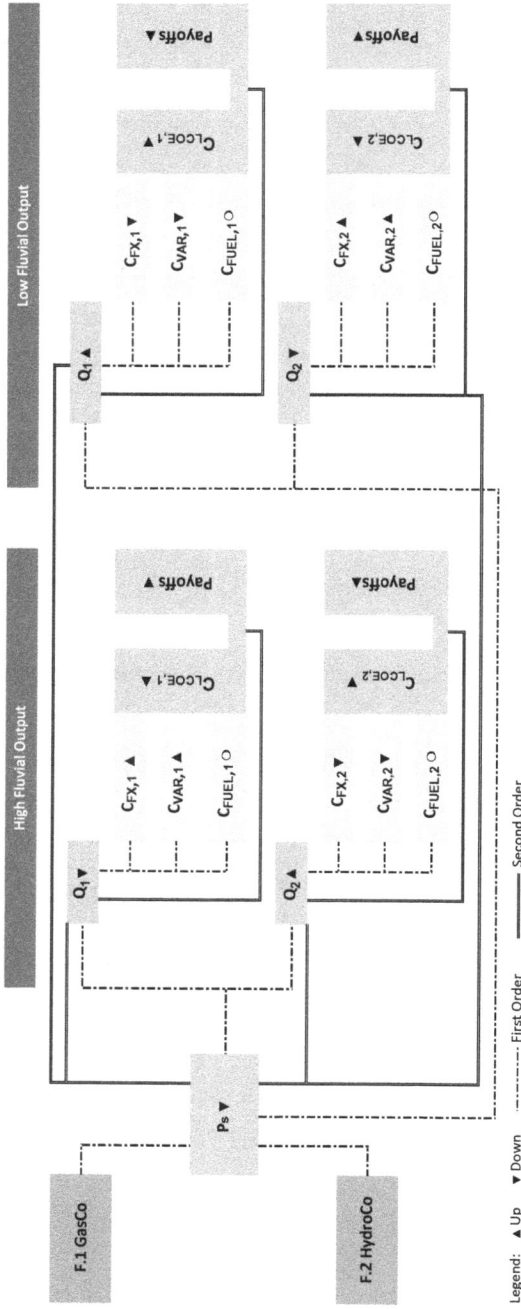

Chart 6.7: Interacting Supply Decisions and Volume Re-allocation

on the investment's payoffs. The remedy lies in how managers make their choices of technology and how it is integrated into their portfolio of assets, rather than to lock in rigid obligations for the sake of certitude. Here's how this may operate:

Previously operating as a monopolist, or sole source of power, GasCo would supply the full volume given that no alternative could viably compete. Coal by this time is relegated to a minor role when the power system has shifted to gas, as a simplifying condition. The entry of HydroCo introduces a credible substitute to power from gas and a viable rival to GasCo, that could erode its hold on the power market. This is how such a prospect could be realised:

Schematically, GasCo has several individual ACCGTs with varying supply costs. As a monopolist, power prices are most likely set according to the most expensive supply, as a way of maximising GasCo's payoffs. In effect, the "cheaper" ACCGTs would gain "excess" cash margins.

HydroCo's entry, with market volumes remaining similar, could only gain market share by providing a lower cost supply. StoHydro complies with this requisite, hence offering the prospect of substituting GasCo's share with hydro power supplies. In this instance, the most expensive ACCGTs are displaced, resulting in "cheaper" assets setting the market prices.

By leaving the power market to operate freely, market prices are expected to fall as a first-order effect. The consequences for GasCo could be painful financially, particularly when fluvial outputs are high. Lock-in to a cost structure and a need to recoup their investments, the "intrusion" of HydroCo is most unwelcome. Doing nothing, GasCo is exposed to a vicious cycle.

GasCo's falling volumes would imply progressively higher supply costs. Fixed costs (and part of the less flexible) variable expenses are incurred regardless of the volume. Hence, $C_{FX,1}$ and $C_{VAR,1}$ increase while revenues fall as volume, Q_1 and power price, P_s, declines. Fuel costs, $C_{FUEL,1}$, are largely unaffected given that these are incurred subject to the volume produced. The interactions of higher costs of supply, C_{LCOE}, and lower power prices, P_s, are likely to progressively compress the payoffs of GasCo.

Conversely, HydroCo is reaping the bonanza of abundant fluvial supplies, partly offset by a sharper reduction in power prices. That is, as more supplies are met by StoHydro, more of the higher cost supplies from ACCGT are displaced. As HydroCo gains volumes, Q_2, $C_{FX,2}$, and $C_{VAR,2}$ decline accordingly, thereby reinforcing their cost advantage with declining $C_{LCOE,2}$. The full uplift to revenues is tempered by a further reduction in P_s, resulting in a more subdued payoff expansion.

Through repetitive bids for periodic supplies, GasCo may see their market share decline to the point of the residual volume, unmet by HydroCo. The first-round effects — declining P_s and Q_1, is reinforced by the feedback loop that produces the second-round effects. As HydroCo establishes a viable presence, GasCo's payoffs erosion is reinforced and may intensify when growth StoHydro supplies are added.

A reversal of fortunes may occur when the fluvial patterns are altered by seasonal or cyclical weather changes. Under low fluvial output, StoHydro would experience lower Q_2, which in effect expands Q_1 as more of the demand is satisfied by supplies from ACCGT. This has a dual benefit: Q_1 is increased by dispatching the previously idle (and higher cost) supplies, thereby enjoying higher P_s. As a result, the payoff expansion is expected to be greater than the simple multiplication of the change in Q_1 and the prevailing power prices, P_s. In many energy markets, the fluvial patterns may shift volumes from StoHydro by as high as +/- 30% from some long-term mean water reserve levels.

In appreciating these interacting effects, dynamic shifts in prospective payoffs of GasCo and HydroCo are seldom linear or correlated. Far from considering this as a problem, GasCo as an incumbent may respond differently to the perceived threats from HydroCo's entry. Specifically:

A default reaction of the incumbent monopolist, or dominant player, is to frustrate the entry of credible rivals. By taking a bunkered perspective, where an incumbent erects barriers to entry, rivals may be hindered or at best, delay its entry. Meanwhile, the cost of maintaining such barriers may prove costly and seldom sustainable. Some such barriers may occur with permitting and development of new hydro resources, organising community resistance or shaping the regulatory ecosystem (e.g. lax environmental standards).

A more enlightened mindset is to examine the diversification potential of hydro and gas. Clearly, with offsetting patterns in prospective payoffs, combining ACCGT and StoHydro could yield a mutually reinforcing supply portfolio. When fluvial output is in abundance, StoHydro delivers more of the payoffs by offsetting what ACCGT is bound to lose. Conversely, when fluvial patterns are adverse, ACCGT provides the floor to volume, while gaining from higher prices on the overall supplies.

Seen in this light, an astute manager may see StoHydro as a complement, rather than as a threat, to its ACCGT assets. Operated in tandem, the portfolio is likely to be well positioned under either fluvial condition.

Does a similar benefit accrue to HydroCo? Probably not. Starting with a higher return asset, diversifying into stable but lower ACCGT payoffs may erode rather than enhance portfolio returns. While the resulting portfolio mix is similar, the rate of change (or enhancement) is seen to be going backwards — from high to low returns.

A similar process is anticipated with the addition of more wind, and to a lesser extent, PVT_M. However, intermittent supplies and lower outputs may reduce its portfolio benefits to the incumbent GasCo. The excess cost to the network that intermittency may suppose and any decommissioning costs to dispose of wind turbines and solar panels may have to be quantified and considered explicitly.

5
A Strategic De-risking

The conventional notion of avoiding losses by veering away from taking risks may have its roots in human fear. In pursuing a happy life, avoiding misery becomes the goal, as much as achieving happiness is a lifelong pursuit. In both cases, a paradox often results: The more one seeks to avoid misery, mishaps that cause great distress and misery appear to follow.

One of the reasons may be rooted in misdiagnosing the symptoms, from the root causes of what makes people happy or miserable. Being happy is often the result of doing something fulfilling. The satisfaction that often comes with it is to put a smile on a face perceived as being happy.

In translating this to managerial decision-making, profits or losses occur largely because of how managers align their resources to the opportunities that emerge. As markets change, misalignment would naturally occur that managers may have to correct, calling for a realignment of resources and actions. This reality, while obvious, is hidden in plain sight to some managers.

The mantra that guides conventional risk mitigation, however, is to avoid or neutralise volatilities and uncertain outcomes. By following this principle, managers would rely on contractual remedies to offload the perceived risks to other parties. An example is to lock in future payoffs with rigid obligations, such as *take-or-pay* contracts, or its variant, or the increasing popularity of corporate PPAs to strengthen the creditworthiness of solar power.

While stable payoffs may be seen as desirable, at least by some managers, the embedded risks are ignored. As contracted terms deviate from what the dynamic market could offer, the well-crafted balance of risks and payoffs between the contracting parties becomes untenable. As continual renegotiations become a feature, the "security to payoffs" that rigid obligations promise becomes illusory.

A remedy is to examine *de-risking* within the context of a value chain, which extends to how the fuel (or feedstock) market arbitrates in allocating risks and payoffs, to assess how these factors interact with the dynamic processes occurring at the power supply market.

A starting point is to appreciate how past choices influence the scope of managers to act strategically and reap the benefits from operational flexibility. In understanding how rivals are likely to respond and feasible outcomes to anticipate, managers are forearmed by being forewarned.

Strategic de-risking is in a way like pursuing happiness or seeking to navigate adroitly in an ever-changing business landscape to avoid the pains of making losses. To be happy, one does not seek happiness for its own sake, as this is more likely to end in grief. In a similar manner, while trying to avoid making a loss through inaction, which is what one tends to do to avoid making a "mistake," one could produce precisely an adverse outcome. By deeply understanding why adverse outcomes occur, managers could be forewarned, so that they can be forearmed to successfully tackle with adroitness the vicissitudes of life and sustain their firms' sustainability.

Box 6.1: Resolving Indonesia's Geothermal Paradox

In a country that boasts one of the largest geothermal resources, Indonesia could only manage to tap into less than a fraction of its known reserves. "Experts" cite the usual culprits (Barcelona *et al.*, 2019): "Unreliable long-term contracts, ambivalent government support, and lukewarm investors investment appetite." While these are the obvious bogeys, the real solutions to real problems lie elsewhere.

Indonesia's flawed "cheap" energy policy is at the root of the geothermal paradox. Power is sold to consumers at below generation costs. Geothermal, while competitive relative to coal-based power, faces very high exploration risks. Without any prospect of earning a return, under Indonesia's "cheap energy regime," private capital is expected to show "benevolence" in risking their capital to lose more.

A remedy to this paradox is to awaken from this fairy tale that deludes policy and consumers alike. The conditions are created to attract investments when energy prices are brought in line with the economic costs of supplies and eliminate redundant subsidies. By innovating with slim-hole geothermal drilling, costs are reduced, promotes resource insurance, and expands applications.

1. Revolutionising with slim-hole drilling

Inherently beautiful, but out of sight, geothermal is energy's Cinderella. Conventional drilling technologies require large front-end capital commitments, with no visible prospect of success. Before the first drill is sunk, civil works and access infrastructures have to be built. A modest 20 MW exploration and drilling programme could easily setback $93 mln, as shown in Box Table 6.1.1.

Slim-hole drilling technology re-arranges the sequence of the expenditures. Reducing the size of the equipment, the system is easier to transport (usually by helicopter). By eliminating the expensive civil works, the front-end costs are reduced to a third ($60 mln vs. $20 mln).

Excerpting from our research (Barcelona *et al.*, 2019), slim-hole drilling changes the geothermal economics that could adapt better to archipelagic geography characterised by small, often isolated markets (Mackenzie *et al*, 2017). Its more modest

Box Table 6.1.1: Comparative Costs of Geothermal Drilling Technologies

					Costs of Geothermal Steam Supplies						Power Generation — Geothermal Park			
Line	20 MW Equivalent Drilling Program - In $ million	Project Capture	3G Surveys	Exploration/ Delineation	Appraisal	Cost to Final Investment Decision	Exploitation	Total Costs of Steam Supplies	Financial Costs of Steam Supplies $/kWh	Cost Difference %	C_{FX}	C_{VaR}	C_{Steam}	C_{LCOE}
		A	B	C	D	E	F	G	H	I	J	K	L	M
	90% Success Rate													
1	Conventional Drilling													
2	Costs incurred per segment	0.50	2.50	60.00	30.00	93.00	96.00	189.00	0.0379		0.0267	0.0190	0.0530	0.0987
3	Cumulative costs to abandon	0.00	-0.50	-3.00	-63.00	-63.00	-93.00							
4	Slim-hole Drilling													
5	Costs incurred per segment	0.50	2.50	20.00	60.00	83.00	34.00	117.00	0.0234	-38.10%	0.0182	0.0095	0.0328	0.0605
6	Cumulative costs to abandon	0.00	-0.50	-3.00	-23.00	-23.00	-83.00							
	70% Success Rate													
7	Conventional Drilling													
8	Costs incurred per segment	0.50	2.50	77.14	30.00	110.14	96.00	206.14	0.0413		0.0267	0.0190	0.0578	0.1035
9	Cumulative costs to abandon	0.00	-0.50	-3.00	-80.14	-80.14	-110.14							
10	Slim-hole Drilling													
11	Costs incurred per segment	0.50	2.50	25.71	60.00	88.71	34.00	122.71	0.0246	-40.47%	0.0182	0.0095	0.0344	0.0621
12	Cumulative costs to abandon	0.00	-0.50	-3.00	-28.71	-28.71	-88.71							
	40% Success Rate													
13	Conventional Drilling													
14	Costs incurred per segment	0.50	2.50	135.00	30.00	183.00	96.00	279.00	0.0559		0.0267	0.0190	0.0782	0.1240
15	Cumulative costs to abandon	0.00	-0.50	-3.00	-153.00	-153.00	-183.00							
16	Slim-hole Drilling													
17	Costs incurred per segment	0.50	2.50	45.00	60.00	108.00	40.00	148.00	0.0296	-46.95%	0.0182	0.0095	0.0415	0.0692
18	Cumulative costs to abandon	0.00	-0.50	-3.00	-48.00	-48.00	-108.00							

Source: Data: Jacobs (August 2017) and authors' estimates. Lifecycle costs of energy (LCOE) is estimated based on the methods shown in Barcelona (2017). Adapted from Barcelona, de Wilde, and Nagruho (2019).

front-end cash commitments allow small sequential cash disbursements. As a result, small-scale ventures are made feasible, reducing costs of failed wells and lowering financial risks.

By segmenting the cash disbursements, the cost of deciding to proceed or abandon (usually to avoid further losses) is estimated. The developers' performance is likewise compared, with the highly successful needing to drill less wells to satisfy a given supply of steam.

To adapt the costing to Indonesia's costs, the latest estimates (2018) from Jacobs, Iceland's ISOR and North Tech, we highlighted that the "economic advantages of using slim-hole technology lie in the following:

1. Reduced drilling costs minimise the losses from a failed exploration. In this case, conventional drilling could imply a loss of $63 mln (D3) against $23 mln (D6), should the appraisal yield a negative result.
2. Low drilling success rates would increase the costs given that more wells have to be drilled to achieve a similar geothermal steam yield (e.g. 90% success rate).
3. Lower resource use, such as water and above surface installations, reduces slim-hole exploitation costs.

The implications for the financial costs (Column H), particularly for steam supplies, are significant. This could vary from 40% to 46% (Column I) representing the costs reductions by using slim-hole drilling. As this translates into costs of supply (Column M), the costs differences are significant (e.g. M5, M11, and M17)."

2. Reframing risks, rewards, and growth options

Investors in the full value chain face two generic risks: During drilling, the well could be dry when no commercial quantity of geothermal steam is found. Alternatively, the quality of the steam may be poor or inconsistent. In this case, the volume of power derived from the geothermal steam would be below what is required to earn the expected payoffs.

Indonesia has no experience in resource insurance that could provide precedents. To provide comfort to private investors, the government as insurer of first loss may consider the following evolving roles:

1. *Reallocate coal subsidies* to fund a state-controlled resource insurance scheme.
2. *Realign aid or climate subsidies* as seed capital for the scheme.
3. *Evolve as regulator* as insurers gain comfort and expertise in providing resource insurance.

In various studies (IFC, 2013; Rolffs *et al.*, 2017) the first exploratory well incurs the highest risk of failure. The cost could be seen as the price of information to delineate (when successful) or redirect to more promising fields. By disaggregating the costs, two things become apparent:

1. *Front-end uninsured costs are reduced substantially*, hence lowering the capital barriers to initiate pre-feasibility and exploratory work to establish the scope of the drilling program.
2. *Sequential disbursements reduce* drilling-related insurable costs by enhancing success rates by bounding risks with adequate use of new information, thereby embedding options to delay, accelerate, expand, or abort.

With resource insurance de-risking geothermal exploration and exploitation, private capital entry could be facilitated. In effect, by making the exercise costs affordable, private investors may choose to acquire an option for future payoffs by investing in geothermal development and power generation.

In Kenya and Ethiopia (Rolffs *et al.*, 2017), for every $1 in public fund invested, up to $60 of private capital could be harnessed. This results from partially reimbursing the cost of failed wells through the resource insurance schemes.

3. Making resource insurance math work

Resource insurance is an emerging instrument with Germany taking an early lead. On a purely private provision of risk cover, a portfolio of wells may cost in excess of 25% of total drilling costs, assuming 80% of the losses are recovered. To make this affordable, the government steps in to "socialise" the risk coverage costs, to internalise the social benefits of reduced pollution. In reality, this could be a simple reallocation of subsidies to coal into funding a resource insurance policy.

Consider a conventional large-hole drilling for a 55 MW portfolio, costing $30 mln for four wells (or $7.5 mln/well). At an 8% resource insurance premium, the following calculation is made:

1. Insurance premium received is $2.4 mln ($30 mln * 0.08).
2. Cost of two failed large-hole wells is $15 mln ($7.5 mln * 2).
3. Cost recovered in (2) at 85% redemption of costs is $12.75 mln ($15 mln * 0.85).

The private insurer bears $2.25 mln of costs redeemed by the developer, leaving a small surplus of $0.15 mln. Indeed, this is too much effort (or risk-bearing) for minimal return to a private insurer.

Slim-hole drilling would radically change the resource insurance returns. For the same portfolio size, the developer would instead drill 16 wells for $19.2 mln, reducing the costs to $1.2 mln/well. Repeating the calculations, an 8% resource insurance premium would now yield the following:

1. Insurance premium received is $1.54 mln ($19.2 mln * 0.08).
2. Cost of two failed slim-hole wells is $2.4 mln ($1.2 mln * 2).
3. Cost recovered in (2) at 42% redemption of costs is $1.008 mln ($2.4 mln * 0.42).

The private insurer bears $1.392 mln of the redeemed costs, leaving a similar surplus of $0.148 mln. The reduced financial exposure offers significant flexibility to developers and the government. The developer may decide to self-insure against the risk cover provided by the government resource insurance scheme. To accelerate geothermal development, the government may choose to fully cover the first two failed wells (or more). After the first few field developments, the government may opt to open the resource insurance scheme to the private insurers.

4. Harnessing social capital and impact investing

To guard against abuses, the resource insurance premium can be segmented to reward successful developers. A proxy for success is the number of failed wells for each portfolio insured. In effect, by minimising failed wells, developers pay a reduced premium while the insurers pay out less. As a co-insurer, the government could see their pay-outs falling over time as the scheme matures.

In practice, the state-owned utility — PT Perusahaan Listrik Negara (PLN) — is the *de facto* executor of the state's "cheap energy" policy. By aligning power prices to consumers to its economic costs of supply, the government can eliminate its subsidy to PLN. In its place, the government may seed the creation of a geothermal resource insurance fund ("fund") to cover its share of the risk coverage. Managed with transparency, the "fund" could incentivise investors and PLN to pursue a "flight to quality" in their contracting. Hence, drillers with superior performance of getting to the resource with the least failed wells would enjoy lower insurance premiums, on top of reducing total exploration and drilling costs.

PLN's creation of PLN Geothermal (PLN G) may offer a path to rechannelling grants and social capital to co-share in underwriting the redemption from resource risks insurance. In general, aids or grants hold no prospect of earning any return. Once disbursed, the attributed social or economic returns actually achieved could prove random.

To align grant giving with Indonesia's objectives, particularly in alleviating energy poverty among isolated areas, grants could complement public funding in de-risking geothermal by recognising this reality:

Faced with "dry wells," the donors are no worse off financially when their alternative is to give aid to worthy causes. With successful drilling, they may condition their grants so that part of the payoffs replenishes their aid funding. Hence, donors could demonstrate a tangible social and economic impact on employment, local development, and community development.

5. Expanding new market access

Slim-hole drilling is given a boost by the emergence of economically viable small turbine geothermal generation. When both technologies are deployed, a geothermal farm could be scaled according to the size of the energy markets it seeks to serve. This is equivalent to turning accepted wisdom, at least under the American drilling traditions, on its head. This potentially opens the microgrid markets that to date was off-limits to large-hole geothermal power.

Reconfiguring how the steam is delivered, or converted into power, enhances slim-hole technology's competitiveness. Instead of collecting steam using expensive pipes networks, well-heads are redesigned to produce power at well-heads with up to 5 MW generation units. Borrowing from photovoltaic solar farms' playbook, the well-head generators are wired with similar configurations with one major difference: It produces more power per MW than solar farms.

Box 6.2: Recouping Revenue Losses via Social Innovation*

When Nicolette Pombo-van-Zyl, Editor-in-Chief of ESI Africa, suggested that I write about how social innovation could resolve some of the energy industry's ills, I had to reflect and recollect from my past experiences. In framing mundane questions, such as non-payments of energy consumption, as partly a social question, the "solutions" that follow are indeed innovative. It transcends the compulsion that gave debt collectors the undeserved ill-repute. What it achieves, instead, is a prospect of turning adversaries into productive partnerships with the community the firms seek to serve.

The United Kingdom privatised, restructured, and transformed its power industry beyond recognition. The post-privatisation profit surge was attributed to improved efficiency that sharply reduced revenue losses. As a direct participant, I posit that social innovation was, and remains, crucial in delivering these results.

Social innovation is doing good for society while pursuing the utility firms' fiduciary objectives. Long before this was fashionable, Manweb, Liverpool's regional electricity distributor (REC), may have stumbled into this strategic response towards resolving its challenges.

Plagued by high unemployment, Liverpool's poor were blamed for its significantly higher revenue losses. However, the data debunked this convenient excuse. With few exceptions, poor consumers were judicious in their payments. Those that did not could fall under one of two categories: limited financial literacy or "fiddler." The latter, as fraudsters and plagiarists in academe do, believe that electricity thefts are victimless acts, resulting in harmless misappropriation. In the absence of penalties, these acts are perpetrated with impunity.

Separated by 40 years, emerging markets' state-owned utilities suffer from this erroneous pre-conception, as Liverpool did. Stealing from the state is simply socialising the costs to benefit the poor. The rich? They simply misappropriate "public" goods for private use.

Brazil's Eletrobras is a case in point. Energia, a World Bank project, reported that Eletrobras lost 22% of its 2014 generated power to "businesses and residents who take energy without paying for it." Amazonas Energia, a subsidiary, lost 39.2% (vs 11.3% nationally) that cost the system $1 billion. This narrative is repeated unaltered throughout Latin America today.

Africa suffers from chronic revenue losses, where poor infrastructures and obsolete metering are blamed. In a 2016 World Energy Council conference, sponsored by USAID-funded *Power Africa*, energy experts echoed South African Eskom's plea: "Electricity theft is not a 'victimless crime'. The utility's inability to collect revenue for its services makes it nearly impossible to provide reliable electric power."

The obvious question is, why do revenue losses continue to haunt Africa? The answer lies in a question seldom asked: Who benefits from this chronic problem?

Corruption, weak policing, and poor law enforcement are the usual suspects. These institutional imperfections, combined with exorbitant access costs and subsidised power, offer a cocktail that gives impetus to illicit enrichment. Here's how it works:

USAID's *Power Africa* reported in 2017 access costs stood at $400 to $1,200, usually paid as lump sum. To qualify for connection, households need to wire their home. This sets back consumers by 4 to 12 months in terms of GDP per capita (or gross earnings).

A shadow market evolves, where enterprising connected households act as "wholesalers." They tap into wires and bypass the meters to supply for a fee their unconnected neighbours. With few customers on record, blocs of neighbours are well illuminated in otherwise low connection areas.

Utilities have little incentive to resolve this thievery in plain sight. Revenue losses are added back as "costs" under the costs-plus tariff setting. Paying customers are hit with higher bills, while "wholesalers" gain by charging more for their "free" or stolen electricity.

To encourage more legal connections, Kenya Power offers subsidised connection charges at Sh15,000 ($150), within 600 metres of a transformer, payable by instalments over three to five years. The rest pay at the market price of Sh35,000 ($350). With increased demand, Kenya Power was hindered by a lack of transformers to fulfil its pledge. Inadvertently, fixers once again stepped in to bridge the gaps.

Manual readings are prone to human errors. However, whether or not the errors are intentional is not fully known. With organised groups making a lucrative living, threats to life and harassment of utilities' employees may contribute to these phenomena.

To combat these problems, Liverpool's approach remains viable, even 40 years later. They upgraded metering and improved efficiency to reduce technical losses and to provide base data to establish the extent of theft. Revenue losses were seen as payment problems. They resolved this by:

1. converting past due accounts into instalment plans with fixed repayments;
2. installing prepaid meters that customers activate with tokens.

These customer-centric solutions gave clients better control of their cash. Its success made revenue losses a distant memory for the customers and the distribution utilities.

The Philippines and Latin America could offer some examples for Africa to emulate:

Visayan Electric Company (VECO) serves the power needs of Cebu, a province of the Philippines, comprising Cebu City, the country's second largest energy market. The power firm was plagued by excessive non-revenue energy, partly from illegal connections, theft, and poor infrastructures. On taking over the utility, Aboitiz Power instituted a number of measures to stem the financial drain.

In my conversations with Anton Perdices, then VECO's Chief Operating Officer (COO), before becoming COO of Aboitiz Power Distribution Utilities, of which VECO is a part of, he described their three-prong approaches: "We proactively engage the community and our customers, focusing on education to align our interests on ensuring reliable supplies. We follow this by prosecuting thieves, and publicise convictions in local media. This 'name and shame' instil a stigma on electricity thefts. The technological solutions — such as better metering and remote readings — are installed to gain transparency. By having the community on side, they police their ranks and work with us closely."

By 2018, VECO's revenue losses were within the 8.5% mandated by regulation, most of which are from technical losses. Perdices added, "Theft occurs with more sophisticated customers. Realising this, we made our meters tamper proof by reconfiguring the kit to make it difficult for thieves to tap into or manipulate."

In his expanded scope, Anton extended the lessons from VECO to all their power distribution units. He noted: "We continue to lower thefts with the deployment of our HawkEye smart metering. Technology is an essential way to meet the tighter regulatory controls of revenue losses, when the limits were lowered to 5.5%. The COVID-19 restrictions shifted demand to residential consumers, with more people working from home. By 2021, we have made good progress on the industrial side, with the increase in revenue losses among residential users a continuing challenge for us. The cooperation we continue to enjoy from the communities we serve is a factor in containing the problem of theft."

Manila Electric and the Brazilian utilities employed socio-economic means to contain thefts in slum areas. They installed limited capacity transformers to serve blocs organised into "cooperatives" that contract specified volumes. When exceeded, because of illegal connections, the neighbourhood is cut off. They reconnect after paying a fee. Hence, the thefts of the few inflict pains on the many.

What they do to the erring neighbours is a matter for the community to resolve. Within the slums, neighbours have a "code of honour" that they adhere to. Thefts remain but fell to manageable levels.

The lessons are twofold: Corruption and its ills, when given a face and a name, could be resolved by social innovation. This is when community engagement and empowerment are channelled to take concrete actions. Metering and transformer technology and tightened enforcement complete the picture.

****

This article was originally published by ESI Africa, *the online power journal of Africa, as Barcelona (2018). "Recouping revenue losses via social innovation."* ESI Africa, *4, September 27, 2018. The present article updates the original version.*

Bibliography

Barcelona, R. G. (2012). Wind power deployment — Why Spain succeeded. *Renewable Energy Law & Policy*, (2), 146–149.

Barcelona, R. G. (2017). *Energy Investments: An Adaptive Approach to Profiting from Uncertainties*. London: Palgrave Macmillan.

Barcelona, R. G. (2018). Recouping revenue losses via social innovation. *ESI Africa*, 4, September 27, 2018.

Barcelona, R. G., de Wilde, A., and Nagruho, H. (2019). Indonesia's geothermal resource paradox: Unbundling risks, unleashing private capital. *The Indonesian Journal of Development Planning*, III(1), 1–18, April 2019.

Bridle, R., Merrill, L., Halonen, M., Zinecker, A., Klimscheffskij, M., and Tommila, P. (2018). *Swapping Fossil Fuel Subsidies for Sustainable Energy*. Oslo: Nordic Council of Ministers.

Castro-Santos, L., Filgueira Vizoso, A., Muñoz Camacho, E., and Piegieri, L. (2016). Costs and feasibility of repowering wind farms. *Energy Sources, Part B: Economics, Planning, and Policy*, 11(10), 974–981.

Chevalier-Roignant, B. and Trigeorgis, L. (2011). *Competitive Strategy: Options and Games*. Cambridge, MA: The Massachusetts Institute of Technology Press.

Colmenar-Santos, A., Campinez-Romero, S., Perez-Molina, C., and Mur-Perez, F. (2015). Repowering: An actual possibility for wind energy in Spain in a new scenario without feed-in tariffs. *Renewable and Sustainable Energy Reviews*, 41, 319–337, January 2015.

Deign, J. (2020). Why aren't falling renewables costs cutting European energy market prices? *gtm*, November 2, 2020.

Dixit, A. K. and Nalebuff, B. J. (1993). *Thinking strategically: The competitive edge in business, politics, and everyday life*. New York: W. W. Norton & Company.

Driouchi, T., Bennett, D. J., and Simpson, G. (2010). A path-dependent contingent-claims approach to capacity investments. *European Journal of Operation Research*, 201(1), 319–323.

Elshurfa, A. M., Albardi, S. R., Bigerna, S., and Andrea Bellino, C. (2018). Estimating the learning curve of solar PV balance of system for over 20 countries: Implications and policy recommendations. *Journal of Cleaner Production*, 196(20), 122–134, September 2018.

Farnworth, E. (2021). Which businesses are leading the way in reducing emissions? *World Economic Forum*, January 28, 2021.

Frondel, M., Ritter, N., Schmidt, C. M., and Vance, C. (2009). Economic impacts from promotion of renewable energy technologies: The German experience. Ruhr Economic Papers #156, Ruhr-Universität Bochum.

Gazheli, A. and van den Bergh, J. (2018). Real options analysis of investment in solar vs wind energy: Diversification strategies under uncertain prices and costs. *Renewable and Sustainable Energy Reviews*, 82(3), 2693–2704, February 2018.

Hampl, N., Lüdeke-Freund, F., Flink, C., Olbert, S., and Ade, V. (2011). *The Myth of Bankability — Definition and Management of Context of Photovoltaic Project Financing in Germany*. Hamburg, Germany: Goetzpartners & COLEXON.

Handiputranto, Hadinoto & Partners (2018). Indonesian government publishes 2017 cost of electricity generation figures. Global Business Guide, Baker MacKenzie, April 5, 2018.

Hürlimann, C. and Bengoa, D. S. (2017). Corporate finance in renewable energy investments — A review of theory and practice. *Global Business and Economics Review*, 19(5), 592–631.

IER (2018). Global investment in renewable energy stalled due to subsidy cuts. Institute for Energy Research, February 26, 2018.

IFC (2013). *Success of geothermal wells: A global study, June 2013*. Washington, D. C.: International Finance Corporation. https://www.ifc.org/wps/wcm/connect/22970ec7-d846-47c3-a9f5-e4a65873bd3b/ifc-drilling-success-report-final.pdf?MOD=AJPERES&CVID=jYlcyTW.

IRENA (2020a). *Renewable Power Generation Costs in 2019*. Abu Dhabi: International Renewable Agency.

IRENA (2020b). *Renewable energy finance: Sovereign guarantees*. Abu Dhabi: International Renewable Energy Agency.

Jacob, S. and Tönnis, M. (2015). Electricity from the depths of Africa. *Munich Re Topics Magazine*, 2, 24–27.

Jewell, J., McCollum, D., Emerling, J., Bertram, C., Gernaat, D. E. H. J., Krey, V., Paoussos, L., Berger, L., Fragkiadakis, K., Keppo, I., Saadi, N., Tavoni, M., van Vuuren, D., Vinichenko, V., and Riahi, K. (2018). Limited emission reductions from fuel subsidy removal, except in energy exporting regions. *Nature*, 554, 209–233.

Jhawar, P. (2020). Renewable energy: It is crucial to honour signed contracts. *DownToEarth*, June 23, 2020.

Joos, M. and Staffeld, I. (2018). Short-term integration costs of variable renewable energy: Wind curtailment and balancing in Britain and Germany. *Renewable and Sustainable Energy Reviews*, 86, 45–65.

Kemp, D. (2019). PPAs are exploding. But are they safe? *Infrastructure Investor*, March 12, 2019.

Mackenzie, K. M., Ussher, G. N. H., Libbey, R. B., Quinlivan, P. F., Dacanay, J. U., and Jacobs, I. B. (2017). Use of deep slimhole drilling for geothermal exploration. *Proceedings of the 5th Indonesia International Geothermal Convention & Exhibition*, Jakarta, Indonesia, August 2–4, 2017.

Martinez-Cámara, E., Latorre-Biel, J.-I., Jimenez, E., Sanz-Adán, F., and Blanco-Fernandez, J. (2018). Life cycle assessment of a wind farm repowering process. *Renewable and Sustainable Energy Reviews*, 93, 260–271, October 2018.

McGrath, M. (2020). Climate change: COVID pandemic has little impact on rise in CO_2. *British Broadcasting Corporation (BBC)*, November 23, 2020.

Mielke, J. and Steudle, G. A. (2018). Green investment and coordination failure: An investors' Perspective. *Ecological Economics*, 150, 88–95.

Mulder, M. and Scholtens, B. (2013). The impact of renewable energy on electricity prices in the Netherlands. *Renewable Energy*, 57, 94–100, September 2013.

Murray, B. C., Cropper, M. L., de la Chesnaye, F. C., and Reilly, J. M. (2014). How effective are US renewable energy subsidies in cutting greenhouse gases? *American Economic Review*, 104(5), 569–574, May 2014.

Nicolini, M. and Tavoni, M. (2017). Are renewable energy subsidies effective? Evidence from Europe. *Renewable and Sustainable Energy Reviews*, 74, 412–423, July 2017.

Offshore Engineer (2021). Equinor, BP firm up US offshore wind partnerships. *Offshore Engineer*, January 29, 2021.

Repsol (2020). WindFloat Atlantic project starts supplying clean energy in Portugal. Press Release, January 2, 2020.

Richter, M., Vedde, J., Green, M., Jahn, U., and Köntges, M. (2017). *Technical Assumptions Used in PV Financial Models: Review of Current Practices and Recommendations*. IEA-PVPS T13-08-2017, Paris: International Energy Agency.

Rolffs, P., Richardson, J., and Amin, A. (2017). Innovative risk-finance solutions: Insights for geothermal power development in Kenya and Ethiopia. United Kingdom: Working Papers, Climate Development Knowledge Network, February 2017. https://cdkn.org/wp-content/uploads/2017/02/CDKN_Parhelion_Working_Paper_Pr3.pdf.

Rousseau, J. J. (1974). *The Essential Rousseau: The Social Contract, Discourse on the Origin of Inequality, Discourse on the Arts and Sciences, the Creed of the Savoyard Priest*. New York: Mentor Book.

Sinn, H.-W. (2012). *The Green Paradox: A Supply-side Approach to Global Warming*. Cambridge, MA: Massachusetts Instittue of Technology Press.

Torani, K., Rausser, G., and Zilberman, D. (2016). Innovation subsidies vs consumer subsidies: A real options analysis of solar energy. *Energy Policy*, 92, 255–269, May 2016.

Vadillo, J. (2021). Iberdrola y Total se alian para entrar en eólica marina en Dinamarca ("Iberdrola and Total ally for entry to Danish offshore wind"), *Cinco Dias*, January 14, 2021.

Vergne, J. P. and Durand, R. (2010). The missing link between theory and empirics of path dependence: Conceptual clarification, testability issues, and methodological implications. *Journal of Management Studies*, 47(4), 736–759.

Woolf, F. and Halpern, J. (2001). Integrating independent power producers into emerging wholesale power markets. Policy Research Working Paper, 2703, The World Bank, November 2001.

Wyman, O. (2020). Why it's too soon to sunset renewable energy subsidies. *Forbes*, January 14, 2020. https://www.forbes.com/sites/oliverwyman/2020/01/14/why-its-too-soon-to-let-renewable-energy-subsidies-expire/?sh=360999931e02.

Zarnikau, J., Woo, C. K., Zhu, S., and Tsai, C. H. (2019). Market price behaviour of wholesale electricity products: Texas. *Energy Policy*, 125, 418–428.

III
BOUnCE to Win

Chapter 7
Cost of Energy

"Costs" of energy are ubiquitous but could benefit from greater coherence in their economic and financial definitions. The various notions of "costs," how they differ, and how they could be reconciled are examined. Evaluated at a granular level, cost structures provide insights into how endogenous or exogenous cost factors are altered by managerial or policy actions and their limitation as a static measure. To its credit, lifecycle cost of energy (LCOE) provides a structured framework that facilitates the identification of the principal sources of variations. These insights help to reframe subsidies to partially resolve the green paradox, to explicitly estimate the cost of CO_2 reduction via supply substitutions, and to build the basis to value the trade-offs of deferring or accelerating investments. Upon gaining this clarity, managers may formulate differentiated, but inter-related, strategies under a portfolio of supplies to meet business viability conditions.

1
Introduction

Managers would ask: What could be simpler than calculating the costs of supplying energy? Their usual answer: We add all the money costs, divide the sum by the quantity supplied, and we have the unit costs. Add a profit margin, and a unit selling price is set.

This introspective costing exercise creates a minefield for managers and policy to navigate. Irrespective of sources, cash costs are compared with prevailing market prices that ignore competition (and supply substitutions). When "costs" are too high, the state is expected to step up with subsidies to adjust for the differences.

By "socialising" any excess costs, regulatory fiat turns moribund investments into a financially compelling proposition. However, such a stance may prove unsustainable if not economically disastrous. Here's why.

Investments become viable when their cash receipts exceed disbursements from operations to earn positive payoffs. This is feasible when supplies are cost-effective, operated by managers that adapt to how dynamic markets shift. In contrast, subsidies tend to be short-lived revenue sources that are premised on the public's continued acquiescence to policy's preferences.

By entrusting their firm's fate to policy's benevolence and steadfastness, managers abrogate part of their responsibilities as stewards of their stakeholders' fortunes. Inadvertently, managers sleepwalk towards a rose-tinted future and often fall off the cliff. This occurs when policy preferences change or ideological convulsions irreparably change the game to managers' "surprise."

Policy rewards some renewables a premium (e.g. feed-in tariffs) or imposes carbon taxes on fossil fuels, which usually raises energy prices. In this simplified view, renewables enjoy higher prices without incurring the tax, hence expanding their financial gains.

Policy and managers, however, quickly find themselves in a bind. Translating a simple financial notion of costs and returns is proving more nuanced and complex. While finance and welfare economics recognise the value of reducing pollution, they fail to agree just how much is its worth, or pollution's cost, to society.

Recognising these drawbacks, the costing of externalities becomes an exercise in consensus building within a political process. By its very nature, the "correct" levels are contingent upon a shifting consensus that sustains or breaks public acquiescence.

As subsidies' burden takes a toll on public finances, policy's impulse is to cut. When this happens, the firms' trust in a steadfast and benevolent regulator is seriously shaken, leading to significant cuts in investments (IER, 2018). Recognising this dilemma, how could finance and economics meaningfully inform managerial and policy decisions?

Both need to tackle the twin questions of how to correctly ascertain energy's supply costs, and consequently, how to sustain the firm's viability. Under competitive markets, these *business viability conditions* serve as our starting points to test the investment's merits:

1. Is it likely to recover all the financial costs disbursed periodically to sustain an ongoing concern?
2. Will it likely continue to attract capital to affordably fund the investing firm's obligations and growth opportunities?

By adopting a decision-maker mindset, I posit that the notions of costs could influence how an investment is chosen among competing alternatives. More importantly, what is committed initially would lock in the firm to a pattern of costs and operational flexibility. Under a transitioning energy market, this may spell the difference between viability and financial distress.

To illustrate these effects, I start by understanding how financial analysis would derive the periodic costs of supplies, its use to inform decisions, and its limitations by connecting financial with lifecycle costing of energy. In the process, explicit links of strategic actions, policy measures, and technology choices to the firm's financial performance are evaluated. In so doing, managers could test their strategic intents by simulating feasible futures for the firm. Policy action, and how it alters the firms' advantages and society's welfare, could be explicitly assessed via the investment evaluation process.

2
Financial and Economic Costing of Energy

Investment evaluation is performed as a "look-ahead" of the feasible outcomes when a set of assumed conditions comes to fruition. More often than not, managers default on what their financial or economic models prescribe to guide their decisions. Perhaps, without consciously abrogating their fiduciary responsibilities, the humanness of managers is ignored. In its stead, Richard Thaler (2015) points to economists' (and financiers' too) penchant for seeing the world as a well-ordered, rational, and "well-behaved" system of aligned incentives and actions.

When it comes to costing energy supplies, investment evaluation is biased towards rewarding the imagined certainties amidst inherently volatile energy markets. Perhaps, not surprisingly, managers err in their decisions when investments are evaluated under static conditions that clash with market volatilities.

To remedy this, I examine how periodic costs interact with supplies and how demand profiles and variations could asymmetrically alter costs (or competitive advantages). Specifically, managers and policy could influence how dynamic energy markets evolve as described in academic literature and experienced in practice.

Policy, informed by economics, acts through the state (e.g. policymakers and agencies) to assert society's perceived preferences. Through the state's omnipotence, they sequester through taxation (Stigler, 1971), or through subsidies, to rebalance the allocation of benefits or costs. The state's beneficence (or maleficence) creates (or impedes) profitable niches. Consequently, the compliant is favoured, or the recalcitrant is penalised.

Within market economies, managers (in its broadest sense) act as economic agents. They organise, allocate, and create wealth for their stakeholders. Acting as stewards, they sustain wealth by creating economic value consistent with their societal obligations.

Policy and managers interact to pursue a common good, however it is understood. Policy reinforces market benefits when managers are rewarded for their risk-taking to uniquely appropriate the benefits of their honest labour. The minimum conditions for markets to function lie in a commonly accepted notion of what is ethical rather than what is legal. Legality is a construct that approximates a *modus operandi* that facilitates arbitration to reconcile colliding interests.

In this broad conception, energy markets act as allocation mechanisms, where competing interests try to find their niches. In its most basic forms, prices are set to match demand with supplies, as we see with wholesale energy markets (Littlechild, 2001). As a two-sided facet, someone's price is another's cost.

2.1 Perils of incomplete *financial costing*

Seen from the manager's perspectives, money is spent to invest or settle costs incurred to produce an output that could be sold for a profit. Two types of costs come to mind: One is operating expenses that are incurred and often disbursed during a given period. The other relates to lump sum investments that generate cash returns over multiple periods. To match "expenses" to "revenues," accountants impute a non-cash depreciation expense to accrue the expense for the period (Damodaran, 1996). This practice is what accountants refer to as an accrual method of attributing costs pertaining to a period.

Chart 7.1 connects the financial and economic costing of energy.

Financial costing looks at the three principal cost components. The invested capital (A.1) representing the capital expenditures is recovered as financial fixed cost recovery (FFCR) (B). To operate the asset, periodic financial variable costs (FVCs) (C) and financial fuel costs (FFCs) (D) are expensed.

In accounting terms, a portion of the invested capital is allocated as depreciation expenses for each period or (Depn) in (B.1).

Variable operating expenses constitute financial fixed operating and management expenses (FFO&Ms) that relate to administrative expenses and labour, among others. Financial variable operations and maintenance expenses (FVO&Ms) vary with output. Summing up the two (C.1), the FVCs (C) are calculated.

FFCs (D) relate to fossil fuel energy, mostly coal or gas, given that renewables have zero fuel costs.

The sum FFCR + FVC + FFC is the financial periodic cost of energy (FPCOE) (A). By pricing energy at this level, revenues would recover the financial costs of supplying energy without earning a profit (or surplus).

Dynamic Decisions

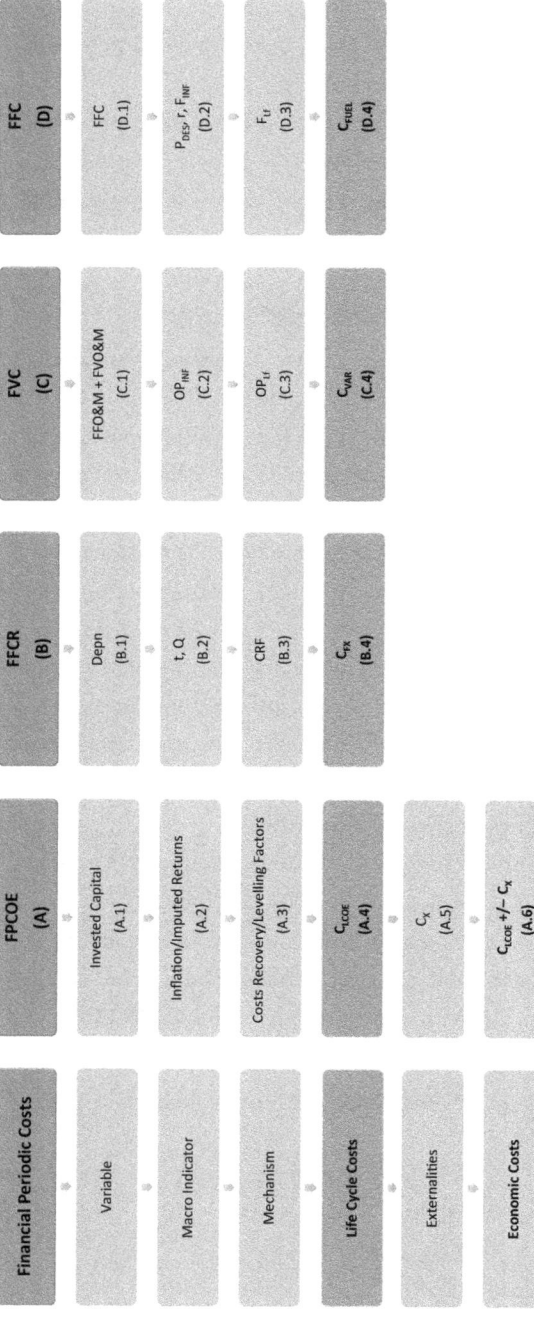

Chart 7.1: Building Blocks of Financial and Economic Costing

Using these variables for financial analysis, managers would need to escalate costs, add a margin and any subsidies or grants. Subsidies and other costs are expressed as C_X (A.5) and added or subtracted to C_{LCOE} (A.6).

What is described is a common financial analysis practice. Managers sum up the financial costs, apply an escalation to FVC and FFC, and a stream of costs is projected over the operating life of the asset. This defines how much the investment should earn in revenues, at a minimum, to break even financially.

At this point, one introspectively "complied" with the first *business viability condition* of recovering the money costs incurred to supply energy. However, any slippages in costs may result in losses as a result of costs under-recovery.

Now the crunch: How much should energy be priced to meet the aspired financial returns?

Investment returns are set to exceed or equal a hurdle rate to pass our second *business viability condition* of attracting sufficient capital to sustain an ongoing concern. In financial terms, this is usually pegged to long bond yields as an alternative security plus some risk premia.

Following this logic, managers encounter two intractable problems: A financial hurdle rate, as proposed, does not distinguish between short or long-life assets, which tends to flatter the value of short duration assets. A linear projection of costs and revenues may deviate significantly if technological advances see rapid falls in costs, with energy prices following suit.

With markets asserting their influence, excessive gains attract new suppliers to erode excess returns. Conversely, persistent losses could force firms to exit prematurely via bankruptcies or divestments.

2.2 Linking to *economic costs–returns nexus*

Extending FPCOEs by employing levelised costing of electricity, LCOEs are employed. Following the Energy Information Administration's (EIA, 2013) usage, it represents the "average revenue (*or costs*) per unit of energy production that would be required … to recover all investment and operating costs. It includes a specified return on investment over a specified project financial life, as well as assumed project utilisation rate." To convert FPCOE into C_{LCOE} in (A.4), the following adjustments are made, as described in Chart 7.2.

Starting with the big-ticket item: How much of the invested capital should be recovered annually?

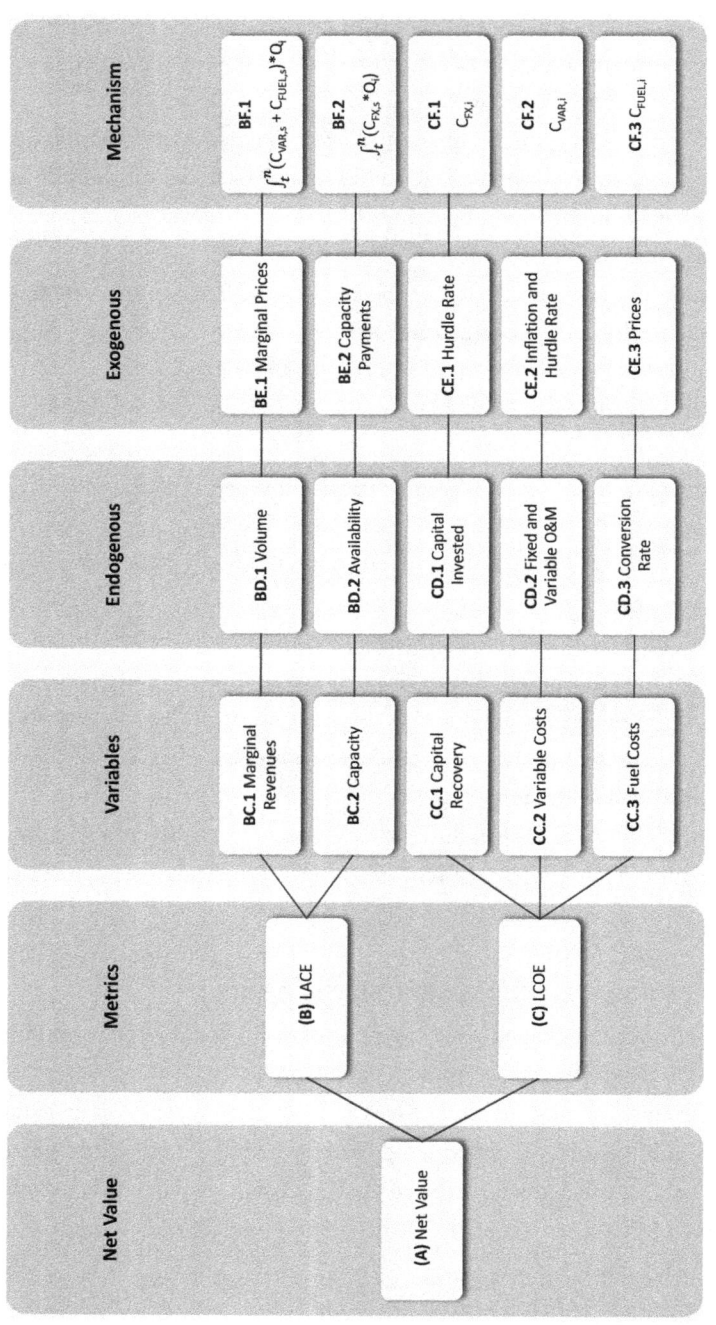

Chart 7.2: Costs–Returns Nexus

Source: Adapted from EIA.

Aside from recovering depreciation expenses, the cost of money adjusted for risks (A.1) is added. Roth and Ambs (2004) provide a capital recovery factor (CRF) to calculate C_{FX}.

Economic cash cost of supply, or marginal price, is the sum of C_{VAR} and C_{FUEL} after adjusting the financial variable and fuel costs for inflation rates (BE.1).

Knowing what the technologies' lifecycle costs look like, how is this translated to revenues?

The lifecycle avoided cost of energy, or LACE, is introduced by EIA (2013) to calculate the "potential revenue… from the sale of energy and generating capacity. This cost is the weighted average of the marginal cost of electricity dispatch during the periods in which the *asset* is assumed to operate, weighted by the number of hours of assumed operation in each time period." In effect, there are two cash streams:

1. *Marginal revenues* are earned from supplying the volume, Q_i, (BD.1) at marginal prices (BE.1). The product in (BF.1) yields the marginal revenues in (BC.1).
2. *Capacity revenues* result from making a volume, Q_i, available to meet a given demand for a fee or capacity payments in BE.2. The product in (BF.2) yields the capacity revenues.

Volumes vary with the load, or demand for power, with power prices fluctuating with demand. By adding the two revenue streams, the potential revenue from a given market of an investment, which is referred to as LACE in (B) is obtained.

2.3 Monetising energy investments

Managers influence directly how much volume (BD.1), and hence capacity (BD.2), they could make available to the system from their fossil fuel and conventional renewable assets. By maintaining their assets in good operating condition, assets could be deployed whenever demand requires their deployment. In contrast, variable renewables availability is subject to the mercy of nature.

Under dynamic markets, system prices are set by the marginal supply that clears periodic demand (e.g. periodic supply equals demand). That is, available supplies are stacked from cheapest to the most expensive until the demand for the period is fully covered.[1]

---

[1] Recall Chart 1.3 in Chapter 1 that describes in detail how a functioning dynamic energy market usually operates.

The volume (BD.1) may be despatched or not, subject to how much demand is needed to be supplied periodically. As volume varies, so would the cost of the marginal supply. As demand falls, or renewables replace fossil fuels, the more expensive supplies are not despatched.

Available supply (BD.2) is where variable renewables differ from fossil fuels and conventional renewables.

The wind blows, or the sun shines, without human intervention. Given their zero fuel costs, they are despatched when available for achieving lower marginal costs than that of fossil fuels. In effect, they are price-takers in the economist's notion of competitive energy markets.

The sums of the marginal revenues (BF.1) and the capacity payments (BF.2) comprise the LACEs of each technology. By subtracting its LCOE from LACE, we have the net value, which "can be thought of as the potential profit (or loss) per unit of energy production for the plant" (EIA, 2013).

For heavily intervened markets, the regulated prices substitute for the marginal cost of supply and its capacity payments. Hence, set "too high," it attracts new supplies that could exceed periodic demand (or vice versa).

3
Informing Managerial Decisions

Knowing how costs are structured and how it influences energy pricing, the way technology choices impact availability and the flexibility (or lack of it) to despatch is examined. Specifically, the diverse technology traits confer the following advantages or limitations:

1. ***Fossil fuels*** confer costs that vary with fuel prices (e.g. coal or gas prices) while gaining in higher capacity utilisation or flexible supply deployment.
2. ***Conventional renewables*** (e.g. hydro or geothermal) are zero fuel cost supply options with despatch flexibility. They often come at higher capital expenditures to build, relative to gas, but benefit from lower operating costs.
3. ***Variable renewables*** (e.g. wind or solar) are less complex to deploy than conventional renewables and confer zero fuel costs supply option while exhibiting more variable and random availability.

Cost of Energy

While the revenues and costs patterns differ, managers tend to ignore these differences when optimising individual investments. To incorporate this thinking, we take a structured approach in using energy costs to inform investment decisions.

3.1 Identifying the financial cost building blocks

Consider a coal-fired power generation investment, designated as $Coal_B$, operated as a baseload capacity. The costs in Appendices 7A–7C and Table 7.1 are used for the subsequent calculations.

$Coal_B$ costs $2,734/kW (A6), or $2.7 mln/MW, to build. Operated as a baseload supply, the asset would operate at 85% of its rated capacity or 7,446 hours a year (A2). Converting this to output, every kW of capacity installed would produce 7,446 kWh annually. Assuming the asset would operate for 30 years (A1), our annual straight-line depreciation expense is $91 (A7) or $2,734/30 (A6/A1). Dividing this by the annual output, we have the annual fixed costs that we need to recover (A8) or $0.0122/kWh.

To operate the plant, we incur operating expenses comprising wages, repairs and maintenance, logistics, and administration. We divided this into the following:

1. FFO&Ms, which are estimated at $31.18 for every kW installed (A9) or $0.0042/kWh (A9/A2);
2. FVO&Ms, which are estimated by EIA (2019) as $0.0045/kWh (A11).

Adding the two (A10 + A11), we have the FVC of $0.0087/kWh (A.12).

FFCs require some math to convert into $/kWh. Coal is sold by its weight, in $/MT, with varying heat rates (mmBTU) and content (MT/mmBTU). We calculate how much coal we need to generate a kWh of power as follows:

1. Coal is purchased at $91.83/MT and incurs a freight of $15.65/MT, costing the plant $107.48/MT (or 0.1076/kg) at destination.
2. The heat rate is 8,800 mmBTU/kWh and heat content of 17,427,005 mmBTU/MT (or 17,427 mmBTU/kg).
3. Dividing the heat rate by its heat content, we have 0.0005 MT/kWh (or 0.505 kg/kWh).
4. Multiplying the coal content (0.505 kg/kWh) by the price of coal ($0.1076/kg), we have $0.0543/kWh, allowing for rounding errors, as shown in (A.13).

Table 7.1: Financial Periodic Costs of Energy

Column/Line	Financial Variables	Units	Acronym	Coal Coal$_B$ A	Gas ACCGT$_B$ B	Nuclear ANuke C	Hydro StoHydro D	Geothermal — Large Hole Geo$_B$ E
	Assumptions							
1	Economic Life of Asset	Years	n	30	30	40	50	30
2	Annual Output per MW	Hours	Q	7,446	7,621	7,884	7,446	8,234
3	Producer Price Index	%	PPI	2.50%	3.10%	2.50%	2.50%	3.00%
4	Interest Rate	%	i	2.50%	2.50%	2.50%	2.50%	2.50%
	Capital Expenditures — CAPEX							
5	Base Overnight Costs	$/MW	BOC	2,734	736	5,224	2,680	2,615
6	Annual Depreciation	$	Depn	91	25	131	54	87
7	Financial Fixed Costs Recovery — Annual	$/kWh	FFCR	0.0122	0.0032	0.0166	0.0072	0.0106
	Operating Expenses — Opex							
8	Fixed Operating & Maintenance	$/MW	FFO&M	31.18	10.30	103.31	40.85	122.28
9	Fixed Operating & Maintenance	$/kWh	FFO&M	0.0042	0.0014	0.0131	0.0055	0.0149
10	Variable Operating & Maintenance	$/kWh	FVO&M	0.0045	0.0021	0.0024	0.0014	0.0000
11	**Financial Variable Costs**	$/kWh	FVC	0.0087	0.0035	0.0155	0.0069	0.0149
	Fuel Costs							
12	Financial Fuel Costs	$/kWh	FFC	0.0543	0.0537	0.0062	0.0000	0.0000
	Costs of Energy							
13	Financial Periodic Costs of Energy (Line 8 + 12 + 13)	$/kWh	FPCOE	0.0752	0.0604	0.0383	0.0141	0.0254

Cost of Energy

Table 7.1: (*Continued*)

Column/Line	Financial Variables	Geothermal — Slim Hole GeoS$_B$ F	Onshore Wind Wind$_{ON}$ G	Offshore Wind — Conventional Platforms Wind$_{OBAP}$ H	Photovoltaic — Tracking PVT$_M$ I	Photovoltaic — Fixed Tilt PVF$_M$ J	Solar — Thermal Solar$_M$ K
	Assumptions						
1	Economic Life of Asset	30	20	20	20	20	20
2	Annual Output per MW	8,234	3,767	4,818	2,891	1,752	1,314
3	Producer Price Index	3.00%	3.00%	3.00%	3.00%	3.00%	3.00%
4	Interest Rate	2.50%	2.50%	2.50%	2.50%	2.50%	2.50%
	Capital Expenditures — CAPEX						
5	Base Overnight Costs	1,700	1,518	4,758	1,876	1,698	4,011
6	Annual Depreciation	57	76	238	94	85	201
7	**Financial Fixed Costs Recovery — Annual**	**0.0069**	**0.0201**	**0.0494**	**0.0324**	**0.0485**	**0.1526**
	Operating Expenses — Opex						
8	Fixed Operating & Maintenance	80.00	48.42	80.14	22.46	22.46	72.84
9	Fixed Operating & Maintenance	0.0097	0.0129	0.0166	0.0078	0.0128	0.0554
10	Variable Operating & Maintenance	0.0000	0.0000	0.0000	0.0000	0.0000	0.0000
11	**Financial Variable Costs**	**0.0097**	**0.0129**	**0.0166**	**0.0078**	**0.0128**	**0.0554**
	Fuel Costs						
12	**Financial Fuel Costs**	**0.0000**	**0.0000**	**0.0000**	**0.0000**	**0.0000**	**0.0000**
	Costs of Energy						
13	Financial Periodic Costs of Energy (Line 8 + 12 + 13)	0.0166	0.0330	0.0660	0.0402	0.0613	0.2081

Source: Raw data: EIA as shown in Appendices 7A–7C.

The financial marginal cost is the sum of FVR (A.12) and FFC (A.13), which amounts to $0.0630/kWh. By supplying, the firm should at least recover its FFCR of $0.0122/kWh (A.8) to fully recover its FPCOE of $0.0752/kWh (A.14).

Having now calculated the cost components, managers will have to decide at what price they would supply. There are two generic approaches:

1. Impute a *cash margin* that would generate cash flows that meet the financial internal rate of return (FIRR) or net present value (NPV) thresholds.
2. Tactically follow *marginal pricing* where the financial cash costs (A.12 + A.13) are recovered.

The resulting prices and volumes supplied determine revenues and costs, and their differences are the cash margins (or payoffs). Repeating this exercise, the FPCOEs are calculated for each energy technology.

At this point, our managerial question needs an answer. By doing the financial costing exercise, are we pricing our energy to ensure our business' viability?

This brings us to the auction prices achieved up to 2019. In various reports, auction prices for wind and PV range from $0.015/kWh to $0.050/kWh for 2023 commissioning. That wind (G.14) and PV (I.14) are becoming cost-competitive with coal (A.14) appears to concur with our FPCOEs estimates.

The business media's enthusiastic reports notwithstanding, a number of managers start to question "how many of these projects would actually be realised," as managers advise caution (Jashari *et al.*, 2018).

Such a cautionary tale is perhaps justified: Along with Germany's CESifo, the International Energy Agency (IEA) asserted that the auction prices do not reflect the full costs. In some cases, price escalations and subsidies are included before they were awarded.

Interestingly, the auction prices for wind and PV are well below the LCOEs, an economic costing estimated by IEA and the European Court of Auditors (ECA) (IEA, 2019; ECA, 2019). This led to a suggestion that the winning bidders may suffer from the "winner's curse" (Léger *et al.*, 2018).

How are these conflicting views on costs reconciled?

Managers anticipate that costs would fall sharply (ECA, 2019) between 2019 and the 2023 commissioning date. By incorporating this into their bids, the auction prices are calculated without any scope for failures. This poses imminent and present dangers to the business.

By converting the expected falls in future costs into an obligation, by offering "lower prices" today, managers have assumed the pricing risks (or deviations from expected costs). If expected falls in costs fail to materialise, and prices are set below costs of supplies, persistent losses will result.

The consequences: Get the sums wrong, and the firm is on track for bankruptcy, as previous variable renewable investors experienced to their grief (Hoium, 2017).

At this point, the first lesson is learned in how financial returns relate to long-term business viability as a precondition to ensuring the firm flourishes financially. *To reap the benefits two generations hence, firms have to earn a profit today.*

3.2 Incorporating economic notions of lifecycle costing

The economic notions of lifecycle costing of energy aim to fulfil the *second business viability condition*: To sustain the firm's access to capital, as an ongoing concern, they must earn in excess of their hurdle rate (or cost of capital). To explicitly incorporate these considerations, one needs to revisit how financial margins can be set and account for costs escalations.

To facilitate subsequent discussions, financial variables are shown as ***bold italics*** in Chart 7.3. Applying the economic adjustments, two objectives are met:

1. ascertain the LCOEs to fully price the output;
2. quantify the financial losses when costs are persistently mispriced.

To illustrate how earning a return equivalent to the financial hurdle rate may fall short, a granular comparison is made for each component of the LCOEs.

3.2.1 Recovery of what was invested

Capital costs recovery, $C_{FX,t}$ (1.2), explicitly accounts for asset life duration, and specific risks, when setting the economic hurdle rates. Specifically, we have the following:

1. ***Depreciation rate*** recovers the annual fixed costs imputed for the period. The estimated rate is the inverse of its operating life, which is 3.33% (e.g. 1/30 years * 100).

Line	Variables	Formula	Endogenous Factors	Exogenous Factors
1	$C_{FX,i}$	$C_{FX} = (I_i + CRF_i)/Q_t$	I_i = Invested capital CRF_i = Capital recovery factor Q_t = Quantity dispatched a year	
1.1		$I_i = C_{OCA} * (1 + X_{CONT}) * (1 + X_{TOF})$	C_{OCA} = Overnight costs of asset, or capex X_{CONT} = Contingency factor, or costs overruns	X_{TOF} = Technology optimism factor
1.2		$CRF_i = [((r_i) * (1+r_i)^p / (1+r_i)^n - (1)]$	$r_i = ARR_i + R_{30} + R_p$ ARR_i = Asset recovery rate	R_{30} = Long bond yield, 30 years R_p = Risk premium
2	$C_{VAR,i}$	$C_{VAR,i} = C_{FO\&M,i} + C_{VO\&M,i}$	$C_{FO\&M}$ = Lifecycle fixed operating expenses $C_{VO\&M}$ = Lifecycle variable operating expenses	
2.1		$C_{FO\&M} = (FO\&M_i/Q_i) * OP_{LF}$	$FO\&M_i$ = Fixed operating expenses	$OP_{LF} = [((r_i) * (1+r_i)^n /(1+r_i)^n - (1)) * (1+OP_{INF})/(r_i - OP_{INF})] *$ $[(1)-(1+OP_{INF})/(1+r_i)^n]$
2.2		$C_{VO\&M} = (VO\&M_i/Q_i) * OP_{INF}$	$VO\&M_i$ = Variable operating expenses	OP_{INF} = Long-term inflation rate
3	$C_{FUEL,i}$	$C_{FUEL,i} = (P_{FUEL,S} * V_{FUEL,i}) * F_{LF}$	$V_{FUEL,I}$ = Volume of fuel used per kWh	
3.1		$P_{FUEL,S} = P_{DES,S} + P_{CONV,i} + P_{FRT,S}$	$P_{CONV,i}$ = Conversion of unit fuel to unit energy $P_{FRT,S}$ = Freight per unit fuel	$P_{DES,i}$ = Price per unit fuel at destination $F_{LF} = [((r_i) * (1+r_i)^n /(1+r_i)^n - (1)) * (1+F_{INF})/(r_i - F_{INF})] * [(1)-$ $((1+F_{INF})/(1+r_i)^n]$
				F_{INF} = Long-term fuel inflation
4	$C_{LCOE,i}$	$C_{FX,i} + C_{VAR,i} + C_{FUEL,i}$	$C_{FX,i}$ and $C_{VAR,i}$	$C_{FUEL,i}$

Chart 7.3: Lifecycle Costs of Energy Calculations

Source: Roth and Ambs (2004).

2. ***Long bond yields*** represent a proxy for the yields one could earn from investing in a risk-free security. A rate of 2.5% is used for the calculations.
3. ***Financial risk premium*** is assumed at 3%, although there is no agreed methodology for deriving this number, which is a potential weakness (Fernandez, 2019).
4. ***Technology risk premium*** varies from 0% to 1%, depending on the maturity of the technology, based on recommended rates by industry engineers (e.g. EIA, 2019). The premium for $Coal_B$ is set at zero as a mature technology.

Adding items (1)–(4) above, 8.83% is the economic hurdle rate. Using the capital recovery formula (1.2), CRF is 9.59%.

The financial capex, or base overnight costs of $2,734 (F.1 or F.2), is now adjusted. By applying the contingency (G.1 or G.2) and technological optimism (H.1 or H.2) factors, the total overnight costs (I.1 or I.2) of $3,013 ($2,734 * 1.07 * 1.03) are the invested capital, 1_i.

By multiplying invested capital, I_i, by CRF, an annual sum of $289.80 for each kW installed is needed to be recovered.

This structured calculation avoids negative CRFs that "negative bond yields" (Ainger, 2019) may erroneously justify. Intuitively, "negative yield" implies that the borrower is paid to use the cash, a "novel" notion that cannot sustain capital-intensive energy business.

How the asset is operated, either as baseload or mid-merit plants, matters. Baseload would yield volumes, Q, of 7,445 kWh annually (e.g. 24 hours/day * 365 days/year * 85% utilisation rate), while mid-merit produces 5,246 kWh (S.1) for each kW. In this case, C_{FX} for $Coal_B$ is $0.0389/kWh (O.1) or $0.0551/kWh (O.2), respectively.

Invested capital clearly predetermines, to a large extent, the costs that are lock-in *a priori* because of the choice in technologies. To recover the investment, the varying capacity factors and the operating life of the assets contribute to its inherent cost advantages (or penalties).

Given these results, what strategic insights do we gain to inform our technology choices?

Technologies are not created equal, as shown in Table 7.2. Given their varying outputs (1.11 to 1.16), we need to compare them on this basis: How much MW is needed to produce similar MWh of output as $Coal_B$ or $ACCGT_B$?

Table 7.2: Comparable Total Overnight Costs Equivalence

Column/Line	Technology	Acronym	Operating Mode	Capex $/kW	Total Overnight Costs (TOC) $/kW	Asset Recovery Rate $/kWh	CRF %
		A	B	C	D	E	F
	Coal						
1	Scrubbed Coal — New	$Coal_B$	Baseload	2,734	3,013	0.0135	9.59%
2	Scrubbed Coal — New	$Coal_M$	Mid-merit	2,734	3,013	0.0191	9.59%
	Gas						
3	Advance Gas/Oil Combined Cycle	$ACCGT_B$	Baseload	736	795	0.0035	9.59%
4	Advance Gas/Oil Combined Cycle	$ACCGT_M$	Mid-merit	736	795	0.0047	9.59%
	Geothermal						
5	Geothermal — Large Hole	Geo_B	Baseload	2,615	2,746	0.0111	9.59%
6	Geothermal — Large Hole	Geo_M	Mid-merit	2,615	2,746	0.0161	9.59%
7	Geothermal — Slim Hole*	$GeoS_B$	Baseload	1,700	1,785	0.0072	9.59%
8	Geothermal — Slim Hole*	$GeoS_M$	Mid-merit	1,700	1,785	0.0104	9.59%
	Stored Hydro						
9	Conventional Hydro — Pumped Storage	$StoHydro_B$	Baseload	2,680	2,948	0.0079	7.71%
10	Conventional Hydro — Pumped Storage	$StoHydro_M$	Mid-merit	2,680	2,948	0.0104	7.71%
	Wind						
11	Onshore Wind	$Wind_{ON}$	Mid-merit	1,518	1,624	0.0216	12.15%
12	Offshore Wind — Conventional Platform	$Wind_{OFCP}$	Mid-merit	4,758	5,495	0.0570	12.15%
13	Offshore Wind — Advance Platform*	$Wind_{OFAP}$	Mid-merit	2,500	2,888	0.0300	12.15%
	Photovoltaic and Thermal Solar						
14	Solar Thermal	$Solar_M$	Mid-merit	4,011	4,292	0.1633	12.15%
15	Photovoltaic — Tracking	PVT_M	Mid-merit	1,876	1,970	0.0388	12.15%
16	Photovoltaic — Fixed	PVF_M	Mid-merit	1,698	1,783	0.0509	12.15%

Table 7.2: (Continued)

Column/Line	Technology	C_{FX} $/kWh G	Operating life Years H	Annual Output MWh I	TOC Equivalence Multiple—$Coal_B$ X J	TOC Equivalence $/MW K	TOC Equivalence Multiple—$ACCGT_B$ X L	TOC Equivalence $/MW M
	Coal							
1	Scrubbed Coal — New	0.0388	30	7,446	1.00	3,013	1.02	3,084
2	Scrubbed Coal — New	0.0550	30	5,256	1.42	4,268	1.45	4,369
	Gas							
3	Advance Gas/Oil Combined Cycle	0.0100	30	7,621	0.98	777	1.00	795
4	Advance Gas/Oil Combined Cycle	0.0134	30	5,694	1.31	1,040	1.34	1,064
	Geothermal							
5	Geothermal — Large Hole	0.0320	30	8,234	0.90	2,483	0.93	2,542
6	Geothermal — Large Hole	0.0462	30	5,694	1.31	3,591	1.34	3,675
7	Geothermal — Slim Hole*	0.0208	30	8,234	0.90	1,614	0.93	1,652
8	Geothermal — Slim Hole*	0.0301	30	5,694	1.31	2,334	1.34	2,389
	Stored Hydro							
9	Conventional Hydro — Pumped Storage	0.0305	50	7,446	1.00	2,948	1.02	3,017
10	Conventional Hydro — Pumped Storage	0.0399	50	5,694	1.31	3,855	1.34	3,946
	Wind							
11	Onshore Wind	0.0524	20	3,767	1.98	3,210	2.02	3,286
12	Offshore Wind — Conventional Platform	0.1386	20	4,818	1.55	8,492	1.58	8,692
13	Offshore Wind — Advance Platform*	0.0728	20	4,818	1.55	4,463	1.58	4,568
	Photovoltaic and Thermal Solar							
14	Solar Thermal	0.3969	20	1,314	5.67	24,321	5.80	24,893
15	Photovoltaic — Tracking	0.0942	20	2,540	2.93	5,775	3.00	5,911
16	Photovoltaic — Fixed	0.1236	20	1,752	4.25	7,578	4.35	7,756

Source: Raw data: EIA 2019 Energy Outlook; Author's estimates marked with *.

To produce the equivalent of 7,446 kWh, which is Coal$_B$'s annual output for each kW of capacity, one would need to build 2.93 kW for PVT$_M$. This is derived by dividing Coal$_B$'s output by PVT$_M$'s (e.g. 7,446 kWh/2,540 kWh). Multiplying this multiple by PVT$_M$'s TOC of $1,970/kW (D.15), the equivalent capital spend for PVT$_M$ is $5,775/kW (K.15), allowing for rounding errors.

Repeating this calculation, using ACCGT$_B$ as the reference capacity, a multiple of 3.0x (L15) and TOC of $5,911/kW is estimated, given ACCGT's better efficiency and higher output.

Under dynamic markets, firms that build assets cheaper than competition, without impairing reliability, embed cost advantages from efficiency. By reducing their C$_{FX}$, higher returns are earned *ceteris paribus*. In contrast, highly regulated systems tend to claw back these efficiency gains, hence eliminating any incentive to build assets cheaply. Consequently, tight regulatory control of costs (e.g. as in cost plus pricing) paradoxically discourages efficiency, which tends to increase costs (and prices).

3.2.2 Keeping the assets running efficiently

It is time to operate the assets and earn revenues. Managers now focus on cost control and operational efficiency. Following the logic of LCOEs and LACEs, managers keep costs low and volumes up.

In both cases, O&Ms are subject to inflationary pressures. The costs are levelised by applying Roth and Ambs's (2004) formulation, OP$_{LP}$ using the assumed long-term inflation rates, OP$_{INP}$ for industrial products (or producer price index (PPI)).

The levelling factor, OP$_{LP}$ is applied to the FVC to derive a levelised cost. The critical variables are the inflation rate that we use to escalate the financial operating costs and the duration, n (or operating life of the asset).

A long-term inflation rate is assumed for Coal$_B$ (equivalent to US PPI) for developed markets. Individual markets may use their specific inflation rates as appropriate by simply changing the data input. Applying Roth and Ambs's (2004) formulation, OP$_{LF}$ is 1.3x. Multiplying OP$_{LF}$ by FVC, C$_{VAR}$ is calculated.

C$_{VAR}$ represents the smallest proportion of LCOEs. While it is tempting to ignore their significance, locational factors may directly influence how it varies. For example, in desert conditions, while the sun may shine brightly to favour PV and solar power, expensive water used for cleaning the panels may push up variable costs to "surprise" managers.

3.2.3 Arbitrage under fuel costs volatilities

To correctly cost fuels and better appreciate its impact on energy prices, two factors are evaluated:

1. inflation's impact on fuel costs and consequently on energy prices;
2. variable fuel prices and how cost rankings of fossil fuels are altered in relation to conventional and variable renewables.

The fuel's levelised factor, F_{LF}, in Table 7.3 (Line 3) could provide an answer. By multiplying F_{LF} for coal (i.e. 1.53x) by the fuel costs of $Coal_B$, C_{FUEL} is $0.0834/kWh, as shown in Table 7.3 (E.4). This assumed a coal price of $91.83/MT.

Over the asset's life, however, coal as well as gas prices have seen highs or lows. The forecasters' capacity to accurately foresee where prices would settle is proven to be limited.

Proportionally, C_{FUEL} accounts for 62.5% of $Coal_B$'s LCOE (or 83.3% for gas — $ACCGT_B$). When coal or gas prices vary, the LCOEs vary, albeit asymmetrically (Table 7.4):

1. Coal (A.1 to A.7) or gas (G.1 to G.7) prices are historically volatile, which we simulate (A.4 for coal, G.4 for gas).
2. Landed costs of coal or gas include less volatile freight and other handling costs, with gas incurring regasification expenses for liquefied natural gas (LNG).

When translated to LCOEs, a 60% increase in coal price (A.1) results in 53.4% in $Coal_B$'s C_{LCOE}. In contrast, a similar increase in gas price shows a 42.9% change in $ACCGT_B$'s C_{LCOE}. In contrast, volatile fuel prices impact renewables' payoffs as follows, given its zero fuel costs:

1. Rising fuel costs increase energy prices that expands cash margins (or payoffs).
2. Conversely, falling fuel costs narrow renewables' payoffs.

To validate these assertions, Table 7.4 simulates how relative LCOEs vary because of fluctuating fuel costs.

Table 7.3: Fuel Costs Volatilities and LCOEs

Column/Line	Fuel Price Variations	Freight Variations	Coal Fired Power Plant					Gas Fired Power Plant						
			Coal DES $/MT	Freight $/MT	Coal Costs $/MT	Fuel Costs $/kWh	C_{FUEL} $/kWh	C_{LCOE} $/kWh	LNG DES $/mmBTU	Regas and Freight $/mmBTU	LNG Costs $/mmBTU	Fuel Costs $/kWh	C_{FUEL} $/kWh	C_{LCOE} $/kWh
			A	B	C	D	E	F	G	H	I	J	K	L
1	60%	15%	146.93	18.00	164.92	0.0833	0.1279	0.1780	10.59	1.74	12.33	0.0814	0.1114	0.1261
2	40%	10%	128.56	17.21	145.78	0.0736	0.1131	0.1632	9.27	1.66	10.93	0.0721	0.0987	0.1134
3	20%	5%	110.20	16.43	126.63	0.0640	0.0982	0.1483	7.94	1.59	9.53	0.0629	0.0861	0.1008
4	0%	0%	91.83	15.65	107.48	0.0543	0.0834	0.1335	6.62	1.51	8.13	0.0537	0.0735	0.0882
5	−20%	−5%	73.46	14.87	88.33	0.0446	0.0685	0.1186	5.30	1.43	6.73	0.0444	0.0608	0.0755
6	−40%	−10%	55.10	14.08	69.18	0.0349	0.0537	0.1038	3.97	1.36	5.33	0.0352	0.0482	0.0629
7	−60%	−15%	36.73	13.30	50.03	0.0253	0.0388	0.0889	2.65	1.28	3.93	0.0259	0.0355	0.0502

Source: Raw data: EIA.

Cost of Energy

Table 7.4: Volatile Fuel Costs and Impact on Relative Costs of Energy

Excess Cash Payoffs from reference LCOE — Δ $/kWh

Column/Line	Fuel Costs $/kWh	C_{FUEL} $/kWh	C_{LCOE} $/kWh	Nuclear ANuke	Hydro StoHydro$_B$	Geothermal — Large Hole Geo$_B$	Geothermal — Slim Hole GeoS$_B$	Onshore Wind Wind$_{ON}$	Offshore Wind — Conventional Platforms Wind$_{OFAP}$	Photovoltaic — Tracking PVT$_M$	Photovoltaic — Fixed Tilt PVF$_M$	Solar — Thermal Solar$_M$
	A	B	C	D	E	F	G	H	I	J	K	L
Coal — Coal$_B$												
0	0.0543	0.0834	0.1335	0.0946	0.0404	0.0524	0.0342	0.0689	0.1603	0.1058	0.1404	0.4746
1	0.0833	0.1279	0.1780	0.0834	0.1376	0.1256	0.1439	0.1092	0.0178	0.0722	0.0376	−0.2966
2	0.0736	0.1131	0.1632	0.0686	0.1228	0.1108	0.1290	0.0943	0.0029	0.0573	0.0227	−0.3115
3	0.0640	0.0982	0.1483	0.0537	0.1079	0.0959	0.1142	0.0795	−0.0119	0.0425	0.0079	−0.3263
4	0.0543	0.0834	0.1335	0.0389	0.0931	0.0811	0.0993	0.0646	−0.0268	0.0276	−0.0070	−0.3412
5	0.0446	0.0685	0.1186	0.0240	0.0782	0.0662	0.0845	0.0498	−0.0417	0.0128	−0.0218	−0.3560
6	0.0349	0.0537	0.1038	0.0092	0.0634	0.0514	0.0696	0.0349	−0.0565	−0.0021	−0.0367	−0.3709
7	0.0253	0.0388	0.0889	−0.0057	0.0485	0.0365	0.0548	0.0201	−0.0714	−0.0169	−0.0515	−0.3857
Gas — ACCGT$_B$												
0	0.0537	0.0735	0.0882									
8	0.0814	0.1114	0.1261	0.0315	0.0857	0.0737	0.0919	0.0572	−0.0342	0.0203	−0.0143	−0.3485
9	0.0721	0.0987	0.1134	0.0189	0.0731	0.0610	0.0793	0.0446	−0.0468	0.0076	−0.0270	−0.3612
10	0.0629	0.0861	0.1008	0.0062	0.0604	0.0484	0.0667	0.0320	−0.0595	−0.0050	−0.0396	−0.3738
11	0.0537	0.0735	0.0882	−0.0064	0.0478	0.0358	0.0540	0.0193	−0.0721	−0.0177	−0.0523	−0.3864
12	0.0444	0.0608	0.0755	−0.0191	0.0351	0.0231	0.0414	0.0067	−0.0847	−0.0303	−0.0649	−0.3991
13	0.0352	0.0482	0.0629	−0.0317	0.0225	0.0105	0.0287	−0.0060	−0.0974	−0.0430	−0.0776	−0.4117
14	0.0259	0.0355	0.0502	−0.0444	0.0098	−0.0022	0.0161	−0.0186	−0.1100	−0.0556	−0.0902	−0.4244

Source: Raw data: EIA and author's calculations.

Line 0 is the starting costs for $Coal_B$ and $ACCGT_B$ (columns A, B, C, line 0). The other technologies' LCOEs are shown under columns D–L, line 0. From line 1 and thereafter, the cost differences are shown by subtracting renewables' C_{LCOE}'s from $Coal_B$ (lines 1–7) or $ACCGT_B$ (lines 8–14). A negative number implies that renewables are more expensive than $Coal_B$ or $ACCGT_B$.

Under a coal-dominated energy system, more renewables could compete with $Coal_B$ when coal trades above our assumed price of $91.83/MT. Using $Wind_{ON}$ as an example, as coal prices trade higher, its excess LCOEs expand (H1 to H7), allowing it to reap a windfall.

As the energy system becomes dominated by ACCGT, power prices falls when cheaper $ACCGT_M$ replaces $Coal_M$ in setting periodic power prices. For $Wind_{ON}$, this shift is proving tougher as it sees its excess LCOE narrow (H8 to H12) to the point of losing its cost competitiveness to $ACCGT_B$ (H13 and H14).

3.2.4 Monetising value with LACE

Volatile prices and volumes, using the LACE framework, impact revenues and payoffs. The patterns of variations are seasonal, with daily peaks or troughs, subject to a market's load factor. The latter fluctuates with how often consumers vary their energy use.

In the four hypothetical markets in Table 7.5, the following dynamics are assumed to be at work that influence $Wind_{ON}$'s revenues and payoffs:

1. $Coal_M$ or $ACCGT_M$ are assumed as the price-setting supplies that set the periodic marginal prices.
2. $Wind_{ON}$ volumes displace less cost-effective $Coal_M$ or $ACCGT_M$ when volume growth is modest, leading to lower power prices.
3. When volume growth is high, as to sufficiently absorb the additional $Wind_{ON}$ supplies, power prices tend to remain neutral.
4. Marginal prices vary periodically according to how $Coal_M$ or $ACCGT_M$'s C_{FUEL} and C_{VAR} fluctuate.
5. Capacity payments for $Wind_{ON}$ are priced as C_{FX} of $Coal_M$ or $ACCGT_M$, which we apply to $Wind_{ON}$'s dispatched volume.

When the wind blows, $Wind_{ON}$ is assumed to be available and despatched, given its zero fuel costs (e.g. lower marginal costs than $Coal_M$ or $ACCGT_M$). The state of

Table 7.5: Location Specificity and LACEs of $Wind_{ON}$

A. Temperate Regions — Average Wind Factor, Low Volume Growth

Season	Time of Day	Marginal Prices $/kWh	Capacity Prices $/kWh	Wind Capacity Factor %	Hours in Period Hrs	Dispatched Hours Hrs	Marginal Revenue Available $	Capacity Payment $	LACE $/kWh
Summer	Day	0.1026	0.0134	0.20	640	128	13	2	
	Night	0.0710	0.0134	0.40	1,100	440	31	6	
	Shoulder	0.0884	0.0134	0.50	460	230	20	3	
Winter	Day	0.0907	0.0134	0.30	460	138	13	2	
	Night	0.0631	0.0134	0.50	1,100	550	35	7	
	Shoulder	0.0828	0.0134	0.30	640	192	16	3	
Spring	Day	0.0868	0.0134	0.30	545	164	14	2	
	Night	0.0615	0.0134	0.40	1,090	436	27	6	
	Shoulder	0.0710	0.0134	0.50	545	273	19	4	
Fall	Day	0.0868	0.0134	0.30	545	164	14	2	
	Night	0.0615	0.0134	0.40	1,090	436	27	6	
	Shoulder	0.0710	0.0134	0.50	545	273	19	4	
Total					8,760	3,422	249	46	0.0860
Implied Capacity Factor and LCOE						39.06%			0.0758
Net Value									0.0102

(*Continued*)

Dynamic Decisions

Table 7.5: (*Continued*)

B. Temperate Regions — High Wind Factor, Low Growth

Season	Time of Day	Marginal Prices $/kWh	Capacity Prices $/kWh	Wind Capacity Factor %	Hours in Period Hrs	Dispatched Hours Hrs	Marginal Revenue Available $	Capacity Payment $	LACE $/kWh
Summer	Day	0.0872	0.0134	0.22	640	141	12	2	
	Night	0.0604	0.0134	0.44	1,100	484	29	6	
	Shoulder	0.0751	0.0134	0.55	460	253	19	3	
Winter	Day	0.0771	0.0134	0.33	460	152	12	2	
	Night	0.0537	0.0134	0.55	1,100	605	32	8	
	Shoulder	0.0704	0.0134	0.33	640	211	15	3	
Spring	Day	0.0738	0.0134	0.33	545	180	13	2	
	Night	0.0523	0.0134	0.44	1,090	480	25	6	
	Shoulder	0.0604	0.0134	0.55	545	300	18	4	
Fall	Day	0.0738	0.0134	0.33	545	180	13	2	
	Night	0.0523	0.0134	0.44	1,090	480	25	6	
	Shoulder	0.0604	0.0134	0.55	545	300	18	4	
Total					8,760	3,764	232	50	0.0751
Implied Capacity Factor and LCOE						42.97%			0.0689
Net Value									0.0062

Table 7.5: (*Continued*)

C. Tropical Regions — Average Wind Factor, High Growth

Season	Time of Day	Marginal Prices $/kWh	Capacity Prices $/kWh	Wind Capacity Factor %	Hours in Period Hrs	Dispatched Hours Hrs	Marginal Revenue Available $	Capacity Payment $	LACE $/kWh
Summer	Day	0.1128	0.0134	0.21	640	134	15	2	
	Night	0.0746	0.0134	0.42	1,100	462	34	6	
	Shoulder	0.1016	0.0134	0.53	460	242	25	3	
Summer	Day	0.0998	0.0134	0.32	460	145	14	2	
	Night	0.0568	0.0134	0.53	1,100	578	33	8	
	Shoulder	0.0911	0.0134	0.32	640	202	18	3	
Monsoon	Day	0.0955	0.0134	0.32	545	172	16	2	
	Night	0.0554	0.0134	0.42	1,090	458	25	6	
	Shoulder	0.0781	0.0134	0.53	545	286	22	4	
Monsoon	Day	0.0955	0.0134	0.32	545	172	16	2	
	Night	0.0554	0.0134	0.42	1,090	458	25	6	
	Shoulder	0.0781	0.0134	0.53	545	286	22	4	
Total					8,760	3,593	268	48	0.0880
Implied Capacity Factor and LCOE						41.02%			0.0721
Net Value									0.0159

(*Continued*)

Table 7.5: (*Continued*)

D. Tropical Regions — High Wind Factor, High Growth

Season	Time of Day	Marginal Prices $/kWh	Capacity Prices $/kWh	Wind Capacity Factor %	Hours in Period Hrs	Dispatched Hours Hrs	Marginal Revenue Available $	Capacity Payment $	LACE $/kWh
Summer	Day	0.1128	0.0134	0.23	640	148	17	2	
	Night	0.0746	0.0134	0.46	1,100	508	38	7	
	Shoulder	0.1016	0.0134	0.58	460	266	27	4	
Summer	Day	0.0998	0.0134	0.35	460	159	16	2	
	Night	0.0568	0.0134	0.58	1,100	635	36	9	
	Shoulder	0.0911	0.0134	0.35	640	222	20	3	
Monsoon	Day	0.0955	0.0134	0.35	545	189	18	3	
	Night	0.0554	0.0134	0.46	1,090	504	28	7	
	Shoulder	0.0781	0.0134	0.58	545	315	25	4	
Monsoon	Day	0.0955	0.0134	0.35	545	189	18	3	
	Night	0.0554	0.0134	0.46	1,090	504	28	7	
	Shoulder	0.0781	0.0134	0.58	545	315	25	4	
Total					8,760	3,952	295	53	0.0880
Implied Capacity Factor and LCOE						45.12%			0.0656
Net Value									0.0224

Source: Raw data: EIA and author's calculations.

the technology dictates how much of the wind is converted into energy. A reality sinks in: When or where or how strong the wind blows is exogenous to human interventions.

Recognising these limitations, we consider the wind capacity factors to vary widely within a period. On average, across seasons it would follow a pattern that mimics the natural climate cycles. Hence, the annual capacity factors tend to be range-bound. Specifically:

Scenario A: We have a market supplied by $Wind_{ON}$ that approximates EIA's (2019) 40% average wind factor, with low volume growth. The LACE is derived by adding the revenues earned from marginal and capacity prices and divided by the volumes despatched.

The resulting LACE is $0.0860/kWh, which is higher than $Wind_{ON}$'s C_{LCOE} of $0.0758/kWh when capacity factor is at 39.06%. The net value is $0.0171/kWh ($0.0860/kWh − $0.0758/kWh), the costs avoided by replacing $ACCGT_M$ with $Wind_{ON}$.

Scenario B: As supplies from $Wind_{ON}$ increase, with higher wind factor and low volume growth, more coal or ACCGT supplies are displaced, exerting downward pressure on power prices. However, the revenues from increased $Wind_{ON}$ volumes are insufficient to compensate reductions in marginal prices.

Paradoxically, a higher share of $Wind_{ON}$ that earned lower marginal revenues end up with a lower LACE of $0.0751/kWh. A higher capacity factor at 42.97%, however, improves $Wind_{ON}$'s LCOE to $0.0689/kWh. Repeating our calculation, the net value is reduced to $0.0062/kWh (when compared to Scenario A).

Scenarios C and D: We now examine an energy market operating in tropical regions, characterised by summer (e.g. hot or hotter) and monsoon (e.g. rain or more rain) seasons. With tight supplies, the market offers higher marginal prices but similar capacity prices. Any addition from $Wind_{ON}$ is absorbed by increasing volumes, hence the effects on marginal prices are minimal.

In both cases, unit LACEs are similar at $0.0933/kWh. Higher despatch would imply higher utilisation rates for $Wind_{ON}$ with the effect of reducing unit LCOEs, respectively, to $0.0721/kWh and $0.0656/kWh (when compared to Scenario A). Consequently, their net values improved to $0.0159/kWh and $0.0224/kWh, respectively.

The comparisons illustrate how costs change with how much supplies are despatched. The technology's performance, and its return, is often contextual or contingent upon prevailing market conditions.

3.2.5 Why getting the costs right matters

Managers would pose the "so what" question: What difference did LCOEs and LACEs make to how investments are decided? A quick reply is: enough to under-recover up to a third of ignored costs, a sizeable difference that could spell prosperity or financial distress.

Going behind the numbers, managers are reminded how smart financial analysts cite copious cash flows to lull them into a state of complacency. For capital-intensive investments, cash is committed upfront and recovered over multiple periods. By its very nature, when outputs are priced adequately to recover operating costs and fixed costs, "cash flows" will indeed be abundant. However, this complacency could lead to misperceiving the investment's economic merits, as illustrated in Table 7.6.

From a decision-making perspective, the cost analysis simply highlighted an inconvenient reality. Managers, with all the best intentions, directly influence less than half of the factors that shape LCOEs and LACEs.

In the rush to outbid rivals, managers may be tempted to flatter their expected returns by relying on incomplete financial costing to achieve lower costs of supplies. To make matters worse, managers tend to ignore factors that they do not control (e.g. volatile prices or volumes). In lieu of explicitly evaluating the impact on costs and expected payoffs, some managers prefer to "sit back and hope for the best" that things will work out according to plan. After all, this is what financial evaluation prescribes when it assumes that predictable cash flows would make the discounting to its present value a reliable way to anchor an investment's value.

Cost of Energy 389

Table 7.6: Comparative Costs of LCOEs and FPCOEs

Column/Line	Technology	Acronym A	Operating Mode B	C_{FX} $/kWh C	C_{VAR} $/kWh D	C_{FUEL} $/kWh E	C_{LCOE} $/kWh F	FFCR $/kWh G	FVC $/kWh H	FFC $/kWh I	FPCOE $/kWh J	ΔFCR $/kWh K	ΔVC $/kWh L	ΔFC $/kWh M	ΔCOE $/kWh N	ΔCOE % O
	Coal															
1	Scrubbed Coal — New	Coal$_B$	Baseload	0.0389	0.0112	0.0833	0.1335	0.0324	0.0087	0.0543	0.0954	−0.0065	−0.0026	−0.0291	−0.0381	39.95%
2	Scrubbed Coal — New	Coal$_M$	Mid-merit	0.0551	0.0135	0.0833	0.1519	0.0459	0.0104	0.0543	0.1106	−0.0092	−0.0031	−0.0291	−0.0413	37.35%
3	Integrated Coal-Gasification Combined Cycle	IGCC$_B$	Baseload	0.0502	0.0183	0.0824	0.1509	0.0418	0.0141	0.0537	0.1096	−0.0084	−0.0042	−0.0287	−0.0413	37.65%
4	Integrated Coal-Gasification Combined Cycle	IGCC$_M$	Mid-merit	0.0711	0.0220	0.0824	0.1755	0.0592	0.0170	0.0537	0.1299	−0.0119	−0.0050	−0.0287	−0.0456	35.10%
5	IGCC with 30% Carbon Sequestration	IGCCCS$_B$	Baseload	0.0671	0.0220	0.0923	0.1814	0.0559	0.0170	0.0601	0.1330	−0.0112	−0.0050	−0.0322	−0.0484	36.38%
6	IGCC with 90% Carbon Sequestration	IGCCCS$_B$	Baseload	0.1051	0.0334	0.1103	0.2489	0.0876	0.0258	0.0718	0.1853	−0.0175	−0.0076	−0.0385	−0.0636	34.34%
	Gas															
7	Conventional Gas/Oil Combined Cycle	CGT$_B$	Baseload	0.0126	0.0071	0.0785	0.0981	0.0110	0.0051	0.0573	0.0734	−0.0016	−0.0020	−0.0211	−0.0247	33.62%
8	Conventional Gas/Oil Combined Cycle	CGT$_M$	Mid-merit	0.0169	0.0078	0.0785	0.1031	0.0148	0.0056	0.0573	0.0777	−0.0021	−0.0022	−0.0211	−0.0254	32.72%
9	Advance Gas/Oil Combined Cycle	ACCGT$_B$	Baseload	0.0100	0.0047	0.0735	0.0882	0.0085	0.0034	0.0537	0.0656	−0.0015	−0.0013	−0.0198	−0.0226	34.47%
10	Advance Gas/Oil Combined Cycle	ACCGT$_M$	Mid-merit	0.0134	0.0054	0.0735	0.0922	0.0114	0.0039	0.0537	0.0689	−0.0020	−0.0015	−0.0198	−0.0233	33.79%
11	ACC with Carbon Sequestration	ACCCS$_B$	Baseload	0.0278	0.0164	0.0838	0.1280	0.0228	0.0119	0.0612	0.0958	−0.0051	−0.0046	−0.0226	−0.0322	33.62%
12	ACC with Carbon Sequestration	ACCCS$_M$	Mid-merit	0.0372	0.0185	0.0838	0.1395	0.0305	0.0134	0.0612	0.1050	−0.0068	−0.0051	−0.0226	−0.0345	32.86%
13	Conventional Combustion Turbines	CCT	Peak	0.0412	0.0145	0.1095	0.1652	0.0360	0.0105	0.0800	0.1265	−0.0052	−0.0040	−0.0295	−0.0387	30.60%
14	Advance Combustion Turbines	ACT	Peak	0.0253	0.0189	0.1091	0.1533	0.0221	0.0137	0.0797	0.1155	−0.0032	−0.0053	−0.0294	−0.0378	32.76%
	Nuclear															
15	Advance Nuclear	ANuke	Baseload	0.0643	0.0212	0.0091	0.0946	0.0530	0.0155	0.0062	0.0747	−0.0113	−0.0057	−0.0029	−0.0199	26.67%

(*Continued*)

Table 7.6: (*Continued*)

Column/Line	Technology	Acronym A	Operating Mode B	C_{FX} $/kWh C	C_{VAR} $/kWh D	C_{FUEL} $/kWh E	C_{LCOE} $/kWh F	FFCR $/kWh G	FVC $/kWh H	FFC $/kWh I	FPCOE $/kWh J	ΔFCR $/kWh K	ΔVC $/kWh L	ΔFC $/kWh M	ΔCOE $/kWh N	ΔCOE % O
	Renewable — Conventional															
16	Geothermal — Large Hole	Geo$_B$	Baseload	0.0321	0.0203	0.0000	0.0524	0.0281	0.0148	0.0000	0.0429	-0.0040	-0.0055	0.0000	-0.0095	22.14%
17	Geothermal — Large Hole	Geo$_M$	Mid-merit	0.0464	0.0294	0.0000	0.0758	0.0406	0.0215	0.0000	0.0620	-0.0058	-0.0079	0.0000	-0.0137	22.14%
18	Geothermal — Slim Hole*	GeoS$_B$	Baseload	0.0209	0.0133	0.0000	0.0342	0.0182	0.0097	0.0000	0.0280	-0.0026	-0.0036	0.0000	-0.0062	22.18%
19	Geothermal — Slim Hole*	GeoS$_M$	Mid-merit	0.0302	0.0192	0.0000	0.0494	0.0264	0.0140	0.0000	0.0404	-0.0038	-0.0052	0.0000	-0.0090	22.18%
20	Conventional Hydro — Pumped Storage	StoHydro$_B$	Baseload	0.0306	0.0098	0.0000	0.0404	0.0270	0.0068	0.0000	0.0338	-0.0036	-0.0030	0.0000	-0.0065	19.32%
21	Conventional Hydro — Pumped Storage	StoHydro$_M$	Mid-merit	0.0400	0.0122	0.0000	0.0522	0.0353	0.0085	0.0000	0.0438	-0.0047	-0.0037	0.0000	-0.0084	19.09%
	Renewable — Variable															
22	Onshore Wind	Wind$_{ON}$	Mid-merit	0.0527	0.0162	0.0000	0.0689	0.0423	0.0129	0.0000	0.0552	-0.0103	-0.0033	0.0000	-0.0137	24.80%
23	Offshore Wind — Conventional Platforms	Wind$_{OFCP}$	Mid-merit	0.1393	0.0209	0.0000	0.1603	0.1037	0.0166	0.0000	0.1203	-0.0356	-0.0043	0.0000	-0.0399	33.18%
24	Offshore Wind — Advance Platforms*	Wind$_{OFAP}$	Mid-merit	0.0732	0.0209	0.0000	0.0941	0.0545	0.0166	0.0000	0.0711	-0.0187	-0.0043	0.0000	-0.0230	32.38%
25	Run of River Hydro*	RivHydro	Mid-merit	0.0484	0.0080	0.0000	0.0564	0.0415	0.0062	0.0000	0.0477	-0.0069	-0.0018	0.0000	-0.0087	18.19%
26	Solar Thermal	Solar$_M$	Mid-merit	0.3989	0.0757	0.0000	0.4746	0.3205	0.0554	0.0000	0.3759	-0.0784	-0.0203	0.0000	-0.0987	26.24%
27	Photovoltaic — Tracking	PVT$_M$	Mid-merit	0.0947	0.0111	0.0000	0.1058	0.0775	0.0088	0.0000	0.0864	-0.0172	-0.0023	0.0000	-0.0195	22.52%
28	Photovoltaic — Fixed Tilt	PVF$_M$	Peak	0.1243	0.0161	0.0000	0.1404	0.1018	0.0128	0.0000	0.1146	-0.0225	-0.0033	0.0000	-0.0258	22.56%
	Battery Storage															
29	Li-On	LN	Peak	0.0664	0.0142	0.0000	0.0805	0.0487	0.0124	0.0000	0.0611	-0.0177	-0.0017	0.0000	-0.0194	31.76%
	Others — Sub-Utilities Scale															
30	Fuel Cells	FCells	Baseload	0.1258	0.0586	0.0973	0.2817	0.0936	0.0466	0.0772	0.2174	-0.0322	-0.0121	-0.0200	-0.0643	29.56%
31	Distributed Generation — Baseload	DG$_B$	Baseload	0.0245	0.0142	0.0937	0.1323	0.0189	0.0111	0.0734	0.1034	-0.0055	-0.0031	-0.0203	-0.0289	27.92%
32	Distributed Generation — Peak	DG$_P$	Peak	0.0691	0.0186	0.1041	0.1918	0.0535	0.0146	0.0815	0.1496	-0.0156	-0.0040	-0.0225	-0.0422	28.20%
33	Biomass	BMass	Baseload	0.0655	0.0270	0.0000	0.0925	0.0526	0.0214	0.0000	0.0740	-0.0129	-0.0056	0.0000	-0.0184	24.89%
34	Municipal Solid Waste	MSW	Mid-merit	0.2432	0.1318	0.0000	0.3750	0.1954	0.1047	0.0000	0.3001	-0.0478	-0.0272	0.0000	-0.0749	24.97%

Source: Raw data: EIA Energy Outlook 2019; Author's estimates marked with *.

Following an economic logic to pricing, managers may isolate the endogenous from exogenous cost factors. This allows managers to formulate multi-layered, but inter-related, strategies to gain a competitive advantage. For this reason, astute managers would most probably manage their investments actively. By adapting, or even shaping, how their markets could evolve, managers effectively adapt to the changing fortunes that policy and markets bestow on them.

4
External Costs and Carbon Emissions Costing

Policy could assert its influence on energy costing and payoffs. What policy bestows, or denies, are examined under the externalities of energy or C_X. Three broad themes are considered as follows:

1. rebalancing "public good, private costs" through subsidies;
2. allocating renewables intermittency's excess system costs;
3. costing carbon emissions and its abatement.

Welfare economics dating back to Pigou (1932) has guided generations of policymakers to examine how investments benefit or cost society socially. Within managerial decision-making, this is incorporated by recognising subsidies as cash receipts (or revenues), or costs, when taxes or penalties are not passed on to consumers.

In energy investments, the grid price parity principle equalises the costs of fossil fuels and renewables. Welfare economists argue that renewables reduce pollution, which is a public good because it cannot be uniquely appropriated by the investing firm. In some cases, renewables' higher costs (e.g. invested capital) "penalise" investors for incurring private costs. By paying subsidies, policy socialised the private costs, thereby encouraging more private capital to invest in renewables (Hurtado Muñoz et al., 2014).

The remedies to date are reliant on policy actions. Granting subsidies, or pricing system's excess costs, tends to focus on technology-specific solutions that presume a "consensus." Hence, by promoting "technology champions," policy would resolve any issues by regulatory fiat. The weight of historical evidence hardly supports this confidence in policy's omniscience. The persistence of green paradoxes, where outcomes often contradict policy's intents, give managers pause. This brings us to an alternative costing of abating carbon emissions as a conscious exercise of managerial economic choices. To compare how this approach differs, we first examine why "welfare-based" costing struggles to gain traction with managers.

4.1 A welfare economist's view

Welfare economics postulates that when social benefits exceed social costs, society is said to benefit from an investment (Florio, 2014). To fund the investment, taxes may be raised to pay for the capital outlays or to transfer cash via subsidies.

Going back to $Coal_B$ investment, we note that its C_{LCOE} under our assumed parameters is \$0.1335/kWh. To equalise PVF_M's C_{LCOE} of \$0.1603/kWh, policy simply pays a subsidy of \$0.0268/kWh to equalise its costs with $Coal_B$.

In theory, by equalising the costs, investing firms are indifferent between investing in PVF_M or $Coal_B$. This works for as long as LCOEs remain stable. However, LCOEs are not, as we have illustrated in Table 7.5.

Consequently, the correct level of subsidies would need to be continually adjusted, making it as volatile as fuel costs. In this context, fixed subsidies may under- or overcompensate private costs. When this occurs, consumers tend to coax regulators to cut subsidies when firms are seen to profit without taking the corresponding risks.

When social benefits are defined too broadly, such as improved health, clean environment, or averting climate crisis, the ability to quantify its value could become intractable. As a result, depending on one's ideological inclinations, the costs of carbon emissions would be set at unrealistically high levels (or vice versa).

Carbon tax, or its variants, is another way of pricing pollution by taxing carbon emissions. In its pure form, the carbon tax is applied to outputs of polluting technologies (e.g. coal or to a lesser extent, ACCGT). The tax raises marginal prices from fossil fuels, benefiting renewables. More importantly, implemented correctly, it alters managerial behaviour by aligning incentives with investments.

Unlike technology-specific subsidies, carbon taxes are said to shift the decision to managers on what to replace polluting supplies with. This freedom of choice has its advantages when managerial decisions are seen as human endeavours. Richard H Thaler and Cass R Sunstein (2008) describe paying carbon taxes as compatible with libertarian paternalism. That is, "liberty is much greater when people are told: 'You can continue your behaviour, so long as you pay for the social harm that it does' than they are told 'you must act exactly as the government says'." By employing this approach, they added: "If a polluter wants to increase its level of activity, and hence its level of pollution, it isn't entirely blocked." It pays until it hurts, at which point some managers may choose to exit polluting supplies as a matter of managerial choice.

4.2   Costs of load intermittency to energy system

The energy system incurs costs to balance the intermittent loads from variable renewables. When its share is residual, fossil fuels absorb its costs, giving variable renewables a free ride (Abbad, 2010). As its share becomes significant, this "come[s] at the expense of reduced utilisation of conventional plants (e.g. *Coal or ACCGT*)… which could be as much as the wind's generating costs" (Ueckerdt *et al.*, 2013).

To reflect the full costs of renewables, Taylor (2013) advocated inclusion of costs of displaced supplies while excluding any subsidies. As experience with intermittency became more widespread, these earlier observations gain greater attention, given that short-term integration costs vary widely (Joos and Staffel, 2018). Since 2010, variable renewables' installed capacity increased five times, with the United Kingdom's system's operating costs increasing by 62% while remaining comparable in Germany. Congestion costs accounted for a significant proportion of the increase (e.g. 74% in the UK, and 14x in Germany).

Spain operates their renewables as a portfolio of supplies within a subsystem. This resulted in supplies that mimic hydro power's volatilities, a familiar trait of the Spanish system. By being able to reward its availability, and price its intermittency, wind power — and to a lesser extent, PV — are fully integrated into the wholesale power market (Abbad, 2010). Perhaps, this is an innovation that was obscured by Spain's cuts in subsidies.

These additional system's costs are often ignored, until too late, by proponents that aggressively push for a low-carbon energy transition. This question is far from resolved and will likely remain an open issue for some time to come.

4.3   Carbon emissions abatement as an investment

An alternative perspective evaluates abating carbon emissions as an investment. Substituting fossil fuels with clean technologies reduce CO_2 emissions. As environmental compliance tightens, carbon taxes (or its equivalent) could escalate following the notions of libertarian paternalism. By avoiding these taxes (or penalties), the savings represent part of the payoffs.

The question is, how much should CO_2 emissions be taxed, or its abatement be subsidised, to encourage private capital to adopt cleaner technologies?

To answer this question, I reframe investment optimisation as deploying supplies that are cost-effective with the least carbon emissions. To do the sums, these steps are followed.

To replace $Coal_B$'s annual output of 7,446 MWh for every MW of capacity, one needs to invest an equivalent MW in renewables, as previously illustrated (recall Section 3.2.1).

For $Wind_{ON}$, one needs 1.98x (B.7) (e.g. A.1/A.7) the MW to match $Coal_B$'s annual output. This implies an invested capital of \$3,210/kW (C.7) (e.g. \$1,624/kW * 1.98). Applying the CRF (D.7), one recalculates the revised C_{FX} and C_{LCOE} for $Wind_{ON}$.

C_{FUEL} (see Appendix 7C) for coal estimates 0.5050 kg coal/kWh or 3,760 MT/MWh/year (E.1) (e.g. A.1 * 0.5050 kg coal). With each kg coal emitting around 1.59 kg CO_2/kWh, $Coal_B$'s annual CO_2 emission is estimated at 5,981 MT/MWh/year.

For ACCGT, 0.436 kg CO_2/kWh is used, resulting in 3,246 MT/MWh/year, based on the estimates of the National Oceanic and Atmospheric Administration (NOAA) (Proctor, 2014). Conventional renewables emit an equivalent of 10% $Coal_B$'s emissions (F.4 to F.6), while variable renewables are assumed at zero.

By substituting $Coal_B$ with an alternative supply, say $Wind_{ON}$, we avoid using coal equivalent to $Coal_B$'s CO_2 emissions or 3,760 MT/MWh/year (E.1) minus zero (E.7). Repeating this calculation, we have the CO_2 emissions abated for each technology in column F in Table 7.7.

At this point, the critical managerial question needs to be asked: How much is the firm gaining to abate the CO_2 emissions through technology substitution?

Use this formula: Deduct C_{FX}, C_{VAR}, and C_{FUEL} of each substitute technology from $Coal_B$'s LCOE cost components (columns H to L). The sum of the differences may result in a negative ΔC_{LCOE}. This implies that the substitute technology is more cost-effective, hence value-accretive (or vice versa).

The final step is to divide ΔC_{LCOE} by the amount of CO_2 abated (column M) to derive the implied cost (+) or value accretion (−) from substituting $Coal_B$.

Clearly, our exercise suggests that abating CO_2 emissions may not have to wait for policy to provide subsidies to get started. ACCGT and conventional renewables deliver significant value even without subsidies. With improved capacity utilisation,

Table 7.7: Implied Costs of CO_2 Abatement

Column/Line	Technology	Annual Output MWh A	Equivalence to $Coal_B$ Output X B	Equivalent Capacity $ mln C	CRF % D	CO_2 Emissions Coal Use MT/MWh/Year E	CO_2 Emissions CO_2 Emitted MT/MWh/Year F	$Coal_B$ Equivalent CO_2 Avoided Coal Use Avoided MT/MWh/Year G	$Coal_B$ Equivalent CO_2 Avoided CO_2 Abated MT/MWh/Year H	LCOE Differences vs $Coal_B$ ΔC_{FX} $ mln I	LCOE Differences vs $Coal_B$ ΔC_{VAR} (3) $ mln J	LCOE Differences vs $Coal_B$ ΔC_{FUEL} $ mln K	LCOE Differences vs $Coal_B$ ΔC_{LCOE} $ mln L	Cost of CO_2 Abated $\Delta C_{LCOE}/CO_2$ Abated $/MT M
	Coal Fired Power													
1	$Coal_b$	7,446	1.00	3,013	8.83%	3,760	5,981	0	0	—	—	—	—	—
	Gas Fired Power													
2	$ACCGT_B$	7,621	0.98	777	8.83%	0	3,246	3,760	2,734	-197	-48	-73	-319	-117
	Nuclear Power													
3	$ANuke_b$	8,322	0.89	5,399	8.00%	0	0	4,202	5,981	166	121	-552	-266	-44
	Conventional Renewables													
4	Geo_B	8,234	0.90	2,483	8.83%	0	1,184	4,158	4,796	-47	68	-620	-599	-125
5	$GeoS_B$	8,234	0.90	1,614	8.83%	0	1,184	4,158	4,796	-124	16	-620	-728	-152
6	$StoHydro_B$	7,446	1.00	2,948	7.50%	0	1,184	3,760	4,796	-45	-10	-620	-676	-141
	Variable Renewables													
7	$Wind_{ON}$	3,767	1.98	3,210	10.50%	0	0	3,760	5,981	71	37	-620	-512	-86
8	$Wind_{OBCP}$	4,818	1.55	8,491	10.50%	0	0	3,760	5,981	625	72	-620	77	13
9	$Wind_{OFAP}$	4,818	1.55	4,463	10.50%	0	0	3,760	5,981	203	72	-620	-345	-58
10	$Solar_M$	1,314	5.67	24,321	10.50%	0	0	3,760	5,981	2,288	480	-620	2,148	359
11	PVT_M	2,540	2.93	5,774	10.50%	0	0	3,760	5,981	340	-1	-620	-281	-47
12	PVF_M	1,752	4.25	7,578	10.50%	0	0	3,760	5,981	530	36	-620	-54	-9

Notes:
* Author's estimates.
(1) kg/kWh for coal, or mmBTU/kWh.
(2) kg CO_2/kg coal, or kg CO_2/mmBTU LNG.
(3) Waste disposal costs are added to C_{VAR} as a fixed operating and management expense.

Source: Raw data and conversion factors: EIA.

Wind$_{ON}$ and some variable renewables could deliver value to investing firms without having to rely on subsidies.

5
Knowing and Using the Numbers

It is not uncommon in C-suites to convert investments to a number game. Without an appreciation for numbers and the logic behind them, managers often err in their decisions. Incorrectly doing the math is as damaging to the firm's financial health as ignoring the costs of taking actions (or inaction).

Specifically, incomplete financial costing could lead to promoting "cheap" sources of energy supply that are seldom viable and fail. While subsidy may flatter returns in the short term, it accentuates regulatory risks as ideological shifts weaken regulatory steadfastness.

These colliding positions are reconciled, *at a logical level*, when energy costing is taken for what it is. Financial periodic costs are building blocks, which, when incorporated into the lifecycle costing of energy, could inform managers' strategic moves. At a granular level, how the costs are structured to how they interact with what managers decide could emerge insights that guide strategic actions.

CO_2 abatement is achieved from technological substitutions of polluting by less or non-polluting supplies. Viewed as such, technologies compete on the basis of their costs of supplies and CO_2 emissions, resulting in minimal reliance (if any) on subsidies.

A useful lesson is for managers to appreciate the extent their actions could alter costs, and how rivals' actions, market forces, or policy measures could spoil their game. In dynamic markets, costs, as well as firm's advantages, seldom stand still.

In the final analysis, correctly costing energy supplies is the first step in a long journey that managers undertake to establish their niche and sustain their firm's viability. Richard Thaler (2015) aptly observed: "Economics started getting highly mathematical. It was basically because economists weren't smart enough to write down models of real behaviour that they started models of highly rational behaviour — and they forgot about humans."

Box 7.1: Geothermal — Evidence from the Field

Geothermal steam is one of the energy resources that is abundant but barely tapped to power the economies where it is found. In places where it is widely used — the United States, the Philippines, and Indonesia — a couple of thousands of MW each in installed capacity place these countries among the top three producers globally. In each case, these countries barely tapped 10% of their known geothermal reserves.

To unravel the mystery, I compared notes with Dr Antonie de Wilde on his experiences in Indonesia and the Philippines. Antonie is acknowledged by the Indonesian government, where he served as adviser to the planning ministry — BAPPENAS — for many years, as instrumental in expanding the country's capacity from 1,190 MW in 2009 to 2,130 MW in 2020.

1. Clearing the confusion

Geothermal steam, a renewable energy resource, differs from hydro, wind, solar, or wave. When one builds a pump storage hydro dam or a river run-off power plant, one can visualise the location where water flows. By measuring the strength of fluvial flows, the site could be established as suitable for a hydro power plant, or not. In a similar way, one can measure the strength of how the wind blows, the intensity of sunlight, or the variations in the waves of the sea, as a way to judge the potential of a site for power generation.

Exploration for geothermal steam has more in common with oil or gas exploration. To its advantage, tell-tale signs of the existence of geothermal reserves are seen from steam spewed from the grounds in some volcanic areas. However, the rich veins of steam reserves have to be explored and located before one can be sure that the correct site is where the drilling is done. This is only established after some physical, chemical, and geophysical surface tests. The test drills are performed to confirm the size of the reserves and the steam's suitability for power generation.

Antonie noted: "Geothermal steam is generated when water comes in contact with the molten rocks heated by the earth's core, or magma. In nature, water comes from springs or water tables beneath the ground. In actual field conditions, the output of steam is enhanced with human nurture and nature. While nature does its wonders, humans do their part in sustaining the life of the geothermal wells."

The outputs of geothermal processes are water in its liquid state and steam. Antonie continues: "The steam is used to drive the generator to generate power. In some cases, the water is not hot enough to produce steam. In this case, low temperature water or steam, say below 180 °C, is pumped to make the steam flow. The water is then fed into a heat exchanger through which it is heated and evaporated into high temperature steam to drive the power generator." In more modern versions, the heat exchanger evaporates a specially designed gas, which then drives a gas turbine which drives the generator.

At this point, the geothermal steam is monetised by selling it as a feedstock to a power generator or as part of an integrated investment from exploring to generating power. This is where the math becomes blurred because what is in theory an expected output may prove as too pessimistic or optimistic in relation to what is achieved in actual field operations.

Antonie cited three factors that influence the monetisation of geothermal steam via power generation: actual power demand sets the volume to be fulfilled; availability of turbines determines how much steam could be converted into power; and the available steam that could be supplied to the turbines.

Starting with the steam supply, Antonie identified the first area of ambiguity: "Geothermal steam is transported via pipes in a conventional system. In theory, the sizes of the pipes are fairly constant. For this reason, economists tend to assume a throughput that is stable, or even constant. The rest is arithmetic, one might think."

From Antonie's experiences, however, the pipes are susceptible to "calcification or silica scaling" that lead to clogging. When this happens, the steam throughput becomes less than what was expected when the well was designed. Over time, if no action is taken to remedy this, developers are surprised to realise that their steam output falls far short of what they projected.

A case in point is the experience of BacMan geothermal field in the Philippines. Fidel Seva See and Christine Marie Espartinez (2015) noted: "After the steam flow increased to its highest level in 1997, the low-boron fluid inflow started to cause mineral deposits in the casings, reducing the steam flows, and steam availability. The Bacman Steam Augmentation Program (BSAP), which involved among others investments in drilling new wells and calcination prevention injection, shows the gradual increase in steam flows to an even higher level in 2013, exceeding the levels reached in 1997."

2. Getting to *actual* power generated

The question of how much power can be generated appears superfluous at first sight, at least for some economists and developers. It is widely believed that once geothermal steam is found, power can be generated at the power plant's rated capacity. The usual assumption is to use 95% capacity factor, or utilisation rate, to calculate the expected outputs.

Antonie and I dive deep into this question. With a number of variables likely to change over the life of the geothermal wells, the prevailing assumptions of project economists and financiers will have to be re-examined. Starting with how much power is expected to be generated, from an installed base, and the eventual comparison against how much is actually produced, it is an interesting journey into convoluted conversations. One way of simplifying the comparisons is to estimate the expected output from the rated capacity of the geothermal power plants against what was actually generated.

From Box Chart 7.1.1, the actual utilisation rates of the two leading geothermal firms in the Philippines and Indonesia are examined. Far from a constant, the outputs vary with the availability of steam. As a result, the output costs over the life of the asset would likewise fluctuate with *actual* outputs. Specifically:

The monthly availability of geothermal steam at EDC's (C) wells varies from 99% to 30%. When Leyte was hit by two strong typhoons, which damaged parts of the geothermal facilities, the geothermal wells had nil outputs for a few months. On average, the annual utilisation rates varied from a low of 63% in 2013 to a high of 85% in 2019 after the wells were refurbished.

Pertamina Geothermal (B) hit a low of 65% in 2016 before settling around 72% from 2017 to 2019. Remediation works are in progress to restore its previous highs of 89%, with newer wells hitting 95%.

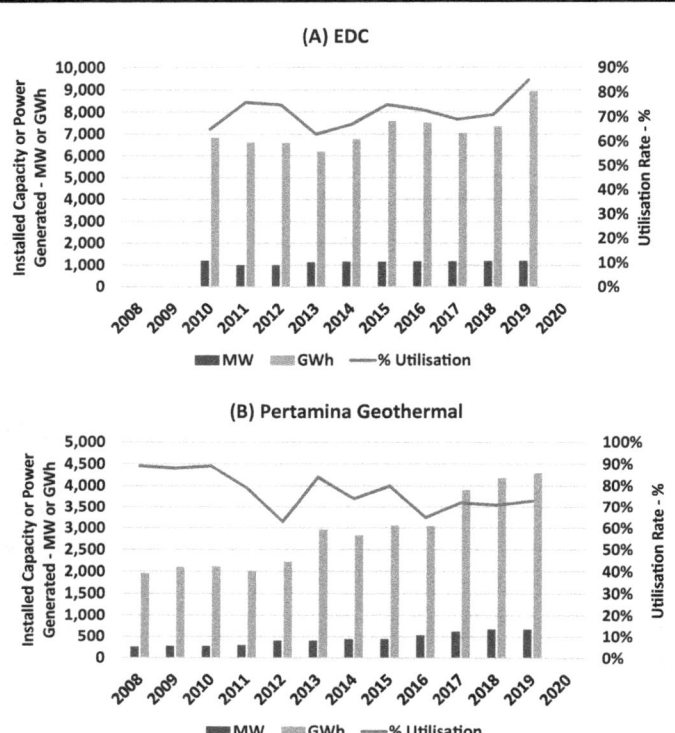

Box Chart 7.1.1: EDC and Pertamina Geothermal Performance
Source: Raw data: Annual Reports of EDC and PT Pertamina.

Antonie noted: "In a number of developing countries, the delineation of costs attributed to feedstock, or steam production, and those accruing to generating power, is a work of art, rather than 'science'. For some integrated projects, cost of distributing power is included, particularly for isolated or unconnected geothermal sites to extant transmission or distribution networks."

The operating costs of steam production vary with the natural characteristics of the fields and specific wells. Antonie cited the following principal factors that influence the level of ongoing operating expenses:

"Flow of water may prove erratic from natural springs or water tables. The water (or brine as engineers would prefer to call it) from other sources may have to be pumped into the geothermal wells in order to produce sufficient steam."

"The best laid out design of manmade geothermal systems are subjected to nature's severe tests. When brine that is super saturated with silica is mixed with mineral rich fluids drawn from the wells, the pipes could become blocked, resulting in diminishing steam outputs."

"To restore its efficiency, mechanical descaling or injecting chemicals are employed to solve this problem, a process called well work-over. Repeated frequently, this process could add to operating costs."

"When pipes are regularly descaled, or undergoing well workover, part of the system experiences downtime. To compensate for this loss of output, extra wells are drilled as 'make-up wells' to produce steam. In some cases, developers try to 'save' by foregoing this expense. As a result, steam outputs progressively decline, accounting for the falling utilisation rates."

With the cost of producing steam delineated, the cost of generating power can be estimated, incorporating the cost of steam as a feedstock (or "fuel"). Just like gas as a fuel, the costs of feedstock and generating power can be clearly delineated, as in gas-fired power plants.

3. Volatile costs – Why it matters

The LCOEs for geothermal vary widely from one official source to another. Aside from varying utilisation rates, differences in assumptions on discount rates and costs of the assets account for the other sources of cost deviations.

When costs are properly delineated, by clearly segregating feedstock and power generation costs, the "true" costs of geothermal power are better appreciated. Following the definition of ORMAT (2019), the rate capacity is calculated as the installed MW multiplied by the hours it could be operated in a year. This is expressed as MW * (24 hours/day * 365 days/year) * Capacity Factor. That is, one MW of capacity operated at 95% would yield 8,322 MWh as an expected output. The *actual* output, when divided by the expected output, would yield the *actual* utilisation rate for the period, as shown in Box Table 7.1.1.

Box Table 7.1.1: Comparative Actual Capacity Factors and Contract Tenors

Column/Line	Location	Plant	Generating Capacity - MW A	PPA Tenor - Years B	Capacity Factor - % C
1	California, USA	Omesa Complex	39	23	72.00%
2		Heber Complex	81	14	
3		Mammoth Complex	29	13	
4		Brawley	13	12	
5	West Nevada	Steamboat Complex	65	18	88.00%
6		Brady Complex	26	16	
7	East Nevada	Tuscarora	18	13	93.00%
8		Jersey Valley	10	13	
9		McGuinness Hills	143	19	
10		Don A Campbell	36	16	
11		Tungsten Mountain	27	24	
12	North West Region	Neal Hot Springs	22	19	92.00%
13		Raft River	11	13	
14		San Emidio	11	19	
15	Hawaii	Puna	38	33	
16	International	Amatilan, Guatemala	20	9	88.00%
17		Zunil, Guatemala	20	15	
18		Olkaria III Complex, Kenya	150	15	
19		Bouillante, Guadeloupe Island, France	15	11	
20		Platanares, Honduras	38	13	

Source: ORMAT Annual Report 2019.

Antonie made these observations: "When utilisation rates are assumed to remain low, the costs would naturally be higher than it could otherwise be. Within this context, geothermal power may be seen as more 'expensive'."

However, in noting from EDC (A) and Pertamina Geothermal's (B) performances, the financial impact of improving the utilisation rate could be significant. For a modest expense in "well work-over" and "make-up wells," raising the utilisation rates of both firms to a creditable level of 90% could yield immediate payoffs. Specifically:

In 2019, EDC's 1,205 MW operated at an actual utilisation rate of 85%, yielding 8,930 GWh of power. If increased to 90%, the output would be 9,500 GWh. This is an annual increase of 570 GWh. At a Philippine wholesale price of $0.0600/kWh, this is an annual incremental revenue of $34 mln.

Pertamina Geothermal's utilisation rate has fallen to 73% by 2019, on an installed capacity of 672 MW, yielding an *actual* power output of 4,292 GWh. To raise the utilisation rate to 90%, which was close to its 2008 level, the *actual* power output is raised to 5,298 GWh or an annual increase of 1,006 GWh. At a regulated price of $0.09/kWh in Indonesia, this is an annual incremental revenue of $90.54 mln.

The attractiveness of keeping the assets well maintained is directly related to the incentive to spend. The incentive is derived from the market demand and the prices that suppliers are paid. Using these simple criteria, trying to "save" on operating costs, while foregoing revenues as utilisation rates decline, would indeed prove to be a manager's folly.

ORMAT Technologies, a leading geothermal resource and power firm, summarised their projects in the United States and a number of countries in Latin America and Africa. With a few exceptions, the scale of their projects is considered small to medium, that is, less than 50 MW.

Antonie offered this observation: "Power purchase agreements (PPAs) remain a fixture in the geothermal resource investment and power generation. In its conventional usage, the PPA's tenor (or maturity) tends to shadow the operating life of the assets.

For example, a geothermal power plant that is expected to operate for 30 years, with some assets assumed to last 40 years or more, some developers would aim to have tenors matching these durations."

Operating under rigid volume and price obligations, geothermal PPAs pose some ignored risks when *actual* outputs are more volatile than managers believed. Declining output may create defaults on delivered volumes, whereas rising costs that come as a consequence may result in cash margins being squeezed or an outright loss.

Recognising these risks, Antonie suggested that "one way of avoiding this exposure is to have a more flexible pricing and volume commitment. When there is a functional wholesale power market, one may find that taking a market risk on volume and price may prove more lucrative. That is, when power prices are higher, firms may benefit if the volumes that they supply remains strong. One thing is true under this more flexible commitment: If power prices are higher than the costs of geothermal supply, the firm can profit by supplying. In contrast, when power prices are depressed, and supplying would incur a loss, the firm has the flexibility to curtail its supply to avoid making a loss."

Antonie continued: "Perhaps, for this reason, ORMAT's PPA tenors (B.1 to B.20) are conspicuously shorter than the asset life. In certain cases, such as accessing project financing, PPAs are often required by lenders to secure the borrowing."

4. New technologies, costs reconfiguration

With geothermal resources' apparent environmental virtues, I posed this question to Antonie: "Why is the uptake for geothermal power lagging behind wind and solar, technologies with less reliable outputs, and what are the prospects for changing this?"

Antonie gave a number of factors: "The frontend costs and risks of finding the geothermal steam can be prohibitive using conventional large hole drilling technologies. However, with slim hole drilling gaining greater acceptance, costs of drilling are substantially reduced. As a result, the financial risks associated with failed exploration is also reduced. More importantly, with the smaller equipment used in slim hole drilling, the frontend costs in civil works such as access roads are avoided by airlifting the equipment to the drill sites."

"A parallel innovation in developing small generating equipment, of less than 5 MW, well-head units are economically installed. This reduces the pipes needed to collect the steam to a centrally generating unit. With less pipes in use, the operating expenses associated with descaling could be avoided. By substituting pipes to collect steam for power generation, wires are used to transmit power instead from wellheads, thereby reducing heat losses while increasing power outputs."

The emergence of slim hole drilling is just the start in giving geothermal power a rightful place in the energy mix of the future. With more innovative financing in place, such as resource insurance and blended finance being made available, Antonie looks forward to a brighter future for geothermal investments.

****

Dr Antonie de Wilde, formerly with the World Bank and International Finance Corporation, was instrumental in expanding the Indonesian geothermal capacity when he was senior adviser to BAPPENAS, Indonesia's planning and development ministry. He combines his formation as an anthropologist and sociologist, and as a mechanical engineer, to devise innovations and solutions that are environmentally and socially sensitive.

Bibliography

Abbad, J. M. R. (2010). Electricity market participation of wind farms: The success story of Spanish pragmatism. *Energy Policy*, 38, 3174–3179.

Ainger, J. (2019). The logic behind the bonds that eat your money. *Bloomberg Businessweek*, July 26, 2019.

Damodaran, A. (1996). *Investment Valuation: Tools and Techniques for Determining the Value of Any Asset*. New York: John Wiley & Sons.

ECA (European Court of Auditors). (2019). Wind and solar power for electricity generation: Significant action needed if EU targets to be met. *Special Report 08-2019*. Luxembourg: European Court of Auditors.

EIA. (2013). Levelized cost of electricity and levelized avoided costs of electricity methodology supplement. *Independent Statistics & Analysis*, U.S. Energy Information Administration, July 2013.

EIA. (2019). *Energy Outlook 2019*. Washington DC: U.S. Energy Information Administration, January 24, 2019.

Fernandez, P. (2019). Valuation and common sense, 7th edn., last revised May 2019. https://papers.ssrn.com/sol3/papers.cfm?abstract_id=2209089. Accessed on October 4, 2019.

Florio, M. (2014). *Applied Welfare Economics: Cost-Benefit Analysis of Projects and Policies*. Oxon: Routledge.

Hoium, T. (2017). Bankruptcies continue in solar industry. *The Motley Fools*, May 19, 2017.

Hurtado Muñoz, L. A., Huijben, J. C. C. M. Boukje, V. B., and Verbong, G. P. J. (2014). The power of grid parity: A discursive approach. *Technological Forecasting and Social Change*, 87, 179–190.

International Energy Agency (IEA). (2019). Have the prices from competitive auctions become the 'new normal' prices for renewables? Paris: International Energy Agency.

Institute of Energy Research (IER). (2018). Global investment in renewable energy stalled due to subsidy cuts. IER Commentary, February 26, 2018.

Jashari, A., Lippelt, J., and von Schickfus, M. (2018). Unexpected rapid fall of wind and solar prices: Background, effects, and perspectives. *CESifo Forum*, 19(2), 65–69, June 2018.

Joos, M. and Staffell, I. (2018). Short term integration costs of variable renewable energy: Wind curtailment and balancing in Britain and Germany. *Renewable and Sustainable Energy Reviews*, 86, 45–65.

Léger, S., Smeets, B., Swysen, T., Tryggestad, C., van Houten, J., and Wodarg, F. (2018). What if the latest wind and solar auction results were the new reality of electricity prices? McKinsey & Company, March 2018.

Littlechild, S. (2001). Competition and regulation in the UK electricity industry (with a brief look at California). *Journal of Applied Corporate Finance*, 13(4), 21–38.

ORMAT Technologies (2019). *Annual Report*. Reno, NV: ORMAT Technologies, Inc.

Proctor, C. (2014). Natural gas power plants emit 40% less CO_2 than coal plants, say study. *Denver Business Journal*, January 10, 2014.

Roth, I. F. and Ambs, L. L. (2004). Incorporating externalities into a full cost approach to electric power generation life-cycle costing. *Energy*, 29, 2125–2144.

Sarmiento, Z. F. (2008). Management of Geothermal Resources in the Philippines. UNU Training Programme, Uganda, November 20–22, 2008.

Seva See, F. and Espartinez, C.M (2015). The BacMan Geothermal Field, Philippines: Geochemical changes and challenges after twenty years of operation. *World Geothermal Conference*, Melbourne, 2015.

Stigler, G. J. (1971). The theory of economic regulation. *The Bell Journal of Economics and Management Science*, 2(1), 3–21.

Taylor, G. (2013). Improving completeness and accuracy of levelized cost of electricity calculations. *Energy Information Administration Workshop on LCOE/LACE*, Washington DC, July 25, 2013.

Thaler, R. H. (2015). *Misbehaving: The Making of Behavioural Economics*. New York and London: W. W. Norton & Company.

Thaler, R. H. and Sunstein, C. R. (2008). *Nudge: Improving Decisions About Health, Wealth, and Happiness*. New Haven and London: Yale University Press.

Ueckerdt, F., Hirth, L., Luderer, G., and Edenfofer, O. (2013). System LCOE: What are the costs of variable renewables? *Energy*, 63, 61–75.

Appendices

7A: Fixed Cost Recovery C_{FX}

Column/Line	Technology	Acronym	Scale and Timing					Capex					Lifecycle Capital Factor								Economic Life and Output			
			Operating Mode	Online Year	Size MW	Implied Lead Time Years	Base Overnight Costs — 2018 Base $/kW	Project Contingency Factor X	Technological Optimism Factor X	Total Overnight Costs — 2018 Base $/kW	Hurdle Rate - r %	Imputed Returns $/kW	Imputed Returns $/kWh	Capex $/kW	CRF %	C_{FX} $/kWh				Economic Life - n Years	Capacity Factor %	Annual Hours in Operation Hrs	Annual Output per MW · Q MWh
		A	B	C	D	E	F	G	H	I	J	K	L	M	N	O				P	Q	R	S
Coal																							
1	Scrubbed Coal — New	$Coal_B$	Baseload	2022	1,300	4	2,734	1.07	1.03	3,013	8.83%	8.87	0.0012	3,022	9.59%	0.0389				30	85.00%	7,446	7,446
2	Scrubbed Coal — New	$Coal_M$	Mid-merit	2022	1,300	4	2,734	1.07	1.03	3,013	8.83%	8.87	0.0017	3,022	9.59%	0.0551				30	60.00%	5,256	5,256
3	Integrated Coal-Gasification Combined Cycle	$IGCC_B$	Baseload	2022	1,200	4	3,525	1.07	1.03	3,885	8.83%	11.44	0.0015	3,896	9.59%	0.0502				30	85.00%	7,446	7,446
4	Integrated Coal-Gasification Combined Cycle	$IGCC_M$	Mid-merit	2022	1,200	4	3,525	1.07	1.03	3,885	8.83%	11.44	0.0022	3,896	9.59%	0.0711				30	60.00%	5,256	5,256
5	IGCC with 30% Carbon Sequestration	$IGCCCS_B$	Baseload	2022	650	4	4,713	1.07	1.03	5,194	8.83%	15.29	0.0021	5,209	9.59%	0.0671				30	85.00%	7,446	7,446
6	IGCC with 90% Carbon Sequestration	$IGCCCS_H$	Baseload	2022	650	4	5,212	1.07	1.03	5,744	8.83%	16.91	0.0032	5,761	9.59%	0.1051				30	60.00%	5,256	5,256
Gas																							
7	Conventional Gas/Oil Combined Cycle	CGT_B	Baseload	2021	702	3	952	1.05	1.00	1,000	8.83%	2.94	0.0004	1,003	9.59%	0.0126				30	87.00%	7,621	7,621
8	Conventional Gas/Oil Combined Cycle	CGT_M	Mid-merit	2021	702	3	952	1.05	1.00	1,000	8.83%	2.94	0.0005	1,003	9.59%	0.0169				30	65.00%	5,694	5,694
9	Advance Gas/Oil Combined Cycle	$ACCGT_B$	Baseload	2021	1,100	3	736	1.08	1.00	795	8.83%	2.34	0.0003	797	9.59%	0.0100				30	87.00%	7,621	7,621
10	Advance Gas/Oil Combined Cycle	$ACCGT_M$	Mid-merit	2021	1,100	3	736	1.08	1.00	795	8.83%	2.34	0.0004	797	9.59%	0.0134				30	65.00%	5,694	5,694
11	ACC with Carbon Sequestration	$ACCCS_B$	Baseload	2021	340	3	1,963	1.08	1.04	2,205	8.83%	6.49	0.0009	2,211	9.59%	0.0278				30	87.00%	7,621	7,621
12	ACC with Carbon Sequestration	$ACCCS_M$	Mid-merit	2021	340	3	1,963	1.08	1.04	2,205	8.83%	6.49	0.0011	2,211	9.59%	0.0372				30	65.00%	5,694	5,694
13	Conventional Combustion Turbines	CCT	Peak	2020	100	2	1,072	1.05	1.00	1,126	8.83%	3.31	0.0013	1,129	9.59%	0.0412				30	30.00%	2,628	2,628
14	Advance Combustion Turbines	ACT	Peak	2020	237	2	658	1.05	1.00	691	8.83%	2.03	0.0008	693	9.59%	0.0253				30	30.00%	2,628	2,628
Nuclear																							
15	Advance Nuclear	ANuke	Baseload	2024	2,234	6	5,224	1.10	1.05	6,034	8.00%	12.07	0.0015	6,046	8.39%	0.0643				40	90.00%	7,884	7,884

7A: (Continued)

		Scale and Timing					Capex				Lifecycle Capital Factor							Economic Life and Output			
							Base Overnight Costs— 2018 Base	Project Contingency Factor	Technological Optimism Factor	Total Overnight Costs—2018 Base	Hurdle Rate-r	Imputed Returns	Imputed Returns	Capex	CRF	C_{vN}	Economic Life-n	Capacity Factor	Annual Hours in Operation	Annual Output per MW-Q
Technology	Acronym	Operating Mode	Online Year	Size MW	Implied Lead Time Years		$/kW	x	x	$/kW	%	$/kW	$/kWh	$/kW	%	$/kWh	Years	%	Hrs	MWh
Column/Line	A	B	C	D	E		F	G	H	I	J	K	L	M	N	O	P	Q	R	S
Renewable — Conventional																				
16 Geothermal — Large Hole	Geo$_B$	Baseload	2022	50	4		2,615	1.05	1.00	2,746	8.83%	8.08	0.0010	2,754	9.59%	0.0321	30	94.00%	8,234	8,234
17 Geothermal — Large Hole	Geo$_M$	Mid-merit	2022	50	4		2,615	1.05	1.00	2,746	8.83%	8.08	0.0014	2,754	9.59%	0.0464	30	65.00%	5,694	5,694
18 Geothermal — Slim Hole*	GeoS$_B$	Baseload	2021	55	3		1,700	1.05	1.00	1,785	8.83%	5.26	0.0006	1,790	9.59%	0.0209	30	94.00%	8,234	8,234
19 Geothermal — Slim Hole*	GeoS$_M$	Mid-merit	2021	55	3		1,700	1.05	1.00	1,785	8.83%	5.26	0.0009	1,790	9.59%	0.0302	30	65.00%	5,694	5,694
20 Conventional Hydro — Pumped Storage	StoHydro$_B$	Baseload	2022	500	4		2,680	1.10	1.00	2,948	7.50%	4.42	0.0006	2,952	7.71%	0.0306	50	85.00%	7,446	7,446
21 Conventional Hydro — Pumped Storage	StoHydro$_M$	Mid-merit	2022	500	4		2,680	1.10	1.00	2,948	7.50%	4.42	0.0008	2,952	7.71%	0.0400	50	65.00%	5,694	5,694
Renewable — Variable																				
22 Onshore Wind	Wind$_{ON}$	Mid-merit	2021	100	3		1,518	1.07	1.00	1,624	10.50%	8.53	0.0023	1,633	12.15%	0.0527	20	43.00%	3,767	3,767
23 Offshore Wind — Conventional Platforms	Wind$_{OFCP}$	Mid-merit	2022	400	4		4,758	1.10	1.05	5,495	10.50%	28.85	0.0060	5,524	12.15%	0.1393	20	55.00%	4,818	4,818
24 Offshore Wind — Advance Platforms*	Wind$_{OFAP}$	Mid-merit	2022	400	4		2,500	1.10	1.05	2,888	10.50%	15.16	0.0031	2,903	12.15%	0.0732	20	55.00%	4,818	4,818
25 Run of River Hydro*	RivHydro	Mid-merit	2022	50	4		2,100	1.07	1.00	2,247	8.83%	6.62	0.0015	2,254	9.59%	0.0484	30	51.00%	4,468	4,468
26 Solar Thermal — Rooftop	Solar$_M$	Mid-merit	2021	100	3		4,011	1.07	1.00	4,292	10.50%	22.53	0.0171	4,314	12.15%	0.3989	20	15.00%	1,314	1,314
27 Photovoltaic — Tracking	PVT$_M$	Mid-merit	2020	150	2		1,876	1.05	1.00	1,970	10.50%	10.34	0.0041	1,980	12.15%	0.0947	20	29.00%	2,540	2,540
28 Photovoltaic — Fixed Tilt	PVF$_M$	Peak	2020	150	2		1,698	1.05	1.00	1,783	10.50%	9.36	0.0053	1,792	12.15%	0.1243	20	20.00%	1,752	1,752
Battery Storage																				
29 Li-On	LN	Peak	2019	30	1		2,067	1.05	1.00	2,170	16.50%	35.81	0.0051	2,206	21.08%	0.0664	10	80.00%	7,008	7,008
Others — Sub-Utilities Scale																				
30 Fuel Cells	FCells	Baseload	2021	10	3		6,250	1.05	1.10	7,219	10.50%	37.90	0.0054	7,257	12.15%	0.1258	20	80.00%	7,008	7,008
31 Distributed Generation — Baseload	DGB	Baseload	2021	2	3		1,501	1.05	1.00	1,576	8.83%	6.96	0.0010	1,583	10.82%	0.0245	20	80.00%	7,008	7,008
32 Distributed Generation — Peak	DGP	Peak	2021	1	3		1,857	1.05	1.00	1,950	8.83%	8.61	0.0028	1,958	10.82%	0.0691	20	35.00%	3,066	3,066
33 Biomass	BMass	Baseload	2022	50	4		3,642	1.07	1.00	3,897	10.50%	20.46	0.0028	3,917	12.15%	0.0655	20	83.00%	7,271	7,271
34 Municipal Solid Waste	MSW	Mid-merit	2021	50	3		8,313	1.07	1.00	8,895	10.50%	46.70	0.0105	8,942	12.15%	0.2432	20	51.00%	4,468	4,468

Source: Raw data: EIA 2019 Energy Outlook; Author's estimates marked with *.

7B: Variable Operating Cost — C_{VAR}

Column/Line	Technology	Acronym	Fixed O&M $/MW-Year	Fixed O&M Levelised Factor X	$C_{FXO&M}$ $/kWh	Variable O&M $/kWh	Variable O&M Levelised Factor X	$C_{VOO&M}$ $/kWh	Opex C_{VAR} $/kWh
		A	B	C	D	E	F	G	H
	Coal								
1	Scrubbed Coal — New	$Coal_B$	31	1.30	0.0054	0.0045	1.30	0.0058	0.0112
2	Scrubbed Coal — New	$Coal_M$	31	1.30	0.0077	0.0045	1.30	0.0058	0.0135
3	Integrated Coal-Gasification Combined Cycle	$IGCC_B$	51	1.30	0.0089	0.0072	1.30	0.0094	0.0183
4	Integrated Coal-Gasification Combined Cycle	$IGCC_M$	51	1.30	0.0127	0.0072	1.30	0.0094	0.0220
5	IGCC with 30% Carbon Sequestration	$IGCCCS_B$	72	1.30	0.0125	0.0073	1.30	0.0095	0.0220
6	IGCC with 90% Carbon Sequestration	$IGCCCS_M$	84	1.30	0.0206	0.0099	1.30	0.0128	0.0334
	Gas								
7	Conventional Gas/Oil Combined Cycle	CGT_B	11	1.38	0.0021	0.0036	1.38	0.0050	0.0071
8	Conventional Gas/Oil Combined Cycle	CGT_M	11	1.38	0.0028	0.0036	1.38	0.0050	0.0078
9	Advance Gas/Oil Combined Cycle	$ACCGT_B$	10	1.38	0.0019	0.0021	1.38	0.0029	0.0047
10	Advance Gas/Oil Combined Cycle	$ACCGT_M$	10	1.38	0.0025	0.0021	1.38	0.0029	0.0054
11	ACC with Carbon Sequestration	$ACCCS_B$	34	1.38	0.0063	0.0073	1.38	0.0102	0.0164
12	ACC with Carbon Sequestration	$ACCCS_M$	34	1.38	0.0084	0.0073	1.38	0.0102	0.0185
13	Conventional Combustion Turbines	CCTP	18	1.38	0.0095	0.0036	1.38	0.0050	0.0145
14	Advance Combustion Turbines	ACTP	7	1.38	0.0037	0.0110	1.38	0.0153	0.0189
	Nuclear								
15	Advance Nuclear	ANuke	103	1.37	0.0179	0.0024	1.37	0.0032	0.0212
	Renewable — Conventional								
16	Geothermal — Large Hole	Geo_B	122	1.37	0.0203	0.0000	1.37	0.0000	0.0203
17	Geothermal — Large Hole	Geo_M	122	1.37	0.0294	0.0000	1.37	0.0000	0.0294

7B: (*Continued*)

Column/Line	Technology	Acronym	Fixed O&M $/MW-Year	Fixed O&M Levelised Factor X	Fixed O&M $C_{FXO&M}$ $/kWh	Variable O&M $/kWh	Variable O&M Levelised Factor X	Variable O&M $C_{VO&M}$ $/kWh	Opex C_{VAR} $/kWh
		A	B	C	D	E	F	G	H
18	Geothermal — Slim Hole*	GeoS_B	80	1.37	0.0133	0.0000	1.37	0.0000	0.0133
19	Geothermal — Slim Hole*	GeoS_M	80	1.37	0.0192	0.0000	1.37	0.0000	0.0192
20	Conventional Hydro — Pumped Storage	StoHydro_B	41	1.43	0.0079	0.0014	1.43	0.0020	0.0098
21	Conventional Hydro — Pumped Storage	StoHydro_M	41	1.43	0.0103	0.0014	1.43	0.0020	0.0122
	Renewable — Intermittent								
22	Onshore Wind	Wind_M	48	1.26	0.0162	0.0000	1.26	0.0000	0.0162
23	Offshore Wind — Conventional Platforms	Wind_OPCP	80	1.26	0.0209	0.0000	1.26	0.0000	0.0209
24	Offshore Wind — Advance Platforms*	Wind_OFAP	80	1.26	0.0209	0.0000	1.26	0.0000	0.0209
25	Run of River Hydro*	RivHydro	16	1.30	0.0046	0.0027	1.30	0.0034	0.0080
26	Solar Thermal — Rooftop	Solar	73	1.37	0.0757	0.0000	1.37	0.0000	0.0757
27	Photovoltaic — Tracking	PVT_M	22	1.26	0.0111	0.0000	1.26	0.0000	0.0111
28	Photovoltaic — Fixed Tilt	PVF_M	22	1.26	0.0161	0.0000	1.26	0.0000	0.0161
	Battery Storage								
29	Li-On	LN	36	1.14	0.0059	0.0073	1.14	0.0083	0.0142
	Others — Sub-Utilities Scale								
30	Fuel Cells	FCells	0	1.26	0.0000	0.0466	1.26	0.0586	0.0586
31	Distributed Generation — Baseload	DGB	19	1.28	0.0034	0.0084	1.28	0.0107	0.0142
32	Distributed Generation — Peak	DGP	19	1.28	0.0079	0.0084	1.28	0.0107	0.0186
33	Biomass	BMass	114	1.26	0.0198	0.0057	1.26	0.0072	0.0270
34	Municipal Solid Waste	MSW	425	1.26	0.1199	0.0095	1.26	0.0119	0.1318

Source: Raw data: EIA 2019 Energy Outlook; Author's estimates marked with *.

7C: Fuel Cost C_{FUEL}

Coal

Column/Line	Technology	Acronym	DES $/MT	Transport (En) $/MT	Fuel Cost $/MT	Heat Rate mmBTU/kWh	Heat Content mmBTU/MT	Coal Volume MT/kWh			Fuel Costs $/kWh	Levelling Factor X	C_{FUEL} $/kWh
			A	B	C	D	E	F	G			K	L	M
	Coal													
1	Scrubbed Coal — New	Coal$_B$	91.83	15.65	107	8.800	1,74,27,005	0.0005			0.0543	1.5354	0.0833
2	Scrubbed Coal — New	Coal$_M$	91.83	15.65	107	8.800	1,74,27,005	0.0005			0.0543	1.5354	0.0833
3	Integrated Coal-Gasification Combined Cycle	IGCC$_B$	91.83	15.65	107	8.700	1,74,27,005	0.0005			0.0537	1.5354	0.0824
4	Integrated Coal-Gasification Combined Cycle	IGCC$_M$	91.83	15.65	107	8.700	1,74,27,005	0.0005			0.0537	1.5354	0.0824
5	IGCC with Carbon Sequestration	IGCCCS$_B$	91.83	15.65	107	9.750	1,74,27,005	0.0006			0.0601	1.5354	0.0923
6	IGCC with Carbon Sequestration	IGCCCS$_M$	91.83	15.65	107	11,650	1,74,27,005	0.0007			0.0718	1.5354	0.1103

LNG

			DES $/mmBTU	Regas (En) $/mmBTU	Transport (En) $/mmBTU	Fuel Cost $/mmBTU	Heat Rate mmBTU/kWh	Heat Content mmBTU/Mcf	LNG Volume Mcf/kWh	mmBTU Conversion	mmBTU/kWh	Fuel Costs $/kWh	Levelling Factor X	C_{FUEL} $/kWh
	Gas													
7	Conventional Gas/Oil Combined Cycle	CGT$_B$	6.79	0.51	1	8.30	7,050	0.0069	1.025	0.0071	0.0573	1.3690	0.0785
8	Conventional Gas/Oil Combined Cycle	CGT$_M$	6.79	0.51	1	8.30	7,050	0.0069	1.025	0.0071	0.0573	1.3690	0.0785
9	Advance Gas/Oil Combined Cycle	ACCGT$_B$	6.79	0.51	1	8.30	6,600	0.0064	1.025	0.0066	0.0537	1.3690	0.0735
10	Advance Gas/Oil Combined Cycle	ACCGT$_M$	6.79	0.51	1	8.30	6,600	0.0064	1.025	0.0066	0.0537	1.3690	0.0735
11	ACC with Carbon Sequestration	ACCCS$_B$	6.79	0.51	1	8.30	7,525	0.0073	1.025	0.0075	0.0612	1.3690	0.0838
12	ACC with Carbon Sequestration	ACCCS$_M$	6.79	0.51	1	8.30	7,525	0.0073	1.025	0.0075	0.0612	1.3690	0.0838
13	Conventional Combined Turbines	CCT	6.79	0.51	1	8.30	9,840	0.0096	1.025	0.0098	0.0800	1.3690	0.1095
14	Advance Combined Turbines	ACTP	6.79	0.51	1	8.30	9,800	0.0096	1.025	0.0098	0.0797	1.3690	0.1091
	Others — Sub-Utilities Scale													
15	Fuel Cells	FCells	6.62	0.51	1	8.13	9,500	0.0093	1.025	0.0095	0.0772	1.2594	0.0973
16	Distributed Generation — Baseload	DGB	6.62	0.51	1	8.13	9,027	0.0088	1.025	0.0090	0.0734	1.2762	0.0937
17	Distributed Generation — Peak	DGP	6.62	0.51	1	8.13	10,029	0.0098	1.025	0.0100	0.0815	1.2762	0.1041

Nuclear

			Units	U_3O_8	Uranium UO_2 Conversion Conversion - U	Transport	Enrichment - SWU	Fuel Fabrication		Power Conversion $/kg	kg/kWh	Fuel Costs $/kWh	Levelling Factor X	C_{FUEL} $/kWh
			kg	8.90	7.50	0	7.30							
			kg	8.90	7.50	0	7.30							
			$/kg	97.00	16.00	0	82.00							
18	Advance Nuclear	ANuke	$/kg – UO_2	863	120	345	599	300		2,227	3,60,000	0.0062	1.47	0.0091

Source: Raw data: EIA 2019 Energy Outlook; Author's estimates marked with *.

Chapter 8
Levers of Value

The valuation process is an artful dialogue that seeks to understand the levers of a firm's value. In approaching financial analysis in this way, managers could reframe how they can use and understand financial information as a way of quantifying the feasible outcomes of their strategic actions. This requires a structured understanding of risks, returns, and how value is appropriated, as a way to highlight what incentives are available, and how competing claims could be reconciled. In the process, how financial analyses support decision-making is transformed: Valuation opens avenues for strategic dialogue to occur rather than a narrow exercise at deriving an expected value that is "unassailable" but often wrong.

1
What Drives Managers to Invest?

"Cash is king" is an accepted wisdom (Koller *et al.*, 2011) that popularly serves as the arbiter of value. To optimise an investment's value, cash flow is maximised presumably by expanding earnings, often assuming that assets are held to maturity (Kim and Kim, 2006). In this construct, managers *invest a sum and receive the expected future cash flows as payoffs*, cementing shareholders' primacy.

Conforming to classic financial economics' optimality, managers choose technologies with sizeable cash margins and minimum capital expenditures (capex), as Myron Gordon and Eli Shapiro (1956) would generally prescribe. To minimise risks, Shapiro (1999) would control for the variance from expected cash flows or risk.

Juxtaposing financial theory with practice, I note that finance managers evaluate investments in a world that they *imagine* real people would inhabit. To fulfil classic financial economics' conditions, managers need to assume an imagined and well-ordered world that is necessary to make valuation work. In holding the assets till maturity, managers would forego any value that accrues if the asset is expanded or retired before the end of its economic life (Kim and Kim, 2006).

Under this well-ordered existence, a hierarchy of cash flows is predicted, valued, and ranked in terms of returns and risks. Inspired by Franco Modigliani and Merton Howard Miller's (1958) capital asset pricing model (CAPM), net present value (NPV) and its twin, internal rate of return (IRR), gained prominence as valuation's gold standard by popular usage. With this acceptance, Irving Fisher's (2012) time value of money, from his *The Money Illusion*, is *de rigour* in employing discounted cash flow (DCF) analyses.

The primacy of shareholder value, however, is successfully being challenged. With advances in corporate social responsibility (Tai and Chuang, 2014) and sustainability (Seuring and Gold, 2013), the Business Roundtable (2019) enshrined the firm's societal obligations. In reframing the firm's purpose, managers will need to rebuild the foundations of the investment ecosystem.

In delivering on the firm's societal obligations, the manager is seen to make decisions as humans. Richard Thaler (2015) posits that perceptions of fairness are powerful impetus to take action. This is because humans are not immune to their social preferences, suggesting that humans are capable of pursuing "irrational" actions if by doing so, they prevent a bigger injustice from being committed. As a result, managers could decide following recursive processes with outcomes that are often tentative while subject to human preferences or frailties.

An imperfect and iterative decision process may iterate as outlined in Chart 8.1. Cognizant that humans perceive fairness, in however way it is defined, the importance that managers give to each factor (or criterion) would shift with the priorities that they happen to hold dear *at the time the decision was taken*.

To institute some order in a chaotic world, managers may weigh the merits of the investment and articulate why one criterion happens to be more important than another:

1. ***Cash flows*** would indicate *mathematically* how feasible and viable an investment is, under specified market conditions, as tested by its ability to internally fund its operational needs.
2. ***Velocity*** springs from old habits (or beliefs) that the faster the invested capital is recovered, the better off are shareholders, as defined by the payback period.
3. ***Value*** is notionally the outcome of prior decisions that form the bases for apportioning returns (or incentives) to stakeholders.
4. ***Allocate*** balances the rewards to competing claimants by reconciling asymmetric contributions, risks, or rewards.

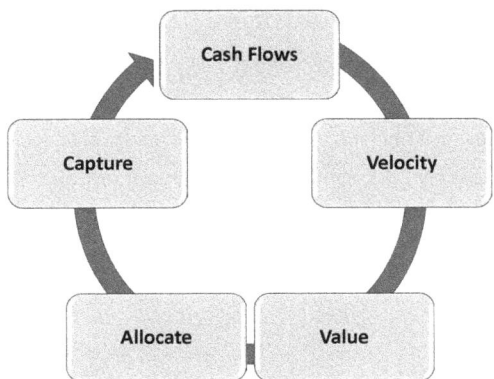

Chart 8.1: Investment Cycle under Static Conditions

5. ***Capture or appropriate*** the rewards (or penalties) that arises as outcomes of operational tactics, strategic decisions on capital structure, and dividend policy.

Chris Argyris (2000) noted the gaps between what the managers believe (e.g. ideas or their ideals) and how they act. As humans, managers espouse what they think is socially acceptable, which some truly commit. Organisationally, rewards may still be skewed to favour a set of accepted wisdom, based on some framework, to guide their actions (e.g. theory in use). In dealing with these internal contradictions, Argyris (2003) reflected: *Humans have become adept at sustaining corrosive features of the decision ecosystem that impedes learning.* One such feature is to defer to financial tools to provide a decision, hence a mathematical answer, that tends to predetermine outcomes. Here's why this could be problematic.

1.1 Era of the earnings multiples

The capital markets match billions of cash daily between sellers and buyers of securities. In my early days at the City of London, money flowed to the equity that sold cheaply or bonds that offer good yields. Value is set by *Price-to-Earnings ratios* (P/E) or its variants, with energy utilities evaluated as bond proxies. That is, by subtracting dividend yields from bond yields, a wide spread favours buying bonds because low dividend yields implied utilities were trading at high share prices (e.g. dividend per share/share price).

For decades, this world was insulated from other real-life experiences. The 1987 "Black Monday" proved two things: analysts' valuation ignored debt, and the effects of macroeconomics on how earnings per share (EPS) are formed.

S G Warburg (eventually became UBS), a few years later, pioneered with the use of "Enterprise Value" (EV). By using EV as the numerator and EBITDA or EBIT as the denominator, EV/EBITDA and EV/EBIT[1] were popularised. By explicitly adding debt, highly leveraged firms would have higher multiples that correctly signal their potential overvaluation.

---

[1] Together with my colleagues, Pablo Diaz and Miko Giedroycz, we calculated EV as the sum of market capitalisation and debt (including pensions and other liabilities), less cash. EBITDA is earnings before interest, tax, depreciation and amortisation, while EBIT is less maintenance capex (using straight line depreciation as proxy) for energy and capital-intensive stocks.

As European equity markets harmonised, EBITDA and EBIT corrected a large part of the accounting distortions associated with provisioning, depreciation, or amortisation policies. The other involves revenue recognition, which is a more subtle earnings distortion to detect from publicly available financial data. EV's ability to rank cross-border stock values added to its popularity among fund managers and equity analysts.

1.2 "New paradigm," old wisdom rules

The City of London seldom stands still. Always on the lookout for opportunities to cash in, the "dot com" posed existential threats to financial analyses. Internet-based businesses sprouted, listed, and traded at astronomical earnings multiples, without as much as earning a single penny. Worst, the more they lose, the higher their multiples went. The only justification?

The "prospects" were naively presumed to be good because the more people view the website, the more popular it gets. Over time, such popularity turns into e-commerce that converts "eyeballs" (or views) into revenues, hence cash flows, in an undefined future. While alluring, this flies against all accepted tenets of corporate finance.

While searching for an answer, my conversations with managers on how capital structures impact valuation, and how returns create value, were informative. Victoriano Reinoso, late Chief Executive of Union Fenosa, Spain, justified his firm's high indebtedness as a way to lower capital costs. He was inspired by CAPM's prescription. In contrast, Feliciano Fuster, late Chief Executive of Endesa, Spain, took a contrary view: With lower gearing, he retained a buffer against adverse events or provided flexibility to gear up should a growth opportunity present itself. In a separate dialogue on corporate structure, Baron Philippe Bodson, then Chief Executive of Electrabel and Tractebel, Belgium, responded to my critique of his cascading holding companies: "We are an industrial group that is managed as a unified structure." He objected to analysts persistently applying a conglomerate discount to their valuation. After some pencil-pushing, we coincided on similar conclusions for a change. The discount matched the value leakages as each corporate layer incurred additional taxes and costs relative to a consolidated entity.

Fortunately, residual income theory re-emerged as shareholder value (Rappaport, 1998) and gained popularity as *Economic Value Added or EVA*® (Stern *et al.*, 1996). In its construct, economic value is created when returns exceed its capital costs. While its predictive power for share prices is mixed (Bridle *et al.*, 2005), I stumbled into a valuation approach that served as a coherent platform to facilitate strategic dialogues, as I did with Chief Executives in Europe.

To my delight, and great discomfort, our analytical exercises yielded answers that were most unwelcome to the "dot com" advocates. Inherently unprofitable, value could only be created when "eyeballs" could show evidence of being monetised as cash. Without this prospect, fund managers were lured into bottomless pits.

With the benefit of hindsight, being referred to as outdated, conservative, old fashioned, and even backward may have turned out as a badge of honour. With reversion to senses having taken place after the "dot com" bubble burst, it dawned on me that the "theory in use" was not a question of methods (e.g. earnings multiples premium). Rather, it was a deep-seated belief in the power of the herd, where highly intelligent individuals are lured by the siren call of a pied piper. Fearful of being seen as a "deviant," one suspends one's own judgement and takes comfort in being wrong with the masses rather than singled out to be vilified or praised.

As valuation tools evolve in sophistication, each method has its critics and avid supporters (Imam *et al.*, 2008). In searching for the right tools, managers are confronted with these dilemmas: Pursue a valuation "holy grail" that singularly give a right answer all the time or extract insights that inform the consequences of one's chosen strategic actions.

I choose to focus on the latter. This choice comes with the obligation to understand how financial tools operate, the premises that guide their use, what their limitations are, and why it could assist managers to do their job well. In framing the decisions in this way, managers engage in conversations that aim to understand not only the outcomes but also why and how such results could come about. This interactive, recursive, and open conversations are what constitute meaningful strategic dialogues.

2
Understanding Financial Data

In one of my visits to Jon Aboitiz, late Chair of Aboitiz Equity Ventures,[2] he handed me his company's annual reports that I requested. Partly in jest, he quipped: "You

---

[2] The company is a major diversified energy and infrastructure conglomerate in Asia, with a primary listing in the Philippine Stock Exchange.

must be one of the few who pores through the accountants' notes with excitement." To which I replied: "Perhaps, foolish enough to try to decipher what accountants try to hide in plain sight."

This banter has a more serious undertone. What excites the financial analyst is the prospect of uncovering insights that become apparent when financial data are rearranged. That is, cash flows to competing claimants are made explicit (Koller *et al.*, 2015).

The cash flow that accrues to the claimant is what (mathematically) determines the investment's value to that party.

Under this premise, cash flow analyses will have to start by making this linkage specific and transparent. At various levels of cash flow, the money is destined for a particular claimant, where the satisfaction of a prior claim conditions what subsequent claimants would receive. As a result, stakeholders such as suppliers or employees take precedence over lenders, with debt providers taking a senior position (in the queue of claimants) over equity providers.

To put this in perspective, knowing what the questions we are trying to answer focuses the mind on the relevant analyses we need to do. I propose we organise the information along the three aspects of their decisions that are strategic, as outlined in Chart 8.2:

1. ***Operationally***, how would the choice of technology lock in the investment's capacity to generate cash, given its cost structure and operational characteristics?
2. In ***funding*** the investment, how would decisions on short- and long-term financing adapt to the shifting needs of specified technologies?
3. In ***monetising*** the expected payoffs, how do the operational and funding decisions translate into cash and the appropriation of value?

To facilitate the mapping, I coded and cross-referenced the variables. For example, earnings after tax (EAT) from *operations* (e.g. profit and loss account), OP7, feed into the cash flow analysis under *monetise*. From *funding* (e.g. balance sheet), the change in working capital requirements (ΔWCR) (BS4) is deducted from CF1 under *monetise*. Additional capex under *monetise* (CF4) increases fixed assets in the balance sheet under *funding* (BS7).

Dynamic Decisions

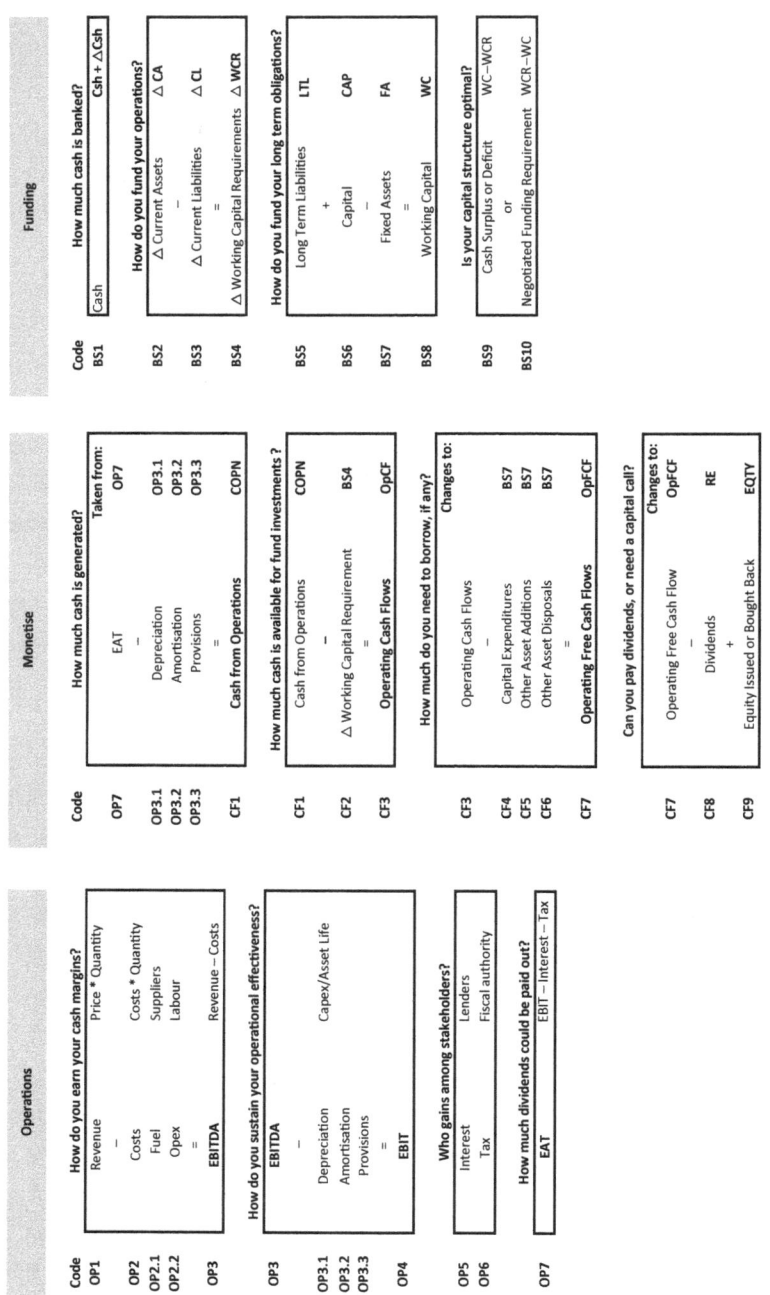

Chart 8.2: Linkages of Financial Information

Source: Author's reframing of financial information.

2.1 Strategic investment and cash flow illusion

While most investments are considered as *strategic*, one of these factors is a necessary condition to qualify:

1. It potentially alters the scale, scope, and course of actions that managers could undertake when exercising their options to commit.
2. Its success (or failure) could propel the investing firm to greater financial prosperity (or misery), with consequences on its ability to grow (or shrink to oblivion).
3. It disrupts extant systems by displacing its infrastructures and logistics, often resulting in the obsolescence of extant models and competencies.

Investments were not always evaluated using cash flow analysis. Fisher's (2012) *time value of money* sits well with evaluating bounded valuation problems such as bond returns. Contractually, lenders disburse the principal (e.g. invest) with borrowers obliged to pay interest and principal (e.g. payoffs for the lender) over an agreed time. There are two ways to estimate the returns to the lender:

The net present value (NPV) of bonds comprise a payoff and the amount lent. However, the cash received today, *ceteris paribus*, could purchase more than cash received a year hence or thereafter. To solve the equivalence, the *time value of money* works in this way:

> Today, $100 is earned, which could be deposited (or invested) at a 10% return. A year later, the cash balance is $110 (e.g. $100 capital plus $10 return). Conversely, tomorrow's $110 is equivalent to today's $100.

Through discounting, the equivalence is calculated by dividing $110 by 1.10, which is the discount factor. That is, 1 + interest rate is raised to time *t*. Hence, for year 1, the discount factor is 1 + 10% = 1.10 when *t* = 1. In year 2, it is (1 + 0.10) ^ 2, which is equivalent to (1 + 0.10) * (1 + 0.10) = 1.21. Repeating this exercise, the yearly discount factors are calculated. As a general rule, the same amount earned farther into the future is worth less in today's money.

The payoffs are the sum of the present value of the future cash flows that are gained by lending. This relationship is the genesis of NPV's decision rule: Lend if NPV is positive, decline if negative.

The mirror image is IRR. Expressed formally:

$$0 = NPV = \sum [(OpFCF_0) + (OpFCF_t)/(1+r)^t \ldots (OpFCFn)/(1+r)^n] \quad (8.1)$$

The discount rate r is the unknown, which is the rate that sets NPV to zero. Being time-sensitive, the loan's repayment schedule gained prominence in determining how much the lender actually earns at maturity.

As the *time value of money* gained traction, NPV and IRR gradually extended their application to equity and physical assets. Transposed intact from bond valuation, the application was far from flawless.

Equity's remuneration is contingent upon how much the firm earns. The same goes with physical asset's cash flows. By applying a bounded valuation to an asset with open-ended cash flows, one can only hope that everything works according to plan. Otherwise, cash flows may fall short (or overshoot) of what was expected. To correct the gaps, NPV inadvertently prescribes what Argyris (2000) is critical of as a "plug the hole" fudge: *Raise the discount rate to penalise with lower valuation volatile cash flows.*

3
Approximating "Cash Flows"

In evaluating the opportunity to build a gas-fired plant, let us examine how conventional earnings analyses differ from what I am proposing. Consider this investment:

$ACCGT_B$[3] is a possible technology to meet our growth in energy supply, requiring 1,000 MW of capacity to be built over three years at a cost of $795,000 for each installed MW. The asset operates in a wholesale energy market, where the power prices are set by the LCOE[4] of $ACCGT_M$, a similar technology but operated as a mid-merit plant.

Armed with the basic data, managers would find the most accurate (or even precise) estimates of prices, costs, and volumes to project earnings for the valuation period. The focus, therefore, is on *what* earnings could be earned for each forecast period.

---

[3] Advance Combined Cycle Gas Turbines operated as a baseload supply, which we designate as $ACCGT_B$.
[4] The lifecycle cost of energy (LCOEs) and how it compares with financial costs of energy (FCOE) are discussed in Chapter 7.

Having finesse the estimates for the projections, managers sit back, decide, and hope for the best that what was planned will be what they get.

Devoid of much strategic insight, the excellent mathematical exercise is number crunching *par excellence*. Unfortunately, with each turn of the market, and each variation in costs, managers would be kept busy plugging the gaps.

3.1 Foundation for strategic dialogues

Working together, we can change this unfortunate situation, and add more meaning to managerial life. *How* things could change starts with understanding *why* earnings evolve the way they do. Forewarned, managers could (hopefully) avoid the pitfalls or prepare to seize opportunities that may emerge.

How a technology's earnings potential could vary is simulated under a specified market structure and pricing. In this way, the conditions that would make things work are identified. Knowing them, managers could monitor market events and be alerted of impending storms or emerging opportunities. Such signals are gleaned from the following:

1. It is *feasible* when power prices are greater than its cost of supply, resulting in positive EBITDA.
2. It becomes *viable* when it earns sufficiently to internally fund ongoing capital expenditures to ensure its operational effectiveness.
3. It can *sustain* itself by securing its credit strength and adequately rewarding equity providers.

Applying this to $ACCGT_B$, managers do a first approximation of earnings potential in Table 8.1.

Revenue (A.1 to J.1) is the product of spot prices, P_s (A.2 to J.2), and the volume sold, Q_j (A.3 to J.3), or $P_s * Q_j$.

The easy part is to estimate the volume. In a day, we have 24 hours, and 365 days in a year, with a leap year every 4 years (e.g. 366 days). For every MW of installed capacity, it could in theory generate 8,760 megawatt hours (MWh) of power if operated at 100% (or 8,784 MWh in a leap year). However, the asset needs to be maintained or allow for some unplanned stoppage, which the industry average estimates at 87%. In a year, $ACCGT_B$ could sell 7,621 GWh (or 7,642 GWh in a leap year).

Table 8.1: Threshold for Financial Feasibility

Advance Combined Cycle Gas Turbine Baseload — ACCGT$_B$ under ACCGT$_M$ Wholesale Market

Column/Line	Profit and Loss	Acronym	Unit	1 A	2 B	3 C	4 D	5 E	6 F	7 G	8 H	9 I	10 J	Normalised Earnings K
1	**Revenues**	Rev	$ mln	**0**	**0**	**0**	**705**	**815**	**928**	**1,040**	**705**	**591**	**479**	**703**
2	Spot Prices	P$_s$	$/kWh	0	0	0	0	0	0	0	0	0	0	0
3	Quantity	Q$_i$	MWh	0	0	0	7,642	7,621	7,621	7,621	7,642	7,621	7,621	7,621
4	**Cost of Fuel (Cost of Goods Sold)**	FFC (CoGS)	$ mln	**0**	**0**	**0**	**460**	**550**	**642**	**734**	**460**	**367**	**275**	**459**
5	Cash Costs	C$_i$	$ mln	0	0	0	438	524	611	699	438	349	262	437
6	Cash Costs per kWh	CFkWh	$/kWh	0	0	0	0	0	0	0	0	0	0	0
7	Quantity	Q$_i$	MWh	0	0	0	7,642	7,621	7,621	7,621	7,642	7,621	7,621	7,621
8	Ancillary Fuel Costs	CAF$_i$	$ mln	0	0	0	22	26	31	35	22	17	13	22
9	Quantity	Q$_i$	MWh	0	0	0	382	381	381	381	382	381	381	381
10	**Gross Cash Profit**	GCP	$ mln	**0**	**0**	**0**	**246**	**265**	**286**	**306**	**246**	**225**	**204**	**245**
11	% Gross Cash Margin	GCM	%	0.00%	0.00%	0.00%	0.00%	32.53%	30.79%	29.43%	34.82%	37.97%	42.61%	34.82%
12	**Operating Cash Costs**	OpCC	$ mln	**0**	**0**	**0**	**30**	**31**	**32**	**33**	**34**	**35**	**36**	**37**
13	Financial Fixed O&M	FO&M	$ mln	0	0	0	11	12	12	12	13	13	14	14
14	Cash Costs per kWh	FO&MkWh	$/kWh	0	0	0	0	0	0	0	0	0	0	0
15	Financial Variable O&M	VO&M	$ mln	0	0	0	18	18	19	19	20	20	21	22
16	Cash Costs per kWh	VO&MkWh	$/kwh	0	0	0	0	0	0	0	0	0	0	0
17	Cash Ancillary Costs	CAC$_i$	$ mln	0	0	0	1	1	2	2	2	2	2	2
18	**Earnings before Interest, Taxes, Depreciation and Amortisation**	EBITDA	$ mln	**0**	**0**	**0**	**215**	**234**	**253**	**273**	**211**	**189**	**168**	**207**
19	% EBITDA Margin	EBITDA%	%	0.00%	0.00%	0.00%	30.51%	28.70%	27.32%	26.23%	29.95%	32.01%	35.03%	29.49%

Source: Author's calculations based on EIA raw data.

The spot prices are set by ACCGT$_M$ with economic costs comprising the recovery of fixed costs (C$_{FX}$), variable (C$_{VAR}$) and fuel (C$_{FUEL}$) costs. As a mid-merit plant, ACCGT$_M$ would spread its fixed costs, which is similar to ACCGT$_B$, over a lower volume (4,954 MWh for each MW in a year).

The fuel cash costs (A.5 to J.5) is the product of the unit financial fuel costs, FFC$_{kWh}$, and the quantity, Q$_j$, supplied. To operate the asset, it produces as well as consumes energy. We expressed this cost as the ancillary fuel costs (A.1 to K.8), which we estimate to be close to 5% of the power generated (e.g. 5% of volume multiplied by unit fuel cost).

Assuming all sales are paid in cash, the *supply spread* (or margin) between power prices, P$_s$, and fuel cost of supply (A.4 to K.4) varies from 33% to 46% equivalent to the *Gross Cash Profit* (GCP) (A.10 to K.10).

Astute managers would recognise, at this early stage, that excellence in procurement is a source of competitive advantage. With fuel suppliers taking 54–67% of the "cash" from revenues, improved terms (e.g. lower prices) and better logistics could reallocate "cash" from suppliers to the firm.

In comparing the cost structures of ACCGT$_B$ and ACCGT$_M$ (which is equal to P$_s$), ACCGT$_B$ gains from lower costs, while partially indexing its volatile financial fuel costs, as illustrated in Chart 8.3. Without any regulatory interventions, where power prices could be cut, fuel cost volatility would shadow power prices, given that ACCGT$_M$'s fuel costs constitute the principal source of price variations.

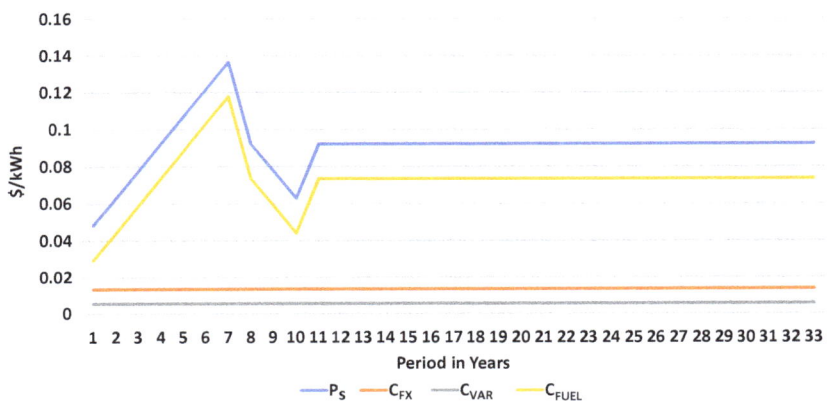

Chart 8.3: Spot Power Prices under Gas System

In contrast, labour and other operating expenses pale in comparison in terms of relative influence on financial costs. Unfortunately, almost by deep-seated reflex, managers follow this dictum: *reduce headcount to raise EBITDA.*

Managers may belatedly regret their actions: The benefits today are miniscule, with inflation eroding tomorrow's gains. Worse, functions or employees that were eliminated may prove critical to making the value chain work. Rebuilding such capabilities could prove more disruptive, expensive, and impair future earnings.

EBITDA's magnitude tests $ACCGT_B$'s financial feasibility where its supply spread and operating cash costs (A.10 to K.10), or *cost of supply*, far exceeds the prevailing range of power prices considered.

3.2 Ignore critical premises at your peril

While much is done to understand power prices, a number of managers assume that capital expenditures are front-end disbursements. Hence, once the initial investment is funded, the asset would run its course and reliably deliver on its promise.

Operating $ACCGT_B$ at its full capacity is indeed planning for success. Experience, however, has taught operational managers (usually with technical expertise) that continual updating is required to sustain the asset's delivered volume. Otherwise, a vicious circle could imperil revenues: *Underinvestment could erode operating efficiency, potentially increasing downtime because of breakdowns or unplanned stoppages. Consequently, revenues fall or operating costs rise, further reducing EBITDA.*

Any erosion in efficiency would reduce volumes and hence imperil revenues. Alerted by our technical colleagues, financially inclined managers incorporate this "long tail" commitment as maintenance capex, as we did in Table 8.2.

Accounting spreads the capex of $795 mln over the operating life of 30 years of $ACCGT_B$, resulting in an annual depreciation expense of $27 mln (A.3 to K.3). This is a non-cash expense, which explains why EBITDA is the preferred "cash flow" of some managers.

I would argue that maintenance capex could be provided for, so that cash could be accumulated to fund its continual disbursements. Similarly, for evaluation purposes, it is equated to depreciation expense to reflect its annual charge to EBITDA. By accepting this premise, EBIT becomes a proxy to test $ACCGT_B$'s capacity to fund maintenance capex with internally generated "operating cash earnings."

Levers of Value

Table 8.2: Threshold for Financial Viability

Column/Line	Profit and Loss	Acronym	Unit	Advance Combined Cycle Gas Turbine Baseload — ACCGT$_B$ under ACCGT$_M$ Wholesale Market										Normalised Earnings
				1 A	2 B	3 C	4 D	5 E	6 F	7 G	8 H	9 I	10 J	K
1	Earnings before Interest, Taxes, Depreciation and Amortisation	EBITDA	$ mln	0	0	0	215	234	253	273	211	189	168	207
	% EBITDA Margin	EBITDA%	%	0	0	0	0	0	0	0	0	0	0	0
2	Depreciation	DPN$_j$	$ mln	0	0	0	27	27	27	27	27	27	33	33
3	Amortisation	AMRT$_j$	$ mln	0	0	0	0	0	0	0	0	0	0	0
4	Provisions	PRVN$_j$	$ mln	0	0	0	0	0	0	0	0	0	0	0
5	Earnings before Interest and Taxes	EBIT	$ mln	0	0	0	189	208	227	246	185	163	135	174
6	% EBIT Margin	EBIT%	%	0.00%	0.00%	0.00%	26.76%	25.45%	24.46%	23.68%	26.20%	27.53%	28.12%	24.78%

Source: Author's calculations based on EIA raw data.

After deducting depreciation expense (A.2 to K.2) from EBITDA (A.1 to K.1), the resulting EBIT is well in excess of ACCGT$_B$'s imputed annual maintenance capex.

The ability to internally fund maintenance capex is a test of viability. This is indicated by positive EBIT, which is sufficiently high to meet its operating and future capital expenditures.

3.3 Continued access to financing

With debt and equity as generic funding, what benefits do borrowings confer if sufficient equity is available?

Our simulation in Table 8.3 prices debt nominally at 3.5% a year for a 20-year term. Interest and principal repayments start on the year after commercial operations. In effect, over a specified period, we are "renting" someone's cash to fund our investments.

In exchange, we "divert" a larger share of EBIT initially to pay interest expenses, which reduces earnings before tax (EBT) (A.6 to K.6). This reduces taxes paid (e.g. 30% on lower EBT) and dividends (e.g. 50% of lower EAT) unless the pay-out ratio is increased.

The flip side: Borrowing reduces the equity invested in the firm. While the probability of financial distress increases with more debt, lenders actually carry a higher default risk for funding up to 70% of capex. To compensate for these risks, lenders are given prior claim than equity in the event of bankruptcy.

In contrast, equity is a permanent (sort of) funding that shareholders provide. As the ultimate claimant (or last in the queue), equity providers assume any residual liabilities or appropriate all unclaimed cash. For this privilege, equity providers earn dividends that, in theory, should exceed the returns on debt.

For managers, this heuristic (or rule of thumb) may come in handy: If debt yields < equity returns, maximise debt that the firm could borrow. By how much is a matter largely influenced by managerial risk aversion and the costs of financial distress.

Taxes are claims by a silent partner, the fiscal authority. The size of the tax claim directly reduces EAT. Hence, low taxes tend to attract private capital by expanding the *EAT* available for dividend increases.

Strengthened credit and adequate equity returns enhance funding access: In "renting" third-party cash, as debt is repaid, a virtuous cycle operates. Reduced interest expenses expand EBT (A.6 to K.6), thereby expanding EAT (A.9 to K.9), which increases dividends and enhances credit strength with lower gearing.

Levers of Value

Table 8.3: Financing and Taxes

Advance Combined Cycle Gas Turbine Baseload — ACCGT$_B$ under ACCGT$_M$ Wholesale Market

Column/Line	Profit and Loss	Acronym	Unit	1 A	2 B	3 C	4 D	5 E	6 F	7 G	8 H	9 I	10 J	Normalised Earnings K
1	**Earnings before Interest and Taxes**	EBIT	$ mln	**0**	**0**	**0**	**189**	**208**	**227**	**246**	**185**	**163**	**135**	**174**
2	% EBIT Margin	EBIT%	%	0.00%	0.00%	0.00%	26.76%	25.45%	24.46%	23.68%	26.20%	27.53%	28.12%	24.78%
3	Interest Income	INTIn	$ mln	3	3	3	1	0	0	1	2	2	3	3
4	Interest Expense	INTEx	$ mln	0	0	0	19	19	19	18	17	16	15	14
5	Others	ORC	$ mln	0	0	0	0	0	0	0	0	0	0	0
6	Earnings before Tax	EBT	$ mln	**3**	**3**	**3**	**171**	**188**	**208**	**229**	**169**	**149**	**123**	**163**
7	% EBT		%	0.00%	0.00%	0.00%	24.19%	23.09%	22.47%	22.04%	24.01%	25.22%	25.63%	23.17%
8	Tax	TAX	$ mln	1	1	1	51	56	63	69	51	45	37	49
9	Earnings after Tax	EAT	$ mln	**2**	**2**	**2**	**119**	**132**	**146**	**160**	**119**	**104**	**86**	**114**
10	% EAT		%	0.00%	0.00%	0.00%	16.93%	16.16%	15.73%	15.43%	16.80%	17.65%	17.94%	16.22%

Source: Author's calculations based on EIA raw data.

What becomes apparent from our simulation are the embedded costs that $ACCGT_B$ locks in. Ignored in plain sight, dynamic interactions of revenues and costs shift thresholds of earnings viability. Thus, without fully understanding how, managers are "surprised" by the consequences of adverse events, often for failing to anticipate its effects on their firm's financial viability. Consequently, managers could stumble from one crisis to another. In gaining a deep understanding of the "what ifs," managers would appreciate how reliant their operating performance is on their prior decisions.

To redirect the "theory in use" from the "safety of the herd," valuation should be seen as an artful judgement in adaptive actions. Instead of betting the farm on a single number (e.g. NPV or IRR), managers weigh the uncertainties, the prize of success, and contingencies to forestall adverse financial impact.

4
Funding Choices and Adaptive Actions

There are two sides to a firm's balance sheet: "what it owns" and "what is owed." Josep Faus's (1995) framing of the financing strategy comprises the following:

1. ***Structural finance*** funds long-term commitments, such as fixed assets, with equity or debt, and any earnings ploughed back into the business, which comprises the *working capital* (WC).
2. ***Operational finance*** pertains to how day-to-day operations are funded, which includes current assets and liabilities, to derive the *working capital requirements* (WCR).

Damodaran (1996) starts us off by defining debt. It is an obligation to pay a defined amount (e.g. interest and principal[5]) at an agreed period (e.g. duration). By

---

[5] A debt payment comprises two cash outflows: Interest expenses deducted from EBIT and repayment of principal deducted from the outstanding balance of the borrowing (or debt).

implication, this would require a future cash outflow (e.g. payment is made) or a loss of future cash inflow *to shareholders* (e.g. paying interest instead of dividends).

By failing to honour this obligation, the firm is in default. Consequently, legal proceedings could incur penalties and costs that the firm may wish to avoid. In effect, the high costs of litigation and defaults, or the prospect of exclusion from a market (e.g. poor credit rating), could make reneging on such obligations expensive if not punitive.

4.1 Knowing funding choices

Going back to our $ACCGT_B$ investment, we examine in Table 8.4 how the simulated earnings could be funded in order to turn the opportunity into a functioning venture. We start with *Working Capital* (WC) and simulate how it could evolve over a decade under the conditions that premised our investing and operating cycle.

Borrowings come in various forms, which we can generically simplify as debt (A.3 to K.3). Provisions constitute future liabilities such as nuclear decommissioning, pensions, or taxes as examples.

Capital (A.5 to L.5) constitutes the equity that shareholders provide (A.6 to L.6) and the portion of EAT that is ploughed back into the business and added to what was previously accumulated (A.7 to L.7). Equity usually remains stable except when new equity is raised or bought back.

4.2 Virtuous cycle of strategic investment

Damodaran (1996) is specific as to what constitutes the firm's assets: It has the "potential to either generate future cash inflows or reduce future cash outflows," where such benefits could be quantified with some precision.

When investing in fixed assets, cash is disbursed upfront to pay for building the asset. Periodically, an annual capital expense is recognised as depreciation deducted from *EBITDA*. It reduces *Fixed Asset* (A.8 to K.8) by increasing accumulated depreciation (A.10 to K.10) when each year's depreciation expense is added to.

To ascertain *WC's* (A.1 to L.1) adequacy for $ACCGT_B$, we note the following:

1. Conforming to the debt repayments, borrowings expand during construction, followed by debt reductions (A.3 to K.3) as EBITs are earned.

Table 8.4: Funding of Long-term Commitments

Advance Combined Cycle Gas Turbine Baseload — ACCGT$_B$ under ACCGT$_M$ Wholesale Market

Column/Line	Balance Sheet	Acronym	Unit	0 A	1 B	2 C	3 D	4 E	5 F	6 G	7 H	8 I	9 J	10 K	Terminal Period L
1	**Working Capital**	WC	$ mln	**265**	267	269	6	83	156	228	307	365	416	265	1,210
2	**Long-term Liabilities**	LTL	$ mln	**186**	**371**	**557**	**557**	**547**	**529**	**501**	**473**	**445**	**417**	**390**	**0**
3	Borrowings	DEBT	$ mln	186	371	557	557	547	529	501	473	445	417	390	0
4	Provisions	PRVLT	$ mln	0	0	0	0	0	0	0	0	0	0	0	0
	Add:														
5	**Capital**	CAP	$ mln	**80**	**161**	**242**	**244**	**304**	**370**	**443**	**523**	**582**	**634**	**677**	**1,726**
6	Equity	EQTY	$ mln	80	159	239	239	239	239	239	239	239	239	239	239
7	Retained Earnings	RE	$ mln	0	2	4	6	65	131	204	284	344	396	439	1,488
	Less:														
8	**Fixed Assets**	FA	$ mln	**0**	**265**	**530**	**795**	**769**	**742**	**716**	**689**	**663**	**636**	**802**	**517**
9	Gross Fixed Assets	GFA	$ mln	0	0	0	0	795	795	795	795	795	795	994	1,590
10	Accumulated Depreciation	ACDPN	$ mln	0	0	0	0	27	53	80	106	133	159	192	1,073
11	Asset under Construction	ACON	$ mln	0	265	530	795	0	0	0	0	0	0	0	0
12	Others	OFA	$ mln	0	0	0	0	0	0	0	0	0	0	0	0
13	Accumulated Depreciation	ACDPN	$ mln	0	0	0	0	0	0	0	0	0	0	0	0

Source: Author's calculations using raw data from EIA.

2. *Fixed assets* (A.8 to K.8) rise as construction progresses, followed by smooth declines because of depreciation, with intermittent lumpy additions from maintenance capex.

WC exhibits a virtuous cycle when internally generated cash expands by accumulating cash surpluses when cash revenues (or inflows) exceed cash expenses (or outflows). As lumpy uses of cash occur, as in funding maintenance capex, it is funded from the firm's cash flows and cash surpluses. When the self-funding stage is reached, asset additions could be financed entirely from the firm's own cash resources.

In optimising capital deployment, debt and capital levels adapt to how fixed assets evolve. Capital is adaptively deployed by employing (flexible) debt with (permanent) equity. As internally generated cash expands, pacing debt repayments or returning cash to shareholders are ways to rebalance *WC*.

4.3 Operating decisions and financing

In markets where all revenues and costs are settled in cash, *EBITDA* and *EBIT* are cash measures, as popular usage would imply.

However, in a world where managers behave as humans would, credit is extended to customers by suppliers in order to grease the wheels of commerce. In this dynamic world, we come face to face with three new acquaintances in Table 8.5:

1. *Receivables* comprise credit to customers where energy sales are invoiced today, with payment promised in the future, say in 20 days (A.3 to L.3).
2. *Payables* are purchases, principally fuels, which we take delivery of the goods today and promise to pay in the future, say in 15 days (A7 to L.3).

In an imperfect world, the delivery of fuel does not always happen in perfect unison with when power is generated. This stockpiling of liquified natural gas (LNG) onsite creates *inventory* (A.4 to L.4).

Other receivables (A.5 to L.5) or payables (A.8 to L.8) relate to expenses that the firm finances or purchases that the suppliers extend credits.

These apparently discrete, tactical decisions, involving how long to finance customers' sales, how much gas to stockpile, or how aggressively to push for longer terms of credit from suppliers would ultimately vary *Working Capital Requirements* (WCR).

Dynamic Decisions

Table 8.5: Working Capital Requirement

Column/Line	Balance Sheet	Acronym	Unit	Advance Combined Cycle Gas Turbine Baseload — $ACCGT_B$ under $ACCGT_M$ Wholesale Market											Terminal Period
				0	1	2	3	4	5	6	7	8	9	10	
				A	B	C	D	E	F	G	H	I	J	K	L
1	Working Capital Requirements	WCR	$ mln	0	0	0	0	77	89	102	114	77	65	53	77
2	Current Assets	CA	$ mln	0	0	0	0	115	135	154	174	115	95	75	115
3	Receivables	RCV	$ mln	0	0	0	0	39	45	51	57	39	32	26	39
4	Inventory	INV	$ mln	0	0	0	0	38	45	53	60	38	30	23	38
5	Others	OCA	$ mln	0	0	0	0	39	45	51	57	39	32	26	39
	Less:														
6	Current Liabilities	CL	$ mln	0	0	0	0	38	45	53	60	38	30	23	38
7	Payables	PYB	$ mln	0	0	0	0	19	23	26	30	19	15	11	19
8	Others	OCL	$ mln	0	0	0	0	19	23	26	30	19	15	11	19

Source: Author's calculations using raw data from EIA.

Recall in Year 4: Revenue of $705 mln is expected which translates into daily sales of $1.92 mln ($705 mln/365 days). Extending 20 days payment period would need to fund $39 mln (E.3) in *receivables*. Increasing this to 30 days would raise receivables to $58 mln, a 58% in cash requirement.

Inventory control and the configuration of logistics impact the inventory that should be carried. In the case of LNG, the delivery cycle relies on the proximity of the source and the speed of unloading the gas. It goes without saying, *without an import facility, LNG is beyond reach for that market.*

We assume that we need 30 days to receive the LNG from the time we ordered. To be on the safe side, we need to stock LNG to avoid supply disruption. We now divide the cost of fuel of $460 mln (or cost of goods sold for other industries) by the days in a year to obtain a daily cost of $1.26 mln. Hence, a 30-day inventory would cost us about $38 mln (E.4).

The role is reversed with suppliers. They extend credit to us when we purchase fuel, but only for 15 days from receipt of goods. We multiply by 15 days the daily fuel cost to estimate our payables. Other payables are estimated in the same way as payables.

Clearly, the build-up in current assets requires the firm to fund this use of cash. As revenues expand, WCR is likely to grow apace unless suppliers discover generosity by offsetting rising current assets with ever longer credit terms.

To correctly reflect the operational funding, *Invested Capital* would need to recognise this by adding *WCR* and *Fixed Assets* (and other assets needed for operations) into its calculation. Hence, for $ACCGT_B$, the invested capital in Year 4 is the sum of $769 mln (E.8 in Table 8.4) and $77 mln (E.1 in Table 8.5) for a total of $846 mln.

An operational perspective examines the operating and cash cycle in terms of the number of days to monetise transactions into cash, as illustrated in Table 8.6.

Loosening credit policy and sloppy inventory control would add to our short-term financing by increasing the operating cycle (A.14 to K.14) or the sum of the inventory and receivables days. Conversely, by negotiating longer payment terms, the cash cycle (A.15 to K.15) is substantially shortened (operating cycle less days payables) by letting suppliers finance partly WCR.

In ignoring operational finance, rapid revenue expansion could create a cash crunch when scant attention is paid to managing WCR. Too loose, expansion of current assets increases calls on cash, in the same way as shortened payment periods would for payables.

Table 8.6: Operating and Cash Cycle

Column/Line	Balance Sheet	Acronym	Unit	Advance Combined Cycle Gas Turbine Baseload — ACCGT$_B$ under ACCGT$_M$ Wholesale Market									
				1 A	2 B	3 C	4 D	5 E	6 F	7 G	8 H	9 I	10 J
1	**Funding to Clients**												
2	Average Inventory	INVAvg	$ mln	0	0	0	19	41	49	57	49	34	26
3	Inventory Turnover	INVT	x	—	—	—	24	13	13	13	9	11	10
4	Days in Inventory	INVDays	Days	—	—	—	15	28	28	28	39	34	35
5	**Credit and Collection**												
6	Average Accounts Receivable	ARAvg	$ mln	0	0	0	19	42	48	54	48	35	29
7	Accounts Receivable Turnover	ART	x	—	—	—	37	20	19	19	15	17	16
8	Days in Receivable	ARDays	Days	—	—	—	7	14	14	14	18	16	16
9	**Suppliers' Funding**												
10	Average Accounts Payable	APAvg	$ mln	0	0	0	9	21	24	28	24	17	13
11	Accounts Payable Turnover	APT	x	—	—	—	49	27	26	26	19	22	21
12	Days in Payables	APDays	Days	—	—	—	7	14	14	14	19	17	18
13	**Operating and Cash Cycles**												
14	Operating Cycle	OpCyc	Days	—	—	—	26	55	63	70	67	50	43
15	Cash Cycle	CshCyc	Days	—	—	—	19	41	49	56	47	33	25

Source: Author's calculations using raw data from EIA.

4.4 Capital rebalancing a core financial strategy

Going beyond conventional financial ratio analysis, we examine, in Table 8.7, how deeper balance sheet analysis could inform when and how to rebalance the capital structure.

The *Liquidity* (A.2/3 to K.2/3) and *Long-term Financing* (A.5/8 to A.5/8) ratios all indicate robust financial strength.

$ACCGT_B$ generates sufficient cash that more than covers its operating liabilities (e.g. current and quick ratios in excess of 1).

Interest cover, where cash earned is in excess of interest expenses, and similar indicators, far exceed its obligations. Over the period, debt gearing (e.g. debt-to-equity ratio) declines rapidly.

With benign neglect, managers could cruise along comforted by the thought that financial distress is a distant prospect if ever. If life works perfectly as the managers planned, more than a billion dollars in cash would accumulate towards $ACCGT_B$'s end of operating life (as a single asset firm).

A mergers and acquisition mindset would see a very different picture. With WC exceeding WCR, cash is accumulating as if it is going out of fashion. While debtors and equity providers take comfort in $ACCGT_B$'s credit strength, the cash pile is far from erecting an impregnable fortress against hostile bids.

Examples are plentiful. Financially constraint Trafalgar House, with no energy expertise, launched a hostile bid for then newly privatised Northern Electric of the United Kingdom (House of Commons, 1995). It was repelled with strong political opposition.

Across the European continent, cash-rich Endesa was a bastion of Spanish commercial pride and success. After leading the economic "reconquest" of Latin America, with its acquisition of Chile's Enersis and other assets in the region, it fell prey to a number of hostile bids. After a few attempts at merging with its Spanish rivals failed, Endesa itself became a target by Germany's E.ON (Forbes, 2007). In the end, Italy's Enel trumped its rivals, with help from Spanish cash-constraint construction firms and the government (Ruano and Dinkloh, 2007).

Regulators are coaxed to claw back excess cash earnings when energy firms are seen to accumulate too much liquidity. Perceived as earning too much at the consumers' expense, the UK regulators were not slow to claw back "excessive" returns by cutting tariffs (Kollewe, 2019; Ambrose, 2019). Two decades after its privatisation, the UK regulator's old habits of rebalancing the largesse of financial success remains intact.

Table 8.7: Cash and Rebalancing Capital Structure

Advance Combined Cycle Gas Turbine Baseload — $ACCGT_M$ Wholesale Market — $ACCGT_B$ under

Column/Line	Balance Sheet	Acronym	Unit	1 A	2 B	3 C	4 D	5 E	6 F	7 G	8 H	9 I	10 J
1	**Liquidity**												
2	Current Ratio	CR	x	—	—	—	3	3	3	3	3	3	3
3	Quick Ratio	QR	x	—	—	—	0	1	2	3	8	12	9
4	**Long-term Financing**												
5	Interest Cover	IntC	x	—	—	—	10	11	12	14	11	10	9
6	Cash Fixed Charges	CshFC	x	—	—	—	0	0	0	0	0	0	1
7	Capex Cover	CpxC	x	0	0	0	—	—	—	—	—	—	1
8	Gearing	DE	x	2	2	2	2	1	1	1	1	1	1
9	**Working Capital**												
10	Working Capital Requirements	WCR	$ mln	0	0	0	77	89	102	114	77	65	53
11	Working Capital	WCR	$ mln	267	269	6	83	156	228	307	365	416	265
12	Cash Surplus	CshS	$ mln	**267**	**269**	**6**	**5**	**67**	**126**	**193**	**288**	**351**	**213**
13	Negotiated Funding Requirements	NFR	$ mln	**-267**	**-269**	**-6**	**-5**	**-67**	**-126**	**-193**	**-288**	**-351**	**-213**

Source: Author's calculations using raw data from EIA.

Managers may pre-empt such unwelcome actions by returning cash to shareholders. They could buy back the shares, if listed, or pay out extra dividends, or do a lump-sum distribution of the excess cash.

While cash is essential to facilitate investment, treating it as kingly treasure may lose a kingdom: Redistribute excess cash by prepaying debt, increase dividends, or buy back shares (if feasible). Accumulating cash is not an objective, it is a result of past actions (e.g. effective cost control or supportive pricing for chosen technology) or managerial inertia (e.g. scrimping on maintenance capex or benign neglect).

5
Creating and Appropriating Cash

By treating cash as an instrument of exchange, how cash flows connect to its purpose and use is readily operationalised. By understanding the roots of the gaps (e.g. between expected and actual outcomes), managers may enhance their capacity to dynamically respond to strategic challenges. Specifically:

1. ***Operating cash flows*** (OpCF) emanate from the managers' prior decisions on what technology to adopt which embeds and locks in a cost structure and its judgement of how supportive the pricing regime could be. How these decisions match up would largely determine how much cash flows could be earned from operations when assets are reasonably managed.
2. ***Operating free cash flows*** (OpFCF) result from the pacing of capital expenditures and how much scope managers have in internally funding future investing or maintenance capex.
3. ***Available cash for disbursement*** (ACD) informs tactical choices for funding temporal shortfalls, or redeploying cash surpluses, that seek to sustain sound capital deployment.

In grounding the conversation around the market and operational realities, the evolving financing requirements are understood for *what* it is and *why*. In some instances, financial tools encourage managers to solve problems by evaluating outcomes for *what it could have been*. For example, had prices been fixed or stable (or even predictable), all transactions were paid in cash, and no interest or taxes are levied, EBITDA and EBIT would come close when estimating cash flows.

However, managers reside in a less hospitable ecosystem. Perhaps, for this reason, managers serve a purpose and remain gainfully employed, with some flourishing by creating wealth.

On commencing operations, revenues are earned, which one hopes are high enough to result in a profit. Hence, we start with EAT in Table 8.8 as the genesis of our cash flow analysis, a measure that explicitly includes all known sources of revenues (inflows) and expenses (outflows), and accruals. It is a mixture of cash and non-cash revenues and expenses. To approximate cash earnings, *Cash from Operations* (A.5 to K.5) results by adding back non-cash expenses, such as *Depreciation* (A.2 to K.2), *Amortisation* (A.3 to K.3), and *Provisions* (A.4 to K.4).

We also know that not all revenues or operating expenses are transacted on a cash basis. However, this is not made apparent when EBITDA or EBIT is used instead.

Excluding cash and securities, credit and collection policies (and practices) impact the changes in WCR (A.6 to K.6) by following these relationships:

- ΔCurrent Assets (ΔCA): An increase is a use of our cash to finance our customers.
- ΔCurrent Liabilities (ΔCL): An increase is a source of financing from our suppliers.
- ΔWCR = ΔCL - ΔCA: If positive, we are generating cash (or vice versa) by reducing current assets or increasing payables from the prior year.

As we learned from WCR, $ACCGT_B$ is extending more generous credit terms to its customers, while being held under shorter leases by its suppliers. Hence, ΔWCR is negative (A.6 to K.6). Deducting this amount from *Cash from Operations* (A.5 to K.5), we have *Operating Cash Flows* (OpCF) (A.7 to K.7). In effect, this is the internally generated cash available to managers to fund their investing prior to any recourse to third-party financing or equity.

5.1   Pacing capital expenditures and its long tail

Investing is considered a discretionary decision by managers. In theory, managers may pursue an expansion, or forego an opportunity, subject to the firm's ability to fund the

Levers of Value

Table 8.8: Operating Cash and Its Genesis

Advance Combined Cycle Gas Turbine Baseload — ACCGT$_B$ under ACCGT$_M$ Wholesale Market

Column/Line	Cash Flow Analysis	Acronym	Unit	0 A	1 B	2 C	3 D	4 E	5 F	6 G	7 H	8 I	9 J	10 K
1	Earnings after Tax	EAT	$ mln	0	2	2	2	119	132	146	160	119	104	86
2	Depreciation	DPN$_j$	$ mln	0	0	0	0	27	27	27	27	27	27	33
3	Amortisation	AMRT$_j$	$ mln	0	0	0	0	0	0	0	0	0	0	0
4	Provisions	PRVN$_j$	$ mln	0	0	0	0	0	0	0	0	0	0	0
5	**Cash from Operations**	COPN	$ mln	**0**	**2**	**2**	**2**	**146**	**158**	**172**	**187**	**145**	**131**	**119**
6	Change in Working Capital Requirements	ΔWCR	$ mln	0	0	0	0	−77	−12	−12	−12	37	12	12
7	Operating Cash Flows "Cash" from Earnings Analysis	OpCF	$ mln	**0**	**2**	**2**	**2**	**69**	**146**	**160**	**175**	**182**	**143**	**131**
8	**Earnings before Interest, Tax, Depreciation and Amortisation**	EBITDA	$ mln	**0**	**0**	**0**	**0**	**215**	**234**	**253**	**273**	**211**	**189**	**168**

Source: Author's calculations using raw data from EIA.

investment (e.g. internal cash flows, borrow, or raise equity). For operational assets, however, capital expenditures are not entirely discretionary. Once an asset is made operational, continual expenditures are needed to keep it operationally efficient (Table 8.9).

To simplify, maintenance capex forms part of capital expenditures (A.2/4 to K.2/4) that are incurred on a five-year cycle. It is deducted from *Operating Cash Flows* (A.1 to K.1) to derive *Operating Free Cash Flows* (OpFCF) (A.5 to K.5).

The mismatch between cash inflows (from earning revenues) and disbursements (resulting from investing) creates temporal gaps in cash flows (A.5 to D.5). In anticipating this lumpy disbursement, managers could plan ahead in funding the next round of maintenance capex (K.5). Fortunately for $ACCGT_B$, *OpFCF* is accumulated (E.5 to J.5) that far exceeds the planned disbursement (K.5).

Forewarned is forearmed when managers come prepared to fund continual and lumpy cash outflows that are otherwise ignored, or managers lose sight of the need to manage maintenance capex.

When starting up the venture, how $ACCGT_B$ could be funded is a strategic decision. Borrowing too much could impair its ability to service future interest and principal repayments. Injecting too much equity may forego some of the benefits of financing the venture with cheaper debt.

The optimal level is an artful judgement that recognises managerial risk aversion, costs of financing, and the state of capital markets. Along the way, project financing has convinced enough managers that 70% debt and 30% equity are optimal for funding capital-intensive investments, such as energy and infrastructure.

For $ACCGT_B$, we simulate project financing's heuristic as a starting point and present the results in Table 8.10. Arguably, the strength of *OpFCF* could comfortably achieve a more rapid deleveraging. Following project financing's logic, where financing with cheaper debt could raise equity returns, $ACCGT_B$ could justify significantly higher borrowings.

The math looks good. After fulfilling its financial obligations, lenders get paid their interest and principal. Equity providers earn dividends that are set at 50% of EAT and any residual cash that accrue to shareholders at the end of the firm's operating life as a single asset entity.

Human preference to avoid facing adverse events constrain, and hence limit, the influence of overly rational urge to borrow to the hilt. I recall my various conversations

Levers of Value — 443

Table 8.9: Investing and Calls on Cash Flow

Column/Line	Cash Flow Analysis	Acronym	Unit	Advance Combined Cycle Gas Turbine Baseload — ACCGT$_B$ under ACCGT$_M$ Wholesale Market										
				0	1	2	3	4	5	6	7	8	9	10
				A	B	C	D	E	F	G	H	I	J	K
1	Operating Cash Flows	OpCF	$ mln	0	2	2	2	69	146	160	175	182	143	131
2	Capital Expenditures	CPX	$ mln	0	265	265	265	0	0	0	0	0	0	199
3	Other Asset Additions	OCPX	$ mln	0	0	0	0	0	0	0	0	0	0	0
4	Other Asset Disposals	ODISP	$ mln	0	0	0	0	0	0	0	0	0	0	0
5	Operating Free Cash Flows	OpFCF	$ mln	0	−263	−263	−263	69	146	160	175	182	143	−67
	"Cash" from Earnings Analysis													
6	Earnings before Interest and Tax	EBIT	$ mln	0	0	0	0	189	208	227	246	185	163	135

Source: Author's calculations using raw data from EIA.

Table 8.10: Appropriating Residual Cash

Advance Combined Cycle Gas Turbine Baseload — ACCGT$_B$ under ACCGT$_M$ Wholesale Market

Column/Line	Cash Flow Analysis	Acronym	Unit	0 A	1 B	2 C	3 D	4 E	5 F	6 G	7 H	8 I	9 J	10 K
1	**Operating Free Cash Flows**	OpFCF	$ mln	0	−263	−263	−263	69	146	160	175	182	143	−67
2	Additional Borrowing	BRW	$ mln	186	186	186	0	0	0	0	0	0	0	0
3	Repayment of Borrowing	RPY	$ mln	0	0	0	0	−9	−19	−28	−28	−28	−28	−28
4	**Available Cash for Disbursement**	ACD	$ mln	186	−78	−78	−263	60	127	132	147	154	115	−95
5	Dividends Paid	DIV	$ mln	0	0	0	0	60	66	73	80	59	52	43
6	Equity Issued or Bought Back	ΔEQTY	$ mln	80	80	80	0	0	0	0	0	0	0	0
7	**Change in Cash**	ΔCsh	$ mln	265	2	2	−263	−0	62	59	67	95	63	−138

Source: Author's calculations using raw data from EIA.

with Feliciano Fuster: He would rather reserve his financial firepower to seize game-changing opportunities that would catapult Endesa as a global energy player. This he achieved while he was at the helm.

Financial strength opens opportunities for growth. In repaying debt, the firm strengthens its credit, thus enhancing its standing in capital markets. With well-remunerated shareholders, and presumably welcoming fiscal authority, future opportunities may benefit from this goodwill.

6
Valuing Stakeholder Returns

We have come full circle in our quest for the "correct" cash flow measure. A pending issue, however, remains. If *EBITDA* and *EBIT* significantly overstate the cash flows an investment generates, how do we reconcile its popular usage to what the firms actually generate?

I propose this reconciliation in Table 8.11 with a utopian presumption.

In selling its energy, $ACCGT_B$ transacts entirely in cash, where no receivables are created. In purchasing, it follows the same mode, hence avoiding any payables. With fuel suppliers fully synchronised with production, delivery is made in perfect coordination with energy production and sales.

In this "cash-only" society, debt or equity are at par where no interest is paid or earned. Taxes are likewise waived given that all public services are paid for when used, with the government operating at no cost to the firm.

In this utopian world, *EAT* (E.1) is adjusted using Year 4 as an example. *Tax* (E.2) and *interest expenses* (E.3) are added back, while *interest income* (E.4) is subtracted. The resulting adjusted *EAT* (E.5) is equivalent to *EBIT* (E.6).

If *depreciation* (E.7) is added back to adjusted *EAT* (E.5), *EBITDA* (E.8) is obtained.

The adjustments to *OpFCF* is more nuanced. Conforming to accounting's accrual system, *capital expenditures* (A.9 to K.9) are added back to *OpFCF* (A.8 to K.8). Given that *current assets* and *liabilities* are all set to zero, ΔWCR is nil. We simply add back ΔWCR (A.10 to K.10), together with the other adjustments we previously made to

Dynamic Decisions

Table 8.11: Reconciliation of "Cash Flows" Measures

Column/Line	Reconciliation	Acronym	Unit	0 A	1 B	2 C	3 D	4 E	5 F	6 G	7 H	8 I	9 J	10 K
				\multicolumn{11}{c}{Advance Combined Cycle Gas Turbine Baseload — $ACCGT_B$ under $ACCGT_M$ Wholesale Market}
1	**Earnings after Tax**	EAT	$ mln	0	2	2	2	119	132	146	160	119	104	86
	Add Back:													
2	Tax	TAX	$ mln	0	1	1	1	51	56	63	69	51	45	37
3	Interest Expense	INTEx	$ mln	0	0	0	0	19	19	19	18	17	16	15
	Subtract:													
4	Interest Income	INT_{In}	$ mln	0	3	3	3	1	0	0	1	2	2	3
5	**Earnings after Tax: Under a Cash-only Transaction, with Zero Interest and Taxes**	EATADJ	$ mln	0	0	0	0	189	208	227	246	185	163	135
	=													
6	**Earnings before Interest and Taxes**	EBIT	$ mln	0	0	0	0	189	208	227	246	185	163	135
	+													
7	Depreciation	DPN_j	$ mln	0	0	0	0	27	27	27	27	27	27	33
	=													
8	**Earnings before Interest, Taxes, Depreciation and Amortisation**	EBITDA	$ mln	0	0	0	0	215	234	253	273	211	189	168
8	**Operating Free Cash Flows**	OpFCF	$ mln	0	−263	−263	−263	69	146	160	175	182	143	−67
	Add Back:													
9	Capital Expenditure	CPX	$ mln	0	265	265	265	0	0	0	0	0	0	199

Table 8.11: (*Continued*)

Column/Line	Reconciliation	Acronym	Unit	Advance Combined Cycle Gas Turbine Baseline — ACCGT$_B$ under ACCGT$_M$ Wholesale Market										
				0	1	2	3	4	5	6	7	8	9	10
				A	B	C	D	E	F	G	H	I	J	K
10	Change in Working Capital Requirements	ΔWCR	$ mln	0	0	0	0	77	12	12	12	-37	-12	-12
11	Tax	TAX	$ mln	0	1	1	1	51	56	63	69	51	45	37
12	Interest Expense	INTEx	$ mln	0	0	0	0	19	19	19	18	17	16	15
	Subtract:													
13	Interest Income	INTIn	$ mln	0	3	3	3	1	0	0	1	2	2	3
14	Depreciation	DPN$_j$	$ mln	0	0	0	0	27	27	27	27	27	27	33
15	**Operating Free Cash Flow: Under a Cash-only Transaction, with Zero Interest and Taxes, with Capex Provided for**	OpFCFADJ	$ mln	0	0	0	-0	189	208	227	246	185	163	135
	=													
16	**Earnings before Interest and Taxes**	EBIT	$ mln	0	0	0	0	189	208	227	246	185	163	135
	+													
17	Depreciation	DPN$_j$	$ mln	0	0	0	0	27	27	27	27	27	27	33
	=													
18	**Earnings before Interest, Taxes, Depreciation and Amortisation**	EBITDA	$ mln	0	0	0	0	215	234	253	273	211	189	168

Source: Author's calculations using EIA raw data.

EAT, to obtain the equivalence of adjusted *OpFCF* (A.15 to K.15) to *EBIT* (A.16 to K.15).

With *capital expenditures* (A.9 to K.9) reported on an accrual basis, their period expense is the straight-line *depreciation* (A.17 to K.17) over its asset life. Adding this to adjusted *OpFCF* (A.15 to K.15), we have *EBITDA* (A.18 to K.18).

Having performed the reconciliation, we can now move back to the real world where managers reside, and make decisions accordingly, to pursue their purpose (whatever that may be).

6.1 Apportioning firm value to debt and equity

In this sub-utopian market reality, the value of $ACCGT_B$ as a firm is premised on *OpFCF*. The value is apportioned to lenders through the interest paid and principal repayments, with equity remunerated with dividends and any residual cash distribution. Other stakeholders had the first bite of the cherry, with fuel suppliers and labour gaining a sizeable share of revenues.

We now address a fundamental question: What discount rate do we use to estimate today's money value for the future cash flows $ACCGT_B$ expects to earn?

The discount rates spark continuing debates that remain unresolved among academe and practitioners. Pablo Fernandez, in his periodic surveys of equity risk premium, a principal component of WACC, persists with a consistent message (Fernandez et al., 2019). The premium varies widely within each cluster (e.g. academics or practitioners), industry, or valuation experts.

Fernandez (2019) attribute this to a failure to recognise that stakeholders have different expectations and risk thresholds. He noted: "There is a schizophrenic approach to valuation. While all authors admit to different expectations of equity cash flows, most authors look for a unique discount rate. It seems as if expectations of equity cash flows are formed in a democratic regime, while discount rate is determined in a dictatorship."

To this, I would add: In a desire for simplicity, some oil and gas majors would go as far as applying a single discount rate based on their treasury's dictate.

The reason is not a lack of intelligence, given that the respondents represent among society's best talents. Quite simply, there is no known methodology that satisfies all needs and hence accepted by theorists and practitioners.

I propose to use WACC as a proxy for expected capital costs, while using the hurdle rate, *r*, as a required threshold for commitment. Here's why.

WACC explicitly recognises the resulting costs from combining debt and equity, albeit the use of risk premium is a point of disagreement among experts. A more serious drawback is its inability to distinguish between long- or short-duration assets. For example, WACC of 3.46%, if used as the rate to recover asset value, would imply 28.9 years to "earn back" the amount invested. While this is within the life of long-duration assets such as $ACCGT_B$, $Wind_{ON}$'s 20 years life may fall short.

Hurdle rates, calculated as the sum of risk-free rate (r_f), risk premium (r_p), and the asset recovery rate (ARR), explicitly consider asset life. This is particularly relevant for shorter-duration assets, where the hurdle rate should be higher to fully recover the asset value (or capital invested). For example, ANuke's 40 years life would have ARR of 2.5% (e.g. 100/40), while PVT_M's 20 years life would require ARR of 5.0% (e.g. 100/20).

We now turn to Charts 8.4(A) and 8.4(B) to examine how $ACCGT_B$'s valuation stack up. In splitting cash flows into a period with explicit estimates (periods 1–10), followed by normalised estimates, we can ascertain the robustness under volatile and stable prices.

$ACCGT_B$ comfortably meet both viability thresholds, following NPV's decision rules. Benefiting from low capex, $ACCGT_B$ is sufficiently cash-generative as to recover its capex in less than a decade from commercial operations under both discount rates. In effect, the period of normalised cash flows provides a sizeable surplus to its NPV.

This is validated by the payback period, as shown in Chart 8.4(C), of less than six years from the start of commercial operations using OpFCF. Including the three years to build the asset, this comprises about the first decade from the initial investment.

The valuation gaps between *OpFCF* and *EBIT*, and how NPVs differ between the two discount rates, have a deeper message for managers. In framing the problem that they aim to solve, applying accepted financial tools without fully understanding its premises, *EBIT* could overestimate the value. Given the differences between *EBIT* and *OpFCF*, it is substantial as to potentially change the decision from commit to reject. Fortunately for $ACCGT_B$, *OpFCFs* are sufficiently robust to make such overvaluation less important to the decision.

Operationally, the implications could be more relevant. *EBIT* conveys a tranquil future without the need to accumulate internally generated cash to fund maintenance capex in period 10. This may encourage a more aggressive debt repayment or generously reward equity providers with bigger dividends.

Dynamic Decisions

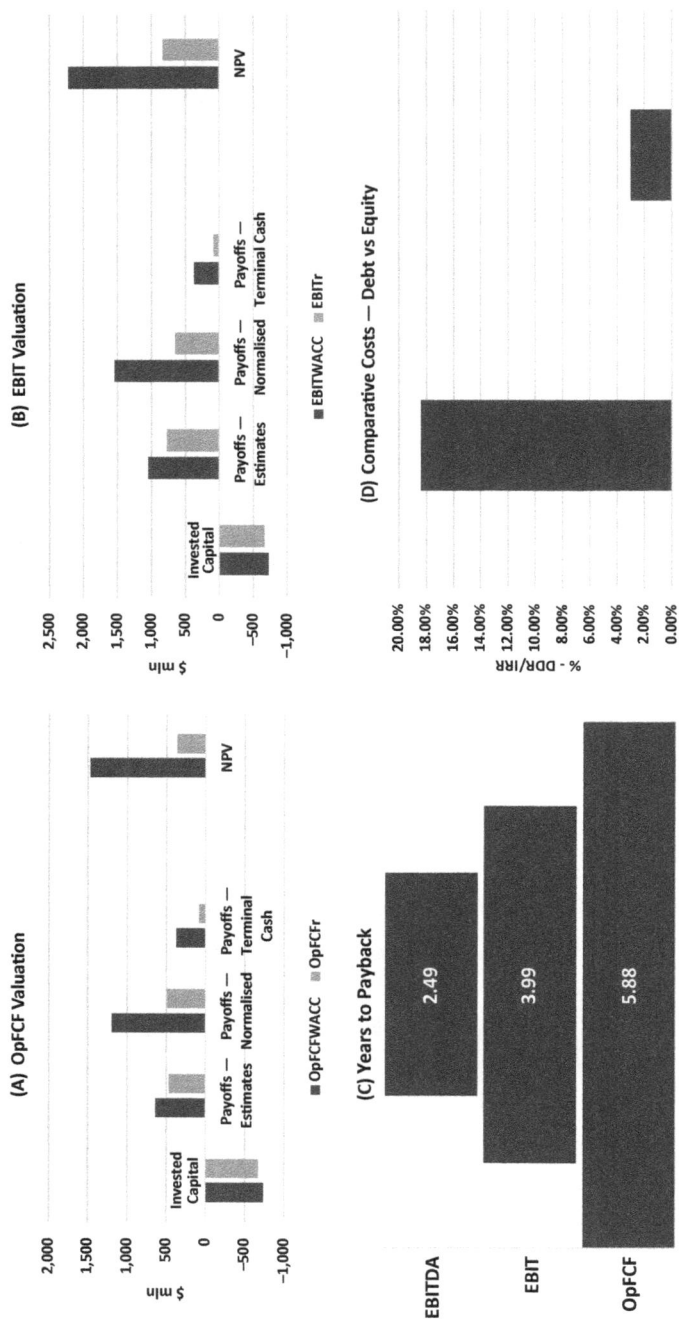

Chart 8.4: Comparative Valuations

Unfortunately, as *OpFCF* reality sets in, managers may be caught by surprise of a cash crunch that was not anticipated or the payback taking longer than the 3.99 years suggested by EBIT.

A way around the problematic discount rates is to use the *internal rate of return* (IRR). This estimates how much lenders and equity providers could earn on their money under project financing's accepted capital structure.

Our simulations show these results in Chart 8.4(D), where bond earns an IRR of 2.98% compared to equity's DDR of 18.38%.

This difference in returns partly answers why shareholders would find borrowing financially attractive. By paying a "rent" for the use of third-party funds, the cash flow that they forego in paying interest and principal is more than compensated by the increase in their DDR.

The disparity in returns may raise questions on project financing's risk–returns allocation. For cash-accretive investments, this may prove a valid concern. One would argue that a struggling investment, where dividends have to be foregone, being the senior claimant has some benefits when interest and principal repayments are secured.

However, with project financed investments structured as special purpose vehicles, a struggling venture may run out of cash as to be unable to secure the obligations to lenders. Without recourse to shareholders, the complex web of contracts to secure lenders' money may have to be re-examined by financiers.

6.2 Creating and managing value

Under *residual income,* value is created when returns exceed its capital costs (e.g. WACC or r). In its unembellished form, residual income can directly relate managerial actions to feasible financial outcomes that are familiar to managers, as illustrated in Table 8.12.

Returns on Invested Capital (RoIC) is the product of the cash margin (D.1) and asset efficiency or the ratio of revenue to *invested capital* (D.6). $ACCGT_B$ is described as a low margin, high asset efficiency asset, which yields RoIC in excess of its WACC and *r*.

A low cash margin implies that the operating costs are higher than competing technologies, such as zero fuel cost renewables. This could offer scope for improvement in cost control that could expand the cash margins.

Table 8.12: Deconstructing Residual Income and Value Creation

Column/Line	Value Creation	Acronym	Unit	Advance Combined Cycle Gas Turbine Baseload — $ACCGT_B$ under $ACCGT_M$ Wholesale Market									
				1 A	2 B	3 C	4 D	5 E	6 F	7 G	8 H	9 I	10 J
1	**Cash Margin on Revenue**	REVMGN	%	26.76%	25.45%	24.46%	23.68%	26.20%	27.53%	28.12%			
2	Earnings before Interest, Tax, Depreciation, and Amortisation	EBITDA	$ mln	215	234	253	273	211	189	168			
3	Maintenance Capex	MNTCAPX	$ mln	27	27	27	27	27	27	33			
4	Operating Profit before Tax	OPBT	$ mln	189	208	227	246	185	163	135			
5	Revenue	REV	$ mln	705	815	928	1,040	705	591	479			
6	**Revenue to Invested Capital**	REV2IC	%	83.42%	98.09%	113.51%	129.47%	95.37%	84.39%	56.12%			
7	Net Fixed Asset	NFA	$ mln	769	742	716	689	663	636	802			
8	Working Capital Requirements	WCR	$ mln	77	89	102	114	77	65	53			
9	Invested Capital	IC	$ mln	846	831	817	803	740	701	854			
10	**Return on Invested Capital — Gross**	GRoIC	%	22.32%	24.96%	27.77%	30.66%	24.98%	23.23%	15.78%			

Table 8.12: (*Continued*)

Column/Line	Value Creation	Acronym	Unit	1 A	2 B	3 C	4 D	5 E	6 F	7 G	8 H	9 I	10 J
							Advance Combined Cycle Gas Turbine Baseload — ACCGT$_B$ Wholesale market						Under ACCGT$_M$	
11	Cash Tax Rate	TAXR	%				23.78%	24.13%	24.68%	25.21%	24.04%	23.64%	21.96%
12	Return on Invested Capital — Net	NRoIC	%				17.01%	18.94%	20.91%	22.93%	18.98%	17.74%	12.31%
13	Weighted Average Cost of Capital	WACC	%				3.35%	3.46%	3.57%	3.69%	3.84%	3.93%	4.04%
14	Residual Income Rate (NRoIC — WACC)	RIRW	%				13.66%	15.48%	17.35%	19.25%	15.14%	13.81%	8.28%
15	Hurdle Rate	r	%				8.83%	8.83%	8.83%	8.83%	8.83%	8.83%	8.83%
16	Residual Income Rate (NRoIC — r)	RIRr	%				8.18%	10.11%	12.08%	14.10%	10.15%	8.91%	3.48%

Source: Author's calculations using EIA raw data.

High asset efficiency implies that the initial asset costs are lower, which when operated under markets with supportive pricing, less capex is needed for similar revenues. This is a structural advantage, given that once invested, that ratio is unlikely to be altered other than achieving higher prices that could raise revenues.

On the side of capital costs, WACC varies with the capital structure, where higher debt within limits would tend to lower the capital cost. Recall: Victoriano Reinoso used this to justify Union Fenosa's higher leverage than Endesa.

Taxes and how the investment could be fiscally optimised is a plank for expanding equity value. By minimising taxes, more value accrues to equity.

In applying residual income analysis to $ACCGT_B$, we can explicitly identify the levers of value with the highest impact to optimise the residual income rate (RIR) (or more popularly, economic value added). In general, positive RIRs increase the value of the *Invested Capital* (IC) (or vice versa).

Critically, operational costs and fuel procurement are the avenues for expanding EBIT, together with timely and effective *maintenance capex*. On the asset side, tight control over capex is a "gift from the past," when assets are built at lower costs than peers without impairing their operational reliability. Control over *WCR* could reduce *invested capital*.

In using either WACC (A.13 to J.13) or hurdle rate (A.15 to J.15), $ACCGT_B$'s *NRoICs* (A.12 to J.12) exceed the cost of capital, implying that it creates value.

Borrowing from NPV, we calculate the present value of the economic profits as follows:

$$\text{Economic Profit (EP)} = (RIR * IC) \tag{8.2}$$

$$\text{Economic Value Added (EVA)} = \sum [(EP_0) + (EP_t)/(1+r)^t \ldots (EPn)/(1+r)^n] \tag{8.3}$$

$$\text{Equity Value} = [(IC + EVA) - (Debt) + (Cash)] \tag{8.4}$$

The equity value, in effect, reconnects residual income to "Enterprise Value." Clearly, set up in this way, how strategic and tactical actions are traced to its outcomes are made transparent, if not readily understood, which facilitates strategic dialogue.

Applying this to $ACCGT_B$, the decision dashboard is likely to focus managerial actions on (a) how to manage operational cash margins by (b) appreciating how the

Levers of Value

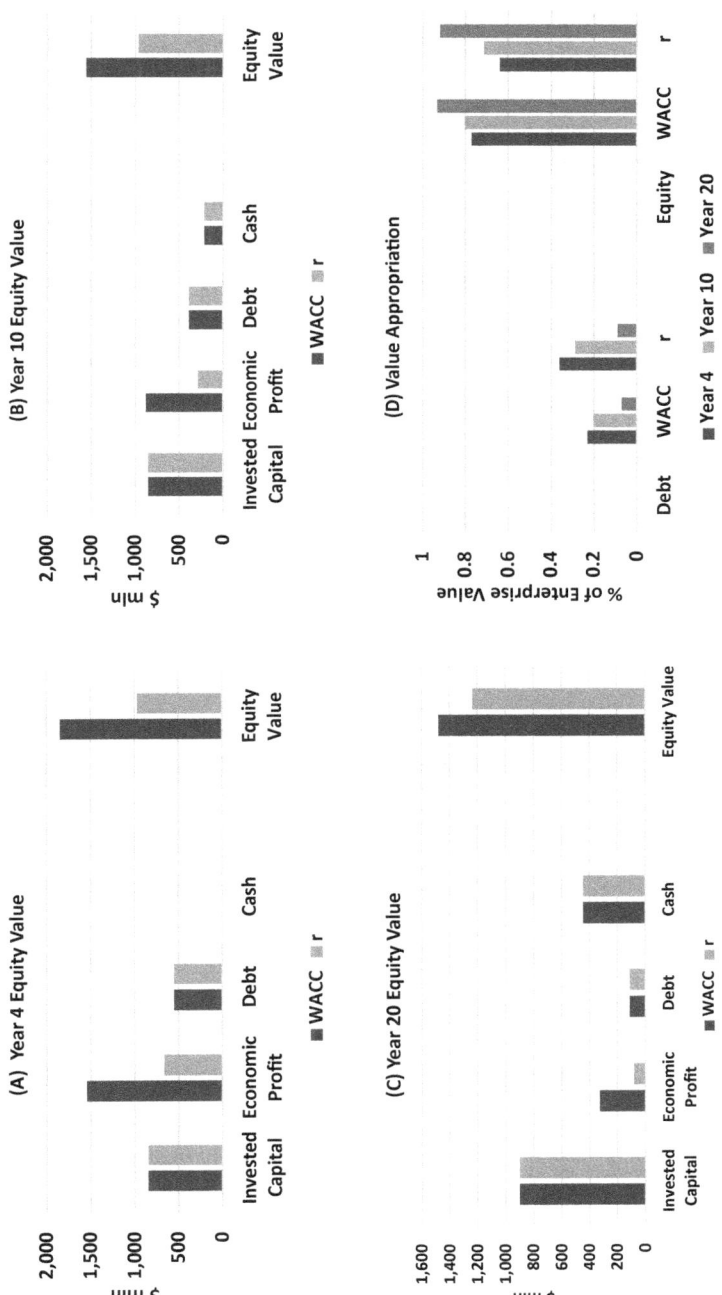

Chart 8.5: Evolution and Appropriation of Equity Value

choice of technology could lock in costs, thus (c) instilling disciplined capex management. On the funding side, WACC and hurdle rates provide a framework that instils coherence in financial strategy.

A simplified dashboard is shown as an example in Chart 8.5. Using WACC and hurdle rates as our reference thresholds for value creation, as fixed assets are depreciated (or eroded), maintenance capex restores its value by keeping it (one hopes) operationally effective (A to C). As the $ACCGT_B$ approaches its end of operating life (C), the remaining value of economic profit diminishes. In its place, declining debt and increasing cash accrue most of the value created to equity providers (D).

The picture is not a pretty one for project financiers. Bearing 70% of the initial funding, it appropriates less than 40% of the enterprise value (D). Over time, equity providers take most of the value created.

7
Incorporating Value and Strategic Dialogue

How financial models are set up to inform managerial decision-making are shown in Appendices 8A–8E. The calculations simulate how the financials of $ACCGT_B$ operating under a power market dominated by gas fired supplies are likely to evolve.

Financial analysis is a core competency of managers that, if used appropriately, could inform how they frame their decisions. By reframing how managers use financial data, and how they are incorporated into strategic dialogues, sound financial analyses become core to informing managerial decisions. Specifically:

1. Operational hurdles derived in earnings analyses could inform how tactical actions (e.g. operating cost control) are prioritised according to their financial impact, and broader stakeholders' interests, to enhance operating viability.
2. Strategic actions that conform to capital deployment are made dynamic and adaptive to how the firms' financial circumstances vary. Informed by early signals from operations, which is largely influenced by how markets evolve, timely actions on capital expenditures, borrowings, and dividends, among others, could prove crucial to sustaining financial performance.

3. Integrating strategic and operational actions into a common framework, monetising and appropriating returns to stakeholders inform how competing interests could be reconciled and made compatible (or vice versa).

Finally, by connecting managerial actions to financial outcomes, residual income analysis may cement how sound financial analyses could facilitate strategic dialogues that enhance performance.

A critical lesson is not only to have a deep understanding of how business works and how its finances reflect the outcomes of decisions that managers took. Argyris (2010) may have stumbled on why managers often fail to achieve what they aspired to when investing.

Argyris noted: "The 'best and the brightest' fail to see problems they are creating. Individuals learn to protect themselves if caught creating or going along with traps. For example, they blame others or the system. They deny any personal responsibility. Next, they deny that they are denying by making the subject undiscussable. In order to make that strategy work, they must make *what cannot be discussed* undiscussable."

To get out of these well-laid traps, managers need to shift the purpose and focus of financial analyses from *what an investment could earn* into a well-informed dialogue on *why* and *how* chosen technologies earn what they earn.

By ignoring the reasons why businesses work the way they do, with managers simply filling the gaps as they emerge, managers would inadvertently set their ventures to fail. This is what Argyris describes as corporate traps that impede learning and innovation. Worse, it encourages managers to hide behind financial tools for the ills that befall them when things do not work out as they expected.

Sounds familiar? A sobering thought to contemplate how billions of cash are entrusted to a herd that finds comfort in numbers.

Bibliography

Ambrose, J. (2019). Energy bills for millions of households to fall after gas prices halve. The Guardian, December 26, 2019.

Argyris, C. (2000). *Flawed Advice and the Management Trap*. Oxford: Oxford University Press.

Argyris, C. (2003). A life full of learning. *Organisational Studies*, 24(7), 1178–1192.

Argyris, C. (2010). *Organisational Traps: Leadership, Culture, Organisation Design*. Oxford: Oxford University Press.

Bridle, G. C., Bowen, R. M., and Wallace, J. S. (2005). Evidence on EVA. *Journal of Applied Corporate Finance*, 12(2), Summer 2005, 69–79.

The Business Roundtable (2019). Business roundtable redefines the purpose of a corporation to promote 'an economy that serves all Americans'. *Business Roundtable*, August 19, 2019.

Damodaran, A. (1996). *Investment Valuation: Tools and Techniques for Determining the Value of any Asset*. New York: Wiley & Sons.

Faus, J. (1995). Operational finance: Analysis and diagnosis. *Technical Notes, FN-386-E 0-296-002*, IESE Business School.

Fernandez, P. (2019). Equity premium: Historical, expected, required and implied. Social Science Research Network, May 18, 2019.

Fernandez, P., Martinez, M., and Fernandez Acin, I. (2019). Market risk premium and risk-free rate used for 69 countries in 2019: A survey. Social Science Research Network, March 23, 2019.

Fisher, I. (2012). *The Money Illusion*. New Haven, Connecticut: Start Publishing, Reprint.

Forbes. (2007). E.ON backs away from Endesa. Forbes Magazine, April 3, 2007.

Gordon, M. J., and Shapiro, E. (1956). Capital equipment analysis: The required rate of profit. *Management Science*, 3(1), 1–115.

House of Commons (1995). *Trafalgar House Bid for Northern Electric*. Tabled January 10, 1995, 1994–1995 Session.

Imam, S., Barker, R., and Clubb, C. (2008). The use of valuation models by UK investment analysts. *European Accounting Review*, 17(3), 503–535.

Itskevich, J. (2020). What Caused the Stock Market Crash of 1987? https://historynewsnetwork.org/article/895. Accessed on March 9, 2020.

Kim, S., and Kim, S. H. (2006). *Global Corporate Finance, 6th ed*. Malden, MA: Blackwell Publishing.

Koller, T., Dobbs, R., and Huyett, B. (2011). *Value: The Four Cornerstones of Corporate Finance*. New Jersey: McKinsey and Company.

Koller, T., Goedhart, M., and Wessels, D. (2015). *Valuation: Measuring and Managing the Value of Companies, 6th ed.* New Jersey: John Wiley & Sons.

Kollewe, J. (2019). Regulator orders water bills in England and Wales to be cut by GBP50. *The Guardian*, July 18, 2019.

Modigliani, F., and Miller, M. H. (1958). The cost of capital, corporate finance and the theory of investment. *The American Economic Review*, 48(3), 261–297.

Rappaport, A. (1998). *Creating Shareholder Value: A Guide for Managers and Investors* (Revised and Updated). New York: The Free Press.

Ruano, C., and Dinkloh, P. (2007). Enel, Acciona bid for Endesa, E.ON takes assets. Reuters, April 3, 2007.

Seuring, S., and Gold, S. (2013). Sustainability management beyond corporate boundaries: From stakeholders to performance. *Journal of Cleaner Production*, 56(1), October 2013, 1–6.

Shapiro, A. C. (1999). *Multinational Financial Management, 6th ed.* New York: John Wiley & Sons.

Stern, J. M., Stewart III, G. B., and Chew, D. H, Jr. (1996). EVA®: An integrated financial management system. *European Financial Management*, 2(2), July 1996, 223–245.

Tai, F.-M., and Chuang, S. H. (2014). Corporate social responsibility. *iBusiness*, 6, 117–130.

Thaler, R. (2015). *Misbehaving: The Making of Behavioural Economics.* New York: W. W. Norton & Company.

Appendices: Comparative Power Generation Financial Analyses

Advance Combined Cycle Gas Turbine Baseload (ACCGT$_B$) under Gas System

8A: ACCGT$_B$ under Gas System — Balance Sheet

Advance Combined Cycle Gas Turbine Baseload — ACCGT$_B$ under ACCGT$_M$ Wholesale Market

Column (A)/ Line (1)	Balance Sheet	Acronym	Unit	0 A	1 B	2 C	3 D	4 E	5 F	6 G	7 H	8 I	9 J	10 K	Terminal Period L
1	Cash and Securities	Csh	$ mln	265	267	269	6	5	67	126	193	288	351	213	1,133
2	Current Assets	CA	$ mln	0	0	0	0	115	135	154	174	115	95	75	115
3	Receivables	RCV	$ mln	0	0	0	0	39	45	51	57	39	32	26	39
4	Inventory	INV	$ mln	0	0	0	0	38	45	53	60	38	30	23	38
5	Others	OCA	$ mln	0	0	0	0	39	45	51	57	39	32	26	39
6	Fixed Assets	FA	$ mln	0	265	530	795	769	742	716	689	663	636	802	517
7	Gross Fixed Assets	GFA	$ mln	0	0	0	0	795	795	795	795	795	795	994	1,590
8	Accumulated Depreciation	ACDPN	$ mln	0	0	0	0	27	53	80	106	133	159	192	1,073
9	Asset under Construction	ACON	$ mln	0	265	530	795	0	0	0	0	0	0	0	0
10	Others	OFA	$ mln	0	0	0	0	0	0	0	0	0	0	0	0

8A: (*Continued*)

Column (A)/ Line (1)	Balance Sheet	Acronym	Unit	Advance Combined Cycle Gas Turbine Baseload — ACCGT$_B$ under ACCGT$_M$ Wholesale Market											Terminal Period
				0 A	1 B	2 C	3 D	4 E	5 F	6 G	7 H	8 I	9 J	10 K	L
11	Accumulated Depreciation	ACDPN	$ mln	0	0	0	0	0	0	0	0	0	0	0	0
12	**Total Assets**	TA	$ mln	265	532	799	801	889	944	996	1,056	1,065	1,082	1,089	1,764
13	**Current Liabilities**	CL	$ mln	0	0	0	0	38	45	53	60	38	30	23	38
14	Payables	PYB	$ mln	0	0	0	0	19	23	26	30	19	15	11	19
15	Others	OCL	$ mln	0	0	0	0	19	23	26	30	19	15	11	19
16	**Long-term Liabilities**	LTL	$ mln	186	371	557	557	547	529	501	473	445	417	390	0
17	Borrowings	DEBT	$ mln	186	371	557	557	547	529	501	473	445	417	390	0
18	Provisions	PRVLT	$ mln	0	0	0	0	0	0	0	0	0	0	0	0
19	**Capital**	CAP	$ mln	80	161	242	244	304	370	443	523	582	634	677	1,726
20	Equity	EQTY	$ mln	80	159	239	239	239	239	239	239	239	239	239	239
21	Retained Earnings	RE	$ mln	0	2	4	6	65	131	204	284	344	396	439	1,488
22	**Total Liabilities and Capital**	TLC	$ mln	265	532	799	801	889	944	996	1,056	1,065	1,082	1,089	1,764

Source: Author's calculations using EIA raw data.

8B: ACCGT$_B$ — Cash Flow Analysis

Advance Combined Cycle Gas Turbine Baseload — ACCGT$_B$ under ACCGT$_M$ Wholesale Market

Column (A)/ Line (1)	Cash Flow Analysis	Acronym	Unit	0 A	1 B	2 C	3 D	4 E	5 F	6 G	7 H	8 I	9 J	10 K
1	Earnings after Tax	EAT	$ mln	0	2	2	2	119	132	146	160	119	104	86
2	Depreciation	DPN$_j$	$ mln	0	0	0	0	27	27	27	27	27	27	33
3	Amortisation	AMRT$_j$	$ mln	0	0	0	0	0	0	0	0	0	0	0
4	Provisions	PRVN$_j$	$ mln	0	0	0	0	0	0	0	0	0	0	0
5	**Cash from Operations**	**COPN**	$ mln	**0**	**2**	**2**	**2**	**146**	**158**	**172**	**187**	**145**	**131**	**119**
6	Change in Working Capital Requirements	ΔWCR	$ mln	0	0	0	0	−77	−12	−12	−12	37	12	12
7	**Operating Cash Flows**	**OpCF**	$ mln	**0**	**2**	**2**	**2**	**69**	**146**	**160**	**175**	**182**	**143**	**131**
8	Capital Expenditures	CPX	$ mln	0	265	265	265	0	0	0	0	0	0	199
9	Other Asset Additions	OCPX	$ mln	0	0	0	0	0	0	0	0	0	0	0
10	Other Asset Disposals	ODISP	$ mln	0	0	0	0	0	0	0	0	0	0	0
11	**Operating Free Cash Flows**	**OpFCF**	$ mln	**0**	**−263**	**−263**	**−263**	**69**	**146**	**160**	**175**	**182**	**143**	**−67**
12	Additional Borrowing	BRW	$ mln	186	186	186	0	0	0	0	0	0	0	0
13	Repayment of Borrowing	RPY	$ mln	0	0	0	0	−9	−19	−28	−28	−28	−28	−28
14	**Available Cash for Disbursement**	**ACD**	$ mln	**186**	**−78**	**−78**	**−263**	**60**	**127**	**132**	**147**	**154**	**115**	**−95**
15	Dividends Paid	DIV	$ mln	0	0	0	0	60	66	73	80	59	52	43
16	Equity Issued or Bought Back	ΔEQTY	$ mln	80	80	80	0	0	0	0	0	0	0	0
17	**Change in Cash**	**ΔCsh**	$ mln	**265**	**2**	**2**	**−263**	**0**	**62**	**59**	**67**	**95**	**63**	**−138**

Source: Author's calculations using EIA raw data.

Levers of Value

8C: ACCGT$_B$ Gas System — Profit & Loss Analysis

Column (A)/ Line (1)	Profit and Loss	Acronym	Unit	Advance Combined Cycle Gas Turbine Baseload — ACCGT$_B$ under ACCGT$_M$ Wholesale Market										Normalised Earnings
				1 A	2 B	3 C	4 D	5 E	6 F	7 G	8 H	9 I	10 J	K
1	**Revenues**	Rev	$ mln	**0**	**0**	**0**	**705**	**815**	**928**	**1,040**	**705**	**591**	**479**	**703**
2	Spot Prices	Ps	$/kWh	0.0482	0.0629	0.0776	0.0923	0.1070	0.1217	0.1364	0.0923	0.0776	0.0629	0.0923
3	Quantity	Q$_f$	MWh	0	0	0	7,642	7,621	7,621	7,621	7,642	7,621	7,621	7,621
4	**Cost of Fuel (Cost of Goods Sold)**	FFC (CoGS)	$ mln	**0**	**0**	**0**	**460**	**550**	**642**	**734**	**460**	**367**	**275**	**459**
5	Cash Costs	C$_j$	$ mln	0	0	0	438	524	611	699	438	349	262	437
6	Cash Costs per kWh	CFkWh	$/kWh	0	0	0	0	0.0688	0.0802	0.0917	0.0573	0.0458	0.0344	0.0573
7	Quantity	Q$_j$	MWh	0	0	0	7,642	7,621	7,621	7,621	7,642	7,621	7,621	7,621
8	Ancillary Fuel Costs	CAF$_j$	$ mln	0	0	0	22	26	31	35	22	17	13	22
9	Quantity	Q$_j$	MWh	0	0	0	382	381	381	381	382	381	381	381
10	**Gross Cash Profit**	GCP	$ mln	**0**	**0**	**0**	**246**	**265**	**286**	**306**	**246**	**225**	**204**	**245**
11	% Gross Cash Margin	GCM	%	0.00%	0.00%	0.00%	0.00%	32.53%	30.79%	29.43%	34.82%	37.97%	42.61%	34.82%
12	**Operating Cash Costs**	OpCC	$ mln	**0**	**0**	**0**	**30**	**31**	**32**	**33**	**34**	**35**	**36**	**37**
13	Financial Fixed O&M	FO&M	$ mln	0	0	0	11	12	12	12	13	13	14	14
14	Cash Costs per kWh	FO&MkWh	$/kWh	0	0	0	0	0	0	0	0	0	0	0
15	Financial Variable O&M	VO&M	$ mln	0	0	0	18	18	19	19	20	20	21	22
16	Cash Costs per kWh	VO&MkWh	$/kwh	0	0	0	0	0.0024	0.0024	0.0025	0.0026	0.0027	0.0028	0.0028
17														
18	Cash Ancillary Costs	CAC$_j$	$ mln	0	0	0	1	1	2	2	2	2	2	2

(*Continued*)

8C: (*Continued*)

Column (A)/ Line (1)	Profit and Loss	Acronym	Unit	Advance Combined Cycle Gas Turbine Baseload — ACCGT$_B$ under ACCGT$_M$ Wholesale Market										Normalised Earnings
				1 A	2 B	3 C	4 D	5 E	6 F	7 G	8 H	9 I	10 J	K
19	**Earnings before Interest, Taxes, Depreciation and Amortisation**	EBITDA	$ mln	**0**	**0**	**0**	**215**	**234**	**253**	**273**	**211**	**189**	**168**	**207**
20	% EBITDA Margin	EBITDA%	%	0.00%	0.00%	0.00%	30.51%	28.70%	27.32%	26.23%	29.95%	32.01%	35.03%	29.49%
21	Depreciation	DPN$_j$	$ mln	0	0	0	27	27	27	27	27	27	33	33
22	Amortisation	AMRT$_j$	$ mln	0	0	0	0	0	0	0	0	0	0	0
23	Provisions	PRVN$_j$	$ mln	0	0	0	0	0	0	0	0	0	0	0
27	**Earnings before Interest and Taxes**	EBIT	$ mln	**0**	**0**	**0**	**189**	**208**	**227**	**246**	**185**	**163**	**135**	**174**
28	% EBIT Margin	EBIT%	%	0.00%	0.00%	0.00%	26.76%	25.45%	24.46%	23.68%	26.20%	27.53%	28.12%	
29	Interest Income	INTIn	$ mln	3	3	3	1	0	0	1	2	2	3	3
30	Interest Expense	INTEx	$ mln	0	0	0	19	19	19	18	17	16	15	14
31	Others	ORC	$ mln	0	0	0	0	0	0	0	0	0	0	0
32	**Earnings before Tax**	EBT	$ mln	**3**	**3**	**3**	**171**	**188**	**208**	**229**	**169**	**149**	**123**	**163**
33	% EBT		%	0.00%	0.00%	0.00%	24.19%	23.09%	22.47%	22.04%	24.01%	25.22%	25.63%	23.17%
34	Tax	TAX	$ mln	1	1	1	51	56	63	69	51	45	37	49
35	**Earnings after Tax**	EAT	$ mln	**2**	**2**	**2**	**119**	**132**	**146**	**160**	**119**	**104**	**86**	**114**
36	% EAT		%	0.00%	0.00%	0.00%	16.93%	16.16%	15.73%	15.43%	16.80%	17.65%	17.94%	16.22%

Source: Author's calculations using EIA raw data.

Levers of Value

8D: ACCGT$_B$ under Gas System — Financial Ratios

Advance Combined Cycle Gas Turbine Baseload — ACCGT$_B$ under ACCGT$_M$ Wholesale Market

Column (A)/ Line (1)	Ratios	Acronym	Units	1 A	2 B	3 C	4 D	5 E	6 F	7 G	8 H	9 I	10 J	Definition
1	**Liquidity**													
2	Current Ratio	CR	x	—	—	—	3.05	2.98	2.93	2.89	3.05	3.15	3.32	CA/CL
3	Quick Ratio	QR	x	—	—	—	0.14	1.48	2.39	3.20	7.63	11.64	9.41	Csh/CL
4	**Long-term Financing**													
5	Interest Cover	IntC	x	—	—	—	9.69	10.74	12.05	13.67	10.84	10.13	8.93	EBIT/IntEx
6	Cash Fixed Charges	CshFC	x	—	—	—	0.44	0.40	0.38	0.36	0.43	0.47	0.54	EBITDA/(FFC + OpCC) or EBITDA/(CoGS + OpCC)
7	Capex Cover	CpxC	x	0.01	0.01	0.01	—	—	—	—	—	—	0.66	OpCF/CPX
8	Gearing	DE	x	2.31	2.30	2.28	1.80	1.43	1.13	0.90	0.76	0.66	0.58	DEBT/CAP
9	**Working Capital**													
10	Working Capital Requirements	WCR	$ mln	0.00	0.00	0.00	77.09	89.37	101.64	113.92	77.09	64.81	52.53	CA − CL
11	Working Capital	WCR	$ mln	266.86	268.72	5.59	82.54	156.38	228.00	306.88	364.82	415.70	265.26	(LTL + CAP) − FA
12	Cash Surplus	CshS	$ mln	267	269	6	5	67	126	193	288	351	213	WC − WCR
13	Negotiated Funding Requirements	NFR	$ mln	−267	−269	−6	−5	−67	−126	−193	−288	−351	−213	WCR − WC
14	**Funding to Clients**													

(*Continued*)

8D: (*Continued*)

Column (A)/ Line (1)	Ratios	Acronym	Units	1 A	2 B	3 C	4 D	5 E	6 F	7 G	8 H	9 I	10 J	Definition
				\multicolumn{10}{c}{Advance Combined Cycle Gas Turbine Baseload — ACCGT$_B$ under ACCGT$_M$ Wholesale Market}	
15	Average Inventory	INVAvg	$ mln	0	0	0	19	41	49	57	49	34	26	(Beginning INV + Ending INV)/2
16	Inventory Turnover	INVT	x	—	—	—	24.40	13.27	13.10	12.98	9.38	10.81	10.43	FFC/INVAvg or CoGS/INVAvg
17	Days in Inventory	INVDays	Days	—	—	—	14.96	27.50	27.86	28.13	38.89	33.75	35.00	365/INVT
18	**Credit and Collection**													
19	Average Accounts Receivable	ARAvg	$ mln	0	0	0	19	42	48	54	48	35	29	(Beginning AR + Ending AR)/2
20	Accounts Receivable Turnover	ART	x	—	—	—	36.60	19.60	19.42	19.29	14.77	16.67	16.34	Revenues/ARAvg
21	Days in Receivable	ARDays	Days	—	—	—	7.24	13.52	13.64	13.74	17.94	15.90	16.22	365/ART
22	**Suppliers' Funding**													
23	Average Accounts Payable	APAvg	$ mln	0	0	0	9	21	24	28	24	17	13	(Beginning AP + Ending Payable)/2
24	Accounts Payable Turnover	APT	x	—	—	—	48.80	26.55	26.21	25.96	18.77	21.63	20.86	(FFC/APAvg) or (CoGS/APAvg)
25	Days in Payables	APDays	Days	—	—	—	7.48	13.75	13.93	14.06	19.45	16.88	17.50	365/APT
26	**Operating and Cash Cycles**													
27	Operating Cycle	OpCyc	Days	—	—	—	26.08	54.98	62.64	70.27	66.93	49.81	42.60	INVDays + ARDays
28	Cash Cycle	CshCyc	Days	—	—	—	18.60	41.23	48.71	56.21	47.49	32.94	25.10	OpCyc − APDays

Source: Author's calculations using EIA raw data.

8E: ACCGT$_B$ under Gas System — Residual Income Analysis

Advance Combined Cycle Gas Turbine Baseload — ACCGT$_b$ under ACCGT$_M$ Wholesale Market

Column (A)/ Line (1)	Value Creation	Acronym	Unit	1 A	2 B	3 C	4 D	5 E	6 F	7 G	8 H	9 I	10 J
1	**Cash Margin on Revenue**	REVMGN	%				26.76%	25.45%	24.46%	23.68%	26.20%	27.53%	28.12%
2	Earnings before Interest, Tax, Depreciation, and Amortisation	EBITDA	$ mln				215	234	253	273	211	189	168
3	Maintenance Capex	MNTCAPX	$ mln				27	27	27	27	27	27	33
4	Operating Profit before Tax	OPBT	$ mln				189	208	227	246	185	163	135
5	Revenue	REV	$ mln				705	815	928	1,040	705	591	479
6	**Revenue to Invested Capital**	REV2IC	%				83.42%	98.09%	113.51%	129.47%	95.37%	84.39%	56.12%
7	Net Fixed Asset	NFA	$ mln				769	742	716	689	663	636	802
8	Working Capital Requirements	WCR	$ mln				77	89	102	114	77	65	53
9	Invested Capital	IC	$ mln				846	831	817	803	740	701	854
10	**Return on Invested Capital — Gross**	GRoIC	%				22.32%	24.96%	27.77%	30.66%	24.98%	23.23%	15.78%
11	Cash Tax Rate	TAXR	%				23.78%	24.13%	24.68%	25.21%	24.04%	23.64%	21.96%
12	**Return on Invested Capital — Net**	NRoIC	%				17.01%	18.94%	20.91%	22.93%	18.98%	17.74%	12.31%
13	Weighted Average Cost of Capital	WACC	%				3.35%	3.46%	3.57%	3.69%	3.84%	3.93%	4.04%
14	**Residual Income Rate (NRoIC — WACC)**	RIRW	%				13.66%	15.48%	17.35%	19.25%	15.14%	13.81%	8.28%
15	Hurdle Rate	r	%				8.83%	8.83%	8.83%	8.83%	8.83%	8.83%	8.83%
16	**Residual Income Rate (NRoIC — r)**	RIRr	%				8.18%	10.11%	12.08%	14.10%	10.15%	8.91%	3.48%

Source: Author's calculations using EIA raw data.

Chapter 9
Price Taker

Operating under competitive markets, classical theory suggests that each firm has limited influence on prices, given that their volumes are too small to move markets. In this context, each firm's investments are similarly price-neutral. For this reason, managers rely on quantitative analytics espoused by capital budgeting to inform their choices. However, instead of sailing through with ease, the decision process is nuanced, if not contorted. An alternative approach is to employ the *BOUnCE* framework, which serves as a way to integrate human biases and preferences into managerial decision-making. It validates and continually reframes investment approaches by simulating feasible futures. In understanding why and how energy markets transition, actions are adapted to respond to shifting strategic intents, potentially altering the firm's financial prospects.

1
Introduction

In my years as an investment practitioner, mostly in investment banking and energy, I observe that finance and strategy appear to operate in parallel universes. These are disturbing phenomena, given that both espouse their best intentions to serve the common good in whatever way it is understood. This divergence has a tangible impact on how managers tackle their challenges and how they pursue solutions to their perceived problems.

Three examples illustrate why this divergence needs to be tackled head on:

On one extreme, a number of finance managers aspire for numerical precision. They demand "precise" estimates of critical inputs (e.g. costs, prices, volumes, among others). This obsessive drive could tie the team for months on end, often at great expense in crunching numbers of all shapes and forms. All of these efforts are directed at achieving one goal: to arrive at an "objective" value that stands the test of time.

On another plane, managers take a "big picture" approach. They take comfort in being guided by their *beliefs*, *outlook*, and *understanding* (or lack of) of their current realities and future challenges. Inadvertently, by relying on what is accepted (or acceptable), few would question how such consensus came about in the first place. Consequently, managers follow the herd because it is the popular thing to do.

A broader tendency is to rely on experience which afflicts a number of successful managers, particularly founders of great enterprises. Their achievements set them apart for unquestioned authority. This has parallels in the military: Commanders tend to fight today's wars with tactics borrowed from the last battles they fought. In particular, the ones they won.

In the commercial world, what succeeded before, surely could be replicated successfully, some managers would claim. However, when markets are transitioning, what succeeded before may be the very source of today's failures. Nokia swallowed this bitter pill when they ceded their dominance to Apple's smartphones, and Samsung, and many more that followed. As the horsewhip maker did, in the era of horse carriages, Nokia aimed to build the best phone in a world moving into multimedia and multipurpose gadgets.

How ironic life is. Nokia, the forestry giant that disrupted telephony, was in turn eased out of the market it helped create!

While the contexts may differ, there is a common element in these experiences. In focusing on the *now* and relying on what is "proven and tested" by popular acclaim, managers may continually err in the prognoses of their realities and challenges. Repeated often, such misdiagnoses take on *faux normalcy* that reinforces accepted wisdom, thereby threatening the firm's very viability. Here's why.

Aswath Damodaran[1] (1996), in his earlier works, identified six myths that developed with advances in the art of valuation that persist to this day. In the energy industry, the bias for quantification is premised on its objectivity (Myths 1 and 4), reinforced by capital budgeting's demand for precision and predictability (Myth 3) that should prove timeless (Myth 2).

In this world of quantitative precision, producing that singular number that surpasses the hurdle for acceptance (Myth 6) is primordial. It comes in various guises that converge around net present values (NPVs) or internal rates of return (IRRs).

What appears amiss is to try to understand the very bases for such calculations. Uncorrected, managers assume rather than validate the types of risks or opportunities that they choose to emphasise. Worst, they overlook, hence ignore risks or opportunities that are not made apparent by their chosen evaluation tools.

In these worlds of parallel realities, the strategy relies on their "vantage" perspective of an all-knowing strategic insight that marks the pathways to achieving an ascribed vision. Financial evaluation is supposed to "validate" the higher purpose of such strategic wisdom.

This brings us to Damodaran's presumption that "the market (for listed shares) is correct. It is the analyst's job to convince oneself (and others) that one's valuation offers a better estimate of value than the market price" (Myth 5).

While the "collective view" of the equity market agents is decisive in setting a periodic share price, the jury is still out on the belief that the "market is always right." I learned this abject lesson when I joined JP Morgan in London, weeks prior to 1987 Black Monday.

Known for their structured investment evaluation, based on dividend discount rates (DDR), I came across the novel notion of *negative risk premium*. For several months, DDRs were below the long bond yields. This implied that lower-risk bonds

---

[1] Professor of Finance, Leonard N Stern School of Business, New York University. At times referred to as the Dean of Valuation for his works on corporate finance.

are earning higher returns than high-risk equity, an idea that was anathema to accepted financial wisdom.[2]

Exuberant equity buyers push share prices ever higher, widening the negative risk premia globally, which was plain for all (who did their sums) to see. While our portfolio managers sold, a few subscribed to a "new paradigm" of momentum investing, akin to what analysts called the drunken sailor[3] (or "greater fool theory"). As share prices collapsed, JP Morgan was heavily into cash in most of their managed portfolios.

The privatisation of the water utilities in the United Kingdom in the late 1980s provided my next learning experience in being a reluctant contrarian.

As the first utility sector to be included in the FTSE Index,[4] the privatisation advisers priced the listed water utilities as "bond proxies." In theory, by pegging the expected total returns (e.g. dividend yield + growth) to long bond yields, share prices were expected to go up when bond yields fall to restore a yield parity (of some sort). By keeping the spread within narrow range, the water utilities were supposed to perform with some uniformity, so the advisers claimed.

This simplistic approach caused great discomfort to us. Schooled in a structured valuation approach, we spent time to understand how the water business works, how they form their profits, and how cash is generated to support their capital expenditures, debt servicing, and dividends. Far from a homogenous sector, their financial fortunes, hence the estimated DDRs, varied widely (e.g. 14–22%), I recall.

Two possibilities dawned on us: We were mistaken and so off the mark from consensus, or the adviser mispriced the deal. After alternating between elation at spotting bargains and fear of being the odd person out, we chose to trust our evaluation. Trusting the outcomes of our structured valuation, we invested in top-tier DDR water shares. Fortunately, enough investors came to a similar conclusion, took action, and revalued the shares to most analysts' surprise.

The capital market, in theory, is efficient at correcting misperceptions of value. In buying or selling equity, fund managers are spectators to what managers do or fail

---

[2] Financial theory suggests that investors are rewarded with higher return to compensate for taking higher risk. For this reason, equity usually earns higher returns than bond, resulting in positive risk premium (e.g. equity returns — bond yields).

[3] A "drunken sailor" is an investor that pays over the odds, in the belief that the good times will roll on and asset values will continue to go up.

[4] FTSE Index is the benchmark to measure the periodic Stock performance for the London Stock Exchange, published regularly by the *Financial Times*.

to do. With few exceptions, fund managers acquire shares, wait, and take profits, or cut losses as share prices adjust.

When investing in physical assets, managers decide how the technologies are chosen and how the assets are operated in order to monetise the payoffs. As active participants, managers make things happen, adapt to changing markets, and aim to create value.

Ignoring this reality, valuation tools are transposed with minimal adaptations to value financial and physical assets. A *faux normalcy* becomes the accepted norm: Managers evaluate investments to conform to ideals of bounded risks and value, that works well with bonds, to assets with otherwise unbounded risks or returns.

I concur with Richard Thaler and Cass Sunstein's (2008) proposition that managers, as humans, make the decisions, not the algorithm that predetermines outcomes. Under this world, financial analyses build a body of evidence (or knowledge) to inform managerial decisions. The purpose is to challenge or validate how the potent mix of *beliefs*, *outlook*, and *understanding* of the managerial challenges could shape strategic decisions. These human emotions (or biases) are influenced by data and expected outcomes as well as how these interacting factors are understood to shift within transitioning energy markets.

2
Investing under Transitioning Markets

Vaclav Smil (2010) observed that muscle power moved the world, using almost exclusively animals to move things or get things done. In the pre-industrial world, donkeys were used to turn the stone wheel that grounded cereals to produce wheat or flour for human consumption. Industrial processes replaced animals with mechanical energy to fulfil similar generic tasks, albeit at greater speed and volumes. The skills to care for animals, a highly valued competency, I would presume became obsolete except for specialised situations. In their place, technicians were sought after for their ability to keep machines running.

Transitioning energy systems imply a shift in how resources are priced and how infrastructures are used and valued. Consequently, how the state plays its cards significantly shapes how managers respond and eventually organise their resources and strategy.

In a world of regulated regimes, policy would set prices and often dictate the investments in new supplies (Pollitt, 2012). As a reward, regulation enables the investing firms to recover their investments with an allowed margin, giving rise to a "cost-plus" system. That is, costs are incurred, certified for recovery under a given tariff, and a percentage of the allowed costs is set by the regulator as a return. In effect, by turning firms into a contractor to the state, they are guaranteed some levels of returns (Holmes, 1992) as part of this "social contract."

In this "command and control" system, managers evaluate investments as bounded problems. Following the pricing formulae, the investment's prices, costs, and volumes are readily solved to obtain a return, sort of. Nurtured under this predictable state, managers grew up to focus on maximising returns by expanding costs and volumes. In a number of systems, standard costs were applied as in Spain. To thrive in this system, I recall what Feliciano Fuster[5] explained in one of our conversations: With power prices largely set, we focus on beating the standard costs by delivering at a cost that is less than what is allowed by the regulator. By keeping the savings, Endesa could enhance its returns.

In this game of *fronton*, a Spanish ball game, you keep hitting the ball against the wall to score, Feliciano would say with a wry smile.

The era of liberalised energy markets introduced variable prices and costs, thanks to the wholesale power market (Littlechild, 2001). Adopted by several European markets, some form of competitive supplies emerged. With price volatility now being a feature, Fuster's Endesa had to change tack, as European energy firms had to, over time.

This is the point where finance and strategy diverge more prominently. While strategy prepares for life in a competitive world, hence adapting how they market their wares, finance was busy reasserting the perceived benefits of a stable pricing regime that was fast disappearing.

---

[5] Chief Executive, Endesa. During his long tenure, he oversaw Endesa's transformation from a state-owned peripheral energy supplier to Spain's leading integrated power group. In his later years, he grew Endesa into one of the major energy companies globally, with dominant positions in Spain, Latin America, and Southern Europe.

The breakdown of the "social contract" was a schizophrenic time for some managers. Lenders demand managers restore predictable cash flows. Managers respond by committing to long-term supply obligations, often with fixed volume obligations and minimal pricing flexibility (Masten and Crocker, 1985) under the expectation of securing their revenues to access financing. However, as contracted prices could diverge from what the market is offering, human calculations come into play. When market prices substantially exceed what was contracted, suppliers may be tempted to renege or renegotiate on their commitments (or vice versa for buyers). Paradoxically, what was designed to secure revenues had become the source of continual renegotiations with its consequent risks.

Clearly, for financial analyses to inform managerial decisions, it needs to go beyond the mathematical calculations to arrive at a reasonable valuation. The belief system that underpins conventional investment evaluation is seldom made explicit, insofar as managers are concerned.

Let me surface what are implicit and what are kept out of sight, when managers decide to accept or reject an opportunity across multiple choices under transitioning energy markets. In this conversation, I am guided by the framework presented in Chart 9.1.

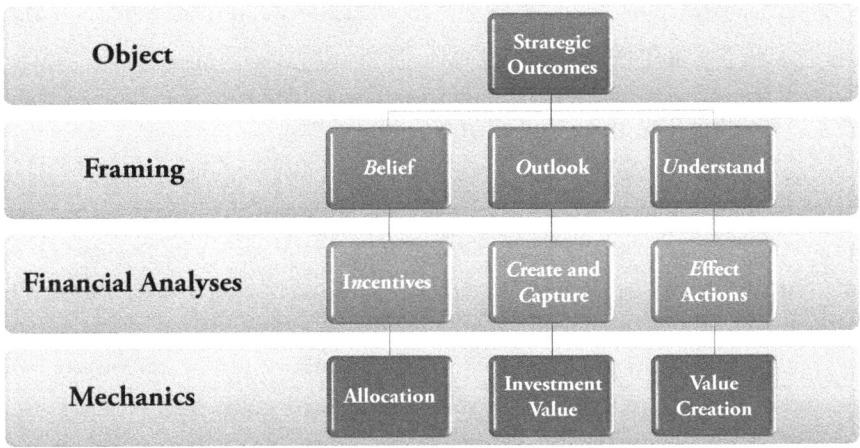

Chart 9.1: *BOUnCE* **and Financial Analyses**

Recall NPV: Invest if the payoffs exceed the investments (Gordon and Shapiro, 1956) among mutually exclusive opportunities. To maximise value, reduce cash flow volatilities (Shapiro, 1999). In effect, managers entrust the firm's future to their ability to forecast outcomes, encapsulated in a single number.

This article of faith is embedded in the *belief* that the firm that invests deserves to earn a payback commensurate to the risks they take. What is left unsaid is the unreserved trust in the managers' foresight and policy's unassailable commitment to fulfil its promises. Both assumptions are heroic and perilous to the firm's financial health.

Inadvertently, when managers *understand* their relevant challenge as avoiding risks (e.g. volatilities), rather than innovating viable solutions, the firm's fate to underperform is sealed. As managers abdicate their powers to decide, the algorithms of financial models take over in apportioning value (e.g. NPV, DDR, or IRR). Without exercising judgement, the managers may just be asking to be replaced by machines that spew decision algorithms.

This alluringly simple approach has drawbacks: While it quantifies, under specified conditions, some notions of value, the model fails to integrate strategy and finance into decision-making. To avoid this trap, strategy and finance need to be reacquainted.

Managers can start by making their *beliefs*, *outlook*, and *understanding* of their realities explicit. In this way, managers can expose and challenge their preconceived ideas of what a transitioning energy system may entail. Informed, at the very least, as to where managers differ or could agree, some aligned views are made explicit on what it is they are trying to resolve if any.[6]

2.1 Setting the meeting place

Policy, strategy, finance, and economics, are divided by a common *intent* to do good. Partly for this reason, a cacophony of well-meaning discourses is espoused without producing melodies that inspire people to actions. In this society's segment of gifted and intelligent people, as leading business schools would claim, why this apparently irreconcilable divergence?

In the policy milieu of the 21st century, energy transition to a low-carbon economy and sustainability have become intertwined. Climate advocates look to 2050 with a

---

[6] This is discussed in detail in Chapter 8, where the *BOUnCE* decision framework is applied to analysing an investment in $ACCGT_B$. The approach is replicated in this chapter to compare the value of competing technologies under a market that is transitioning from $Coal_M$ to $ACCGT_M$.

singular objective of achieving carbon neutrality (UN, 2018). Success is achieved when fossil fuels are replaced by renewables.

To place this in a firm's strategic context, the strategy needs to articulate granular aspirations as to where managers want to take their firms, how they would open feasible pathways, and what the aspired endgame would imply to stakeholders. To be part of this recursive process, finance will have to make explicit linkages as to how actions could lead to, or impede, possible aspired outcomes. This requires policy, strategy, finance, and economics to bridge what divides them by working on what unifies them: *the strategic outcomes they seek to advance, and aspire to credibly deliver, within their lifetime.*

This places managers in a more complex world, where their strategy and decision-making have become more challenging (and exciting). This is because, as Adam Douglas Henry (2009) observed, managers would be navigating through terrains that attenuate between normative belief and value divergence that are deeply rooted in ideological conflicts. This challenge is made intractable when sustainability means different things to different people. In those cases when there is some shared meaning, it is not always clear how to get there, Henry added.

After more than a decade, Henry's (2009) observations are made even more relevant: "Many realms of environmental policy are characterised by political stalemate despite massive amounts of scientific evidence that policy change is required." The United Nations call to arms is indicative of this hardening of positions: It calls for more aggressive CO_2 emission cuts as nations lag in delivering on their promised targets (UN, 2018) *again*. To make up for politicians' inactions and by extension, managers, UN prescribes bigger and more rapid emission cuts, employing principally similar failed approaches.

High-profile forays such as *Energiewende* have proved painful, financially and socially, with more future challenges likely to emerge (Beveridge and Kern, 2013). If this aggressive policy is designed to offer learning opportunities, it comes with a very high tuition fee. As Thomas Cunningham observed, the lessons are German-specific and are unlikely to be replicated elsewhere (Cunningham *et al.*, 2018).

An accepted policy view is distinguished by emphasising the apparent conflicts between pursuing human economic welfare and protecting the environment, as William C Clark (2007) highlighted. With sustainability's ascendancy, business is moving away from Milton Friedman's (1970) shareholder primacy towards a purpose that recognises the firm's societal obligations (The Business Roundtable, 2019).

Taking these policy and market developments into account, I can foresee that energy investments will have to demonstrate how they will deliver on these managerial aspirations. In making the firm's societal purpose explicit, the measures by which managerial performance is evaluated will have to form part of the criteria for investing.

This is where strategy and finance will have their work cut out. Lofty ideals are no longer adequate. For this reason, managers would have to approach sustainability questions away from the deep-seated ideological divides that political advocacies tend to purvey.

2.2 Crossing the chasm to take actions

Managers are realistic about the decisions that they are tasked to make. They work on incomplete information, with little prospect that the data will ever be adequate. They commit enormous cash by exercising wisdom and prudence in making judgements. Recognising this, a decision framework will have to link knowledge to action, and that action occurs at the level of the firm to make it relevant to managers.

To bridge this need, the information that financial analyses proffer should be salient, timely, and legitimate in the eyes of managers individually and collectively as a decision unit. How firms interact with rivals, or economic agents, will be governed by some rules that make markets workable. Examined from this level of granularity, an otherwise intractable ambition to *solve world hunger* becomes specific, actionable, and measurable.

This is where the challenges of energy transitions and sustainability, sooner or later, will have to be understood within a financial economics framework. I attempt to make this connection, using Chart 9.2, to focus on these strategic areas for action: (a) How could market prices shift and reallocate resources? (b) How could supplies or technologies thrive? (c) How are logistics and infrastructures going to be reconfigured? and (d) At what speed and direction will change take place?

The past gives some guidance, albeit incomplete. The emergence of climate change as a policy imperative initially recognised gas as a viable substitute for coal (IEA, 2019). This evolved into a policy push for renewables and even for reviving nuclear energy. The world, polarised as ever, remains as divided in the political and academic spheres as far as advocacies are concerned.

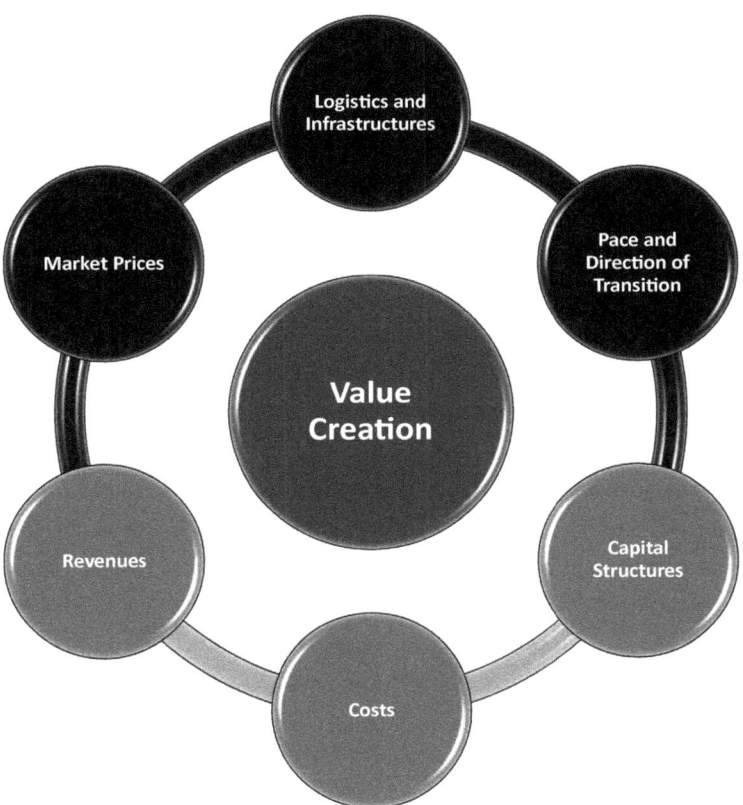

Chart 9.2: Iterative Interactions of Value Creation

This is where, ironically, the much-maligned managerial ranks (by environmentalists, that is) could inject realism. Managers could strategically position their firms for what is in store under transitioning energy markets. By understanding how firms may thrive or flounder, managers could largely mark the way it could meaningfully move forward.

What is known is how gas replaced coal as Europe's dominant fuel for power generation. Cheaper to build, and more flexible to operate, the nascent combined cycle gas turbines (CCGT)[7] replaced coal-fired supplies. As European wholesale power

---

[7] Advances in the technology developed into more advanced versions, the ACCGTs, which is used as the basis for costing gas-fired supplies in this chapter and elsewhere in this book.

markets were adopted, CCGTs replaced mid-merit coal in setting periodic power prices. Its tangible effects on extant and new supplies are the same: Both experienced lower prices and hence lower revenues for similar volumes supplied.

The emergence of gas as a preferred fuel coincided with more infrastructure being built. Gas is delivered using gas pipelines (e.g. for Russian and North Sea gas) or received through import terminals (e.g. Zeebrugge in Belgium, United Kingdom, and various points in Spain) for liquified natural gas (LNG). On the supply side, oil and gas companies invested in liquefaction plants and shipping. With marketing and trading added to the mix, gas evolved as a globally traded and fungible commodity. To those markets that are connected with infrastructures and logistics, gas is a viable fuel that is readily available, affordable, and has lower CO_2 emissions than coal.

How these market changes crept into managerial decision-making was a process of trial and error. Intuitively, declining prices would lead one to expect lower revenues and perhaps lower fuel costs. However, before gas reached some tipping point, a long period of gas to coal (and back) substitutions occurred, with no clear trend towards a decisive shift to gas. For this reason, early adopters of CCGT reaped the benefits of higher power prices, combined with its lower costs of supply, to earn high returns.

As CCGT's benefits were demonstrated, and fuel and power markets were accommodating, more independent power producers (IPPs) entered the market. Financing was equally accommodating, with lenders seeing gas as the growth opportunity in an otherwise *sleepy*, *solid* but *stolid* power generation industry bundled under energy utilities.

In simulating how energy transition could progress, managers could translate how "qualitative factors" could impact any one of the variables identified in Chart 9.2. Without aiming to be exhaustive, the exercise could allow managers to connect their notions of what drives energy transitions, as a source of some knowledge, to how it impacts specified valuation inputs.

The objective of managers is more modest. Without going for humanity's salvation singlehandedly, managers could shed light on the economics and how the value chain could vary as one resource substitute for another (e.g. gas for coal). How quickly and to what direction such transition could occur would be informed by how technology could reconfigure the logistics or even disrupt extant networks. Ultimately, things happen because managers as humans decide to take actions. They respond to policy or market impetus, or pre-empt rivals and policy by reshaping the markets.

Apple's successful reshaping of the mobile phone market is a stark reminder as to how transient market dominance is.

Let me now turn to how *BOUnCE* could shed light on how real-life investment decision-making could be reframed, and made more transparent, in order to facilitate meaningful strategic dialogues.

3
Coal to Gas Transition

Let me consider the world where Jocelyn Chalmers[8] inhabits. A geologist by profession, she started her career in the fields prospecting for oil and gas, and other energy resources. She progressed as an economist, undertook several commercial roles, before becoming the Chief Executive of a major oil and gas company. While contemplating her firm's future, the question of sustainability looms large.

For Jocelyn, this is a double-edged sword: She needs to demonstrate continued leadership in sustainable business practices where her firm staked its reputation. At the same time, a sustainable economy is seen by climate advocates as a world with no place for fossil fuels. Was this to be where the world is heading, is 80% of her business *today* going to be obsolete sooner or later?

To narrow the scope, Jocelyn entrusted Roy Barron, her trusted adviser, to oversee a strategic exercise involving her multifunctional team. Her mandate was specific: Should the firm decide to embark into power generation globally, how would they focus their resources and presence?

After several weeks of working with the technical and commercial teams, Roy presented in Chart 9.3 the team's summary of the competing technologies' costs and their operating profiles. The data are derived from the Energy Information Administration (2019), which serves as a first look.

In simulating how prices and costs could vary, Roy assumed a competitive wholesale market is in place. This would mean that power prices are periodically set by matching

---

[8] The names of some characters mentioned in this section are disguised, unless when actual companies are mentioned.

Dynamic Decisions

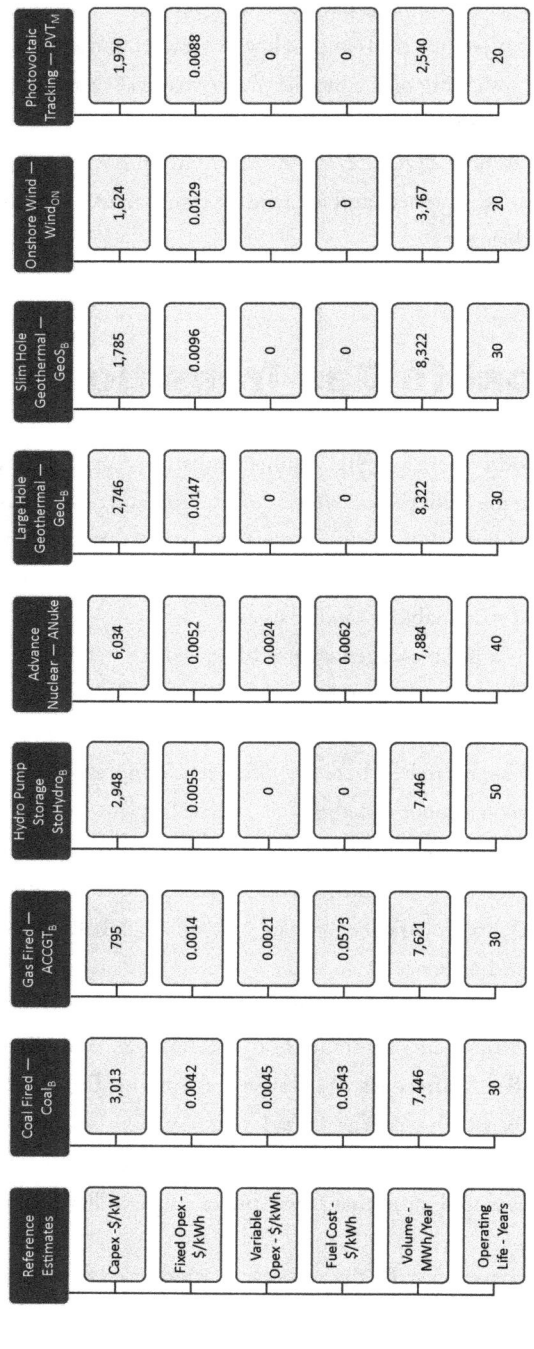

Chart 9.3: Comparative Costs and Profiles

Source: Author's calculations using EIA raw data.

the available supplies to demand, with the marginal supply that clears demand, setting the price for that period. That price is equivalent to the lifecycle cost of energy (LCOE) of the marginal supply. In this context, the competition is between $Coal_M$ and $ACCGT_M$ as the mid-merit supplies that would set prices.

Under competitive energy markets, each firm is too small to influence volume or prices. Hence, each supplier would aim to maximise their despatch by enhancing their cost efficiency. To achieve this, each asset aims to operate as a baseload supply where higher volumes result in lower unit costs.

Roy is having this conversation with Jocelyn and the rest of the team:

In using the data from Chart 9.3, financial analyses were conducted for each technology under two power pricing systems: One assumes $Coal_M$ as the marginal supply, and the other uses $ACCGT_M$ for setting prices, once gas has replaced coal as the dominant fuel. As a short hand, they refer to these systems as $Coal_M$ or $ACCGT_M$ pricing regimes.

What becomes apparent from Roy's cost comparisons in Chart 9.4 are the intrinsic disadvantages of coal. Managers, who were accustomed to seeing coal as the dominant fuel, were slow to accept this changing market. One would recall Bar-Lev and Katz (1975) trying to demonstrate the virtues of expensive but stable price gas as a hedge against volatile coal prices. However, with advances in technology, the emergence of advanced gas technologies saw $ACCGT_M$ surpass $Coal_M$ in terms of achieving lower cost of supplies (A).

Prices of gas and coal tend to vary similarly because their prices are either peg to oil (as substitutes) or shadow oil prices as the most widely traded fuel in the global markets. This is why some managers tend to confuse coal's cheapness as a fuel with coal-fired plants' cost advantages as power suppliers. By breaking down the costs, as Roy did in (B), $Coal_B$'s higher capex and operating costs account for its disadvantages against $ACCGT_B$.

Undoubtedly, the financial environment under $Coal_M$ regimes is more benign than the new world under $ACCGT_M$. Jocelyn confers with Felicity Carpenter, Chief Executive of a major European power generator, on her market's transition from $Coal_M$ to $ACCGT_M$.

Felicity concurs with Roy's estimates of the extent the EBIT margins are eroded (D) from the revenues originally estimated under $Coal_M$ (C). On full transition, the earnings carnage is in full view.

484 Dynamic Decisions

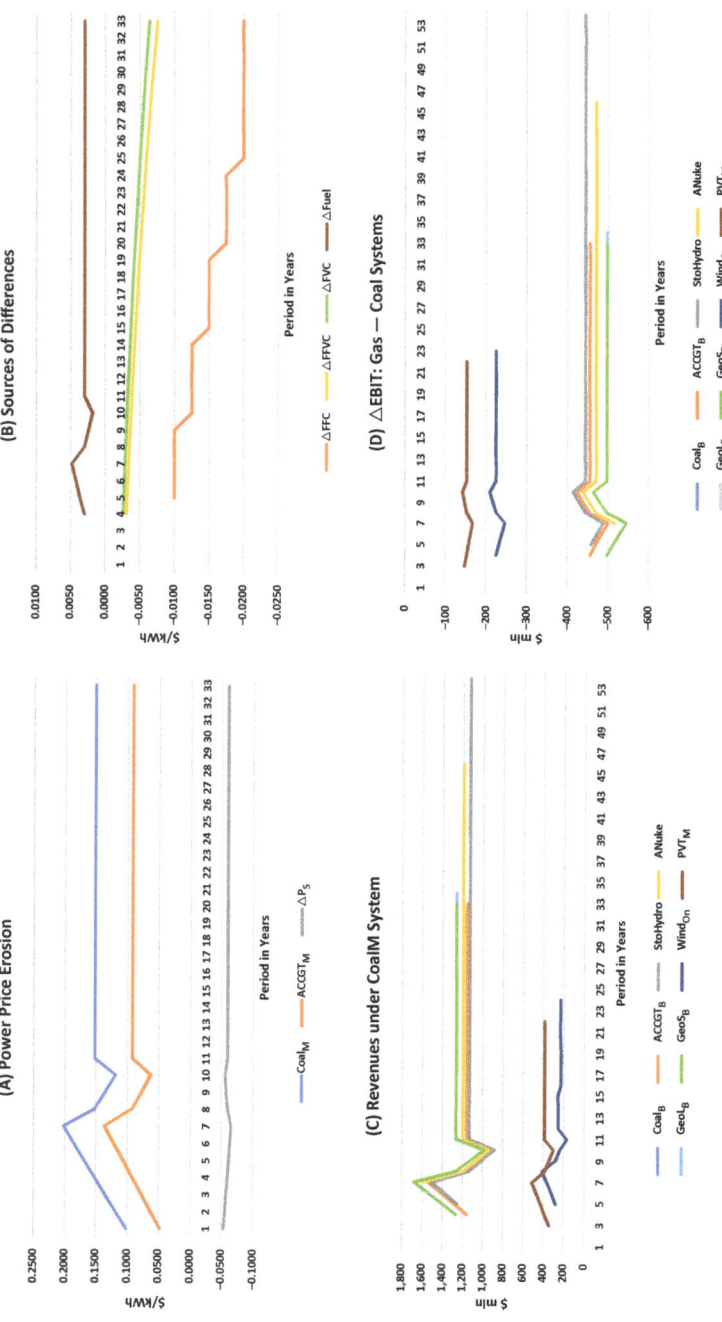

Chart 9.4: Comparative Power Prices and Cash Margins

Having done a similar analytical exercise, Felicity focused on three technologies where she experienced the most pain during the $Coal_M$ to $ACCGT_M$ transition. While the power price erosion adversely impacted all technologies, $Coal_B$, ANuke, and PVT_M are worth focusing on.

Felicity recalled the "dash for gas" that UK deregulation initiated (Littlechild, 2001). While incumbent coal-fired power generators were at first sceptical, the full impact of the power price erosion reached a stage when gas achieved a critical mass. In effect, there was enough power supplied by gas to consistently outbid coal in setting periodic market prices. The process of substitution evolved in the following manner, as shown in Chart 9.5:

1. EBIT margins were gradually eroded (A) when $Coal_B$ is embedded with structural cost disadvantage. With more than half of its cost of supply accounted for by fuel, $ACCGT_B$ lower capex embeds an irreversible edge in spite of its marginally higher fuel costs than $Coal_B$.
2. $Coal_B$'s capex is estimated at \$3,013/kW against $ACCGT_B$'s \$795/kW. With OpFCF squeezed by generally lower power prices (B), $Coal_B$ struggles to finance without borrowing more. This is a reversal of fortunes with $Coal_B$ hardly able to repay its debt until the end of its operational life (C).
3. Consequently, with $Coal_B$'s cumulative losses, it foregoes paying dividends, resulting in negative DDR that contrasted to its previous returns of 13.2% in $Coal_B$'s "good old days" (D).

A closer examination of $Coal_B$'s capacity to pay down their debt may yield some light on some financial entities' decision to curtail their lending. The European Investment Bank is an example (Fleming and Hook, 2019). While presented principally as the Bank's (EIB) commitment to meeting the Social Development Goals (UN, 2015), the parlous cash flows may provide an economic argument in favour of EIB's lending policy. With losses expected to accumulate in later years of its operating life, greater pressure on its cash flows could mount with more stringent standards on environmental quality (e.g. reduce CO_2 emissions).

Returning to the "dash for gas," Felicity highlighted that as the new kid on the block, gas DDR of 40.0% was simply beyond most managers' belief. As she recalled,

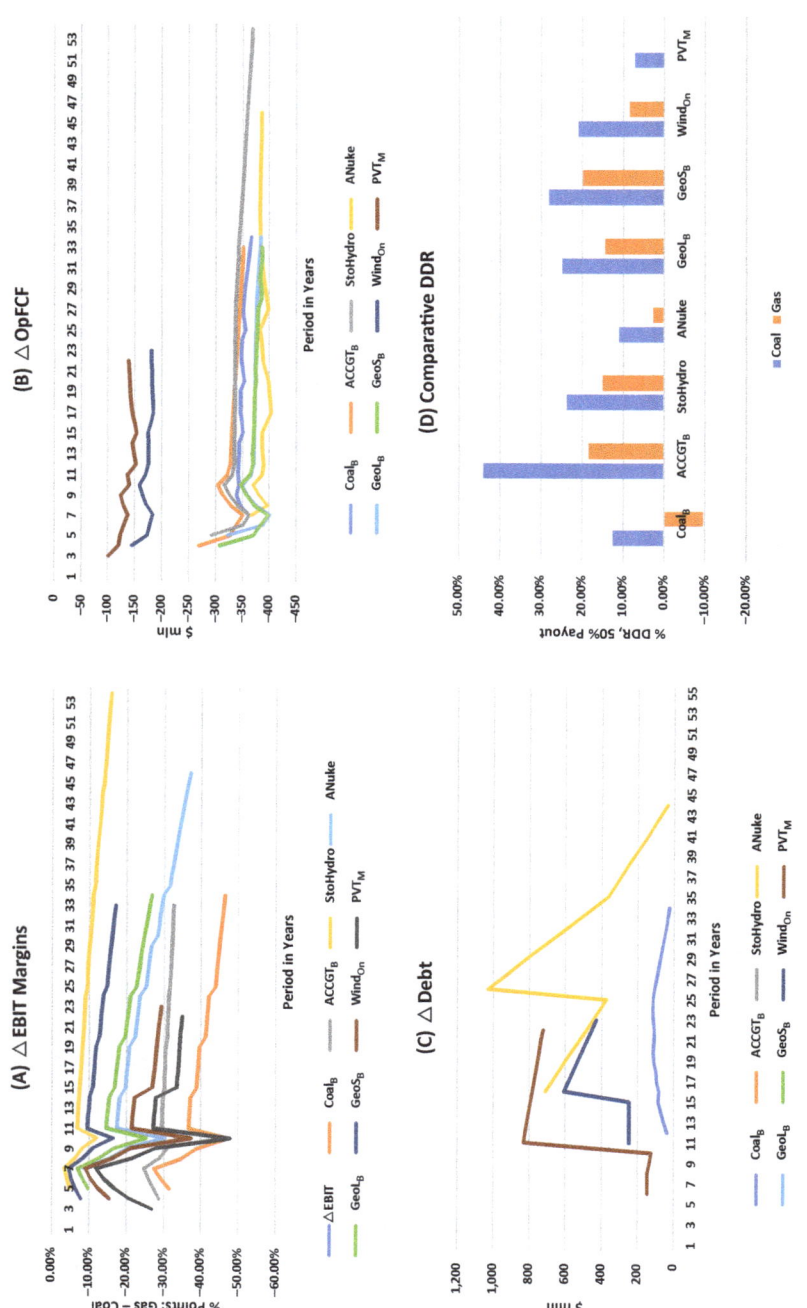

Chart 9.5: Comparative Financial Indicators — Coal$_M$ vs ACCGT$_M$ Systems

new independent power producers (IPPs) were offering precisely such ventures, as they benefited from high power prices under $Coal_M$, but with substantially lower capex.

Advance Nuclear (ANuke) is an inflexible supply, with very high front-end capex in excess of $6,034/kW. It experiences at least two drawbacks: It takes a long time to build (e.g. six years with luck), posing significant risks that the asset becomes obsolete before it operates as competing technologies become cheaper. Complex and inflexible to operate, it requires substantial costs to maintain (e.g. maintenance capital expenditures) and has to run at constant load. A tail-end decommissioning and nuclear waste disposal add to its cost uncertainties. To its merit, its operating costs are stable and it enjoys a long operating life (e.g. 40 years).

In observing the fate of British Energy, a privatised UK nuclear power generator, nuclear power faces three existential threats to its financial survival under the wholesale energy market:

1. Volatile power prices, and fairly fixed operating costs, would tend to squeeze its margins when prices are persistently low (or vice versa).
2. Volume is constant given the high costs of ramping up or down. Without this operational flexibility, during trough demand (e.g. off peak or mid-night) it is cheaper to run at a loss.
3. While it sells the volume that it generates, it may end up paying customers to take up the volumes to keep the plant running.

I recall being in the minority in valuing British Energy before it went bust in 2002 (House of Commons, 2007). Self-assured equity analysts followed a common narrative towards the late 1990s: British Energy was throwing up cash, reinforced by a stable volume because what it produces, it sells. What was amiss is the qualifier that power prices and demand were on an upswing. Under these conditions, it was seen as a safe bet, with no risk to its dividends.

A number of portfolio managers beg to disagree with some analysts' optimism. Working closely with them, I came to the view that the good times could end at some point. What would trigger a reversal in cash flows would be a cut in power prices or persistent low power prices. In such price scenarios, cash flows would trickle or dry up.

Unfortunately, this came sooner than most analysts thought possible. Insolvency became extreme financial distress before bankruptcy and renationalisation were resorted to.

Changing continents, PVT_M enjoys high prices pegged to $Coal_B$ in Asia. In spite of this, Asian regulators follow the examples set by Europe and the United States. Power prices were kept high, thanks to *feed-in tariffs* (FiT), a form of subsidies to encourage investments in photovoltaic technologies. The subsequent removal of FiTs has similar effects as the price erosion in the $Coal_M$ to $ACCGT_M$ transition. Power prices paid to PVT_M were effectively reduced.

In a world without subsidies, PVT_M's virtues of using "free energy that is readily accessible," because the sun shines almost everywhere (for part of the day), could turn into a disadvantage. With little cost to cut, PVT_M is the quintessential price-taker in a competitive market. As Chart 9.5(A)–(D) would illustrate, PVT_M struggles to stay afloat without continued subsidies, even as its costs have been falling sharply since 2008. Low volumes, intermittent and inflexible supplies, plague PVT_M with similar malaise as nuclear power, but none of the benefits that high volumes could occasionally mitigate when power prices are high.

4
Renewables' Disruptions in Unexpected Places

Renewables are often seen as disrupting fossil fuels by replacing them and, in theory, rendering them obsolete. If the experts' views are to come true, various long-term forecasts would show a significant and long tail for fossil fuels, in particular for gas (IEA, 2019). What is more realistic is a coexistence of renewables and fossil fuels, at least in the lifetime of many managers today.

In this hybrid system, what would renewables most likely disrupt? This question is particularly relevant to Jocelyn, given that pushing for more renewables may only result in disrupting her own business while gaining little from her new ventures into renewables.

Taking Felicity's experiences to heart, Jocelyn now focuses on understanding how investing in renewables would alter her firm's strategic advantages. As a fossil fuel supplier, her firm is accustomed to evaluating investments as a financial exercise. Over the years, her firm prides itself as an excellent operator of the logistics that connects their extractive activities (e.g. exploration, production, and mining), through their pipelines, transmission lines, and transport, to places where their customers would need the fuels (e.g. depots, petrol stations, and power generators).

Jocelyn mentally navigates the pathways to a low-carbon future. To inform their moves, Jocelyn is digesting what Roy presented in Chart 9.6 in an attempt to understand how the different technologies could thrive under a more stringent $ACCGT_M$ pricing regime.

Roy added in a note to Jocelyn: Felicity's experiences with a $Coal_M$ to $ACCGT_M$ transition offers some lessons that can be generalised:

1. *Cheaper energy supplies are bound to erode prices* that adversely impact returns, the *severity* of which could *accelerate a transition* as it did with coal to gas in power generation.
2. *Pace* is dictated by how quickly *infrastructure and logistics* would *adapt* to accommodate the new supply (e.g. gas), conferring early movers with excess returns as $ACCGT_B$'s 40% DDR would indicate.
3. As *substitution* gathers momentum, $ACCGT_M$'s dominance *progressively erodes* gas-fired asset's excess *returns*, while diminishing Coal's financial viability and *impairing* inflexible supplies' *economic attractiveness* (e.g. ANuke and PVT_M).

Going back to Roy's comparisons, revenue differs largely because of the volumes that each technology could deliver. This is endowed by the way it generates power. Intermittent $Wind_{ON}$ and PVT_M lag its peers, such as fossil fuels, renewables such as StoHydro and geothermal, and ANuke (A).

The EBITDA (B) comparison yields less obvious insights. More than half of $Coal_B$ and $ACCGT_B$'s costs are fuel. How fuels are procured and how suppliers are brought in as strategic partners are critical to sustaining the investment's viability. The network of infrastructures and logistics, and its configuration, would be decisive to accessing fuel and in delivering the power output. Control of access to resources and operational

Dynamic Decisions

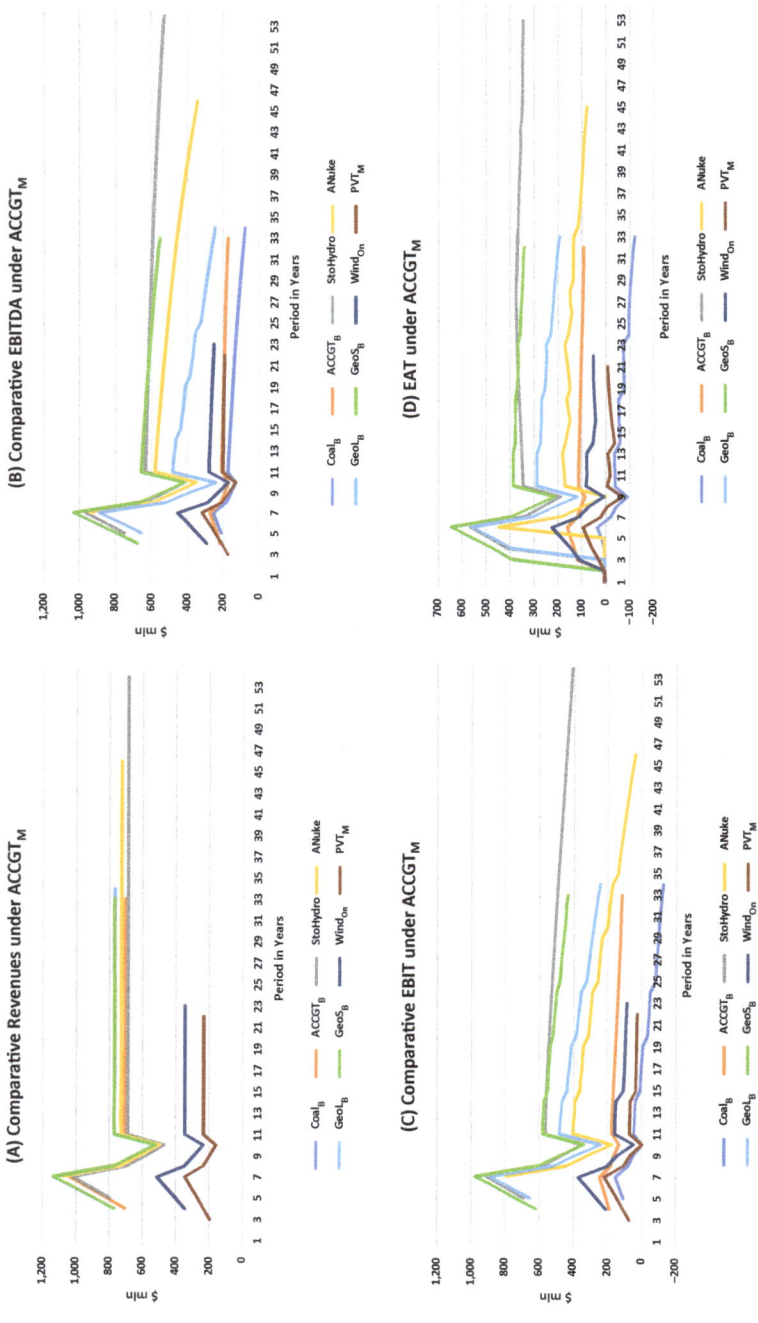

Chart 9.6: How Revenues and "Cash Margins" Differ

competence, therefore, are sources of strategic advantages in determining who plays and who is excluded from the energy market.

In contrast, such advantages become peripheral when a decisive move towards renewables is made, insofar as access to fuels is concerned. Access to networks to supply power output, and its operational control, however, remains of strategic importance. This is where renewables' intermittency impact costs to the energy system, but are seldom imputed specifically. Such costs include, but are not limited to, how the variable loads are balanced by fossil fuels, in power systems where intermittent renewables' penetration is low.

Believing that "time is money," having the asset operational sooner surely would yield better value when EBITDAs are earned earlier. This is where some maintenance capex will need to be incurred to keep the assets operational efficient. By minimising downtime, the assets could deliver the volumes assumed in the financial model. Assuming depreciation is equivalent to the maintenance capex, comparing EBIT margins is a more insightful exercise (C).

Adjusting for maintenance capex, EBIT margins diverge significantly among low-carbon technologies. While $Coal_B$ and ANuke's high capex is dragging its EBIT margins, hydro and geothermal energy sources pose some paradox. Identified as the most cash-generative technologies, Jocelyn wondered why power generators are not investing more, judging by their tepid growth in installed capacity.

In posing this query, Jocelyn's team provided this accepted narrative from energy financial experts:

Water and geothermal steam, as "fuel sources," are location-specific (or geocentric). Water is impounded by building a dam, which could be environmentally hazardous and increase geo-hazards when water overflows or the dam bursts because of poor design, construction, or maintenance.

Geothermal drilling and exploration are highly uncertain and costly. Hence, unlike coal or gas, where a global market operates with supportive infrastructures, geothermal steam has to be found first before any power could be generated. Its high front-end expense has to be committed before the drillers know with certainty that they are in the right location. For the decision-maker, this is a high-stake roulette to put down a bet, with career-limiting prospects for the manager.

Unconvinced, Jocelyn saw in these arguments tell-tale signs that managers are missing the essential points, particularly for geothermal exploration and drilling. Instead, she sees the massive front-end exploration and drilling costs and uncertainties as offering a space for technological and financial innovations to disrupt the energy market.

Privately, Jocelyn toys with this idea: If she could find a way to reduce the scale of exploration and drilling costs, and engineer a financing approach that reduces the risks to developers, this problem could be turned into an opportunity. She made a mental note to explore this farther.[9]

Instead, Jocelyn's team extolls the virtues of using "free energy" to generate power. Installed with less technical complexities, $Wind_{On}$ and PVT_M should be a no brainer. However, observing how the EBIT margins evolve, PVT_M in particular is made vulnerable to prolonged bouts of low power prices. $Coal_B$, ANuke, and PVT_M's rapidly shrinking EBIT margins are not lost on Jocelyn.

In examining the EAT margins, Jocelyn raises two strategic points:

1. Why does she need debt to finance the investment, when her firm is well capitalised and enjoys copious cash flows?
2. Why is tax planning done as an afterthought, when the fiscal authority takes about a third of its earnings before tax without doing much for the business?

These are very legitimate questions that need some answers. Aside from its obvious redistributive effects, where cash is allocated to lenders and the fiscal authorities, the basic premises are addressed in the funding approach that the firm decides to take.

Suffice to say at this stage, while often ignored, the fiscal authority is a silent partner that gets remunerated by legislative fiat. Seen in this light, the dynamics of how business relates to the state, and how the state interacts with business, could be better understood through the process of setting taxes and incentives.

Doing a mental note, Jocelyn noted this preliminary insight:

In her previous foray into power generation, the strategic narrative was rather straightforward and compelling, so her senior leadership colleagues thought. As a major producer of gas, integrating downstream into power generation was a natural next move as an add-on business. In part, this was right, except that as fuel prices fell, power prices also fell, thereby eliminating any hope for arbitrage (e.g. power prices

---

[9] Jocelyn was presented with slim-hole drilling to replace large-hole geothermal drilling. Designed with smaller equipment, slim-hole drilling reduces costs by eliminating heavy civil work expenditures that are otherwise made before knowing that they are drilling in the right place.

would be more resilient). Lacking in scale, Jocelyn recalled the split identity they have to endure: They are dominant in oil and gas, but a puny player in power generation. The latter is inhabited by incumbent giants, who happened to be their best customers for gas.

Renewables bear little resemblance to what they pride themselves to be good at. As a dispersed resource, it needs none of the massive infrastructures and logistics that her firm is best at. There is no fuel (e.g. gas) to power spreads to arbitrage her cash margins. To build a business to a competitive scale, this is committing huge sums that will ultimately cannibalise her oil and gas business.

But then, doing nothing could mean 80% of her business will be gone in a generation, should policy and climate advocates achieve their objectives.

5
In Search of Viable Pathways

The finance managers in Jocelyn's strategic review are perplexed by her questions. In the deep recesses of their thoughts, they wondered why she could not fathom the advantages of borrowing?

In attempting to give Jocelyn a credible answer, they embarked on examining the capital requirements and the comparative cash flow earnings of the different technologies. To recall, following Josep Faus's (1995) formulation, this split into *working capital* (WC) to fund the long-term commitments and *working capital requirements* (WCR) to fund day-to-day operational financing.

The finance managers break down WCR into its current assets and liabilities. Accustomed to evaluating large investments, most of the finance managers were rather dismissive of spending time in understanding how WCR works. However, to come prepared, they would rather have their answers ready in case Jocelyn would choose to "cross-examine" them as part of the routine.

To their surprise, Ian Walsh, a newly hired economist, raised a number of interesting questions that seasoned managers opted to ignore. In going through Chart 9.7, Ian pointed out the following:

"We are accustomed to seeing receivables, inventory and payables, as part and parcel of our working capital requirements. Except for receivables, our foray into renewables would eliminate inventory and most of the payables (A and B). Without

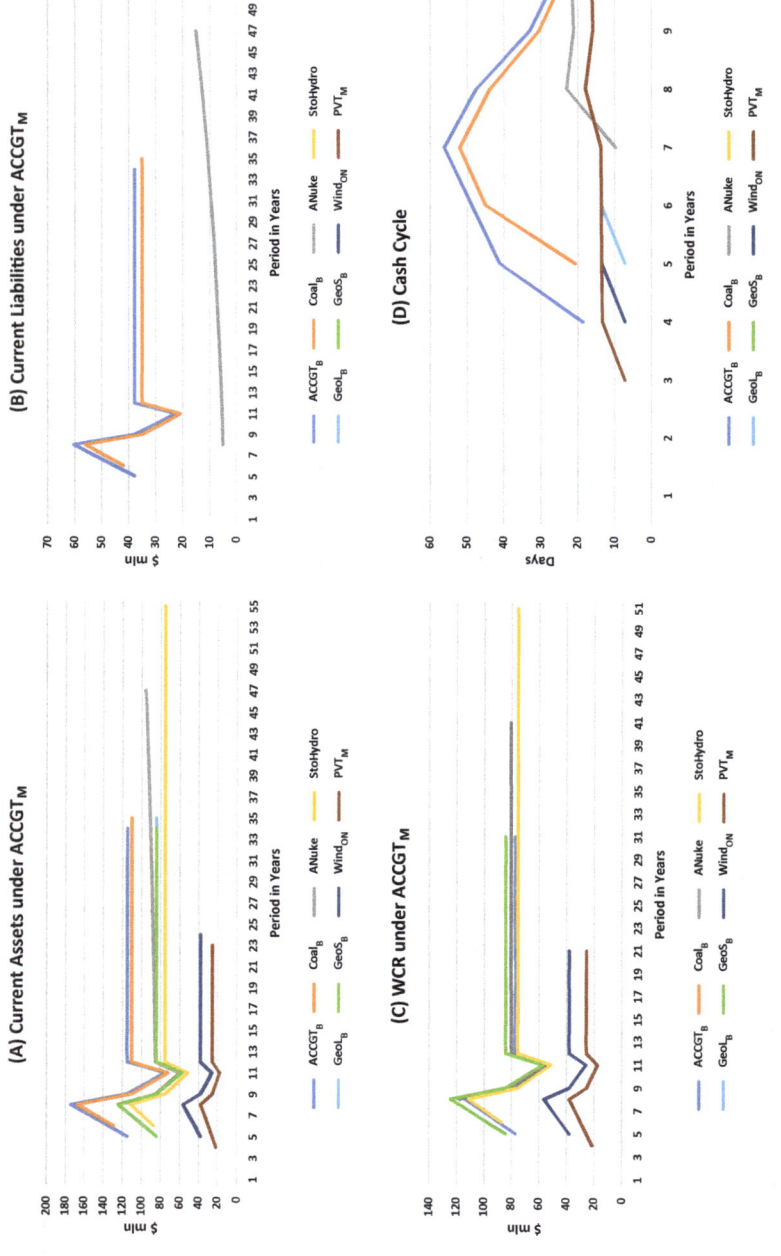

Chart 9.7: Working Capital Requirements under $ACCGT_M$

inventory, renewables have no fuel costs, payables are practically non-existent. WCR in this case is down to managing the collection of receivables in a timely manner (C). We now connect this to our cash cycle, which clearly shows us how much shorter it is for renewables (D)."

Intrigued by this, seasoned finance managers could only admire Ian's simple but powerful message. Operational finance for renewables differs from oil and gas, or fossil fuel power generators. By implication, what marked an oil and gas firm for excellence, such as inventory control, logistics, and infrastructure operations (e.g. pipelines, storage, and transport), loses its importance in a world that shifted to renewables.

Encouraged by this rediscovery of the power of basic financial analysis, they seek to replicate this with working capital. Again, deconstructing, WC looks at the two sides of the balance sheet. On the asset side, there is the fixed asset that makes the production of power possible. It is funded by borrowings and equity, representing the liabilities and capital. Any EAT ploughed back to the business is shown as retained earnings, which is part of the capital (e.g. equity and retained earnings).

Consulting with their colleagues in technical and operations, Roy incorporated their inputs to their financial analyses. One revision that altered their views is the explicit inclusion of maintenance capital expenditures (or maintenance capex). This is the long tail on ongoing commitments that recur periodically as lumpy expenditures to sustain the assets' operational effectiveness. Roy appreciated that without making this expenditure, the efficiency of the assets would deteriorate over time. In this case, the assumption of operating flat out at full capacity over the assets' lives would be heroic and unrealistic.

Just like Ian, Roy pointed out that not all renewables are made equal as Chart 9.8 would illustrate. Under specified market conditions, some would continue to thrive as they did under $Coal_M$, while others could flounder. Working backwards, investing in fixed assets involves front-end cash outlays and a continuing expenditure that explains the "sawtooth" pattern in (D).

While all technologies are assumed to borrow to fund 70% of their capital expenditures, the financing needs diverge drastically when capital expenditures are explicitly evaluated. Cash-generative assets accumulate capital by partially retaining earnings (e.g. $ACCGT_B$, $StoHydro_B$, $GeoL_B$, and $GeoS_B$) (C). In contrast, technologies that struggle to earn sufficient returns would rely on new equity to stay afloat or continue

496 Dynamic Decisions

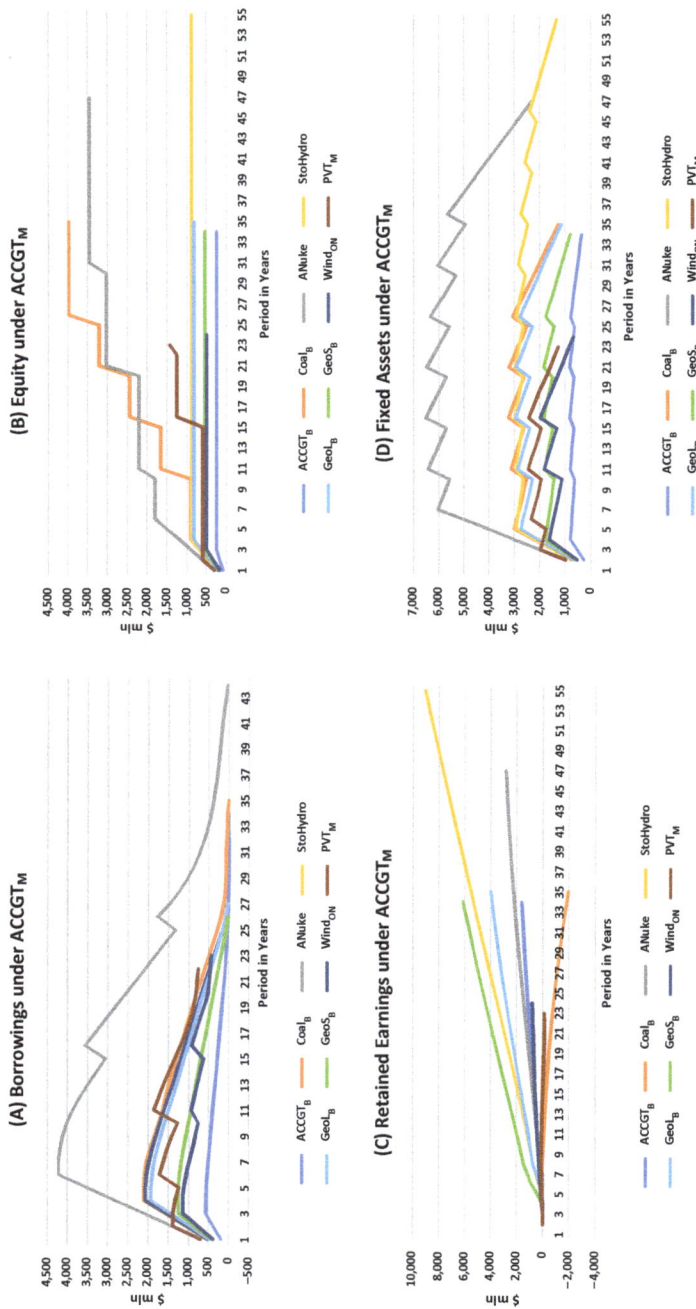

Chart 9.8: Working Capital under ACCGT$_M$

to gain access to debt (B) and (A). This is what investors in ANuke, $Coal_B$, and PVT_M are expected to face, a recurring cash call to keep the business going.

These diverging fortunes come as a bit of a surprise to some managers. Accustomed to making their financials work, by assuming prices and costs that would result in acceptable returns, what the simulation shows is disconcerting.

Josep Faus's (1995) working capital framework came to mind. By following a standard capital ratio comprising 70% debt, and 30% equity, project financing would accept the investment as bankable (e.g. amenable to be funded). However, extending the analysis, Roy noted the following insights:

With cash earnings diverging, differing cash flows would result in different borrowing needs. In examining Chart 9.9, a standard capital structure may prove excessive for some (e.g. cash generative assets), while creating financing gaps for others (e.g. $Coal_B$, ANuke, and PVT_M) (A). Hence, to satisfy lenders about their continued financial viability, assets such as $Coal_B$, ANuke, and PVT_M would need more equity to fund the financing gaps while restoring their credit strength.

To have a quick look, Faus suggested that cash surpluses arise when WC exceeds WCR (C) Conversely, firms would need to *negotiate financing requirements* (NFR), or line up credit facilities, if WCR exceeds WC (D). What Roy observed is simply a validation of what he already suspected to be the case.

In aiming to gain a better perspective, Roy revisited the cash flow analyses that they have previously discussed with Jocelyn (Recall: Chart 9.5). Going deeper, Roy began to appreciate why the diverging fortunes surprised some of his colleagues, all seasoned finance managers. These are his thoughts:

Aside from planning for success, where managers assume prices and costs that make their investments "work," they may inadvertently oversimplify their cash flow analyses. For those that go beyond using EBITDA as proxy for cash earnings, they usually stop at deriving operating cash flows. How they differ is illustrated in Chart 9.10.

By adding back depreciation, provisions, amortisation, and other non-cash expenses to EAT, cash from operations is calculated (A). This is adjusted by the changes in WCR in order to recognise how increases in current assets or current liabilities are requiring the firm to fund. Conversely, how much of the operating finance is funded by suppliers is shown through changes in payables (B).

Without going any farther, managers could be blindsided by the copious cash flows that energy investments generally earn at the operating cash flow level. This

Dynamic Decisions

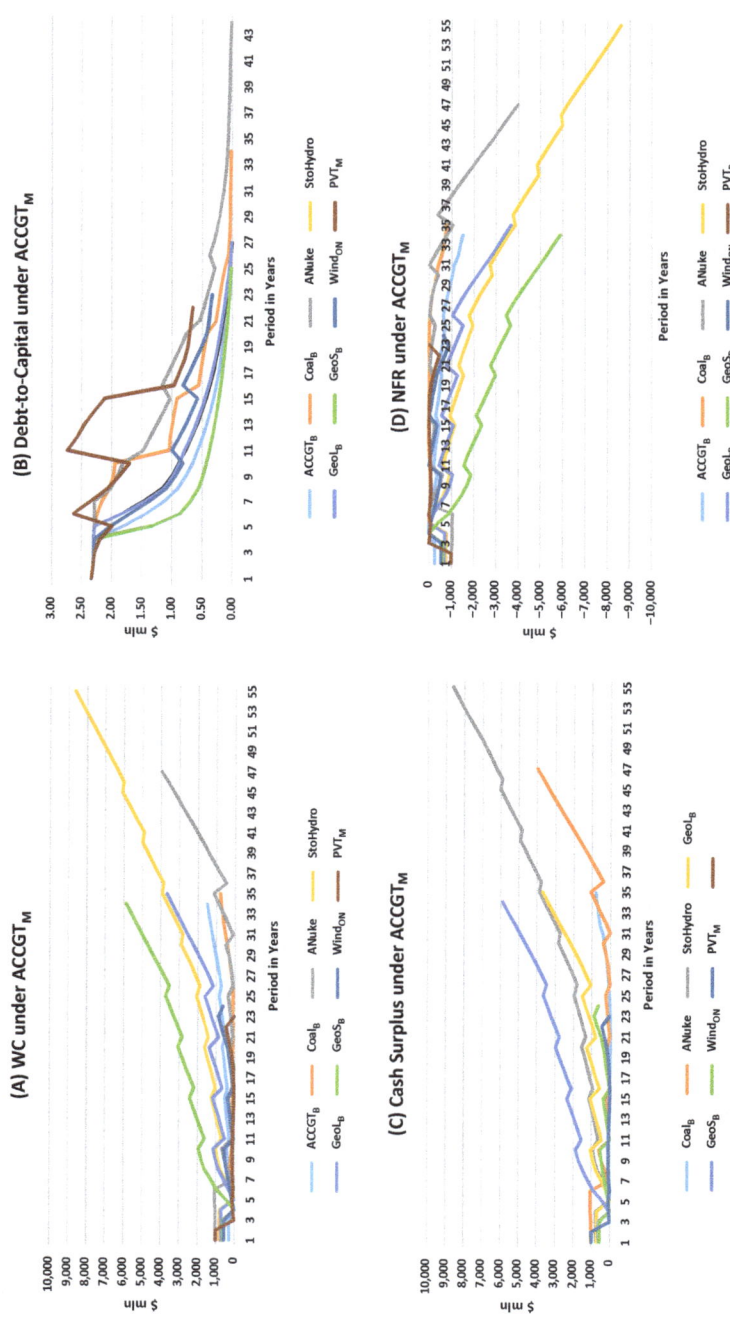

Chart 9.9: Credit Strength and Cash Accumulation

Price Taker

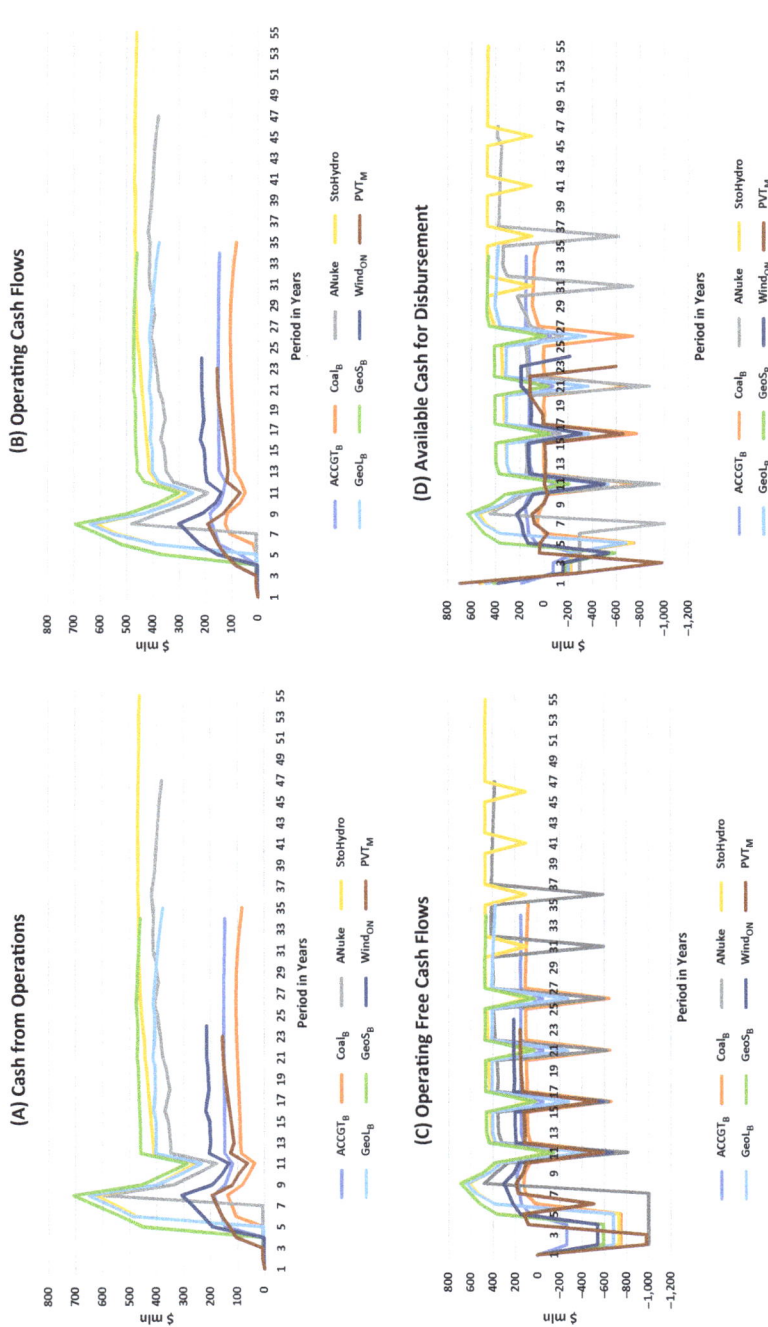

Chart 9.10: Comparative Cash Flows and Profiles

stands to reason: Even for a slightly loss-making firm (e.g. negative EAT), adding back a large amount of depreciation could mask the losses by showing positive operating cash flows (OpCF) or EBITDA when used as a proxy.

The picture changes completely when operating cash flows' sufficiency is judged against any continuing expenditures. By deducting capex and maintenance capex, operating free cash flows (OpFCF) show markedly divergent paths to achieving financial viability. In the firms' language, financial viability is achieved when an investment could self-finance its continuing obligations, which includes maintenance capex as a necessary element to meeting its volume assumptions.

The same message comes back to Roy, with added clarity in Chart 9.10(C) and(D): High capex requires greater cash flows to sustain the investment as an ongoing concern. This is where declining power prices could place cash flows under pressure when costs are inflexible to alter or adapt. Such is the case for $Coal_B$, where its higher costs to supply compared to $ACCGT_M$ would lock it under a cycle of persistent losses. ANuke is in a slightly better position, although its OpFCF is unlikely to be sufficient to meeting periodic calls on its cash to fund its maintenance capex. PVT_M suffers from low volumes, which is an inherent trait of the technology as an intermittent supply dependent on the sun shining to generate power (hence revenues and cash flows).

Consequently, with parlous cash flows, what remains after capex is funded, is a constrained ability to fund the repayment of its debt and interest expenses. To ease this burden, more equity will have to be provided so as to reduce the cash calls from borrowings. However, as in the case of $Coal_B$, with little left as *available cash for disbursement* (D), it becomes doubtful for shareholders to be keen on investing more equity with little prospect of earning any returns.

A closer examination of $Coal_B$'s capacity to pay down their debt may yield some light on some financial entities' decision to curtail their lending. The parlous cash flows provide an economic argument to curtail lending to Coal. With losses expected to accumulate in later years of its operating life, greater pressure on its cash flows could mount with more stringent standards on environmental quality (e.g. reduce CO_2 emissions).

The transition from $Coal_M$ to $ACCGT_M$ lengthens the wait for firms to recover what they invested. Again, this is where some confusion arose when seasoned managers use different cash flow metrics to calculate payback periods. To align, Roy explained

Table 9.1: Comparative Payback Periods under Coal$_M$ and ACCGT$_M$

			Payback Period from Start of Commercial Operation in Years					
			Coal$_M$			ACCGT$_M$		
			OpFCF	EBITDA	EBIT	OpFCF	EBITDA	EBIT
Column/ Line	Technology	Acronym	A $ mln	B $ mln	C $ mln	D $ mln	E $ mln	F $ mln
1	Advance Combined Cycle Gas Turbine	ACCGT$_B$	2.59	1.17	1.21	6.00	3.50	4.00
2	Coal Fired Power	Coal$_B$	8.87	3.27	4.41	—	18.00	—
3	Advance Nuclear Power	ANuke	10.07	5.43	6.62	31.60	10.30	16.10
4	Pump Storage Hydro Power	StoHydro$_B$	3.14	2.98	3.32	7.76	3.41	3.92
5	Geothermal — Large Hole Drilling	GeoL$_B$	3.22	2.25	2.74	7.60	2.89	3.76
6	Geothermal — Slim Hole Drilling	GeoS$_B$	2.50	1.45	1.53	3.93	1.51	2.65
7	Onshore Wind Farm	Wind$_{ON}$	6.57	2.66	3.59	15.87	4.34	7.38
8	Photovoltaic Tracking	PVT$_M$	18.59	6.82	9.50	—	12.42	—

Source: Author's calculations using EIA raw data.

that OpFCF is the correct basis, given that what the firm could appropriate is the cash flow that remains after meeting its operating obligations, which includes providing for maintenance capex.

As Roy illustrated in Table 9.1, using EBITDA and EBIT as proxies for cash flows would flatter the pace at which the capex is recovered. In effect, by overstating the cash flows, managers may err in planning for a shorter payback period and assume a more aggressive gearing that could impair the investment's financial viability.

In this simulation, it appears that this advertency holds true for Coal$_B$ and PVT$_M$. Incurring losses and sub-optimal cash flows, both assets are unlikely to recover what is invested with their OpFCF.

Jocelyn reconvened the team and focused on extracting insights from the valuation presented in Table 9.2 under both systems. With the debate unresolved, the valuation is premised on the weighted average cost of capital (WACC) and hurdle rate (r) as the discount rates for OpFCF. At this point, what the math showed is no longer a surprise after the inputs to the financial analyses were widely discussed. Roy offered a number of insights:

Table 9.2: Comparative NPVs

Column/Line	Technology	Coal$_M$ NPV ∫S−X A $ mln	Invested Capital X B $ mln	Payoffs E SE C $ mln	Payoffs N SN D $ mln	Terminal Cash STC E $ mln	ACCGT$_M$ NPV ∫S−X F $ mln	Invested Capital X G $ mln	Payoffs E SE H $ mln	Payoffs N SN I $ mln	Terminal Cash STC J $ mln
	Hurdle Rate										
1	ACCGT$_B$	3,285	673	1,715	1,882	361	368	673	468	492	81
2	Coal$_B$	187	2,449	1,020	1,417	198	−2,530	2,449	−65	−56	40
3	ANuke	−56	4,649	1,029	3,296	268	−3,128	4,649	239	1,178	105
4	StoHydro$_B$	4,811	2,468	2,519	4,440	321	1,444	2,468	1,356	2,344	214
5	GeoL$_B$	3,409	2,232	2,300	2,868	474	371	2,232	1,124	1,294	186
6	GeoS$_B$	5,505	1,511	3,135	3,221	660	2,199	1,511	1,717	1,667	326
7	Wind$_{ON}$	712	1,334	1,038	796	212	−495	1,334	443	343	53
8	PVT$_M$	−602	1,698	440	529	127	−1,614	1,698	−90	174	1
	WACC										
9	ACCGT$_B$	7,276	736	2,320	4,216	1,476	1,465	736	639	1,190	372
10	Coal$_B$	3,311	2,739	1,412	3,621	1,017	−2,739	2,658	−119	−88	125
11	ANuke	6,523	5,285	1,425	8,547	1,836	−2,278	5,070	295	2,145	352
12	StoHydro$_B$	12,516	2,680	3,248	9,997	1,951	4,662	2,615	1,666	4,703	909
13	GeoL$_B$	9,888	2,496	3,199	6,926	2,259	2,258	2,422	1,447	2,592	642
14	GeoS$_B$	12,431	1,654	4,191	7,196	2,698	4,830	1,614	2,172	3,227	1,045
15	Wind$_{ON}$	2,940	1,504	1,493	2,083	868	30	1,468	570	760	168
16	PVT$_M$	653	1,860	607	1,396	509	−1,589	1,826	−159	393	3

Source: Author's calculation using EIA raw data.

Technology disruptors, when successful, confer the early adopters with excess returns, as $ACCGT_B$ is contemplated to do under $Coal_M$. With its significant cost advantages, investing in $ACCGT_B$ creates an arbitrage: For as long as $Coal_M$ continues to set the price, $ACCGT_B$ would reap returns that are above the "normal" NPV (A.1). That is, the "safe and proven" choice is to invest in $Coal_B$ that is tantamount to indexing costs to supply with the price-setting capacity. The resulting NPV is more modest (A.2).

Such excess returns, however, are unlikely to be sustained. Under competitive markets, new entrants would invest in more $ACCGT_B$, thereby shifting the price-setting supply to $ACCGT_M$. As power prices are eroded, because $Coal_M$ is displaced, $ACCGT_B$ would become the "safe and proven" choice under $ACCGT_M$. As a result, the NPV would also set some "normal" returns (F.1).

The next phase of a transition could be the potential dominance of renewables. The question is, which of the technologies, known or emerging, would dominate?

The jury is still out, but Jocelyn would have to provide strategic guidance *now*, if not a decision, as to where she aims to take the firm going forward. In contemplating her next moves, Jocelyn decided to spend some quiet time before putting forward a proposed strategy.

6
Making Choices

Jocelyn contemplates the feasible scenarios that energy may evolve into. On the extremes, there is a world that climate advocates worked and hope to make into a reality, a market where renewables fully replaced fossil fuels. The other is transitioning into multiple supplies world, with renewables and fossil fuels (principally gas) coexisting, as IEA is projecting (2019). How the market will eventually pan out is unknown, and this is where Jocelyn's judgement will make a difference to her firm's future.

By a process of elimination, Jocelyn examines how much of the future performance would depend on their choice of technologies, using the analysis in Chart 9.11. Focusing on renewables, geothermal and hydro sources caught her attention. They share traits that are attractive to her: The EBIT margins are high, with reasonable asset efficiency (e.g. revenue/invested capital). Combined, they do deliver returns (e.g.

Dynamic Decisions

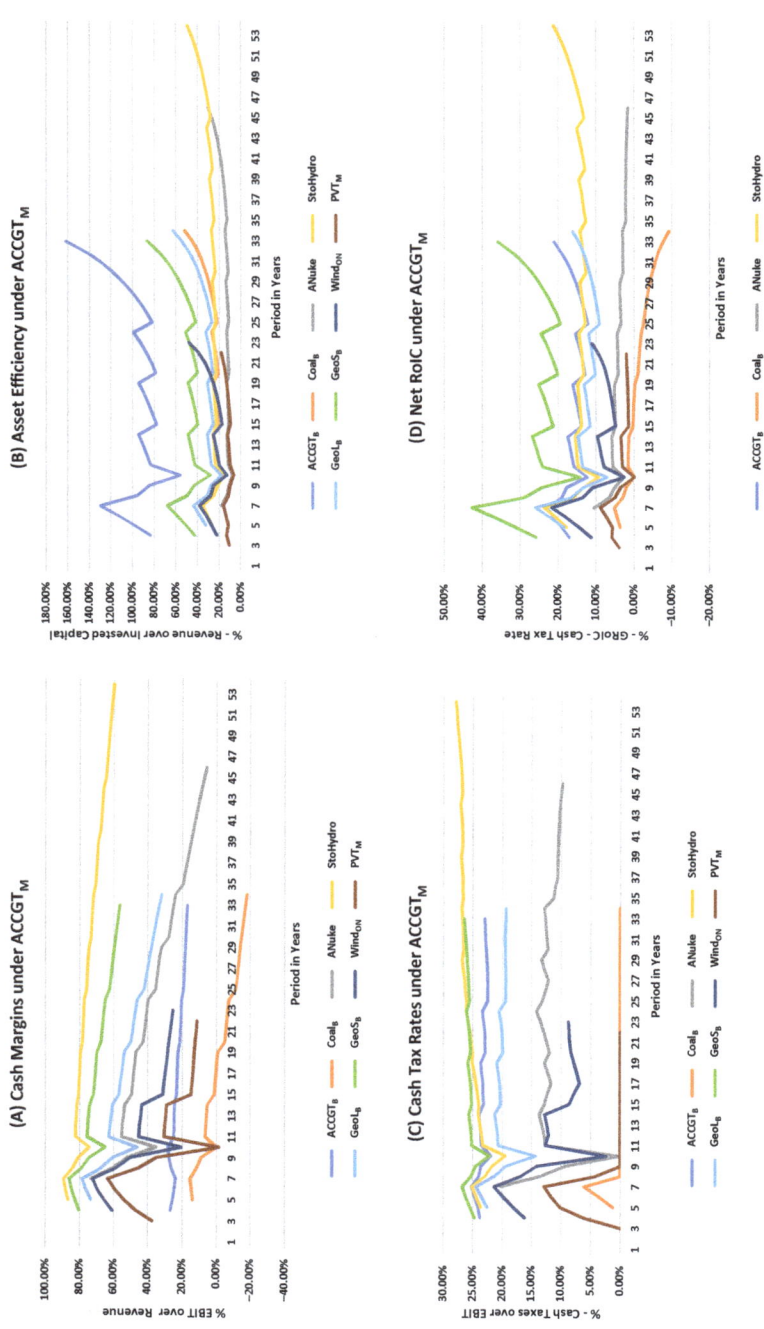

Chart 9.11: Levers of Returns

product of EBIT margins and asset efficiency) that are comparable to $ACCGT_B$, which is thus far the most familiar and compatible with their gas business.

Recalling how $ACCGT_B$ disrupted $Coal_B$, slim-hole geothermal ($GeoS_B$) caught her attention. While economics would imply $GeoS_B$ as offering the highest potential returns, industry statistics fail to support this. This is where her optimistic briefings are so disconnected from the realities on the ground. Jocelyn thought out loud: Are my industry colleagues so blinded that they fail to see the virtues of $GeoS_B$ in plain sight?

Her notes shed some light. While $GeoS_B$ is a compelling energy conversion technology, to make it work, one has to find geothermal steam first. This is where the crux of the problem lies. With geothermal steam, investors have to find the steam supply in a similar way that firms looking for oil and gas have to incur exploration costs without any certainty of striking successful wells.

Large-hole geothermal (Geo_B) is a conventional well drilling technology employing bulky equipment that has to be transported to the site. In many cases, infrastructures and civil works will need to be in place before one really knows that it is the right place to drill. Without sufficient capital and technical competency, a failed drilling would be too much to bear. For this reason, few firms would venture into geothermal exploration and drilling.

Jocelyn's meeting with a slim-hole geothermal driller intrigued her. With equipment made smaller, sizeable expenditures on civil works and infrastructures can be avoided. By substantially cutting the costs, $GeoS_B$ is a potential disruptor: Low-cost steam, combined with reduced capex, may provide a narrow window (as $ACCGT_B$ did) where excess returns could be possible.

To digress, Tim Koller *et al.*'s (2011) "best owner" proposition posits that assets deliver the value that is contemplated by how they are managed. Similar assets could perform differently, depending on how they are managed often as a function of any initial endowments and competencies enjoyed by the firm.

This managerial reality is not lost on Jocelyn. She wondered: What advantages are endowed in her firm, and how can these be turned to create profitable niches in a decarbonising energy market?

Ample capital and access to technologies and talents come to mind. Following this intuition, it appears that low capital, low technical complexities may not be the place to start. In this segment, the barriers to entry of new entrants are low, and to

Dynamic Decisions

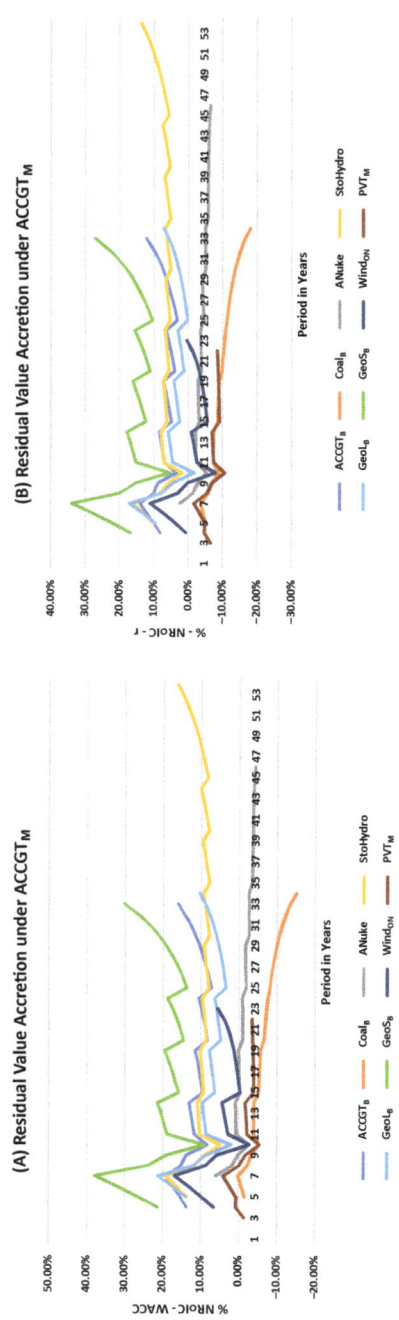

Chart 9.12: Comparative Residual Value Accretion

add, its low returns may not prove compelling. Clearly, moving into PVT_M which the business press popularised is not an obvious niche.

Across the technological spectrum, slim-hole geothermal is a curiosity. One of the most value-accretive technologies, as Chart 9.12 would suggest, is the energy market, ignoring the potential havoc it could wreak as a disruptive investment.

Jocelyn recalled her earlier foray into gas-fired power as an independent power producer. There are some parallels: As an early entrant, it could potentially reap excess returns, largely because of the unrecognised disruptions of reduced exploration and drilling costs, and lower capex for power generation.

By substantially reducing front-end costs, the financial costs of failed exploration and drilling are converted into manageable risks, at least for well-capitalised firms. In effect, the risks are now of a scale that is similar to oil and gas exploration, something that Jocelyn professionally as a geologist understands. Admittedly, developing an oil or gas field requires certain specialised skills, which may differ from geothermal steam fields, the technical discipline to explore for resources may have more in common than generally thought.

Chevron, a major geothermal power producer in Indonesia and the Philippines, and its exit, looms large in Jocelyn's mind (Chevron, 2016). A glimmer of optimism is noted: Chevron was wedded to large-hole geothermal drilling, where the scale of investment and the market it could serve were limited by a minimum demand threshold. By implication, geothermal could only work when there is a large enough market to serve, which makes the technology highly dependent on infrastructure and interconnection to markets. With slim-hole geothermal being made viable at smaller scales, its market scope is greatly expanded, particularly in archipelagic or fragmented markets that were beyond reach.

To prepare for her board presentation, she summarised what she now knows from their collective contributions to frame their strategy. As energy markets transition from $Coal_M$ to $ACCGT_M$, eroding power prices could impair the financial viability of $Coal_B$, ANuke, PVT_M, while setting some floor prices to make $Wind_{ON}$ thrive. Among the alternatives, $ACCGT_B$, $StoHydro_B$, $GeoL_B$, and $GeoS_B$, appear to be the viable options to invest in. For other emerging technologies, such as offshore wind and wave, high capex continues to be barrier for wide-scale investment. However, as the efficiency and costs improve, there may be a place for them, if she is planning for her firm's future for the next generation.

This last thought stopped Jocelyn in her tracks: Why should I make a commitment now and lock-in my firm's future in a *now or never* decision when the market remains very fluid?

Jocelyn contemplated: Surely, there must be a value in injecting some flexibility into how they phase their strategic investments, given the uncertainties as to how the technologies and markets would evolve five years hence? With their ambition to be a global power player, are they indeed large enough to impact prices, and supplies, as they wade in to reshape the market?

She picked up her phone: "Roy, can we spend the remainder of the day to see how we can phase our investments and adapt it as technologies, markets, and policies develop?"

How Jocelyn and Roy tackle these strategic issues would question the very premise that their present valuation stands, following economics' pure competition assumptions and capital budgeting's accepted wisdom.

Bibliography

Bar-Lev, D. and Katz, S. (1976). A portfolio approach to fossil fuel procurement in the electric utility industry. *The Journal of Finance*, xxxi(3), June 1976, 933–947.

Beveridge, R. and Kern, K. (2013). The Energiewende in Germany: Background, developments, and future challenges. *Renewable Energy Law and Policy*, 4(3), 3–12.

The Business Roundtable (2019). Business Roundtable Redefines the Purpose of a Corporation to Promote "An Economy that Serves All Americans". *The Business Roundtable*, August 19, 2019.

Chevron (2016). Chevron Announces Sale of Geothermal Operations. Chevron Press Release, December 23, 2016.

Chevron (2020). https://www.chevron.com/stories/geothermal-energy. Accessed on April 10, 2020.

Clark, W. C. (2007). Sustainability science: A room of its own. *Proceedings of the National Academy of Sciences*, 104, 6, 1737–1738.

Cunningham, T., Hedberg, A., Nzakat, S., and Yao, L. (2018). *Assessing the Energiewende: An International Expert Review*. Berlin: Konrad Adenauer, March 2018.

Damodaran, A. (1996). *Investment Valuation: Tools and Techniques for Determining the Value of Any Asset*. New York: Wiley & Sons.

EIA (2019). *Energy Outlook 2019*. Washington DC: US Department of Energy, Energy Information Administration, April 2019.

Faus, J. (1995). Operational Finance: Analysis and Diagnosis. *Technical Notes, FN-386-E-O-296-002*, IESE Business School.

Fleming, S. and Hook, L. (2019). EIB to phase out lending to fossil fuel projects by 2021. *Financial Times*, November 15, 2019.

Friedman, M. (1970). The social responsibility of business is to increase its profits. *The New York Times Magazine*, September 13, 1970.

Gordon, M. J. and Shapiro, E. (1956). Capital equipment analysis: The required rate of profit. *Management Science*, 3(1), 1–115.

Henry, A. D. (2009). The challenges of learning for sustainability: A prolegomenon to theory. *Human Ecology Review*, 16(2), 131–140.

Holmes, A. (1992). *Privatising British Electricity: Restructuring and Resistance*. London: Financial Times Publications.

House of Commons (2007). *The Restructuring of British Energy: Forty-third Report of Session 2006–07*. London: Committee of Public Accounts. The House of Commons, July 9, 2007.

IEA (2019). *World Energy Outlook*. Paris: International Energy Agency.

Littlechild, S. (2001). Competition and regulation in the UK Electricity Industry (with a brief look at California). *Journal of Applied Corporate Finance*, 13(4), 21–38.

Masten, S. E. and Crocker, K. J. (1985). Efficient adaptation in long term contracts: Take-or-pay provisions for natural gas. *The American Economic Review*, 75(5), 1083–1093.

Pollitt, M. (2012). The role of policy in energy transitions: Lessons from the energy liberalisation era. *Energy Policy*, 50, 128–137.

Shapiro, A. C. (1999). *Multinational Financial Management, 6th Edition*. New York: John Wiley & Sons.

Smil, V. (2010). *Energy Transitions: History, Requirements, and Prospects*. Sta Barbara, CA: Praeger.

Thaler, R. H. and Sunstein, C. R. (2008). *Nudge: Improving Decisions About Health, Wealth, and Happiness*. New Haven and London: Yale University Press.

United Nations (2015). The 2030 Agenda for Sustainable Development. Accessed on April 9, 2020. https://sustainabledevelopment.un.org/?menu=1300.

United Nations (2018). Secretary General's statement on climate change. Accessed on October 11, 2018. https://www.un.org/sg/en/content/sg/statement/2018-09-10/secretary-generals-remarks-climate-change-delivered.

Chapter 10
Oligopolistic Rivalries

Oligopoly differs from pure competition in substantive ways. As oligopolists, each rival firm asserts its influence on prices, costs, or volumes. As their actions interact, their market shares as well as their costs vary, thereby altering the value of their firms. To adaptively respond, managers would need to "look forward, reason backwards" and glance sideways when aiming to profit from changing markets. Avinash K Dixit and Barry J Nalebuff (1993) succinctly describe what the managerial purpose is. They understood strategic thinking as an "art of outdoing an adversary, knowing that the adversary is trying to do the same to you." By understanding the dynamic decision contexts, managers could identify adaptive pathways and the levers of value to inform their next strategic moves.

1
Introduction

Financial analyses have instilled in managers a simple decision rule. Invest when you are earning more than what you are spending. Formally, analysts would project their cash flows over multiple periods, discount the flows to estimate the present value, and estimate the payoffs (or the discounted cash flows). If the present value is greater than the amount spent on building the assets or its capital expenditure, the investment is said to be a good one and should be funded. This is how the net present values (NPVs) are used, a simple way of ranking competing opportunities from highest to lowest amounts in hierarchical order.

To make NPVs work, it assumes an almost perfect foresight to predict what the future could bring. In this static world, managers tend to ignore what their rivals may do or could do to spoil their game. For this reason, Anil Arya and his colleagues (Arya *et al.*, 1998) warned against NPV's penchant to lead managers to make sub-optimal decisions, a tendency that persists today. Inadvertently, this is reinforced when achieving target is amply rewarded. Thus, the managerial mantra of "promising low, delivering high" has formed part of the "accepted wisdom."

Astute managers would encourage in rivals this self-centric behaviour. After all, to what end does an enterprise serve when it is set to fail by repeated managerial errors?

Oligopoly comprises rivals whose actions could directly alter prices, volumes, and markets. With each supply added, shortages are eased or worsen oversupplies. How astute managers could tackle these decisions, I defer to the guidance of Avinash K Dixit and Barry J Nalebuff (1993):

"Think of the difference between the decisions of a lumberjack and those of a general. When the lumberjack decides to chop wood, *one* does not expect the wood to fight back; *the* environment is neutral. But when the general tries to cut down the enemy's army, *one* must anticipate and overcome resistance to *one's* plans. Like the general, you must recognise that your business rivals, prospective spouse, and even your child are intelligent and purposive people. Their aims often conflict with yours, but they include some potential allies. Your own choice must allow for the conflict, and utilise the cooperation. Such interactive decisions are called strategic, and the plan of action appropriate for them is called a strategy." I would add: The competence to carry out such a strategy adaptively comprises the elements of strategic actions underpinning *dynamic decisions*.

This is as true in politics as in the realms of management. As I started my investment banking career in the City of London, then Prime Minister Margaret R Thatcher was scaling up her privatisation of vital industries. The very idea of handing strategic firms to private capital was anathema to a brand of "nationalist" ideology of state capitalism. While the merits or ills of her era await history to render its judgement, little is said about Thatcher's contribution to strategic actions. Ignored by a number of critics till today (Niemietz, 2013), managers may learn a few lessons on exercising strategic actions.

To reshape British industries, Thatcher had to wean them off state subsidies. She first had to reverse state capitalism's penchant to subsidise ailing firms, hoping against hope that they will recover. What Thatcher inherited was an economy teetering on bankruptcy, a fact that is forgotten or taken for granted today.

In executing her strategic actions, Thatcher followed this playbook (Matthews and Minford, 1987): "Rather than launching an immediate and grand assault on all fronts, Mrs Thatcher picked off enemies one by one, each victory consolidating her position for the next attack. Only when inflation was clearly under control could more radical supply-side measures be introduced." They added that "once serious supply side policies were introduced, they had significant effect on productivity, growth, and equilibrium rate of employment."

To sustain her reforms, Thatcher shied away from accelerating adjustments by injecting fiscal stimulus and loosening monetary policy. Such moves would have brought privatised firms back to heavier dependence on government spending for support. Instead, Thatcher "advocated farther supply side measures and deregulation to help markets achieve this transition" towards a functioning market economy, Matthews and Minford concluded.

In tackling a complex array of change, human virtues are essential for success. Tim Koller *et al.* (2020) said as much when they noted: "As business leaders wrestle with this challenge (*on sustainability*), not to mention the broader questions about purpose and how best to manage the coalescing and colliding interests of myriad owners and stakeholders in a modern corporation, they will need a large dose of humility and tolerance for ambiguity. They'll also need crystal clarity about problems their communities are trying to solve. Otherwise, confusion about objectives could inadvertently undermine capitalism's ability to catalyse progress as it has in the past, whether lifting millions of people out of poverty, contributing to higher literacy rates, or fostering innovations that improve quality of life and lengthen life expectancy."

To assist managers in this undertaking, Thatcher's incremental approach could be formalised. I propose combining binomial processes to model how volatilities could be tracked with real options and game theories to value managerial flexibility and the interactions of rival firms. Starting by disentangling a mosaic of dynamic interactions amidst the rivalry of firms, the complexity is partly simplified. This is where a large dose of humility and tolerance for ambiguity is helpful. As past beliefs (and comfort) are growing more untenable, managers must be ready to embrace untried approaches to confront future challenges today.

2
Understanding (Some) Decision Contexts

Under transitioning markets, NPVs continue to imagine a world that could be made predictable by managers. Persisting in their beliefs, managers would focus on employing the means to make their cash flows as precise and predictable as their analytical tools would allow. Ignoring how oligopoly markets and rivals are changing their game, NPV advocates err in at least two aspects in their prognosis of the managerial challenge:

1. Outcomes result from one-off "now or never" decisions often undertaken in isolation. Under oligopoly, however, decisions are contingent upon what rivals do or forego.
2. "What one produces, it can sell" is generally assumed for power under pure competition. With oligopoly, volumes are reallocated, which often strands some supplies.

Power as an output is generally considered as a commodity that cannot be stored. For this reason, power has to be produced and supplied in quantities that at least match the demand for a given period. While this is generally the case, fossil fuels, pump storage hydro, and geothermal power resolved this "storage" problem by storing energy in its raw form. For instance, coal or gas is stored as inventory. With the adequate logistics, coal or gas is fed to power-generating assets for conversion into power at relatively short lead times. Similarly, this is the case for pump storage where water is collected in a reservoir or geothermal steam kept underground for ready conversion to power when needed.

Centrally collected and converted, power from these energy sources could be varied at minimal costs to meet periodic fluctuations in demand. Their integration into extant power distribution networks is proven to work. This contrasts with wind and photovoltaic energy resources, which are dispersed and intermittent. While storage technologies are progressing, costs remain an issue with more scope for rapid improvements in store.

Under these dynamic contexts, a linear projection of costs, prices, and volumes that ignore how rivals would respond often lead managers to err in valuing investments. To remedy, managers would need to reframe their decision premises by explicitly evaluating the effects of rivalries on outcomes and how it shapes the strategies that managers may adapt. This notion is revisited in the following section. For now, let us examine why NPVs may have outlived their usefulness in informing oligopolists as they plot their next moves.

Some managers aspire to cut down their adversaries but choose to behave like a lumberjack. By ignoring a rival's response, the lumberjack chops wood and assumes they could sell what they cut. To maximise profits by expanding volumes, they focus on sharpening their axe (or tools), with less attention paid as to why they are chopping wood.

This resonates with maximising payoffs under NPVs. To restore efficiency, after experiencing volume erosions, managers instinctively spend on maintenance capex, or MCPX, to restore maximum available supply to its previous level. Managers happily imagine a future of riches, counting the incremental volumes as gold.

In contrast, an astute manager would take a page from the general's playbook. One may opt to invest in a more cost-effective technology. By displacing the lumberjack's incremental volumes, it becomes potentially worthless. As a result, the unsuspecting lumberjack could suffer irretrievable damage.

To avoid this fate, the general would first re-examine the contours of the battlefield to understand how oligopoly is changing their game. Instead of picking to fight with all guns blazing, the general chooses the battles that matter the most.

In the context of energy supplies, on what bases are rival firms actually competing?

Energy as a commodity is fungible and indistinguishable as an output. They compete on volumes, where the cheapest supply is dispatched first, followed by the next least expensive, until the demand is fulfilled for a given period (Lundin and Tangeras, 2020). The volume that completes the demand is the marginal supply, usually fulfilled by $Coal_M$ or $ACCGT_M$. In theoretical terms, oligopoly energy markets follow Cournot volume competition (Kreps and Scheinkman, 1983; Trenblay, 2011) in allocating supplies among rivals.

When supplies exceed periodic demand, the more expensive volumes are not sold. Unless stored at minimum costs, as pump storage hydro power does, their revenue is nil, earning no returns. This reallocation of volumes is the result of how rivals interact. What each firm does impacts the other and would tend to elicit a reaction. As humans, managers would tend to react differently, with the following consequences:

Accustomed to sharpening their axe as an instinctive response, the lumberjack is likely to ask for more data, or even seek expert advice, on how to get a better axe.

Opting for an easy life, the lumberjack defaults to what one is accustomed to. That comfort is provided by NPV. By relegating judgement to NPV's algorithm, invest when NPV > 0, the efforts begin in earnest to "fine-tune" the inputs to "prove" contrary evidence "wrong."

With financial evaluation out to reinforce the entrenched *beliefs* purveyed by "experts," the lumberjack gains comfort in numbers. "Validating" what was "believed," opinions take on the weight of "accepted wisdom." The late Colin Powell, former Chair, US Joint Chiefs of Staff, may have foreseen this when he offered this advice: "Don't be buffaloed by experts and elites. Experts often possess more data than judgement. Elites can become so inbred that they produce haemophiliacs who bleed to death as soon as they are nicked by the real world."

In assessing the contours of the battlefield, the general would break down their battle plans into a combination of skirmishes, diversions, advances, or tactical retreats. In outdoing her powerful adversaries, Thatcher manoeuvred her way to outflank Arthur Scargill during the 1984–1985 Coal Strike (BBC, 1984).

Richard Rumelt (2011) prescribes deep analyses and disciplined thought processes to choreograph strategic actions. Residing in a messy and chaotic world, managers would adapt their actions as new information becomes available. It may clarify the nature of the uncertainties or discard what were entrenched as beliefs but invalidated by data. To make this happen, the lumberjack's mindset needs to morph into one that could combine intellect, humility, and wise judgement, to make managers fit for command as a general.

3
Purposive Dynamic Decisions

In a managerial context, most managers already possess these qualities. What is missing are dynamic thought processes that could formally structure how interacting strategies among rivals would impact valuation. The logic of *purposive dynamic decisions* is handy. It applies knowledge to inform judgement when solving relevant business problems.

In orchestrating the skirmishes, diversions, advances, or tactical retreats, to achieve one's purpose, a general employs intelligence to inform on rival's movements. Armed with information, one assesses the resources and capabilities of the troops, complements or substitutes as needed, before engaging rivals. As battles progress, the general adapts, alters, accelerates, or aborts one's prior moves. Such flexibility in actions could lead to gains or avoid losses when it is executed with minimal costs, a sentiment reinforced by Avinash K Dixit and Barry J Nalebuff (2010).

Financial economics formalise these adaptive moves under real options and game theories. To apply this to energy investments, the binomial processes following the *Cox-Ross-Rubinstein* (2003) genre is employed. It converts the intricacies of oligopolistic interactions into serial binary events, as illustrated in Box 10.1.

3.1 What value do binomial processes enhance?

NPVs reward predictability in cash flows with lower discount rates. This differs from binomial processes, as Chart 10.1 summarises, that engender diametrically opposed managerial behaviour to produce radically different outcomes. Specifically:

1. NPV sees volatilities as risks to minimise, while binomial processes explicitly evaluate variations for the options embedded and their call (or put) value.
2. Managers aim to accurately predict (or pay for forecasts) and fix obligations to reduce uncertainties to "maximise" NPVs. In contrast, binomial processes value operational and strategic flexibility, employing real options reasoning.

Dynamic Decisions

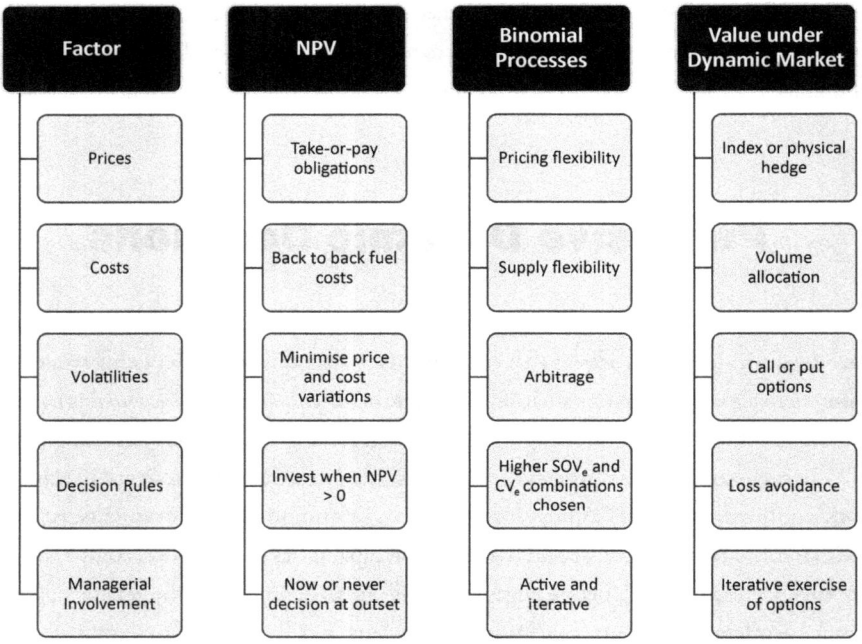

Chart 10.1: Comparative Approaches of NPV and Binomial Processes

3. NPV introspectively moves managers to invest in isolation. In contrast, binomial processes via game theory aim to comprehend rival's actions to outdo them or extend the hand of cooperation.

Recalling how the decisions differ, binomial processes, employed under *purposive dynamic decisions*, could remedy NPV's limitations. It adds value by identifying arbitrage opportunities arising from volatilities as outcomes deviate positively. This is conferred when excess value is created when there is pricing or volume flexibility. By quantifying the payoffs from arbitrage, managers can value the options embedded in the manager's chosen actions.

Asymmetric information and access to resources almost always are part of the card generals are dealt with. How they turn a weak hand into a strong suit is part of exercising judgement. They take stock of their situation and humbly submit to what they could change and those that they cannot.

Acting nimbly, they adaptively move from pounding on the enemy or waltz the night away even with rivals. The choices managers make are informed by their purpose, their human virtues (or lack of it), and principles. For this reason, dynamic actions are bounded by certain principles, as opposed to unfettered liberty to change course or renege on obligations:

1. To sustain a business, it has to earn returns that are sufficient to remunerate its stakeholders, to fund any required reinvestments, and to compensate for risk-taking.
2. Rivals choose to compete or cooperate to promote mutual gains, a point at which "notional equilibrium" is achieved, as a transient pause or prolonged stability.
3. For each action, there is likely to be a reaction. Rivals may opt to set the pace or to follow, subject to the managers' judgement of their advantages (or the best way to avoid losses).

To incorporate these principles, Benoit Chevalier-Roignant and Lenos Trigeorgis (2011) combine under *option games* the strength of real options in valuing operational and strategic flexibility with games theory. Set up as *games*, the effects of rivalry and competing strategic moves on the firms' values could be quantified.

In promoting mutual gains, *games* are set up to expand payoffs or to minimise pains from losses. This "notional equilibrium" is akin to what John Forbes Nash Jr formulated. The "equilibrium" is reached and sustained for as long as any other moves would erode value. That is, by deviating, the rival is made worse off value-wise (Abada *et al.*, 2013).

The "notional equilibrium" may be transient or prolonged. While academic theory sets out to present humans as rational, Richard Thaler (2015) strongly disputes this premise. He instead posits that humans seldom act rationally (in an economic sense, that is). Instead, managers may act contrary to what financial theories would prescribe for the following reasons:

1. Asymmetric valuation leads to divergent (from economic optimum) actions, as the lumberjack and the general would pursue different paths.

2. Increasing pains, or above-normal gains, take time for managers to recognise and react to, prolonged when managers are obstinate or choose to live in blissful ignorance.
3. Managers rely on their gut instead of doing the sums and opt to imagine certainty that only exists in the managers' minds.

While there is no silver bullet to overcome these human tendencies, it can be informed and redirected following the logic and intuition behind what I call *dynamic thought processes*.

3.2 *Dynamic thought processes* and actions

Dynamic thought processes break down complex interactions into binary *up* or *down* moves. Prices are up or down by certain magnitudes as are costs and volumes. Performed as separate binomial trees, each component's moves are quantified with the results recombined to yield a range of outcomes.

Capital-intensive investments, such as mining, resource exploration, refineries, power plants, or infrastructures, monetise their outputs subject to volatile commodities prices and volumes. To make the results tractable for managerial decisions, managers label their estimates as P90 (high estimate), P50 (equally likely up or down), or P10 (low estimates). By picking three possible prices or volumes, the resulting valuations are given.

Richard Thaler (2015) asserts that humans' ability to estimate a "correct range" is limited, often clouded by the most recent prices or volumes and observed volatility, σ. Within a "narrow range," disruptions from technological change (e.g. coal to gas transition) or of a pandemic nature (e.g. transient or prolonged loss) are ignored as low probability events. While this is often true, a strategic mind would instead aim to understand how disruptive events could change the *games* in their favour or work against extant competitive positioning. Juxtaposing a familiar strategic schema, against the questions *dynamic thought processes* would raise, the purpose and strategic pathways are usually made clearer and actionable:

1. *Where are you, where do you want to go?*: Know the terrain, articulate what you are trying to change and why.
2. *How do you get there?*: Know yourself and your rivals, and understand how your actions could coalesce or collide with your rivals' ascribed purpose.

3. ***What and how do you need to navigate adaptively?:*** What events could frustrate or facilitate your journey? How do you recognise it and what could you do about it?

What makes disruption fearsome is the unknown, as to its timing, nature, or magnitude. Fearful of losing "authority," some managers instinctively look for a "new normal" to buy time to formulate a credible narrative. This is where humility could serve as the font of wisdom.

Managers, acting with humility, articulate with integrity what they do not know, identify those who may know, or at worse, appreciate what is collectively unknown. With prior assessment of "low probability" events, managers may have gained some inkling of what extremely low prices, or volumes, or spiralling costs could inflict on their business. By working their way to connect these factors to the nature of the disruptions, managers may (re)gain insights on the contingencies that they may have planned for, but readily forgot because of its remoteness from their daily chores.

In the final analysis, if rising tides lift all boats, even those with leaks, a pandemic would hasten the decline of the weak and moderately prepared. Paradoxically, one could prepare the least when managers focus on predicting what and when a pandemic would hit them. With once in a decade as a likely answer, inaction may result.

A better stance would be to examine how one could recover from a shock of disappearing volumes, interrupted supplies, or obsolescing assets. This strategic exercise involves dynamic thought processes that start with a structured articulation of purpose and contexts, as outlined in Chart 10.2.

To spend or not on MCPX is a question that faces managers periodically. Applying *dynamic thought processes*, I propose a six-step deconstruction of the problem in the following sections.

3.2.1 First identify the areas of uncertainties

The size of the pie is determined by the market volume, which may grow, contract, or remain stable. Rivals make their supplies available, where the maximum is a function of their installed capacity, available feedstock (e.g. fuel, water, wind, steam, or sunlight), and operating efficiency. The uncertainties revolve around the pace of volume erosion from natural wastage or lax routine maintenance, volatilities of feedstock supplies, or the pace (e.g. stable, expansive, or declining) and shape (e.g. symmetric or asymmetric) of volume growth.

Dynamic Decisions

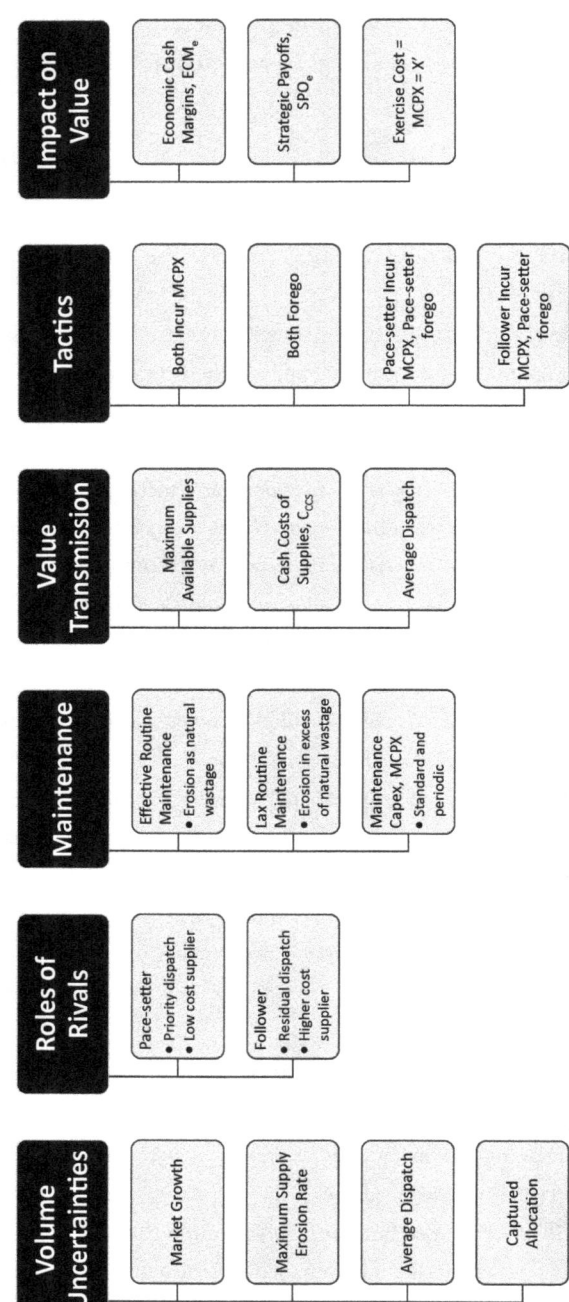

Chart 10.2: A Feasible Dynamic Thought Process

Combined, the uncertain factors impact how much a rival could supply and at what costs. The cash cost of supply, C_{CCS}, would position the rival as the first or the last to supply.

3.2.2 Understand how market allocates volumes to rivals

The duopoly rivals are pace-setters or followers. As pace-setters, they are the first to supply as the low-cost supplier. The follower takes what remains from what the pace-setter could not supply.

The C_{CCS} is locked in as initial endowments of the chosen technology, with declining volumes tending to increase the costs (or vice versa). Operated under flexible volumes and prices, a rival may avoid losses by curtailing supplies when market price, $P_s < C_{CCS}$, is below the cash cost of supply.

Regulation may confer priority dispatch to intermittent renewables and nuclear, regardless of their C_{CCS}. Hence, PVT_M or ANuke supplies first, ahead of $ACCGT_B$, even when the lifecycle costs are higher.

3.2.3 Evaluate what maintenance capex, MCPX, contributes

A well-executed maintenance programme is one way to slow the erosion rate, and this costs money. Routine maintenance relates to day-to-day operations that comprise the operations and maintenance costs included in C_{VAR}.

A well-managed routine maintenance could slow the erosion to the rate of natural wastage of an asset. In contrast, by being lax, erosion rates could increase, resulting in higher volumes lost and foregoing revenues. Over time, the volumes lost (or eroded) accumulate to a tidy sum.

To restore the lost volume, the asset may have to be refurbished from time to time. The expense associated is the maintenance capex, MCPX. By incurring MCPX, more volume is made available, adding to the maximum available supply for the rival that spends.

3.2.4 Variable volumes and the rivals' value

The simple answer is, volume can be monetised when it is sold at a price greater than its cash cost of supply. That is, the power price P_s is greater, so that $P_s > C_{CCS}$.

Prices are set by the lifecycle cost of energy (LCOE) of $ACCGT_M$, which is based on a mid-merit volume of 5,694 MWh (see Box 10.1). If volume is growing fast, it is possible that the mid-merit supplier may achieve higher volumes. In this case, $ACCGT_M$ would yield a marginal cost that is lower when fixed costs embedded in LCOE are spread over higher MWh. To simplify, when volumes fall below 5,694 MWh, $ACCGT_M$'s LCOE is retained for setting power prices. This would imply that the supplying firms would absorb the excess costs, thereby reducing its economic cash margin, ECM_e.

This connects the analysis back to the average dispatch of each rival. As an intuitive rule of thumb, if average dispatch persistently falls below the maximum available supply, there is excess supply.

3.2.5 Pairings of rivals and contingent moves

Rivals tend to respond with every action initiated by a competitor. The outcomes are quantified as strategic option values (e.g. SOV_{e1} and SOV_{e2}) and valued as their call values (e.g. CV_{e1} and CV_{e2}) for Firm 1 and Firm 2, respectively. The pairings may take any one of the following forms:

1. Both Firm 1 and Firm 2 act in symmetry, where they both spend on MCPX periodically to boost their maximum available volume.
2. Only Firm 1, as the pace-setter, invests while Firm 2, the follower, foregoes the opportunity. With this action, Firm 1 is expected to gain volumes with Firm 2 possibly losing some.
3. Only Firm 2 invests while Firm 1 foregoes, leaving the field open to its rival, where both firms retain their roles.
4. Both Firm 1 and Firm 2 forego MCPX.

In each of these pairings, volumes are reallocated, thus altering C_{CCS}. Both firms receive a common market power price, P_s, for each period, for their fungible volumes. Unsubsidised, as revenues and costs are altered, so are ECM_e and strategic payoffs, SPO_e.

3.2.6 Formalise quantifiable outcomes using binomial processes

Employing the binomial processes, following the methods in Box 10.1, how ECM_e varies could be estimated under each pairing. SPO_e, or the present value of ECM_e, is weighted as risk-neutral payoff when discounted by the risk-free rate. By deducting

MCPX as X' from terminal SPO_e, SOV_e is calculated for each node for the terminal period. Working backwards, CPX as X is then deducted as the exercise costs to build the asset.

Now that the quantifiable outcomes could be estimated, positivist financial economics and behavioural aspects of managerial decisions could be made to complement. In challenging or validating entrenched beliefs, managers may connect their insights to turn adversity into opportunities through purposive actions.

4
Adaptively Reshaping Markets

"To innovate is to flourish" encapsulates a managerial belief to solving business problems. Left as an aspiration, it remains as such unless managers could articulate why they want to innovate and with what levers they could turn ideas into action. In choosing among prospective energy technologies, addressing these questions may help crystallise actionable ideas:

1. How did the ***shrinking carbon space*** emerge, and why does it matter to managers?
2. Is disruption played out under similar contexts where the disruptor emerges triumphant, or is it a transient passage of a ***disruptor set up for prospective disruption***?
3. In a world of continual change, how would managers decide whether to ***set the pace*** or ***follow rivals*** in embarking on their future course?
4. Dissatisfied with what one sees, what could managers do to ***change the course*** of their business and ***outdo their rivals***?

To tackle these questions, I propose we reconnect with Roy Barton, adviser to Jocelyn Chalmers, Chief Executive of a major oil and gas company. In offering his advice, Roy uses a simple case of *spend or forego* decision on MCPX to drive home his proposed strategic actions. Using the terminologies of managers, Roy describes an investment as "in the money" when its SPO_e > X or SOV_e > 0. Otherwise, when SOV_e < 0, it is "out of the money" because it incurs a loss, hence value is nil.

As a discretionary decision, MCPX is "in the money" when the incremental volume earns SPOe > X', or MCPX. Vice versa, it is "out of the money" where its call value, CV_e, is nil. The CV_e, when positive, indicates the value of the investment at a given node, as described in Box 10.1.

4.1 Shrinking carbon space

Two rivals, $Coal_B$ and $ACCGT_B$, compete under a coal-dominated power market, where $Coal_M$ sets the power prices. Coal and gas prices may move *up* or *down* at similar magnitudes and direction, or gas prices may be more volatile than coal.

To access their payoffs, $Coal_B$ would need to spend about fourfold compared to $ACCGT_B$, with MCPX showing similar divergence.

With higher SPO_e and lower CPX and MCPX, $ACCGT_B$ enjoys the best of both worlds when power prices are set by $Coal_M$. This gives $ACCGT_B$ significant economic incentives to expand its volumes, at the expense of the more expensive $Coal_B$, as indicated by higher SOV_{el} and CV_{el} across all pairings of actions considered (Table 10.1).

What the math signals is a rivalry that seeks mutual gains through an accommodative *modus vivendi* when both have symmetric cost volatilities under stable volumes. Specifically:

1. $Coal_B$ gains the most by leaving the field open to $ACCGT_B$ and foregoes MCPX (Column E). By spending, it elicits $ACCGT_B$ to spend as well, resulting in $Coal_B$ losing more (Column C).
2. $ACCGT_B$ gains by spending on MCPX, at the expense of $Coal_B$ because the more it supplies, the less the demand is left for $Coal_B$ to fulfil.

Through substitution, gas displaces coal. However, it is in $ACCGT_B$'s interests to keep $Coal_B$ sufficiently healthy financially to sustain supportive power prices pegged to coal. By prolonging coal's presence, $Coal_B$ managers have been granted a relief from sudden death.

Jocelyn recalled her first foray into the power market as an independent power producer, using gas as her preferred fuel. Those were days when "spark spreads" (or the difference between gas and power prices) made previous versions of $ACCGT_B$ lucrative assets to own. With some regrets, Jocelyn thought that this was indeed too good to last.

Table 10.1: ACCGT$_B$ and Coal$_B$ under Symmetric Cost Volatilities and Stable Volumes

Dynamic Volume Allocation with Flexible Pricing under Coal$_M$ as Price-setter — Symmetric Costs Volatilities

Column/Line	Duopoly		Power Prices A $/kWh	Both Incur MCPX SOV$_{e,1}$ B $ mln	Both Incur MCPX SOV$_{e,2}$ C $ mln	ACCGT$_B$ Only SOV$_{e,1}$ D $ mln	ACCGT$_B$ Only SOV$_{e,2}$ E $ mln	Coal$_B$ Only SOV$_{e,1}$ F $ mln	Coal$_B$ Only SOV$_{e,2}$ G $ mln	Both Forego MCPX SOV$_{e,1}$ H $ mln	Both Forego MCPX SOV$_{e,2}$ I $ mln	Notional Equilibrium SOV$_{e,1}$ J $ mln	Notional Equilibrium SOV$_{e,2}$ K $ mln
1	F1: ACCGT$_B$	F2: Coal$_B$	0.2290	11,102	3,331	11,165	3,908	9,364	3,331	8,787	2,962	11,165	3,908
2	F1: ACCGT$_B$	F2: Coal$_B$	0.1971	10,434	2,862	10,497	3,805	8,817	3,235	8,448	2,922	10,497	3,805
3	F1: ACCGT$_B$	F2: Coal$_B$	0.1717	9,909	1,831	9,972	3,379	8,387	2,848	8,181	2,801	9,972	3,379
4	F1: ACCGT$_B$	F2: Coal$_B$	0.1514	9,497	717	9,560	2,636	8,049	2,158	7,954	2,600	9,560	2,636
5	F1: ACCGT$_B$	F2: Coal$_B$	0.1353	9,167	0	9,230	1,739	7,778	1,285	7,705	2,373	9,230	1,739
6	F1: ACCGT$_B$	F2: Coal$_B$	0.1223	8,731	0	8,794	969	7,479	450	7,346	2,201	8,794	969

Column/Line	Duopoly		Power Prices $/kWh A	Both Incur MCPX CV$_{e,1}$ B	Both Incur MCPX CV$_{e,2}$ C	ACCGT$_B$ Only CV$_{e,1}$ D	ACCGT$_B$ Only CV$_{e,2}$ E	Coal$_B$ Only CV$_{e,1}$ F	Coal$_B$ Only CV$_{e,2}$ G	Both Forego MCPX CV$_{e,1}$ H	Both Forego MCPX CV$_{e,2}$ I	Notional Equilibrium CV$_{e,1}$ J	Notional Equilibrium CV$_{e,2}$ K
7	F1: ACCGT$_B$	F2: Coal$_B$	0.1971	10,656	3,234	10,717	3,809	8,992	3,247	9,032	2,888	10,717	3,809
8	F1: ACCGT$_B$	F2: Coal$_B$	0.1717	10,042	2,757	10,103	3,697	8,489	3,143	8,703	2,846	10,103	3,697
9	F1: ACCGT$_B$	F2: Coal$_B$	0.1514	9,559	1,748	9,621	3,271	8,094	2,755	8,437	2,726	9,621	3,271
10	F1: ACCGT$_B$	F2: Coal$_B$	0.1353	9,178	675	9,240	2,541	7,782	2,075	8,165	2,529	9,240	2,541
11	F1: ACCGT$_B$	F2: Coal$_B$	0.1223	8,829	0	8,890	1,670	7,510	1,225	7,822	2,309	8,890	1,670

As an observer of history, Roy wonders out loud: "What could have pushed managers to embark on paths leading towards mutual value eroding moves?"

Jocelyn offered her insights: "Managers, as humans, may prove unwilling to cede volumes to rivals. This is compounded when investments are evaluated by ignoring rivalries, and are undertaken when NPV > 0. On this criterion, both $Coal_B$ and $ACCGT_B$ would justify spending on MCPX."

Going back to the math, as both $Coal_B$ and $ACCGT_B$ spend, $Coal_B$ progressively observes their shrinking SOV_{e2} until it's "out of the money." These points are reached when power prices fall below \$0.1223/kWh (A.6), resulting in nil SOV_{e2} (C.5 and C.6).

Roy now moves to examine how asymmetric cost volatilities could change the decision, if at all, based on the math shown in Table 10.2. While the general decision remains unchanged, asymmetric cost volatilities could ease the pressure on $Coal_B$'s SOV_{e2} and CV_{e2}. Counterintuitively, these diverging trends in SOV_{e1} and SOV_{e2} are of particular interest:

1. $Coal_B$ earns more when coal prices are high (and vice versa), with SOV_{e2} and CV_{e2} declining as power prices fall.
2. $ACCGT_B$ earns more when power prices decline, as shown by expanding SOV_{e1} and CV_{E1}.

The power price threshold when $Coal_B$ would be "out of the money" is lowered to \$0.1223/kWh, when both decide to spend on MCPX.

Delving deeper into its causes, Roy illustrated in Chart 10.3 how fuel costs, the principal cost for $Coal_B$ and $ACCGT_B$, when their volatilities are symmetric or asymmetric.

Symmetric fuel cost volatilities (10.3(A)) yield similar spreads (10.3(B)) between coal and gas prices. In effect, $Coal_B$ tends to experience supply costs disadvantage relative to $ACCGT_B$ over the range of power prices considered. In contrast, as gas prices become more volatile than coal, $Coal_B$ is cheaper than $ACCGT_B$ when power prices are above \$0.1717/kWh (10.3(C)). However, below these power prices, gas prices fall faster than coal, thereby widening the coal–gas prices spread (10.3(D)).

Roy explained: "While coal and gas prices, and how they evolve, are in itself uncertain, plotting the series of binary moves allow managers to build scenarios and

Oligopolistic Rivalries 529

Table 10.2: ACCGT$_B$ and Coal$_B$ under Asymmetric Cost Volatilities

Dynamic Volume Allocation with Flexible Pricing under Coal$_M$ as Price-setter — Asymmetric Costs Volatilities in Stable Demand

Column/Line	Duopoly		Power Prices A $/kWh	Both Incur MCPX		ACCGT$_B$ Only		Coal$_B$ Only		Both Forego MCPX		Notional Equilibrium	
				SOV$_1$ B $ mln	SOV$_2$ C $ mln	SOV$_1$ D $ mln	SOV$_2$ E $ mln	SOV$_1$ F $ mln	SOV$_2$ G $ mln	SOV$_1$ H $ mln	SOV$_2$ I $ mln	SOV$_1$ J $ mln	SOV$_2$ K $ mln
1	F1: ACCGT$_B$	F2: Coal$_B$	0.2258	6,453	3,722	6,453	4,288	5,624	3,722	4,981	2,962	6,453	4,288
2	F1: ACCGT$_B$	F2: Coal$_B$	0.1971	8,998	3,249	8,998	4,184	7,708	3,625	7,272	2,922	8,998	4,184
3	F1: ACCGT$_B$	F2: Coal$_B$	0.1717	10,336	2,212	10,336	3,756	8,803	3,235	8,530	2,801	10,336	3,756
4	F1: ACCGT$_B$	F2: Coal$_B$	0.1514	10,929	1,091	10,929	3,008	9,288	2,540	9,126	2,600	10,929	3,008
5	F1: ACCGT$_B$	F2: Coal$_B$	0.1353	11,016	77	11,016	2,142	9,103	1,700	9,311	2,330	11,016	2,142
6	F1: ACCGT$_B$	F2: Coal$_B$	0.1223	10,484	0	10,484	1,521	9,057	935	9,245	2,004	10,484	1,521

Column/Line	Duopoly		Power Prices $/kWh A	Both Incur MCPX		ACCGT$_B$ Only		Coal$_B$ Only		Both Forego MCPX		Notional Equilibrium	
				CV$_1$ B	CV$_2$ C	CV$_1$ D	CV$_2$ E	CV$_1$ F	CV$_2$ G	CV$_1$ H	CV$_2$ I	CV$_1$ J	CV$_2$ K
7	F1: ACCGT$_B$	F2: Coal$_B$	0.1971	6,964	3,615	6,964	4,180	6,034	3,628	6,304	2,888	6,964	4,180
8	F1: ACCGT$_B$	F2: Coal$_B$	0.1717	9,130	3,135	9,130	4,067	7,807	3,523	8,188	2,846	9,130	4,067
9	F1: ACCGT$_B$	F2: Coal$_B$	0.1514	10,240	2,119	10,240	3,639	8,716	3,132	9,177	2,726	10,240	3,639
10	F1: ACCGT$_B$	F2: Coal$_B$	0.1353	10,685	1,030	10,685	2,905	9,013	2,450	9,599	2,527	10,685	2,905
11	F1: ACCGT$_B$	F2: Coal$_B$	0.1223	10,608	72	10,608	2,069	8,869	1,632	9,673	2,262	10,608	2,069

530 Dynamic Decisions

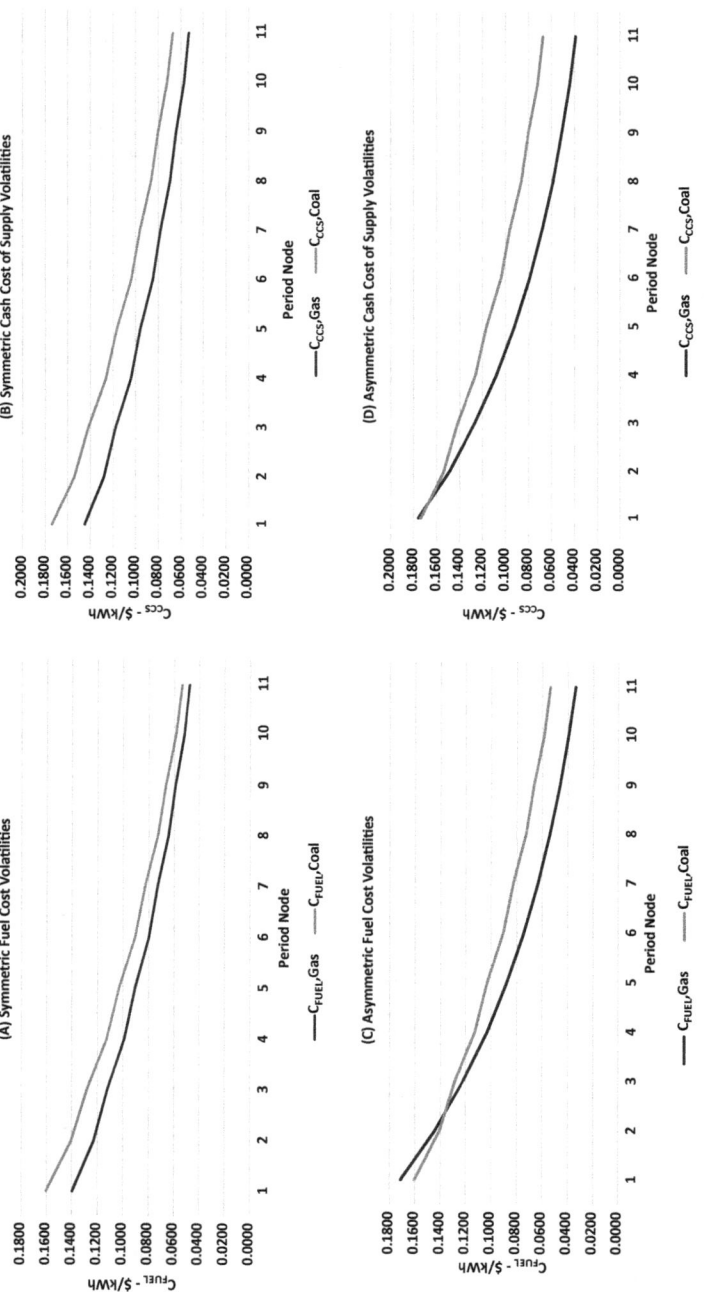

Chart 10.3: Comparative Cost Volatilities

quantify the feasible outcomes. Having done this exercise, one comes to a view that a dynamic energy market tends to favour $ACCGT_B$."

In Jocelyn's mind, this question arises: What would sustain a "steady state" to persist? If the math is there for all to see, why do $Coal_B$ managers continue, at least for a while, to pursue actions that could only lead to auto-destruction?

Dealing with Jocelyn's first question, Roy stuck with the math and use "notional equilibrium" he previously showed in Tables 10.1 and 10.2:

1. By foregoing MCPX, $ACCGT_B$ would leave $Coal_B$ to spend and add to its maximum available supply, expanding its SOV_{e2} compared to foregoing (10.1 and 10.2, Columns I). While SOV_{e1} remains high (10.1 and 10.2, Columns F), $ACCGT_B$ could gain more if it spends (10.1 and 10.2, Columns D).
2. $Coal_B$ spending may uplift SOV_{e2} if $ACCGT_B$ does not. However, this is unrealistic, given that $ACCGT_B$ stands to gain by spending whatever $Coal_B$ does.
3. What deters $Coal_B$ from aggressively expanding is the prospect of being "out of the money." This occurs when both $Coal_B$ and $ACCGT_B$ spend and power prices fall below $0.1363/kWh.
4. By leaving the field to $ACCGT_B$ and seeking an accommodative *modus vivendi*, both $ACCGT_B$ and $Coal_B$ optimise SOV_{e1} and SOV_{e2} and their respective CV_{e1} and CV_{e2}.

What is driving these outcomes is each rival's ability to monetise, or not, any incremental volumes that are made available. $Coal_B$'s decision to seek an accommodative *modus vivendi* with $ACCGT_B$ is strengthened by how volume is reallocated, as shown in Chart 10.4.

(A) shows that $ACCGT_B$ is likely to monetise the incremental volumes, where it tracks closely the maximum available supply. With $Coal_M$ providing premium pricing, the math makes the decision to spend for $ACCGT_B$ straightforward.

By foregoing MCPX, average volumes of $ACCGT_B$ would continue to track its declining maximum available supply (B). This is unlikely to be sustained as the foregone SOV_{e1} could prove too high to ignore.

$Coal_B$ is in an entirely different position. As a residual supplier, it gets to supply the demand that $ACCGT_B$ is unable to fulfil. The consequence is persistent

Dynamic Decisions

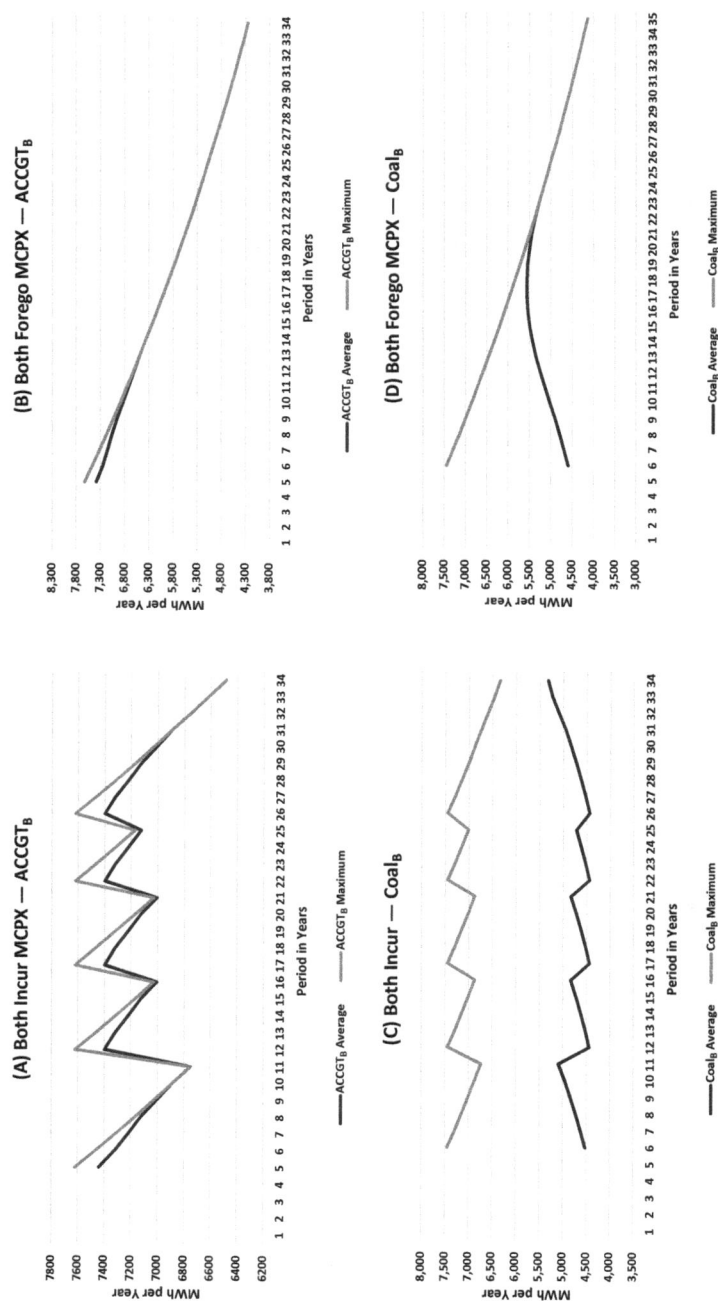

Chart 10.4: Volume Reallocation and Value of MCPX — ACCGT$_B$ and Coal$_B$

underutilisation, as (C) would show. The gaps between maximum available and average supplies are potentially closed when $Coal_B$ does not add to its available volumes (D).

The *modus vivendi* could become less accommodating for $Coal_B$ as $ACCGT_B$ dominates supplies. As $ACCGT_M$ replaces $Coal_M$ in setting power prices, the need for $ACCGT_B$ to accommodate $Coal_B$ is less compelling. The shift, while gradual, radically reshapes the power market as follows:

1. Power prices are substantially lower under $ACCGT_M$ ($0.1519/kWh vs $0.0922/kWh).
2. $Coal_B$ volumes become residual and persistently underutilised, facing the prospect of closure.
3. Cash costs of supplies progressively increase as volumes fall, which would kickstart a vicious cycle of making $Coal_B$ less and less competitive.

Recalculating, $Coal_B$ under a regime of $ACCGT_M$ as price-setter would hardly remain economically viable. With nil SOV_2 under all power price scenarios, the dynamic energy market is left clear for $ACCGT_B$ to dominate. The results are shown in Appendix 10C.

Roy now turns to Drax Group PLC in the United Kingdom to respond to Jocelyn's next query: Why do managers inadvertently embark on a path towards "self-destruction?"

National Power, a privatised power generator, was required to divest Drax Power Station, its largest coal-fired facility, to clear its acquisition of Midland Electricity, a regional privatised power distributor.

As a new entrant, AES sees in Drax Power Station a rapid way of scaling up their UK operations. After a couple of ownership changes and a public listing, Drax was reputed to have the most efficient coal-fired asset. Fast forward to 2020, Drax decided to end the use of coal ahead of its 2025 target closure (Gross, 2020). They are progressively replacing coal with pellets and refocusing their fuel on biomass. Over the past 15 years, Drax's share prices peaked at 800 pence before slumping to about 240 pence in early 2020 (Drax, 2020).

To an outside spectator, this is puzzling. Drax Power Station has done the right things in making its operations as efficient and cost-effective as coal-fired assets could achieve. Its difficulties were largely attributed to a bankruptcy of a major customer. With its stable volume offtake gone, Drax required a major refinancing that was not readily forthcoming.

Roy returned to the analogy of the lumberjack and the general to make his point.

From hindsight, the UK's dash for gas coincided with Drax Power Station's irreversible plunge towards obsolescence. During the 1990s, coal was progressively displaced by gas (Winskel, 2002). This was aided by supportive regulations that allowed the use of gas for power generation (Bocse and Gegenbauer, 2017). As a cheaper supply than coal, gas became the preferred fuel to generate power.

The general would assess this changing terrain by gaining a deep understanding of the battlefield, and the options it offers. The general could opt for benign neglect by foregoing MCPX or tactically withdraw by divesting.

Coincidentally, National Power did just that by "swapping" Drax Power Station, an obsolescing asset, for Midlands Electricity that repositioned the group into an integrated energy supplier.

The lumberjack took a very different route. Without changing tactics, the lumberjack continues to expand and commit judiciously to spending on MCPX to maximise available supplies. The lumberjack, as Drax did, realised belatedly when its volumes progressively shrunk that management blamed on intense competition that drove power prices down.

While one cannot be too definitive, an introspective perspective engendered by NPV does not help. This was what stopped Jocelyn short from endorsing the initial ranking of opportunities by her team before she called for a break.[1] With the binomial processes, the factors influencing the decline of $Coal_B$ amidst $ACCGT_B$ ascendancy are made apparent in Table 10.3.

The shrinkage of the carbon space is partly because of an obsolescing $Coal_B$ when paired with $ACCGT_B$. What displaces $Coal_B$ is likely to be multiple competing sources, other than gas, a phenomenon already seen in Western Europe (IEA, 2019).

4.2 Upsetting the $ACCGT_B$ apple cart: $StoHydro_B$ and geothermal

Roy highlighted how the carbon to renewables transitions could take two distinctive pathways. Modulated renewables comprise StoHydro and geothermal power (Geo_B

---

[1] This refers to the discussions of Jocelyn Chalmer with Roy Barton and her team, when they examine their strategic options. This is covered in Chapter 9.

Oligopolistic Rivalries

Table 10.3: $ACCGT_B$ and $StoHydro_B$ with Asymmetric Costs under $ACCGT_M$, Stable Volumes

Dynamic Volume Allocation with Flexible Pricing under $ACCGT_M$ as Price-setter — Asymmetric Costs Volatilities in Stable Demand

Column/ Line	Duopoly		Power Prices $/kWh A	Both Incur MCPX		$ACCGT_B$ Only		$StoHydro_B$ Only		Both Forego MCPX		Notional Equilibrium	
				SOV_1 B $ mln	SOV_2 C $ mln	SOV_1 D $ mln	SOV_2 E $ mln	SOV_1 F $ mln	SOV_2 G $ mln	SOV_1 H $ mln	SOV_2 I $ mln	SOV_1 J $ mln	SOV_2 K $ mln
1	F1: $ACCGT_B$	F2: $StoHydro_B$	0.1900	700	1,977	700	3,088	837	1,859	995	4,365	995	4,365
2	F1: $ACCGT_B$	F2: $StoHydro_B$	0.1408	700	1,563	700	2,684	837	1,455	995	3,669	995	3,669
3	F1: $ACCGT_B$	F2: $StoHydro_B$	0.1063	700	1,309	700	2,437	837	1,207	995	3,176	995	3,176
4	F1: $ACCGT_B$	F2: $StoHydro_B$	0.0820	627	1,226	627	2,329	825	1,126	966	2,802	966	2,802
5	F1: $ACCGT_B$	F2: $StoHydro_B$	0.0649	86	1,331	203	1,970	590	1,228	712	2,192	712	2,192
6	F1: $ACCGT_B$	F2: $StoHydro_B$	0.0527	0	1,331	0	1,129	71	1,228	473	1,267	473	1,267
Column/ Line	Duopoly		Power Prices $/kWh A	Both Incur MCPX		$ACCGT_B$ Only		$StoHydro_B$ Only		Both Forego MCPX		Notional Equilibrium	
				CV_1 B	CV_2 C	CV_1 D	CV_2 E	CV_1 F	CV_2 G	CV_1 H	CV_2 I	CV_1 J	CV_2 K
7	F1: $ACCGT_B$	F2: $StoHydro_B$	0.1408	786	1,767	786	2,855	941	1,586	1,083	4,323	1,083	4,323
8	F1: $ACCGT_B$	F2: $StoHydro_B$	0.1063	786	1,426	786	2,522	941	1,252	1,083	3,704	1,083	3,704
9	F1: $ACCGT_B$	F2: $StoHydro_B$	0.0820	783	1,245	783	2,335	940	1,076	1,082	3,256	1,082	3,256
10	F1: $ACCGT_B$	F2: $StoHydro_B$	0.0649	696	1,237	700	2,132	915	1,068	1,046	2,774	1,046	2,774
11	F1: $ACCGT_B$	F2: $StoHydro_B$	0.0527	96	1,298	265	1,594	663	1,128	799	2,037	799	2,037

and GeoS$_B$). They differ from intermittent renewables, comprising Wind$_{ON}$ and PVT$_M$, in two aspects:

1. StoHydro$_B$, Geo$_B$, and GeoS$_B$, in theory, enjoy high utilisation rates, where volumes could be varied according to how demand fluctuates.
2. Power output is reliant on flows of water or steam rather than on installed capacity.

In relation to ACCGT$_B$, the positioning is radically turned on its head. As the cheaper supplies, StoHydro$_B$, Geo$_B$, and GeoS$_B$ would set the pace in gaining volumes, often at the expense of ACCGT$_B$ as follower or residual supplier.

StoHydro$_B$ can vary supplies according to demand. However, maximum available supply follows seasonal patterns or changing climate. Counterintuitively, Table 10.3 indicates that a "notional equilibrium" is achieved when both ACCGT$_B$ and StoHydro$_B$ forego spending on MCPX. There are two reasons for this:

As described in Box 10.1, renewables and nuclear inversely impact power prices. That is, the more they supply, the lower power prices are likely to be. In effect, their volumes follow inverted binomial moves, where *up* is negative, while *down* is positive.

StoHydro$_B$, Geo$_B$, and GeoS$_B$ supply more volumes when power prices are low, while ACCGT$_B$ benefits from higher prices and volumes.

The more volatile volumes are, the wider are the gaps between maximum available supplies and average volumes sold as shown in Charts 10.5(A) and (C). Consequently, the incremental volumes gained by spending may not earn enough to recover MCPX.

In contrast, by foregoing MCPX, natural wastage would close the gaps over time (Charts 10.5(B) and (D). Guided by the math (Table 10.4), ACCGT$_B$ may consider divesting when power price expectations are in excess of $0.0820/kWh. Its call value, CV$_e$, is at a maximum.

Roy now turns to describe how the ACCGT$_B$ and StoHydro$_B$ would yield different strategic responses under growth-biased markets with lax routine maintenance (Table 10.4). With more growth to go for and higher volume erosions, to forego MCPX could imply foregoing more revenues.

Paradoxically, at high power prices when StoHydro$_B$ tends to be underutilised, foregoing MCPX enhances SOV$_{e1}$ and SOV$_{e2}$. As power prices fall below $0.0649/kWh, increased volumes would be more than sufficient to offset low prices with higher volumes for StoHydro$_B$.

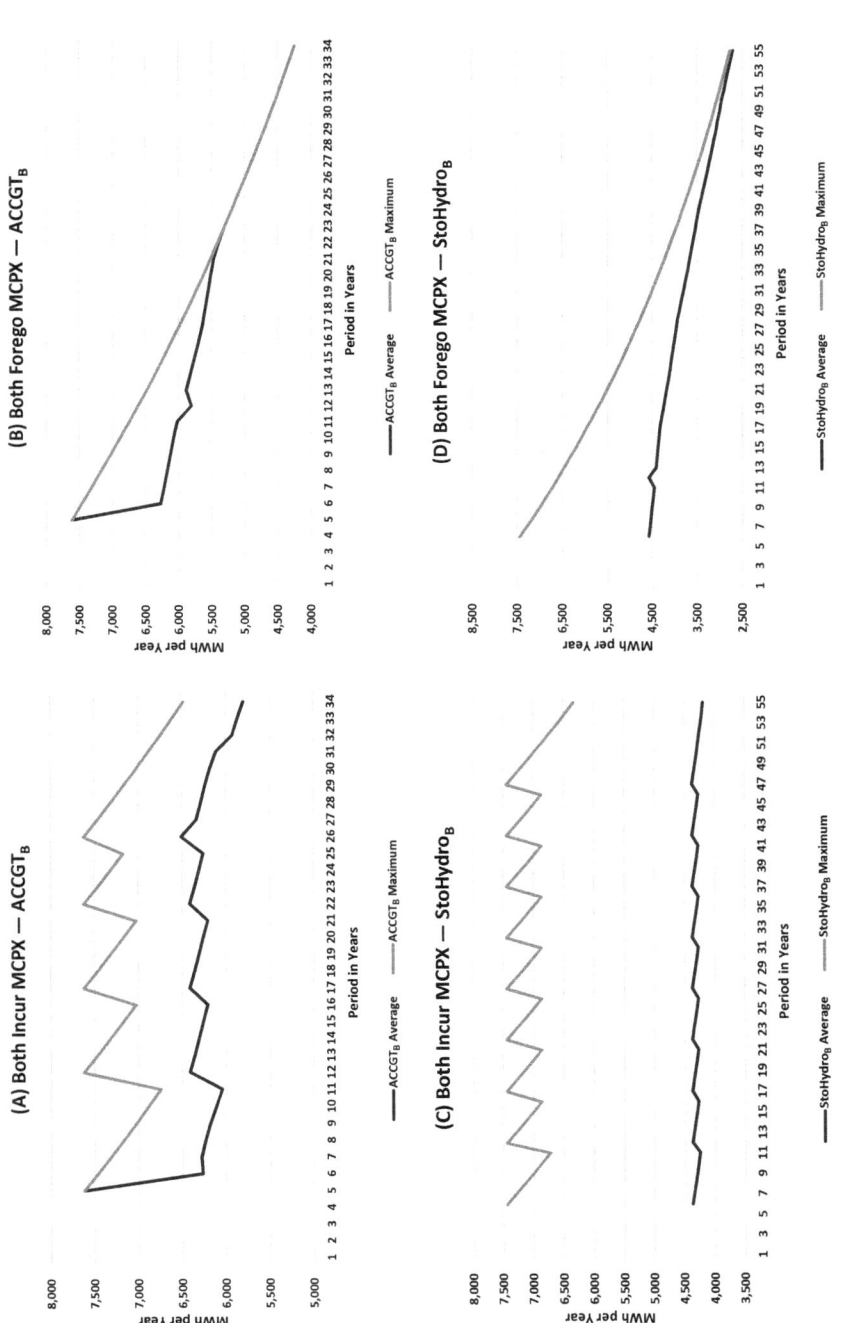

Chart 10.5: Volume Reallocation and Value of MCPX — ACCGT$_B$ and StoHydro$_B$

Table 10.4: $ACCGT_B$ and $StoHydro_B$ with Asymmetric Costs under $ACCGT_M$, Growth-Biased Volumes

Dynamic Volume Allocation with Flexible Pricing under $ACCGT_M$ as Price-setter — Asymmetric Costs Volatilities in Growth-biased Demand

Column/Line	Duopoly		Power Prices $/kWh A	Both Incur MCPX			ACCGT$_B$ Only			StoHydro$_B$ Only			Both Forego MCPX			Notional Equilibrium		
				SOV$_1$ B $ mln	SOV$_2$ C $ mln		SOV$_1$ D $ mln	SOV$_2$ E $ mln		SOV$_1$ F $ mln	SOV$_2$ G $ mln		SOV$_1$ H $ mln	SOV$_2$ I $ mln		SOV$_1$ J $ mln	SOV$_2$ K $ mln	
1	F1: ACCGT$_B$	F2: StoHydro$_B$	0.1900	335	847		385	1,712		541	847		666	2,704		666	2,704	
2	F1: ACCGT$_B$	F2: StoHydro$_B$	0.1408	335	536		385	1,236		541	536		666	1,937		666	1,937	
3	F1: ACCGT$_B$	F2: StoHydro$_B$	0.1063	335	346		385	768		541	346		666	1,238		666	1,238	
4	F1: ACCGT$_B$	F2: StoHydro$_B$	0.0820	335	284		385	299		541	284		666	588		666	588	
5	F1: ACCGT$_B$	F2: StoHydro$_B$	0.0649	68	360		278	0		446	360		561	0		446	360	
6	F1: ACCGT$_B$	F2: StoHydro$_B$	0.0527	0	27		117	0		142	27		410	0		142	27	

Column/Line	Duopoly		Power Prices $/kWh A	Both Incur MCPX			ACCGT$_B$ Only			StoHydro$_B$ Only			Both Forego MCPX			Notional Equilibrium		
				CV$_1$ B	CV$_2$ C		CV$_1$ D	CV$_2$ E		CV$_1$ F	CV$_2$ G		CV$_1$ H	CV$_2$ I		CV$_1$ J	CV$_2$ K	
7	F1: ACCGT$_B$	F2: StoHydro$_B$	0.1408	422	713		469	1,489		642	592		748	2,670		748	2,670	
8	F1: ACCGT$_B$	F2: StoHydro$_B$	0.1063	422	454		469	1,036		642	332		748	1,930		748	1,930	
9	F1: ACCGT$_B$	F2: StoHydro$_B$	0.0820	432	312		479	588		652	190		737	1,259		737	1,259	
10	F1: ACCGT$_B$	F2: StoHydro$_B$	0.0649	402	296		463	192		632	174		742	640		742	640	
11	F1: ACCGT$_B$	F2: StoHydro$_B$	0.0527	78	240		358	0		516	119		638	0		516	119	

By not spending on MCPX, losses from lax routine maintenance are estimated to make StoHydro$_B$ "out of money." By spending MCPX, increased volumes enhance CV$_{e2}$ (G.11 vs I.11). In contrast, ACCGT$_B$ erodes CV$_{e1}$ (B.11 vs. F.11) but is better off foregoing rather than spending on MCPX.

Jocelyn was curious if Geo$_B$ and GeoS$_B$, given that steam flows are less volatile than water, would prove a bigger challenge to ACCGT$_B$, to which Roy responded by going through the math in Table 10.5 for GeoS$_B$. The comparative calculations for Geo$_B$ are in Appendices 10A and 10B.

Roy started, assuming that geothermal steam is located and available, about how steam flows for GeoS$_B$ vary less than StoHydro$_B$. As a result, GeoS$_B$ would tend to supply more volumes, thereby eroding significantly the volumes that are left for ACCGT$_B$ to supply. The volume squeeze would cause ACCGT$_B$ to opt for benign neglect where it allows its asset to erode gracefully.

By spending on MCPX, ACCGT$_B$ invites GeoS$_B$ to spend as well, thereby hastening ACCGT$_B$'s economic obsolescence (e.g. power prices persistently below $0.0820/kWh). By foregoing MCPX, ACCGT$_B$ may withstand GeoS$_B$'s onslaught. At this point, however, GeoS$_B$ may switch from *forego* to *spend* to expand SOV$_{e2}$ and CV$_{e2}$. When this happens, ACCGT$_B$ is expected to be "out of money" if power prices are persistently below $0.0527/kWh.

Jocelyn queried: How about in emerging markets, where there is volume growth bias, but lax routine maintenance?

Roy pulled out Table 10.6. He observed that lax routine maintenance is indeed a feature in a couple of Asian geothermal areas where volumes could erode up to 7% per year. Operating under these conditions, GeoS$_B$'s decision is made simpler: By foregoing MCPX, foregone revenues are substantial as to render the investment "out of money" when power prices remain below $0.0527/kWh.

To optimise SOV$_{e2}$ and CV$_{e2}$, GeoS$_B$ would proceed to spend on MCPX. This leaves ACCGT$_B$ to either follow suit and risk being "out of money" when power prices are below $0.0820/kWh. By opting to leave the field to GeoS$_B$, it could remain economically viable for longer.

At this point, Jocelyn saw the penny drop: "When ACCGT$_B$ is relegated to a follower, its continued role in the supply mix mimics that of Coal$_B$ with one difference. ACCGT$_B$ is cheaper to build, and remains viable at power prices above $0.0820/kWh, when both rivals spend. With GeoS$_B$ facing a prospect of a similar fate when power

Table 10.5: ACCGT$_B$ and GeoS$_B$ with Asymmetric Costs under ACCGT$_M$, Stable Volumes

Dynamic Volume Allocation with Flexible Pricing under ACCGT$_M$ as Price-setter — Asymmetric Costs Volatilities in Stable Demand

Column/Line	Duopoly		Power Prices A $/kWh	Both Incur MCPX		ACCGT$_B$ Only		GeoS$_B$ Only		Both Forego MCPX		Notional Equilibrium	
				SOV$_1$ B $ mln	SOV$_2$ C $ mln	SOV$_1$ D $ mln	SOV$_2$ E $ mln	SOV$_1$ F $ mln	SOV$_2$ G $ mln	SOV$_1$ H $ mln	SOV$_2$ I $ mln	SOV$_1$ J $ mln	SOV$_2$ K $ mln
1	F1: ACCGT$_B$	F2: GeoS$_B$	0.1900	700	15,837	700	16,704	837	15,837	837	16,704	837	16,704
2	F1: ACCGT$_B$	F2: GeoS$_B$	0.1408	514	11,741	550	12,308	797	11,741	797	12,308	797	12,308
3	F1: ACCGT$_B$	F2: GeoS$_B$	0.1063	190	8,695	320	8,952	656	8,695	658	8,952	658	8,952
4	F1: ACCGT$_B$	F2: GeoS$_B$	0.0820	0	6,445	106	6,390	411	6,445	495	6,390	411	6,445
5	F1: ACCGT$_B$	F2: GeoS$_B$	0.0649	0	4,733	0	4,425	93	4,733	351	4,425	93	4,733
6	F1: ACCGT$_B$	F2: GeoS$_B$	0.0527	0	3,151	0	2,895	0	3,151	237	2,895	0	3,151

Column/Line	Duopoly		Power Prices A $/kWh	Both Incur MCPX		ACCGT$_B$ Only		Geo$_B$ Only		Both Forego MCPX		Notional Equilibrium	
				CV$_1$ B	CV$_2$ C	CV$_1$ D	CV$_2$ E	CV$_1$ F	CV$_2$ G	CV$_1$ H	CV$_2$ I	CV$_1$ J	CV$_2$ K
7	F1: ACCGT$_B$	F2: GeoS$_B$	0.1408	719	14,792	754	15,529	856	14,792	908	16,021	908	16,021
8	F1: ACCGT$_B$	F2: GeoS$_B$	0.1063	533	11,002	581	11,442	815	11,002	849	11,818	849	11,818
9	F1: ACCGT$_B$	F2: GeoS$_B$	0.0820	199	8,189	343	8,327	675	8,189	697	8,614	697	8,614
10	F1: ACCGT$_B$	F2: GeoS$_B$	0.0649	0	6,094	113	5,948	430	6,094	522	6,169	522	6,169
11	F1: ACCGT$_B$	F2: GeoS$_B$	0.0527	0	4,401	0	4,120	99	4,401	366	4,291	99	4,401

Table 10.6: ACCGT$_B$ and GeoS$_B$ with Asymmetric Costs under ACCGT$_B$, Growth-biased Volumes

Dynamic Volume Allocation with Flexible Pricing under ACCGT$_M$ as Price-setter — Asymmetric Costs Volatilities in Growth-biased Demand

Column/ Line	Duopoly		Power Prices $/kWh A	Both Incur MCPX		ACCGT$_B$ Only		GeoS$_B$ Only		Both Forego MCPX		Notional Equilibrium	
				SOV$_1$ B $ mln	SOV$_2$ C $ mln	SOV$_1$ D $ mln	SOV$_2$ E $ mln	SOV$_1$ F $ mln	SOV$_2$ G $ mln	SOV$_1$ H $ mln	SOV$_2$ I $ mln	SOV$_1$ J $ mln	SOV$_2$ K $ mln
1	F1: ACCGT$_B$	F2: GeoS$_B$	0.1900	404	11,979	407	7,879	541	11,979	566	7,879	541	11,979
2	F1: ACCGT$_B$	F2: GeoS$_B$	0.1408	404	8,658	407	5,214	514	8,658	566	5,214	514	8,658
3	F1: ACCGT$_B$	F2: GeoS$_B$	0.1063	339	6,110	393	3,257	438	6,110	552	3,257	438	6,110
4	F1: ACCGT$_B$	F2: GeoS$_B$	0.0820	105	4,121	332	1,817	320	4,121	491	1,817	320	4,121
5	F1: ACCGT$_B$	F2: GeoS$_B$	0.0649	0	2,562	258	752	189	2,562	427	752	189	2,562
6	F1: ACCGT$_B$	F2: GeoS$_B$	0.0527	0	1,333	181	0	85	1,333	365	0	85	1,333
Column/ Line	Duopoly		Power Prices $/kWh A	Both Incur MCPX		ACCGT$_B$ Only		Geo$_B$ Only		Both Forego MCPX		Notional Equilibrium	
				CV$_1$ B	CV$_2$ C	CV$_1$ D	CV$_2$ E	CV$_1$ F	CV$_2$ G	CV$_1$ H	CV$_2$ I	CV$_1$ J	CV$_2$ K
7	F1: ACCGT$_B$	F2: GeoS$_B$	0.1408	437	11,359	500	7,765	574	11,359	656	8,107	574	11,359
8	F1: ACCGT$_B$	F2: GeoS$_B$	0.1063	437	8,222	492	5,189	546	8,222	648	5,440	546	8,222
9	F1: ACCGT$_B$	F2: GeoS$_B$	0.0820	371	5,811	454	3,296	471	5,811	610	3,480	471	5,811
10	F1: ACCGT$_B$	F2: GeoS$_B$	0.0649	118	3,932	373	1,901	352	3,932	530	2,038	352	3,932
11	F1: ACCGT$_B$	F2: GeoS$_B$	0.0527	0	2,464	280	862	222	2,464	447	958	222	2,464

prices fall below $0.0527/kWh, by foregoing MCPX, $GeoS_B$ may choose to keep $ACCGT_B$ as a passive follower for longer, but under a tight lease."

4.3 Unified by symbiotic interests: $ACCGT_B$ and ANuke

Prior to Jocelyn's ascendancy into the executive ranks, she was one of those that explored for uranium in Australia. It was a time when nuclear was seen as humanity's saviour. The energy it generated was too cheap to meter, according to Lewis I Strauss, Chair, US Atomic Energy Commission (Smil, 2016). In her three decades with the firm, she saw the group exiting uranium mining, with nuclear power a hazy aspiration long forgotten. With talks of a nuclear resurgence, Jocelyn is of two minds about ANuke's comparative merits to $ACCGT_B$.

Roy pointed out that ANuke's "cheapness" is not borne out by the calculations (Box Table 10.1.1; EIA, 2019). In terms of CPX, it is among the most expensive and takes the longest to build. Once operational, it is an inflexible asset given that it has to run continuously to bring its costs into line with other supplies.

This is where the regulator lends a hand. ANuke, while not the cheaper supply compared to $ACCGT_B$, is given preferential dispatch. That is, it is supplied whenever it is available. With $ACCGT_B$ as a follower supplying the residual volumes, ANuke sets the pace in gaining volumes at $ACCGT_B$'s expense. With ANuke's low volume volatilities, the squeeze on $ACCGT_B$ could be tremendous.

Notwithstanding the advantages endowed to ANuke, Table 10.7 indicates a number of economic challenges when ANuke is paired with $ACCGT_B$:

1. Volume squeeze on $ACCGT_B$ results in underutilisation that does not warrant spending on MCPX to gain incremental volumes that it could not sell.
2. ANuke's high capex, X and MCPX, X', far outweigh what it could gain from incremental volumes.
3. To mutually flourish, both forego MCPX while keenly hoping power price remains above $0.1063/kWh.

This prospect is more likely to be realised when supplies are tight, which could happen when ANuke exits if power prices persist below $0.0649/kWh.

Repeating the simulation under growth-biased markets with lax routine maintenance, the relative positioning is similar, with both firms foregoing MCPX as the

Table 10.7: ACCGT$_B$ and ANuke with Asymmetric Costs under ACCGT$_M$, Stable Volumes

Dynamic Volume Allocation with Flexible Pricing under ACCGT$_M$ as Price-setter — Asymmetric Costs Volatilities in Stable Demand

Column/Line	Duopoly		Power Prices A $/kWh	Both Incur MCPX		ACCGT$_B$ Only		ANuke Only		Both Forego MCPX		Notional Equilibrium	
				SOV$_1$ B $ mln	SOV$_2$ C $ mln	SOV$_1$ D $ mln	SOV$_2$ E $ mln	SOV$_1$ F $ mln	SOV$_2$ G $ mln	SOV$_1$ H $ mln	SOV$_2$ I $ mln	SOV$_1$ J $ mln	SOV$_2$ K $ mln
1	F1: ACCGT$_B$	F2: ANuke	0.1900	602	8,727	643	11,129	833	9,306	746	13,331	746	13,331
2	F1: ACCGT$_B$	F2: ANuke	0.1408	371	3,805	483	6,069	774	4,456	664	7,597	664	7,597
3	F1: ACCGT$_B$	F2: ANuke	0.1063	128	422	318	2,619	648	1,001	576	3,515	576	3,515
4	F1: ACCGT$_B$	F2: ANuke	0.0820	0	0	159	61	457	0	483	602	483	602
5	F1: ACCGT$_B$	F2: ANuke	0.0649	0	0	9	0	231	0	388	0	388	0
6	F1: ACCGT$_B$	F2: ANuke	0.0527	0	0	0	0	55	0	290	0	290	0

Column/Line	Duopoly		Power Prices A $/kWh	Both Incur MCPX		ACCGT$_B$ Only		Geo$_B$ Only		Both Forego MCPX		Notional Equilibrium	
				CV$_1$ B $ mln	CV$_2$ C $ mln	CV$_1$ D $ mln	CV$_2$ E $ mln	CV$_1$ F $ mln	CV$_2$ G $ mln	CV$_1$ H $ mln	CV$_2$ I $ mln	CV$_1$ J $ mln	CV$_2$ K $ mln
7	F1: ACCGT$_B$	F2: ANuke	0.1408	605	6,456	671	8,742	894	7,051	828	11,314	828	11,314
8	F1: ACCGT$_B$	F2: ANuke	0.1063	375	2,298	513	4,478	812	2,903	749	6,214	749	6,214
9	F1: ACCGT$_B$	F2: ANuke	0.0820	132	235	355	1,485	665	558	662	2,578	662	2,578
10	F1: ACCGT$_B$	F2: ANuke	0.0649	0	0	203	34	465	0	572	411	572	411
11	F1: ACCGT$_B$	F2: ANuke	0.0527	0	0	12	0	263	0	478	0	478	0

Source: Author's calculations.

"notional equilibrium." The volume reallocation illustrates in Chart 10.6, the extent to which regulatory distortion damages the economic prospects of both firms when power prices are declining (Table 10.7). To offset the persistent volume underutilisation, high power prices are among the few ways that could offer immediate economic relief.

4.4 Intermittent supplies and its dichotomy

$Wind_{ON}$ and PVT_M comprise the two intermittent renewables Roy uses as examples. The business press heralds both technologies as humanity's best hope for a decarbonised energy system. The patterns have become far too familiar: Initial euphoria (The Economic Times, 2020) on bagging a "cheap" offer, hailing innovations (Kerr, 2019) as breakthroughs, only to face obstacles (gtm, 2018) in what was hailed as groundbreaking project in a Saudi Arabian desert, to eventual bankruptcies (Hook, 2013) that continues to this day (Eavis et al., 2021).

Regardless of their cost competitiveness, their intermittency confers a preferential dispatch. Not knowing when the next wind will blow adequately or the sun to shine sufficiently to produce enough power, supplies are dispatched whenever available.

Reliant on wind flow or sunlight, they exhibit similar volatilities as $StoHydro_B$, while enjoying ANuke's preferential dispatch. That is where the similarities end. With the low conversion of feedstock to energy, volumes are substantially lower. For this reason, their eroding effects on power prices are substantially less.

By pairing $ACCGT_B$ with $Wind_{ON}$, in spite of its preferential dispatch, $Wind_{ON}$ may opt to take its cue from $ACCGT_B$. While it is tempting to push for maximum available volumes, $Wind_{ON}$ is constrained by two factors that are not entirely within managers' control, from benefiting as a pace-setter:

1. By spending on MCPX, in theory, $Wind_{ON}$ could gain from the volume uplift. However, how much is monetised would depend on the wind flows which tend to vary widely. In practice, $Wind_{ON}$ tends to supply on average below its maximum available supply.
2. Partly as a function of the technology, high MCPX would deter spending when payoffs from low volume utilisation would result in nil SOV_{e2}. This occurs when power prices fall below $0.0820/kWh when both spend.

These insights are gained from the simulation results shown in Table 10.8. Repeating the simulation for the growth-biased market with lax routine maintenance,

Oligopolistic Rivalries 545

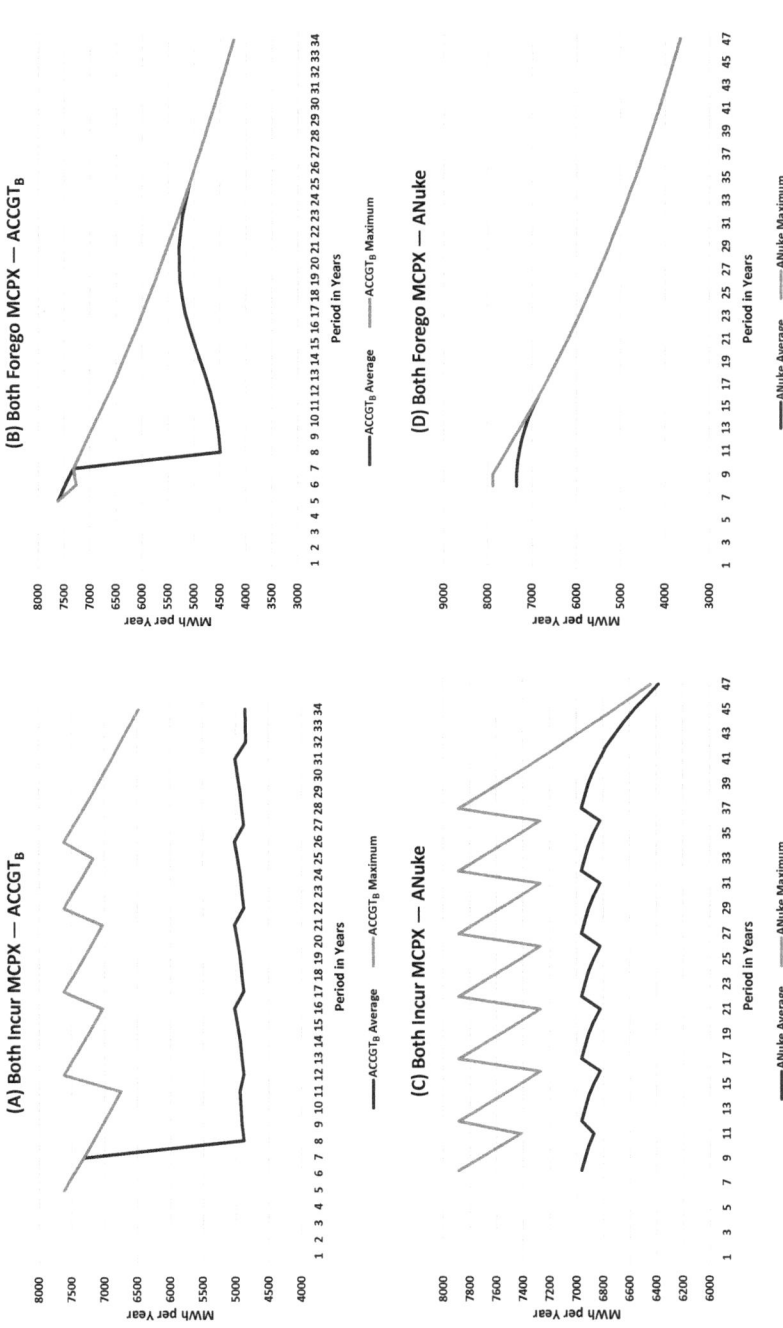

Chart 10.6: Volume Reallocation and Value of MCPX — ACCGT$_B$ and ANuke$_B$

Table 10.8: $ACCGT_B$ and $Wind_{ON}$ with Asymmetric Costs under $ACCGT_M$, Stable Volumes

Dynamic Volume Allocation with Flexible Pricing under $ACCGT_M$ as Price-setter — Asymmetric Costs Volatilities in Stable Demand

Column/ Line	Duopoly		Power Prices $/kWh A	Both Incur MCPX		$ACCGT_B$ Only		$Wind_{ON}$ Only		Both Forego MCPX		Notional Equilibrium	
				SOV_1 B $ mln	SOV_2 C $ mln	SOV_1 D $ mln	SOV_2 E $ mln	SOV_1 F $ mln	SOV_2 G $ mln	SOV_1 H $ mln	SOV_2 I $ mln	SOV_1 J $ mln	SOV_2 K $ mln
1	F1: $ACCGT_B$	F2: $Wind_{ON}$	0.1900	691	953	691	2,258	837	938	837	2,261	837	2,261
2	F1: $ACCGT_B$	F2: $Wind_{ON}$	0.1408	691	345	691	1,649	837	330	837	1,654	837	1,654
3	F1: $ACCGT_B$	F2: $Wind_{ON}$	0.1063	691	0	691	1,186	837	0	837	1,192	837	1,192
4	F1: $ACCGT_B$	F2: $Wind_{ON}$	0.0820	691	0	691	830	837	0	837	836	837	836
5	F1: $ACCGT_B$	F2: $Wind_{ON}$	0.0649	691	0	691	439	837	0	837	445	837	445
6	F1: $ACCGT_B$	F2: $Wind_{ON}$	0.0527	641	0	675	0	826	0	826	3	826	3

Column/ Line	Duopoly		Power Prices $/kWh A	Both Incur MCPX		$ACCGT_B$ Only		$Wind_{ON}$ Only		Both Forego MCPX		Notional Equilibrium	
				CV_1 B	CV_2 C	CV_1 D	CV_2 E	CV_1 F	CV_2 G	CV_1 H	CV_2 I	CV_1 J	CV_2 K
7	F1: $ACCGT_B$	F2: $Wind_{ON}$	0.1408	777	1,141	777	2,413	920	1,126	920	2,225	920	2,225
8	F1: $ACCGT_B$	F2: $Wind_{ON}$	0.1063	777	473	777	1,792	920	452	920	1,651	920	1,651
9	F1: $ACCGT_B$	F2: $Wind_{ON}$	0.0820	777	0	777	1,319	920	0	920	1,213	920	1,213
10	F1: $ACCGT_B$	F2: $Wind_{ON}$	0.0649	777	0	777	949	920	0	920	832	920	832
11	F1: $ACCGT_B$	F2: $Wind_{ON}$	0.0527	768	0	769	545	913	0	913	418	913	418

the relative positioning of $ACCGT_B$ and $Wind_{ON}$ remains broadly similar. That is, both would forego spending on MCPX.

In comparing the fate of PVT_M when paired with $ACCGT_B$, it suffers worse outcomes. What is simulated in Table 10.9 for PVT_M is far from encouraging. In all power prices considered, managers that choose PVT_M are expected to be "out of the money."

High capex and MCPX would practically eliminate any prospects for recovering the investments, much less to sufficiently earn adequate returns. Jocelyn was thinking out loud when she said to Roy: "What did the press and the advocates of PVT_M know that EIA (2019) did not?"

Sifting through the math, when one strips out the tax credits and subsidies, solar and photovoltaic power remains one of the most expensive in spite of the 70% fall in panel prices since 2010 (Atwell, 2018). Roy added: "The headline bid prices often anticipate how solar panel and installations would fall in three to four years. With three to four years to build from award, and about two years to build, an aggressive bidder would assume future solar costs would fall substantially. With solar costs having fallen in excess of 20% a year since 2016, bidders in 2020 would only need to commit on their panel suppliers and contractors by 2022. If everything works according to plan, PVT_M may be 40% to 50% cheaper."

Jocelyn raises a question: How would the low bids in a number of auction rounds expect to recoup their investments, and what would drive future declines in LCOEs?

Roy started: "In theory, PVT_M could increase volumes which would require major technological breakthroughs such as a substitution of silicon with materials of superior capacity to convert light to power. The other, where most of the cost declines has been delivered, is to substitute expensive with cheaper materials to reduce CPX. Installation costs have seen great strides to deliver costs declines in excess of 20% a year.

In my estimates, if capex falls from $1,922/kW to $275/kW, and MCPX from $1,621/kW to $232/kW, PVT_M may be in the running if it could sustain its 28% conversion of sunlight to power. The latter is already above what most PV schemes are achieving, with new materials "breakthroughs" delivering substantially less.

$Wind_{ON}$ has a brighter prospect. A fall in capex from $1,585/kW to $932/kW, and MCPX from $1,337/kW to $786/kW, would get $Wind_{ON}$ into "in the money" territory. A 41% reduction may look challenging. However, with declines in excess of 10% a year, this is a possibility within the next five years or less.

Table 10.9: $ACCGT_B$ and PVT_M with Asymmetric Costs under $ACCGT_M$, Stable Volumes

Dynamic Volume Allocation with Flexible Pricing under $ACCGT_M$ as Price-setter — Asymmetric Costs Volatilities in Stable Demand

Column/Line	Duopoly		Power Prices $/kWh A	Both Incur MCPX		$ACCGT_B$ Only		PVT_M Only		Both Forego MCPX		Notional Equilibrium	
				SOV_1 B $ mln	SOV_2 C $ mln	SOV_1 D $ mln	SOV_2 E $ mln	SOV_1 F $ mln	SOV_2 G $ mln	SOV_1 H $ mln	SOV_2 I $ mln	SOV_1 J $ mln	SOV_2 K $ mln
1	F1: $ACCGT_B$	F2: PVT_M	0.1900	700	0	700	0	837	0	837	0	837	0
2	F1: $ACCGT_B$	F2: PVT_M	0.1408	700	0	700	0	837	0	837	0	837	0
3	F1: $ACCGT_B$	F2: PVT_M	0.1063	700	0	700	0	837	0	837	0	837	0
4	F1: $ACCGT_B$	F2: PVT_M	0.0820	700	0	700	0	837	0	837	0	837	0
5	F1: $ACCGT_B$	F2: PVT_M	0.0649	700	0	700	0	837	0	837	0	837	0
6	F1: $ACCGT_B$	F2: PVT_M	0.0527	700	0	700	0	837	0	837	0	837	0

Column/Line	Duopoly		Power Prices $/kWh A	Both Incur MCPX		$ACCGT_B$ Only		Geo_B Only		Both Forego MCPX		Notional Equilibrium	
				CV_1 B	CV_2 C	CV_1 D	CV_2 E	CV_1 F	CV_2 G	CV_1 H	CV_2 I	CV_1 J	CV_2 K
7	F1: $ACCGT_B$	F2: PVT_M	0.1408	786	0	786	0	920	0	920	0	920	0
8	F1: $ACCGT_B$	F2: PVT_M	0.1063	786	0	786	0	920	0	920	0	920	0
9	F1: $ACCGT_B$	F2: PVT_M	0.0820	786	0	786	0	920	0	920	0	920	0
10	F1: $ACCGT_B$	F2: PVT_M	0.0649	786	0	786	0	920	0	920	0	920	0
11	F1: $ACCGT_B$	F2: PVT_M	0.0527	786	0	786	0	920	0	920	0	920	0

PVT$_M$ has a steeper fall to deliver. With materials largely replaced with cheaper ones, with silver largely removed, technological breakthroughs in conversion rates and materials may remain its best hope to be self-sustaining."

In parting, Jocelyn concluded: "In effect, Roy, if the costs for PVT$_M$ stalls, or even spikes as Wind$_{ON}$ previously did from 2004 to 2010, these low bids may never be delivered, as SoftBank and Saudi Arabia (Dvorak and Jones, 2019) belatedly learned to their grief."

5
Chief Executive's Reflections

The broader insights that a dynamic thought process uncovers go beyond simplifying complex mathematics. In a structured and sequential assessment, my simulations on the pairings of competing technologies provide a nuanced view of how strategic actions could vary with the contexts of the decision.

Jocelyn shares her notes, as shown in Chart 10.7, on how she sees her leadership team could think as a general does. She added her reflections and insights as follows:

"Taking stock of our advantages, interests, and contexts of the market, and the circumstances rivals find themselves under, you may choose to confront our adversaries with massive force, offer a hand of cooperation, or seek some form of *accommodative modus vivendi* that we both could gain from. For this reason, comprehending the conditions that lead to some *notional equilibrium* is a basic information that we need to acquire through deep analyses, or insights.

Strategically, the implications in an age of no subsidies, managers would choose different strategies under each pairing. For ACCGT$_B$, it gains under Coal$_M$ by keeping Coal$_B$ alive and well to profit from the supportive power prices set by Coal$_M$. Under ACCGT$_M$, it could perhaps displace as much supplies from Coal$_B$.

The game changes for ACCGT$_B$ when confronted with StoHydro$_B$, Geo$_B$ and GeoS$_B$. As owner of ACCGT$_B$, you may choose to waltz away the night by co-existing with our rivals. We do complement in a strange way: When rivals' supplies are plentiful, power prices are low, with ACCGT$_B$ hardly operating at volumes considered economic.

Dynamic Decisions

Duopoly Rivals			Stable Volume Market		Growth-biased Volume Market	
	F.1	F.2	Notional Equilibrium	Strategic Actions	Notional Equilibrium	Strategic Actions
				Under Coal$_M$ as Price-setter		
1	ACCGT$_B$	Coal$_B$ Asymmetric	Spend	F.1 Maximises volumes at premium prices; F.2 Seeks accommodative *modus vivendi*	Spend	F.1 Maximises volumes at premium prices; F.2 Seeks accommodative *modus vivendi*
2	ACCGT$_B$	Coal$_B$ Symmetric	Spend	F.1 Maximises volumes at premium prices; F.2 Seeks accommodative *modus vivendi*.	Spend	F.1 maximise volumes at premium prices; F.2 Seeks accommodative *modus vivendi*.
				Under ACCGT$_M$ as Price-Setter		
3	F.1 ACCGT$_B$	F.1 Coal$_B$	Forego	F.1 Maintains volume and costs advantage; F.2 Opts for benign neglect or exits.	Forego	F.1 Retain volume and cost advantage; F.2 Manages decline or exits.
4	ACCGT$_B$	StoHydro$_B$	Forego	F.1 Follows and acts contingent upon F.2; F.2 Opts for routine maintenance excellence.	Forego / Spend	F.1 Follows and acts contingent upon F.2; F.2 Switches from forego to spend as volumes tighten.
5	ACCGT$_B$	GeoS$_B$ / Geo$_B$	Forego/ Spend	F.1 Follow sand acts contingent upon F.2; F.2 disrupts F.1 and switches to spend when volumes tighten.	Spend	F.1 Follows and acts contingent upon F.2. F.2 maximises volumes at F.1's expense.
6	ACCGT$_B$	ANuke	Forego	F.1 and F.2 Act symbiotically to keep power prices up. F.2 perpetuates preferential dispatch by regulatory fiat.	Forego	F.1 and F.2 Act symbiotically to keep power prices high. F.2 perpetuates preferential dispatch by regulatory fiat.
7	ACCGT$_B$	Wind$_{ON}$	Forego	F.1 Index payoffs via physical hedge; F.2 Perpetuates preferential dispatch by regulatory fiat.	Forego	F.1 Index payoffs via physical hedge; F.2 Perpetuates preferential dispatch by regulatory fiat.
8	ACCGT$_B$	PVT$_M$	Forego	F.1 Index payoffs via physical hedge; F.2 Perpetuates preferential dispatch by regulatory fiat.	Forego	F.1 Index payoffs via physical hedge; F.2 Perpetuates preferential dispatch by regulatory fiat.

Chart 10.7: Summary of Dynamic Interactions of Rivals

As rivals' supplies fall, as they seasonally do, $ACCGT_B$ gains by supplying more at higher power prices.

ANuke and $ACCGT_B$ are reluctant dancing partners but share a symbiotic interest. Both gain when power prices are high. As adept dancers, we can orchestrate our steps by keenly watching what our rivals do, not what they say.

As for $Wind_{ON}$ and PVT_M, the future could be bright for their successors, when CPX falls substantially below present levels or efficiency rises significantly. $Wind_{ON}$ is closer to this reality, with PVT_M living out a hope to be 'in the money' — if only news headlines could turn promise into cash."

The insights transcend the interests of managers directly investing in energy. For the broader industries that make a living out of energy, such as equipment manufacturers, suppliers, and service contractors, the implications are far-reaching. For example:

Under tighter power pricing, equipment manufacturers and service providers, particularly for maintenance, may have to rethink their strategy. With the challenges lying in cutting the costs of CPX and MCPX, future equipment may have to be reconfigured.

Ideally, Jocelyn observed, "equipment could sustain their operating efficiencies with a minimum need for MCPX. If this is to be the future, a substantial service revenue from re-equipping could disappear. Coupled with reduced CPX, compounded by obsolescing technologies, the product cycle for energy equipment may prove a lot shorter than suppliers presently contemplate. Consequently, long-term contracts, such as power purchase agreements, requires a serious rethink.

Repowering or portfolio rotations would be essential components of asset management. Holding assets to maturity may become an option, but not as the norm.

After all, energy investments and the challenges managers aim to resolve, would impact stakeholders well beyond its immediate vicinity. As a general would fully appreciate, their success would involve 'looking forward, and reason backwards'. To fully appreciate disruptive events, astute managers do need to look sideways beyond their familiar stomping ground for guidance."

Box 10.1: Binomial Model and Processes

Volatile prices, costs, and volumes are modelled following binomial processes. These involve estimating the value of an *up* or *down* move of the specified variable as binary events. Repeated over several time periods, risk-neutral values are iteratively estimated as Avinash K Dixit and Barry J Nalebuff (1991) advised: "Look forward, and reason backward" when quantifying payoffs.

The binomial model explicitly considers how actions of rival firms interact and alter each firm's valuation. Managers can break down their analyses to understand how changes in specific variables could lead to different outcomes. Binomial processes and their logic provide a coherent framework to decipher how rival firms and their actions impact each rival's strategic position and economic fortune.

As a result, their strategic responses prioritise what matters by linking resource deployment to monetising value accretion.

1. Preliminary calculations

In committing to invest, managers aim to monetise the economic payoffs that accrue to each asset. Under dynamic markets, payoffs vary as power prices, volumes, and costs fluctuate. How managers adeptly respond spells a difference between profit and loss.

1.1 Lifecycle costs of energy (LCOE)

Energy costs are usually estimated over its lifecycle, where inflation, imputed returns on assets, operating life, and its assumed volumes influence the "levelised" costs. The comparative LCOEs that I calculated, using raw data from U.S. Energy Information Administration (EIA), are shown in Box Table 10.1.1.

Lifecycle avoided costs of energy (LACE) calculates the potential revenues by multiplying LCOE with the varying volumes in a day in a given market to obtain a volume-weighted average. I extend this approach by explicitly adjusting LCOE, when deriving the cash cost of supplies, C_{CCS}, according to the volume supplied. By doing

Box Table 10.1.1: Comparative Lifecycle Costs of Energy and Assumptions

Column/Line	Acronym	Technology Type	Operating Mode	C_{LCOE}	C_{FX}	C_{FOM}	C_{VAR} C_{VOM}	C_{LGX}	C_{FUEL} C_{CADIT}	MWh/Yr	Capex — $/kW	Operating Life — Years	Time to Build — Years	Maintenance Capex — Lifetime Frequency	WCR — As % of Revenue
				A	B	C	D	E	F	G	H	I	J	K	L
				\$/kWh											
				Assumptions											
				Price Setting Supply — $/kWh											
1	$ACCGT_M$	Advance Combined Cycle Gas Turbine	Mid-merit	0.0922	0.0134	0.0024	0.0029	0.0132	0.0603	5,694	795	30	3	4	10.00%
2	$Coal_M$	Coal Fired Power Generation	Mid-merit	0.1519	0.0551	0.0077	0.0058	0.0117	0.0716	5,694	3,013	30	4	4	10.00%
				Technology Choices and Life Cycle Costs of Energy — $/kWh											
3	$Coal_B$	Coal Fired Power Generation	Baseload	0.1334	0.0389	0.0054	0.0058	0.0117	0.0716	7,446	3,013	30	4	4	10.00%
4	$ACCGT_B$	Advance Combined Cycle Gas Turbine	Baseload	0.0883	0.0100	0.0019	0.0029	0.0132	0.0603	7,621	795	30	3	4	10.00%
5	$StoHydro_B$	Pump Storage Hydro Power	Baseload	0.0405	0.0306	0.0079	0.0020	0.0000	0.0000	7,446	2,948	50	4	8	9.00%
6	Geo_B	Geothermal — Large Hole	Baseload	0.0524	0.0321	0.0203	0.0000	0.0000	0.0000	8,234	2,746	30	4	4	9.00%
7	$GeoS_B$	Geothermal — Slim Hole	Baseload	0.0342	0.0209	0.0133	0.0000	0.0000	0.0000	8,234	1,785	30	3	4	9.00%
8	ANuke	Advance Nuclear Power	Baseload	0.0945	0.0643	0.0179	0.0032	0.0009	0.0082	7,884	6,034	40	6	6	9.00%
9	$Wind_{ON}$	Onshore Wind	Mid-merit, Intermittent	0.0689	0.0527	0.0162	0.0000	0.0000	0.0000	3,767	1,624	20	3	2	9.00%
10	PVT_M	Photovoltaic Tracking	Mid-merit, Intermittent	0.1058	0.0947	0.0111	0.0000	0.0000	0.0000	2,540	1,970	20	2	2	9.00%

Source: Author's estimates and calculations using EIA raw data.

1.2 Market volume and allocation

We have two rivals in duopoly: $GeoS_B$ and $ACCGT_B$. As described in Box Table 10.1.2, $GeoS_B$ supplies at a maximum 8,234 MWh, with $ACCGT_B$ supplying 621 MWh, giving an available market supply volume of 15,855 MWh per year. This is eroded by 2% yearly from the start of commercial operations, unless maintenance capex, MCPX, is incurred. In which case, available volumes are reset to their initial maximum.

The initial demand of 11,826 MWh (A.6) varies at +/– 2%. *Up* volume = 12,063 MWh (C.5) or *down* move = 11,589 MWh (C.7) in period one results. Repeated, each node's value is estimated and populated. The probability for each node is compounded. For period two: On an even probability of *up* or *down* move, there is a 25% chance of an *up* move, followed by another *up* move (e.g. 50% * 50% = 25%) (F.4), which is similar for *down–down* moves (F.8). The middle value (F.6) is the sum of 25% *up–down* move and 25% *down–up* move.

$Geos_B$ costs $0.0342/kWh to supply, hence $GeoS_B$ is likely to supply prior to "expensive" $ACCGT_B$, which costs $0.0883/kWh. As volumes are reallocated, prices and costs would also fluctuate. Taking the cue from Janina C Ketterer's work (2014), power prices tend to fall as more renewables are supplied, a phenomenon similar to my findings and other studies (Parachiv *et al.*, 2014). To reflect this, $GeoS_B$'s volume varies along an "inverted binomial tree." This co-exists with $ACCGT_B$'s conventional volume fluctuations, making $GeoS_B$ and $ACCGT_B$ volume moves complementary.

In practice, $GeoS_B$'s initial volume of 8,234 MWh (A.30) would move *up* with an 8% fall (7,575 MWh in C.29) or move *down* by rising 10%, capped by its maximum available supply of 8,234 MWh in C.31. In contrast, $ACCGT_B$ would fulfil the residual periodic demand. Hence, the *up* volume is 3,592 MWh or 12,063 MWh (C.5), that is, 7,575 MWh less than that $GeoS_B$ already supplied, which falls far short of $ACCGT_B$'s available supply of 7,621 MWh (C.24).

1.3 Market power prices – P_s

Periodic power prices, P_s, mimic the costs of supplies of $ACCGT_M$ as the price-setter. Assuming a mid-merit volume of 5,694 MWh, $P_s = C_{LCOE,s} = C_{FX,S} + C_{VAR,S} + C_{FUEL,S}$. Box Table 10.1.3 shows the calculation results.

Box Table 10.1.2: Market and Rival Firms' Volumes

Column/Line	Market Demand Assumptions	Variable	Unit	Value		0 A	p B	1 C	p D	2 E	p F	3 G	p H	4 I	p J	5 K
					Market Volume — MWh											
1	MWh Equivalent per Year		MWh	11,826												13,057
2														12,801	6%	12,545
3	Volatilities			Multiplier (X)								12,550	13%	12,299	25%	12,053
4	Up Move	u	%	2.00%	1.02					12,304	25%	12,058	38%	11,817	38%	11,580
5	Down Move	d	%	2.00%	0.98			12,063	50%	11,821	50%	11,585	38%	11,353	25%	11,126
6						11,826	100%	11,589	50%	11,358	25%	11,131	13%	10,908	6%	10,690
7	Probabilities															
8	Up Move		%	50.00%	0.50											
9	Down Move		%	50.00%	0.50											
10																
11	Risk-free Rate	r	%	2.50%	1.03											

(Continued)

Box Table 10.1.2 (Continued)

| Column/Line | Supply | Variable | Unit | GeoS_B | ACCGT_B | \multicolumn{11}{c}{Volume with Maintenance Capex — ACCGT_B} |
						0	p	1	p	2	p	3	p	4	p	5
12	Installed Capacity		MW	1,000	1,000											7,469
13	Rated Capacity per Year		MWh	8,760	8,760									6,902	6%	6,646
14	Maximum Supply per Year		MWh	8,234	7,621							6,138	13%			
15	Erosion Rate per Year		%	2.00%	2.00%					5,335	25%			5,887	25%	5,641
16	Starting Supply per Year		MWh	8,234	7,621			4,487	50%			5,088	38%			
17						3,592	100%			4,246	50%			4,847	38%	4,611
18	**Volatility**							3,355	50%			4,010	38%			
19	Up Move	u	%	8.00%	2.00%					3,124	25%			3,778	25%	3,551
20	Down Move	d	%	10.00%	2.00%							2,897	13%			
21														2,674	6%	
22	**Multiplier**					\multicolumn{2}{l}{*Maximum Annual*}									2,620
23	Up Move	u	X	0.92	1.02	\multicolumn{2}{l}{*Supply — ACCGT_B*}									
						7,621		7,621		7,621		7,621		7,621		7,469
24	Down Move	d	X	1.10	0.98											

Oligopolistic Rivalries

Box Table 10.1.2 (*Continued*)

Column/Line		Cost of Supplies — Baseload Volume				Volume with Maintenance Capex — GeoS$_B$					
		Variable	Unit	GeoS$_B$	ACCGT$_B$	0	p 1	p 2	p 3	p 4	p 5
25	Lifecycle Cost of Energy	LCOE	$/kWh	0.0342	0.0883						5,427
26										5,899	6%
27	Fixed Costs Recovery	C_{FX}	$/kWh	0.0209	0.0100				6,412	13%	5,899
28										6,412	25%
29	Variable Costs	C_{VAR}	$/kWh	0.0133	0.0048		7,575	50%			6,412
30	Fixed Operating & Maintenance (O&M)	$C_{FO\&M}$	$/kWh	0.0133	0.0019	8,234	100%		6,969	38%	
31	Variable O&M	$C_{VO\&M}$	$/kWh	0.0000	0.0029		8,234	50%		6,969	38%
32								8,234	25%	7,575	25%
33	Fuel Costs	C_{FUEL}	$/kWh	0.0000	0.0735				8,234	13%	7,575
34	Commodity Prices	C_{CMDT}	$/kWh	0.0000	0.0603					8,234	25%
35	Logistics	C_{LGX}	$/kWh	0.0000	0.0132						8,069
36						Maximum Annual Supply — GeoS$_B$					
37						8,234	8,234	8,234	8,234	8,234	8,069

Source: Author's estimates and calculations using EIA raw data.

Box Table 10.1.3: Power Prices under $ACCGT_M$

Column/Line	Calculation Assumptions — $ACCGT_M$ as Market Price Setting Supply			0		1		2		3		4		5
								Power Prices — $ACCGT_M$						
	Variable	Unit	Value	A	p B	C	p D	E	p F	G	p H	I	p J	K
1	Reference Volume	MWh/Yr	5,694											0.1900
2												0.1630	6%	
3	Volatility Multiplier — Fuel (C_{CMDT})									0.1405	13%			0.1408
4	Up Move	X	1.20					0.1215	25%			0.1219	25%	
5	Down Move	X	0.83			0.1056	50%			0.1059	38%			0.1063
6				0.0922	100%			0.0926	50%			0.0929	38%	
7	Volatility — Logistics (C_{LGX})	%	Multiplier			0.0813	50%			0.0817	38%			0.0820
8	Up Move	X	1.10					0.0722	25%			0.0725	25%	
9	Down Move	X	0.95							0.0645	13%			0.0649
10												0.0581	6%	
11	Probabilities													0.0527
12	Up Move	%	50.00%											

Oligopolistic Rivalries

Box Table 10.1.3: (*Continued*)

					Fuel Commodity Prices — ACCGT$_M$										
					0	p	1	p	2	p	3	p	4	p	5
13	Down Move		%	50.00%											
14	Risk-free Rate	r	%	2.50%											0.1500
15	Reference Power Prices	P$_S$		0.0922									0.1250	6%	
16	Fixed Costs Recovery	C$_{FX}$	$/kWh	0.0134							0.1041	13%			0.1037
17									0.0868	25%			0.0864	25%	
18	Variable Costs	C$_{VAR}$	$/kWh	0.0053			0.0723	50%			0.0720	38%			0.0717
19	Fixed O&M	C$_{FO\&M}$	$/kWh	0.0024	0.0603	100%			0.0600	50%			0.0598	38%	
20	Variable O&M	C$_{VO\&M}$	$/kWh	0.0029			0.0500	50%			0.0498	38%			0.0496
21									0.0415	25%			0.0414	25%	
22	Fuel Costs	C$_{FUEL}$	$/kWh	0.0735							0.0345	13%			0.0343
23	Commodity Prices	C$_{CMDT}$	$/kWh	0.0603									0.0286	6%	
24	Logistics	C$_{LGX}$	$/kWh	0.0132											0.0237

Source: Author's estimates and calculations using EIA raw data.

C_{FUEL} comprises a volatile commodity cost, C_{CMDT}, and logistics expenses, C_{LGX}, to get fuel to market. Natural gas, $ACCGT_M$'s principal fuel, varies *up* 20% or *down* 17%. In contrast, C_{LGX} varies *up* 10% or *down* 5%. With initial $C_{CMDT} = \$0.0603/$ KWh and $C_{LGX} = \$0.0132/kWh$, individual binomial trees are populated by following a binomial *up* or *down* process for each node. Adding the values for the corresponding nodes gives us C_{FUEL} for each node.

C_{VAR} comprises two sets of operating and maintenance costs (O&M), a fixed, $C_{FO\&M}$, and variable, $C_{VO\&M}$. As the latter varies directly with volumes, $C_{VO\&M}$ is unaltered by volume variations. However, costs captured under $C_{FO\&M}$ are expensed to meet a given volume, say 5,694 MWh.

For the price-setter, when volumes for $ACCGT_M$ fall below 5,694 MWh, $C_{FO\&M}$ and C_{FX} would tend to go up, and I use the lower of the two which equates to \$0.0024/kWh (line 19, reference cost). As a result, power prices would reflect the most competitive supply, recognising that LCOEs are calculated using the median costs. Within similar technologies, there is a range of values.

For cash costs of supplies, C_{CCS}, which is the sum of C_{VAR} and C_{FUEL}, the revised volumes are used to reflect the higher costs when volumes fall below the mid-merit level.

$C_{FO\&M} = \$0.0024/kWh$ for $ACCGT_M$ is recalculated as (\$0.0024/kWh * 5,694 MWh)/periodic volume.

C_{FX} follows similar principles and calculations as $C_{FO\&M}$. For the same node, the revised $C_{FX} = (\$0.0139/kWh * 5,694\ MWh)/(2,620\ MWh) = \$0.0212/kWh$. For this reason, as $GeoS_B$ dynamically crowds out $ACCGT_B$, the initial market power price may increase to \$0.1014/kWh, instead of the reference price of \$0.0922/kWh. However, within competing ACCGTs, varying supply costs would pave the way for more expensive ACCGTs towards obsolescence. At this point, supplies from $GeoS_B$ would reassert its eroding effects on power prices.

1.4 Economic cash margins – ECM_e

The economic cash margins, ECM_e, are the difference between periodic power price, P_s, and the periodic cash costs of supply, or $C_{CCS} = C_{VAR,j} + C_{FUEL,j}$ for firm j. For perfectly indexed supplies, $ECM_e = C_{FX,j}$ which is possible but more of an exception.

Deviations are more common, which give rise to arbitrage opportunities (e.g. cost over-recovery) or risks of stranded costs (e.g. costs under-recovery).

Taking period four in Box Table 10.1.4, which is the initial year of operation for $GeoS_B$ and $ACCGT_B$, a power price $0.1630/kWh (I.2, Box Table 10.1.3) corresponds to a volume of 5,899 MWh (I.26) for $GeoS_B$ (from Box Table 10.1.2), giving a revenue of $962 mln. $ACCGT_B$'s revenue is $1,125 mln ($0.1630/kWh * 6,902 MWh).

$GeoS_B$ has zero fuel costs, C_{FUEL}, and $C_{VO\&M}$, with $C_{FO\&M}$ of $0.0133/kWh as its economic cash costs, based on 8,234 MWh per year (from Box Table 10.1.1, C.7). Adjusted, the revised $C_{FO\&M}$ is $0.0186/kWh or ($0.0133/kWh * 8,234 MWh)/(5,899 MWh), giving a cash cost of supply of $110 mln. Deducted from revenue of $962 mln, ECM_e = $852 mln.

Dynamic power markets are perceived by some managers as adding to $ACCGT_B$'s risks. Volatile prices and fuel costs make ECM_e "volatile." While this belief persists, this half-truth is re-examined.

ECM_e = $95 mln (I.2) is derived from revenue of $1,125 mln, less C_{FUEL} = $996 mln and C_{VAR} = $34 mln.

C_{FUEL} comprises the sum of C_{CMDT} = $0.1250/kWh and C_{LGX} = $0.0194/kWh, resulting in C_{FUEL} = $0.1444/kWh. Multiply this by the volume 6,902 MWh, fuel cost is $996 mln.

C_{VAR} is the sum of $C_{VO\&M}$ = $0.0029/kWh and the revised $C'_{FO\&M}$ = $0.0021/kWh, given the lower volume of 6,902 MWh (instead of the reference 7,621 MWh). At this volume, the variable cost is $34 mln.

Now, assume that gas prices fell by 20%, with volumes and logistics expenses remaining at the same level. The resulting values are compared (previous amounts in parentheses) as: P_s = $0.1381/kWh ($0.1630), giving revenue of $953 mln ($1,125 mln). With C_{VAR} as it was, ECM_e = 95 mln is unchanged.

There is no financial sleight-of-hand. Indexed to power prices, the decline of $172 mln in fuel costs is passed on entirely to consumers, as an equivalent amount in revenue reductions. With this physical hedge, fuel costs volatility is not $ACCGT_B$'s principal worry.

Being crowded out by $GeoS_B$ in a stable volume market is what gives managers sleepless nights (and days).

Box Table 10.1.4: Economic Cash Margin

Economic Cash Margin with Maintenance Capex — ACCGT$_B$ under ACCGT$_M$

Column/Line		Calculation Assumptions				0	p	1	p	2	p	3	p	4	p	5
	Variable		Unit	GeoS$_B$	ACCGT$_B$	A	B	C	D	E	F	G	H	I	J	K
1	**Volatility — Economic Cash Margin**															104
2	Up Move	u	%	7.33%	2.70%									95	6%	
3	Down Move	d	%	11.67%	3.00%							0	13%			91
4										0	25%			79	25%	
5	**Probabilities**							0	50%			0	38%			75
6	Up Move	u	%	50.00%	50.00%	0	100%			0	50%			62	38%	
7	Down Move	d	%	50.00%	50.00%			0	50%			0	38%			58
8										0	25%			45	25%	
9	**Multiplier**											0	13%			42
10	Up Move	u	X	1.11	1.03									28	6%	
11	Down Move	d	X	0.87	0.99											27

Box Table 10.1.4: (*Continued*)

	Risk-adjusted Probabilities				Economic Cash Margin with Maintenance Capex — GeoS$_B$ under ACCGT$_M$											
						0	p	1	p	2	p	3	p	4	p	5
12	Up Move	u	%	62.70%	85.78%											921
13	Down Move	d	%	37.30%	14.22%										6%	
14														852		721
15	Risk-free Rate	r	%	2.50%	2.50%					0	25%	0	13%		25%	
16								0	50%					672		572
17						0	100%			0	50%	0	38%		38%	
18								0	50%					538		462
19										0	25%	0	38%		25%	
20														440		382
21												0	13%	369	6%	
22																316

Source: Author's estimates and calculations based on EIA raw data.

1.5 Risk-neutral strategic payoffs

The strategic economic payoff (SPO_e) is the present value of ECM_e comprising two parts. There is an explicit point estimate up to period five and a terminal value of payoffs, TVP_e, from period six till the asset's *end-of-life*. The two "discrete" periods are discretionary divides in order to simplify the analyses.

Binomial model starts from the endpoint and works back to period zero, which is in theory the point when the decision is taken.

The first point of encounter is to estimate TVP_e for each power price level. Extending the model, prices, costs, and volumes are assumed at a steady state for each power price point in period five. ECM_e for each period is extended till *end-of-life*, with volumes revised up after each MCPX is incurred. Discounted at the risk-free rate, r, TVP_e is calculated with period six as the initial year.

By using a risk-free rate to discount ECM_es, binomial processes are spared from the conflicting prescriptions purveyed for estimating risk premium. To guard against "flattering" the present value, Cox *et al.*, (2003) recalibrate the *up* moves by applying risk-neutral probabilities according to the following:

$$p_u' = ((1 + r) - (d)) / (u - d) \qquad (10.1.1)$$

Hence, the *down* move is:

$$p_d' = 1 - p_u' \qquad (10.1.2)$$

Starting with the end period t = 5,

$$S_{t=5} = (TVP_e)/(1 + r) + (ECM_{t=5})/(1 + r) \qquad (10.1.3)$$

This binomial process now calculates the value for each node by moving back from period t=5 to period t = 4, as follows:

$$S_{t=4} = (ECM_{e,t=4})/(1 + r) + p_u' * S\_\{u,t=5\} + p_d' * S\_\{d,t=5\} \qquad (10.1.4)$$

As an example, Box Table 10.1.5 shows at M.1 TVP_e = $1,984 mln for $ACCGT_B$. Given pricing and volume flexibility, supplies are curtailed when its cash costs of

Oligopolistic Rivalries — 565

Box Table 10.1.5: Payoffs and Strategic Option Value

Payoffs ($) and Call Option Value With Flexible Volume Obligations — $ACCGT_B$ under $ACCGT_M$

Column/Line	Discount Factor	Calculation Assumptions	Variable	Unit	$GeoS_B$	$ACCGT_B$	0 1.03 A	Strategic Option Value B	1 1.03 C	Strategic Option Value D	2 1.03 E	Strategic Option Value F	3 1.03 G	Strategic Option Value H	4 1.03 I	Strategic Option Value J	5 1.03 K	Strategic Option Value L	Terminal Value M	X' =MCPX N	Strategic Option Value O
1																	1,475	700	1,984	575	1,409
2		PV Capex	$P_0 = X$	$ mln	1,741	775									1,506	657					
3		PV Maintenance Capex	$P_0 = X$	$ mln	1,178	521							1,439	613			1,289	514	1,806	575	1,231
4											1,372	569			1,289	456					
5		Implied Volatilities Multiplier — Economic Cash Margins							1,306	526			1,212	404			966	190	1,490	575	915
6		Up Move	X		1.11	1.03	1,241	483			1,137	357			957	159					
7		Down Move	X		0.87	0.99			1,065	314			886	133			633	0	1,165	575	590
8											819	112			616	0					
9		Risk-adjusted Probabilities											557	0			307	0	848	575	273
10		Up Move	u	%	62.70%	85.78%									295	0					
11		Down Move	d	%	37.30%	14.22%											78	0	628	575	53

(Continued)

Box Table 10.1.5: (*Continued*)

Payoffs (S) and Call Option Value with Flexible Volume Obligations — GeoS$_B$ under ACOGT$_M$

Risk-free Rate r 2.50% | 2.50% | 2.50%

	Strategic Option 0 / 1.03	Value	Strategic Option 1 / 1.03	Value	Strategic Option 2 / 1.03	Value	Strategic Option 3 / 1.03	Value	Strategic Option 4 / 1.03	Value	Strategic Option 5 / 1.03	Value	Terminal Value	X' = MCPX	Strategic Option Value
12															
13											17,578	15,837	18,397	1,301	17,096
14									16,491	13,960					
15							14,709	12,305			13,482	11,741	14,399	1,301	13,098
16					13,135	10,845									
17			11,742	9,558			11,368	9,118			10,437	8,695	11,426	1,301	10,125
18	10,507	8,420			10,187	8,034			9,888	7,664					
19			9,135	7,071			8,885	6,750			8,187	6,445	9,230	1,301	7,929
20					7,978	5,925			7,793	5,665					
21							6,987	4,936			6,474	4,733	7,555	1,301	6,254
22									6,100	4,042	4,892	3,151	6,000	1,301	4,699

Source: Author's estimates and calculations based on EIA raw data.

supply, $C_{CCS} < P_s$, in order to avoid making a loss. Assuming no penalties or costs, curtailing supplies results in $SPO_e = 0$. To acquire this payoff, MCPX is continually incurred. To reflect this, MCPX is deducted from TVPe, where strategic option value, SOV_e, is used instead as "terminal payoff."

In period five, the terminal SOV_e = $1,409 mln (O.8) and the period's ECM_e = $104 mln (K.1, Box Table 10.1.4) are added. Discounted by 1.025, the node value is $1,475 mln (K.1).

Period t = 4 starts applying the risk-neutral probabilities to derive the node SPO_es. For example, p(u)' = 85.78%, where the numerator is ((1+025) − (0.9855)) = 0.0392 and the denominator is (1.0315 − 0.9855) = 0.0457. Hence, p(d) = 1 − 0.8578 = 14.22%.

Period four's payoffs, S, at node I.9 of $1,506 mln becomes a walk in the park. The weighted sum of $1,475 (K.8) * 0.8578 and $1,289 mln (K.10) * 0.1422 = $1,448 mln. Adding the period's ECM_e = $95 mln (I.2 from Box Table 10.1.3), and discounted by 1.025, the node value is $1,505 mln.

2. Making choices with option valuation

Real-life managerial decisions are often contingent, reserving the option to change course when the evidence from market warrants. This managerial flexibility confers a right, but not an obligation, to continually supply (Dixit and Pindyck, 1994). The objective is to gain payoffs that exceed what was invested or $SPO_e > X$ (e.g. capex and MCPX).

This option is valued using option pricing, popularised in finance as Black–Scholes–Merton (Damodaran, 1996; Duffie, 1998). Generically, option value is created when the present asset prices deviate from the value of future payoffs. Both are premised on expectations, which could vary over time.

To trade on this, "investors can create an arbitrage position, that is, a position that requires no investment, involves no risk, and delivers positive returns" (Damodaran, 1996). In effect, this requires a replicating portfolio that mimics the payoffs (and risk profile) of the underlying asset, with deviations creating arbitrage or option value.

Practice, however, is divided on its use for physical assets. An example is the critique of Espen Gaarder Haug and Nassim Nicholas Taleb (2011). In creating a replicating portfolio, finding passive financial assets that mimic closely the underlying assets poses challenges. This problem is heightened with physical assets. Trying to capture the subtleties of dynamic managerial actions, essential to differentiate among feasible SPO_es, the task becomes intractable.

As practical people, I propose that the "best" replicating portfolio is the asset itself, where binomial processes provide greater latitude to model a decision as closely to its context. In this formulation, the strategic option value (SOV_e) is the *call option*. The present "price" is the initial capex's present value, discounted at the risk-free rate. For example:

Period t = 5 gives a node SOV_e = $700 mln (L.8, Box Table 10.1.4) or terminal SPO_e = $1,475 mln (K.8) minus the present value of initial capex = $775 mln, as "current price." Repeated, the remaining SPO_es are calculated, where negative SOV_es are set to zero. That is, assets that are *out of the money* have zero *call option* value.

If at any time prior to the asset's *end-of-life*, managers decide to exit, how much would an option be worth? This brings us to evaluating the *call value*, CV_e, with the results shown in Box Table 10.1.5. The node values for CV_e are derived using the general form expressed as:

$$CV_e = (S_t * \Delta) - ((1 + r) * (B)) \quad (10.1.5)$$

With two unknowns to solve, two equations are needed to derive the number of shares, Δ, and the amount to borrow or lend, B, as replicating portfolio.

Using the SPO_es for *up* or *down* moves of "current price," the two unknowns are solved by substituting node values (from Box Table 10.1.4) to Box Eq. (10.1.5) for the prior period's *up* or *down* values for SPO_e and SOV_e:

(1) $SOV_{e,u}$ = ($1,475 mln * Δ) - (1.025% * B) = $700 mln; and
(2) $SOV_{e,d}$ = ($1,289 mln * Δ) - (1.025% * B) = $514 mln.

Solving the two equations simultaneously, we have Δ = 1.000 and B = $757, from N.1 and O.1, respectively, at Box Table 10.1.6. Substituting these values to Box Eq. (10.1.5), CV_e = $719 mln (M.1). This implies that to achieve similar portfolio payoffs, investor may purchase 1.000 share of $ACCGT_B$ and borrow/lend at 2.5% the sum of B = $757 mln.

Box Table 10.1.6: Call Value with Maintenance Capex

Call Value with Maintenance Capex — ACCGT$_B$ under ACCGT$_M$

| | Calculation Assumptions | | | | Call Value | Δ | B | Call Value | Δ | B | Call Value | Δ | B | Call Value | Δ | B | Call Value | Δ | B |
| | | | | | 0 | | | 1 | | | 2 | | | 3 | | | 4 | | |
Column/Line			GeoS$_B$	ACCGT$_B$	A $ mln	B	C $ mln	D $ mln	E	F $ mln	G $ mln	H	I $ mln	J $ mln	K	L $ mln	M $ mln	N	O $ mln
1	PV Capex	X	1,741	775													**719**	1.0000	757
2	PV	X	1,301	575															
3	Maintenance Capex				**483**	0.8788	607				**569**	0.9205	694				**533**	1.0000	757
4								**526**	0.9033	654				**404**	0.8924	678			
5	Call Value:																		
6	COV$_c$ = (S$_t$ +1 * Δ) − (1 + r) * B							**314**	0.7697	506	**357**	0.8309	588	**133**	0.4682	282	**199**	0.5719	353
7											**112**	0.4048	220						
8	Risk-free Rate	r	%	2.50%										**0**	0.0000	0	**0**	0.0000	0
9																	**0**	0.0000	0

(*Continued*)

Box Table 10.1.6: (*Continued*)

Call Value with Maintenance Capex — GeoS$_n$ under ACCGT$_M$

	Call Value $ mln	0 Δ X	B $ mln	Call Value $ mln	1 Δ X	B $ mln	Call Value $ mln	2 Δ X	B $ mln	Call Value $ mln	3 Δ X	B $ mln	Call Value $ mln	4 Δ X	B $ mln
10													**14,792**	1.0000	1,699
11										**12,305**	0.9536	1,722			
12							**10,845**	0.9536	1,680				**11,002**	1.0000	1,699
13				**9,558**	0.9537	1,640				**9,118**	0.9536	1,722			
14	**8,420**	0.9539	1,603				**8,034**	0.9538	1,682				**8,189**	1.0000	1,699
15				**7,071**	0.9544	1,648				**6,750**	0.9543	1,728			
16							**5,925**	0.9558	1,700				**6,094**	1.0000	1,699
17										**4,936**	0.9590	1,764			
18													**4,401**	1.0000	1,699

An intuitive way of thinking about Δ is to take the ratio of the differences of SOV_e and SPO_e. In this case, we have from Box Table 10.1.5, ($700 − $514)/($1,475 − $1,289) = 1.000. [(L.1 − L.2)/(K.1 − K.3)]. With Δ = 1.000 and substituting into Box Eq. (10.1.1)–10.1.5, B = $757 mln.

While $GeoS_B$ is "in the money," given its positive call value, CV_e, $ACCGT_B$ would have nil CV_e when power prices fall below $0.725/kWh. At low power prices and low volumes, $ACCGT_B$ would be worthless when paired with $GeoS_B$.

3. To spend or not to spend

Maximising volume is accepted as a sound investment strategy under the economics of pure competition. Assuming what firms could supply are despatched, this is roundly questioned under oligopoly. This question needs an answer: Is incurring maintenance capex, MCPX, a necessity to optimise payoffs? I propose a quintessentially economist reply: It depends.

Let us examine the results from the simulation:

Box Chart 10.1.1 illustrates in four charts my take on the virtues (or waste) from MCPX. It is an option to acquire the incremental volumes, and as a result, any accretive SOV_e. Box Charts 10.1.1(A) and (B) both confirm there are significant volumes to be gained by $GeoS_B$ and $ACCGT_B$. By letting the assets to erode, the gaps widen between volumes from with and without MCPX.

To monetise the incremental volume, there should be a need for it. Taking the average and the maximum volumes deployed, $GeoS_B$ and $ACCGT_B$ diverge in their economic fortunes. With $GeoS_B$, being despatched ahead of $ACCGT_B$, its incremental volumes are more likely to be monetised. In contrast, as indicated by $ACCGT_B$'s widening gaps between what it could supply and what it is supplying, the incremental volumes are stranded. That is, by adding to its underutilised supply, it incurs MCPX with little prospect of seeing any payoffs.

This explains the contrasting outcomes shown in Box Charts 10.1.1(C) and (D). $GeoS_B$ makes money by supplying more to offset declining power prices. This is the curse $GeoS_B$ lives with: The more available its volumes are, the more it undercuts itself by eroding prices. To compensate, it supplies more so that revenues are sustained.

Expecting prices to remain above $0.0858/kwh, MCPX is more than covered by incremental SPOe. $ACCGT_B$ would struggle at all power price levels. Implication? $ACCGT_B$ may divest or exit or run down its asset rather than reinvest its payoffs.

Dynamic Decisions

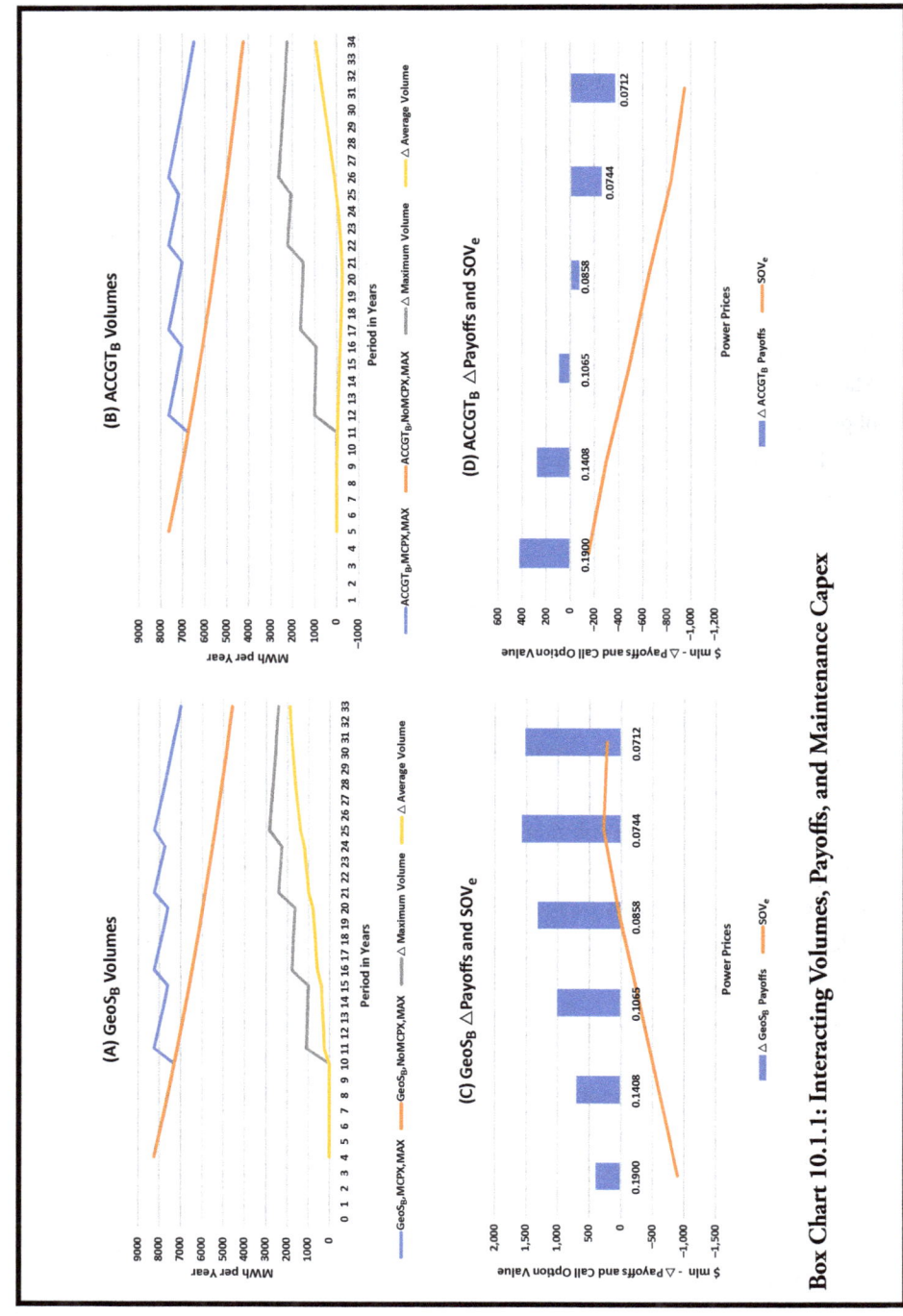

Box Chart 10.1.1: Interacting Volumes, Payoffs, and Maintenance Capex

4. Residual economic value

Residual Economic Value (REV$_e$) serves as a dashboard for an initial screening of technology pairs. Calculated under binomial processes, REV$_e$ provides the contours and patterns of how economic value evolves as power prices, costs, and volumes interact.

Starting with its economic return-on-invested capital (RoIC$_e$), hurdle rate, r_h, is recalibrated to align with the use of risk-free rate for option valuation. This is now the sum of risk-free rate, r, and the depreciation rate for the asset, DPN$_{r,e}$.

RoIC$_e$ is simplified as ECM$_e$/invested capital, where invested capital is the sum of capex, MCPX, and the working capital requirement (WCR). WCR is estimated as a percentage of revenues, with the tax rate applied to RoIC to derive the net returns. With all variables previously calculated, binomial trees are employed to iteratively estimate the changing REV.

Box Table 10.1.7 establishes the economic viability of GeoS$_B$ and ACCGT$_B$, across the power prices considered. While this masked the counterintuitive insights on MCPX, this suffices for an overview to "pre-qualify" certain technologies for investment consideration. At low power prices and low volumes, ACCGT$_B$ is value eroding, which is a similar assessment that nil call value gave.

Where REV$_e$ serves its purpose lies in the enterprise value (EV) calculations. By adding REV$_e$ to invested capital (IC), the valuation is now reconnected to financial analyses. Knowing EV, a decision on debt and equity as sources of funding facilitates the understanding of how value could be allocated among fund providers.

****

The counterintuitive insights from binomial processes are disconcerting for some managers. That volumes are gained or lost, in the same way as market shares, is well accepted. However, embedded beliefs may prove persistent in seeing maximising volumes as a virtue in energy investments.

When macroeconomists and strategists get together, a collision course is in the offing. Imagine a pure economic theorist expounding on the virtues of perfect competition. Dismantling barriers that impede entry or exit, or squeeze surplus to nil, are lifelong mantras for the purists. With Michael E Porter's *Five Forces of Competition*

Box Table 10.1.7: Residual Economic Value

Column/Line	Residual Economic Income Calculation	Variable	Unit	GeoS$_B$	ACCGT$_B$	0 A	p B	1 C	p D	2 E	p F	3 G	p H	4 I	p J	5 K	Terminal Value L
										Residual Economic Value — ACCGT$_B$ under ACCGT$_M$							
1	**Enterprise Value**			10,372	1,875									597	6%	603	588
2	PV Invested Capital	IC	$ mln	3,096	1,405							566	13%			509	500
3	PV Residual Economic Value	REV	$ mln	7,276	470					534	25%			480	25%		
4						470	100%	502	50%			437	38%	259	38%	297	293
5	**Risk-adjusted Probabilities — Economic Cash Margin**									396	50%						
6	Up Move	u	%	62.70%	85.78%			357	50%			219	38%	19	25%	64	66
7	Down Move	d	%	37.30%	14.22%					181	25%						
8												(14)	13%			(173)	(165)
9	**Risk-neutral Hurdle Rate**	rh	%	**5.83%**	**5.83%**									(216)	6%		
10	Depreciation Rate	DPNr	%	3.33%	3.33%											(342)	(328)
11	Risk-free Rate	r	%	2.50%	2.50%												

Box Table 10.1.7: (*Continued*)

						Residual Economic Value — GeoS$_B$ under ACCGT$_M$							
Working Capital Requirements	WCR	%	9.00%	10.00%		0	p	1	p	2	p	3	p	4	p	5	Terminal Value
Cash Tax Rate	TAXCR	%	22.00%	22.00%													

	0	p	1	p	2	p	3	p	4	p	5	Terminal Value
12											12,743	12,445
13												
14									11,823	*6%*	9,569	9,347
15							10,466	*13%*	8,886	*25%*		
16					9,268	*25%*	7,877	*38%*			7,209	7,044
17	7,276	*100%*	8,211	*50%*								
18			6,192	*50%*	6,985	*50%*	5,953	*38%*	6,707	*38%*	5,467	5,343
19					5,273	*25%*			5,084	*25%*		
20							4,483	*13%*			4,139	4,045
21									3,773	*6%*		
22											2,914	2,840

Source: Author's estimates and calculations based on EIA raw data.

(Porter, 2008), corporate strategists are most likely to erect *barriers to entry* to *dominate* a profitable niche. Beyond the initial niceties, strategists (and finance) come to realise that what in their eyes are legitimate pursuits are under threat. Competition *purists* promote policies to dismantle such *market imperfections* that managers sought to strategically erect or reinforce. Policy's resolve to intervene in two-sided markets appears to have weakened, partly for its complexity to regulate.

The $ACCGT_B$ maintenance capex paradox, on closer examination, is a product of unquestioned beliefs. It took a housewife, former UK prime minister Margaret R Thatcher, to remind managers and policy of what is obvious to her "household economics": *Spend less than what you could earn.*

Resolving $ACCGT_B$'s dilemma: *Why spend to add to volumes that would remain idle, earning no payoffs?* After all, decisions are made within some given contexts, where judgement is valued over delegating decisions to the algorithm of financial or economic models.

Bibliography

Abada, I., Gabriel, S., Briat, V., and Massol, O. (2013). A generalized Nash–Cournot model for the Northwestern European natural gas markets with a fuel substitution demand function: The GaMMES model. *Network Spatial Economics,* 13, 1–42.

Arya, A., Fellingham, J., and Glover, J. C. (1998). Capital budgeting: Some exceptions to the NPV rule. *Issues in Accounting Education*, 13(3), 499–507, August 1998.

Atwell, C. (2018). The true cost of solar energy. *Power Electronics*, February 7, 2018.

BBC — British Broadcasting Corporation (1984). 1984: The beginning of the end for British coal. http://news.bbc.co.uk/onthisday/hi/dates/stories/march/12/newsid_3503000/3503346.stm. Accessed on June 19, 2020.

Bocse, A.-M. and Genebauer, C. (2017). UK's Dash for Gas: Implications for the role of natural gas in European power generation. *EU Centre for Energy Resources and Security*, King's College London, February 2017.

Chevalier-Roignant, B. and Trigeorgis, L. (2011). *Competitive Strategy: Options and Games*. Cambridge, M.A.: Massachusetts Institute of Technology Press.

Cox, J. C., Ross, S. A., and Rubinstein, M. (2003). The Cox-Ross-Rubenstein model. In *Mathematical Finance and Probability*. Birkhauser, Basel: Springer Basel.

Damodaran, A. (1996). *Investment Valuation: Tools and Techniques for Determining the Value of any Asset*. New York: John Wiley & Sons.

Dixit, A. K. and Nalebuff, B. J. (1993). *Thinking Strategically: The Competitive Edge in Business, Politics, and Everyday Life*. New York and London: W. W. Norton & Company.

Dixit, A. K. and Nalebuff, B. J. (2010). *The Art of Strategy: A Game Theorist's Guide to Success in Business and Life*. New York: W. W. Norton and Company.

Dixit, A. K. and Pindyck, R. S. (1994). *Investment under Uncertainty*. Princeton, NJ: Princeton University Press.

Drax (2020). https://www.drax.com/investors/share-price/. Accessed on June 30, 2020.

Duffie, D. (1998). Black, merton and scholes: Their central contributions to economics. *The Scandinavian Journal of Economics*, 100(2), 411–423, June 1998.

Dvorak, P. and Jones, R. (2019). SoftBank's bid to build a solar-power empire founders. *The Wall Street Journal*, August 10, 2019.

Eavis, P. and Penn, I. (2021). Home solar is growing, but big installers are still losing money. *The New York Times*, September 8, 2021.

EIA (2019). *Energy Outlook 2019*. Washington DC: U.S. Energy Information Administration.

Gross, A. (2020). Drax to end use of coal at UK's biggest power plant 3 years early. *Financial Times*, February 27, 2020.

Haug, E. G. and Taleb, N. N. (2011). Option traders use (very) sophisticated heuristics, never the Black-Scholes-Merton formula. *Journal of Economic Behaviour & Organization*, 77(2), 97–106, February 2011.

Hook, L. (2013). Top solar panel maker goes bankrupt. *Financial Times*, March 21, 2013.

IEA (2019). *The Role of Gas in Today's Energy Transitions*. Paris: International Energy Agency.

Ketterer, J. C. (2014). The impact of wind power generation and the electricity price in Germany. *Energy Economics*, 44, 270–280, July 2014.

Kerr, E. (2019). The future of solar is bright. *Science in the News*, Harvard University, March 21, 2019. https://sitn.hms.harvard.edu/flash/2019/future-solar-bright/#.

Koller, T., Goedhart, M., and Wessels, D. (2020). *Valuation: Measuring and Managing the Value of Companies*. New York: John Wiley & Sons.

Kreps, D. M. and Scheinkman, J. A. (1983). Quantity pre-commitment and bertrand competition yield cournot outcomes. *The Bell Journal of Economics*, 14, 326–337.

Littlechild, S. C. (2001). Competition and regulation in the UK electricity industry (with a brief look at California). *Journal of Applied Corporate Finance*, 13(4), 21–38.

Lundin, E. and Tangeras, T. (2020). Cournot competition in wholesale electricity markets: The Nordic Exchange, NordPool. *International Journal of Industrial Organisation*, 68, 1–21, January 2020.

Matthews, K. and Minford, P. (1987). Mrs Thatcher's economic policies 1979–1987. *Economic Policy*, 2(5), 52–101, October 1, 1987.

Niemietz, K. (2013). Thatcherism and British living standards. *Institute of Economic Affairs*, April 18, 2013.

Parachiv, F., Erni, D., and Pietsch, R. (2014). The impact of renewable energies on EEX day-ahead electricity prices. *Energy Policy*, 73, 196–210, October 2014.

Porter, M. E. (2008). *Competitive strategy: Techniques for analysing industries and competitors* (with new introduction). New York: The Free Press.

Powell, C. and Persico, J. E. (2003). *My American Journey (Revised Edition)*. New York: First Ballantine Book.

Rumelt, R. P. (2011). *Good Strategy, Bad Strategy: The Difference and Why it Matters*. London: Profile Books.

Smil, V. (2016). 'Too cheap to meter' nuclear power revisited. *IEEE Spectrum*, September 26, 2016, The Institute of Electrical and Electronics Engineers.

Thaler, R. (2015). *Misbehaving: The Making of Behavioural Economics*. New York: W. W. Norton & Company.

Trenblay, C. H. (2011). The Cournot-Bertrand model and the degree of product differentiation. *Economic Letters*, 111(3), 233–235, June 2011.

Tulonen, A. (2020). On China, COVID-19, and Coal: Can the EU convince China not to lean on coal for its economic recovery from the Covid 19 crisis?. *The Diplomat*, April 3, 2020.

Winskel, M. (2002). When systems are overthrown: The 'Dash for Gas' in the British Electricity Supply Industry. *Social Studies of Science*, 32(4), 563–598, August 2002.

Appendices

10A: ACCGT$_B$ and Geo$_B$ with Asymmetric Costs under ACCGT$_M$ as Price-setter — Asymmetric Costs Volatilities in Stable Demand

Dynamic Volume Allocation with Flexible Pricing under ACCGT$_M$ as Price-setter — Asymmetric Costs Volatilities in Stable Demand

Column/Line	Duopoly		Power Prices A $/kWh	Both Incur MCPX		ACCGT$_B$ Only		Geo$_B$ Only		Both Forego MCPX		Notional Equilibrium	
				SOV$_1$ B $ mln	SOV$_2$ C $ mln	SOV$_1$ D $ mln	SOV$_2$ E $ mln	SOV$_1$ F $ mln	SOV$_2$ G $ mln	SOV$_1$ H $ mln	SOV$_2$ I $ mln	SOV$_1$ J $ mln	SOV$_2$ K $ mln
1	F1: ACCGT$_B$	F2: Geo$_B$	0.1900	700	14,203	700	15,853	837	14,203	837	16,216	837	16,216
2	F1: ACCGT$_B$	F2: Geo$_B$	0.1408	222	9,849	544	11,207	797	10,002	797	11,731	797	11,731
3	F1: ACCGT$_B$	F2: Geo$_B$	0.1063	190	7,061	306	8,046	656	7,061	657	8,312	657	8,312
4	F1: ACCGT$_B$	F2: Geo$_B$	0.0820	0	4,812	84	5,530	411	4,812	484	5,706	484	5,706
5	F1: ACCGT$_B$	F2: Geo$_B$	0.0649	0	3,115	0	3,599	89	3,115	330	3,709	330	3,709
6	F1: ACCGT$_B$	F2: Geo$_B$	0.0527	0	1,563	0	2,098	0	1,563	203	2,161	203	2,161

Column/Line	Duopoly		Power Prices $/kWh A	Both Incur MCPX		ACCGT$_B$ Only		Geo$_B$ Only		Both Forego MCPX		Notional Equilibrium	
				CV$_1$ B	CV$_2$ C	CV$_1$ D	CV$_2$ E	CV$_1$ F	CV$_2$ G	CV$_1$ H	CV$_2$ I	CV$_1$ J	CV$_2$ K
7	F1: ACCGT$_B$	F2: Geo$_B$	0.1408	759	12,131	770	13,626	908	12,192	908	15,427	908	15,427
8	F1: ACCGT$_B$	F2: Geo$_B$	0.1063	292	8,504	599	9,681	849	8,593	849	11,167	849	11,167
9	F1: ACCGT$_B$	F2: Geo$_B$	0.0820	0	5,998	352	6,853	692	5,998	695	7,922	695	7,922
10	F1: ACCGT$_B$	F2: Geo$_B$	0.0649	0	4,022	97	4,630	434	4,022	570	5,450	570	5,450
11	F1: ACCGT$_B$	F2: Geo$_B$	0.0527	0	2,424	0	2,917	94	2,424	421	3,556	421	3,556

10B: $ACCGT_B$ and Geo_B with Asymmetric Costs under $ACCGT_M$, Growth-biased Volumes

Dynamic Volume Allocation with Flexible Pricing under $ACCGT_M$ as Price-setter — Asymmetric Costs Volatilities in Growth-biased Demand

Column/ Line	Duopoly		Power Prices A $/kWh	Both Incur MCPX		$ACCGT_B$ Only		Geo_B Only		Both Forego MCPX		Notional Equilibrium	
	F1	F2		SOV_1 B $ mln	SOV_2 C $ mln	SOV_1 D $ mln	SOV_2 E $ mln	SOV_1 F $ mln	SOV_2 G $ mln	SOV_1 H $ mln	SOV_2 I $ mln	SOV_1 J $ mln	SOV_2 K $ mln
1	F1: $ACCGT_B$	F2: Geo_B	0.1900	404	10,538	407	7,423	566	10,683	566	7,445	566	10,683
2	F1: $ACCGT_B$	F2: Geo_B	0.1408	43	6,973	407	4,496	566	7,232	566	4,700	566	7,232
3	F1: $ACCGT_B$	F2: Geo_B	0.1063	36	4,474	393	2,488	552	4,661	552	2,682	552	4,661
4	F1: $ACCGT_B$	F2: Geo_B	0.0820	14	2,706	312	1,061	440	2,735	475	1,197	440	2,735
5	F1: $ACCGT_B$	F2: Geo_B	0.0649	0	1,209	219	0	251	1,186	396	100	251	1,186
6	F1: $ACCGT_B$	F2: Geo_B	0.0527	0	10	125	0	61	0	318	0	318	0

Column/ Line	Duopoly		Power Prices A $/kWh	Both Incur MCPX		$ACCGT_B$ Only		Geo_B Only		Both Forego MCPX		Notional Equilibrium	
	F1	F2		CV_1 B	CV_2 C	CV_1 D	CV_2 E	CV_1 F	CV_2 G	CV_1 H	CV_2 I	CV_1 J	CV_2 K
7	F1: $ACCGT_B$	F2: Geo_B	0.1408	466	9,006	500	6,340	656	9,359	656	7,514	656	9,359
8	F1: $ACCGT_B$	F2: Geo_B	0.1063	135	5,917	492	3,768	648	6,263	648	4,814	648	6,263
9	F1: $ACCGT_B$	F2: Geo_B	0.0820	14	3,747	453	1,988	607	3,954	609	2,827	607	3,954
10	F1: $ACCGT_B$	F2: Geo_B	0.0649	17	2,137	354	708	473	2,191	562	1,365	473	2,191
11	F1: $ACCGT_B$	F2: Geo_B	0.0527	0	794	242	120	267	791	485	120	267	791

10C: ACCGT$_B$ and Coal$_B$ with Asymmetric Costs under ACCGT$_M$, Stable Volumes

Dynamic Volume Allocation with Flexible Pricing under ACCGT$_M$ as Price-setter — Asymmetric Costs Volatilities in Stable Demand

Column/Line	Duopoly		Power Prices	Both Incur MCPX		ACCGT$_B$ Only		Coal$_B$ Only		Both Forego MCPX		Notional Equilibrium	
			$/kWh	SOV$_1$ $ mln	SOV$_2$ $ mln	SOV$_1$ $ mln	SOV$_2$ $ mln	SOV$_1$ $ mln	SOV$_2$ $ mln	SOV$_1$ $ mln	SOV$_2$ $ mln	SOV$_1$ $ mln	SOV$_2$ $ mln
			A	B	C	D	E	F	G	H	I	J	K
1	F1: ACCGT$_B$	F2: Coal$_B$	0.1900	694	0	684	0	837	0	837	0	837	0
2	F1: ACCGT$_B$	F2: Coal$_B$	0.1408	694	0	684	0	837	0	837	0	837	0
3	F1: ACCGT$_B$	F2: Coal$_B$	0.1063	694	0	684	0	837	0	837	0	837	0
4	F1: ACCGT$_B$	F2: Coal$_B$	0.0820	694	0	684	0	837	0	837	0	837	0
5	F1: ACCGT$_B$	F2: Coal$_B$	0.0649	634	0	624	0	830	0	827	0	827	0
6	F1: ACCGT$_B$	F2: Coal$_B$	0.0527	478	0	468	0	816	0	787	0	787	0

Column/Line	Duopoly		Power Prices	Both Incur MCPX		ACCGT$_B$ Only		Coal$_B$ Only		Both Forego MCPX		Notional Equilibrium	
			$/kWh	CV$_1$ $ mln	CV$_2$ $ mln	CV$_1$ $ mln	CV$_2$ $ mln	CV$_1$ $ mln	CV$_2$ $ mln	CV$_1$ $ mln	CV$_2$ $ mln	CV$_1$ $ mln	CV$_2$ $ mln
			A	B	C	D	E	F	G	H	I	J	K
1	F1: ACCGT$_B$	F2: Coal$_B$	0.1408	712	0	703	0	856	0	856	0	856	0
2	F1: ACCGT$_B$	F2: Coal$_B$	0.1063	712	0	703	0	856	0	856	0	856	0
3	F1: ACCGT$_B$	F2: Coal$_B$	0.0820	712	0	703	0	856	0	856	0	856	0
4	F1: ACCGT$_B$	F2: Coal$_B$	0.0649	712	0	703	0	856	0	856	0	856	0
5	F1: ACCGT$_B$	F2: Coal$_B$	0.0527	653	0	643	0	846	0	846	0	846	0

IV
Winning Actions

Chapter 11
PIVOT and *BOUnCE* to Profit

After formulating the playbooks to **PIVOT** and **BOUnCE**, managers are seldom endowed with complete information. This is where chance, or *luck*, asserts its influence on how people choose to tackle their challenges and opportunities. In preparing to act, managers are confronted with two opposing tendencies: Some (or a vast majority) would leave nothing to chance and plan for every conceivable contingency. A few equip themselves to recognise opportunities from the unexpected and adaptively act on their *lucky breaks*. The latter are often the lucky managers, not because they wait for a chance to come their way. They create their own luck by building the ability to seize an opportunity when it presents itself. In creating the arenas for emerging opportunities, managers could engage in three levels of **PIVOT** and an adaptive **BOUnCE**: *Foundational* shifts involve building resilience by *repurposing* resources and capabilities as the firm's initial endowment. *Transitional* moves create pathways by exercising options (and closing some), where choices are *reframed* and tested. *Transformational* pivot seeks to *reconfigure* extant networks and relationships to shift the sources of competitive advantages to the firm.

1
Introduction

Business leaders are at times portrayed as omnipotent managers that command enormous resources that can make things happen at will. While this makes good copy for mystery novels or corporate dramas embellished when made into films, the boardroom realities may prove too mundane in comparison.

C-suites are inhabited by *real people*, even in unlisted energy firms or start-up ventures. Managers seldom operate with complete information and absolute control of their resources. To demystify managerial decision-making as well as policymaking, most strategic moves are made under ambiguous and uncertain conditions. Judgements fill in the gaps when the unknowns (or partly known) rear their head.

Managers succeed with "luck" in a Napoleonic sense. Napoleon Bonaparte asserted: "Ability is of little value without opportunity, I had rather my generals be lucky than able." Adopting this to the C-Suite, Charles Vallance, Chair of advertising agency VCCP, describes how ideas are turned into actions (Vallance, 2014):

> "The best ideas tend to evoke the response 'I wish I'd thought of that'. Bold leadership, therefore, should create the conditions where these ideas have the best chance of happening most frequently. I often find that the boldest thing is to let the common sense prevail. As Emerson said, it's as rare as genius."

What sits well, however, with policy and managers is evoking a semblance of omniscience. "Empirical evidence" and the "categorical answers" from science elevate beliefs into the realms of unassailable "truths." Luck, therefore, is ignored simply because nobody planned for it. Consequently, decision-makers expend enormous resources to leave nothing to chance, with contingencies over contingency plans becoming a cottage industry. With a constituency built around this process, decision-makers would find comfort in abdicating judgement to decision rules prescribed by financial models. This rewards, unfortunately, mediocrity and risk aversion to the detriment of innovation and the business' viability. Obvious as this may seem, "mediocrity and risk aversion are surprisingly powerful forces that get their way more often than not," Charles Vallance asserted. This is, however, only half of the story. In going through the list of energy giants in 1900, their demise is presided in equal measure by managers seen to be "mediocre and risk-averse" as well as the "adventurous and the brave."

Perhaps, Napoleon Bonaparte may have a point about ability and luck.

Richard Wiseman, in his book *The Luck Factor*, observed (2003): "People have searched for an effective way of improving the good fortune in their lives for many centuries. Lucky charms, amulets, and talismans have been found in virtually all civilisations throughout recorded history." However, in spite of its persistence, in some cases forming part of the management rituals, "superstition doesn't work because it is based on outdated and incorrect thinking. It comes from a time when people thought that luck was a strange force that could only be controlled by magical rituals and bizarre behaviours" (Wiseman, 2003).

In doing his research on luck, Wiseman observed these attitudes to explain why some people are blessed with good fortunes, while others (perhaps a vast majority) toil under the weight of repeated misfortunes. To wit:

> "Take the case of chance opportunities. Lucky people consistently encounter such opportunities, whereas unlucky people do not. I carried out a very simple experiment to discover whether this was due to differences in their ability to spot such opportunities. I gave both lucky and unlucky people a newspaper, and asked them to look through it and tell me how many photographs were inside. On average, the unlucky people took about two minutes to count the photographs whereas the lucky people took just seconds."

The explanation was simple and hidden in plain sight. Wiseman placed a message in bold type face on the second page of the newspaper: "Stop counting — There are 43 photographs in this newspaper." The lucky people spotted it, while the unlucky ones were too focused on counting the photographs. To spice up the exercise, Wiseman placed another message halfway through the newspaper: "Stop counting, tell the experimenter you have seen this and win $250." Wiseman noted that the "unlucky people missed the opportunity because they were still too busy looking for photographs."

In the realms of the managerial world, it is not uncommon for managers (and policy as well) to blame the stars for their misfortunes and stand as a godparent for success. However, when presented with strategic challenges, some revert to behaviours that resonate with the unlucky ones. How people respond to these challenges is encapsulated by Julian Rotter (1966) in his works on locus of control. I used this to examine why the green consumers remained elusive.

A decade ago, following Julian Rotter's categories, I examined how people's actions are predisposed along two general preferences: The internally oriented (in terms of their perception of control) "believe their actions have a strong, reinforcing impact on events around them." The externally oriented "see themselves as exerting little influence over their environments and put things down to powers beyond their control" (Barcelona, 2011). Applied to decision-making, I posit that Rotter's social learning theories are "significant because they avoid taking an overly deterministic or automated approach to human behaviour. Rather, they seek to account for how individual personality types might interact with and influence their environments — all of which is extremely relevant when considering corporate activities in the context of sustainable marketing and procurement, which lie at the dynamic intersection of economic, social and environmental value creation."

Connecting this to Wiseman's work on luck, how people get lucky is often a result of their attitudes, which influence how they respond to the unexpected. By embracing the unthinkable, managers ***PIVOT*** by acting on a hunch or gut feel, tested against alternate scenarios. The notions of what could constitute an opportunity are continually subjected to evolving streams of information, know-how, and learning. The evolving moves set the stage for firms to ***BOUnCE*** adaptively, under ambiguities and incomplete information, where the element of chance (or luck) is explicitly recognised as part of the uncertainties.

Energy transition is a recursive and tentative process that does not happen overnight. Unlike a linear process, where a start and an end point are clearly delineated, a recursive process would take firms to pathways different from what was initially planned. In connecting decision-making to this reality, managers could pragmatically start with

repurpose rather than from the textbook prescription of *frame*, *analyse*, and *solve* in problem-solving. The reasons are pragmatic:

In a transitioning energy market, the future is likely to be different. With this change, today's sources of strengths, capabilities, and competitive advantages may be as dead as a dodo or even a burden to incumbents that fail to *repurpose* and *redeploy*. How that future will be energised is uncertain. Extant networks and technologies, however, may provide some clues as to what is feasible and what needs disrupting to facilitate a profitable transition. Given that present actions are seldom divorced from what already exists, except in the imagined world of net present values (NPVs), the *initial endowments* of firms and society will influence the choices managers make. For this reason, understanding what to *repurpose*, often informed by hunches, influences how managers could *reframe* the contests they choose to win and *reconfigure* accordingly as to how that contest could be waged.

Played out over reasonably long durations, managers embark to profitably transform their business by breaking down their strategic moves into *foundational PIVOT* to lay a resilient base. This sets the stage for a *transitional PIVOT* to open pathways to tomorrow's perceived profitable niches. In this phase of experimentations, innovations are tested and emerging opportunities are identified, with an eye on the unexpected to open or close feasible options. As opportunities mature and a foothold is established on a more solid footing, firms may take a decisive stand to execute a *transformational BOUnCE*.

In defaulting to rewarding risk aversion, adhering to the *controller's mindset* is problematic. The opposite tendency is equally perilous when managers take leave of their good sense and act on pure gut feel. *PIVOT* and *BOUnCE* are frameworks that balance these opposing tendencies by promoting strategic dialogues. Taking Charles Vallance's advice to his managers to heart: "Embrace *uncertainties*, and make it something that your competitors fear. The most self-actualised people are the ones who are most open to change." Also, those that adaptively *transform* will inherit the future, I would add.

2
Foundational *PIVOT*

A *controller's mindset* is manifested by this oft-repeated but flawed approach: Cut costs by making people redundant when times are bad, inadvertently losing the best talents first through defection. Recruit them back when business turns a corner. Delay or cut capital expenditures to conserve cash.

The uplift to earnings is short-lived, but the impact to business is dire but hidden from plain sight. The costs pile up with "double-handling": Redundancies cost money, hiring new talents often comes at a premium, while losing out on the accumulated learning. Defunding pivotal investments also set back advances made by the teams, often giving lagging rivals time to catch up or peers to overtake to reap the benefits from innovations.

There is no shortage of technologies to convert feedstock into useful energy. The question of why some are adopted while others fall by the wayside lies with economics, logistics, and reliability. Within dynamic systems, the relative preferences vary, making any competitive advantages at best transient. While less dramatic than the shift from animal to mechanical energy, accidentally averting London being buried in nine feet of manure, today's innovations are no less important. With climate advocates and managers learning from history, today's reliance on big mandated "solutions" may extract valuable lessons from the 19th century "Horse Manure Crisis" that never materialised.

Gaining some insights from these "close calls," modern economies with their greater technological and resource endowments curiously struggle to find effective routes to decarbonisation. I attribute this to schizophrenia among managers. This results in strategic insights overridden by a penchant to conform and to avoid the unknowns. In ignoring the influence of this mindset on how managers decide, one can be stuck with "outdated and incorrect thinking" that Richard Wiseman warned people against. A remedy is to replace "managerial superstitions" with a mindset that enables *dynamic decisions*.

To recall, *dynamic decisions* are undertaken by humans employing their judgements. By its very nature, humans differ in how they perceive their challenges, hence in their way of solving problems as well. On a deeper level, these perceptions as the basis for forming their judgements are influenced by how humans come to understand what matters to them. For some, they hold dear the customs and traditions whose purpose or origins are blurred or embellished by memories. Experience is seen as a proxy for ability and competence, with success measured as accumulation of wealth (and perhaps, power) to judge material well-being. The transient nature of wealth (and power) poses serious problems to managers stuck in these "managerial superstitions." Specifically:

Holding oil and gas reserves is the way to ensure the long-term viability of the super majors, among oil and gas companies. In singularly raising the ratio of reserves over annual production, the reserve replacement ratio was a harbinger of expanding equity value. Taken to extremes, creative accounting in recognising proven reserves cut short Philip Watts' executive career as Shell plc's Chief Executive (Harrison, 2004).

Subsidies to renewables, in theory, would encourage wide-scale deployment. By the operation of the "learning effects," managers assume installation costs would fall sharply. This logic is flawed on two counts: In "securing" subsidies to buoy their investments' payoffs, managers ignore that governments do renege in subtle ways by cutting subsidies. In moving first, the early movers lock in what are likely to be expensive supplies that represent a permanent penalty.

Policy's focus on growing installed capacity for wind and solar (Evans, 2021), inspired by the *learning effects*, ignores the tight profit margins (or losses) that investing firms experience (Williams and Hittinger, 2020) and the contingent cost of disposing toxic panels on decommissioning (Bates, 2020). That cost is estimated at 10 times the revenues (Tao *et al.*, 2020), but are nowhere part of the lifecycle cost estimates.

Customs and traditions, in theory, serve as anchor to what people stand for and value. When managers fail to examine why things work in the past, but can be a liability today, erroneous strategies are pursued. With energy transition gathering pace, hitching one's fortunes with a "tried and tested" technology may be foolhardy. Technologies that fuelled yesterday's prosperity may prove to be the firms' undoing today, as the technology obsolesces.

Maintaining an asset in tip-top efficiency is a virtue when maximising volume is the way to optimise payoffs. This volume maximisation justifies continued expenditure on maintenance capex. Under dynamic markets, when coal is displaced by ACCGT, Coal suffers from persistent underutilisation. Continuing to expend on MCPX may prove suicidal financially.

A shift in the mindset could turn these flawed approaches into potential opportunities. The continual re-examination of the business mix, as Repsol undertook in its various stages of transformations (Box 1.1), led to a shift in its capital allocation focus. Instead of getting a head start over its rivals in finding oil in Latin America, to replicate its former position, it shifted its portfolio to Europe after YPF was sequestered by the Argentine government. The unexpected bonanza was the payment it received for YPF's shares. With cash and a portfolio no longer saddled with high-risk assets, it shifts its focus to developed markets from the allure of emerging areas. What started out as an effort to mend its damaged balance sheet, Antonio Brufau Niubó, Respol's Chairman, presided over a period of radical transition. Strategically, Repsol is better positioned to reap the opportunities presented by a push for a low-carbon energy future.

When one talks about mobility and transport, the business media could only portray a future where vehicles are powered by electricity. Tesla, the most visible electric vehicle company, is rewarded with a premium rating that made its founder, Elon Musk, vying for top honours in the Forbes Global Rich List. To a casual observer, this places the whole future of gas storage companies in doubt.

This is when Michael Laengle, Chief Finance Officer, RAG of Austria (Box 1.2) debunks this pessimism. In a recursive and tentative journey to find a low-carbon future, Michael poses a relevant question: Is battery storage a cost-effective way of turning curtailed power from wind farms and renewables into an economic good?

A simple *reframing* of the problem led RAG of Austria to consider the potential of hydrogen as a fuel. In their hydrogen experiments, RAG of Austria's scientists may have stumbled into their "chance opportunities" when they were presented with their "Dom Perignon" moment: By adding hydrogen to their abandoned gas caverns, CO_2 levels declined. The mystery is not fully resolved, although scientists suspected natural bacteria may be at work to produce this effect. Time will tell if this is a flux or indeed the start of an inexpensive way to decarbonise gas.

In the midst of the excitement in popular conversations, the real opportunities may not be in installing solar panels. Handling and disposing toxic waste from decommissioned solar panels is wide open for firms to explore and perhaps profit from. In shifting the mindset from achieving growth in a known business to one that rewards new business development, emerging opportunities are more likely to be recognised and acted upon. To do this, intelligence and the courage to act with integrity become essential.

This brings me back to Philip Watts, Shell plc's former Chief Executive hailed as the champion of sustainable energy and later vilified for his role in the oil reserves scandal (Harrison, 2004).

I am not privy to Philip Watts' thought processes. What I surmise, the resulting pivot to the spiritual sphere could only result from deep re-examination. To *repurpose* his skills and vast executive experiences, he first qualifies himself as a pastor by acquiring his theology degree from Ripon College. In taking on the responsibility as pastor-in-chief of Waltham St Lawrence in east Berkshire, United Kingdom, he became a fisher of souls in the Judeo-Christian context of the Church of England (Owens, 2013).

Within the managerial realm, such re-examination is facilitated by employing the **PIVOT** framework I propose. Here's how:

Contrary to how managers learn their financial evaluation, at least most that I know, managers seldom start with a blank slate. Incumbent energy firms start with distinct advantages in terms of market positioning, resources, and capabilities that start-ups may find daunting to overcome. In contrast, in a transitioning energy market, start-ups may experience greater freedom of action as they are not burdened by potentially obsolescing resources and capabilities. In both cases, they start with their *initial endowments* that open or deter managers from pursuing certain options.

In starting with these *initial endowments*, managers would recognise what among the resources they can access, which are gifts *from the past* or *burdens from prior decisions*. The following realities become apparent:

A dominant position in fossil fuels, either as supplier or user, implies the firm is heavily invested in extant markets that are about to change. The uncertainties, given the range of actions managers could take, lie in the choices of technologies to replace fossil fuels, how quickly this could happen, and what options are available for their assets. At a strategic level, managers would simulate what rival firms could do, and what resources are within their reach, to scope their feasible choices.

In moving too early, such as divesting fossil fuel assets to rivals, one may unload a burdensome resource. However, caught wrong-footed, disposing assets that are potentially of value (at least to the buyer) could alter its competitive positioning. This could happen if the pace of transition proves to be a drawn-out process, allowing the new owner to profit from the acquisition.

In some cases, the selling firm may prove lucky with their timing, particularly when obsolescence sets in much earlier. An example is Drax in the United Kingdom: Acquired for its dominant coal position, modernisation of its coal-fired assets appeared to usher in a new lease of life in the 1990s. By the dawn of the 21st century, the deteriorated prospects for Coal resulted in Drax's early shutdown. To pivot to renewables, Drax employed acquisitions to beef up its portfolio with renewables assets through a series of deals (Drax, 2021).

Two Philippine energy firms — ACEN Corporation and Semirara Mining and Power Company — operate from vastly different *initial endowments*. On deeper examination, both came to a similar view of what resources are of real value to them:

ACEN Corporation, a subsidiary of Ayala Corporation, is perceived to benefit from access to its parent's strong balance sheet. However, on closer examination, financial capital has become commoditised. Its success in entering a market competing against entrenched rivals, and the extent it moved regionally in Asia Pacific, has more to do with its ability to structure projects, leverage on the strengths of its industrial and local partners, and ability to raise funding competitively (Box 11.1). By chance or by design, ACEN Corporation's "inexperienced and untested" team proved most observers wrong. Within a decade, it has become Asia's major player in renewables, as investor and as operator, with an orderly drawdown of its coal assets.

Semirara Mining and Power Company enjoys the support of its major shareholder, DMCI Holdings, a well-capitalised conglomerate. Coal is clearly not an obvious place to find optimism in a world bent on decarbonising energy. The location of its coal mine, the largest in the Philippines, and its environmental compliance record, offers the potential to *repurpose* the site into an energy hub and tourism destination. The latter is within the competence of the group, underpinned by construction and property development. As a miner, the company has the project management capabilities to *repurpose* its systems to engage in mining other mineral resources (Box 11.2) to support the rapid pace of renewables adoption.

In framing the foundations upon which future energy systems are likely to evolve, resource ownership is not the principal source of competitive advantage. In using this perspective, managers could appreciate where their real strengths lie. This is a realisation that I come to appreciate in my conversation with Rama Velamuri, Dean and professor, Mahindra School of Management in India (Box 5.1).

In posing the question on contrasts in transitions, Rama pointed to Kodak and Fujifilm. While Kodak saw their strength in making photographic films and products, they respond to the threat of digital cameras by playing catch up with more agile and technologically advanced competitors. In contrast, Fujifilm framed its response as a redeployment opportunity. In effect, while Kodak was working to re-establish dominance in a much-evolved photographic market, from a position of weakness, Fujifilm recognised this drawback. Instead, they pose a different question: What can they do with the resources and capabilities that they possess as a firm? After some iterations, Fujifilm recognises their real strength was in chemicals processing and imaging. Armed with this insight, Fujifilm proceeds to pivot into cosmetics and medical diagnostic imaging. The end results? Kodak went into Chapter 11 bankruptcy, while Fujifilm reinvented itself into a profitable player in their chosen competitive arenas (Box 5.1).

3
Transitional *PIVOT*

When energy firms *repurpose* their resources, they engage in creating options by restructuring their capital and business. In divesting assets that have become peripheral, retooling skills, or redeploying resources, managers judge the trade-offs when executing such moves. The motivations could range from raising cash, realising value by selling assets that could be valued more by another owner, or as a way to enable surplus labour to find an alternate home where their talents are valued.

As managers move to the next stage, some choices are made early, while others are created by acquiring new skills, accessing new technologies, or building footholds in extant or new market niches. To the task of creating options, managers start to exercise some options that lock in future choices within the evolving *initial endowments*. In this *dynamic decision* ecosystem, managers will have to employ adaptive moves, with an eye on what rivals are likely to respond to and how the value of their firms could be altered. Clearly, managers with *static mindsets* that see the world as moving in a linear and predictable progression could be dead wrong and err in their decisions. The alternative is to employ real options and option games reasoning, as proposed in the ***BOUnCE*** framework as a complement to ***PIVOT***.

Seen in this light, the managers' tasks do not revolve around getting a categorical answer to what the future will be, which unfortunately is what some would spend their waking hours figuring out. In a counterintuitive way, managers are more likely to preside over flourishing businesses by adopting a portfolio mindset, combined with option games reasoning, within a portfolio context.

In my simulations of how European energy systems generally operate, a portfolio mindset under dynamic markets would yield vastly different strategic insights. What one combines is as important as how and when specific assets are brought into the portfolio. Specifically:

Starting with the initial endowments, a coal portfolio diversifying with cheaper ACCGT is likely to create value. Reversing the sequence, albeit ending with the same mix, erodes portfolio value when returns are likely to deteriorate. Adding StoHydro or Geo to ACCGT embeds *call* options, where value is enhanced under volatile power prices. The resulting portfolio profits from rising prices, while ACCGT cash margins cushion against very low prices, when ACCGT is the price setting supply (thus indexing its fuel cost variations to power price volatilities). $Wind_{ON}$ has a similar effect, albeit to a lesser extent given its lower volume output. The case for adding PVT_M is less clear cut. Moving too aggressively and early, portfolio risks increase with the prospect of obsolescence (or vice versa). By deferring, managers may reserve PVT_M as a future option when costs are substantially reduced further or efficiency is upgraded (Barcelona, 2017).

This contrasts with how NPV would prescribe a decision. Without differentiating, the sequence and the initial endowments are ignored as irrelevant. For new entrants or incumbents, an investment that produces sufficient cash flows with positive NPVs should warrant access to capital. This is where managers err, particularly when the nuances of valuation are overly simplified as "cash is king." I would argue, it probably is, but is it a robust ruler or a weakling on the throne?[1]

The logic of *dynamic decisions* may shed some light on the moves energy firms are making. From a spectating perspective, managers appear to try to fulfil policy's aspirations while "doing exactly the opposite." For example:

The unthinkable was executed by two German energy behemoths: RWE and E.ON. After years of bulking up and integrating partly from fuels to power, policy moves to renewables as encapsulated under *Energiewende*. In

---

[1] I attempted to provide answers in Chapters 8, 9, and 10. The short answer is: When renewables exert downward price pressures, cash margins are compressed. In particular, PVT_M may continue to generate positive cash flows because its variable costs are very low. The resulting cash flows, however, are insufficient to recoup the investments. With early obsolescence considered, its financial value is questioned.

response, the two reversed course and split their businesses. RWE retains its nuclear, gas, and coal power while spinning off renewables to Innogy (Morris, 2016). E.ON retained renewables, energy networks, and energy efficiency while spinning off to Uniper its fossil fuel assets, hydro, and energy trading (Amelang and Wettengel, 2016; Timperley, 2016). The realignment of businesses was followed by complex asset swaps that "drastically reshape Germany's energy landscape, already in turmoil as the country's phaseout of nuclear power and transition to renewable sources is wrecking old business models, and new competitors enter the frame" (Appunn, 2018). The hope is, as reported by the German media, the reshaping could produce in RWE a leader in renewables and security of supply services with a broadly diversified portfolio of renewable and conventional generation assets. E.ON, for its restructured business, would be Europe's largest power retail company (Proctor, 2020).

Investors are divided on the benefits of RWE/E.ON reshaping the energy industry, initially in Germany, with likely consequences globally. Perhaps, not surprisingly, Gero Lücking, Managing Director of LichtBlick, Germany's largest renewables supplier, observed: "There has never been such a concentration of power in the German energy market." A study LBD consultancy did for LichtBlick argued that "by taking over Innogy's grid assets makes E.ON Germany's dominant electricity provider, with its electricity grid covering two thirds of the country, and 70% of its consumers in its grid areas." Potentially, and in practice, E.ON can control competition and prices in those regional markets (Knight, 2019).

One can deduce, from the actions that are made apparent publicly, RWE and E.ON's moves may signal the following strategic intents:

A reaction to policy actions arises from Angela Merkel's decision, then Germany's Chancellor, to abandon nuclear power after Japan's Fukushima nuclear disaster in 2011. Accounting for a large part of their power generation portfolios, separating the assets under threat from the rest of the business was one way of containing the risks. Hence, both companies, practically comprising the German energy industry, are "forced to radically restructure to survive" in the midst of major plant shutdowns and billions of Euros in losses (Steitz and Käckenhoff, 2018).

The *theory in use*, I would argue, has changed little. The deep-seated belief that "big is beautiful" is alive and well. While this is as valid a place to start, previous attempts have been far from stellar. To start with, diminishing margins from intense competition for customers, unleashed by deregulation, E.ON's precursors, VEBA and VIAG opted for consolidation (Boston, 1999). While scaling up worked for a while, making extant business facing competitive threats more cost-effectively, it fell short in averting continued margin and volume erosions.

On a more optimistic note, Rolf Martin Schmitz, RWE's Chief Executive is unto something that battle-hardened managers may have always known about the pragmatic side of their job. The addition of fossil fuels back into its power generation portfolio, after doing a split to separate renewables, may be perceived differently: With a fleet of flexible and conventional power stations, a reliable bridge *is built* to the new energy era, and with energy trading, RWE is conferred the expertise to seize opportunities on global energy markets (Proctor, 2020). In contrast, E.ON opts for bulking up on the "safer" regulated assets under a "benign regulatory environment." In my view, this logic resonates more with what my portfolio simulations highlighted.

From a decision-making standpoint, I can sympathise with the optimism of both E.ON and RWE in pinning their hopes on streamlining investments. My own experiences in shepherding investment proposals taught me a few nuggets of realities:

A strong financial base, in theory, offers possibilities to pursue decisively the opportunities for the future. In one company, investments were evaluated using a single discount rate on the premise that a portfolio mix was decided *a priori*. By focusing on the payoffs, it was assumed that the "best" opportunities among competing alternatives would fall into place.

Simple as it may sound, the investment hurdle inadvertently favoured higher risk assets over producing assets. That is, with ample cash flows that are visible, some smart managers argued that "risk" is recognised by risk adjusting the cash flows rather than applying higher discount rates. One can only imagine how the investment evaluation degenerates quickly into an academic treatise on the "correct" way of calculating NPVs. Without a *mindset* transition on what constitutes risks, and how one can move forward while optimising the value of extant businesses, managers are confronted with these flawed decisions:

In overly focusing on making the NPVs work, while assuming the world would remain predictable, the opportunities that could create tomorrow's profitable niches would lose out. Always struggling to meet the investment hurdles, new ventures get funded as "strategic commitments" or "exceptions to the rules." This exposes them to vacillating priorities or "regime changes" as sponsoring managers gain or lose favour. Projecting cash flows beyond the immediate periods where managerial remunerations are set, managers are likely to place lower priorities on these ventures than they would on today's payoffs. This economically logical response may imperil the very viability of a transitioning business operating under great uncertainties.

A streamlined business, one presumes, would allow capital to be allocated among comparable investments with "homogenous" risks. I would question this "accepted wisdom." In persisting to evaluate investments as "undifferentiated risks and opportunities," a tacit acceptance that "predictable is good" would direct capital to the "proven and tested," whatever that may mean. Under this decision ecosystem, new ventures outside the known businesses are unlikely to be given a chance. Ignored for their merits, firms may miss the opportunity...again and again.

A more feasible way to orchestrate a *transitional PIVOT* is to examine the lessons from these two approaches:

Technology Solutions: Shell plc's GameChanger programme started by funding innovation ideas from employees and contractors. It expanded its scope to help early-stage technologies to develop into commercial ventures. The company evaluates investments in four areas: novelty in terms of the technology's fundamental difference from existing processes or services, albeit unproven; potential to create substantial value if it works; relevant to Shell and the energy future; testing would prove the technology quickly and affordably (RDS, 2021a). In focussing on new technologies or approaches for tomorrow's energy market, the programme joined forces with the National Renewable Energy Laboratory, US Department of Energy, to initiate GCxN, an incubator for low-carbon technologies. In a practical and commercially focussed way, GCxN seeks to reduce technology risk and accelerate the tech-to-market phase (RDS, 2021b).

Business Services: Enel X was created by Italy's ENEL in recognising that "companies are changing the way they buy energy, manage it, and track usage, integrating sustainability goals and leveraging new technologies and business models to reduce risks, lower energy costs, and lower greenhouse gas emissions" (ENEL, 2021). To achieve this, ENEL lends their expertise in energy supplies and logistics and automation. The latter incorporates the increasing use of digital technologies, such as described by Anjaney Borwankar and Guido Toscani (Box 11.3).

In both cases, Shell plc and ENEL recognise the need to access and broaden their scope to deploy the fruits of innovation to the market. In undertaking innovation within a commercial framework, the ways new ideas could be monetised are potentially accelerated.

I came across Shell plc's *GameChanger* in its earlier incarnation. The record of success is creditable, with embryonic ideas of capturing CO_2 and turning it into a product for greenhouses in the Netherlands being an example. The business where I spent my time most, Shell Gas & Power, started as a project to replace revenues from the closure of South African coal mines at the height of the struggle against apartheid (Conlon, 1988). It started as the smallest business unit in the Shell Group. By the first decade of the 21st century, gas developed into the second largest unit, with Shell plc gaining leadership in liquefied natural gas (LNG). Through a number of acquisitions, the most prominent of which was BG of the United Kingdom, the company cemented its global leadership. However, as the push for green energy benefits from declining costs and policy push (McFarlane, 2021), Shell plc is re-emphasising the power business once again.

ENEL itself was a product of the combination of two former state-owned power utilities: Italy's ENEL took control of Spain's Endesa in 2007 and acquired the remaining shares by 2010 (Ash, 2010). After a few rounds of restructuring, ENEL adaptively evolves to fulfil the changes required by changing regulation. The unbundling of the power industry is an example. The competitive power generation and retail businesses coexists with the regulated transmission and distribution activities. Renewables fall under a special regime, particularly in Spain where a subsystem operates all intermittent power supplies as a portfolio.

One can note that the explicit strategies to decarbonise are presented, at least by most European incumbents, as trying to resolve the following strategic dilemmas:

In moving away from fossil fuels, managers weigh the potential revenue and returns erosion as the firm builds up a position in the "new" businesses. The expected magnitude and pace that such erosion may materialise would influence the speed at which divestments, acquisitions, or new investments would be undertaken.

Digitalisation of information could revolutionise the way low-carbon products and services could be offered. Consumers, in most cases, are not fully conscious of their carbon footprint, although the intent may be there. With real-time feedback or systematic tracking, energy suppliers and consumers would be able to validate the claims that each offering purports to deliver. In this new world, the pitch for green offerings would shift from *trust me* to *show me the goods*, placing the whole bases on an honest and verifiable footing.

Decisively exiting the energy business, as managers know it today, is not common among incumbent firms. None that I am aware of are contemplating on replicating what Fujifilm did in response to an obsolescing photographic film product (Box 5.1). That is, instead of working to protect a dwindling market, Fujifilm *repurposes* their expertise in processing chemicals, then *reframes* their future business into a pharmaceutical and cosmetics company.

In tackling these three areas, I posit that a *mindset transition* will have to precede the actions that managers take in reassessing their technological needs in order to reposition their firms in their chosen markets. I would suggest the following:

In recognising the element of luck, investments involve the judgement to explicitly evaluate the trade-offs within portfolios (Barcelona, 2015), how assets and resources could be combined, and how rivals' actions would alter the value of firms. This *reframes* investment as an option that managers can continually exercise with managerial flexibility.

The millennials and those that follow are shown as highly conscious of their carbon footprint (Mavrokefalidis, 2020). This shifts green offerings from a *nice to have* to a *precondition to operate*, with a preference for ecological food influencing choice for low-carbon energy (Penz et al., 2019). Unhindered by company practices, policy, or availability, this is a strengthening of an earlier tendency I noted: When people practice recycling at home, they are likely to practice the same thing at work (Barcelona, 2011). Aided by digital technology to enable real-time feedback, this self-reinforcing loop may accelerate a low-carbon transition at the individual level (Box 11.3).

Policy would come under greater pressure to resolve a contradiction in renewables, as the large spending spree promised comes face to face with fiscal prudence. Intermittent renewables cannot claim to outcompete fossil fuels and continue to want to retain subsidies. The "border tax for carbon" is reviving what Michael Wagoner (2009) proposed as an alternative to cap and trade. The bigger moves will have to come from a fundamental question: How are top performers in delivering sustainability rewarded?

Faced with ambiguous and evolving markets, managers that opt for the categorical answers are predestined to fail. Unfortunately, the desire for certainty is hardwired in some managerial psyche. One can learn from the US military: Prepare the troops to effectively respond to the unexpected, particularly to bounce back from adverse events quickly and safely. One cannot predict where and when the next attack will come from. However, standing ready for such an event, the troops know how to respond and survive (Box 4.2). Pointless exercises and manoeuvres? There is order in the "chaos," Charles Payne II would respond to me in jest.

4
Transformational *BOUnCE*

Firms execute their transformational ***BOUnCE*** when a path is offered for greater commitment to an idea or a "vision." Recalling ***P W One*** that Bas Kloppenborg adopted with aplomb (Box 3.1), a coalition of the willing and the committed would have rallied around a *cause*, in however way it is generally understood. Sustainability in one form or another becomes a way of life, as Terry Möllner (Chapter 3) showcased during his time at Ben & Jerry's.

Within the contextual ecosystem of decision-making, managers would have advanced in their prior commitments to establish new and repurposed *initial endowments* from where change could be pursued. A prior transition from coal to gas illustrates this point.

When the power market was deregulated and gas was emerging as a viable alternative to oil and coal, it unleashed new opportunities in power generation. Freed from the constraints of regulated markets, and former utilities were finding their ways to compete in this brave new world, the power market was seen by oil and gas companies as a new growth market. The logic was simple and compelling:

Gas needs a minimum volume to make the infrastructure worthwhile to build. A 1,000 MW combined cycle gas turbine (CCGT, or its more advanced form, ACCGT) creates demand large enough to generate the needed revenues for new gas markets to be started. On the market side, power prices were seen as offering good margins, compared to the volatile cash flows from gas. Hence, by integrating forward to power generation, oil and gas firms would benefit from secure volumes and cash margins for as long as power prices vary within a specified range. The former utilities, in hoping to secure their gas supplies, because gas-fired power assets were proving cheaper to run, power companies find acting as a buyer serving their need for stable costs. In this apparent symbiotic relationship, oil and gas companies entered the power market, with local utilities acting as ready buyers.

In some cases, oil and gas companies acquired interests in local energy or power firms (Box 1.1), such as Repsol's controlling stake in Gas Natural (precursor of Naturgy) or Veba (predating E.ON) and RWE's interests in oil companies, Veba Oel and DEA.

Today's push for electrification, as it takes hold, would most likely reduce the demand for coal or gas. Under this scenario, the previous logic of integrating fuels and power takes on a different path. Specifically, I see the following as their pros and cons:

Merging dominant power and oil and gas firms, in theory, create ready access to customers and infrastructures. However, with unbundling of the power industry, one can gain access through a functioning market without the need to own the assets. This enables firms to focus on what they can do best and work with others who are best at operating logistics or infrastructures.

Incumbents benefit from established market positions and revenue streams. These are seen as "secure and stable" sources of cash flows that a start-up struggles to achieve at the outset. However, obsolescing assets may saddle incumbents, making their transition more complex. Managers will have to *repurpose* their extant resources before they can sensibly move to commit to new businesses that could put at risk the "goose that lays the golden eggs." This balancing act is easily tipped one way or the other by human preferences, non-economic reasons, or pure luck. In contrast, new entrants may bypass this stage and focus on capturing value from emergent opportunities.

This is where I see the virtues of *reframing* the investment mindset of managers. In its neutral context, risks are technically deviations from an expectation, however that was set. Using the *dynamic decisions* framework I propose, transformation takes on a different approach. For instance:

Recalling how diversification could be executed differently, a coal-dominated firm invests in ACCGT to enhance its payoffs with cheaper supplies. In contrast, ACCGT-dominated firms may invest in renewables, particularly StoHydro, Geo, or Wind$_{ON}$, to acquire *call* options. Under dynamic prices and volumes, volatile cash margins from renewables provide the prospect of higher payoffs under rising prices, with ACCGT achieving stable cash margins through indexation. However, as renewables become dominant, the "protection" that ACCGT confers may no longer suffice, as it comes under threat of being displaced by StoHydro (or Geo if available) and Wind$_{ON}$ as Spain demonstrated when volumes fell sharply during the COVID-19 lockdowns (Chapter 1; Chapter 10).

Forward integration by acquiring oil and gas companies by power generators, or a backward integration to fuels supplies by utilities, may prove unworkable. While such moves accelerate building dominant markets in fuels and power, it also saddles the merged entities with legacy assets at risk of obsolescence.

Pacing and the value of waiting are illustrated with the value erosion of early movers in solar power. With low foregone revenues, the cost of waiting is more than offset by savings in capital expenditure. To make matters worse, by going in first, early movers erode their own value while favouring the latecomers. A double loss (Chapter 7; Chapter 10).

Ownership of reserves, as in oil, gas or coal, may no longer assure a sustainable energy business. To avoid this predicament, managers are rewarded for what they can *repurpose* their resources for, including fossil fuel reserves, or adaptively create new niches where their capabilities are at a premium (Box 5.1). Recall Fujifilm and Nokia's moves from forestry to "creating the mobile phone market." Written off after struggling to keep pace with Apple and Samsung in Smartphones, Nokia transformed itself into a network services firm (Finley, 2016) and is flourishing (Hardesty, 2021).

Rival firms interact within their markets as well as respond differently to policy impetus. Each move alters how an individual firm's payoffs are impacted, eliciting some response by choice. Under these dynamic interactions, financial and economic models serve to simulate a range of scenarios and feasible outcomes. Models do not prescribe a decision, it informs managers and policy on what could or may not occur as well as the uncertainties around these expectations. How such shifts could impact firms and the market is the better focus and use of financial and economic analyses, not getting the forecasts right to the last decimal point (Chapter 7).

This brings financial and economic analysis, as well as the bases for decision-making, closer to the realities of the markets. Partly for this reason, policy that works in one market may fail singularly in another when managers and policy fail to grasp the very purpose, the mechanics, and degree of support a policy measure enjoys.

As energy firms embark on a transformation journey, the ability to time and execute divestments or acquisitions take on central roles. The motivations may also change. For example:

Divestments become a portfolio restructuring exercise, where profitable assets judged to become obsolete in due course are sold to maximise proceeds rather than sold under duress when its diminishing prospects are too obvious for everyone to see.

Recognising the incumbents' inherent advantages as their capital, access to talents and markets, they can be the incubator of emerging businesses. Acting as agile followers, incumbents may opt to incubate *game changers* while providing support to start-ups. By separating the funding to these ventures from the mainstream business, greater focus could be achieved, hence minimising the distractions to operating businesses that provide today's profits, from those whose payoffs may be a few years away.

Transitioning to a low-carbon energy future is often assumed to comprise a continued presence in a business that managers are familiar with. In certain instances, exiting is as much as an explicit choice as well as doing nothing.

Inaction presumes the future would continue to sustain the incumbent's present business.

Acquisitions are likely to be undertaken as modular moves, where building blocks to a future portfolio may be configured. In testing the waters, energy firms may acquire a firm or asset to gain experience or partner to complement its capabilities.

Technology adoption takes a different approach with digital systems, machine learning, or artificial intelligence. As if tackling *energy transition* and sustainability are not complex enough, the value of how these technologies will contribute to the business agenda will come under increasing focus. As a tool for operational effectiveness, real-time operational and market information will most probably intensify the need to tangibly demonstrate any low-carbon promises. With an enhanced capacity to measure, the ability to validate claims also becomes transparent (Box 11.3). Put into good use, managers and policy's creative capacity to innovate will be tested. With this demand placed on their shoulders, firms and society will operate under a "show me the goods" mindset, because "trust me" will no longer suffice. Ronald Reagan, former US president, in responding to Mikhail Gorbachev's plea for trust, pointed the way to the future: "Trust but verify."

5
Making Counterintuitive Moves

The notion of differentiation is well embedded in strategy and most areas of business. To outcompete rivals or even collaborate with partners, managers are asked the "so what" question: Why are you the natural owner of this opportunity?

This elicits discomfort from battle-tested managers. Proven for winning their battles, managers often presume that the "tried and tested" would work, negating the need to venture into paths less taken. Operating under the ambiguities of transitioning energy markets, managers are blindsided, often at the peril of the firm's future viability. Recognising this, I offer four reflections on how *dynamic decisions* could alter a firm and the managers' fortunes. At the very least, managers may achieve better results with the following insights:

1. Going against the herd adaptively: One cannot hope to distinguish one's firm by following the herd, neither defy nature nor the constraints of the physical world. One *reconfigures* by knowing how the extant systems could be done better by doing it differently. Specifically:

The obvious problems are not the best place to start to plot a path to a prosperous future. Strong financials and smart managers are supposedly unbeatable, but many failed ventures are backed with both. Luck and ambiguities are sources of chance opportunities. Paraphrasing Napoleon Bonaparte, able managers are of little value if they cannot create luck and act on it when choosing battles they would fight to win.

One cannot aspire to change the world, but revert to evaluating the virtues of one's investments as if the world will remain the same. This makes managers live in schizophrenia. An astute mind can turn turmoil into arenas for emerging opportunities when resources are allocated with an *enlightened mindset*.

In a curious way, when managers admonish people to "think out of the box," I have my doubts if the call for "innovative approach" is fully understood. I reserve judgement for now.

2. Probe and know before you jump: This brings me to my discomfort with "innovation" and "science" as cures to everything that ails managers and policy. In an unfortunate way, some decision-makers find speed as decisive.

Establishing the facts is not akin to paralysis by analysis. Going back to "think outside the box," it was a novel idea that propelled firms to financial success, until it became part of the mainstream business lexicon. This is when the problem starts: By its very nature, one needs to understand how the extant system works in *reality* before one can sensibly orchestrate meaningful change. Without this prior knowledge of "what is inside the box," simply doing something different could be a stab in the dark. When one does not understand what they are looking for, it would be inconceivable to find an answer to questions one fails to ask. **PIVOT** can help remedy this dire situation (Chapters 3–6).

"It's the science" is now the default retort when one disagrees on anything from climate change to pandemics. Indeed, the "science" is categorical because eminent persons are in broad consensus. A superficial probing as to what "science" they refer to and how their "science" is relevant to the issue at hand, one draws a blank from advocates. Unsurprisingly, the conversation turns into heated exchanges among advocates of all stripes.

This strikes at the heart of the fallacy: Scientific facts are accepted through validation, regardless of the popular consensus. The world did not become flat by disregarding Galilei Galileo's contrarian view, at that time anyway, because the prevailing "consensus" thought otherwise. For this reason, one steps back and reexamine the premises before accepting "unassailable (half-) truths" as "facts." Otherwise, plunging into actions "decisively" could result in disaster (Chapters 1 and 2).

Gary Steel and Paul Collin encouraged people to go up and down their "ladder of inference" (Box 4.2). This comprises breaking down the premises that form an "accepted fact." With few simple questions, biases and folklore are separated from lessons of past actions and from experience. At a strategic level, what Bas Kloppenborg achieved with *P W ONE* is an open ecosystem that surfaces *real problems* that lead to a resolution where *real people* coalesce to act coherently (Box 3.1).

3. "Luck" begets good fortunes to those who seek to create it: It is not uncommon for people to react with surprise at this assertion. In polite company, I am described as "counterintuitive" or "contrarian" but seldom as "mainstream." In other circles, I suspect they greet this view as an oxymoron. I offer this food for thought:

In dealing with *energy transitions* and executing their *sustainability agenda*, brilliant minds and gifted amateurs expend energy and money to get things right. This constitutes *knowing* what the *unknowable future* could bring, so that a "roadmap" or "action plan" is created as "template" for actions. Once agreed, managers are supposed to align and march in lockstep with policy. Uncertainties or unplanned occurrences, or *luck*, are ignored as irrelevant because "consensus" had made policy or managerial decisions "unequivocal." In pursuing this course of action, firms and societies are predestined to fail.

I propose a different approach that departs from these policy and strategic conventions. By recognising *luck* as a form of ambiguity, *lucky breaks* happen when firms exercise managerial flexibility. Managers can seize on *chance opportunities* when circumstances prove opportune. One can create *luck* and profit from it by standing ready when it comes knocking.

This brings me to two human predispositions: One dreams for better things to fall their way. The other is to act without a dream and let fortune takes its course, akin to a sailor steering a rudderless boat. To bridge the missing link, one can **PIVOT** and **BOUnCE** to know what to do when *luck* casts its smiles. Charles Payne II may just have pointed a way to profit from one's *luck* by enabling people to deal with the unexpected: Build the capabilities to respond positively in the face of the unexpected (Box 4.2).

4. *Unity of life* and *purpose* simplify decisions, expand opportunities: The separation of life and work, the personal from the professional, is a useful context to achieve focus, albeit a tenuous construct. Imperfect humans act, often in consonance with their beliefs, values, and biases, that often permeate all spheres of their life. In a corporate context, ignoring this reality may spell the conditions for *energy transitions* and *sustainability* to persist as wicked problems that are intractable.

The collision between the *expansive and creative mindset* that drive strategists, and the generally risk-averse *controllers' mindset,* is well rehearsed. In expanding their horizons, strategic dialogues of the genre promoted by Chris Argyris (Chapter 8) are frustrated by a preference for the "tried and tested" and aversions to the *unknowns*. Often, this persists when analytical tools, limited in their scope to explicitly evaluate uncertainties, default into making the *uncertain certain*. Policy finds itself in a similar bind: Judged under amorphous criteria, they erroneously equate equitable with equal distribution of benefits, in whatever form it is understood.

Fortunately, leading thinkers such as Amartya Sen *reframes* development as an expansion of freedom by expanding equitable access to opportunities. One access opportunities by building capabilities rather than by equally distributing wealth. Richard Thaler reinforces the notion that individuals respond to choices, and people's ability to work for achieving higher social ideals, at times at personal expense, as a human behavioural reality. Elinor Ostrum, in debunking greed as a human predilection, offers pathways for managers and policy to work for the common good. Modern finance, with its greater openness to question "accepted wisdoms," has come to embrace, albeit reluctantly, how the ambiguities when recognised could serve as sources of value (Chapters 7–9). This is manifested by the explicit evaluation of options and the effects on portfolio value of rivalries among competing firms or technologies (Chapter 10). Benoit Chevalier-Roignant and Lenos Trigeorgis' works, as well as Tarik Driouchi, have contributed to its adoption by managers.

****

The misfortunes of firms and managers do not lie with the stars nor should managers (and their peers) be too quick to appropriate credit for the good things that happen in their firms. It is often a combination of *luck* presenting itself, with capable managers who can recognise and act as opportune, when opportunities come knocking. The capability and the exercise of judgement are what distinguishes the *good* from the *excellent*. It separates those that worry about what the future would bring from those that orchestrate the means to make their future happen.

Policy, in exercising its due care for achieving the common good, may also rethink its whole purpose and *raison d'etre*. In working to make society sustainable and equitable, policy does not work to compel compliance to its "one political solution fits all." That is an exercise of *tyranny by creep* that is often resisted or frustrated by the very people they assumed to serve. Worst, the collision of interests is predestined, as not all interests can be made compatible to everyone's satisfaction.

Policy enables *a thousand flowers to bloom*, with my apologies to Deng Xiaopeng. Policy achieves this by expanding equitable access to opportunities and enabling people to exercise their choices. With all its imperfections, I view a market economy offers greater scope to fulfil these conditions, at times under what Richard Thaler promotes as *paternalistic libertarianism*.

In exercising *humility* and a *generosity* of spirit, humans may just recognise there is no *monopoly to wisdom* or knowledge. With a dose of integrity, the wicked and intractable problems of *energy transition* and *sustainability* may, with some *luck*, just produce the *unexpected*.

This is enabled by *trust* that underpins all human relations that matter!

****

Box 11.1: ACEN Corporation — New Entrant's Pivot to Green Value

Eric Francia, President and Chief Executive Officer (CEO), Eric to colleagues and friends, sees himself as a most unlikely "disruptor." The Philippines, ACEN Corporation's home market, is characterised as an energy system fragmented by its archipelagic terrain, coal-dominated, with weak power infrastructures. When ACEN Corporation was set up in 2011, equity analysts wondered: What got into Ayala Corporation, a venerable proponent of sustainable development and renowned Asian leader in responsible corporate citizenship? A decade later, with an imminent initial public offering, equity analysts redirected their queries: With the makings of a renewable powerhouse in Southeast Asia, how will ACEN Corporation profitably pivot to a low-carbon future?

Through several months of conversations, Eric and I went through a process of examining what makes a "new entrant" not only prosper but gain strategic advantage over incumbents a decade hence. *Complementation through effective partnerships* is a recurring theme that binds the group's approach to business — a notion that opens pathways to a future beyond coal. In evolving energy markets, a capacity to acquire skills and adaptively combine technologies is valued, Eric added as the core to moving forward.

1. Building a "home" market

Banking on Ayala Corporation's financial strength, the group is committed to meaningfully contributing to Philippine development. With growing prospects of another power crisis befalling the country, the Group faced a dilemma in 2011: Reluctant to enter regulated markets, Ayala Corporation focused on property development, operating commercial centres, and financial services as its core. The dire need for new power supplies was seen as an emerging challenge that a well-capitalised business group could turn into an opportunity. The imperative for economic development outweighed the broader concerns on coal as "dirty" but perceived as "cheap" fuel.

Banking on its parent's financial strength, Eric embarked on replicating what worked for the group: "We partnered with competent power developers to venture into energy. With gas supplies fully committed, importing LNG was not an option, albeit its image as a cleaner fuel. Without import facilities, the country has no access to LNG. Wind and solar were then expensive. While ACEN Corporation was supportive of the government's Feed-In Tariff program (a form of subsidy) to jump start the renewable energy sector, it was clearly not going to solve the imminent need for reliable and affordable power. This left us with coal as the only viable option."

In forming a partnership with GNPower (2021), "We gained a ready pipeline of projects and expertise. In a way, we bought a position in the market that is falling short of power," Eric added. "With the GNPower portfolio, we enabled 2,520 MW of which 1,336 MW were supercritical coal-fired plants. The plants were mostly located at Bataan, an industrial centre, with one plant in Lanao del Norte in southern Philippines (552 MW). This gave us a favourable if not an advantageous locational critical mass," Eric reflected on GNPower's pipeline, most of which were greenfield projects.

By 2016, or five years of building its portfolio, ACEN Corporation had crossed 1,000 MW of attributable capacity (adjusted for its equity share in projects). All projects were in the Philippines, with more than 90% of its capacity in coal and the balance in renewable energy.

2. Setting sights on transitioning markets

When one talks of Philippine banks, they are better known for their consumer lending. Project type financing is a secondary business. However, excess liquidity became a feature among Philippine banks, driven by strong dollar inflows from overseas remittances and business process outsourcing. For ACEN Corporation, its parent's financial strength and corporate reputation gave it some leeway for innovating. This also opened the doors for ACEN Corporation, as the company began its international foray in 2016. In successfully bidding for Indonesia's Darajat and Salak geothermal fields in West Java, with 637 MW of steam and power, Eric explains:

> "The geothermal bid in Indonesia entailed a proven operating plant with a long-term off-take contract. In other words, the winning bid would be driven by who has the lowest cost of capital and who can manage costs most

effectively. We were up against Japanese-backed competitors with strong project financing support from Japan Bank for International Cooperation (JBIC). Meanwhile, our consortium was receiving financing offers from international banks that were priced expensively and had relatively short tenor. We then sought the support of our Philippine banking relationships. To our delight, while not as superior as JBIC financing, the Philippine banks were able to provide project financing that allowed us to compete and eventually win, especially after incorporating synergies with our local partner."

ACEN Corporation's minority stake (20% of the geothermal venture) was a cost-effective entry into a technologically complex and highly regulated energy market such as Indonesia. In choosing its terrain, "we bring our financial muscle and structuring capabilities, to complement the technical competence of our partners. This division of labour appears to mutually benefit us. We gain credibility as an energy investor, our partners ensure that the investment works and operated profitably," Eric explained.

The direction towards returning to our sustainability roots was set "with our first foreign greenfield wind farm, a 75 MW Sidrap project, with UPC Renewables Indonesia." This partnership started with UPC Renewable's 81 MW wind farm in Ilocos Norte, Philippines, in 2013.

In my conversations with Eric, a few things became clear. ACEN Corporation differed in substantive ways from some of their larger, more entrenched rivals in the energy market. The firm starts with building expertise in areas where they lack the capabilities. Partnering with credible technical partners and bringing their financial and project structuring advantage, the joint venture has a stronger basis for sustaining itself. Credibility is gained with each success, with which the partnership can scale to achieve its regional ambitions. In this context, Eric contends that "being the largest in a market is not an objective, we content ourselves to having a large and growing share of our region's opportunities where renewables are rapidly gaining grounds."

The initial market entry in Indonesia was quickly followed by a successful expansion in Vietnam in 2018, as the country was embarking on a bold transition to renewables.

By continuing to leverage strategic international partners, ACEN Corporation also quickly moved into other international markets, such as India, Myanmar, and Australia.

As of 2021, ACEN Corporation's 10th anniversary, the company has grown to approximately 2,900 MW of attributable capacity. Of this installed capacity, 1,800 MW are renewables, mostly wind and solar power, with some geothermal presence. By 2025, ACEN Corporation aims to surpass 5,000 MW of renewables with an aspiration to be the "largest listed renewables platform in Southeast Asia," Eric reiterating their commitment to becoming a leader in the region.

Judging from how ACEN Corporation's asset portfolio has changed, as illustrated in Box Chart 11.1.1(A), the greater focus on renewables is well underway. On a cumulative basis, the cash received by its parent, Ayala Corporation, in the forms of dividends and return of capital (B), ACEN Corporation disclosed that it amounts to equivalent annual returns of about 16%.

3. Reframing arenas of strategic advantages

At this point, my conversation with Eric turns to sceptics among equity analysts and peers in Philippine business. Perceived as an upstart with "unproven" capabilities, rigid markets accustomed to "doing things their way," what did they miss?

I offered my own conjectures: In an evolving energy market, with renewables gaining ground rapidly in some areas, the obsolescence of extant businesses is the farthest from incumbents' strategic scenarios. In building or even reinforcing extant competencies, incumbents may lose sight that the bases for future competitiveness are shifting away from them. This was how coal was caught off-guard when petroleum became the dominant fuel. Coal coexisted with oil and gas and other fuels for the past century. However, the firms' financial performance had a clearer divide: *Coal floundered as oil, and latterly gas flourished to dominate the fuels and power generation segments.*

To these observations, Eric shared his thoughts on how ACEN Corporation took a different view on how its competitive advantages are deployed to solidify their early edge: "As a small player in coal, we do not have the 'curse' of a large installed coal capacity, considered the 'cheapest' power supply in the Philippines. When incumbents diversify into renewables, they have a difficult time justifying their moves. The incremental additions of renewables do not 'move the needle' value-wise for them."

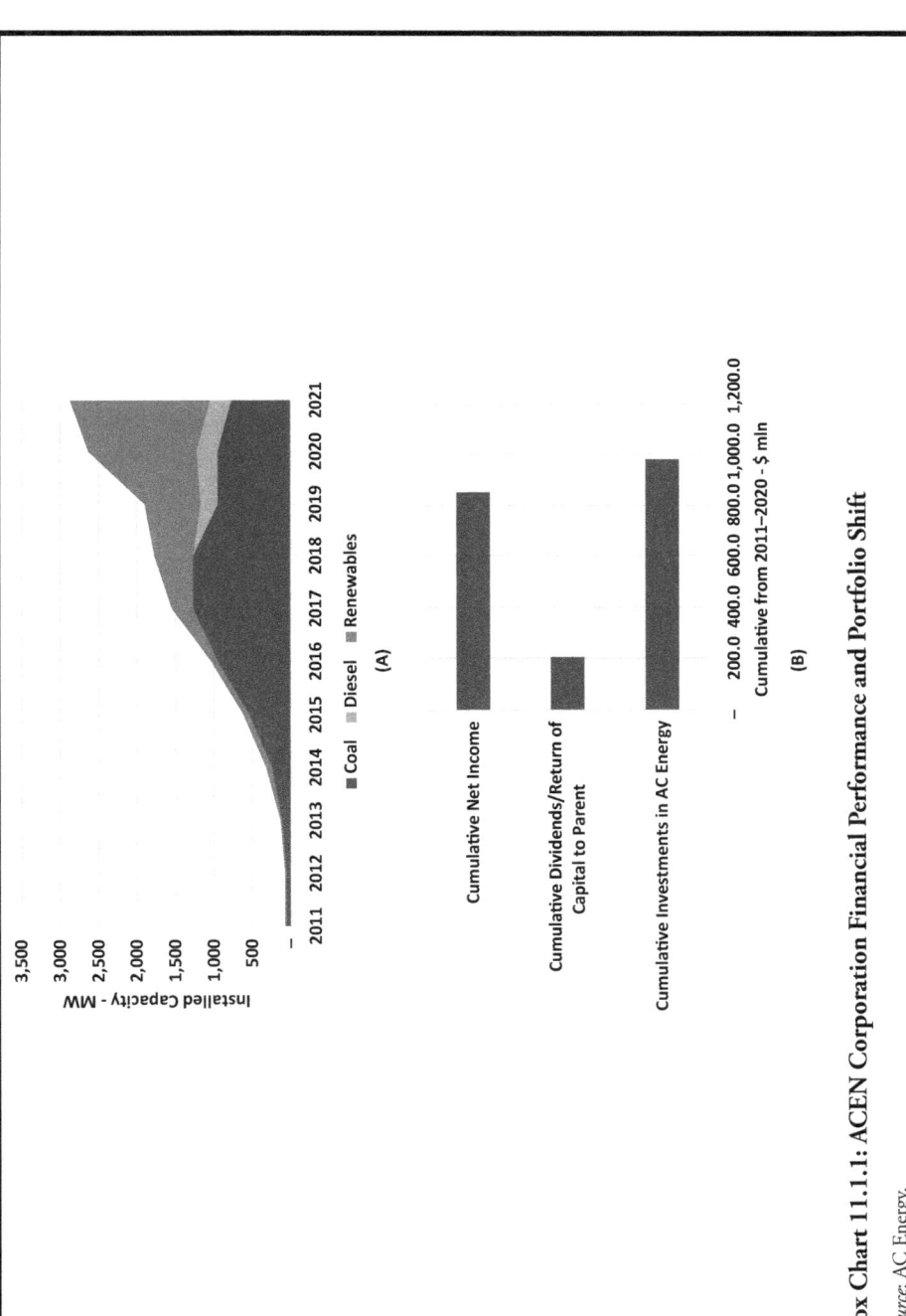

Box Chart 11.1.1: ACEN Corporation Financial Performance and Portfolio Shift

Source: AC Energy.

Eric asserted: "In contrast, we have a fresh perspective. We did not have set rules or entrenched positions to protect. By experimenting with different ways of getting things done, we learned how best to optimise our resources. Even in dealing with partners, we customise what would work for the partnership. We are not cookie cutter, where a template is applied to all ventures. In an evolving market, with ever changing cost advantages for specified technologies, our small scale makes us flexible and nimble."

Eric noted: "As we grow in scale, Ayala Corporation's reputation for good governance and corporate citizenship is an advantage for ACEN Corporation. The structure and discipline are welcome for an otherwise highly 'entrepreneurial' albeit 'chaotic' (to some) working environment. The challenge for us lies in encouraging creative spurts from such 'chaos', while applying some operating standards to operational assets."

4. Consolidate to pivot

In reflecting on how ACEN Corporation came to be decisively committed to renewables, Eric recalled: "In 2017, we faced a strategic choice. We can remain as a multi-fuel power supplier, by keeping coal and our pioneering investments in Philippine wind farm. Dependent on feed-in tariffs (FiT), the subsidised segment of renewables is small. Without FiT, wind and solar are at significant cost disadvantages to make the investment financially viable."

Unlike coal-fired power, however, there are no entrenched incumbents in wind or solar power in the Philippines or in our focus region (i.e. Indo-Pacific). Eric pointed out: "For AC Energy, we see this as an opportunity for us to deploy our financial muscle and growing credibility, by co-investing with capital scarce but technically capable partners. As early as 2017, we began to see the momentum shift towards renewables with the rapid decline in cost and increasing efficiencies in solar and wind technologies. At the same time, there was an increasing concern on coal globally, and we thought that it was just a matter of time before the momentum of the renewables push would strengthen in our shores. Clearly, Southeast Asia was going to need thermal power for decades to come, so in a way it was a leap of faith for us to begin divesting our coal investments and reinvest the capital into renewables."

The pivot to renewables was complemented by ACEN Corporation's decision to expand beyond the Philippines and to transform itself from being an investment holding company to a full-pledged industrial concern. This would entail consolidating our development and operating capabilities, in combination with our strengths in financing and structuring investments.

Acquiring Bronzeoak Clean Energy in 2017 was the first step in ACEN Corporation's corporate transformation. Bronzeoak is one of the pioneers in developing renewable energy projects, having developed at the time over 250 MW of solar and biomass power plants. This was followed in 2019 with the acquisition of PHINMA Energy, a Philippine firm with mostly legacy coal and diesel assets but with some renewable assets: a 54 MW wind farm and 30 MW geothermal plant.

In parallel, ACEN Corporation continues to work with development partners to complement its internally developed pipeline of projects. "The renewables opportunity is enormous in the Philippines and around Indo Pacific. We have a very strong balance sheet that can enable not only our own projects, but other developers as well. This strategy is rapidly turning a vision into reality at ACEN Corporation three years after its first acquisition." Eric cited these subsequent moves as contributing to the accelerating pace of transformation:

"In 2020, ACEN Corporation signed a joint venture agreement with Citicore, followed by an agreement with Solar Philippines in 2021. Both developers have sizeable development pipelines in the Philippines."

"Our cooperation with UPC Renewables started in 2013 with our investment in their Ilocos wind mills in northern Philippines. We extended this cooperation to Indonesia, Vietnam, India and Australia."

Eric added: "We are fortunate to cement these partnerships at a time when there is significant appetite from 'green capital', or equity looking to invest in low carbon opportunities, but a scarcity of viable projects in our focus region." This was partly the reason for the strong demand for ACEN Corporation's green bond offering in 2021, a reality not lost on Eric:

"The combination of abundant capital, robust pipeline and strong network of partners plays to our strength. We can accelerate our renewables expansion in the Philippines and around the region as co-investors offering capital and management, as needed."

At this point, I queried Eric: The success to date is an encouraging start for ACEN Corporation's next pivot. I have been privileged to get to know some truly successful companies and the people behind their success. One theme is recurring: *They learn more and valued the lessons even more, from their failures.* In your successful run to date, would you like to share some of these *learning moments*?

Without hesitation, Eric replied: "Our failure to qualify and win a competitive selection process (CSP) for a major power supply procurement by a large Philippine distribution utility is a case in point. In our view, we had a compelling offer that should differentiate us from those provided by suppliers using coal-fired and gas-fired power. We were disappointed for being disqualified on a technicality. However, in our *after action review* (AAR), we gained deeper lessons that would otherwise be lost." Specifically, Eric describes the bidding process and their bid as the following:

"The terms of reference were designed for supplies for baseload coal or gas-fired power. To qualify, the technical parameters require a minimum scale for a new power plant, with the ability to operate and supply on 24-hour daily cycle. These requirements immediately place intermittent wind and solar at a disadvantage. Unfazed, we decided to put in an offer that is innovative and new to the customer."

"The solution was built on the 'round the clock' approach consisting of wind, solar and storage technologies across a portfolio of power plants in several interconnected locations. In our mind, this diversified portfolio balances resource risk for wind and solar, with offsetting volume variations to achieve a more stable power supply. Battery storage is brought in as its costs become affordable. Periodic excess production can be sold to the wholesale power market."

"We were banking on the rapid cost reductions of battery power storage. We had four years to build the power generating assets, which coincides with the development cycle of new coal-fired or gas-fired power plants.

Should our prognoses prove accurate, customers could have enjoyed close to fix prices given that our hybrid portfolio has nil fuel costs. Our production shortfall or *de facto* outages, where we were allowed some downtime, would coincide with the off-peak hours (when the sun is down, while wind continues to blow). We believe that predictable production shortfalls during off-peak hours as with the case of the renewables round-the-clock solution was superior to unforeseen thermal plant outages that could happen in the middle of peak summer demand."

Eric reflected as an afterthought: "One stark lesson to me is the asymmetry between our excitement to innovate, and the market's readiness to accept a new and untested approach. An incremental introduction may have faced less resistance and could tilt the balance in our favour. This was probably not the opportunity to be 'adventurous'. After all, a bureaucrat faces career limiting consequences if the lights went out, because the untested approach fails to live up to its promises."

On looking into the future, Eric expresses a lot of excitement and optimism. "The renewable energy transition is just getting started. As older coal plants get decommissioned and storage technologies become more cost competitive and scalable, renewable energy can only expand and replace fossil fired power plants. AC Energy is accelerating its shift towards a low carbon portfolio and by the 2030's, it is quite possible for the company to get to a zero-carbon portfolio. We are grateful for the opportunity to play a leading role in the renewable energy transition in the region, and AC Energy shall continue to work closely with its partners to help build a sustainable future for all."

****

Eric Francia is the President and CEO of ACEN Corporation (PSE: ACEN). Under his leadership, Ayala Corporation established its energy platform from a standing start in 2011 to become one of the largest renewable platforms in Southeast Asia, with over 1800 MW of renewables capacity as of early 2021. Prior to founding ACEN Corporation, Eric was the Chief Strategy Officer of Ayala Corporation, one of the largest and most respected Philippine business groups.

Box 11.2: Semirara: Adaptive Pivot by Redeploying Strengths

In a coal-free world, the Philippines' largest coal mine could become redundant, and with it, goes the coal-fired power assets of Semirara Mining and Power Corporation (SMPC). The Philippine government would forego royalties and taxes as well. SMPC's social initiatives, working with communities, turned the town of Caluya into an oasis of economic well-being, achieving less than 6% poverty incidence in Semirara Island. This is in stark contrast to Antique province's poverty incidence of 19.1% (PSA, 2019) or the World Bank's projection of 18.7% for the Philippines for 2021 (PNA, 2019).

Jorge A Consunji, a member of the SMPC Board of Directors, shared: "The government has issued a moratorium on endorsing greenfield coal-fired power assets. However, committed coal-fired power projects and operating complexes, which already have firm expansion plans and landsite provision are exempted from this moratorium. This is in line with the country's goal of improving energy sustainability and security."

While the 2018–2040 Philippine Energy Plan (DoE, 2018) still sees more than 50% of the power supplies generated from coal by 2030, calls for a major redraft are echoed by environmental groups to incorporate the impact of COVID-19 pandemic into the long-term energy outlook.

In this context, I posed this query to Jorge: "While one cannot ignore what the government aspires, or what present realities deem as reasonable, one possibility cannot be ignored. What happens if we are all proven wrong and the market transition away from coal sooner?"

1. What are Semirara's strengths?

A little-known island prior to DMCI Holdings' acquisition and management takeover of SMPC (formerly Semirara Coal Corporation), Semirara offers picture-perfect marine habitats right next to a major coal mining operation. One could be forgiven for mistaking its landscape as belonging to Boracay Island, a globally renowned resort that Conde Nast' readers (Morton, 2020) named as second among the world's best.

To an outside observer, coal mining and environmental preservation do not mix very well. However, Semirara's operations may offer a counterfactual evidence to the contrary. Thriving giant clams and pristine beaches, both requiring clean and unpolluted water, are realities for the island. The island is also home to the Semirara Marine Hatchery and Laboratory, a biodiversity facility established by SMPC in 2010.

Maria Cristina C Gotianun, SMPC President and Chief Operating Officer, shares further insights into the company's history:

"SMPC has been through cycles of growth and decline because of market volatility and operational headwinds. Our commitment to our stakeholders has remained constant. Through our investments, royalties, taxes and dividends, we are able to contribute meaningfully to the Philippine economy and to our host communities."

"In an evolving energy market, where competition is getting more intense, SMPC is working hard to enhance its environmental sustainability performance through its reforestation and biodiversity programmes, and active mine rehabilitation efforts."

In examining the data disclosed by SMPC, I shared my observations on SMPC's historic performance as shown in Box Chart 11.2.1:

"While the Philippines still import coal, SMPC's ability to serve the local, as well as the global markets, provided the firm a flexibility to arbitrage on coal price differences. By integrating into power generation, SMPC gained a physical hedge, as well as securing its own coal supply. The hedge of course is not perfect, as Chart (A) would illustrate. Volume (B) and price swings still impact SMPC's cash margins (C), albeit tempered within its coal–power asset portfolio."

"The government benefits with a share of SMPC's cash earnings through its royalties and taxes (C). The value added of power generation, a principal user of SMPC's coal, presents an interesting advantage (D) as the integrated value is retained within the group. This reflects an inherent edge of mine-mouth power generation, over stand-alone coal-fired assets, where fuel supply is secured at lower cost."

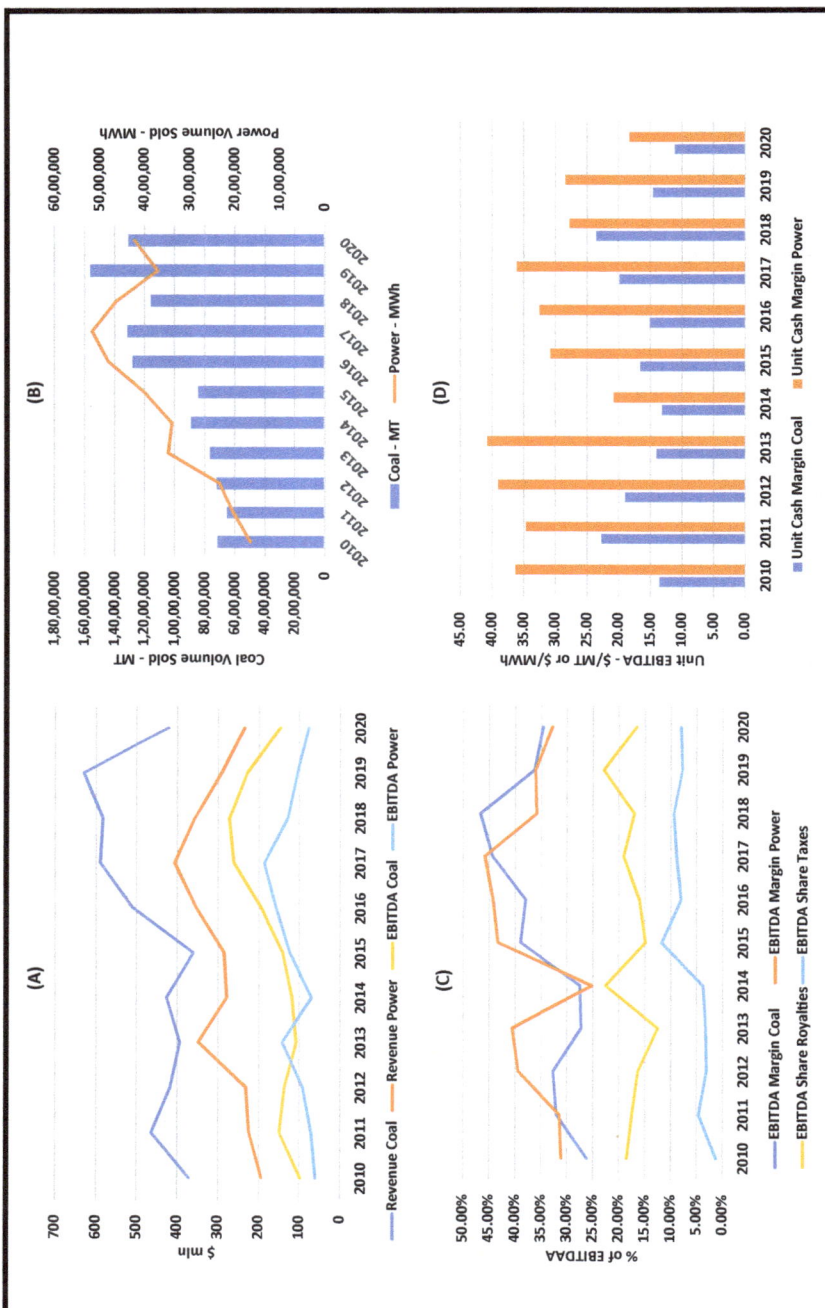

Box Chart 11.2.1: Semirara's Historic Performance

Source: Semirara Mining and Power Corporation; SEM-Calaca Power Corporation; Southwest Luzon Power Generation Corporation; and Author's calculations.

On a broader strategic view, I shared my observations as to how resource companies are often underestimated by environmental advocates and equity analysts. Their ability to pivot when faced with adverse policy moves could be significant. In SMPC's case, they face similar challenges as many coal mining operations were confronted: "SMPC, just like other similar companies, has gained solid experience in mining, and because of the most recent policy changes, it can use this expertise to diversify into mining other minerals. SMPC can leverage its mining know-how and assets to mine minerals that are in demand but not seen as harmful to the environment." Within DMCI Holding's capabilities as a group, its foothold in Semirara island, I would say, could offer opportunities beyond coal mining and power generation.

2. Positioning for inter-connected national grid

Semirara island's location offers some advantages within a fragmented power system that an archipelagic terrain would dictate. With the exception of Luzon grid, the Philippine power system cannot optimise its load because of limited transmission inter-connections. Hence, excess supply in Mindanao, the southern island, cannot offset shortages in Luzon, as the two systems are not yet connected.

To provide a context, the Philippine archipelago comprises in excess of 7,200 islands. Luzon is the largest power market, comprising more than half of the country's volume demand. Mindanao is the next largest landmass, with abundant hydro resources, but unconnected to the Luzon or Visayas grids. Visayas is home to geothermal power, with limited interconnections among its major islands of Negros and Leyte, principal sources of geothermal power, with the demand centres in Iloilo and Cebu. The proposed links shown as (7) and (9) would ease the bottlenecks that presently curtail excess solar power from Negros Island, the *de facto* solar power capital of the Philippines.

Given this reality, I offered my description, partly in jest, to Jorge: "Energy 'experts' often err in thinking that the Philippines suffer from excess supplies. However, an 'excess' in Mindanao does not help Luzon that suffers from tight supplies, often resulting in rolling power outages in some parts of Metro Manila and other industrial hubs."

On a more serious note, I highlight a number of my thoughts on what Semirara's strategic locational advantage could offer potential investors: "With the reduction of submarine cable costs, the proposed national grid interconnection could position SMPC's mine-mouth coal-fired power plants as a basis for building a power generation

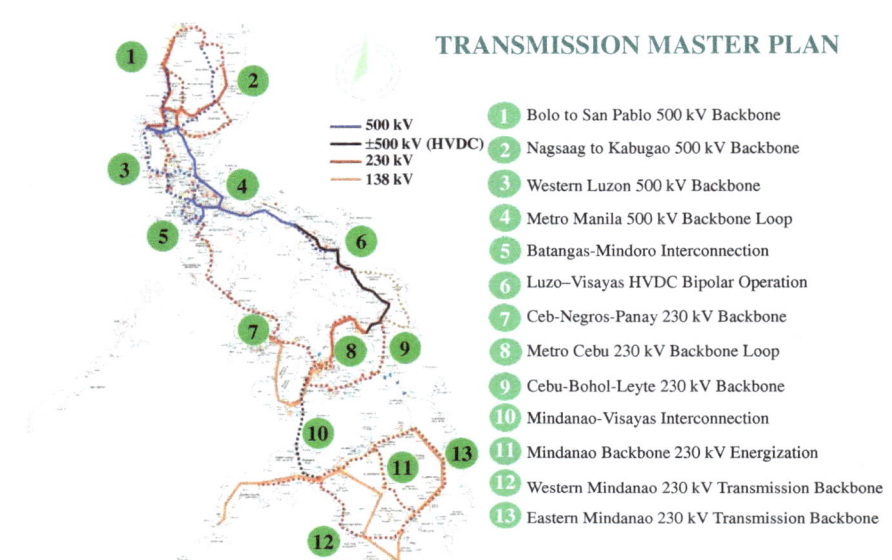

Box Chart 11.2.2: Proposed National Grid Interconnections
Source: National Grid Corporation of the Philippines (2016).

hub. That grid is in the works for a few years now, with government pushing to connect Mindanao to Visayas and Luzon grids (NGCP, 2020). The power grid map, shown in Box Chart 11.2.2, published in the 2016–2040 plan (NGCP, 2016), remains broadly unchanged insofar as major planned inter-connection projects are concerned. Under this plan, Semirara Island can be connected to Mindoro (5), an off-grid system, as Mindoro could be connected to the Luzon grid through Batangas City by investing in a submarine cable."

Limited transmission capacity may render any advantages from solar farms, as a clean source of energy, hypothetically. I added: "Negros Island is a major producer of geothermal power, which is well in excess of local demand. To make geothermal viable, the Negros production has to be sold to neighbouring demand centres in Cebu and Iloilo. Transmission capacity, however, is limited and booked to its limits by geothermal. The island also hosts two of Asia's largest solar farms (when it was built). Without sufficient transmission capacity, solar power experiences the occasional shedding of load, leaving solar operators without revenue and no subsidies. Solar power is paid subsidies (or their feed-in tariff) on actual delivery of power to customers, not on production."

3. Supply security and net zero waste coal

On a longer term, rising population, shifting growth to regional centres (away from congested Metro Manila), and inroads of electric vehicles may spur demand. With focus on COVID-19 and its adverse effects on industrial production, power volumes experienced declines in 2019 and 2020. However, as restrictions are relaxed, power and energy demands are likely to resume their high growth trajectory.

While the aspiration to achieve a wider role for renewables and cleaner fuels such as gas is a stated government policy, weak infrastructures and transmission connectivity may slow this pace significantly. To import cheap natural gas, usually in its liquefied form, import and regasification facilities are needed. The Philippines has none. Until one is built, access to cheaper world gas supplies and hence expansion of gas-fired power generation capacity is not within the country's feasible alternatives. This is particularly true, with local gas reserves expected to reach depletion towards the end of 2030 or earlier.

Faced with this reality, even the most committed technocrat in government to phasing out coal may struggle to reconcile such a move. Such heavy-handed policy action would trade people's economic prosperity, which is linked to secure energy supplies and has an immediate effect, and a coal-free future whose benefits for the country will have to be proven. The political fall-out may see any support for a coal-free future to become untenable, I would opine.

With coal likely to be around for longer, even the government admits that much, I see the Philippines as facing these dilemmas: "Introduce technologies and processes that reduce CO_2 emissions, by making the use of coal cleaner, while enhancing power usage and generation more efficient. The latter makes strengthening of an interconnected power grid a priority. A national grid reduces wasted energy from load shedding. Stronger interconnections reduce the need for higher reserves to keep fragmented grids reliable."

4. Feasible future niches to pivot

In the end, SMPC will have to look at what is best for its stakeholders including the shareholders, the employees, and the community in which it operates. While development in solar and wind technology has greatly advanced, coal is still the cheaper, preferred, and more consistently available source of energy, within the Philippine archipelago.

Jorge appreciates as much: "As a developing country, we have to be pragmatic about our options, strengths and weaknesses when it comes to power generation." One, however, cannot always rely on policy and the energy market to evolve as planned. For this reason, Jorge turned around and posed this question to me: "In your view, what areas do you see as feasible ways forward for SMPC and the Philippine energy industry?"

To which I offered my observations on what we can learn from others' experiences. While not an exhaustive list, I propose the following as starting points:

"Coal is vilified as a 'dirty fuel' but the Philippines may not have a clear path, at least in a generation, to move into gas or renewables, such as pump storage hydro, mini or midi hydro, or expand its geothermal supplies. The enhanced connectivity of the power grid offers Semirara island the opportunity to evolve into an energy hub. A two-prong approach may be considered: *Reduce its CO_2 footprint by employing more environmentally benign processes that are emerging*, and *repurpose depleted coal mines to host future diversified energy hub.*"

"Leveraging on capabilities to mobilise resources for large scale projects, SMPC and similar firms may cast their sights more broadly than mining. Within energy, civil works expertise may come useful in scaling down the economic size of pump storage hydro power, so that it could serve smaller systems. Emerging offshore wind and wave energy may offer opportunities for inclusion within an energy hub."

"The civil works involve in pump storage hydro would play into the strength of DMCI as a group. With some retooling, DMCI Holdings could play as an investor or through DM Consunji Inc as contractor, working with international groups."

"As a property developer DMCI Homes could extend its credibility as an environmentally responsible company to open for tourism selected areas of Semirara Island. Boracay Island started with a lot less in terms of infrastructure. The access by sea or air could be facilitated by expansion of existing Semirara facilities."

In our exchanges over time, I explained my premise: "As a low-cost power generator, within the present Philippine context, SMPC can consolidate its extant position to meet the Philippine energy system's imperative for supply security. To a practical mind, half of the power market will still need to be served because intermittent renewables, such as wind and solar, are unlikely to fulfil. In positioning for a future with stronger interconnections, SMPC can play to its strengths in terms of its location, group capabilities, and endowments. This balanced approach that recognises geography, societal needs, and capacity to execute, may shift the balance of opportunities and risks to its favour."

****

Jorge A Consunji is President and Chief Executive Officer of DM Consunji Inc and a member of the Board of Directors of Semirara Mining and Power Corporation.

Cristina Consunji Gotianun is President and Chief Operating Officer of Semirara Mining and Power Corporation and a member of the Board of Directors of DMCI Holdings, Inc.

Ricardo S Consunji coordinated the provision of data, its validation, and my exchanges with group companies and their team. In particular, I appreciate his efforts in providing me with sound feedback to ensure I am within the realms of market realities in expressing my views relating to SMPC and the Philippine energy prospects.

Box 11.3: Getting to Low Carbon with Data Analytics

Blockchain and data analytics are gaining space in conversations around energy firms' pivot to low-carbon systems. This is perhaps not surprising. When managers are given real-time insights on how their carbon footprint is evolving, at what cost to them and their communities, they are provided with immediate feedback on *actions* and *outcomes*. Prior to these tools being made available and the increasing ease of extracting data, managers and policy operate with opacity when monitoring the effectiveness of carbon-related measures or initiatives. Without digitally enabled real-time data gathering, collection costs could run into a tidy sum, while providing insights that may have become outdated with the passage of time. With very minimal costs, at least on an ongoing basis, mining information from pools of data become possible and are economically of value.

As it relates to energy transition, data analytics and the role it could play is an evolving art. To situate myself, I draw on the experiences of Anjaney Borwankar, a serial entrepreneur based out of Singapore, and Professor Giulio Toscani, a digital transformation expert, who resides in Barcelona, Spain and lectures globally in leading academic centres.

1. What changed with data science?

In Anjaney's mind, the hype around blockchain and its association with polarised views on "bitcoin" did not help to demystify the tool. As the name implies, Distributed Ledger Technologies (DLT), of which blockchain is a subset, is simply a digital way of organising and distributing data across computer networks. With the ability to audit all revisions and provide a secure way of sharing data digitally, one can simplify the certification and validation of the source and uniquely identify the document. At a high level, this has the potential to reduce transaction costs, minimise frauds, and improve transparency. Anjaney explains as summarised in Box Table 11.3.1:

"The data contained in a document, say a certificate, is interpreted by the computer as just a series of 0s and 1s. These data are input into a unique algorithm or mathematical function (a.k.a. the *hashing function*), which in turn churns out a fixed length of unique characters (called *the hash value or hash*). The hashing function is constructed in such a way that it is impossible to guess the contents of the original document by looking at the output hash value. If any part of the original document changes, even slightly, the hash will change completely and in an unpredictable way. Thus, the hash can serve as a proxy for the document data, alerting if any change takes place. Hashes from one document or data field can be input again into the hashing function and combined with other data (say from another document) to create a new hash value. This hashing of the hashes creates *chaining* of the data and guarantees immutability."

Box Table 11.3.1: Comparison of Conventional Database and Blockchain

Comparison of Key Attributes	Conventional Database	DLT/Blockchain
Data Privacy	Raw data i.e. human interpretable information (for example, a person's name and address) is stored on servers. Data privacy is compromised if the database is hacked.	Cryptographic hashes are stored that are proxies for the original raw data. This in turn facilitates data privacy. (The person's name and address can be converted into a hash e.g. 12yuzdfkjksldf67oz which can't be understood by a human.)
Storage	Data is stored on centralised storage systems that can be brought down relatively easily.	Distributed storage of transaction records. High resiliency as multiple copies of the records are created on computer networks.
Immutability	Data can be deleted or modified by the database or network owner.	Records on the blockchain cannot be deleted. Writing to the blockchain needs an agreement (consensus) from the majority of actors on the blockchain network.

Source: Navozyme.

One drawback of digitalising is the phenomenon of "double spending." In the physical world, Anjaney continued, "your $5 bill, once spent, is gone to somebody else. In the digital world, you could pay $5 in 'digital currency' for your coffee. You can also duplicate the same $5 digital currency infinitely, hence allowing you to use $5 duplicates to pay for other things. In these endless rounds of replication, at almost nil marginal costs, one could 'double spend' and, in theory, acquire twice (or multiple factors) what a physical $5 would otherwise purchase."

One would have thought, is this not a wonderful way to consume with little money? That may be, but without a seller taking the other side of the trade, no transaction is possible. With its "advantages" highly hypothetical (or even speculative), some form of order has to be instilled. This is where blockchain comes into the scene as the tool to rescue a nascent digital technology from oblivion.

Anjaney explained: "Blockchain is the use of existing technologies (such as cryptography and peer-to-peer networking) to put together a system of digital codes that would enable data to be *hashed*, *distributed*, and made *immutable*. In effect, what a verification system does to paper documents, blockchain tools perform a similar function, to prevent *double spending* with the $5 bill. That is, by making 'duplicates' traceable, 'digital money' takes on a similar limitation as a physical $5 bill. In theory, this 'uniqueness' bestows a trustworthiness that the 'digital money' used to pay for the goods or services as the original issue, and not worthless duplicates. Just like the Central Bank or the notary, as the certifying entity, gives credence to the veracity of the paper bill or document, the blockchain codes can give authenticity to the digital money or for that matter any digital asset."

2. Digitalising verifiable documents

People are trusted for their reputation and reinforced by repeated demonstration of integrity. As a general notion, trust is enhanced when people can verify what is claimed is indeed true or the person (or the entity) certifying is known to be upright and qualified. The same is true with digital data, which differs partly from physical documents, because of an indistinguishable difference of the duplicates from the original. Anjaney shared his work on how the maritime industry resolved this dilemma:

> "Reporting on waste volumes that ships generate for disposal is problematic: The amount of waste accumulated is at best an estimate, and reported by

the ship's captain, using handwritten submissions as per the international Marine Pollution (MARPOL) regulations. To prevent unauthorised dumping of waste in the oceans, MARPOL Operators issue Waste Delivery Receipts (WDRs) when the waste is collected and disposed of at the port. One can imagine how unreliable the data provided by even the most trustworthy captains are. It is simply a heavy and labour-intensive endeavour to check the accuracy of the waste collected, with little prospect of cost-effectively verifying the actual waste generated and properly disposed of."

"Navozyme recently demonstrated to maritime authorities in Spain, Singapore, and the Philippines, how Blockchain Enabled E-certificates (BEEs) simplifies the verification and maritime processes. With all BEE data stored as cryptographic hashes in a common platform, multiple anchoring could consolidate all the data giving the full cycle waste disposals. This largely helps with MARPOL compliance tracking and disincentivises unauthorised disposals."

"The authenticity of e-certificates is readily verified using a special QR code imprinted with the issued document. The QR code is generated from the hash values of the original data fields contained in the certificate. If the data changes, the QR code will not match with the original certificate. This ensures that the certificates can be verified by anyone in real-time."

The potential of this digital verification is substantial to enhance pollution control and inter-agency information exchanges among regulatory bodies of cooperating governments. A regional cooperative effort may extend beyond controlling verification of waste disposals to a broader monitoring of maritime traffic, safety, and compliance.

3. Transformative potential for energy

The energy industry is known for its advanced automation. Characterised as lumpy investments, with stringent safety and environmental controls, the gains from efficiency even from incremental improvements could prove substantial. Decarbonisation of energy systems poses specific challenges, particularly when intermittent renewables are heralded as the industry's future.

Intermittent renewables, such as wind, solar, or emerging technologies such as wave energy, differ from dense sources of energy such as coal, oil, and gas, and renewables such as pump storage hydro and geothermal steam. The feedstock used to produce energy is dispersed, experiences wide variability in loads, and is often randomly available. The implications to managing the networks and the costs involved to balance the loads could be significant. To ensure a sustainable transition to networks that could handle more intermittent supplies, a few questions need to be answered. I describe these challenges in a tangible way, as a manager would likely see it:

"In many systems today, intermittent renewables enjoy privileged positions of being the first to supply, when available, with no obligation to bear the costs of load fluctuations. The few that levy a charge is Spain, where a system of measuring the costs and how it could be allocated is introduced some years back (Rivier Abbad, 2010). Without a transparent way of measuring the effects of load variability, and how much it costs the system, in real time, it would be difficult to apportion the costs to the parties that created the expense. On a larger scale, this asymmetric cost burden, usually borne by coal and gas-based power supplies, exit of coal or gas would simply have to shift the full cost of operating the future system to renewables (or surviving supplies). This may come as an unpleasant surprise."

I pose this query: How would digital technologies address this emerging economic challenge to both policy and managers, as the energy system increasingly shifts to more intermittent renewables?

The benefits of digital technology extend beyond this fundamental challenge. Here are a few concrete examples:

Equipment maintenance using the predictive facility of data analysis to anticipate downtime or unplanned interruptions could lower the costs of supply disruptions.

People's patterns of use to vary offers, a practice that is partly being done now to optimise the load of the network. With inputs from data analytics on consumer preferences, utilities may offer services that reconcile consumers' preference for flat rates (because the cash demand is predictable in advance) and any benefits from variable pricing based on time of use. Iberdrola in Spain, among others, provides this choice to consumers to opt for a fixed price or variable billings of their utility service.

Real-time feedback on operating costs based on the energy usage of industrial processes (oil or gas plant operations or networks). Carbon footprint, when measurable, could alter carbon taxation. Policy can fine-tune tax on actual emissions, enabling it to focus on imposing penalties on polluters in a targeted way.

To conclude, revenues from hardware are not tied anymore to a simple sales transaction of the device, but to performance *optimisation-based less downtime and more hours performed over the course of a period.* Increasingly, companies are investing in software that will incorporate increased connectivity, intelligence, and platform functionality in their equipment.

4. Focus areas for data analytics

Data analytics are making energy operations scalable and automated, positively impacting energy production, whose performance varies with market demand, delivery and consumption. Scalability is based on predictions from digitally collected data, industrial sensors for production and delivery, and by collecting people's preferences for energy consumption.

Blockchain can ensure the authenticity of the quantity measured to allow variable pricing or real-time pricing like the example of Data Gumbo, a blockchain application that offers detailed real-time bills for water usage in the oil and gas industry.

General Electric (GE) employs digital sensors on its wind turbines and equipment to gather data. The information extracted is used to optimise equipment performance, utilisation, and maintenance. To demonstrate the value of GE's technology, GE now charges a percentage on the improved output instead of generating revenues from equipment sales. As a result, while selling less equipment, they earn more on services and develop a mutually profitable relationship that tightens the network of suppliers, distributors, and developers of related products and services. Indeed, a potentially formidable relationship that a rival will find challenging to break into.

Google Nest positively influences energy production by collecting preferences of home temperatures in time and space. This is the consumer equivalent of sensors in production, but applied to sensing temperature preferences in the workplace and at home. By devising ways to adjust the temperature, as needed, usage is optimised even without the people having to continually adjust the gauge. In this way, energy usage is reduced while people can focus on doing their work or enjoy their leisure time undisturbed. As adoption gains scale, the data collected offers scope for informing energy suppliers on market and usage profiles, and at the community level, a more targeted consumer-centric offer becomes feasible. These offers may take the forms of dynamic pricing or managing any excess own production from their rooftop solar panels, as a few examples (Iansiti and Lakhani, 2014).

Microgrid applications can benefit from offering smart grids, as a way to offer enhanced services that extant power grids would not be in a position to, at least for now. For a small community or new developments, smart grids system can optimise production and storage and variable supplies more efficiently. Supply planning is aided with real-time inputs on weather, demand patterns, and real-time supply variations to an extent that it could inform more broadly decisions on onsite selection, network configuration, and future expansion (or contraction). More broadly, asset planning could be made more cost-effective and efficient for most network operations (Zhou *et al.*, 2016).

5. Reflections

Without experimentation, it is difficult to find out what may be possible. One of the keys to innovation is to experiment. The costs for experimenting, also termed as piloting or creating proofs-of-concept, have never been so low. Experimenting with digital technology does not require huge capital investments, rather it requires a mindset shift amongst the decision-makers. Try an idea and see how the data can inform the validity of one's assumptions and indicate how the pilot delivered on its intended output. Fail fast and fail cheap, but always learn why it failed to enhance the odds to succeed, next time around.

Scalability is only the next step after experimentation. Many newcomers in the digital world forget that predictions based on collected digital variables have started on a small scale. Also, data analytics require pilot tests both for industrial and domestic applications. Industrial data prototyping for production's industrial sensors and delivery is as important as in digitally "coding" people's preferences for energy consumption. Scaling up those models is the step further, not the first.

Technology should always act as the enabler. The problem worth solving needs to be understood well in advance before any technology solution is adopted. Usually, a lot of different technologies are needed to work in harmony to solve a real problem. That is, applying data analytics and blockchain technology in isolation would not create value.

The art is in how different technologies and tools are deployed to support the execution of strategies that result in a different, perhaps, superior way of delivering results that matter to its user. GE sells less equipment, but may have built a revenue-enhancing network of interlocking interests that erects formidable barriers to rivals. In effect, by changing the way the game is played, rivals are potentially locked out from today's profitable niches and of the future.

****

Anjaney Borwankar is Co-founder and Chief Executive of Navozyme. Anjaney leads some of the world's pioneering blockchain initiatives for the maritime industry. He designed the popular Blockchain for Maritime Decision-makers' Programme which has been ongoing since 2019. A special edition was also conducted for the IMO, the highest international maritime body. A former navigating officer with Maersk, Anjaney is an alumnus from IESE Business School (MBA) and Oxford University (Blockchain & Fintech certification from Said Business School).

Giulio Toscani is Professor at Universidad Pacifico, Perú. He is also Member, Advisory Board, Navozyme, and Professor and Academic Director, Artificial Intelligence for Business, ESADE Business & Law School, Spain, and is an expert on Digital Strategy and Strategic Leadership. Giulio lives between Barcelona, Spain, and Lima, Perú, where he teaches at Pacifico Business School. His background as chemical engineer and patent attorney has been an asset to keep himself actively involved in the energy sector and its data analytics, most recently with Repsol.

Bibliography

Amelang, S. and Wettengel, J. (2016). E.ON shareholders ratify energy giant's split. *Clean Energy Wire*, June 9, 2016.

Appunn, K. (2018). Deal between utilities E.ON and RWE set to reshuffle German energy market. *Clean Energy Wire*, March 12, 2018.

Ash, N. (2010). Enel growing through acquisition. *Power Technology*, February 3, 2021.

Barcelona, R. G. (2011). Reviving a revolution: New tools to capture the elusive green consumer. *IESE Insight*, 8, First Quarter 2011, 21–28.

Barcelona, R. G. (2015). Renewable energy with volatile prices: Why NPV fails to tell the whole story. *Journal of Applied Corporate Finance*, 27(1), 101–109.

Barcelona, R. G. (2017). *Energy Investments: An Adaptive Approach to Profiting from Uncertainties*. London: Palgrave Macmillan.

Bates, A. (2020). Solar panels are starting to die. What will we do with the megatons of toxic trash? *Grist*, August 13, 2020.

Boston, W. (1999). Veba and Viag Agree to Merge in $14 billion Stock-Swap Deal. *The Wall Street Journal*, September 28, 1999.

Conlon, P. (1988). *South Africa Coal Report*. New York: United Nations Centre Against Apartheid.

DoE — Department of Energy (2018). *Philippine Energy Plan, 2018–2040*. Metro Manila, Philippines: Department of Energy.

Drax (2021). *History of Drax*. https://www.drax.com/about-us/our-history/. Accessed on July 24, 2021.

ENEL (2021). *ENEL X — Solutions for Businesses*. https://www.enelx.com/n-a/en/for-businesses/products. Accessed on July 27, 2021.

Evans, S. (2021). "Exceptional new normal": IEA raises growth forecast for wind and solar by another 25%. *Carbon Brief*, May 11, 2021.

Finlay, K. (2016). Hey, Nokia isn't just a company that used to make phones. *Wired*, April 27, 2016.

Gita-Carlos, R. A. (2019). PH poverty projected to be at 18.7% in 2021: WB. Philippine News Agency, October 17, 2021.

GNPower (2021). https://www.gnpower.com.ph/about-us-new/#corp-profile. Accessed on February 25, 2021.

Hardesty, L. (2021). Nokia plans to boost its full year 2021 guidance. *FIERCE Telecom*, July 13, 2021.

Harrison, M. (2004). Philip Watts to quit early as chairman of Shell. *Independent*, January 13, 2004.

Iansiti, M. and Lakhani, K. R. (2014). Digital ubiquity: How connections, sensors, and data are revolutionizing business. *Harvard Business Review*, 92(11), 19.

Knight, S. (2019). Is RWE — E.ON deal creating a "Google of the Grids". *Wind Power Monthly*, October 31, 2019.

Kritz, B. (2020). Rethinking the Philippine energy plan. *The Manila Times*, October 11, 2020.

Mavrokefalidis, D. (2020). Two-thirds of consumers support carbon footprint labelling on products. *Energy Live*, April 28, 2020.

McFarlane, S. (2021). As the shift to green energy speeds up, Shell's Big Natura-Gas Bet is at risk. *The Wall Street Journal*, March 27, 2021.

Morris, C. (2016). RWE splits into two. *Energy Transition: The Global Energiewende*, April 1, 2016.

Morton, C. (2020). The best Islands in the world: 2020 readers' choice awards. Condé Nast Traveller, October 6, 2020.

NGCP (2016). *Transmission Development Plan 2016–2040: Final Report, vol 1*. Metro Manila, Philippines: National Grid Corporation of the Philippines.

NGCP (2020). *Transmission Development Plan 2020–2040: Consultation Draft, vol 1*. Metro Manila, Philippines: National Grid Corporation of the Philippines.

Owens, M. (2013). Sins from the past: Shell boss turned reverend to begin new church post. *Maidenhead Advertiser*, February 8, 2013. https://royaldutchshellplc.com/2016/02/13/phil-watts-oil-man-turned-spaceman-turned-holy-man/.

Penz, E., Harth, B., and Hoffman, E. (2019). Explaining consumer choice of low carbon footprint goods using the behavioural spill over effect in German-speaking countries. *Journal of Cleaner Production*, 214(2019), 429–489.

Proctor, D. (2020). RWE, E.ON deal will reshape energy markets. *POWER Magazine*, July 1, 2020.

PSA — Philippine Statistics Authority (2019). http://rsso06.psa.gov.ph/antique. Accessed on March 19, 2021.

RDS (2021a). *Shell GameChanger*. https://www.shell.com/energy-and-innovation/entrepreneurs-and-start-ups/shell-gamechanger.html#vanity-aHR0cHM6Ly93d3cuc2hlbGwuY29tL2VuZXJneS1hbmQtaW5ub3ZhdGlvbi9lbnRyZXByZW5ldXJzLWFuZC1zdGFydC11cHMvc2hlbGwtZ2FtZWNoYW5nZXIuaHRtbBWw. Accessed on July 27, 2021.

RDS (2021b). *GCxN — Shell + NREL: A Global Energy GameChanger*. https://gcxnrel.com/#!/about. Accessed on July 27, 2010.

Rivier Abbad, J. (2010). Electricity market participation of wind farms: The success story of Spanish pragmatism. *Energy Policy*, 38, 3174–3256.

Rotter, J. (1966). *Generalised Expectancies for Internal versus External control of Reinforcement*. Washington, DC: American Psychological Society.

Steitz, C. and Käckenhoff, T. (2018). RWE, E.ON reshape German power sector in Innogy asset swap deal. *Reuters*, March 11, 2018.

Tao, M., Fthenakis, V., Ebin, B., Steenari, B.-M., Butler, E., Sinha, P., Corkish, R., Wambach, K., and Simon, E. (2020). Major challenges and opportunities in silicon solar module recycling. *Progress in Photovoltaic*, July 22, 2020.

Timperley, J. (2016). E.ON completes split of fossil fuel and renewable operations. *The Guardian*, January 4, 2016.

Vallance, C. (2014). Interview at annual conference — Resetting the agenda. *The Marketing Society*, November 26, 2014.

Waggoner, M. J., The House Erred: A Carbon Tax is Better than Cap and Trade (September 1, 2009). *Tax Notes*, p. 1257, September 21, 2009, *University of Colorado Law Legal Studies Research Paper*, 9–18.

Williams, E. and Hittinger, E. (2020). Wind and solar profits: The race between falling costs and declining revenue. *gtm*, May 15, 2020.

Wiseman, R. (2003). The luck factor. *Skeptical Inquirer*, 27(3), May/June 2003, 1–5.

Zhou, K., Fu, C., and Yang, S. (2016). Big data driven smart energy management: From big data to big insights. *Renewable and Sustainable Energy Reviews*, 56, 215–225.

Glossary

Accepted wisdom: A set of beliefs or ideas, or correct ways of doing things, that are widely held by a majority of people, or expert opinions accepted as the truth in a field of study or within organisations.

Accrued costs: All costs of goods and services expensed during a period, including those received but not paid (e.g. receivables or payables), or previously incurred and allocated for the period (e.g. depreciation).

Acronym: Abbreviated description of a term, such as those describing power generation and energy technologies, economic and financial variables, or organisations (see appendices of Chapters 7, 8, and 10).

Adaptive moves: The manager's ability to affordably alter prior decisions (or commitments) as market circumstances change, such as deferring or accelerating actions, following *real options reasoning*.

Agency: A relationship where the agent acts on behalf of another party with superior decision-making authority as principal, whereby the agent is obliged to act in the principal's best interest.

Ambiguous conditions: A market where a set of outcomes and the conditions through which they arise cannot be fully known *a priori*, are shifting, or are uncertain.

Anchors of policy: Systemic factors that influence how policy is formulated and adopted, hinging on societal, individual, and economic values, that shape the ideological basis of organising a system:

> **Market system:** Operates under a rule of law that recognises individual initiatives and rewards as a basis for allocating resources, as well as economic and social benefits and costs.
>
> **Policy-directed system:** Premised on the hegemony of experts, the state takes on a dominant role in setting societal priorities, through policy measures such as subsidies or taxation.

Anchoring bias: A bias where a notional number is accepted as a correct "anchor", often as a manager's guess, from which subsequent estimates are adjusted or negotiated.

Arbitrage: Price differentials of an asset that one could buy or sell in different markets, locations, or times.

Articulate: An ability to express coherently a set of ideas, connecting a firm's purpose and actions.

Asymmetric costs: Uncorrelated costs of competing supplies, or opposite of **symmetric costs**.

Behavioural economics: A study of how economic decisions are influenced by psychological, cognitive, emotional, cultural and social factors, which at times deviate from rational economic criteria.

Behavioural finance: A sub-field of behavioural economics that analyses how psychology influences investor behaviour, influencing how firms' outcomes could differ or how market anomalies could occur.

Binomial processes: A system of evaluating variables with random moves, under specified periodic probabilities and volatilities, to estimate an investment's risk-adjusted payoffs and embedded options.

Glossary 643

Binomial tree analysis: An analytical method that represents how the option's intrinsic value varies at each node, subject to compound probabilities of outcomes derived from volatilities' binary up or down moves.

Biofuels: A form of renewable fuel that is derived from biomass such as plant, algae, or organic waste.

Blended finance: A combination of social and commercial funding, usually provided by development financial institutions and foundations taking one or a combination of the following forms:

> **Direct investments:** Concessional capital to complement private capital.
>
> **Credit lines:** Short-term financing extended to local banks for relending to specified social niches.
>
> **Green bonds:** Long-term financing backed by development financial institutions for renewables to provide cover for specified risks and funding.
>
> **Guarantees and insurance for credit enhancement:** Instruments that seek to safeguard private investors against certain types of commercial or political risks, or resource risks.
>
> **Grants and technical assistance:** Financial assistance provided to projects to fund feasibility studies and access to other technical capabilities to enhance a project's chances of success.
>
> **Local currency loans and investments:** Local funding sources that better align financial costs with expected revenue sources that are usually denominated in local currency.

BOUnCE: A complement to *PIVOT*, the structured thought process guides managers to connect strategic insights to the feasible scope of actions. Specifically:

> *B*eliefs and *O*utlook: Shape the choices one would consider as perceived by managers based on the best available information, preferences, or risk appetite.

*U*nderstand: Translate and interpret observed data or information, gained by learning from their experiences, experimentation, or from what they observed from others' circumstances.

I*n*centives: Align the financial rewards, based on outcomes of the firm's performance, with the contributions of stakeholders.

*C*reate and capture: Identify and appropriate value created by the firm's performance (see also **wealth creation**).

*E*ffect actions: Convert ideas into tangible actions that explicitly **articulate** how certain purposes (or objectives) could be achieved under ambiguous conditions.

Taking *PIVOT* and *BOUnCE* as a strategic framework, *BOUnCE* translates the managers' aspirations, at times articulated as "nebulous" ideals, into forms that are actionable and measurable.

Black–Scholes model: A pricing model used for valuing (financial) option's call or put, according to how the underlying asset value varies based on its duration, strike price, and typology.

Build-operate-transfer (BOT): A state concession extended to a private firm to build and operate privately funded asset, with an obligation to transfer at expiry to the government.

Burden from prior decision: Embedded costs or consequences from prior actions that may determine the available pathways for the present options available to a firm (also referred to as path dependency).

Business of energy: A commercial activity that converts raw feedstocks into fuel or energy to fuel mobility, provide warmth, energise work processes, or communications, among others.

Business viability conditions: A set of conditions that facilitate how a firm could fully recover what it invested with the cash it earns, at a level to affordably fund its obligations and growth opportunities.

Calibrate: An iterative process of testing assumptions and estimating feasible outcomes under specified conditions, with explicit recognition of ambiguities and their possible sources.

Capital budgeting (or investment appraisal): A process that managers undertake to evaluate, compare, and allocate resources to projects, usually for capital-intensive investments, among others.

Capital-intensive investments: Assets that require significant upfront cash commitment that is costly to reverse, while producing the outputs that are subject to volatile prices, costs, or volumes.

Carbon intensity: The amount of CO_2 emitted for every unit volume of energy produced.

Carbon space (prescribed): This refers to the amount of energy supplied by carbon-intensive sources within a system, as it impacts the desired level of CO_2 emission without causing environmental damage.

Cash costs or revenues: Costs incurred or revenues received as cash, which excludes all non-cash expenses (e.g. payables, depreciation, or amortisation) or receipts (e.g. receivables).

Ceteris paribus: A common assumption in classical economics where the future is assumed to remain unchanged from present market conditions.

Changing climate: Measurable changes in weather patterns over a long period from both natural sources, and human activities, alternating between cooling and warming cycles.

Choice architecture system: In policy or decision-making contexts, this involves the way choices are presented to people, where incentives tend to mobilise actions while mandates often elicit resistance.

Classical economics: Rooted in the 18th and 19th centuries, a school of economic thought that focussed on growth, freedom, and laissez-faire principles, underpinned by free competition.

Climate change: Quantified variations in moving averages in temperatures and weather patterns, usually measured over 30 years periods globally, that are attributed directly or indirectly to human activities.

Climate policy–expected outcomes matrix: An analytical mapping of how policy impacts a firm's feasible responses and expected performance, based on a specified matrix of indicators.

CO_2 abatement costs: The quantity of CO_2 emissions reduced divided by the incremental cost (or cost savings) of replacing fossil fuel with renewables, using LCOEs to compare estimated costs.

Common good: Outcomes of actions that orient people to societal good, to motivate people when necessary to sacrifice personal interests in favour of achieving higher ideals, facilitated by these virtues:

Humility: A behaviour that recognises what one knows, what one does not, and what one is capable of.

Integrity: A behaviour that exhibits consistency with what one does, in private as well as in public life, against what one professes.

Generosity: A behaviour that demonstrates openness to accept the gift of feedback, as well as to provide one, as a basis for improving the individual as a person.

Competitive process: An open process for firms or individuals to access equitably available goods, services, political influence, or benefits, with known selection criteria *a priori* to minimise favouritism.

Confirming evidence bias: "Shared views" are misconstrued as evidence of managerial alignment, particularly when only like-minded people constitute the management team.

Contingent move: Using *game-theoretic reasoning*, the actions of a firm depend on the moves that a rival firm is anticipated to make, and how such moves are perceived to impact on a firm's value.

Contractual renegotiations: Action (or request) by one or both **contracting parties** to change certain provisions of a contract that result in some reallocation of costs or benefits to the counterparties.

Controller's mindset: A managerial preference for control, as they aim to achieve predictable outcomes with minimal deviations between expected and actual performance.

Costs of supplies: Attributed costs to supply a unit or a given volume of energy, measured in cash or accrual terms.

Counterparties (or contracting parties): The other side to a contract, where the buyer (acquirer) is the other party to the seller (provider), with both sides comprising the contracting parties to an agreement.

Custom and tradition: Custom pertains to practices commonly accepted within a community, that turns into **tradition** when such customs are transmitted from one generation to the next.

Dark spreads: Difference between the unit costs of coal (as input) and power (as output) for every unit of power supplied.

Decarbonise: A transition from fossil fuel to renewables technologies that reduce carbon or carbonaceous materials resulting from producing products or performing services.

Decision rule: A prescribed action subject to fulfilling specified criteria set *a priori*.

Decision-tree analysis: Alternative pathways are drawn from binary branches of decisions, with an indicated financial impact and its probability, to assess the effectiveness of alternative courses of action.

Decision-switching: A managerial action that changes a decision, such as replacing an originally preferred technology with another championed by policy, by virtue of receiving subsidies or incentives.

Decommission: The process of withdrawing from active use, dismantling and decontaminating an energy-producing asset and its logistics, which are usually performed at the end of an asset's operational life.

Default risks: The probability that one of the **counterparties** fails to fulfil their obligations, resulting in possible quantifiable losses to one or both parties.

Deregulation (or market liberalisation): A transition to competitive markets with state regulation shifting focus from direct interventions to strengthening market institutions, monitoring, and policing compliance.

De-risking: The contingency to avoid losses from adverse events, or profiting from better-than-expected outcomes, by embedding and exercising managerial flexibility to vary prior commitments.

Dispatch volume: In the power market context, this is the volume of available electricity that is called to supply (hence sold) to the wholesale power market.

Disruption: An abrupt, radical, or gradual interruption of a status quo that changes the trajectory of markets and firms, usually because new technologies, systems, or capabilities are introduced.

Disruptive innovation segment: Niches in markets that are too small to serve by incumbents, requiring less resources for new entrants to develop and potentially dominate with new products or services.

Dom Perignon moment: A discovery that is often unplanned, with a potential to *reframe* an experiment or strategic direction of **R&D** efforts (also known as chance opportunities).

Dynamic decisions: A decision-making ecosystem that recognises how people's interactions alter market, requiring managers to identify pathways and levers of value to profitably adapt their strategic moves.

Dynamic and functional market: A system that freely trades goods, services, and other assets, under predefined rules, where regulation expands access to opportunities for most participants.

Dynamic thought process: A way humans simplify complex interactions by breaking down each decision component, quantify its impact, and recombine probable interacting results into a range of outcomes.

Dynamic volume reallocation: A dispatch hierarchy within wholesale energy market where cost-effective or preferred supplies fulfil periodic demand first, followed by less competitive or residual supplies.

Erosion rate: The rate at which a technology's actual maximum capacity declines annually from wear and tear, or poor maintenance of asset, usually reversed by periodically expending maintenance capex.

ESG: A set of guidance on the firm's environmental and social obligations and how they achieve transparency by practising sound governance principles.

Ethics: A mode of behaviour grounded on moral principles and the individual's virtues that guide the actions that they choose to undertake.

Emerging opportunities: A business idea that serves a market niche or need that a new technology, a different way of supplying or producing a good or service, may potentially satisfy profitably.

Energiewende: A German transition into low carbon, environmentally sound, reliable, and affordable energy supply, which seeks to phase out fossil fuels and nuclear fuel, and replace them with renewables.

Energy transition: A recursive and tentative displacement, over an extended period, that sees some predominant sources of energy or system being substituted by another with superior features or qualities.

Equality: A notion of fairness as an equal division of output produced among members of the collective.

Equator Principles: A set of principles adopted by most lenders for project financing as a risk management framework that guides how **ESG** related risks are assessed and managed.

Equilibrium: Following **game-theoretic reasoning**, this condition is reached and sustained for as long as any other moves would erode value, such that by deviating, the rival is made worse off value-wise.

Equitable access: In a system where freedom is expanded with development, people are enabled to exercise their choices with their capabilities that enhance their well-being and those around them.

Error of commission: A decision error that could arise when managers knowingly commit to rigid obligations that have no way of being known *a priori*.

Error of omission: A decision error that could arise when managers assume away any effects of volatilities or uncertainties on value.

Estimating and forecasting errors: A common error in conventional investment evaluation that linearly projects the future performance of firms based on *ceteris paribus*.

Feedback: Information that describes a person's behaviour, which may be positive or negative, how such behaviour impacts others, and its consequences to the individual as well as team performance.

Feed-in tariff: A payment to some renewables as a way to "equalise" the costs of fossil fuels and intermittent renewables, often used as an incentive for early adoption.

Firm (theory of): A notion of an entity that resources, contracts, and holds assets and resources, with a purpose to optimise its financial profits while meeting its societal obligations that evolved as follows:

> **Neo-classical:** A self-contained producer of goods and services for others, whereby price is what moves supply and demand, the firm being precluded from self-consumption.
>
> **Transaction cost or specialisation:** Under perfect information, resource use can be ranked with specialisation to optimise value. With uncertainty, the firm's role turned into a reallocator of risks.
>
> **Stakeholder theory and community relations:** The firm's stakeholders and the interests of each group are joint hence the firm must consider how value is created for each stakeholder.

As a **juridical person**, a firm is endowed by law with a personality that bears legal rights and obligations, distinct from human managers and their owners.

Fossil fuel energy: Energy derived from **carbon-intensive** minerals such as coal, oil or gas, which when converted into energy, produces pollutants or greenhouse gases such as CO_2, SO_x, or NO_x, among others.

Framing a problem: A way of defining or articulating the problem that is worth solving by managers.

Free will: A capacity to act using one's own judgement, premised on a set of virtues that one adheres to, whilst recognising the consequences and responsibility for one's actions.

Freedom: The ability to choose freely, by providing people with real opportunities, what they really value, which are often manifested in exercising these categories of freedom:

> **Economic freedom:** Ability to choose how to create and allocate resources, or appropriate the benefits from one's labour or capital, within the rules of a functioning market.
>
> **Political freedom:** Ability to exercise one's rights, participate fully in the political process, where individual freedom is protected from infringement by government or regulatory overreach.

Funnel process: A structured process of converting ideas into prospects, prioritising and allocating resources, to form a portfolio of opportunities that usually follows this sequence of activities:

> **Business idea:** A concept or notion where a potential for financial gain is identified, although requiring further structuring, testing, or validating, on how such an idea could be monetised.
>
> **Prospect:** A conversion of business ideas into real options, potential niches, or pathways to arenas of opportunities.

Portfolio of opportunities (opportunity set): Possible combinations of risky assets that produce a range of explicit risk–rewards potential from which managers may make their choice(s).

Choice: A selection of opportunities that optimises the overall returns within an acceptable level of risks, exercised under conditions of managerial flexibility.

Game changer: A new factor that alters to the new entrant's benefits, the sources of a firm's competitive advantages that are often found in the technological or organisational reconfiguration of extant firms.

Game-theoretic reasoning: An evaluation of how rival firms interact, and how their actions potentially alter the value or position of others, as prices, costs or market shares vary as they alternate as:

Pace-setter: Initiates a game with a more favourable position to capture an opportunity, such as a capacity to fulfil a given demand first by virtue of its cost competitiveness or availability.

Follower: Reacts to the pace-setter's action, by doing nothing, curtailing its supplies, or taking up the volume slack, as feasible ways of optimising its value under a less advantageous position.

Geothermal resource insurance: An insurance against predefined thresholds of losses arising from failed steam exploration, failed wells, or steam resource shortfall, in a portfolio of geothermal wells.

Gift from the past: Advantages that a firm enjoys today, derived from past policy or managerial actions or events, that continues to deliver ongoing benefits (see **initial endowment**).

Gold plating: A practice where assets are over-specified or over-insured against some perceived risks, which may have a low probability of occurring.

Goods and services: The output from an economic activity that results from a "division of labour" between the state and firms, whose costs or benefits could be allocated and appropriated accordingly:

> **Public:** Create benefits (or positive externalities) that cannot be uniquely appropriated by firms or individuals, thereby relegating its provision to the state as an agent acting for the people.
>
> **Private:** Costs are directly related to benefits (as revenues or income) of the provider, conforming to private capital's risks — returns criteria to commit.
>
> **Social:** Social benefits are significant albeit ambiguous as to their appropriability by the provider, making its provision conditional on the competence of the state or private capital, or as a hybrid.
>
> **Common pool resources:** Scarce resources that confer tangible benefits to the users, although nobody has an exclusive claim or obligation to its upkeep or conservation.

Green dilemma: A prevailing mantra among some managers that by helping the environment, one hurts business, or irreparably harm business while protecting the earth.

Green paradox: Generous subsidies to renewables achieve diametrically opposed outcomes to policy objectives, such as achieving wide-scale deployment, affordable supplies, or sustainable ventures.

Grid price parity principle: Subsidy is estimated as the difference between the LCOEs of a reference (and cheaper) fossil fuel technology and the preferred (but expensive) renewable sources of energy.

Horse Manure Crisis: A 19th century "existential threat" that forecasted London and other cities would be buried with horse manure, in an era when horse-drawn carriages were the predominant mode of transport.

Human innovation: The ability of humans to resolve societal or individual challenges by doing things differently, in the ways they recombine resources, people and technologies.

Impact investing: Investments made with the intention to generate positive, measurable, social and environmental impact alongside a financial return.

Income distribution: A statistical measure that indicates how a nation's income is distributed by showing who, or which group of people, receives how much of the pie.

Index (or physical hedge): This involves matching the cost of supply, and how it varies, with how the commodity (or asset) is going to be priced in a transaction, to achieve stable returns.

Initial endowment: The extant characteristics that shape a business that managers start with, in terms of costs, flexibility or available options, that are embedded by prior decisions or investments.

Innovation system: As technology evolves, and markets change or get disrupted, resources and capabilities are re-arranged to respond to shifting needs or competitive advantages.

Internal combustion engine: Device powered by fossil fuels, this is an engine commonly used for motor vehicles that use heat released during combustion to drive the engine.

Investment: A cash outlay that is committed upfront, with an expectation to recover at a profit the initial cash outlay, whose present values are evaluated using the following variables:

> **Capital expenditure (or capex):** Initial cash outlay to fund acquisition or building the asset.
>
> **Maintenance capex (or MCPX):** Continual cash outlays that are periodically disbursed to keep the asset in adequate operational efficiency.
>
> **Cash payoffs (profit or earnings):** Cash earned from selling energy as revenues, less any cash expenses related to supply.

Discount rate: The rate that is used to convert a future income stream to today's (or present) value.

Hurdle rate: A minimum return to recover the capex over the investment period including an opportunity cost for the use of capital.

Iterative exercise of options: The ability to continually exercise or defer options optimally, when there is flexibility to do so before its expiry date, such as supplying or curtailing energy supplies.

Judeo-Christian context: A western liberal notion that rests on a religious consensus premised on Christianity and the Jewish traditions, and the natural law, that is at times associated with conservative principles.

Ladder of inference: A thinking process that checks against "jumping into conclusions". Going down the ladder is a way of validating assumptions, contexts, and perceptions, against data, before concluding.

Late-mover's benefits for energy: Applies to energy technologies where the costs are falling sharply while foregone cash earnings by delaying investment are less than the expected savings in capex.

Learning effects (or experience curves) for energy: In theory, as more of an energy asset is deployed, its unit cost tends to fall at an estimated rate with each doubling of the installed capacity.

Libertarian paternalism: An economic school of thought that recognises how private initiatives and state interventions could alter behaviour of economic agents to achieve aspired ends within **dynamic markets**.

Licence to operate: Compliance with prevailing laws and ethos to legally operate as a business, whilst fulfilling the accepted social norms of the communities it seeks to serve.

Lifecycle avoided cost of energy (LACE): The "avoided costs" are revenues displaced from extant supplies, that accrue to a new power generation asset, estimated as LCOE divided by its dispatched volume.

Lifecycle cost of energy (LCOE): An average cost of supplying energy from a power-generating asset over its lifetime, at assumed volumes, adjusted for inflation and its attributable return.

Locus of control: An individual belief on the extent that they can control their destiny (internally oriented), or the extent that they are at mercy of outside forces such as fate, or luck (externally oriented).

Logistics: A system of managing how goods, services, or information are conveyed, usually involving storing, moving through networks, security, and delivery from source to use.

Loss avoidance: A strategy that curtails supplies when the cost of supplies exceed the potential revenue that could be earned by supplying.

Luck: Unplanned events usually with a connotation of bringing good fortunes or positive outcomes, or **misfortune** when an unplanned event that occurs leads to adversity or misery.

Malthusian theory: A notion that as population growth outstrips food production, famine is predetermined, a notion revived in modern day energy economics as resource scarcity, peak oil or peak demand.

Manager: A person who has authority to allocate resources, responsibility for controlling and administering the entirety or part of a firm, and to direct its strategic direction.

Managerial flexibility: The ability to affordably reverse prior commitments or decisions when justified by changing market conditions.

Market and structure: An organised system for the exchange of goods and services, with varying degrees of competition according to the following relationships between buyers and sellers:

> **Pure competition:** Each firm is too small on its own to singularly influence market volumes where the matching of supply and demand sets a price when market is in equilibrium.

Oligopoly: Comprises a small number of rivals whose actions could directly alter prices, volumes, and markets, whereby each supply added could ease shortages or worsen over-supplies.

Monopoly: Sole supplier of a unique product or service with control over pricing and supply.

Mindset transition: A different way of framing a decision, mobilising resources, and optimising value, often questioning **accepted wisdom** that could lead to new profitable niches being created.

Moral commitment: Premised on individual values and beliefs, these are conditions that are important for people to meet in order to act with integrity in ways that affirm one's vows, promises, and obligations.

Mutatis mutandis*:** A notion in economics that prescribes a change in the firm's approach when a status quo is altered in order to flourish or avoid adverse consequences (opposite of ***ceteris paribus).

Natural owner of opportunity: A firm with specified traits or capabilities that could uniquely optimise the feasible outcomes of a given investment.

Natural law: A social or juridical order which enables every individual, endowed with inalienable rights, to attain one's fullest or integral development, as a premise for achieving **common good**.

Net present value (NPV): The present value of the expected cash payoffs (or earnings) less the present value of the cash invested (or capex), which could be alternatively evaluated as a ***real option*** as follows:

> **Exercise price:** The capex managers choose to commit to gain access to the expected cash payoffs.
>
> **Expected cash payoffs:** See **Cash Profit**.

The flipside is the internal rate of return (IRR), which is the discount rate that equates NPV to nil.

Net zero agenda: Popularly, this refers to replacing fossil fuels with renewables or low-carbon energy sources. In some policy circles, this is extended to decouple economic growth from resource utilisation.

NIMBY: "Not-in-my backyard" is a syndrome where people object to locating a project within their vicinity even without questioning the costs or benefits of the investment to their community.

Obsolescing bargain: A bargain struck initially favouring the investing firm, with advantages shifting to the host government as fixed commitments are subjected to taxation, regulatory actions, or sequestration.

Omniscience: An assumption that policy (or strategy) is formulated under known conditions, with policymakers (or decision-makers) endowed with complete knowledge of the aspired outcomes.

Omnipotence: All-powerful ability that is uniquely endowed to the state to command acquiescence or compliance from the people or firms (e.g. taxation, sequestration, or public spending).

Operational flexibility: The managerial ability to continuously exercise periodic options to supply, in order to avoid losses under adverse conditions, or gain when expected outcomes are more favourable.

Opportunity cost: An expected foregone return on an alternative investment or security on the cash employed to fund capital expenditures.

Option: An instrument that gives a right but not an obligation to exercise a commitment, whose value is dependent on the performance of the underlying asset. This may be a:

> **Financial option:** Holder is a passive investor that exercises their right to acquire or sell a given quantity of security on the basis of the specified holding period(s), the strike price(s), and share price(s).

Real options: Managers actively and continuously exercise their flexibility to supply or curtail, as a way to optimise cash flows, avoid adverse events, or incur financial losses.

A **call** gives a right to acquire while a **put** confers a right to sell a given quantity of the underlying asset, the value of which is referred to as **call or put value**.

Option games: A valuation of the firm that combines how oligopoly rivalries (game theory) and options under managerial flexibility (real options) could influence the firm's value under ambiguities.

Option premium: A flexibility value for waiting that rapidly erodes upon entry of credible rivals because the fear of losing out when pre-empted by rivals could encourage earlier exercise by an oligopolist.

Organisational agility enablers: Endows managers, as the orchestrator of resources and capabilities, to coach and cheerlead the team are often undertaken and reinforced by these factors:

Governance: A predefined *modus operandi* that confers managerial agility by providing clarity of one's scope of authority.

Structure and competency: A repository of pools of talents, competency is built whilst providing capable people to support conversion of ideas to opportunities.

Processes: Rules of engagement, interfaces, and interactions, ease the way to do the right things, not to restrict actions.

Organisational agility and innovation: An analytical matrix that helps inform managers on how to focus their resources to deliver the innovation outcomes. Specifically:

Command-and-control: Specialised assets and capabilities are optimised with operating efficiency under stable demand and markets.

Outsource or divest: With limited capability, managers may opt to acquire the services of specialised providers or divest their own assets to an owner that can do better.

Special forces: Work on small opportunities, or low hanging fruits with high potential payoffs, to experiment, learn, or scale to gain insights and internal capabilities.

Bounded empowerment: Involves the deployment of cross-functional teams, with a specified mandate, to undertake new ventures, usually outside the mainstream firm structure.

Organisational learning (or strategic dialogue): Divergent–convergent processes of gaining insights, rectifying prior errors, or experimenting with new ways of getting things done. Specifically:

Single loop learning: Focus is on identifying and correcting errors which could encourage managers to pursue a problem's solution to perfection while sustaining the status quo.

Double loop learning: Focus is on re-examining the premise and how human behaviour influences outcomes, encouraging managers to employ dialectic tensions to discover alternative futures.

Out of the money: An option or an investment that is making a loss when the exercise price is greater than the value of the payoffs to be received.

Outcome–variation matrix: A risk analysis tool that maps a range of expected outcomes, how it could vary and the nature of uncertainties, and some feasible responses firms could employ. Specifically:

Certain outcomes (known) — identified (known) variations: Predictable extant world that rewards operational efficiency under stable prices and costs with guaranteed cost recovery.

Unknown outcomes — known sources of variations: Operating under managerial flexibility, simulation or scenarios inform decision-making to avoid adverse outcomes.

Known outcomes — unknown sources of variations: Managers insure against known consequences such as natural disasters but of unknown timing or magnitude.

Unknown outcomes — unknown sources of variations: Managers may adapt their moves, contingent upon competitors' **games** and flexibility accorded under **real options thinking**.

P W One: "Partnerships that win" employs storytelling as a technique to articulate how cooperating stakeholders could reinforce each other's leadership in their respective market niches.

Pareto optimality: A situation where society's well-being can no longer be made better by reallocating resources to make at least one party better off without making another worse off.

PIVOT: A thought process that facilitates **strategic dialogues** among stakeholders with diverse interests, priorities, or often opposing views, that may follow this structured approach:

---

*P*urpose and *I*nsights: Defines why the firm does what it aims to do, and explicitly describes what the bases are for considering certain priorities as important, and why it matters.

*V*eer: Recognises managers can change course or prior decisions when circumstances change, following ***real options and game-theoretic reasoning***.

*O*utcomes: Under ambiguous conditions, managers simulate outcomes and their impact on value, by employing scenarios to map rivals' potential actions and their firm's feasible responses,

*T*ake action: Managers work at a granular level on how they can convert their strategic ideas (or bets) into emerging opportunities to create tomorrow's profitable niches today.

Pivotal investment: Investments that are critical to embed options or capabilities for a firm to transition into a profitable niche from its extant position.

Policy allocation: The state decides, in its presumed omniscience, what benefits (or costs) and to whom it should be provided (or borne), usually through the state's power to tax, subsidise, or sequester.

Policy (and relation to energy regulation): Comprises a set of principles that guide the course of actions of the state, business, political party, or individual that evolves with changing supply and market's agility:

Command-and-control: State regulation sets prices and volumes, under limited supply diversity, with suppliers converted into sub-contractors to the state that rewards operational efficiency.

Benevolent paternalist: State regulation favours policy-mandated supplies under diverse sources while undertaking some reforms and restructuring prior to introducing competition.

Libertarian paternalist: State regulation transitions into a "visible but benign hand" in handing over more freedom to firms, while asserting some influence through subsidies or fiscal incentives.

Dynamic markets: State regulates by exception, shifting its priorities to institutional building. See **Deregulation (or market liberalisation).**

Collectively, policy may be used to refer to policymakers or the state sector in some chapters.

Policy instruments and market orientation matrix: A framework that explicitly evaluates how policy and strategy interact that informs how managers adapt to changing business landscapes. Specifically:

> **Policy push and champions:** Policy employs its presumed omniscience and omnipotence to push for adoption of technology champions.
>
> **Policy-enabled market pull:** As an enabler, policy uses taxation as an instrument to encourage the adoption of non-polluting technologies.
>
> **Policy-enabled competitive process:** Policy employs competitive mechanisms such as auctions for firms to access permits, concessions, or rights.
>
> **Markets with regulatory intervention by exception:** Policy actions are focussed on correcting market failures, or building supportive institutions to strengthen dynamic markets.

Politics: The domain that studies how ideology influence the ways states or communities are governed, how they arbitrate conflicts, or allocate power, with ideological inclination categorised as:

> **Conservatism:** Seeks to sustain institutions, rule of law, and traditions, while promoting individual and market initiatives to expand access to economic and social opportunities.
>
> **Progressivism:** Aims to achieve social progress through reforms as a way to improve human society, where collective actions are facilitated through state interventions or support.
>
> **Populism:** Focus to appeal to a working or middle class that popularly believed their concerns are ignored by a political and governing elite.

Moderates: Avoid extreme views where adherents tend to subscribe to mainstream political views representing a centre ground between conservatism and progressivism.

Portfolio mindset: A strategic thought process that seeks to dynamically evaluate the resulting valuation from what assets one combines, how and when specific assets are included to form part of the portfolio.

Portfolio risk and returns: An explicit evaluation of how interacting volatilities among different assets are correlated, enabling managers to diversify or alter their mix to achieve their aspired returns and risks target.

Power purchase agreement (PPA): Long-term rigid contract that obliges a buyer to purchase a specified quantity of power at given prices from a supplier with an obligation to supply.

Profitable niches: A market segment or niche where the firm could optimally deploy for profit, its resources and advantages to outcompete its rivals (or competitors).

Purpose: A unifying expression of principles that managers adhere to, coherent with their personal virtues, that guides how firms formulate their strategy and how managers act.

R&D: Mobilise resources to undertake research and development efforts aimed at formulating new ways of doing things, through innovations, technological or process reconfiguration, among others.

Rational economic agents: Decision-makers are entirely reliant on reason and logic (often assumed as devoid of emotions) in making their choices with a view to optimise their benefits.

Rebound effect (or Jevon's paradox): Improved resource efficiency raises real income and accelerates economic growth, which is achieved by using fewer resources to produce more goods sold at a nice profit.

Red-hot stone phenomenon: An illustration of objective reality: "A red hot stone, when touched with one's bare hands, is bound to burn the hand badly", regardless of how one would think otherwise.

Redistributive justice: A process of allocating fairly the burdens and benefits of collective efforts among people with differing interests, as they compete to fulfil their needs and claims.

Regulatory risk: A change in law or rules that materially alter the firm's (or asset's) value or performance.

Reliability: The ability to perform according to specified criteria and technical specifications within acceptable deviation from a standard measure.

Renewables: A source of energy from natural sources such as water, geothermal steam, sunlight, wind, or biomass, which can be readily replenished and emits minimal or no pollutants. The types of energy supplies are as follows:

> **Modulated:** Energy supplies that could be readily varied or dispatched according to the demand, such as hydro and geothermal power with high **reliability**.
>
> **Variable (or intermittent):** Energy supplies vary with the availability of wind or sunlight, and given its intermittency, is usually considered non-dispatchable with low **reliability**.

Reserve replacement ratio: In the oil and gas industry, this is the volume of proven reserve divided by the annual production, as a way of estimating the number of years the proven reserves may last.

Residual economic value: See **wealth creation**.

Residual supplier: The marginal or the last to supply energy in a dynamic wholesale energy market, at times referred to as the **price-setting supply**.

Resource scarcity fallacy: A counter-argument to finite resources logic that posits minerals such as coal are displaced, not because the world is running out of supply, but because better and more affordable fuel had become available.

Risk: As a financial metric, it measures the deviation from an expected outcome which could be higher or lower. Popularly, it connotes erroneously an exposure to danger or adverse outcomes.

Risk aversion: A "virtue" that some managers equate to preserving the value of the asset (or firm) by avoiding making a loss, or not taking any exposure to adverse outcomes.

Risk-neutral strategic payoffs: The adjusted present value of economic cash margin (economic cash revenue less cash cost), at times estimated as point forecasts plus a terminal value of payoffs, employing LCOEs.

Risk-taking: An act that some managers see as essential to growing or pivoting away from an obsolescing business, as a way to create or preserve wealth.

Sarbanes Oxley: A U.S. law enacted in 2002 that was intended to protect investors from fraudulent accounting practices or disclosures by companies such as Enron, a bankrupt gas major.

Schizophrenia (managerial): A disconnect between how policymakers and managers perceive reality, and what their toolkits prescribe as decision criteria, often leading to erroneous valuation and decisions.

Second best, General theory of: A second best option is considered when Pareto optimality conditions cannot be satisfied, thereby constrained optimisation becomes the best alternative for managers.

Shareholders: Owners of a firm that coordinate, orchestrate, and organise, either directly or through their agents, to harness resources for the firm and society's benefits by expanding stakeholders' prosperity.

Social cost and benefit analysis: Extending net present value (NPV) analysis, a policy's social impacts are evaluated where its social costs are compared to its social benefits.

Social enterprise: A firm organised with a social objective that serves as its guiding purpose as well as the manner in which profits are allocated or distributed to stakeholders.

Social innovation: An approach where firms extend stakeholder engagement by harnessing the cooperation of the communities they serve as partners in resolving problems.

Social responsibility of firms: Acts of business entities, through their policies and performance, that seek to promote the well-being of their communities by lessening the adverse impact of their activities.

Social utility: Through trading, one sells less desired good or service to someone who values it more, and acquires a good or service that one desires more, which could result in an aggregate expansion of utility (or welfare).

Socio-environmental impact: Pertains to how a firm's (or people's) activities alter the livelihood, physical and communal environment, within the specified geographic area.

Spark spreads: Difference between the unit cost of gas as fuel (input) and the price of power (as output) for every unit of power supplied.

Stakeholders: A range of parties, including shareholders, that have direct interests in the firm's performance, or those who are affected by the firm's actions.

Status quo trap: A predisposition of managers to do things as they have always done, thereby perpetuating extant systems and processes even as the needs are changing.

Strategic actions: A sequential plan connecting purpose and aspired objectives with an array of initiatives, defining who owns them, when and how they are executed, and how they reinforce the next moves.

Strategic flexibility: A managerial capability to identify relevant market changes, quickly adapts to commit resources to ***repurpose***, ***reframe***, and ***reconfigure*** the firm's **strategic actions**.

Strategic initiatives (or responses): The means that a firm undertakes to achieve its aspired goals or objectives. Specifically, managers adapt their moves by employing one or more of the following:

> **Operating efficiency:** A firm with specific capabilities dominate a stable niche where barriers to entry are high, reinforced by the scale and operating efficiency.
>
> **Sustaining innovation:** Agile firm under stable markets improves their energy offering, such as combining fossil fuels and renewables to improve cost-effectiveness while reducing CO_2 footprint.
>
> **Disruptive innovation:** Agile firm in rapidly transitioning markets evolves unnoticed in ignored segments to build an ecosystem that potentially displaces the incumbent's offering.
>
> **Retool/Divest:** A firm with specific capabilities are threatened by obsolescence as markets rapidly transition, giving managers the option to retool or divest (or exit earlier).

Strategic insights: Insights gained from *PIVOT* and *BOUnCE* are turned into actionable ideas that comprise the firm's strategic moves. Specifically:

> ***Repurpose:*** Labour, capital, processes, or intellectual properties are deployed for alternative use. This often involves reskilling people, redeploying and recombining resources, or divesting assets.
>
> ***Reframe:*** Adapts how a firm may choose to achieve its purpose (or objectives) under changing or ambiguous markets.
>
> ***Reconfigure:*** Reorganises how a firm produces, meets or delivers, its customer's needs in response to policy actions or changing markets.

Strategic move: An action taken by a rival outside the confines of a game, that differentiates a firm that a competitor may find difficult to match or overcome.

Strategic option value (SOV): The value of outcomes measured as the payoffs that are altered as a result of the interactions of rival firms' actions.

Strategic thinking: A thought process that seeks to combine resources with actions to outdo an adversary, while anticipating how the adversary would respond under dynamic decision contexts.

Subsidies (or Pigouvian tax): A public funding of private costs as a way of recognising positive external benefits, which effectively socialises part of the cost of provision of a service or good, categorised as:

> **Demand-pull policy:** Measures that create demand by penalising by taxing polluting technologies, such as carbon tax on fossil fuels.
>
> **Supply-push policy:** Measures creating supplies by socialising the excess costs of technologies such as **feed-in tariffs**.
>
> **Pigouvian tax** incorporates the measures included in **policy instruments and market orientation matrix.**

Sunk costs trap: A decision error that favours making choices today to justify prior commitments when good money chases bad as managers continue to fund irreversibly failing investments.

Superstition: A set of beliefs, often unvalidated, that influence policymakers and managers in attributing a cause-and-effect causation of events or actions, often leading to outdated and incorrect judgement.

Sustainability or sustainable practices: A set of actions that enables firms or communities to meet their present needs without hindering future generations to meet theirs, often guided by **ESG** principles.

Tactical move: The specified steps or actions that a manager undertakes to get a job done or to achieve a strategic objective.

Take-or-pay contracts: See **power purchase agreement** (PPA).

Technology alternatives: This refers to the different ways of converting raw materials into useful energy to fuel mobility, provide warmth, or energise work processes. Among which are:

> **Fossil fuels:** Converts coal, oil or gas into fuels or power, usually operated as baseload or mid-merit supplies that could be ramped up or down as demand varies.
>
> **Nuclear:** Converts uranium into power, usually operated as inflexible baseload supply.
>
> **Conventional (modulated) renewables:** Converts hydro or geothermal into power with minimal CO_2 emissions, with the flexibility to ramp up or down as baseload or mid-merit power supplies.
>
> **Variable or intermittent renewables:** Converts disperse wind, solar radiation or waves into power, where supplies availability is reliant on the weather.

TECOP risk analysis framework: A multi-disciplinary approach to examining the clusters of risk factors that facilitates an assessment of overall investment (or project) risk, such as:

> **Technical:** Choice of technology, logistics and scale, and its impact on networks configuration, development, and operational risks.
>
> **Economics:** Scope of costs and expected payoffs, as well as risks and uncertainties, over the lifecycle of the asset.
>
> **Commercial:** Strategies around pricing and market access, and managing risks around a network of relationships.

Organisational: Gaps in resources, competencies, or required leadership skills, towards delivering the aspired objectives of the investment (or project).

Politics (or policy): Shifts in regulatory or stakeholder relationships, and identifying contingencies, to enable the investment (or project) to fulfil its societal obligations.

Transition or transformation of firms: In transitioning towards a low-carbon energy system, firms may undertake a transformation following these phases:

Foundational shift: The initial phase involves building resilience by *repurposing* resources and capabilities as the firm's initial endowment.

Transitional moves: The next phase creates pathways by exercising options (and closing some), where choices are reframed and tested.

Transformational pivot: With clarity of purpose, firms aim to *reconfigure* extant networks and relationships to shift the sources of competitive advantages to favour them.

Triple bottom line: Firms are evaluated based on their performance based on their profit, impact on the environment and people (at times referred to as profit, people and planet).

Unity of purpose and actions: With the firm's purpose as a unifying principle, managers adhere to it when there is a minimum alignment with their personal virtues, beliefs or necessity, to guide their actions.

Value chain risk assessment: A risk evaluation approach that specifically identifies risk factors, their impact, and *reframing*, in order to *reconfigure* the value chain to embed options to facilitate capital flows.

Wealth creation: In financial economics, this occurs when RoIC exceeds WACC, under the following conditions:

Returns on Invested Capital (ROIC): Is positive, when revenues exceed the cash costs incurred to supply specified goods or services, less any taxes due, divided by the capital invested.

Weighted average cost of capital (WACC): Refers to how much is attributed as cost for the use of equity, debt (after tax), and any other form of capital.

Economic profit (EP) or residual income (RI): The difference between RoIC and WACC after tax.

Economic value added (EVA) or residual value added (RVA): The present value of EP or RI which could be simplified by dividing EP or RI with the discount rate.

Welfare: This represents the economic surplus that an economy produces from its activities, and how this surplus is allocated, popularly known as **income distribution**, **equality** or **equitable access** to benefits.

Index

A

Aboitiz, Jon, 418
accepted wisdoms, li, liv–lv, 7, 58, 77, 138, 274, 283, 289, 414, 471, 512, 516, 600, 611, 641
ACEN Corporation, 613–621
    home market, building, 613–614
    pivot, consolidate to, 618–621
    strategic advantages, reframing arenas of, 616–618
    transitioning markets, setting sights on, 614–616
acronym, 86, 377, 455, 476, 509, 526, 641
adaptation, xlv, 35, 39, 335
adaptive actions, by real people, xlii–xlv
adaptive moves, xlvi–xlix, 641
adaptive value chain de-risking, 309–310
    divergent risks or opportunities, 310–314
    resolving contradictions and geothermal paradox, 314–317
after action review (AAR), 224, 235, 620
Archer, Léonie J, 47
Argyris, Chris, 250, 416, 422

Arrow, Kenneth J, 104, 276
articulation, purpose, 137, 642
    Chief Executive's next moves, 172–175
    firms and markets exist, 141–145
    inspiring commitment with purpose, 164–166
Arya, Anil, 512
Asian Development Bank, lx, 117
Asia-Pacific Financial Forum, lx
asset recovery rate (ARR), 449
autonomous group market operator (AGMO), 115
available cash for disbursement (ACD), 439
Awerbuch, Shimon, xli, 102, 277

B

Badaracco, Joseph L, Jr, 198
Bar-Lev, Dan, xli, 277
battery power storage, 58
behavioural economics, 246, 642
behavioural finance, 642
Benevolent Paternalist, 107, 662

Bentham, Jeremy, 104
binomial model and processes, 552–576
   binomial processes, 642
   binomial tree, 277, 643
   making choices with option valuation, 567–571
   market volume and allocation, 554
   to spend or not to spend, 571–572
biofuels, 118–119, 643
Biofuels Act of 2006, 118
Black–Scholes model, 644
Blanco, Herib, 60
blended finance, 123–124, 643
blockchain, 630, 635
Blockchain Enabled E-certificates (BEEs), 633
Bochum, Ruhr-Universität, 298
Bollinger, Mark, 99
Borwankar, Anjaney, liii–liv, 601
Bossel, Ulf, 40
Botts, Tom, 180
BOUnCE, xlix–liii, 469, 475, 585, 588, 643
bounded empowerment, 219, 660
bounded possibilities, 189
   strategic dialogue, CFO's role in, 225
   unpacking policy uncertainties, 204–211
British Energy, 487
Brufau, Antonio Niubó, xlvi, lx, 45–57
build-operate-transfer (BOT), 113, 644
burden from prior decision, 644
business idea, 651
business of energy, 156–161, 644
Business Round Table (BRT), 149, 414
business viability condition, 359, 361, 365, 373, 644

C
calibration, 241, 645
   creative power of humans, harnessing, 245–246
   decision traps, managers fall into, 246–250
   managers' odds at succeeding, 250–253
   judgements and financial discipline, 263
      ambiguous conditions, valuation under, 271–273
      complex choices, calibrating value creation under, 263–271
      improving odds, 283–284
   prioritising opportunities, ecosystem for, 254–256
cap-and-trade, 103
capital asset pricing model (CAPM), 414, 417
capital budgeting, 155, 251, 273, 317, 471, 645
capital costs recovery, 373
capital expenditure (capex), 654
capital-intensive investments, 264, 296, 388, 442, 520, 645
capital recovery factor, 19, 367
carbon emissions costing, 391–392
carbon intensity, 645
carbon-intensive assets, 258
   minerals, 651
carbon space, 24–25, 27, 534, 645
   shrinkage of, 526–534
Carbon Strategy, 49
carbon tax, 105, 108, 203, 207, 266, 392

Index

cash flow, 415, 419, 422–423, 446–447, 499
    financing, continued access to, 428–430
    ignore critical premises, 426–428
    strategic dialogues, foundation for, 423–426
cash flow illusion, 421–422
cash margin, 25, 266, 271, 273, 279, 329, 372, 451, 484, 490
ceteris paribus, xl, 7, 645, 650, 657
changing climate, 645
Charnley, Anthony, 177
cheap energy policy, 314–315, 341, 346
Chevalier-Roignant, Benoit, xl, lix, 299
Chief Executive Officer (CEO) seeks, 190–191
Chief Finance Officer (CFO), 67, 190–192, 215
choice architecture system, 645
circular economy, 61
City of London, xxxvii, li
civil society, xliii–xliv
Clark, William C, 477
climate change, 646
Climate Change Unit, 49
Climate Finance Access Network, 127
climate policy-expected outcomes matrix, 646
CO_2 abatement costs, 646
Coase, Ronald Harry, 144–145, 148
CO_2 emissions, 13–16, 51, 165, 297
Cohen, Ben, 150–151
Collin, Paul, xlvii
Collins, Jim, 172

command-and-control approach, 22, 32, 91, 103, 219, 474, 659, 662
common good, 646, 657
comparative power generation financial analyses, 460–461
competitive process, 210, 646
Comstock, Stephen, 13
confirming evidence bias, 646
conservatism, 663
conservatives, 76, 160
Consunji, Jorge, liii, lxi, 622, 629
contingent move, 524, 646
contracting parties, 340, 647–648
contracting strategy, comparative values of, 319
contractual renegotiations, 647
controller's mindset, xxxvii, xl, 589–590, 611, 647
conventional renewables, 117, 368, 394, 670
core financial strategy, capital rebalancing, 437–439
corporate power purchase agreement (Corporate PPA), 126, 155, 211, 304–306, 314, 340
cost-benefit analysis (CBA), xxxix–xl
cost minimisation strategy, 277
cost of equity, 266
costs of energy, 359–361
    numbers, knowing and using, 396
costs of production, 147–149
costs of supplies, 647
counterintuitive and contrarian moves, xxxvi–xlii
Cox–Ross–Rubinstein binomial tree, xlii, 277, 517

credit enhancement, guarantees and insurance for, 124, 643
credit lines, 124, 643
credit strength, 423, 428, 498
Crossboundary Energy Fund (CBE), 125
cross-cultural cooperation, 180–183
Cunningham, Thomas, 477

D

Damodaran, Aswath, 430, 471
dark spreads, 647
data analytics, 630, 635–636
data science, 630–632
decision-making ecosystem, 214
    approach, 251
decision rule, 647
decision-switching, 647
decision-tree analysis, 647
deep uncertainties, 213
    managerial responses to, 212–216
        recombining resources, 221–224
        uncertain outcomes, organising adaptively for, 216–221
default risks, 648
demand-pull policy, 669
Demsetz, Harold, 144, 146–148
Department of Environment and Climate Change (DECC), 324
depreciation rate, 373
deregulation, 648
de-risking energy, 295–300, 648
    adaptive moves to, 317–320
        pacing and counterintuitive learning effects, 328–332
        unlocking exogenous bottlenecks, 324–328
        inadvertent consequences, 300–301
        ignored risks under rigid obligations, 302–306
        secure revenues/embedded default risks, 306–309
    notion of, 299
Development as Freedom, 78
direct investments, 124, 643
discounted cash flow (DCF), 288, 414
discount rate, 655
disruptive innovation, 169–172, 668
disruptive innovation segment, 648
dividend discount rates (DDR), 471–472
Dixit, Avinash K, xlviii, 242, 252, 299, 511–512, 517
Dom Perignon moment, 59–60, 592, 648
Dormann, Juergen, 227
double loop learning, 245–247, 282, 660
Drax Power Station, 533–534
dynamic decisions, xxxv, xliii, 608, 648
dynamic market, 107–108, 154, 189, 655, 662
dynamic thought process, 520–525, 648
    areas of uncertainties, first identifying, 521–523
    binomial processes, formalise quantifiable outcomes using, 524–525
    market allocates volumes to rivals, 523
    pairings of rivals and contingent moves, 524
    variable volumes and the rivals' value, 523–524
dynamic volume reallocation, 649

Index

E

earnings after tax (EAT), 419
earnings per share (EPS), 416
EBITDA, 416–417, 426, 431, 440, 445, 489, 491, 501
economic cash margins (ECM$_e$), 560–563
economic costs of energy, 362–363
    economic costs-returns nexus, 365–367
    monetising energy investments, 367–368
    perils of incomplete financial costing, 363–365
economic freedom, 651
economic profit (EP), 672
economics, xxxvi, 197, 645
economic value added (EVA), 263–264, 417, 672
economies of scale, 36, 42, 91, 332
Econs, 88
Electric Power and Industry Restructuring Act (EPIRA), 113
electric vehicles (EV), 5, 52
Ellsworth, Richard R, 198
ENEL, 601–602
Energia Do Portugal Renewable (EDPR), 54
Energiewende, 477, 649
energy, lxii
    static lifecycle costs of, 20
    transformative potential for, 633–635
energy ecosystem, rethinking, 157
energy firms, 152–156
    changing roles of, 161–163
Energy Information Administration (EIA), 19, 21, 102, 314, 552

energy investments, xl, 76, 105, 367–368
energy *PIVOT*, xliv–xlvi
Energy Regulatory Commission (ERC), 116
energy system, 191
    costs of load intermittency to, 393
energy TECOP framework, 195, 199
energy transition, xxxv–xxxvi, xlii, xlv, liii–liv, 3, 5, 7, 29, 32–33, 588, 649
engineering mindset, 36
Enterprise Value (EV), 416
environmental, social, and governance (ESG), 37, 649
environmental virtues, 110–111
equality, 649, 672
Equator Principles, 110, 649
equitable access, 650, 672
erosion rate, 649
error of commission, 253, 650
error of omission, 253, 650
Espartinez, Christine Marie, 398
estimating and forecasting errors, 650
Esty, Daniel C., 18
European Alliance for Social Responsibility, 49
European Environmental Agency (EEA), 16
exercise price, 657
expected cash payoffs, 657
Expected Outcomes–Variations Matrix, xlvii, 199–200
external costs, 391–392
    investment, carbon emissions abatement as, 393–396
    welfare economist's view, 392–393

F

Faaij, André, 60
Faus, Josep, 493, 497
faux normalcy, 471, 473
feed-in tariff (FiT) scheme, 64, 94–95, 107, 117, 488, 618, 650, 669
Ferns, George, 48
final investment decision, 260, 262
financial cost building blocks, 369–373
financial costing, 363–365
financial costs of energy, 362–363
financial data, 418–420
financial economics, 274
financial fixed cost recovery (FFCR), 363
financial fixed operating and management expenses (FFO&Ms), 363
financial fuel costs (FFCs), 363
financial option, 658
financial payoffs, 319–320
financial periodic cost of energy (FPCOE), 363, 365, 370–372, 389–390
financial ratios, 465–466
financial risk premium, 375
financial variable costs (FVCs), 363
firm, 139, 141–145, 650
    minimise costs of production, 147–149
firms' rivalry, 273–283
Fitzgerald, F. Scott, 245
fixed asset, 431, 433, 435
fixed cost recovery, 408–409
floating regasification and storage units (FRSU), xxxix
fossil fuel, 368, 670
fossil fuel energy, 651
foundational *PIVOT*, liii, 589–596, 671
framing a problem, 651

Francia, Eric, liii, 613
Freeman, R Edward, 151–152
Friedman, Milton, 138, 148, 477
Frondel, Manuel, 298
FTSE Index, 472
fuel cost, 412
fuel cost minimisation, xli–xlii
Fujifilm, 287–288
funding choices, 430–431
    knowing funding choices, 431
    operating decisions and financing, 433–436
    strategic investment, virtuous cycle of, 431–433
funding renewables projects, 128–129
funnelling process, 258, 651

G

game changer, 652
game-theoretic reasoning, 646, 649, 652
gas-to-liquids, xxxix
General Theory of Second Best, 104, 666
generosity, xxxvii, xliii, 646
geocentric energy resources, 160, 328
geothermal, 397–405
geothermal drilling technologies, 39, 491
    comparative costs of, 342
geothermal paradox, 314–317
    expanding new market access, 346–347
    harnessing social capital and impact investing, 345–346
    making resource insurance math work, 344–345
    reframing risks, rewards, and growth options, 343–344
    revolutionising with slim-hole drilling, 341–343

geothermal resource insurance, 652
geothermal steam, 397–399
global warming, 159
Gotianun, Cristina C, liii, lxi, 623, 629
governance, 220, 659
Government Commission for GOCC (GCG), 115
Graham, John, 263
grants and technical assistance, 643
graphite, 40
Great Recession, 148, 151
green bonds, 124, 643
green dilemma, 653
Greenfield, Jerry, 150–151
greenhouse gases, 158
green paradoxes, l, 93, 95–99, 297, 653
   actually gains, 94–95
Gregorek, Jerzy, 237
Grenadier, Steven, 281
grid price parity, 95, 97, 105, 276, 306–308, 391, 653
gross cash profit (GCP), 425
Group of Seven (G7), 16
Gruber, Rudolph, 66–67
Guterres, Antonio, 14

H

Hair, Jay D, 47
Hamburger, Philip, 81–82
Hammond, John S, 247, 283
Hansen, Harry Louis, 191, 197, 209
Hardin, Garrett, 77
Harrabin, Roger, 4
Harvey, Campbell R., 263
Haug, Espen Gaarder, 567
Helm, Dieter, 10, 16, 24
Henry, Adam Douglas, 477

Heukampf, Franz, lix
Hirschmann, Winfred B, 99
Horse Manure Crisis, lvii, 5, 7, 11, 43, 590, 653
human-centric investment funnelling process, 255, 283
human innovation, 6, 654
human judgement, 260–263
humility, xxxvii, xliii, 646
Humphreys, H Brett, 277
hurdle rate, 655
hydrogen, lxvi, 40–42, 59, 65, 262
Hyman, Leonard S, 91

I

impact investing, 345–346, 654
   learning from, 121–127
income distribution, 654, 672
Independent Electric Market Operator of the Philippines (IEMOP), 116
independent market operator (IMO), 115–116
independent power producers (IPPs), 487
industry coupling, 41
informing managerial decisions, 368–369
initial endowment, 33, 191, 201, 299, 310, 505, 523, 589, 593–594, 596, 604, 654
innovation system, 282, 654
institutional investors, xxxvii, 125
integrity, xxxvii, xliii, 646
intermittent renewables, 117–118, 160, 314, 634
internal rate of return (IRR), 414, 451, 471
International Energy Agency (IEA), 5, 19, 372, 503

International Petroleum Industry Environmental Conservation Association (IPIECA), 49
invested capital (IC), 268–271, 435, 454
investment evaluation, 33, 109, 193, 246–247, 288, 362, 471, 475

J

Jacob, Stephan, 325
Jevon's paradox, 664
Jevons, William Stanley, 11
Joos, Michael, 326–327
Judeo-Christian context, 655

K

Katz, Steven, xli, 277
Kennedy, John F, 149
Kloppenborg, Bas, xlvii, 176, 183, 604, 610
Kluth, Andreas, 160
Knight, Frank Hyneman, 146, 148
Koller, Tim, 513
Koonin, Steven E, 9, 18
Kyoto Protocol, 49

L

Laengle, Michael, xlvi, lx, 58–59, 61–67, 592
Lagac, Joyce Marie P, 117
late-mover's benefits for energy, 655
Leadership and Performance (LEAP), 176, 226
learning effects, xlii, 31, 36, 99–103, 160, 211, 591, 655
levers of value, 413
    creating and appropriating cash, 439–440

incorporating value and strategic dialogue, 456–457
investing, managers to, 414–416
    earnings multiples, era of, 416–417
    new paradigm, old wisdom rules, 417–418
libertarian paternalism, 78, 103, 108, 655, 662
licence to operate, 655
lifecycle avoided cost of energy (LACE), 21, 655
lifecycle costing, incorporating economic notions of, 373–391
    arbitrage under fuel costs volatilities, 379–382
    monetising value with LACE, 382–388
    recovery of what was invested, 373–378
lifecycle cost of energy (LCOE), l, 19, 94, 305, 359, 552–554, 656
liquefied natural gas (LNG), xxxviii, 161
local currency loans and investments, 643
locus of control, 656
logistics mindset, 36
long bond yields, 375
long-term inflation rate, 378
loss avoidance, 656
Lotilla, Raphael PM, xlvi, lx, 113
low-carbon future, 54, 65–67
low-carbon policy, 205
low-carbon prosperity, pathways to, 55–57
luck, 610–611, 656
The Luck Factor, 587
Lücking, Gero, 588

M

maintenance capex (MCPX), 426, 433, 442, 454, 500, 554, 556–557, 569, 592, 654
Malthusian theory, 656
managerial flexibility, 656
marginal revenues, 367
market disruptions, diverging paths in, 287–288
market-friendly policies, 207
market liberalisation, 648
market orientation matrix, 210, 663
market power prices, 554–560
market pull transition, 209
market structures, 103–108, 656
market transition, 32
Markowitz, Harry M, xli, 276
Martin, Roger L, 243–244, 268
McClain, Katherine T, 277
mean variance portfolio optimality (MVPO), 277
Michalak, Bob, 138
Mielke, Jahel, 334
Miller, Merton Howard, 414
mindset transition, xxxix, 3, 8–9, 657
    managers' strategic responses, 12–16
    policy and climate advocates' imperatives, 9–12
Mine-resistant Ambush Protected Buffalo (MRAP Buffalo), 233
moderates, 664
Modigliani, Franco, 414
modus vivendi, 182, 526, 531, 533
monopoly, 657
Morgenstern, Oskar, 280
Multilateral Investment Guarantee Agency (MIGA), 124
Murray, Brian C, 298
mutatis mutandis, 7, 12, 657

N

Nagruho, Hanan, xlix
Nalebuff, Barry J, xlviii, 242, 299, 511–512, 517
Nash, John F, 280
National Aeronautics and Space Administration (NASA), 158
National Economic Development Authority (NEDA), 113
natural gas, lxv–lxvi, 161
natural law, 657
natural owner of opportunity, 657
Nederlandse Aardolie Maatschappij (NAM), 178
negotiate financing requirements (NFR), 497
neo-Malthusian theory, 282
net present values (NPVs), xxxix, l, lii, 247, 274, 276, 288, 414, 421, 471, 502, 512, 516, 657
Net Zero by 2050, 5, 8, 13, 658
Newberry, David M, xli
not-in-my-backyard (NIMBY), 164, 312, 658
notional equilibrium, 519, 531, 536, 544, 549
Nuclear Energy Agency (NEA), 19
Nussbaum, Martha C, 81, 83, 85
Nuttal, William, xli

O

obsolescing bargain, 153, 658
Offshore Operations Academy, 178

oligopolistic rivalries, 511–514
  adaptively reshaping markets, 525–526
  intermittent supplies and dichotomy, 544–549
  shrinking carbon space, 526–534
  Chief Executive's reflections, 549–551
  decision contexts, 514–517
  purposive dynamic decisions, 517
    binomial processes, 517–520
oligopoly, 105, 281, 511, 657
omnipotence, 209–210, 362, 658
omniscience, xxxvii, 6, 205, 210, 586, 658
ONEgas offshore academy, 177–180
operating cash flows (OpCF), 439
operating free cash flows (OpFCF), 439, 442, 448, 500
operational flexibility, 318, 658
option games, 280, 334, 519, 596, 659
option premium (OP) formulation, 105, 659
option valuation, 567–571
organisational agility, 212, 215, 218
  enablers, 659
  and innovation, 659
organisational learning, 660
ORMAT Technologies, 403
Ostrum, Elinor, xlii, lvii, 77, 80, 86, 611
outcome-variation matrix, 660

P

Pacific Islands Renewable Energy Investment Program, 126
pacing capital expenditures, 440–445
Pareto optimality, 104, 661
Pareto, Vilfredo, 104–105
Paris Agreement, lxiv, 49, 159, 161
Payne, Charles II, xlvii, 232, 237, 604, 611
payoffs, 39, 95, 193, 212–213, 241, 271, 296, 306, 312, 317, 320, 340, 372, 421, 515, 564–567
Pérignon, Fray Pierre, 60
Perusahaan Listrik Negara (PLN), 315, 346
Peszko, Grzegorz, 94
Pew Research, 204
Philippine Electric Market Corporation (PEMC), 114
Pigouvian tax, 669
Pindyck, Robert S, 252
PIVOT, xlvi, xlviii, l, 3, 7, 585, 588, 609, 661
  create niches to, 28–29
    market ambiguities, 29–32
    rethinking tactical and strategic moves, 32–43
  foundational, 590–596
  priming for, 51–54
  shifting worlds, profitably adapting to, 43–44
  transitional, liii, 589, 596–604
policy, xliii, 84–86, 297, 662
  normative anchors of, 89
policy allocation, 210, 662
policy and managerial actions, 75–81
  feasible policy, 108–112
  freedom and choices, 81
  firms and policy, innate strengths of, 84–86
  and spheres of influence, 81–84
  reframing policy and managerial actions, 87

common pool resources,
   governing, 87–91
   deregulation, glacial pace to,
   91–93
policy-directed system, 88, 207, 642
policy-enabled competitive process, 211,
   663
policy-enabled market pull, 211, 663
policy instruments, 210, 663
policy process, under ambiguous
   conditions, 113–120
   colliding aspirations and political
      realities, 113–114
   competitive supply procurement,
      119–120
policy push and champions, 210–211, 663
policy push transition, 209
political freedom, 651
political uncertainties, 204
politics, 18, 56, 153, 211, 513, 663, 671
populism, 663
portfolio diversification, 273–283
portfolio mindset, 664
portfolio of opportunities, 652
portfolio risk and returns, 664
power purchase agreement (PPA), 101,
   249, 301–302, 316, 403, 404, 664
   revenues and risks, 303
power-to-gas, 59, 61–62, 66
Prahalad, C K, 138
price-setting supply, 665
price taker, 469–473
   coal to gas transition, 481–488
   investing under transitioning markets,
      473–476
      crossing the chasm, 478–481

meeting place, setting, 476–478
making choices, 503–508
unexpected places, renewables'
   disruptions in, 488–493
viable pathways, in search of, 493–503
price-to-earnings ratios (P/E), 416
private goods, 86
private governance, 114–116
profit & loss analysis, 463–464
progressivism, 663
project financing, xxxix, 404, 442, 451, 615
prospects-to-opportunities funnel, 256–261
public regulation, 114–116
pure competition, 656
Purisima, Cesar Antonio V., lx
P W One, xlvii, 166–168, 176–183, 610,
   661
pyrolysis, 40–41

R
RAG Austria AG (RAG), 58–67
Ramos, Fidel V, 113
Rappaport, Alfred, 263–264
rational economic agents, 664
real-life markets, xxxv
real options reasoning, 641
real options theory, 276, 659
real people, 138, 175, 242, 414, 586, 610
   adaptive actions by, xlii–xlv
rebound effect, 11, 664
receivables, 182, 433, 435
reconfiguration, 40–43, 668
red-hot stone phenomena, xlvii, lv, 150,
   152, 154, 665
redistributive justice, 665
reframing, 36–40, 668

regulatory risk, 75, 665
renationalisation, 33, 50, 488
renewables, 16, 30, 94, 121, 124–126, 300, 306, 312, 665
repurpose, 35–36, 668
research and development (R&D) phase, 37, 664
reserve replacement ratio, 665
residual economic value, 573–576, 665
residual income (RI), 451, 467, 672
residual value added (RVA), 672
resource scarcity, 11
resource scarcity fallacy, 666
return on invested capital (RoIC), 264, 266, 451, 472, 672
risk, 36, 666
risk aversion, 241, 253, 442, 586–587, 666
risk-neutral strategic payoffs, 564–567, 666
risk reductions, 145–147
risk-taking, 253, 295, 362, 666
risk-weighted returns, 222
Ronney, Paul, 42
Roques, Fabien A, xli, 277
Rotter, Julian, 588
Rousseau, Jean Jacques, 333
Ruben, Peter Paul, 48
Rubinstein, Mark, xlii
Rumelt, Richard, 33, 516

S
Salkhit Wind Farm, 125–126
Sarbanes–Oxley, 110, 666
second business viability condition, 365, 373
Securities and Exchange Commission (SEC), 115

Semirara
  feasible future niches to pivot, 627–629
  inter-connected national grid, positioning for, 625–627
  strengths, 622–625
  supply security and net zero waste coal, 627
Sen, Amartya, lvii, xlii, 77, 82–83, 107, 611
sequential value capture, 322
shareholder value, 264
shareholder value added (SVA), 264
Sharpe, William F, xlii, 277
Shellenberger, Michael, 173
Shell plc, 4, 12, 213, 593, 600–601
ship-or-pay, 304–305, 314
Simons, Tony, 193
single loop learning, 245–247, 263, 282, 660
Sinn, Hans-Werner, 297
Slater, Martin, 145
slim-hole drilling, 314, 324, 341–343, 346
Smil, Vaclav, 473
Smith, Adam, 104, 146
social capital, 109
social contract, 474–475
social cost and benefit analysis, 666
social innovation, 327, 348–351, 667
social responsibility of firms, 667
social utility, 104, 667
solar power, 31, 329–330
spark spreads, 667
Staffeld, Iain, 326–327
stakeholder theory, 149–152, 650, 667
state-preference portfolio theory, xlii, 277
state's control, 107–108
status quo trap, 247, 667

Steel, Gary, xlvii
Steudle, Gesine A, 334
strategic de-risking, 339–340
strategic dialogue, 660–661
strategic economic payoff (SPO$_e$), 564
strategic flexibility, 318, 667
strategic investment, 421–422
strategic move, 3, 29, 31, 34, 38, 299, 586, 669
strategic option value (SOV), 669
strategic thinking, 299, 511, 669
strategic uncertainty, 299
Strauss, Lewis, 154
Subnational Climate Fund (SnCF), 125
subsidies, 6, 24, 30, 32, 94–97, 105, 117, 155, 210, 266, 276, 297–298, 307, 309, 359–361, 365, 372, 391–396, 591, 669
sunk costs trap, 249, 669
Sunstein, Cass R., 92–93, 103, 109, 249, 256, 392, 473
supply mix transition, 25
supply-push policy, 669
sustainability, xxxv–xxxvi, xlv, 28, 43
    environmental remediation to, 16–17
        green dilemmas, 17–18
        grips with dynamic markets, 22–28
        meaningful and relevant questions, 18–22
    sustainable practices, 669
sustaining innovation, 668

T

take-or-pay, 154–155, 195, 199, 272, 305, 670
Taleb, Nassim Nicholas, 567
Taylor, G, 393

technology risk premium, 375
TECOP risk analysis framework, xlvii, 670
Thaler, Richard H, lviii, xlii, 88, 92–93, 103, 109, 151, 246, 249, 256, 392, 396, 414, 473, 611
Thatcher, Margaret R, 91, 513
The Heritage Foundation, 81
Tichy, Noel M, 176
Tirole, Jean, 333
Tönnis, Matthias, 325
Toscani, Giulio, liv
transformational BOUnCE, 589, 604–608
Trigeorgis, Lenos, lvii, 299
The Triple Bottom Line, 139, 671

U

uncertainty, 195–199
    insurable consequences, 202–203
    learning through options and games, 203–204
    predictable extant world, 199–201
    strategic/operational flexibility, 201–202
Underground Sun Conversion and Storage Initiative, xlvi
United Nation's Intergovernmental Panel on Climate Change (UN IPCC), 14
unity of purpose and actions, 671
uranium, 152, 156, 158, 310, 312, 542
US Agency for International Development (USAID), 125

V

value chain risk assessment, 671
value chain, strategically adapting across, 320–324
value creation, iterative interactions of, 479

value-risk trade-off framework, 278–279
valuing stakeholder returns, 445–448
    creating and managing value, 451–456
    debt and equity, apportioning firm value to, 448–451
variable operating cost, 410–411
variable or intermittent renewables, 670
variable renewables, 304, 306–307, 368, 373, 393
Velamuri, Rama, xlviii, 285, 290, 595
Villegas, Bernardo M, lviii–lvix, 80, 141, 145
volatile costs, 401–404
volatile volumes, 21
von Neumann, John, 280
vox populi, 81

W
Wagoner, Michael, 603
wealth creation, 671

Wealth of the Nations, 104, 146
weighted average costs of capital (WACC), 35, 264, 266–267, 448–449, 454, 501, 672
welfare economics, 392–393, 672
welfare economic theories, 105
wholesale electricity spot market (WESM), 113–116
Wilde de, Antonie, xlix, l, lx, 397, 405
Williamson, Kevin, 76
Wiseman, Richard, 587
Wiser, Ryan, 99
working capital (WC), 430, 493–495
    under $ACCGT_M$, 496
working capital requirements (WCR), 430, 433–434, 493
World Bank, 118, 124, 154, 348, 622
Wriston, Walter, 198–199

Y
Yap, Joseph, 117

CPSIA information can be obtained
at www.ICGtesting.com
Printed in the USA
BVHW091239170922
647108BV00002B/6